MODELING AND ROLE-MODELING:

A VIEW FROM THE CLIENT'S WORLD

MODELING AND ROLE-MODELING:

A VIEW FROM THE CLIENT'S WORLD

Helen L. Erickson, PhD, RN, AHN-BC, FAAN
Editor

Unicorns Unlimited
Cedar Park, Texas.

MRM Logo Reprinted with Permission of EST Co.

Library of Congress Cataloging-in-Publication Data

**Modeling and Role-Modeling:
A View From the Client's World**

Helen L. Erickson (1936-), Editor.

Includes bibliographic references and index.

ISBN: 0-9779203-0-5

1) Energy 2) Mind-body-spirit 3) Healing
4) Health 5) Holism 6) Self-care

Development Editor: Geeta Erickson, M.A.
Copy Editor: Geeta Erickson, M.A.
Cover and Interior Design: Lance Erickson, M.A.
Graphics: Lance Erickson, M.A.

Distributed by
Unicorns Unlimited
406 Trail Ridge Dr.
Cedar Park, TX. 78613
unicornsunlimitedbooks@yahoo.com

Printed in the United States by BookSurge.com

CONTENTS

CONTRIBUTING AUTHORS

Linda S. Baas, PhD, RN, ACNP
Professor and Coordinator of the Acute Care Graduate Program, University of Cincinnati
College of Nursing; Nurse Practitioner.
University Hospital Heart Failure Center
Cincinnati, Ohio

> *I am honored to be able to contribute to this book. In my roles as educator, researcher, and nurse practitioner I have been able to examine components of the Self-care model and demonstrate how Self-care relates to quality of life. For more than 15 years, I have been interested in Self-care Knowledge and intrigued with how people come to know their body and recognize the early signs and symptoms when something is "not right."*

Diane Benson, RN, EdD
Associate Professor of Nursing
Humboldt State University
Arcata, California

> *While a nurse/nurse educator/clinical nurse specialist for almost 40 years, I became interested in Modeling and Role-Modeling when I joined the faculty at HSU. This interest blossomed for my doctoral dissertation, which expands the application of The Adaptive Potential Assessment Model to groups.*

Mary Brekke, PhD, RN, CHTP, AHN-BC
Metropolitan State University, School of Nursing
St. Paul, Minnesota

> *I am very grateful for this opportunity to articulate, via an energetic framework, the depth and power of Modeling and Role Modeling. I have "resonated with" the framework for more than 15 years as I have taught the framework to RN-BSN students and used it in my private Healing Touch practice.*

Da'Lynn Kay Clayton, PhD, RN
Imagine Nursing Consultant
Associate Professor
College of Nursing
Harding University
Searcy, Arkansas

> *As a holistic nurse consultant I focus on facilitating holistic, theory-based nursing practice, education, and research. MRM theory and Ericksonian strategies have been essential aspects of my professional practice for over two decades. They integrate with my personal philosophy of Nursing and inform all aspects of my work—Nursing practice, nursing education, and research methods.*

Margaret E. Erickson, PhD, RN, AHN-BC
Executive Director, American Holistic Nurses' Certification Corporation
Imagine Nursing Consultant
Cedar Park, Texas

> *Based on this theory, I facilitate health promotion, healing, and wellness in my work with individuals and institutions interested in implementing and improving holistic health care for their clients, patients, employees, and students.*

Judith E. Hertz, PhD, RN
Associate Professor
Director of Graduate Studies
School of Nursing, Northern Illinois University
DeKalb, Illinois

> *I am so pleased to contribute to the expansion of MRM theory and to this book. My passion and research based on MRM theory is to support autonomy and Self-care in older adults as a means to health promotion. On a daily basis, I strive to incorporate MRM concepts in my interactions with students, colleagues, family, and friends.*

Betty Ayotte Jensen, PhD, RN
The University of Texas at Austin

> *As a student of Helen Erickson, I was excited to find a theory that fit my philosophy of nursing. Since then it has had a major impact on my practice, research, and teaching.*

Carolyn K. Kinney, PhD, RN, AHN-BC
Integrated Health Care Therapist and Wellness Consultant
Associate Professor of Nursing
The University of Texas at Galveston (Retired)
Austin, Texas

> *Modeling and Role-Modeling Theory has been integral to my private practice, scholarship, and teaching for 25 years. It is an honor to contribute to the expansion and application of the theory through this book.*

Sharon Rogers, PhD, RN
Imagine Nursing Consultant
Assistant Professor
Patty Hanks Shelton School of Nursing
A Consortium of Hardin-Simmons University
Abilene Christian University and McMurry University
Abilene, Texas

> *MRM informs my practice as a nurse, educator, and human being.*

Ellen D. Schultz, PhD, RN, CHTP
Professor of Nursing
Metropolitan State University
St. Paul, Minnesota

> *My interest in Modeling and Role-Modeling developed several years ago as our nursing faculty searched for the appropriate nursing theory to serve as the foundation for our curriculum. The theory has continued to enrich my life as it has grown from a theoretical framework to a way of being.*

Marsha Jelonek Walker, PhD, RN, AHN-BC, RMT
Mindbody Health
Educator and Private Practice
Austin, Texas

> *My fascination with the power of our thoughts and feelings to affect change in the body took me to graduate school in the late 1980's. There I attended a Modeling and Role-Modeling class with Helen Erickson where I first learned that healing occurs when people receive what they believe they need to heal. I also learned that stressors affect people differently depending on the resources they bring to the situation. These principles continue as cornerstones in my exploration of the mind, body, spirit relationship, guiding my professional and personal journey.*

ACKNOWLEDGEMENTS

Acknowledgements inadequately express my appreciation to those who have contributed to my understanding of human nature and, therefore, contributed to this book. Nevertheless, a few must be recognized. First, on behalf of my colleagues and myself, I wish to recognize the hundreds of clients, colleagues, and students who stimulated our thoughts, challenged our beliefs, and mandated that we clarify and articulate our ideas. Thank you. You are our inspiration.

To all the contributing authors, who diligently articulated their thoughts, inspired my heart, and challenged my mind: Without you, this book would not have happened. You are the best and I am blessed to have had this time to work with you. Thank you.

To the members of the Society for the Advancement of Modeling and Role-Modeling: Thank you for your belief in MRM, your encouragement to write this book, and your willingness to let me do it in my own time. Without you, there would not be a need for this book.

To my family: Thank you for Being You. You are my love; you give me joy, hope, and assurance that what has been written is valid. Without your willing participation, I would never have had the will or fortitude to put this book together. You are my heart.

To Geeta Erickson for her willingness to "stick with it," read, re-read, correct, and then read again: Thank you for your persistence and patience, your willingness to challenge content and concepts, and for your inspirations. And to Lance Erickson, Jr., Thank you for your inspiration, cover design, creation of figures and tables, formatting, changing spaces, and managing all the little details. You have been a blessing. You two have made a difficult task a pleasure and given words a life of their own.

Thank you to each and every one of you.
Helen Erickson, Editor

DEDICATION

For years I have had the following dream: As I walk along a beautiful country lane, I suddenly find myself in front of an interesting, but mysterious house. As I approach it, I note that the door is ajar. I knock, but no one seems to be at home. However, the door swings open. I hesitate, but then enter and begin to explore. The house is delightful! There are many rooms, with all the doors open, so I continue to explore one room after another until I reach the back of the house. There I find a door that is closed. The doorknob turns, but the door is locked. I turn around and go back outside through the front door, once again viewing the beauty of the outdoors.

This dream persisted for years. It got to be an old friend; I knew exactly what I would see in each room and where each hallway would take me, until I reached the locked door. For years, I left wondering what was behind that door.

About one month after I started writing this book, "my dream" visited me again. Only this time, as I stood in front of the door, it suddenly swung open. I was astounded! I stepped into the room and saw my husband standing there waiting for me. Our children (all eight of them) and all eight of our grandchildren were there, too! I was flabbergasted! When I asked my husband how he had done that, he held up a key and said, "Here, I have always had the key. You just never asked!" Now I know that the key is always available, we just have to learn to ask—and to receive.

I dedicate this book to my husband, who "holds the key." I know he will share this dedication with those who "shared" the space with him: my beloved children and grandchildren. They are my teachers, my inspiration, the light of my life, and the gifts I will always treasure.

PREFACE

In the early 1980's I was fortunate to be part of a group that met in monthly seminars with authors Erickson, Tomlin, and Swain, prior to the publication of their seminal work, *Modeling and Role-Modeling: A Theory and Paradigm for Nursing* (1983). The participants were nursing faculty, students, and practicing nurses interested in learning, growing, and sharing our ideas about nursing, stretching our views, and digging deeply into what we knew as we explored the foundational elements of the theory. We knew then that the Modeling and Role-Modeling (MRM) theory synthesized an important new way of thinking about and implementing nursing that was on the frontier of conceptualizing nursing. Yet, it also embraced truths about human needs and behavior that were both universal and timeless.

Health care and the world at large have changed significantly since the publication of MRM in 1983. Yet, one thing remains the same. In spite of the tremendous advances in treatment options and increasing acceptance of adjunctive, alternative, and integrative types of care, nursing's focus remains on the human being receiving the care. MRM has been steadfast in its emphasis on understanding all dimensions of the individual client's perspective (modeling his or her world) as a prerequisite to providing nursing care.

This book's goal of expanding and elaborating upon the underlying philosophical foundation and the concepts and components of the MRM theory challenges us to push even further the boundaries of what Nursing is and can be. With Helen Erickson's inspiring and untiring guidance, the contributors provide direction for contemporary nursing practice and scholarship and for the next era in nursing's unfolding history. Some of the most expansive and thought-provoking ideas in the field are explicated, along with elaboration of nurses' roles as facilitators of our clients' growth, development, and transformation of mind, body, spirit, and soul. As a result, this work provides guidance for what it means to be human, personally and professionally, and for sustaining nursing's holistic and comprehensive approach to fulfilling our commitment to our clients and our contract with society.

Carolyn K. Kinney, PhD, RN, AHN-BC
Integrated Health Care Therapist and Wellness Consultant
Associate Professor of Nursing
The University of Texas at Galveston (Retired)
Austin, Texas

PROLOGUE

It was 1989 when I was first introduced to the Modeling and Role-Modeling Theory. I was about to take a new position as Chair of the Department of Nursing at Humboldt State University (HSU) where the faculty were engaged in curricular revision and were about to make Modeling and Role-Modeling the basis of all of their teaching. One of my colleagues gave me a copy of the 1983 book and said "Here, you have to read this. You'll see that it really makes sense. It explains exactly what we've all been doing all these years, and it if isn't what we've been doing – it is what we should have been doing!"

I considered myself a rather diligent student of nursing theory and I was surprised that there was a theory about which I knew nothing. I was intrigued and very impressed that *an entire faculty* was so committed to this particular point of view. Needless to say, I did read the book and not only did it make immense sense, it gave me a new perspective on care and new language to use in describing important nursing observations and activities. Modeling and Role-Modeling is a theory that helped me put nursing in perspective, particularly in relationship to our clients. It includes concepts of adaptation, adaptive states, human development, basic human needs, growth, and healing. It sets out guidelines for nursing practice–the five aims of intervention. It explores the concept of nurturance as a basic nursing intervention and gives voice to the distinction between nurturance and care. The theory provides a structure and framework for care that is easily understood and that can be practiced intuitively. There is an easy 'fit' between what we know as experienced nurses and what Modeling and Role-Modeling says. There is also an easy 'fit' between what novice nurses want desperately to do (care for and help others) and this theory, as every sophomore student at HSU found when they learned nursing from this model. They were immediately able to apply it to their beginning nursing practice.

The theory also requires something I'll call *faith* for lack of a better descriptor. We have to *believe* in the process, we have to *trust* that the client knows deep down why he or she is sick and what he or she needs to get better. We have to *believe* that the human being innately strives for health and healing. We have to *believe* it is appropriate for professional nurses to give up control and render control to the client. We have to *believe* that we can assist best by asking the client what he or she needs and then listen and act on the client's responses. The theory directs nurses to be humble, compassionate, responsive, nurturing, knowledgeable, and courageous human beings–people who are willing to enter into nurse-client relationships that will inevitably leave both the nurse and the client changed for having had the personal encounter with one another. From my perspective, that means the theory requires commitment to holistic nursing– providing care that has one and only one main goal: healing the whole person.

This new text: *Modeling and Role-Modeling: A View from the Client's World,* is a long-awaited book that enhances the original work. It is not an 'updating' of a theory, nor is it an attempt to bring the theory into a modern, contemporary context in ways that would change the basic tenets of Modeling and Role-Modeling. Further, and quite thankfully, it is not an attempt to place Modeling and Role-Modeling in competition with other current theories for purposes of 'finding its place' in our current array of nursing theories. This is a book that provides depth, science, and grounding for each of the constructs of the original theory.

My first impression of the theory was that it made sense and that it could be practiced intuitively. Practicing by intuition and applying the theory by intuition will work for both nurse and clients. But, our current environments emphasize evidence-based practice, the need to know, evaluate and prove efficacy, and need to demonstrate and explain outcomes through data or theory. These environments make it essential that nurses understand the depth, the data, and the practice decisions they make while putting this theory into use. For me, that is exactly what this text does.

This book explores the concept of holism–the nurses' and the clients' ways of being. It explores the body-mind-spirit connections and the connections between two people – one the healer, the other the person striving to be healed. In reading, we are compelled to explore the human spirit and to understand the spiritual drive at the core of every person. We are provided with the science and the data that underpin energy theories, psychoneuroimmunology, and the physiology of the human heart. We are asked to take a new look at human development. Also, we are asked to review our notions about stress, stress states, self-care knowledge, self-care actions, and role of the body as an unconscious memoir for all past history and events in a person's life. The reader will explore the differences between development and growth, connections and relationships, nurturance and facilitation, holistic care and complementary modalities, presence and professionalism, and spirituality and emotions and thoughts.

This new text is by no means a replacement for the original work on the theory. Quite the contrary, basic knowledge of the theory is required to understand the chapters that follow. Without basic knowledge of the theory, and even with it, reading this book may seem for some like coming into a movie that has already begun. Each chapter stands alone providing important content. Together they stand as a thorough exploration of the meanings of Modeling and Role-Modeling. This text provides a summary of pertinent data, theories, constructs and concepts that guide holistic nursing care. Each chapter contains personal stories and narratives of client situations illustrating the ideas set forth. Helen Erickson writes "this book is about helping people grow, develop, and, when needed, heal" (Chapter 14). This book is also about the growth, development, and healing of contemporary nursing. Read it with pleasure!

Noreen Frisch, PhD, RN, FAAN, APHN-BC
Cleveland State University
Cleveland Ohio
2006

INTRODUCTION

My professional life has been dedicated to the development and expansion of the art and science of holistic care, with an emphasis on the interface among body, mind, and spirit. To this end, a holistic theory and paradigm was articulated and published in 1983 that emphasized the client's world-view as the primary source of information. A Society was established the following years to promote the advancement of this way of thinking.

In recent years, members of the Society for the Advancement of Modeling and Role-Modeling (SAMRM), students, colleagues, and others have requested and encouraged the publication of a follow-up book that would expand on or clarify the concepts conveyed in classrooms, presented at conferences, discussed during SAMRM meetings, and communicated in general discussions.

This book is the first of four planned in response to these requests. The next will focus on the research methods and measurements used to study this theory (2007). The third will provide guidelines for those who teach or practice MRM (2007). And the fourth book will present detailed information about a research project undertaken to study the effects of applying MRM in the care of persons with Alzheimer's disease and their caregivers.

Some of you will ask if this book is intended to replace the work presented in the first book. The answer is no, it is not. That book stands alone and will continue to be in print, as-is. SAMRM has designated it as a classic, one of a kind. Since it stands on its own and is the reference source for this book, you can use it without ever opening this book or use it as a reference.

I know there will be a mixed response to what is presented in this book. Some readers will not agree with what has been proposed; some will, but with qualifications, and others will say, "It's about time!" We know some readers, not having read the original, will be confused and have difficulty with concepts presented in this book. To that extent, we encourage you to read the original before delving into this book.

Section I starts with a chapter describing my current thinking on the search for meaning in life. It was inspired by those who have asked about Modeling and Role-Modeling, my role in conceptualizing this theory, and why I have pursued these ideas for so many years. My answer to you is that I believe it is my Soul-work. I could leave it at that, but I decided it is important to explicitly state what we think, so others will understand where we come from and why we say what we do. For example, although the original book described a spiritual drive that permeates the entire human being, we never described what that spiritual drive meant to us. While I remember feeling passionately that it needed to be illustrated as the core of the human being, we minimally discussed the significance of this notion. The first chapter in this book describes my view on this issue. The co-authors (Evelyn Tomlin and Mary Ann Swain) of the first book may have differing opinions and views (see Appendix F, A Note from Evelyn Tomlin).

The ideas expounded in the second and third chapters of this book were also implied or presented in the original, but were not clarified. These chapters expand on what is meant by energy and mind-body relations. Authored by colleagues, they have been carefully edited so the content is consistent with my current way of thinking. Again, the other authors of the first book may have differing opinions.

Several chapters of the next two sections of this book have also been authored by colleagues who have studied and applied Modeling and Role-Modeling and are now ready to present their ideas in written format. As in section 1, I have edited their work to ensure it is consistent with my current thinking on Modeling and Role-Modeling. I have also interspersed my own comments throughout the book. I hope you will read our words, challenge our beliefs, study our proposals, and join with others to clarify and add to these words.

I also invite you to visit the website of the Society for the Advancement of Modeling and Role-Modeling: mrmnursingtheory.org

Sincerely,

Helen L. Erickson

SECTION 1

SECTION I

MIND, BODY, SPIRIT CONNECTIONS

The life you know is a thin layer of events covering a deeper reality. In the deeper reality, you are part of every event that is happening now, has ever happened, or ever will happen. In the deeper reality, you know absolutely who you are and what your purpose is. There is no confusion or conflict with any other person on earth. Your purpose in life is to help creation expand and grow. When you look at yourself, you see only love. The mystery of life isn't any of these things, however. It's how to bring them to the surface. If someone asked me how to prove that there really is a mystery of life, the simplest proof would be just this enormous separation between deep reality and everyday existence.

Deepak Chopra (2004). *The Book of Secrets: Unlocking the Hidden Dimension of Your Life* (p. 5).

This section includes three chapters designed to expand the philosophical underpinnings of the Modeling and Role-Modeling theory and paradigm first presented in Erickson, Tomlin, and Swain (1983), *Modeling and Role-Modeling: A Theory and Paradigm for Nursing.* Chapter 1 addresses issues related to the spiritual drive proposed in the holistic model (Erickson et al., 1983, p. 45) including linkages among the Soul, spirit, and the biophysical body, our Reason for Being, and Life Purpose.

Chapter 2 discusses energy concepts relevant to the Modeling and Role-Modeling Theory and Paradigm. The ideas that we are energy first and that all energy comes from a Unified Field are proposed. Chapter 3 discusses mind-body-spirit relations. Relations between body chemistry, human energy fields, and Universal Consciousness are also addressed.

CHAPTER 1

SEARCHING FOR LIFE PURPOSE: DISCOVERING MEANING

HELEN L. ERICKSON

He was just a little boy, perhaps five years old, when he looked at me and asked, "Where is myself?" Looking down at him, I pointed and said, "Right there; you ARE yourself." He responded, "No, that is Me. Where is my SELF?" We had recently moved, so I interpreted this as symptomatic of some nervousness about the move and where his "things" might be. Some were still in boxes waiting to be unpacked. The other possibility was he wanted to know, "What is myself?" In either case, it seemed important I ease his anxiety.

With a glint of humor in my voice, I pulled him closer, placed my palm on top of his head, and said, "This little boy, this person you call Me, this person I love, IS your self. You are right here, by me. Your toys and other things are still in boxes waiting for us to unpack them. We'll do that soon."

With great patience he gently pushed me away, looked me straight in the eye, and slowly said, "I know where my stuff is, that's not my problem. I want to know WHERE IS MY SELF?" Looking into his eyes, I remember being a bit unsettled. What in the world was he talking about? Did he really mean, "Where is my SELF?" Our little boy had asked a question I had never thought about! One I'd never discussed with anyone, and one I didn't know how to answer. Maybe I had misinterpreted his response. Certainly this 5 year-old couldn't be thinking more profound thoughts than me at my age! After all, I was the parent! So, to clarify, I asked, "What do you mean?" And again, in a statement I will never forget, he said, "I want to know where my Self is so I'll know what I'm supposed to BE when I grow up."

OVERVIEW

Now I know we all ask questions about our Self and our Reason for Being. Some are direct; others are more rhetorical. Some are sophisticated and difficult to understand; others are simple and to the point. I also know answers to these questions do not lie in another person's response. Each of us has to discover our own Reason for Being. Others can only help us along the way by encouraging, supporting, and sometimes guiding us.

Answers to our questions come gradually as we learn to find meaning in day-to-day life. Each new understanding offers a glimmer of who we really are, a glimmer of our Self. Over time, information derived from looking within helps us discover a pattern in our process. As we make choices, attribute meaning to experiences resulting from these choices, and think about our responses to each, themes emerge. Woven together, they create a pattern—the pattern of our life. As we contemplate the patterns we've woven across time, we can see our Life Purpose and gain awareness of why we are on earth.

This chapter is about searching for meaning *in* life and finding the meaning *of* life. It is about discovering linkages among our Soul, Spirit, and Self. It is also about recognizing our Life Purpose and determining our Reason for Being. The first part presents some philosophical considerations; the second presents an overview of my life journey.

My comments are my views on life. I know they are consistent with the work of Deepak Chopra (2000, 2004), Elizabeth Lesser (1999), Thomas Moore (1992), Gary Zukav (1989), and others. Nevertheless, I don't expect everyone to agree with them or accept them. I hope you read this chapter for enjoyment if not for clarifying your thinking. I also hope you come away with something of importance as you continue on your journey and search for meaning in your life.

SOUL-WORK

Most people believe we have a Soul. Some believe we live many life times; others believe we only live one. No matter what a person believes, there has to be a reason for our having biophysical-psychosocial bodies. I think it is because we can only do Soul-work when we are with others, in human form.

Reason for Being

It has taken me years to discover my Reason for Being and realize it is my Soul work! This discovery was a peak experience; it reoriented me and changed my life-view! As long as I can remember, I've tried to make decisions based on "being true to my values." I used to think being true to my values was the same as "connecting with my Soul." I thought the body, which came before birth with genetic, physical, cognitive, and psychological predispositions, was influenced *after* birth by society, significant others, and life experiences. I also thought the Soul entered the body sometime before birth or shortly after. This orientation implies we start as a body, and then somehow, our Soul merges with it. Now I know I was looking at it upside down. I know there are two ways to think about the relationship between body[2] and Soul, and each has a significant impact. The overall question is, "Are we body or Soul first?"

Are We Body First?

One possibility is the body comes first, and sometime during the lifetime the Soul connects with it. In this scenario, the underlying assumption is that we grow as human beings, but our Soul doesn't change. So, our life work as biophysical-psychosocial beings is to grow, and someday we link up with our Soul. From this perspective, the journey of life might include a search for the Soul, but the emphasis is on the growth of the biophysical-psychosocial being. Connection with the Soul is important, but not the emphasis of the journey. Instead, we focus on biophysical, social, cognitive, and emotional growth and development.[3]

Or Soul First?

An alternative perspective is that our *Soul needs to grow, it has work to do,* and that is why we are here! That is, we are Soul first, and the body is selected to carry out the Soul's work! This perspective changes the way we view the world.[4] Rather than a body that connects at some point along the way with the Soul, we are Soul first–which chooses a body so it can further its work. This suggests that, as a Soul, we may choose relationships that will enhance the Soul's work; we integrate with the body for this reason. From this perspective, we have a body so we can have interpersonal relationships, relationships necessary to enhance growth of the Soul.

> If our Soul comes first, then there must be a reason for us to exist in human form. I think our reason for becoming a human being is to continue a specific aspect of our Soul-work. It is our Reason for Being!

Life Purpose

Creating Holistic Beings

Our Soul is composed of energy vibrating at a very high level. To connect with a human body, it has to transform into energy that vibrates at a much lower level. Soul energy converted to lower level vibrations becomes Spiritual energy.[5] Spiritual energy synchronizes its vibrations with the human body so the two can integrate. The integration of biophysical, psychosocial, cognitive, and spiritual energy fields produces a *holistic being*, unique to this lifetime, and here for a reason.

Inherent Spiritual Drive

If we are Soul first, and the body is chosen as a "home" for us to do the work of the Soul, to carry out our Reason for Being, then there must be a force that pulls the two, the Soul and the body, together. The work of this force is to fulfill our inherent need to integrate Soul and body. I think this force is the spiritual drive (see Figure 1.1).

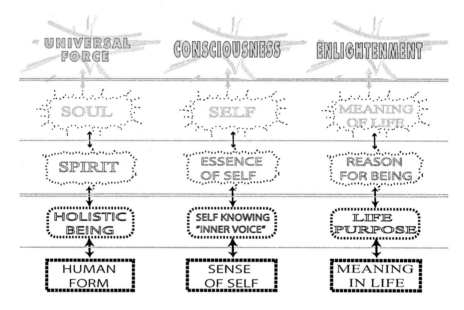

Figure 1.1 Relations among Soul, spirit, holistic being and human form.

This spiritual drive starts before our biophysical existence, continues through our lifetime, and culminates during Transformation.[6] It is always present, and pervades our subsystems even though we may not be consciously aware of it. It inspires us to search for our Life Purpose.

That is, we become holistic beings because we have to do Soul-work within the *context of this lifetime;* this is our Life Purpose. While Life Purpose is linked to the Soul and our Reason for Being, it is different. *Our Life Purpose is the work we have to do in human form in this lifetime to enhance the Soul. Our Reason for Being is why the Soul chooses to integrate with a human body.*

> We convert from Soul energy to Spiritual energy to live as holistic human beings and accomplish our Life Purpose. Spiritual energy (spirit) integrates with the human body, creating holistic human beings. Our spirit, then, is the link between our Soul and our human form. It pulls the parts together, bringing with it meaning.

Going back to the example of the five-year-old, our son had alluded to the orientation of Soul first when he said, "No, that is Me. Where is my SELF? I want to know where my Self is so I'll know what I'm supposed to be when I grow up." He called it his Self. He was trying to discover his Soul's reason for taking on a human form–his Reason for Being. He wanted to know what he should do with his life, so he could fulfill his Soul-work.

If I had been wiser at the time, I might have said he needed to find his Life Purpose before he could understand his Reason for Being. While he would have been too young to understand, I might have added that he was asking the right questions, he just needed time. What I did know was that he would learn to know his Self if we facilitated him to be true to himself.

<u>Essence of Self.</u> It is always interesting to watch young children who are facilitated to be themselves. These children seem to have 'free spirits.' They know what they need and how their needs are best satisfied, providing their caregivers don't interfere! It is as though they have an inner 'voice' that says, 'You need quiet,' or 'You need to be nurtured,' or 'You need stimulation,' and so forth.

These children often ask questions that surprise adults. Sometimes their questions seem disassociated from reality,[7] so adults are challenged to answer them. Interestingly, because these children perceive secure affiliation, they are comfortable with their individuation.[8] Although some people may think them 'loners,' they are not. They are children eager to be connected with others, but don't have to be with someone at all times to feel safe. They often seem to transcend their biophysical bodies and grasp beauty where others fail to see it. They feel more deeply, think more creatively, and experience life more richly than others. Let me give you an example:

I remember one such free spirit, a child who did something unexpected with his blocks and toys. Perfectly content to explore his world, he always found something to do, something to play with, and something of interest. He was a happy little boy with a sense of humor. But he also noticed the beauty in a flower, a colorful sunset, or a butterfly's flapping wings. At the age of three, he was enrolled in a playgroup so he could make friends.

Within a few weeks, the teacher commented that he seemed happy playing with other children, but also seemed happy playing alone. She wondered if he needed to be evaluated! Maybe he needed some "help" learning to get along! His mother asked if there was a problem, and the teacher said, "Not really, he just didn't seem to need to play with others all of the time." She just wanted to help him! The decision was to wait and see.

At the next conference, the teacher again reported he was different from the other children, but this time she said he was also more perceptive. She described, as an example, the day she came to school after experiencing a very difficult situation at home. She was upset, but tried to cover it. None of the children seemed to notice, except this one small child.

He went to her during playtime, put one hand on each side of her face and said she looked very sad and he was sorry. She explained that he did that while all the other children were running around, laughing and playing, unaware of his actions. Not only was she astounded by the depth of his perception, she was also touched by his gentleness and kindness. To think she had believed this child might possibly be unaware of how others felt!

Our Essence of Self *is our* spirit, *derived from our* Soul, *and our way of* Being *within this lifetime. It is who we are, without the influence of others.* Defined by the context of this lifetime*, it does not change, but* it does evolve in how it is expressed. The child described above was connected with his spirit, and minimally aware of the opinions of others. He was a *'free spirit'; he marched to his own drum.* He was aware of his needs, found ways to meet them, and interacted with others in meaningful ways. He listened to his "inner voice," his connection with his Self.

> Our Self is who we are, across time; it is the nature of our Soul.
> Our Essence of Self is the nature of our spirit within a given lifetime.

We learn about our Essence of Self through spiritual experiences,[9] which may sometimes last for only a second, and sometimes longer. In any case, we never really forget these experiences; we just file them away, often discounting their significance. They stay with us only to resurface as we search for our Life Purpose, look for our 'Essence,' try to find meaning in our lives, hope to understand our life choices, and wish to justify our existence. But, discovery is evasive. Just as we think we understand, the significance slips away.

I think this is normal. Most of us try too hard! We often ignore the moment-to-moment opportunities for spiritual enlightenment. We are too busy getting our work done to notice the beauty of the day, the twinkle in the eye of a child, the sadness on the face of a stranger, or even our own desire to have a quiet moment or to hear a song.

Not only do we often fail to open ourselves to personal experiences, we often fail to recognize interactions with others as important. Sometimes people say things to us, trying to express their inner feelings about who we are or how they have experienced time with us. Instead of recognizing these statements as opportunities to learn about our Self, we hear them as off-hand statements or someone else's thoughts. They may be perceived as documentation for the self as defined by others, but not as a reflection of our "Soul-in-action" as experienced by another! As a result we lose opportunities to better understand the Essence of our Self and our Life Purpose.

Sense-of-self. We also have a sense-of-self, formed as we interact with others. As children move from the protection of the family circle into society, responsible adults usually think they have to be socialized. That is, they have to be taught to listen to others, to pay attention to the needs of others, and to follow the rules of society.

Often these social lessons are learned at the cost of stifling the "inner voice." This is probably because entry into the developmental stage of Initiative coincides with an expansion of a social network,[10] and it is important to learn social protocols in order to develop meaningful relationships. However, it is also important to stay in touch with our inner nature, to maintain a healthy sense of affiliated-individuation. But, some children find themselves in a position where they have to sacrifice some of their individuation in order to maintain affiliation. As a result, they learn to accept the image of their self as others frame it. This type of self emerges as we take on or accept how others see us, experience us, and think of us. We have a sense of our selves formed by the opinions, values, and attitudes of others.

This sense-of-self, influenced by our relations with others, can change over the lifetime, depending on our relationships. On the other hand, the Essence of Self, our spiritual Self, may become obscured by the sense-of-self, but in reality, never changes during a lifetime.

> Our sense-of-self is how we perceive ourselves, based on the perceptions and attitudes of others. It may be closely linked to our Essence of Self, but not necessarily.

Merging the Selfs. Our vocabulary is filled with words about how we perceive others. Rarely do we indicate that a child, as in the story above, is self-actualized! Instead, such children are usually described as 'self-involved,' or as they grow older, 'selfish,' 'self-centered' and so forth.[11] The child in the story above, now a teenager, is often described as self-contained, one who doesn't need much to be happy, one who rejects conformity for the sake of conformity, and one who marches to his own beat.

Still, that young adult's insight into the needs of others exceeds the observations of most adults around him. He is interested in socializing with others, but is not influenced by social pressures. I think he knows how to stay tuned to his inner voice (his connection with his Self) even as he attends to the self influenced by society. The first will help him find the meaning of his life; the second will help him find meaning in his day-to-day life in socially acceptable ways. Integration of the two will help him accomplish his Life Purpose.

A String of Pearls. We might think of life as a string of single-colored pearls. The core of each pearl represents an important experience and the outer layer represents the life decision made about the experience. Some decisions are proactive; others are reactive. Some are purposeful steps taken to initiate action; others are secondary to life events we unexpectedly experience. How we interpret these experiences, how we react, and what we do with what we've learned, determines the color of the pearls. Some are bright and shiny; some are not.

Each pearl has significance; each adds to the one before and paves the way for the next. When examined individually, we see multiple, single-colored pearls (or life experiences), some more interesting than others, and some more fulfilling. Examined as a whole, however, a new picture emerges. A string of unmatched pearls, previously seen as separate and unrelated to one another, suddenly reveals a pattern.

> Initially viewed as individual life experiences with momentary meaning, the pearls can now be perceived differently. The relationship among the individual experiences creates a clearer picture of what is and is not meaningful in our lives. With this insight, we gain awareness of our Essence of Self, which we are able to compare with our sense-of-self. The closer the two match, the closer we are to understanding our Life Purpose, a precursor to finding our Reason for Being. Actualizing our Life Purpose, or Self-Actualizing, requires merging our sense-of-self with our Essence of Self.

The Reservoir

Some people have told me finding meaning in their lives is so evasive they cannot hope to find a purpose for their existence. They do not expect to ever really comprehend their Essence of Self or be connected with their Soul. Some are afraid to look deep within themselves, fearful of finding their inner self a disappointment, or worse. Some are afraid they will find their inner self empty, a void.

They have forgotten the Soul is our Reservoir. It contains information about who we are, what makes us unique, what drains us, what fulfills us, and what gifts we have to offer. This reminds me of a client I worked with a number of years ago.

> *We had worked together for several months. Initially, she had minimal positive residual and lots of negative residual.[12] She had a dreadful sense-of-self. During our time together, she had grown considerably, had achieved positive residual in Trust and Autonomy, and had decreased her Mistrust, Shame, and Doubt. One day she stated she was afraid. When asked to clarify, she expressed concern that "if she got any better, something bad would happen"; she was worried about what she would learn about herself. I said something to this effect: "Most of us are worried about looking too deeply into ourselves. We fear what might be there. It is like opening a can with a tight lid. We are afraid to look inside; we worry we might find worms." She agreed, so I went on. "But, what if you look twice at those worms and discover they are really caterpillars? (Pausing) You do know caterpillars go through a wonderful growth process and come out as butterflies!" She seemed amazed to think she could discover something "good" about herself, something that would help her grow and actualize more of her Self. With that discovery, she was able to move on and into the next stage of development, Initiative.*

We have an inherent drive to know our Self, and to be connected with others in fulfilling ways. We search for meaning in our lives, hoping to find a purpose for our existence. But, sometimes we forget we can only discover our Life Purpose by finding meaning in day-to-day experiences. Sometimes our experiences are fulfilling and sometimes not. Our search takes a lifetime. Often, we look back on previous experiences, hoping to put them in context. Sometimes we are successful in this endeavor and sometimes not. Usually, persistence pays off! When we give ourselves time to discover, assimilate, and understand, our Life Purpose becomes obvious.

However, life is like a kaleidoscope: just as the picture becomes apparent, the scenery changes! And with each change, a new picture emerges. We are constantly evolving; our grasp of purpose evolves with our day-to-day experiences. Tomorrow we will be different from what we are today. We will have new experiences and find new meaning in them. Nevertheless, it is possible to discover our life journey has direction and purpose. We just have to stay true to our inner voice.

The Inner Voice

Each of us has an inner voice which speaks to us, sometimes when we ask for insight, and at other times when we least expect it. I have referred to it earlier as our connection with our Soul and the Universe. Our inner voice doesn't always deliver messages we understand, so we often ignore or pass these messages off as irrelevant thoughts.[13]

My very good friend talks about waking up to a message from her inner voice, listening to the message, acting accordingly (Kinney, 996), and talking about her experience with health care providers who discounted her "knowing." She also discusses the importance of her following through with her 'instincts'. Her story, published in 1996, carries important messages for all of us.

> I think all of us yearn to be connected with our Soul, so we search for ways to reconnect! If that is the case, all we have to do is remember to listen to our inner voice.

Some 'listen' more than others. I think many people learn, when very young, to ignore their inner voice. Perhaps, this happens because children are socialized to be concerned about others, or they learn to be concerned about others to get their needs met. Since a person's inner voice cannot be experienced by others, no one else can really know what is best for us. Yet, we often listen to others rather than to our own Self. Maybe, it is because we emphasize the biophysical world and what is "real." For many people, nothing is real unless it can be experienced by one of the five sensory organs.

Nevertheless, the inner voice remains. Some talk about learning to listen to their unconscious or paying attention to their intuition.[14] They are probably all talking about the same thing, which is learning to listen to messages from the Self and the Universe; messages about who we are, what we need, and what we know. These messages are drawn from our personal reservoir of knowledge as well as from a greater resource, the Universe or God. This is our Self-knowing.

> Our Self-knowing comes from listening to our inner voice which draws from our Soul and the Universe.

<u>Self-Knowing.</u> Our inner voice is not our conscience; it is not massaged or shaped by society or social norms. It comes directly from our Soul. It draws energy (and, therefore, knowledge, or intelligence) from the Universe and imparts energy, created by our holistic being, back to the Universe. *Our inner voice is an aggregate of knowledge drawn from our Soul and knowledge drawn from the Universe.*

LIFE IS A JOURNEY

A Search for Meaning

Most of us agree Life is a Journey. However, our view of the journey varies. Some argue we simply live our lives and that is the journey. For them, wherever life takes us is where we are supposed to be. Others argue that fulfilling our Life Purpose is the journey. They believe there is a purpose to life, and we make choices and follow specific pathways in order to find it.

The position we take depends on many things, including the one posed above: which comes first, body or Soul? If the body comes first, then living our life creates the journey. We might compare this position with marking footsteps in the sand. After we have walked through the sand, we can look back and see the pathway. While the pathway did not exist until we took the steps, it is obvious in hindsight. On the other hand, if the Soul comes first, then there is a purpose for the journey! That is, we take the journey so we can fulfill our Life Purpose!

Going back to the footsteps in the sand analogy, there are multiple pathways laid out for us to choose from. Some will help us achieve our Life Purpose; others will have less impact. Nevertheless, we have a choice. For this model, we not only have multiple pathways ahead of us, but we can also look back and assess the ones we have taken, compare them with others, and determine how our choices have helped us accomplish our Life Purpose.

But, we all know pathways aren't quite so obvious most of the time. Even though the decision to take one over the other might be very important in the big picture, it is not always easy to "see" the best pathway, to know what to do, how to do it, or even why it is important. Sometimes, it seems life is just a matter of coincidence, so the choices we make are based on luck. I know. I've had those experiences. However, I now think there are no coincidences. Instead, there are "guides," if and when we are wise enough to pay attention. Through the years, I've come to trust my guides and inner voice. I've learned to follow intuitive pathways.

Intuitive Pathways

Since I've learned to trust myself, I've often chosen pathways based on intuition (or inner voice) rather than logic. Although I use logic to sort out alternatives, when logic cannot distinguish between them, intuition is the better choice. This is because my intuition connects my Reason for Being with my Life Purpose at an unconscious (or even out of conscious) level.[15] When I let my intuition guide me, I've unearthed my capabilities, strengths, and interests. But, most importantly, I've learned what fulfills my life on a day-to-day basis. I've learned more about *the purpose for the journey.*

On the contrary, when I've ignored my 'intuition,' I've also learned important lessons. Frequently, the lessons are about what I *can do*, but don't want to! I've learned there are many things in life I can do well, and others may confirm my abilities, but they are not fulfilling. They do not help me fulfill my Life Purpose. (It is like creating a multicolored pearl).

In any case, life experiences have taught me what is and isn't important in my life work. It is so obvious when I look back! I have learned what I can do (or do not want to do) that will be personally satisfying. I've learned to distinguish pathways that will be fulfilling from those with less promise. I've discovered patterns in the process, and now know it is important to follow my intuition and to make logical decisions. We can only uncover the pattern when we have something for comparison. I had to see both sides of the issue before I could truly know the Essence of my Self and discover my Life Purpose. This discovery has helped me connect with my Soul and better understand my Reason for Being.

<u>Disconnection.</u> The need to be connected with our Soul, find meaning in our life experiences, and understand our Reason for Being is inherent in the human being. This "search" floats to our consciousness and disappears, sometimes forgotten for weeks, months, or even years. Nevertheless, it resurfaces as we go about day-to-day, living, and doing. Our inherent drive exists across time. We cannot extinguish it, but we can deny it. We have multiple opportunities, but, often failing to recognize them as spiritual experiences, we stay disconnected.

Sometimes, these opportunities (for spiritual experiences) come as joyous events and at other times, as tragedies. Sometimes, they are just moments in time when someone asks something, when we make eye contact with another person, or become connected with all that is around us: the beauty of the sky, trees, and flowers. Sometimes we recognize these opportunities for what they are— opportunities to resonate with our Soul. But, often they seem fleeting and therefore insignificant, and so we move on.

And then there are times when we choose to ignore an experience because *the meaning of the experience* is inconsistent with how we think of ourselves. That is, when the implications of some experiences seem to be in conflict with our ego, our sense of who we are, or what we want to be. When this happens, we tend to disconnect or ignore our Self and instead, accept *versions of our self* imposed by others, our sense-of-self. We may deepen our *understanding of how others see us*, but in doing so, we may lose touch with our Self. When we do this, we have trouble defining our Life Purpose.

I now believe our journey starts with our Soul, continues through this lifetime, and culminates when we transform.[16] We need to find meaning in day-to-day events so we can discover our life patterns. When we do this, our Life Purpose presents itself and our Reason for Being is obvious. The following paragraphs describe some of my life experiences and their outcomes. I hope you enjoy my story.

> Life is a journey. There are many pathways to choose from, each with an opportunity for learning. What we do on the journey determines the meaning we derive from the experiences.

Learning to Learn

I grew up in a small mid-western town, in a middle-income family. My parents worked hard to provide a home and teach us important life lessons. I learned hard work pays, goal setting is important, breaking tasks into small parts helps one achieve success, and goal achievement requires staying focused. I also learned about myself as a human being. Although shy as a child, I saw my "real self" emerge when I focused on others. I had something to offer, but first, I had to realize my own worth.

One day, when I was 5 or 6 years old, a girl in my school told me I was "poor" because my mother made my clothes and because we didn't live in town! I didn't understand her, but knew it was deprecating, so I told my mother. She told me, "Don't worry about that. Just know that you are just as good as anyone else, but no better!" She went on to say what we wear and where we live are not nearly as important as how we act and think about ourselves and others. Her advice rings in my ears to this day. It prepared me for nursing.

I first *knew I would be a nurse* when I was about 5 years old. Never questioning the decision, I practiced 'nursing' on my sisters, dolls, and animals during childhood, took necessary courses in high school, and proclaimed I would attend nursing school. While most of my friends talked about getting married or finding jobs, these distractions were not on my mind. If anyone had asked me *why* I wanted to be a nurse, I don't know what I would have said. I just knew.

I loved nursing school;[17] I seemed to find my life purpose. I discovered aspects of myself and my abilities to help people heal in multiple ways. One memory stands out.

I had been in nursing school about 3 months when my instructor decided I needed to learn to provide "total care" for a comatose patient. I was assigned to Mrs. Cook, an elderly lady dying of cancer. During report, I learned Mrs. Cook was non-responsive, moaned continuously, was not taking nourishment, had a catheter, and was expected to die any time. She needed a full bed bath and total care. I asked about her family and was told no one came to see her.

Immediately after report, I went to the treatment room, prepared my "treatment tray" and started toward her room. Halfway down the hall, I could hear her moaning. Entering her room, I called her by name, explained what I was going to do and did it. She moaned the entire time. When I finished, she was still moaning—a sad, lonely sound of grief and agony. Leaving her room, I, too, felt sad. I knew I had given her good physical care, but it seemed so empty. So I went to her, took her hand gently, and stroked it. Once again, I called her name and told her we had the same last name since my maiden name was Cook. I told her I was with her and would be back to see her several times that day. Stroking her forehead and hair, I quietly hummed 'Amazing Grace'. Much to my amazement, she squeezed my hand slightly and stopped moaning.

Throughout the morning, she was very quiet. All the nurses on duty stopped to see if she was okay and always came out of her room surprised that she was still breathing, but quietly and without suffering. The wrinkles were gone from her forehead, and she seemed to be at peace. Later that morning, I went back to check her vitals. When I called her name and told her I was there, she reached for me. I took her hand, and she took one last breath. She looked so peaceful as she passed that it was hard to believe she was the same lady I had seen only a few hours earlier.

That was my first experience with Transformation. (Although we used to call it dying, I now know better.) I had begun to learn the joy of nurturing growth. A simple act of kindness, a simple expression of compassion, and Mrs. Cook was able to move on; she was able to transform. Death was not the issue. Being able to move on with peace and tranquility was *what was* important.

That experience taught me many things about nurturing growth and about myself. I had started to learn that I could learn about previously unknown things! This was an important step in my evolution. However, sometimes the most important things we learn, we don't understand until much later. While we accumulate the "pearls," we don't always see the pattern! Therefore, we ignore new information. Much of what I learned through this experience I stashed away in the back of my mind until much later in life.

Being Nurtured

I met Lance, my husband-to-be, about one year before I finished nursing school. When his parents attended a conference at a nearby city, Lance arranged for me to meet them. I've written elsewhere (Erickson, 1988) about that meeting, so I won't repeat it. It was an experience which altered my way of thinking about learning, about my potential, and myself.

Prior to that meeting, I had been an avid learner of any and all information regarding nursing and medicine. But I had been misguided. I believed that what was written in books, taught and tested in classes, and prescribed in the clinical laboratory was the *right* way to think about people, their health and sickness, and their lives in general. I didn't understand that people live in a *context*, which is the key to understanding their world views.

Seeding[18]

My father-in-law, Milton Erickson, taught me that people live in a context. Subtly, he helped me learn new ways of thinking about human nature, of knowing myself, and of relating to others. More importantly, he helped me learn to fully appreciate the context of a person's life. He said to understand another human being, it is necessary to step into their world, to model their world before trying to plan interventions. All people have social roles, he said, which they wish to fulfill. It is our job, as health professionals, to help them. We do this by nurturing growth and facilitating development. We do it by helping them discover themselves.[19]

He never seemed to "teach" me anything; he simply helped me learn what I was eager to know. I will always be grateful to him for nurturing my curiosity, my need to discover my Self, and become what I had a natural propensity to be. He seeded possibilities and then nurtured my natural tendencies to grow. He was instrumental in my future learning.[20]

Learning to Know

I married Lance; we had children and moved several times. Each step gave me new opportunities to experience life from a different perspective and explore how my values interfaced with my life experiences. By the time I was in my thirties, I had learned my view of nursing was a little different from some of my colleagues. I had *discovered* our role was to facilitate growth and healing in others, not fix or control their physical health.[21] I knew this meant paying attention to how the mind and body worked together, rather than just focusing on the subsystems.[22]

Practicing

During the late 1960s and early 1970s everyone talked about stress. Stress was the big thing! Friedman and Rosenman (1975) had been studying the behavior of persons with coronary heart disease and had concluded that a primary predisposing factor was stress. They defined a pattern of behavior they called Type A Behavior. People who had Type A Behavior were highly stressed and considered high risk for myocardial infarcts. While I totally agreed with this view, I soon decided the key issue for nurses was not whether someone was stressed or not, but how well the person could handle stress.[23]

I also knew understanding one's ability to handle stress was the basis for assisting patients in their Self-care. Furthermore, to understand Self-care, we had to understand the person's view of the world. How they experienced life, what was important to them, what helped them, and what troubled them. For a number of years, I practiced this philosophy as a nurse, mother, friend, and member of society. But, I rarely shared it,[24] never wrote about it, and was unwilling to change it! I knew what I knew, and vowed to be true to what I believed.

Priorities

I had determined that my family was my priority. Although I continued to work part-time as a nurse, nurturing growth in my family seemed to be my purpose. My children needed me to stay focused on them, and to be their mother—to nurture them so they could discover their true nature. My husband also needed support and care; he, too, was building a career and needed a respite from the stress of life.

New Pathways

And then a series of events occurred, which built on previous life experiences and opened new horizons. Another pathway in the sand. At the time they seemed insignificant, but as I look back, I know we have numerous points in our journey where our path intersects with the pathways of others. When this happens, we make decisions about what happens next. Sometimes these choices seem incidental, so we walk parallel pathways until something else changes the course of our journey.

Parallel Pathways

My husband introduced me to a new colleague and his wife. While we had four children at the time, they were newly married and just finishing graduate school. His wife (Mary Ann Swain) had accepted her first professional position in the Research Center at the University of Michigan (U of M) School of Nursing. I was a staff nurse at U of M's Medical Center. She was eager to learn about nursing, and I was willing to share my version. We became fast friends immediately. Soon, Mary Ann an avid learner, began to ask why others didn't share my view of nursing.[25] I told her I believed they retained a medical model of nursing and I didn't support that view.

<u>Resistance to Direction.</u> She repeatedly encouraged me to go back to school, suggesting nursing needed me. I thought this was silly. I *was* nursing, I was at the bedside, I was attending to people, and *they* needed me. I knew nurses I worked with didn't like what I had to say and didn't want me to 'preach' to them. So, I scoffed at her suggestions of returning to school.

<u>Reframing.</u>[26] One day, she said, "If you could only find some way to help nurses think like you, you'd make an important contribution." Never before had I even considered helping nurses think like me! My view of nursing was based on a belief system about people and life—I had always thought of that as a way to feel about life and nursing. Besides, whenever I talked about my views, nurses often seemed puzzled or put out. I had decided the best thing to do was to keep quiet and do my own thing. After all, nursing was between my patients and me, not between my colleagues and me!

Confirmation. Not long after that exchange, a life changing experience at work built on what Mary Ann had said.[27] Discussing this experience with my husband, I described what was wrong with the way a client had been treated, and shared my frustration, anger, sadness, and helplessness. I decided I needed to quit nursing. He confirmed my feelings, reassuring me that such an experience would certainly change how a person thought about life, but insisted that nursing needed me and, furthermore, I probably needed nursing! We concluded that I should go back to school in order to learn to articulate what I knew to be true, how I thought about nursing, and how to practice nursing from my view. This was a big decision. We had four young children, he had just completed his Ph.D., and we were trying desperately to build stability for our children. The decision for me to return to school had many implications for us as a young family. Nevertheless, we both knew it was the "right" one.

Merging Paths

So, I started on a new pathway, expecting a BSN would help me articulate what I knew. It didn't take long to realize the BSN was a way to legitimize what I knew, but it did not give me 'the right' to talk about nursing differently from others! To do this, I needed to have a Master's degree. And so the next decision was made, and with it a new colleague was found.

I had decided, at this point, that a degree in Medical-Surgical (Med-Surg) Nursing was appropriate for me, but U of M organized their graduate programs around medical specialties at that time. I approached the chair of the Med-Surg area, explained my belief system, and asked permission to combine the Med-Surg program with the Psychiatric Nursing program, so I could study the 'whole person'. My request was initially denied. However, after seeking approval from the Chair of the Psychiatric Nursing program, I was granted permission to combine the programs. Naturally, this made me the 'odd duck;' I didn't really fit in either program. The other students were either true Med-Surg students or Psych students! Nearly all of them seemed confused about my need to know about mind-body relations! Only one other Medical-Surgical graduate student, Evelyn Tomlin, understood what I was talking about.

Within a few weeks of our first semester, Evelyn also combined her programs. Now I had three other people who believed in what I was trying to articulate—my husband, Mary Ann Swain, and Evelyn Tomlin. It is amazing what happens when someone else believes in you, encourages you to "follow your bliss" or "think outside the box."

Expanding Horizons

Evelyn and I graduated in 1976. My master's thesis was the first articulation of the APAM model (Erickson, 1976; Erickson & Swain, 1982; Erickson et al., 1983). Mary Ann invited me to participate with her and Susan Steckel in a research study, proposing two models that would be considered as ways of dealing with hypertension. Susan was interested in contracting and I was interested in applying the concepts I had derived from my clinical practice; ideas that were soon labeled as Modeling and Role-Modeling concepts. I requested Evelyn's participation and Mary Ann agreed. A number of us worked closely together, studying the effects of our nursing models on the well-being of our clients. Within a few years, I was being asked to do guest lectures and then keynotes, and to describe my model of nursing. I began to travel within and outside Michigan.

Challenges

In the early 1980's, Evelyn Tomlin was asked to author a chapter in Introduction to Person-Centered Nursing (Lindberg, Hunter, & Kruszewski, 1983) entitled 'Nursing Concepts of Self-Care'. She briefly mentioned Orem and Kinlein[28] and then expanded on what she called Helen Erickson's Concept of Self-Care (pp. 54-57). She provided a preliminary overview to what would later become Modeling and Role-Modeling.

With each invited lecture, I became more uncomfortable with a single question and comment that seemed to end the Question/Answer portion of the presentation: "Where is this written? I want to read more about it!" My discomfort grew; my colleagues were saying they wanted to learn more about this way of thinking! But, I was so busy with work, school, and my family it seemed impossible to take time off to write! Evelyn insisted; it had to be done! She and Mary Ann wanted to help. Now the project seemed less formidable.

Self-care Action

The decision was made. A book would be written. It was time to reach down deep, to explore my reservoir, and put into words what *I* knew to be true about people and nursing. Once the decision was made to start on one more pathway, to speak out, the words simply flowed. Within a few months, a book was written and published. A new theory and paradigm were born; the ideas took on a life of their own.

In the interim, my children were growing and becoming independent. While they still needed me, the demands had changed slightly. My world had expanded. While I still focused on nurturing growth in my family, my family had expanded! Now, nurses and colleagues were included. My Reason for Being seemed to be to nurture growth in others, including my family!

Self-Actualizing

When we wrote, *Modeling and Role-Modeling (MRM): A Theory and Paradigm for Nursing* (1983), we decided some concepts were so important they had to be presented in figure form: Adaptation, Health, Holism, Affiliated-Individuation, Self-care, Nurturance, Facilitation, and Unconditional Acceptance. (Erickson et al., 1983) Articulation of these concepts served as a description of my view of nursing (see Figure 1.2). Relations among them created a theory. Application of the theory created a paradigm. Repeatedly, we stated that a model of the client's worldview is the base for applying these concepts and our job is to nurture growth and facilitate development.

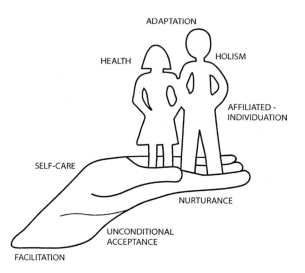

Figure 1.2 Major concepts in MRM theory and paradigm. Reproduced with permission, *Modeling and Role-Modeling: A Nursing Theory and Paradigm,* 1983, EST Co: TX.

Self-Care and Holism

<u>Self-Care.</u> Two concepts presented in MRM were Self-Care and Holism. We argued that Self-care was not the ability to manage activities of daily life, but the ability to take care of oneself in multiple ways–ways that facilitate holistic growth and development. We proposed that people know what they need, but don't always have the *resources* to bring their "knowledge" to conscious awareness or to articulate it. People also don't always have the *resources* to take the *action* necessary to satisfy their needs. While we have an inherent drive toward Self-actualization, we often have difficulty getting in touch with what we know about our Self and exploring what we know, *but aren't aware we know!*

<u>Holism.</u> We also talked about holism as a factor in our ability to connect with our Self. We argued that human beings are holistic with mind, body, and spirit interactions that influence how we think about ourselves and affect our well-being (see Figure 1.3).

> *A person is not just a head and a body, a thinking mind without feelings, or physiological needs...the human is a biophysical, psychosocial, spiritual being...the human is a holistic, multisystem being...When needs are not met within one subsystem (to some significant extent and from the person's perspective), a potential exists for the individual to draw energy from another subsystem...to maintain himself...As a result, individuals have a propensity to become physically sick when experiencing psychosocial stressors or emotionally distressed when experiencing biophysical stressors* (Erickson et al., 1983, p. 55).

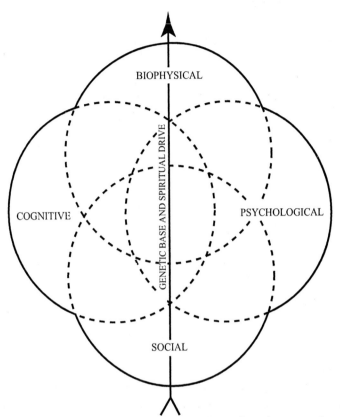

Figure 1.3 Holism as defined in the MRM nursing theory and paradigm. Reproduced with permission, Modeling and Role Modeling: A Nursing Theory and Paradigm, 1983, EST Co: TX.

Self-Knowledge. Throughout our work we indicated Holism and Self-care were intertwined. The body and mind were inseparable; what affects one affects the other. We emphasized an individual's perspective, beliefs, and expectations as the key to understanding biophysical observations. The implications were that an individual's "knowledge" about Self was invaluable in understanding what would help that person grow.

Spiritual Drive. Our figure (see Figure 1.3) depicting Holism showed an inherent spiritual drive permeating all aspects of the human being. This model was purposefully chosen over a model that indicated the spirit was another subsystem of the person, interacting equally with all others. I personally believed our spiritual drive is greater than any of the subsystems (or drives related to them) and has a bigger influence on our total well-being. This view differed from some of the other nursing depictions of holism at that time. I believed it essential we be clear about this difference.[29] I wanted to be certain a model of the holistic person illustrated the difference between the subsystems and the spiritual drive, and showed the spiritual drive expand beyond the confines of the subsystems. It was important to show the spiritual drive drew from the Universe and gave back to the

Universe, and permeated all the subsystems, influencing their processes. At the time, I did not know the importance of this decision, but I did know it had to be! I could not agree with any other model of holism.

Only with time have I been able to see the larger picture. While the entire original book was written to help nurses comprehend the importance of viewing life from another person's perspective, several key decisions were made, helping me discover my own purpose in life. I will address two of these decisions. The first was to specify Aims of Nursing and the second was to write the last chapter, "What Do You Need to Practice Nursing?"

Aims of Nursing

Prior to MRM, nursing theorists talked about Goals of Nursing, but did not differentiate between Aims and Goals of Nursing, perhaps because nurses focused on what we do *to or for* our patients or clients. Some believed the process was more important than the outcome and some believed the outcome was more important. Others agreed the process might well predict the outcome, but couldn't distinguish between the two. Most considered the skills, techniques, and strategies learned in nursing school and polished with experience, the essence of nursing. While I recognized the importance of such knowledge, I thought our *intention*, was more important than our "bag of skills." Our *intention* determines how we interact with our clients, which affects their holistic well-being.

It was very important to me that we clearly express the difference between intent and goals. Goals are specified in respect to what a patient can do within a given time, while intent focuses on our own motivation as we help people meet their goals. Since MRM is about helping people grow, develop, heal, and self-actualize, I believed *the intent had to be connected with the outcome.*

The aims gave us direction for the process—what we needed to think about as we aspired for the outcome. The goals gave us ways to assess our relationship with our client as we worked toward our goals. We specified five aims of nursing: build trust, promote client's positive orientation, promote client's control, affirm and promote client's strengths, and set mutual goals that are health directed (p.170). The relationship between these Intervention Aims, the Principles of MRM, and the Intervention Goals are described in the original book (pp. 160-222).

What was not specified was the relationship between the Aims and finding one's Self. Interestingly, one might argue it was implied! For example, our Aim, *Promote client's positive orientation* was linked to our Intervention Goal, *Facilitate a self-projection that is futuristic and positive.* The related Principle was that *Affiliated-Individuation is contingent on the individual perceiving that he or she is an acceptable, respectable, and worthwhile human being.*

In our discussion on Promoting Positive Orientation (pp.186-195) we discussed issues related to this aim and possible solutions. For example, we suggested nurses might use statements such as "Thank you for being you," "I enjoy our interactions," or "The world is a better place to be in just because you have been here." We went on to state:

The intervention, 'Thank you for being you,' is sometimes followed by the client's asking the question, 'What's so great about me?'...Some answers we have found useful have related to the client's model and strengths. 'Your gentleness makes it a nice world to live in.' 'Your art adds beauty to the world.' 'Your smile brightens my day.' 'Your courage gives me strength.' 'Your love for life is delightful.' 'You are! That makes you special and important to me' (p.187).

We stated our goal was to help people feel they are acceptable, respectable, and worthwhile human beings. We might have added that these are the attributes of a self-actualized person—a person who "dares to listen to himself, his own self..." (Maslow, 1982, p. 46).

Nurturing Growth in Nurses

As the work approached completion, I realized every time I talked about this way of thinking, someone would ask a simple question: "What do I need to do to practice this kind of nursing?" They didn't want to know more about the theory. They wanted to know how to move outside the box. How to think differently. How to grow and have confidence needed to be more of what they want to be. And so, the last chapter in our book was written overnight! I wanted to encourage nurses to have a foundation for understanding themselves and with that foundation search within themselves for answers. We stated:

When we talk about a philosophy and a belief system...we mean an in-depth searching in your heart, mind, and soul of what you really believe...As you work on this task, you will want to remember that you are human and that you will probably change some of your beliefs over time. Perhaps, you won't change the essence of your philosophy, but you may change the way you operationalize it...To hold different views does not mean you devalue yourself for the views you held five years ago. Those changes directly reflect that you, like all other humans, have an innate need to know, to grow and to develop. Rejoice in your development and in what lies ahead (pp. 225-226).

Later we said: "Believe in yourself....You are an essential, valued human being....We believe in you; believe in yourself" (p. 231). It was important to help nurses discover their gift to their clients—their gift of themselves. While their purpose in life may not be to nurture growth in others, many of them had a "calling" to be a nurse and many were drawn to our way of thinking about nursing. They just needed to be nurtured, so they could be more of what they had a natural propensity to Be. Nurturing growth in these nurses was another way for me to fulfill my Reason for Being!

What's In a Name?

When it was time to title the book we'd just written, several ideas were discussed, including "Erickson's Self-Care as presented in Lindberg, Hunter and Kruszewski" (1983). I vetoed all possibilities, except Modeling and Role-Modeling. I wanted to be sure readers remembered the ideas, not the conceivers of the ideas! In my view, it all came down to truly believing that nurses help people uncover their sense-of-self and discover their Essence of Self, a Self that is spiritually-based and has an inherent drive toward Self-actualizing.[30] We do that by stepping into their world, trying to understand the implications,[31] and then facilitate them to fulfill their desired life roles. This helps people fulfill their Life Purpose; and when we fulfill our Life Purpose, we find Meaning.

I had learned as a young nurse that *being with* people helped them connect spirit with body, so they could articulate what they needed in order to grow and heal. I had also learned a spiritual connection gave life meaning, and often, with meaning came healing. The title for our work was determined; it would be "Modeling and Role-Modeling."

Higher Integration

My String of Pearls

My journey over these past 20 some years has led me to believe we have an inherent need (or motivation) to connect our Soul with our biophysical-psychosocial being. This is what our spiritual drive does—it pulls us toward *Integration* of body, mind, and Soul. It draws from the Universe (where all intelligence exists) bringing Universal Energy[32] to our subsystems. *This facilitates our ongoing need to find meaning in our life experiences. It starts before birth and continues throughout the lifespan. I call this spiritual enlightenment.* Spiritual enlightenment helps us uncover our Reason for Being or our Soul-work for this lifetime. When we encounter a conflict between needs, so that satisfaction of one type of need mandates sacrifice of another, there is greater harm done when Soul-related needs are unmet than when biopsychosocial needs are unmet. It is more devastating, in the long run, to lose sight of the Soul than it is to be hungry! I learned this a number of years ago, when I had the privilege of speaking with Viktor Frankl (1984).

A Self-Actualized Man

Viktor Frankl talked about his experiences as a concentration-camp prisoner. Describing the horror of the experience, including the deaths of many of his family, friends, and neighbors, he insisted he did not hold animosity toward those who selected who should die, or toward the executioners. He stated, instead, that these experiences and losses were part of his journey. He did not deny the difficulty of the losses, or the pain and suffering of the journey, and said he had been able to make meaning of the experiences, even as he was having them. He went on to say he "knew" they were a part of his life journey, and they had helped him to fully understand the Meaning of Life.

> *Man's search for meaning is the primary motivation in his life and not a 'secondary rationalization' of instinctual drives. This meaning is unique and specific in that it must and can be fulfilled by him alone; only then does it achieve a significance which will satisfy his own will to meaning...Man...is able to live and even to die for the sake of his ideals and values* (Viktor Frankl, 1984, p. 121).

I have often thought of his attitude and demeanor. We were at a conference where world-famous icons were speaking. There was a crowd of nearly 8000 people. Everyone wanted to hear him talk, catch a glimpse of his face, or just be in the same room as he. Yet, he was untouched by all this attention. Patient, kind, and respectful of questions sent his way, he was also unflappable. Some would challenge him saying they didn't believe anyone could possibly live through such an experience and not have animosity toward those who caused the suffering. He simply responded with a patient discussion about learning to *find meaning in our life experiences, no matter how difficult.*

He had transcended experiences that would have driven many of us to giving up or left us with the strength to do little more than survive. He had not only survived; he had thrived. He had sought meaning from his experience rather than trying to make the experience have a purpose. Because he was able to find meaning in the moment, meaning in the experience, he was able to grow and help us grow. He clearly knew the difference between finding meaning in life and knowing the Meaning of Life.

Frankl's life and life-work are a testimony to possibility. He exemplified Being. I suspect he knew his Reason for Being. He knew how to stay in touch with his Soul-work, and allow others to travel their pathways in their own time. He was a truly Self-Actualized man.

My Life Purpose

As I reflect on my writing and think about numerous life experiences, some reported here, some not, I realize a few concepts repeatedly emerge. First, Nurturance, Facilitation, and Unconditional Acceptance have always been key words in my view of nursing. Over and over, I have made life decisions (sometimes not popular with significant others) based on a simple truth. *It is more important to be than it is to do.* Doing is important, I grant you that! But, being is more important. Key concepts in holistic nursing such as Centering, Empathy, Unconditional Acceptance, Facilitating and Nurturing, Affiliated-Individuation, Mutuality (and others) all require Being. They all require that we think, feel, and act from our spirit, that we are present spiritually as well as physically, emotionally, cognitively, and socially. *Doing without Being is empty, it lacks Presence.* Being can be Doing, because Presence can help people feel cared about, mobilize their resources, and grow. These things can happen without us taking any other actions other than to Be.

> To Be is to emanate spiritual energy; Being is to be spiritually present; to Become is to achieve maximum integration of body, mind, and Soul.

Second, I believe we *need* to be connected with others (or other energy sources) as well as be individuated, that is, we need to experience affiliated-individuation. I don't think we can have affiliated-individuation without Being. Being mandates we stay connected with our Self even as we connect with another. This is a type of transcendence of the physical environment. Transcendence can happen whenever we become fully connected: Self with another, Self with Environment, or Self with a Higher Power.

Reflection on these beliefs and my "string of pearls" has led me to conclude that my Life Purpose is to nurture growth in others. When I first thought about this, it seemed so insignificant I decided an entire life could not be about that. Clearly, there must be something more important, something more profound! However, looking back on my life, revisiting my "string of pearls," attaching meaning to significant experiences and memories, I've concluded that *nurturing growth is tantamount to facilitating self-actualization or finding-of-Self* in others. I have decided this is a worthy purpose for living.

I am satisfied this is my Life Purpose; it is my Soul-work. My Reason for Being is to learn that Unconditional Acceptance of others precedes nurturing growth. With this in my mind, I now understand the Meaning *of* my life.

> When we find meaning in our daily life, we catch a glimmer of our Life Purpose. Frequent "glimmers" help us view the bigger picture and capture the Cosmic View. With this comes an understanding of our Reason for Being. When we are able to capture the Cosmic View and understand the implications, we can make Meaning of our Lives. We know why we are here and what we need to do to continue our Soul-work.

My Gift to You

Discovering one's Reason for Being and Life Purpose does not happen overnight. It comes with years of introspection, years of searching for meaning in experiences sometimes too painful to think about, sometimes too trivial to be important, and at other times, too joyous to have deep meaning. It is a personal, private experience, which happens as you interact with those you love, those you don't like, and those you don't know. It is not a metamorphosis, but more of an unfolding. It happens when you listen to your inner voice and be true to your Self. It doesn't come with a big ah-h-h, but with a gentle seeping of nourishment into your Soul until it awakens with new knowledge.

> As I found meaning in my individual experiences, I was able to view my Life Purpose. As I did this, I was freed to become more completely who I was meant to be, and in doing so, I found my Reason for Being and the Meaning of my Life.

Which Gem Do You Wish to Pass On?

You have read about many ideas in this chapter and will read more in the following chapters. Some ideas you will enjoy and embrace. Others you will put aside. Some you will fully disagree with. This is an important part of the process—learning what is you and what is not. Learning where you interface with others and where you don't. In any and all cases, it is my hope that you discover your Self and come to know the beauty of that discovery. This is my hope for you. My gift to you is this: I know the True You, your Self, is quite remarkable; it has many treasures to be shared with others, and as you discover those gems—those parts of your Self that are you and only you—you will pass them on. Only as you pass them on will they continue to grow. As they grow, they will light the path for others.

> The True You, your *Self*, serves as a glowing light for others as they take their journey.

ENDNOTES

[1] As a young unknowing mother, now fully unsettled, but eager to ensure he didn't need to worry about such things at his age, that he had a whole lifetime ahead of him, I tried to respond to the *reason he gave for asking the question, not the question itself.* I automatically changed the meaning of his question! I told him he had lots of time to decide what to *do* with his life, that he was just a little boy and someday when he was much older, he would know what he wanted to *do*, but first he had to go to school and then college. I assured him he'd know what to do when he finished college, but he didn't need to worry about that now. Although he accepted my response, he seemed a little disappointed. I hadn't given him any new information. I hadn't responded to his question. I'd just reaffirmed he needed to go to college and then assured him he'd know what to do. I didn't tell him that we can't *find* our Self; we have to *discover it!* Nor did I tell him *discovery of Self is a gradual process, one he had already initiated, but one that would take a lifetime.*

He'd asked a question about how to *create a fulfilling life*, and I'd responded that he had to *do things* first, but I didn't tell him that by doing, he would learn about himself. I didn't tell him life is a process of making *choices*, *living experiences* (that result from the choices), *and attributing significance to the experiences.* I didn't tell him *we could only discover our Life Purpose by finding meaning in our life experiences.* He'd asked about finding the Essence of his Self, so he would know how to BE, how to have a fulfilling life— to do his *Soul-work*—and I had reassured him he had to go to college first. No wonder he was disappointed!

At some level, our son understood *life is a journey with optional pathways.* He knew we have to make decisions about which path to take, and that our decisions influence what happens next. My response may have diverted his attention and sent him down an alternative path for a period of time. I may have encouraged him to put aside his yearning to "find his Self." But true to human nature, he, just like everyone else, would revitalize his search as he traveled the pathways of life.

[2] I still believe our biophysical, psychological, cognitive predispositions are genetic.

[3] A natural question to ask when we view life like this is where does the Soul come from? And how does it know it has the right body?

[4] For example, I recently talked with a young acquaintance, who said she was going to her parents' home for the Christmas holidays. Her tone of voice was rather reserved, so I asked her if she looked forward to it. She replied she enjoyed seeing everyone, but it didn't last long, so she didn't look forward to their time together. She then stated her family had never accepted her. They criticized how she looked, acted, thought, and so forth. She said she either had to go into her "shell" or defend herself the entire time.

When I asked her if she had any idea why she had chosen her mother, she was taken aback, and said she never thought she had any choice; she was just born and that was all there was to it. I asked her what would happen if she discovered she had chosen her mother because she needed to help her mother learn something important or she had something important to learn from her mother? What if she was here to help her mother learn to have fun? She immediately teared up, proceeded to tell me how her mother and sister had recently told her they wished they were more like her, that they envied her ability to have fun and be happy.

A few days later she talked about going home for the holidays, and taking a new game with her. She said she planned on staying for three days and just having fun. She said she had decided maybe she was here to help her mother, and all these years she had thought her mother was supposed to be here to help her! I suggested maybe it was a bit of both, and that left the door open for many possibilities.

[5] See Chapter 2. Soul energy vibrates at a level too high for it to connect with the human body, therefore, some of it needs to separate into energy that vibrates at a lower level. This is Spiritual energy.

[6] See Chapter 5, Developmental Process, for a discussion about Transformation, the final stage of human development in a given lifetime.

[7] Too often our reality is about doing and thinking what others say is okay or is important! Reality, usually, does not mean thinking outside the box. It means thinking, talking, and acting within the norms of society, as others would want us to be, or as others will accept us.

[8] If this is a new word for you, I recommend you visit the original MRM book and read the sections discussing affiliated-individuation. Then, read Chapters 6 and 7 in this book.

[9] When we have fulfilling experiences in our lives, we energize our spirit, transcend the human body, and connect with our Soul. Transcending is a dynamic, ongoing, ebb and flow of energy, with high and low points of understanding. It happens over a few seconds or minutes in time. It does not last long, but when it happens, it helps us understand our Self in new ways. We are able to connect with our Self, to experience Self-actualizing.

[10] *Keep in mind a social network is not the same as a social support system!* (Erickson et al., 1983, pp. 125-132).

[11] When I reviewed words in the Random House Dictionary that started with self (e.g., self-abasement), I was astounded to discover there are several pages of such words, but self-actualized was not one of them! There were many that could be construed to be a compliment, such as self-taught, self-starter, but the majority of the 'self' words had a pejorative meaning, e.g., self-serving, self-conceit, self-centered.

[12] I'm referring to developmental residual. If you are new to this theory, you might want to review pp. 54-70, 86-92 in the original book, and then read Chapter 5 in this book

[13] My daughter exhibited an interesting behavior a number of years ago that demonstrated her willingness to 'sometimes' listen to her inner voice. Her brother came home from a great day rollicking in the river near his home. He had left his car at the river, because he had lost his keys. He said he'd looked and looked, but simply couldn't find them. He also commented that everyone else there at the time had helped him, but he thought they were gone. His sister suggested going back with him and helping him search; he said there was no point, but he would appreciate a ride back to get his car. We drove to the site. She immediately got out of the car, walked into the river, waded past her waist, bent down, and picked up the keys! We stood there with our mouths open! I

had barely gotten out of the car. When asked how she knew where they were, she simply said, "My inner voice told me!"

[14]My Father-in-law, Milton Erickson, taught me to attend to my Reservoir! He taught me ways to listen to my inner voice, to connect with my Self, and to enjoy my knowing.

[15]The idea of an unconscious level suggests that our understanding is buried somewhere in the brain or body, while the out of conscious notion implies understanding may be at a spiritual level.

[16] Transformation is described in Chapter 5, Developmental Processes.

[17] I went to Saginaw General Hospital School of Nursing, a training program. We started our clinical rotations 6 weeks after school started.

[18] This is an important technique used to help people learn about themselves. It is discussed in Chapters 10-12.

[19] This is the essence of Modeling and Role-Modeling, first told to me by Milton Erickson, MD, in the early 1960's.

[20] While Dad, i.e., Milton Erickson, was instrumental in my learning about hypnosis and myself, Mom, i.e., Elizabeth Erickson was instrumental in my learning about Unconditional Acceptance. Her ability to find good in everyone and to accept people as they are sets a standard I have always tried to meet. I will always be grateful to her for her open arms and unconditional acceptance of me

[21] Keep in mind, in hindsight, I learned this in part from Milton Erickson, but remember he didn't really teach. He facilitated learning and as a result, only with hindsight was I aware of the source of my learning! So, I had many discoveries. I will never know how many of them were initiated by my father-in-law. Perhaps, none of them; perhaps, all of them. At the least, I know he 'turned on my learning engine' and from there I took off!

[22] I had also learned that colleagues didn't always want to hear what I thought, so I kept my insights to myself.

[23] Later this led to my work on the APAM and the first study in 1976.

[24] You have to remember in those days, a practitioner who thought out of the box was considered a radical and was often ostracized by coworkers. I have written about these experiences in Lynn Keegan's book on Nurse Healers (1998).

[25] Keep in mind Mary Ann was interacting with faculty and graduate students at this time and I was a diploma prepared nurse providing bedside care.

[26] In essence, reframing is a communication technique in which we help someone think about something from a different perspective. It is discussed in more detail in Chapters 10-12.

[27] We had a D.O. admitted to our unit for diagnosis of stomach pain. He soon learned he had cancer. He was told he had to have a gastrectomy and bowel resection. The night before surgery he told me he wished he had known what he had before he came to the hospital. He said he would never have allowed it to go this far. He didn't want his wife and son to see him sick and suffering. He thought it would have been better to have 'just lived until I couldn't any more.' After surgery he did poorly, infected and had to have debridment surgery. But he didn't recover; the doctors told him he needed to have a colostomy. He wouldn't sign for surgery, so the doctors coerced his wife to do it.

After that surgery, he again infected and had to go back for one more surgery. Neither his wife nor he would sign, so the doctors cornered his son and told him he would be responsible for his father's death if he didn't sign. So he did, tears running down his face, hands shaking, and totally distraught. A few days later the patient was comatose, gurgling from lung infection, terminal. The doctors wanted to do a tracheotomy. The wife and son refused to sign the permission paper. The doctors came out to the workstation and talked it over. They decided they could insert a temporary breathing tube to suction him, knowing he would have difficulty when they withdrew it. This would create an emergency, giving them permission to do a tracheotomy with signed permission. Throughout this patient's admission, I had tried to discuss the ethical and humanistic issues with the doctors. They would have nothing to do with it. I lacked the language and scientific research to be able to communicate appropriately. By the time the discussion regarding the tracheotomy emerged, I was fed up and told them that. I will always remember their response—they laughed! The next evening when I came to work, I found my patient with a tracheotomy and his family in despair. His last few days were miserable; his family had been traumatized in ways we will never fully know. I felt a complete failure. I had not been able to comfort my patient or his family, and I had not been able to communicate what I knew to be 'true' to those who had the power —to let nature take its course.

[28] Orem (1959; 1971) presented the concept of self-care to nursing as early as 1959, but didn't widely distribute her ideas until 1971. Kinlein (a former student of Orem) followed in the mid seventies (Kinlein, 1977). These authors presented ways of thinking about my earlier (but unpublished) orientation to nursing. Orem talked about self-care from a nurse's perspective, including activities of daily life, need assets and need deficits (all accessed within the context of the nurse's view of the sick client's world). Kinlein, on the other hand, talked about those who were healthy and reached out for nursing assistance. She argued that client's could verbalize what they wanted as she attended to their expression of needs. Neither of these seemed to be fully consistent with what I had decided about nursing. For example, Orem had mentioned needs as a basis for nursing practice, but then went on to discuss nursing care as though the mind and body had nothing to do with one another! Kinlein implied mind-body relations, but didn't bring in the holistic possibilities. She emphasized that what nurses attend to must come from the client, but didn't mention how this interfaced with medicine or other nurses. As the first modern day private practicing nurse in the United States, she focused on problems healthy persons brought to her attention, not mind-body relations, understanding of the past and predictions for the future, or how we needed to work together as a health care team.

[29] As I write this chapter, I realize this was one of *those choices* made as we continue our journey— a choice that prepared the way for today's writing. I also realize this choice and many others like it were made because I had learned to trust my Inner voice.

[30] According to Maslow, Self-Actualizing (or Being) is the process we use to become Self-Actualized. He describes Self-Actualization as "...experiencing fully, vividly, selflessly, with full concentrating and total absorption.... At this moment of experiencing, the person is wholly and fully human. This is a self-actualizing moment...Self-actualization is an ongoing process....It implies that there is a Self to be actualized (Maslow, 1982, p. 45).

[31] Another publication that might help you better understand this view was published in 1990: Erickson, H. (1990). Theory Based Practice. In Modeling and Role-Modeling: Theory, Practice and Research; Vol. 1, No. 1, pp.1-27.

[32] We will discuss this further in Chapters 2 and 3.

CHAPTER 2

ENERGY THEORIES:
MODELING AND ROLE-MODELING

MARY BREKKE AND ELLEN D. SCHULTZ

A human being is a part of the whole, called by us the Universe, a part limited in time and space. He experiences himself, his thoughts and feelings as something separated from the rest- a kind of optical delusion of his consciousness. This delusion is a kind of prison for us, restricting us to our personal desires and to affection for a few persons nearest to us. Our task must be to free ourselves from this prison by widening our circles of compassion to embrace all living creatures and the whole of nature in its beauty. Nobody is able to achieve this completely, but the striving for such achievement is in itself a part of the liberation and of a foundation for inner security. —Albert Einstein, *N.Y. Post*, November 28, 1972.

OVERVIEW

When nursing students, introduced to Modeling and Role-Modeling say, "I really *resonate* with this theory!" what do they really mean? Do they mean the philosophy behind the theory is consistent with their way of thinking? Do they mean they are attracted to the concepts in the theory? Or, do they mean they *feel* the theory? Does some part of the model interface with something in them that seems to "strike a bell"? That is, does something about the model "echo" the way these students think and feel? And, if so, does this "echo" (in one subsystem) cause subtle, but recognizable changes in other subsystems? And does this then change their way of thinking, feeling, and relating? Perhaps people who *resonate* with concepts experience an energy shift somewhere in their body-mind-spirit— an energy shift that affects the whole being.

When nurses seek to fully understand their clients' model of the world are they attempting to match the vibratory level of the client? What do they mean when they say that they are trying to "get on the same wave length" with their clients? According to Gerber (1988), during the process of resonance, electrons move to a new vibration in order to be consistent with energy fields surrounding them. Expressions such as, "I really resonate with that theory" and "We're on the same wave length" are used in daily conversations. Perhaps they indicate we not only *experience energy* and *changes in energy levels*, we also possess an "inner knowing" (not always consciously identified or articulated), which changes how we experience our lives. How exciting it would be if we were able to consciously, proactively use these ideas to make differences in our lives as well as the lives of those with whom we live and work!

Energy concepts are implied in the Modeling and Role-Modeling theory and paradigm (Erickson, Tomlin & Swain, 1983), but never fully explicated. The authors suggest positive interpersonal relationships can enhance one's energy level while negative ones have the potential to deplete energy. They use the words "invigorating" and "draining" (p. 160) and encourage nurses to assess the client's perceived relationships with others to determine if they "restore or diminish resources" (p. 161). Their assumption that energy is related to Self-care is threaded throughout the work. For example, they state:

> *...Sometimes the client will deplete energy stores trying to maintain a support system when instead he or she should be acquiring, building, and storing energy by interacting with the support system. An impoverished person does not have the energy to invest in maintaining others without further depleting his or her own internal resources* (pp. 125-126).

> *...Projection into the future, for some, can be overwhelming, especially if they feel that all interactions tax them, rather than energize them* (p. 189).

Not only do Erickson et al. (1983) indicate energy is inherent in relationships between or among people, they also imply energy is related to the internal, holistic interactions of the mind, body, and spirit. In the introduction to the original book, they discuss their hope for the reader and state, "We hope...that you will *find our ideas stimulating, challenging and energizing"* (p. 2*)*. Later, when discussing holism, they state:

> *...A person is not just a head and a body, a thinking mind without feelings or physiological needs...the human is a biophysical, psychosocial, and spiritual being....This...encompasses the belief that the human is a holistic, multisystem being....When needs are not met within one subsystem (to some significant extent, and from the person's perspective), a potential exists for the individual to draw energy from another subsystem in order to maintain himself or herself* (p. 55).

While this work suggests energy levels determine one's ability to cope, grow, heal, and develop, the authors did not define what they meant by the word *energy,* nor did they describe how energy concepts relate to the Modeling and Role-Modeling theory or paradigm.

This chapter helps clarify some of these issues. We start by briefly describing what we mean by energy, energy fields, and some related concepts common to nursing. We then extend our discussion to include Modeling and Role-Modeling concepts and how they relate to energy theories. We hope you enjoy exploring our ideas and find ways to incorporate some of them into your daily lives.

ENERGY THEORIES

Nurses often talk about *energy fields.* They are probably talking about electromagnetic or bioelectric fields. While theories about both are important, they are far too complex to present in detail. Instead, we offer a basic discussion sufficient to introduce the ideas. We invite the reader to further explore the areas of Newtonian and Quantum physics for details and offer a range of references in the bibliography for this purpose.

What is Energy?

Simply stated, energy is the capacity to do "work," and "work" occurs when something changes. According to Sarter (2002),

> *Energy is the capacity to create change. Whenever there is change, or the potential for change, there is energy. By this definition, energy is not only a physical phenomenon. It is also the foundation of the emotional, mental, social and spiritual spheres* (p.1).

Energy is categorized as either potential or kinetic. Potential energy is stored, such as energy in batteries or food. Kinetic energy is moving, such as light derived from a flashlight, sound from a drumbeat, and so forth. Energy can be found in numerous forms such as chemical, electrical, thermal, light, mechanical, and nuclear. While it cannot be created or destroyed, it can be transformed from one type to another. For example, toasters change electrical energy into light and heat energy; televisions change electrical energy into light and sound energy; our body changes chemical energy (food we eat) into electrical energy (energy derived from the creb cycle), mechanical energy (lifting your arm), and so forth.

Energy, as the capacity to do work and create change, is constantly evolving and, although unpredictable, *has a tendency toward order* (Greene, 2003).

> *One overarching lesson we have learned during the past hundred years is... the known laws of physics are associated with principles of symmetry* (Greene, 2003, p. 374).

Four Forces

There are four known[1] types of forces that create energy: electromagnetic, nuclear, weak, and gravitational. Electromagnetic forces occur between electric charges such as movement between electrons and protons. Nuclear forces occur between subatomic particles, that is, particles within the protons and neutrons. Weak forces arise from radioactive decay, and Gravitational forces occur between masses.

Each is important to understand. However, when talking about energy, nurses rarely talk about weak forces or gravitational forces although gravitational forces are part of everyday nursing! Instead, they often use terminology such as energy exchange, energy fields, or universal energy. This is because we have not applied energy theories to everyday nursing. While we teach nurses to read EKGs (electromagnetic forces), be careful with patients receiving radioactive medications (nuclear forces), and lift properly (gravitational forces), nursing students are not usually introduced to the basic theories of energy as a way of[2] *thinking about nursing.*

This chapter is not intended to alleviate this problem, but we do hope to offer some insight on how energy concepts relate to nursing in general and, more specifically, the Modeling and Role-Modeling theory and paradigm. We will start with a discussion about three ways of thinking about energy and then discuss transformation of energy. We recognize these do not match the four known forces one-on-one. Nevertheless, our discussion extrapolates information and applies it in the areas most relevant for health care providers:

1) Electromagnetic energy;
2) Quantum energy (subatomic particles); and
3) Subtle bioenergy.

Types of Energy

Electromagnetic Energy

Matter is made up of atoms and atoms are made of particles called protons, neutrons, and electrons. Protons have a positive charge, neutrons a neutral charge and electrons a negative charge. When there is an imbalance in the number of protons and electrons, the positive charges attract the negative, moving toward a balance. The movement of the electron (negative charge) to the proton (positive charge) creates a *current of electricity.*

Electrical currents move more easily through some matter than other. When movement is facilitated, the power is increased; when there is resistance, the power is decreased. Metals such as copper and aluminum are known to be good conductors of electricity, increasing power, while rubber, plastic, cloth, and dry air are known to resist the movement of electrons from one atom to another, thus decreasing the power (*Energy story*, 2002).

Electric fields are created by the build up of positive and negative electric charges—the greater the build up, the stronger the electric field. As the electric field increases, the potential for movement increases. Since all matter is made up of atomic particles (neutrons, protons, and electrons) that attract and repel one another, electric fields are created wherever there is matter.

Magnetic fields are produced when the electric current flows—the greater the flow, the stronger the magnetic field. Since electric fields are created where there is matter, and a magnetic field is created when the electric current flows, there are electromagnetic fields (EMF) inside and outside our bodies, in the environment, and in the universe.

The earth has a magnetic field (called a *geomagnetic field*), which is thought to be created, in part, by the convection of molten iron and nickel within the earth's core, coupled with the earth's rotation. The strength of this geomagnetic field varies depending on its interface with other electromagnetic fields such as those created by lightning strikes around the world[3] (Oschman, 1997, p 185) and electromagnetic pollution caused by computers, color TVs, microwave ovens, and other man-made machines that create electric fields (Gerber, 2001, p. 41).

The earth's geomagnetic field can pass through walls and, therefore, interface with those created by our body and immediate environment. While World Health Organization studies (2005) have indicated geomagnetic fields from the environment are not harmful, further study is needed to determine their true effect on our health and well-being.

> The geomagnetic field is reinforced by electrical currents, which exist in the earth's outer core. It is currently believed that deep within the Earth's inner core there are two magnetic poles with opposite charges, one more or less opposite the other—one more or less directly north and one directly south. The two fields (the electrical currents in the earth's outer core and the magnetic field in the earth's inner-core) merge creating a self-sustaining geomagnetic field that extends tens of thousands of kilometers into space as the magnetosphere.

Quantum Energy[4]

While we used to think protons, neutrons, and electrons were the smallest atomic particles, we now know better! The theory of quantum physics holds that protons and neutrons *are each made up of* very small particles called quarks. They are held together by even smaller particles called gluons, which collect together to make glueballs! They are so small we cannot observe them directly—they are subatomic particles.

A subatomic particle is a "quantum," which means a quantity of something. Precisely what these particles, these quanta, consist of is a matter of speculation. Quantum mechanics views subatomic particles as "tendencies to exist" or "tendencies to happen." (Gribben, 1995). How strong these tendencies are is expressed in terms of probabilities. These subatomic particles are very resourceful and can manifest as a particle or a wave.[5] *Since at the subatomic level mass and energy change unceasingly into each other*, these particles can manifest as mass or energy. Particle physicists are so familiar with the phenomenon of mass becoming energy and energy becoming mass, they routinely measure the mass of particles in energy units.

> *If we could examine these particles with even greater precision—a precision many orders of magnitude beyond our present technological capacity—we would find that each is not point like, but instead consists of a tiny one dimensional loop. Like an infinitely thin rubber band, each particle contains a vibrating, oscillating, dancing filament that physicists...have named a string* (Greene, 2003, p. 14).

Subtle Bioenergy
Western science typically talks about energy in terms of force, fields, or as metabolic and/or bioelectrical energy (Gerber, 2001, p. 22). However, traditional healing systems define energy in a different way. Although both Western science and traditional healing systems talk about transmission of forces, those involved with energy *as a way of healing* also talk about *characteristics of consciousness* such as "nonlocality" (Dossey, L. 1993, pp. 84-87; Gerber, 2001, pp. 382-383; Jonas, 2002, p. 198) and subtle energy (Gerber, 2001, pp. 22-36). Pert (2003), also talks about subtle energy. She argues that "energy" is nothing more than the "free flow of information" and says,

> *What is this energy that is referred to by so many alternative healers who associate it with the release of emotion and the restoration of health?...It is my belief that this mysterious energy is actually the free flow of information carried by the biochemicals of emotion, the neuropeptides and their receptors* (p. 276).

This view seems to ignore the fact that the interaction between neuropeptides and their receptors might be facilitated or impeded by the flow of energy.[6]

> Subtle energy may be the spiritual-energy of the holistic human being.

Gerber (2001) discussed known energy systems and the significance of subtle energy in health care. He states:

> *The neuroelectrical and biochemical energy systems of the body are fairly well established in scientific circles and in time, the bioelectrical and biophotonic or light-based, energy systems of the body will be validated by further scientific research. Most conventional medical practitioners acknowledge at least some of these energy systems. Perhaps certain doctors will be comfortable accepting these specific energy systems as components of a new vibrational-energy systems involving the*

flow of specific types of energy that have not yet been accepted by conventional or 'scientific' medicine. These other types of energy systems are perhaps even more critical to life than the afore mentioned energies, yet they still lack 'official' recognition by most Western physicians. These other energy systems we have been referring to are the important life-energy and spiritual-energy systems of the multidimensional human being. Much of our knowledge of such 'unconventional' energy systems, sometimes referred to as 'subtle-energy' systems, comes from the sacred and spiritual knowledge of the Far East and India (p. 16).

Trivieri (2001) argues that the multiple perspectives of energy serve as a basis for a wide range of therapies utilizing energy concepts. According to him,

...subtle bioenergetic techniques and the use of both conventional and experimental microcurrent and magnetic energy devices...may become one of the most important aspects of holistic medicine in the twenty-first century due to its ability to diagnose and treat disease in the human bioenergy field, often before it manifests physically in the body (p. 288-289).

Universal Life Force. Ancient cultures believed there was an energetic "life force" (Bruyere, 1989) or a "life energy" (Gupta, 2001) that came from the Universe, was necessary for human life, and returned to the Universe upon physical death.

Qi produces the human body just as water becomes ice. As water freezes into ice, so qi coagulates to form the human body. When ice melts, it becomes water. When a person dies, he or she becomes spirit (shen) again. It is called spirit, just as melted ice changes its name to water (Wang Chong, AD 27-97).

Many believed that two opposite ends of the spectrum—yin, the energy of earth, and yang, the energy of heaven—combined in humans to create this vital force. There were various names for this "life force." It was known as Mana in Polynesia; Prana in India; Ki in Japan; Chi, Chee or Qi in China; Ruach in Hebrew and Barraka in Islamic countries. Despite the difference in terms used among these cultures, they shared a common belief: "...one thing underlies existence...there is a vital energy (or force) unique to and inherent in things..." (Todaro-Franceschi, 1999, p. 14). Some call this *subtle* energy (Eden & Feinstein 1998; Gerber, 2001).[7] Gerber stated we are energy first and subtle energy is an expression of the Soul. Pert (2003), describes it like this:

In a very real sense, our soul, our 'true self,' expresses itself through a physical body that is subtly influenced and molded by these various spiritual bodies. Each of our spiritual bodies is formed from vibrating life-energy fields of progressively higher and finer levels of energy and matter. The first of these higher spiritual bodies, known as the etheric body, is actually a highly structured energy field that is invisible to the naked eye...It provides a unique form of energetic information to the cells of the body that helps to guide human growth and development (p. 23).

Since there was so much confusion among the experts about the different kinds of energy, L. Dossey and others convened the Samueli Conference on Definitions and Standards in Healing Research. Their goal was to reach a level of consistency in the way concepts are defined in healing research. They concurred that bioenergy is a "Force or influence believed or hypothesized to flow through and off living systems" (Dossey, 2002, p. A10) Today, many, building on these beliefs, practice therapies such as Reiki, Therapeutic Touch, Acupuncture, tai chi, qi gong, yoga, sound therapies, and body work such as massage and rolfing.

Transformation of Energy

Transformation of energy can be thought of in two ways: a simplistic exchange of energy from one form to another (such as chemical, electrical, thermal or mechanical energy transformation), or energy as information. The first, transformation of energy, is easy to understand. It happens all the time. For example, we know we can mix two chemicals together and they will generate heat (chemical to thermal). We also know our body sends electrical messages to our muscular-skeletal system and from those messages our muscles contract.

A slightly more difficult concept to understand is transformation of energy into information. Gerber (2001) described it as follows:

Our cells communicate through coded messages carried by hormones and biochemicals, as well as through electrical signals (such as those carried by the nerves of the body) and also through weak light signals. The cells of the body appear to have their own inherent intelligence that allows them to understand and use this coded information in its many forms in order to maintain the body in a state of health (p. 11).

Energy can be transformed and stored as information.

Pert (2003), when describing the function of receptor sites in our body and how those serve as receivers of information, stated:

Basically, receptors function as sensing molecules—scanners. Just as our eyes, ears, nose, tongue, fingers, and skin act as sense organs, so, too, do the receptors, only on a cellular level. They hover in the membranes of your cells, dancing and vibrating, waiting to pick up messages carried by other vibrating little creatures...which come cruising along—diffusing is the technical word— through the fluids surrounding each cell. We like to describe these receptors as 'keyholes,' although that is not an altogether precise term for something that is constantly moving, dancing in a rhythmic, vibratory way (p.23).

Oschman (2003) asserted that all chemical communication in the body and all physiological processes in the body-mind have an electrical counterpart or component. Pert (2003) calls this the body's information system or the body-mind. Others (Chopra, 1990; Gerber, 2001; Rossi, 1986) using similar terminology, agree with the concept that the body is informed on how to function through exchanges of chemical and electrical energy. *Energy as information is the basis of mind-body-spirit relations. It is the basis of holism.*

Cellular Memory

A related aspect of energy transformation occurs when chemical molecules stored after a specific life experience are later excreted during similar life experiences, flooding the body with chemicals that create feelings similar to those experienced during the first life event. This is called *cellular memory* (Pearsall, 1998). This type of stored energy provides information about the "memories" and is an ongoing, dynamic process that provides insight into mind-body relations. Mind-body relations and cellular memory are further discussed in Chapters 3 and 4 in this book.

SIGNIFICANCE OF TRANSFORMATION OF ENERGY

In the preceding paragraphs we talked about three types of energy: electromagnetic, quantum, and subtle bioenergy. We also discussed the possibility that energy can be transformed from one type to another. The significance of such an idea can alter the way we look at the world. In the first chapter, Erickson posed the question, "Which comes first, body or Soul?" She indicated the Soul is an energy field that connects with the energy field of the body. In this Chapter we pose another question, "What if the body was an energy field *before it took the form of matter?*" Einstein's theory of Relativity has demonstrated that energy and matter interact, so that energy can become matter and matter can become energy. We support this view. *So, what if we are energy before we are matter?*

We Are Energy First

Gerber (1988) described research undertaken to validate the existence of energy points in rabbits, salamanders, frogs, and chick embryos, stating that embryonic chick meridian ducts were formed within 15 hours of conception, well before the formation of rudimentary organ structures. Some say all things start as energy first—that our existence comes from energy, which dictates how our cells grow, and from the energy comes matter (Bruyere, 1994; Chopra, 1990; Emoto, 2004; Gerber, 2001; Pert, 2003; Hunt, 1995.) Research with the "Kirlian phantom-leaf-effect" has demonstrated that the energy field of leaves (taken from trees) remains even after half the leaf is amputated (Gerber, 2001, p. 26). This idea of energy first is quite intriguing when you think of the implications. Energy before matter suggests there is something to us before we become biophysical-psychosocial beings!

> *The genes create structures, but the genes do not control them; the vital force directs them* (Claude Bernard, 1839).

But, if we are energy first, where does it come from? Many from the healing professions have argued that there is Universal Energy (Chopra, 1990; Dyer, 1989, Grayson, 1997) or a Life Force (Gordon, 2002). Gerber (2001) calls it "life energy" or "spiritual energy" (p16-17).

Unified Field

Another way of thinking about a common source of energy is derived from those who argue for a Unified Field of Energy that reconciles the four types of energy forces, bringing them together in a common space where they simply transform (or change) into one of the four forces. Einstein first proposed this idea, but was unable to provide evidence. Nevertheless, many have continued to pursue the idea. Greene (2003) stated, "Einstein was simply ahead of his time. More than half a century later, his dream of a unified theory has become the Holy Grail of modern physics" (p. 15).

Some argue that the solution to this question of a Unified Field lies in a better understanding of the Zero Point Field. McTaggart (2002) describes it like this:

> *The Zero Point Field is a repository of all fields and all ground energy states and all virtual particles—a field of fields. Every exchange of every virtual particle radiates energy. The zero-point energy in any one particular transaction in an electromagnetic field is unimaginably tiny— a photon's worth* (p. 23).

It is called the Zero Point Field because fluctuations are still detectable in the lowest possible energy state, absolute zero. Within the Zero Point Field, all matter in the universe (including humans) is interconnected by waves, spread out through space and times. "This energy exchange is so constant and so indispensable for all living organisms that it can be regarded as a universal field effect" (Karagulla & Kunz, 1989, p. 12). Quantum fields are mediated by exchange of energy, an intrinsic property of particles. This energy is redistributed in a "dynamic pattern." Anderson (2005) posed a theory that mass comes from the interaction of matter with the quantum vacuum that pervades the universe—the Zero Point Field.

> Is it possible Zero Point Energy exists?

While this theory is not widely accepted by physicists, Haisch, Rueda and Puthoff have published several papers advocating for the Zero Point Field (1994, 1994, 1997) Arthur Clarke, famous for his science fiction books on space, wrote about the zero point field in the acknowledgements of his recent work, *3001: The Final Odyssey* (1997). According to him, the work of Haisch, Rueda, and Puthoff would one day be regarded as a landmark. To quote:

> *It addresses a problem so fundamental that it is normally taken for granted...the question asked is: 'What gives an object mass (or inertia) so that it requires an effort to start moving, and exactly the same effort to restore it to its original state? Their provisional answer depends on the astonishing...little known fact that so called empty space is actually a cauldron of seething energies—the Zero Point Field...(They) suggest that both inertia and gravitation are electromagnetic phenomena resulting from interaction with this field* (p. 255-257).

The implications of such a theory are nearly boundless. At the least, it supports the notion that we might be energy first, that there could be a Universal Force not yet scientifically identified, but nevertheless, a fifth force that would unify the other four described above.

Implications

We know from physicists that self-organizing fields are the substance of the universe. We briefly discussed this issue above when we talked about the electromagnetic and geomagnetic fields. Some animals have acute bioelectric sensors that are highly sensitive to magnetic fields. These capabilities help them find their way around the world. For example, migratory birds follow common flight patterns, which they navigate based on the earth's magnetic field (Sheldrake, 1999). Whales do the same thing. So do salmon and other animals. Dogs are able to sense when their masters plan to return home (Sheldrake, 1999). The list goes on and on. We repeatedly see self-organizing abilities in animals that are thought to be due to electromagnetic and geomagnetic fields. Why would we think animals have these capabilities, but not humans? We think we are just beginning to understand the implications of energy theories to the well-being of human beings. As this field of knowledge grows, nurses will be better able to apply the theories to their practice. Currently we talk about concepts such as Presence, Intentionality, Unconditional Acceptance, and Holism. All of these are energy-based. Some of these will be discussed below as we talk about the Caring Field.

Implications of a Unified Energy Field are endless. It implies we are all connected, one with another, perhaps by a Universal force.

Bache (2000) described 'learning fields' that develop under certain conditions and accelerate learning. Physiologists talk about biorhythms, chronobiology, and other natural rhythmic cycles found within the human being. Others, such as Russek and Schwartz (1996), described how the cardiovascular system communicates throughout the body using energy messages. Clearly, energy fields can be discussed from the very small to the grandiose and within the context of all animals, including human beings. For example, energy fields are created with the electronic action within and between atoms, molecules, human organs and organ systems; between people, and among groups of people; in the environment with plants, animals, and everything else in the environment made of matter, which includes the earth and universe. There are energy fields everywhere! Since nurses, nursing students, clients, families, and others we live and work with are all humans, these theories apply to us in our professional and personal lives.

We have our energy fields and we join those of others. We create systems when we do that. That is, multiple fields create systems. We live in energy systems; we create them, draw from them, and contribute to them. Some systems are more powerful than others; some are natural and some man-made. Probably the one that affects people the most is the earth's geomagnetic field. But, then, let's not forget the smaller systems—such as the human energy fields that create a system.

Perhaps, most important of all is the idea that there is a Unified Field of Energy, the source of all energy and from which we can draw. It contains a Universal Force which some would describe as subtle energy and others as zero-point energy. It is in us, around us, in the universal space, and everywhere.

We hope to show you how Modeling and Role-Modeling uses many of these ideas. But, first, we will discuss concepts important to nursing at large. That is, we think these ideas and ways of thinking about energy theories are applicable to the practice of nursing in general. We cannot address all possibilities. Instead, we will focus on the human energy system and then discuss the nurse's caring field and the healing field as they relate to the human energy system.

APPLYING ENERGY FIELDS TO NURSING

The Human Energy System

The human energy system has been understood as consisting of three primary energetic structures that interact with one another: *meridians, chakras,* and *aura*. As our knowledge increases, additional energetic structures are being identified. According to Oschman (2000),

There is no single 'life force' or 'healing energy'. Instead there are many systems in the body that conduct various kinds of energy and information from place to place. Different energetic therapies focus on different

aspects of this multiplicity, and each of these therapies presents a valuable set of clues and testable hypotheses about how human energy systems work (p.2).

Eden (1998) described the individual as "...a constellation of energy systems" (p. 95). The energy consists of vibrations that are in constant exchange with the environment. The individual can also be described as a system of "interdependent force fields" (Karagulla & Kunz, 1989, p. 26) characterized by patterns that are responsive to changes in consciousness.

Our discussion covers the most commonly accepted energy system. We start with the meridians—energy pathways that connect the parts of the body with each other and with the universe. We then move to the chakras—vortices within the body where meridians intersect, and end with a discussion of the aura—the energy field that surrounds the body. While these three—the meridians, chakras, and the aura are all part of the human energy field, we describe them here as a system because their structure and function are interdependent. For example, the meridians and chakras deliver energy to the organs of the body as well as energize the field surrounding the body. The energy system responds to various types of feedback from the body including biochemical, emotional, and cognitive.

Meridians

Are they real? Meridians, first described by the Ancient Chinese, are *energy pathways* that run throughout the body, connect all parts of the body with each other, and connect the body with the universe. *It is believed subtle energy* moves along these pathways; it is of low intensity and moves fast—perhaps as fast as the speed of light. Just as gases cannot be seen in the air we breathe, the subtle energy cannot be seen upon direct inspection. Because scientists lack technology to measure subtle energy directly, some argue it doesn't exist (Napier, 2004). Others argue that it does exist; we just need more sophisticated technology to be able to study it (Benor, 2001, 2005). Since we cannot see or measure subtle energy directly, some argue there is no such thing as meridians. We disagree with this position. We accept the arguments and research findings that support the presence and movement of energy along pathways throughout the body, body to universe, and universe to body.[8]

What are they? While some talk about meridians as channels or vessels (Gupta, 2001), it might be more accurate to think of them as a system of points connected to one another by their ability to receive and forward *subtle energy*. These points, when located near the outside of the body, are called pressure points. Deeper points are called acupoints. Both are thought to have elevated sensitivity to the conduction of electricity when compared to other parts of the body.

Gerber (2001), describing the way in which energy points work, asserts that energy points are, "energetic pore(s) in the skin through which subtle energy from the surrounding environment is carried throughout the body via the meridians, supplying nutritive chi (energy) to the deeper organs, blood vessels, and nervous system" (p. 522).

> We can describe meridians as pathways created by energy points that interconnect organs within the body; pathways that can be mapped just as one might map a highway connecting a series of cities.

Although there are probably hundreds of meridians, most agree that within the body there are twelve *primary* pathways, each related to a specific organ. There are also at least two (perhaps as many as eight) *central and/or governing* meridians. For simplicity's sake, our discussion will take the position that there are twelve primary and two central, governing meridians.

<u>Where are they?</u> Each primary (or organ related) meridian runs down one side of the body and back up the other, so it seems like they are a matching pair—the right reflecting the left and the left reflecting the right. Each key meridian has many pathways that branch off, creating smaller and smaller pathways, always moving toward the outside of the body, and then they reverse their direction, and move back in toward the center of the body. They form a crisscross network throughout the body, connecting organs with muscles, bones, skin, and so forth.

<u>What are they for?</u> A simple way to describe meridians is to draw an analogy with the cardiovascular system. Both the meridians and the cardiovascular system seem to have no real start and stop point. Instead, they constitute a continuous cycling process, with each segment of the system extremely important for the functioning of the whole system. The cardiovascular system takes nutrients to the cells so they can live and grow, and moves waste products away from the cells to prevent the build up of a toxic environment. The same holds true for the meridians: the meridians deliver energy to the cells, so they can function; they also remove excessive electrons from the cells, as needed, for a harmonious balance.

The central, governing meridians differ from the primary meridians in two significant ways. First, they do not run in pairs, cycling from within the body to the outside and back upon themselves. Instead, they run along the inside of the body, paralleling the internal paths of the primary meridians. Another difference is their purpose. While the primary meridians serve as a pathway for energy movement to and from the cells throughout the body, the central, governing meridians serve as a reservoir for the distribution of energy to the primary meridians. They give off energy when needed and store energy when excess exists. While the primary meridians consist of charged energy points that create pathways, the governing meridians have no pressure points of their own. Their connection is with the primary meridians and the universe.

The governing meridians serve as regulators of the primary meridians, bringing energy into the human energy system (i.e., primary meridians) from outside the body and giving off energy from the human. This differs from the primary meridians whose function is to distribute energy within the human system. When the energy flows freely (through the meridians), the person is healthy and balanced. When the energy becomes blocked, weakened, or stagnated, it can result in a decline in health and well-being.

Chakras

Are they real? As with pressure point meridians, chakras have been measured objectively by researchers. Using human subjects, Dr. Valerie Hunt, a professor at the University of California (UCLA), and Dr. Hiroshi Motoyama, Director and President of the California Institute for Human Science, used electromyographic (EMG) electrodes to measure waves of energy over chakras. The frequencies recorded over the chakras were higher than any previously recorded frequencies of any part of the human body (muscles, bones, brain) (Slater, 2005).

Motoyama also recorded chakra energy in three groups of people: control subjects, advanced meditators, and people with histories of psychic experiences. "Chakras that the meditators believed were 'awakened' showed electrical readings of increased frequency and amplitude when compared to control subjects' chakras" (Slater, 2005, p. 185).

What are they? The concept of the chakra originated in India (2000-600 B.C.).

> *According to the Vedic seers, whenever two or more channels of subtle energy meet, there is a vortex (of spinning energy), which they named 'chakra'. The word chakra, derived from Sanskrit, means 'wheel'* (Lilly & Lilly, 2004, p. 168).

The ancient Indians also used it as a metaphor for the sun, which they considered to be the eternal wheel of time and energy. The Vedics also considered the chakras as psychic centers of consciousness (Chopra, 1989, p. 184). More recently, the chakras have been identified as regulator and communicator sites.

> *Chakras regulate, maintain, and manage the physical, emotional, mental, and spiritual aspects of our being on the physical plane (earth). Chakras themselves serve as revolving doors or portals between our body, mind, and soul* (Dale, 2003, p. 15).

Gerber (1988) described chakras as follows:

> *The chakras are specialized energy centers which connect us to the multidimensional universe. The chakras are dimensional portals within the subtle bodies, which take in and process energy of higher vibrational nature so that it may be properly assimilated and used to transform the physical body* (p. 370).

Gerber (2001), when discussing the seven in-body chakras, added to his earlier description by stating:

They are actually considered emotional and spiritual-energy processors. Each... is individually linked to small nerve bundles known as ganglia. Each ganglion is like a little brain center. It appears that each of the seven chakras (and their associated nerve centers) processes and 'remembers' different emotional events and traumas that affect us throughout our lifetime. We seem to store specific types of emotional memories in these centers. Perhaps this is one of the reasons we remember things not only with our brains, but with our bodies as well (pp. 18-19).

Today, several (Brofman, 2003; Dale, 2003; Gerber, 2001) link the two views, stating that Chakras are both vortices of spinning energy and centers of consciousness. Consciousness, thought to be the interchange of subatomic particles, is what makes it possible for all living things to connect with one another (McTaggart, 2002, p. 104).

<u>Where are they?</u> There are seven primary in-body chakras aligned along the spine from the base of the spine to the crown of the head, five out-of-body chakras, and more than 360 minor chakras throughout the body. Figure 2.1 shows the location of the seven major in-body chakras and 3 major out of body chakras.[9]

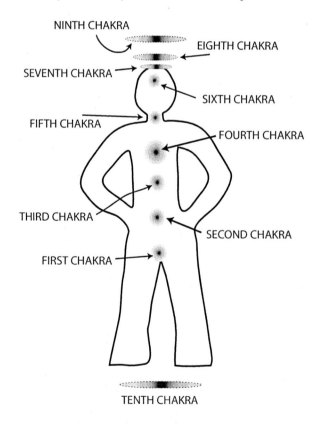

Figure 2.1 Seven in-body and 3 out-of-body chakras.

Chakras have "regional responsibilities." That is, each chakra regulates energy flowing from the universal energy field to a specific area of the body-mind-spirit. This regional responsibility allows experienced practitioners to facilitate holistic well-being by enhancing energy flow to specific areas of the person. While some energy therapists take a more intuitive approach, most express considerable agreement as to the location of the chakras and the areas of the body-mind supported by each chakra. Chakra energy can be heard, felt, seen, and otherwise perceived by some healers.

What are they for? Brennan (1987) stated that chakras have three functions. They

1) Energize and support the auric field and, in turn the physical mind-body-spirit;
2) Facilitate the development of consciousness and spiritual awareness; and
3) Transmit energy between the layers of the auric field.

Gerber (2001) states that "chakras are specialized energy centers throughout our bodies where a unique form of subtle environmental (life) energy is absorbed and distributed to our cells, organs, and body tissues" (p.17). While we accept this view, we wish to reemphasize the notion that chakras also connect mind and body with spirit. Dale (2003) said,

Because chakras dictate or assist with physical, mental, emotional and spiritual processes, they function like revolving doors between these four dimensions of our humanness....Therefore, the chakras serve a communication function. Basically, each chakra can communicate with our internal and external worlds... (p.29).

Dale (2003) also pointed out that chakras serve the function of storing memories. She said it is similar to our brain's ability to record memories—only it is different. "To record is to imprint; to store is to hold the energy of something intact" (p. 27). She pointed out that storing energy preserves the memory, so we can learn from it. That is, we can hold on to it and preserve it until we are ready to deal with it at a later time. She explains by saying the soul is affected by all stored memories, and *if* our soul doesn't fully trust our body, then the mistrust can impede our ability to discover our purpose (i.e., Life Purpose).

To summarize, the chakras have many purposes. Their key functions are to serve as: communication centers (of energy), regulate physical and emotional functions of the body and mind, store information of the holistic person, and enhance our ability to connect with higher sources of energy.

Development of Chakras. It is believed chakras develop as one deals with life challenges and, thus, gains knowledge and wisdom. Bruyere (1994) identified particular life issues for each chakra, which correlate with human growth and development. The ideal situation is for all chakras to develop fully and completely in their sequential time. When this does not happen, chakras can be undeveloped, setting the stage for mind-body-spirit problems. According to Page (2000), "The degree to which each chakra is open, and therefore active, is dependent upon the level of soul consciousness of the individual and of mankind as a whole" (p. 74).

Page (2000) suggests that as we as a people have been increasing our consciousness, our higher-level chakras have been activated. Motoyama's (2001) continuing research has demonstrated that awakened chakra energy charges the auric field and related meridian.

Dale (2003) builds on the notion that we are energy first. She states that all our chakras, open before conception, play an active role in creating our energy template, and then "go to sleep during the conception process so as not to interfere with the development of the physical body" (p.82). She, too, argues for a sequential awakening of the chakras, with the first stage of prebirth. Her stages of awakening are age-consistent with the stages of development proposed by Erik Erikson and discussed in Chapters 5 and 11 of this book. Dale also says that while there are specific times for the awakening of various chakras, we actually have access to all of them at all times. She also talks about two cycles of unfolding, which seem to be consistent with Erikson's model of epigenesis (see Chapter 5).

The Auric Field

The human energy field or Aura is the energy "envelope" around the holistic person that supports our physical structure and communicates with the pressure points (along the meridian) and the chakras. This field surrounds and penetrates the body, providing support for our bio-physical functioning. It serves as a conduit for the movement of universal energy into and through the body, and for energy from the holistic person to move into the universe. Excess electrons interfere with optimum flow of energy, and can contribute to congestion in the fields and, correspondingly, diminished well-being.

> The energy field contains interpenetrating subtle energy bodies, contained within one another. The first, the etheric body, is closest to the physical body. Each successive body extends further out. While these are often called layers, they aren't like layers that can be peeled off because they co-exist in the same space. They each have a different frequency of vibration and perform different functions, so they can occupy the same space even though they seem to be layers. The three innermost *layers*, like the three lower chakras, are strictly associated with our life as human beings—the physical, emotional, and mental aspects of our being while the three outer layers, like the three upper chakras, are associated with the spiritual aspects of our being. The fourth layer, associated with the fourth chakra (at the heart), is the mediator between the inner and outer layers (Bruyere, 1994; Dale, 2003; Gordon, 2002).

While not within the realm of normal vision, the aura can be experienced or perceived. According to Bruyere, "It is an energy system that keeps body and mind alive and healthy, and may in actuality create them" (1994, p. 18). There are at least 7 layers of the aura, which correspond to the 7 chakras. Bruyere (1994) described the aura as "generated by the spinning of the chakras" (p. 61). As each chakra spins, an electromagnetic field is generated. As the different electromagnetic fields created by the spinning chakras combine, the aura is created. Hunt (1995) and Gerber (20001) describe research findings that support the presence of the aura.

Oschman (1990) provides (p. 76) an interesting way to think about the linkages between the body and the human energy field. His biomagnetic grid depicts the flow of energy around and through the body and is a representation of the human energy field. Figure 2.2 provides an example of the relationship of the inbody chakras and the human energy field.

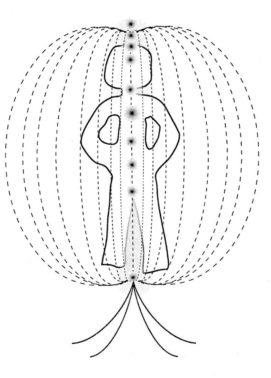

Figure 2.2 Human energy field and auric body.

According to Oschman (1990), the "…overall shape of the field results mainly from currents set up in the body, particularly in the heart, which produces the strongest biomagnetic field" (p. 77). Muscles, vascular structures (arteries), and body fluids are the primary carriers of the energy throughout the body. The field becomes weaker as it moves away from the body. The grid depicts a size of an average aura, that of an arm's length or 2 feet around the body (Oschman, 2000).

Since it is not uncommon for human energy fields to extend 2 feet or more from the edge of our bodies, our fields often overlap and we share one another's energy field. When people share energy fields, information can be exchanged via the field, without a word being spoken. Sometimes this information is received and perceived at an unconscious level, but sometimes it reaches our consciousness. This information can be perceived as both positive and negative "information," depending on the nature of the electrical charge of the other's energy field. Because the human is composed of multiple energy fields, we think of it as a human energy system.

The Nurse's Caring Field

The relationship between nurse and client can also be expressed in terms of an energy field. Watson (1999), one of health care's key leaders in holistic nursing, stated that when the nurse is fully present with the client, nurse and client connect on an energetic level, creating what she describes as a Caring Field, a new field of consciousness and possibilities. She states, "The transpersonal caring field resides within a unitary field of consciousness and energy that transcends time, space, and physicality (unity of mind-body-spirit nature universe)" (2005, p. 222).

Nurses can influence the caring field through their intentions, actions, thoughts and feelings (Dossey, L. 1992). Edwards (2005) proposes that healing occurs when a resonance is set between the client and healer as they meet in *The Field.*

> *The nurse has a profound effect on the patient and we need to assume responsibility for awareness of this effect. As we become increasingly aware of this oneness, this interconnectedness, we can view the nurse-patient encounter as a dynamic, open, ever-changing energy system. There is a continuous multilevel exchange of energy between nurse and client* (McKivergin and Daubenmire 1994, p. 76).

We believe a Caring Field is the basis for helping people grow, develop, and heal. Others such as Chopra (1994), Dossey (1999), Gerber, (2001), and Oschman, (1997) have all talked about combining the natural electromagnetic fields or the universe and humans to create a *healing field.* Various studies (Byrd, 1988; Grad, 1965; Targ & Karta, 1999) on plants and humans using distant healing support the idea that the Zero Point Field may serve to maintain our own health or to facilitate healing in others. Dossey, L. (1999) refers to these distant healing events as "nonlocal." They are unmediated (they do not require a go-between), unmitigated (increasing distance does not diminish the strength), and immediate. Nonlocal energy will be further discussed in the next chapter as we talk about distant healing.

McTaggart (2002) states The Zero Point Field may be used as a healing field in two different ways. First, one person may "...act as a healing conduit, allowing The Field to realign another person's structure" (p. 181). The second way is that information held in The Field may be a "...collective memory of healing spirit" (p. 194) that can be tapped to facilitate healing. The implications for nursing are enormous. Oschman (1997) said:

In terms of healing, important rhythms have been discovered by medical researchers who are employing magnetic pulses for 'jump starting' the repair of a wide spectrum of tissues and for treating diseases. While a variety of signals are being tested, medical interest has especially focused on pulsing magnetic fields of low energy and extremely low frequency (ELF). (The ELF range is arbitrarily defined as frequencies below 100 HZ, [Miller, 1986]). Similar frequencies emanate from the hands of practitioners of therapeutic touch and related methods. Moreover, the fields emitted by practitioners are not steady in frequency, but 'sweep' or 'scan' through the range of frequencies that medical researchers are finding effective in facilitating repair of various soft and hard tissues (p. 180).

Nurses have always known they have the capability of facilitating healing in their clients, but haven't always been able to substantiate their 'knowing' or link healing to energy theories. Martha Rogers' work, first published in 1970 and refined in 1982 to include energy fields, has provided the basis for extensive research (Wirth, 1990). Today, we know *the intent to care* or enhance healing is what is important (Quinn, 1989). Waters and Daubenmire (1997) talk about *Transformational Healing,* stating intentionality is key. They extrapolate from a number of sources and state:

Intentionality is a critical idea that merits increased exploration in nursing. Bohm (1980) states that every action starts from an intention...Intention is the behavior that can move one into conscious relationships. Chopra (1992) indicates that 'intention is the active part of attention; it is the way we convert automatic processes into conscious ones' (p. 19). We define intent as 'one's focused will.' Involving spirit, mind and body. The nurse can center and intend to be present, to be a healing force for the patient...There is an emerging awareness of the importance of connecting, of understanding unitive consciousness—that we are not separate, that we are all one. Physicists state that the universe is an inseparable whole, a vast web of interacting, interweaving probabilities (p. 62).

Intentionality and distant intentionality will be further discussed in the next chapter as we discuss the mind-body-spirit interactions.

APPLICATION OF ENERGY CONCEPTS TO MODELING AND ROLE-MODELING

The previous section briefly described some of the concepts frequently encountered when discussing energy theories. This section describes how some of these relate to major concepts in the Modeling and Role-Modeling Theory and Paradigm.

Holism

One of the key concepts in the Modeling and Role-Modeling theory and paradigm is holism. The authors argued there is a difference between wholism, where the sum of the parts creates a whole, and holism, where the sum of the parts is greater than the whole. They stated:

> *Human beings are holistic persons who have multiple interacting subsystems. Permeating all subsystems are the inherent bases. These include genetic makeup and spiritual drive. Body, mind, emotion, and spirit are a total unit (that) act together. They affect and control one another interactively. The interaction of the multiple subsystems and the inherent bases creates holism* (pp. 44-45).

Holism at the Cellular Level

While this discussion of holism states that the subsystems of the person are in continuous, dynamic interaction, it does not describe how interaction *within* a subsystem works. Oschman's (2000) theory on Energy Medicine provides an interesting description of dynamic interaction that starts at the cellular level, moves out to the subsystems, and into the entire *body* of the person. He called this the "living matrix."

> *The living matrix is a continuous molecular system that simultaneously conducts energy and information throughout the body, and that regulates growth, form, and wound healing. Every part of the body is a part of this continuous living matrix. It is a system of systems. Memories are stored within this system, and the totality of its operations gives rise to what we refer to as consciousness. This system is accessed by acupuncture and other complementary medical approaches* (Oschman, 2003, p. 141).

The Old Model: A Membrane Bound Bag. Oschman (2000) stated that scientists have viewed cells as membrane-bound bags, meaning that each cell contains certain kinds of molecules and is encapsulated by a bag, or cell membrane. Particles within each cell, such as enzymes, amino acids, sugars, etc., interact randomly to carry out cellular functions.

The cell is not filled with specific structures, but has empty space, which is filled with a type of "molecular soup." Oschman stated,

> *Physiologists seized the bag-of-solution model of cell structure and conducted decades of research in which an underlying assumption was that substances crossing a layer of cells, such as the intestinal wall, simply diffuse through the fluid compartments inside the cells* (p.45).

As techniques such as electron microscopy have developed, scientists have discovered a variety of intracellular structures. These intracellular structures contribute to a continuous body structure that is "simultaneously a mechanical, vibrational or oscillatory, energetic, electronic, and informational network" (Oschman, 2000, p. 49).

<u>The Living Matrix.</u> Oschman (2000) described an alternative view of biophysiology, the "living matrix." He described the interior of the cell as being filled with fibers, tubes, and filaments, collectively called the cytoskeleton (of the cell) or the cytoplasmic matrix. He goes on to say that integrins (i.e., "linkers") extend across the cell surface, connecting cells within a molecule, and then connecting those molecules with others in a system. Systems connect with one another in the same way. With this model, Oschman argues that the "living matrix" is a continuous and dynamic supramolecular webwork, extending into every nook and cranny of the body.[10] He stated:

> *In essence, when you touch a human body, you are touching a continuously interconnected system, composed of virtually all of the molecules in the body linked together in an intricate web work. The living matrix has no fundamental unit or central aspect, no part that is primary or most basic. The properties of the whole net depend upon the integrated activities of all the components. Effects on one part of the system can, and do spread to others* (p. 48).

Oschman's "living matrix" view of holism is very consistent with Modeling and Role-Modeling. It helps further our understanding of the linkages between chemical and electrical energy, mind-body relations, and the importance of Self-care Knowledge as the primary source of information.

Holism at the Subsystems Level

The model of the holistic person in Modeling and Role-Modeling theory presents a template for describing the person as bioenergy. This model, shown in Figure 1.3, demonstrates both the energy exchange that occurs within the holistic person and the energetic interaction of the individual with the environment.

This model shows a spiritual drive that runs through the subsystems, arising from the universal energy field. Accordingly, spiritual energy permeates and unifies the dimensions of the person. As shown in the model, the spiritual drive draws from the universe and gives back to the universe, representing the continual exchange of energy. "This constant exchange is an intrinsic property of particles, so that even 'real' particles are nothing more than a little knot of energy which briefly emerges and disappears back into the underlying field" (McTaggart, 2002, p. 22).

This orientation is consistent with the view that the spirit is first; the molecules are second. "Consciousness precedes matter" (Pert, 2002, p.27), that is, the spirit (or subtle energy as described above) comes first and is manifested in the biophysical, cognitive, psychological, and social dimensions of the holistic person. Weiss (2002) describes human beings as a "continuum between energy and matter" (p. 104).

> This model also makes an important point regarding the significance of the spirit. A person's spirit is not a dimension of the person, as represented in some nursing theories (Alligood & Tomey, 2002, Tomey & Alligood, 2002), nor is it an object that can be assessed and treated (Wright, 2005). The spirit is the energy that transforms purposefully, is manifested in the dimensions of the person, and transcends person. It is drawn from the Universal life force and becomes individualized for each human being during the process of becoming. This is consistent with the notion of consciousness, described above.

The Subsystems and the Aura. The auric layers correspond to the dimensions of the holistic person as presented in the Modeling and Role-Modeling theory and paradigm. Each layer of the auric field has its own structure, function, and vibrational frequency; each is also associated with a specific chakra. Energy permeates each successive layer. A description of the human energy field, or auric field, was presented earlier in this chapter. Table 2.1 provides an overview of how the auric field, based on Brennan's (1994) work, relates to the subsystems described in Modeling and Role-Modeling.

Table 2.1 Relationships between MRM subsystems and the human energy field.

MRM Subsystems	Energy Field Levels	Purpose/ Function
BioPhysical	Level 1	Associated with physical functioning and sensation. A strong first level is related to a healthy physical body.
Psychological	Level 2	Relates to feelings and emotions about Self. A strong second level is associated with feeling comfortable with self.
Cognitive	Level 3	Connected to rational mental processes and state of mind. A strong third level relates to a clear mind and harmony of rational and intuitive functioning.
Social	Level 4	Associated with relationship with others and the Universe, including feelings about others. It is also a "bridge between physical and spiritual worlds" (Brennan, p. 24). A strong fourth level is related to positive relationships.

(Compiled from various sources, including Brennan, 1994; Erickson et al., 1983)

While energy is described as being manifested in each of the subsystems, the MRM theory also states that not only are these dimensions of the holistic person in constant interaction with each other, they are also in constant interaction with the spirit of the human being. As stated (Erickson et al., 1983), in "holistic persons who have multiple interacting systems…(b)ody, mind, emotion and spirit are a total unit and they act together. They affect and control one another interactively" (pp.44-45). These mechanisms of interaction are energy-based and include the energy movement and exchange through the auric field, chakras, the meridians and the entire living matrix. Since knowledge about energetic systems and structures continues to develop, our understanding of holism also continues to develop and evolve.

> All things come from a single source of energy; all things continually interact with that source, and all things feed back into that source. Human beings interact with the Universal Field by way of the Human Energy system, which consists of three key components: meridians, chakras, and aura.

Health

Health is defined by Erickson et al. (1983) as a "state of physical, mental and social well-being…It connotes a state of dynamic equilibrium among the various subsystems" (p.46). The word *dynamic*, defined as "pertaining to energy," implies continuous change. When describing health from the perspective of energy, balance is a key concept, just as homeostasis is a key concept in biology. Eden (1998) described this dynamic process in this way: "In this exquisite alchemy, energies are built up, stored, spent, transformed, harmonized and brought into balance" (p. 22).

As shown in the holistic model of the person in Figure 1.3, the spiritual drive permeates and integrates the multiple dimensions of the person. Sarter's (2002) description of high-level health reinforces the importance of spirit as demonstrated in this model. Sarter states, "High level health is present when the spiritual dimension of the person is vital and strong enough to integrate and harmonize all aspects of the being" (p. 20).

In the energy world, all things vibrate and possess a characteristic frequency, or wave-length and height. A higher frequency of vibration indicates a higher level of energy. According to Sarter (2002),

An individual is a complex field of vibrations of many different frequencies. In the average person, more often than not, these physical, organic, emotional, mental and spiritual vibrations are in harmony. Perfect health is when all of the vibrations of one's being are in harmony or equilibrium (p.22).

"Vibrations underlie virtually every aspect of nature...Virtually all that we know about living systems is based on the analysis of vibrations" (Oschman, 2000, p. 121). When relating the "living matrix" to the concept of "health" as defined by Erickson et al. (1983), the parallels are obvious. Oschman (2000) stated,

> ...all parts of the living matrix set up vibrations that move about within the organism, and that are radiated into the environment. These vibrations or oscillations occur at many different frequencies, including visible and near visible light frequencies...Each molecule, cell, tissue and organ has an ideal resonant frequency that coordinates its activities (p.62).

When there is coherence, surrounding tissues and organs come to vibrate more closely with each other. A more coherent living matrix reflects a healthier person. The dynamic interaction described by Erickson et al. (1983) is required in all dimensions of the human energy systems as well as in the continual interaction with the universal energy field. McTaggart (2002) speculates that illness may be isolation, "a lack of connection with the collective health of The Field and the community" (p. 194).

One goal of energy healing may be to connect a person to the vibrations of the earth. Geopathic stress is caused by alterations in earth energy. Schumann resonance of 7.8 cycles/second is most constant earth energy. "Since the earth's magnetic field is already weaker than it was a few thousand years ago, and since all living things are dependent upon daily exposure to the geomagnetic field, it looks as if anything that blocks or further weakens earth magnetism could be potentially deleterious in its effects upon human health. Conversely, anything that can help maintain an appropriate level of exposure to earth's geomagnetic field should be advantageous to humans" (Gerber, 2001, p. 270).

Understanding the client's model of the world may be expressed in terms of vibrations as well—as the nurse attempts to match the vibratory level of the client, or to "get on the same wave length."

Adaptation

One underlying belief of Modeling and Role-Modeling theory is that individuals possess an inherent drive toward growth, development, and holistic health. "Adaptation occurs as the individual responds to external and internal stressors in a health and growth-directed manner" (Erickson et al., 1983, p. 47). Expressed energetically, energy is constantly changing and transforming. Scientists are recognizing the underlying patterns within systems and their inherent ability to self-organize. When applied to the person, it is described in this way: "Man is a system of interdependent force fields, within which energy patterns are not only appropriate to the particular field, but are also ordered by special processes and mechanisms" (Karagulla & Kunz, 1989, p. 26).

The ability to adapt or respond in a growth-directed manner can be expressed in terms of the concept of vibration:

> *...once energy reaches a certain threshold, molecules begin to vibrate in unison, until they reach a high level of coherence. The moment molecules reach this state of coherence, they take on certain qualities of quantum mechanics, including nonlocality. They get to the point where they can act in tandem* (McTaggart, 2002, p.49).

While the person many be making conscious attempts to change in a growth-directed manner, or to adapt, this process is also occurring at the energetic level. Adaptation is not a state, but a process.

Affiliated-Individuation

Energy adds a new perspective to Modeling and Role-Modeling's concept of affiliated-individuation. "Affiliated-individuation occurs when a person perceives himself or herself as simultaneously close to and separate from a significant other" (Erickson et al., 1983, p. 68). The auric field can be used to explain affiliated-individuation at the energetic level. Because we are in constant interaction with the environment, it is difficult to identify a specific point where a person's auric field ends and the "Universe" starts. However, we can perceive the boundaries of the auric field.

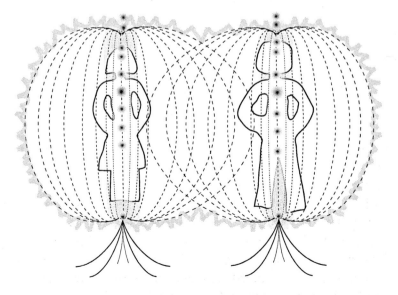

Figure 2.3 Energy fields and aura of two people positively interacting with one another.

As we interact with others in our daily lives, our auric fields are in contact with the fields of others. Brennan (1992) described it in this way:

> *On the fourth level of the auric field, everything we do with each other shows up in a living, moving constantly changing display of colored fluidlike light, or bioplasma....Bioplasmic displays reveal that we are connected to each other in many ways that our psychological and sociological theories have not included. They show an interdependence between all living creatures far beyond what we have previously understood* (p. 177).

This coming together is described as communion, and it is through communion that we are able to "move apart into individuation" (p. 178).

When we respond with thoughts such as "You are in my space" or, "this is too close for comfort" we may be experiencing an uncomfortable level of interaction between auric fields. In other situations, closeness may be desirable. Figure 2.3 shows the energy exchange in the auric field of two people positively interacting with one another.

Affiliation is important in our lives, as it is through relationships that spiritual growth occurs (Brennan, 1994). When there is a healthy level of affiliated-individuation, the energy exchange with others is appropriate and meets the needs of the people involved in the relationship. When interactions are positive, they nourish the field through a positive feedback loop. In contrast, an isolated person (see Figure 2.4) may not receive the personal or energetic interaction necessary to sustain holistic balance.

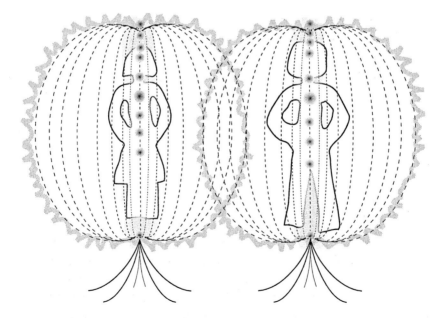

Figure 2.4 Energy fields of isolated individuals.

Lifetime Growth and Development

One assumption in Modeling and Role-Modeling is that individuals have the capacity to grow and develop over the life span, and a desire to fulfill their potential. From an energetic perspective, growth and development also occur in the human energy field. One is not fully developed energetically at birth. As one moves through stages of life, there are corresponding higher vibrations and, at the same time, the person has an increased ability to "sustain higher levels of vibrations/ energies/consciousness coming into and through her vehicles, her auric bodies and chakras" (Brennan, 1987, p. 61). Higher levels of vibration allow for new learning and expansion of the personality. As the individual grows and develops, the activity of the chakras increases.

Self-care

Application of energy can enhance our understanding of the concept of self-care as presented in Modeling and Role-Modeling theory. Self-care is comprised of three parts: Knowledge, Resources, and Actions. The three aspects of Self-care work together much like the human energy system described above. Self-care Knowledge is the repository of "knowing." It is active, dynamic, constantly changing and based on new input. It is much like the energy flowing through the meridians. Self-care Resources are the repository of "energy" or resources needed to contend with ongoing life and new stressors. We might compare it to the governing meridians; it provides new resources when needed. Some of these are specific to the "need"; some are adapted. Nevertheless, they are mobilized in response to the "need" of the holistic person. The process of mobilizing the resources is Self-care Actions.

Self-care Knowledge

Self-care knowledge, or "self-knowing," is described by Erickson et al. (1983) as follows:

> *At some level, a person knows what has made him or her sick, lessened his or her effectiveness or interfered with his or her growth. The person also knows what will make him or her well, optimize effectiveness or fulfillment (given the circumstances) or promote his or her growth* (p. 48).

We often think of "knowledge" as information that can be acquired through traditional learning experiences—through formal and informal educational processes and through daily life experiences. This type of knowledge can often be categorized or isolated as cognitive, psychological, or social knowledge. But, using such an understanding of Self care Knowledge minimizes the notion that people are holistic. When something is learned, it is learned throughout the person, it is remembered at the multiple levels of consciousness; it is remembered in the cells (Pert, 2003) and even in the DNA (Rossi, 1986). This is why the definition above states, "At some level, a person knows..." While people may not be consciously aware of what they need, at some level they "know." Their self-knowing (described by Erickson in Chapter 1) is drawn from their current life experiences, spiritual energy resources, as well as Universal knowledge.

Energy theories embrace the notion of "energy of consciousness," described as a field of intelligent information expressed energetically. As with all energy fields, consciousness is not limited to time and space. Through the phenomenon of nonlocality, we have access to this information through energy exchange within the field of universal energy. Chopra states: "Pure consciousness is pure potentiality; it is the field of all possibilities and infinite creativity" (1994, p. 12).

Another way of understanding Self-care Knowledge is cellular memory theory. We have learned from the study of biology that some cells are especially good at storing coded information and, therefore, have strong memories. Cellular memory theory supports the idea that the cells in the body have "various levels of stored information left there by the heart's conduction of 'L' energy..." (Pearsall, 1999, p. 221). Pearsall's interest in cellular memory was sparked by his work with heart transplant patients who recalled forms of their donor's memory. According to him, "Since information is a form of energy and...cannot be destroyed, cellular memories are infinite" (p. 221). Pearsall's work reinforces that we are energy first because it has been reported that some personality traits are transferred from donor to recipient of a heart transplant. For more information regarding cellular memory (or stored memories), see Chapters 3 and 4.

Self-care Resources.

Self-care resources are the internal and external resources the client can use to promote health and healing. While some Self-care Resources are not easily mobilized, if and when they can be mobilized, they serve the same purpose—to promote health and healing. Erickson et al. (1983) discuss depletion of resources,[11] restoring resources,[12] and resource potential.[13] Modeling and Role-Modeling differentiates between external[14] and internal resources.[15] This chapter is not intended to replace this earlier work, but to expand on it—to describe how energy concepts interface with the theory.

When using energy theory, we talk about therapists using their energy fields to activate their clients' fields. Since we are holistic beings, our energy field is influenced by how we think and feel, how well-balanced our biological system is, and how well we are connected to the Universal Field. Research shows the "intent to help" has an important effect on our ability to mobilize energy in others. We are interacting energy fields; the well-being of one affects the well-being of another. Energy therapists know that it is important to center themselves, consciously think of the other person with the "intent to care," and focus on the process while interacting. They know when they do this, the two energy fields interact in a way that maximizes energy flow within each of the individuals, between them, and the universe.

Application of energy concepts to Nursing at large and to the theory of Modeling and Role-Modeling proposes that Unconditional Acceptance, Facilitation, and Nurturance are all energy-based concepts.

The Nurse's Role

Modeling and Role-Modeling lists five major Principles of Nursing. Specific aims of interventions and intervention goals are associated with each Principle (See Table 2.2) Threaded through these directives are three major concepts also common in energy field discussions. These are Unconditional Acceptance, Facilitation, and Nurturance.

Table 2.2 MRM principals and five aims of interventions reproduced with permission, Modeling and Role-Modeling: A Theory and Paradigm, 1983, EST Co: TX.

Principal	Aim
1. The nursing process requires that a trusting and functional relationship exist between nurse and client.	Build trust.
2. Affiliated-individuation is dependent on the individual's perceiving that he or she is an acceptable, respectable, and worth-while human being.	Promote client's positive orientation.
3. Human development is dependent on the individual's perceiving that he or she has some control over his her life, while concurrently sensing a state of affiliation.	Promote client's control.
4. There is an innate drive toward holistic health that is facilitated by consistent and systematic nurturance.	Affirm and promote client's strengths.
5. Human growth is dependent on satisfaction of basic needs and facilitated by growth-need satisfaction	Set mutual goals that are health-directed.

Unconditional Acceptance

H. Erickson states that unconditional acceptance of the person, as a human in the process of Be-ing and Be-coming, is basic to the Modeling and Role-Modeling paradigm. It is prerequisite to facilitating holistic growth and movement toward eudemonistic health. "Unconditional Acceptance of the person as a human being who has an inherent need for dignity, respect from others, and for connectedness—that kind of Unconditional Acceptance is based on Unconditional Love. When we have Unconditional Love, it is only one step more to Unconditional Acceptance" (H. Erickson, personal communication, December 20, 2005).

Love is an inherent aspect of the energy system. In fact, the fourth chakra is the center of love. Brofman (2003) stated:

(This) chakra is involved with relating, the area of relationships in our lives, and with our perceptions of love. It terms of relationships, it can be about partnerships, or about relating with anyone close to our heart...It can also be experienced as being in a shared space in which the love is felt, and just flows, with a sense of inclusion, and not necessarily a sense of giving or receiving (p.183).

This statement emphasizes the need for nurses to be centered, to attend to the balance of their own energy fields so that they are able to express their love, compassion and stay centered. Without this balance, it becomes difficult for nurses to facilitate or nurture their clients. Instead, they have the potential to become "effectors" and emphasize controlling rather than nurturing the client's sense of control (Erickson et al., 2005, pp. 169-222).

Facilitation

The Modeling and Role-Modeling (1983) philosophy states that the nurse is a "facilitator not an effector" (p.48). The authors stress that our work is to help people become the most they can be, to work toward higher levels of well-being. They defined facilitations as "making easier or less difficult; helping forward. The nurse-client relationship is an interactive process that helps the individual to identify, mobilize, and develop the individual's own strengths in his or her own movement toward health." (p. 252).

The process of facilitation is enhanced by resonance. The interactive process described above occurs at an energetic level as well as on a personal level. Resonance occurs when independent systems begin to vibrate in unison. A given person (the client) as a vibrating body is capable of achieving resonance with another human, the nurse, establishing a complementary relationship. The MRM view of facilitation is very consistent with roles defined by energy therapists. However, since there are many ways for people to heal, it is important clients identify and pursue modalities and strategies that suit them.

Nurturance

(The) nurse-client relationship is an interactive, interpersonal process that aids the individual to identify, mobilize, and develop his own strengths...Nurturance fuses and integrates cognitive, physiological and affective processes, with the aim of assisting a client to move toward holistic health...Being accepted as a unique, worthwhile, important individual—with no strings attached—is imperative if the individual is to be facilitated in developing his or her own potential (Erickson et al., 1983, pp. 48-49).

This fusing and integrating of multiple processes occurs at an energetic level when the nurse intervenes to balance and integrate the client's energy system. This is the basis of nurturance.

The Enduring Nurse-Client Relationship

Nurses may claim their fast-paced work situations do not offer the time required to provide theory-based care. Practicing nursing from a theory base that incorporates energy concepts, such as MRM, can enhance the time spent with clients. Consider the concept of Intention. By taking a minute to set an intention for a positive outcome for the client prior to entering the room, the nurse has already set into motion the energy of that thought pattern.

Although the nurse-client relationship may be limited by rapid discharges characteristic of the current health care system, the effect of the relationship is not limited. Nonlocal energy connections help maintain a lasting bond that exists despite separation by time and space.

On a practical level, most nurses know they have impacted the lives of their clients. They may assume the client is applying knowledge learned during a teaching session or know the client will be reminded of their relationship through the use of a transitional object. Bell's theorem demonstrates that the relationship endures at an energetic level as well. "Bell showed that objects, once in contact, both change if there is a subsequent change in the other, no matter how far apart they are" (Pearsall, 1998, p. 166). Pearsall later adds, "all connections exist at some level forever, everywhere, and for all time" (p.229).

> The nurse-client relationship, an intertwining of energy fields, is based on a heart-to-heart connection that continues even in the absence of physical presence.

ENDNOTES

1 Some people argue there is a fifth force—a Universal force that incorporates subtle energy.

[2] Take for example, the lifting of patients, moving of beds, back strain, and so forth.

[3] According to Oschman (1997), *"While you may be experiencing calm weather where you are now, there are, on average, about 200 lightning strikes taking place each second, scattered about the planet. To use the physics terminology, lightning pumps energy into the earth ionosphere cavity and causes it to vibrate or resonate at frequencies in the ELF range"* (p. 185).

[4] This work is based on Quantum Physics theory. For interesting reading, you might want to check the website, newscientist.com.

[5] These waves vibrate, creating "resonance." You will find more information in the next chapter regarding resonance.

[6] It is interesting that in the last chapter of her book Pert talks about the linkage between her search for Truth, i.e., her work as a scientist, and God. She states, *"some of my best insights have come to me through what I can only call a mystical process. It's like having God whisper in your ear..."* (p. 315).

[7] For very interesting reading on this matter, go to the The International Society for the Study of Subtle Energies and Energy Medicine's website.

[8] See Benor, D. (2005), www.ijhc.org, and wholistichealingresearch.com for more information.

[9] For more information regarding in-body and out-of-body Chakras, Dale provides interesting reading.

[10] In Chapter 3 the authors talk about neuromodulation. You will be interested to notice how the two relate.

---

[11] Please see Erickson, Tomlin, and Swain (1983), pages. 2, 47-48, 58, 80, 82, 92, 110, 122, 125-28, 122-24, 128-29, 159.

[12] Please see pages 125-27, 122-24, 128, 152-62, 176.

[13] Please see pages . 86, 91-92, 96, 119, 125-29, 124, 127-29, 148, 150, 152-162.

[14] Please see pages 48, 125-28, 124, 128, 158-59, 162.

[15] Please see pages 48, 126, 128-29, 124, 128, 158-162, 176.

CHAPTER 3

MIND-BODY-SPIRIT RELATIONS

MARSHA J. WALKER AND HELEN L. ERICKSON

Lou, a surgical nurse of 35 years, tells this story:

When my twin grandchildren were born at 25 weeks gestation, doctors informed us they had little chance of surviving, and if they did, they would have numerous mental and physical problems. I decided differently.

I attended an energy-based therapy workshop where I asked the class to help me use what we had learned to help the twins. We focused our thoughts on them, envisioned them healthy, and sent them love. My classmates gave me the red dots from their nametags as reminders that they were thinking of the twins and me. I put them on the twins' incubators. Both babies were on ventilators, had feeding tubes, and bilateral chest tubes. They had no eye lashes, eyebrows, or nipples, and no finger or toe nails. Jacob's colon ruptured when he was 5 days old, and an emergency colostomy was done. According to the doctors, he had almost no chance for survival.

I created a plan for the twins and shared it with the nurses and family. All negative thoughts about the babies were washed away when people washed their hands. People were encouraged to have only healing, positive thoughts around the babies. Everyone in the family visualized the twins being two years old and running through the bluebonnets, chasing their dog. We did Therapeutic Touch on them, holding our hands in the energy field over their abdomens and lungs, which were the greatest problem areas. The red dots remained on the cribs.

We imaged light and love coming from God, flowing through us, and filling the twins. We sang Amazing Grace, and visualized soothing colors permeating them. The babies were more relaxed after the sessions: their respirations were slower, and they turned their heads toward the person doing the energy work. They needed less insulin, and their elevated blood pressures dropped.

Even though the neonatal unit had a "No Touch" policy, with a little convincing, nurses let the family touch each baby's foot with one finger. At first, their feet were rigid; then they became soft and relaxed. Soft music played in the nursery all the time. I made, for their cribs, pillows that played Brahms lullaby, and continued attending the monthly workshops, never knowing whether the babies would live another day.

With some coaxing, staff let the family hold the babies. We began to give them short massages. The twins began to have neurological and muscular improvement, and gained weight more rapidly. Finally, they came home.

At 2 1/2 years old, the twins, singing Mary Had a Little Lamb, were perfectly normal in every way. Doctors say it's a miracle. I believe it was what I learned in class—how to use my whole self to help others grow. Jacob and Kristin are now chasing their dog through the bluebonnets.

OVERVIEW

The above story is one of hope and positive expectations for the future. It is a story of nurses and family working together to meet the needs of the client and taking advantage of nature's potential to help us grow and heal. This is a story of Modeling and Role-Modeling—how stepping into the world of another helps us plan purposeful interventions.

Chapter 1 discusses the relationship between our spiritual drive and the holistic being. Chapter 2 explains energy theories and their relation to the holistic model proposed by the MRM theory. This chapter describes how the mind, body, and spirit work as an ongoing, dynamic, constantly communicating system, and how these interactions affect our health and well-being. We start with a brief background about neurological functioning. Next, we discuss how cells communicate with one another throughout the body. This is followed by linking the mind and body with the spirit. Finally, we revisit some of these issues and incorporate energy concepts.

The intent of this chapter is not to provide a full review of the published evidence supporting the discussion of how the mind, body, and spirit interface. Instead, we wish to provide sufficient information to stimulate the curiosity of the reader, so you, too, will try to find answers to questions you may have about these relationships. To that purpose, we have included various resources in the bibliography.

BACKGROUND INFORMATION

Neurological Functioning

The functional unit of the human nervous system has about 100 billion neurons differentiated as *sensory, motor,* and *interneurons.* Sensory and motor neurons are located throughout the body while interneurons are found only in the central nervous system. Interneurons, also known as connector neurons, process signals from one or more sensory neurons and relay signals to motor neurons. The space between neurons is called the *synapse or synaptic cleft* (Pinel, 1993).

Basically, there are three key parts to the neuron: cell body, dendrites, and axon. An exceedingly complex communication network within the cell moves messages from the dendrites through the cell body to the axon terminals. These connections are dynamic, occur almost instantaneously, and are necessary for biophysical life. Briefly, the nerve cell receives messages through receptor sites in the dendrite membranes, creates action potentials in the cell body (when the signal is strong enough), and transmits them down the axon and out through the axon terminal nodes to the next cell.[1]

Reception and Transmission of Messages

Neurotransmission is the primary way the central nervous system (the brain) communicates with the peripheral nervous system (the autonomic nervous system). Messages communicated through neurotransmission come from one neuron and affect only one other neuron. Their action can be thought of as neuron-neuron exchange of information.

Dendrites are little fibers with multiple receptor sites that extend out of the cell body and into the synapse. They serve as communication relay stations. These little fibers act like antenna, searching constantly for "messages" coming toward the cell. Some of these "messages" are excitatory and some are inhibitory. When messages approach the dendrites, the *receptor sites* determine whether the "message(s)" will be accepted. *Receptor sites are discriminating. Each one allows only few kinds of "messages" to connect with it.*

The "message" and the receptor site must be in synchrony before they can bind with one another. However, every "message" has a chance of finding a receptor site that will accept it because each neuron has multiple dendrites with different types of receptor sites. There may be as many as 70 *different types* of dendrites on one neuron, with the number of receptors on a neuron totaling nearly a million!

Receptor Potentials. When a "message" binds to a receptor site, it initiates a "receptor potential." Receptor potentials are weak electrical charges, which lose speed as they move passively down the dendrite into the cell body. Since many *receptor potentials* may be moving toward the cell body at the same time, they integrate. What happens next depends on the ratio of the integrated receptor potentials. Given that "messages" can be excitatory or inhibitory, when there are more inhibitory "messages," the integrated receptor potentials are unable to reach the threshold required to create an electrical impulse. The messages are carried no further.

    <u>Action Potentials.</u> On the other hand, when the integrated receptor potentials have more excitatory messages *and* are able to reach threshold required, an *action potential* results. An action potential creates an *electrical impulse*, which moves from the cell body down the axon (of the nerve cell) and out through the axon terminals. Communication continues; the message moves on to another cell. The electrical impulse initiates the release of neurotransmitters.

> Neurotransmission (which takes milliseconds) can be thought of as a series of neurons creating pathways. If we were to draw a picture, they might look like a pathway made of stepping-stones with a "connector" (neurotransmitter) between the stones. The connecting sites (synapses) can transmit the "message" only because neurotransmitters are there to do the job.

Neurotransmitters

    Neurotransmitters are chemicals that carry "messages" from cell to cell. Every neurotransmitter has a specific molecular make-up, which means it carries a specific "message." "Messages" are carried in small sacs, called synaptic vesicles, clustered at the tip of the axon. When the vesicle receives the electrical impulse from the neuron body, neurotransmitters are excreted into the synaptic cleft. Some move to adjacent neurons; others enter body fluids and are taken to other neurotransmitter receptive cells throughout the body.

> All neurons simultaneously receive multiple messages. The type of impulse *generated* by these "messages" is determined by the interaction of the excitatory and inhibiting neurotransmitters received by the dendrites. Some impulses are too weak to propagate (or send down the axon); others are strong, so the impulse is sent forth to release neurotransmitters into the synapse. The process goes on and on. No one knows where it starts or ends. It is a continuous, dynamic process from the beginning to the end of biophysical life.

    <u>Classification.</u> Neurotransmitters can be broadly classified into two groups: small-molecule transmitters and neuroactive peptides (or neuropeptides). While several chemicals such as biogenic amine acetycholine, monamines, amino acids and the polypeptides are commonly identified as neurotransmitters, some also include substances such as insulin, carbon monoxide, and so forth. These latter substances are sometimes included as neurotransmitters because they also bind with receptor sites and modulate cell activity. Determining which should be included and which left out depends on how one defines a neurotransmitter. For our immediate purpose, we will include all the above-mentioned substances, since all have the ability to bind with receptor sites and therefore, determine cellular responses. Table 3.1 shows one way of grouping neurotransmitters.

Table 3.1 Classification of neurotranmitters. (Compiled from a variety of sources.)

SMALL MOLECULE NEUROTRANSMITTERS	NEUROACTIVE PEPTIDES OR NEUROPEPTIDES
Biogenic Amine	**Polypeptides**
Acetycholine (Ach)	Bombesin
	Gastrin releasing Peptide (GRP)
Monamines	Gastrins
Pheyalanine and Tryrosine	Gastrin
Dopamine (DA)	Cholecystokinin
Norepinephrine (NE)	Neurophyophyseals
Epinephrine (Epi)	Vasopressin
Tryptophan	Oxytocin
Serotonin (5HT)	Neurophysin I & II
Melatonin (Mel)	Neuropeptide Y
Histadine	Neuropeptide (NY)
Histamine (H)	Pancreatic polypeptide (PP)
	Peptide YY (PYY)
Amino Acids	Opiods
Asparate	Corticotropin (ACTH)
Glutamate (GLU)	Beta-lipotropin
Glycine (Gly)	Dynorphin
GABA	Endorphin
	Enkephaline
Others	Leumorphin
Purines	Secretins
Adenosine	Secretin
ATP	Motilin
GTP	Glucagon
Luetinizing Hormone	VIP
Insulin	GRF
Zinc	Somatostatins
Nitric Oxide (NO)	Somatostin
Carbon Monoxide (CO)	Tachykinins
	Neurokinin A & B
	Neuropeptide A
	Neuropeptide gamma
	Substance P
	Atrial Natriuetic Factor (ANF)

While Table 3.1 lists some of the known neurotransmitters, it should be remembered that scientists continue to uncover even more. No doubt the list will be extended considerably within a few years.

Neuropeptides. Many people use the terms *neuropeptides or peptides* when discussing a *type* of neurotransmitter, the neuroactive polypeptides. This is because approximately 95% of neurotransmitters are neuropeptides (Pert, 2003a, p. 25), the primary neurotransmitters associated with feelings and emotions.

Nevertheless, because other chemicals such as phenylalanine and tyrosine[2] and tryptophan[3] are important in mind-body discussions, but are not neuropeptides, it is more accurate to talk about neurotransmitters as the overall classification. Doing so, we can talk about *neurotransmitters in general,* and we can use the term neuropeptides when dealing specifically with that subgroup.

> Within cells, neurotransmitters are usually packaged in vesicles. When an action potential travels to the synapse, rapid depolarization causes calcium ion channels to open. Calcium then stimulates the transport of vesicles to the synaptic membrane; the vesicle and cell membrane fuse, leading to the release of the packaged neurotransmitter, a mechanism called exocytosis.

MIND AND BODY COMMUNICATION

Cell-to-Cell Communication

We have discussed electrical conduction and chemical transmission as the basis for communication within and between cells. We said electrical conduction occurs between the dendrite receptor sites and the axons and we said neurotransmitters are the "messengers" for chemical transmission of cell-to-cell(s) messages. We mentioned the specificity of receptor sites, which allows (and prevents) the binding of messenger molecules to receptors, and we said *neurotransmission*, the neuron-to-neuron exchange of information, is the primary way the brain communicates with the peripheral nervous system.

What we haven't clearly stated is cell-to-cell(s) communication through body fluids makes it possible for the brain and the rest of the body to interact. This was discussed briefly in Chapter 2 when Brekke and Schultz talked about Transformation of Energy. Our discussion will now focus on how cells communicate through body fluids in what is known as *neuromodulation*.

Neuromodulation
Neuromodulation is the primary way we are able to have a dynamic, interactive web of continuous feedback loops of communication among all parts of the body, organ-to-organ, system-to-system, including the immune system. Rather than affecting a single neuron, neuromodulators tend to impact groups of neurons. For example, the cells in the limbic system are thought to respond as a group of cells rather than as individual cells. Although neuromodulation can happen in milliseconds, it can take longer, sometimes minutes to days. It usually has a longer effect than neurotransmission.

Neuromodulation occurs when neurotransmitters are released directly into one of the body fluids such as the blood, spinal fluid, or lymph fluid. These molecules are then carried throughout the body. In some cases, they connect with cells of other organs, carrying their messages with them. In others, they move into the cellular space around neurons, attach to the receptor sites used in neurotransmission and, therefore, interfere with messages sent neuron-to-neuron. But, remember, receptor sites are discriminating, so how do they decide which messages will be accepted and which rejected? The answer to this question takes us back to our discussion of energy principles presented in Chapter 2.

> Neuromodulation is the movement of neurochemicals from one part of the body to another through body fluids.

Synchrony of Energy Fields. When messenger molecules are released, they move through the body *vibrating and creating energy fields around them*. When they approach a receptor, they gently bounce against the receptor site to test its receptivity. When the two energy fields are able to "vibrate in synchrony,"[4] the messenger molecule is able to bind with the receptor site. Depending on the information carried in the messenger molecule, the function resulting from "binding" can either depress or stimulate cellular function (Pert, 2003a, p. 23).

> *When a peptide or other chemical messenger approaches a receptor, the receptor begins to vibrate, changing its shape. As the receptor begins its "vibrational dance," the messenger responds, touching the receptor to see if it will respond with a vibration that will allow the two to connect. Only if the two can vibrate in synchrony, will the receptor allow the messenger to bind with it. When binding occurs, channels in the membrane of the neuron open and ions move into or out of it...depending on whether the receptor has inhibitory or excitatory effects* (Pert, 2003, p. 27).

The implications of messages being sent throughout the body, cell to cell, organ to organ, and system to system are almost beyond imagination. What we know is we can no longer talk about a dichotomy of mind and body. We now know the human being consists of dynamic, interactive feedback loops that have no clear beginning or endpoint. This kind of thinking has changed science.

Integrating Mind and Body: Psychoneuroimmunology

Historically , most mainstream health care providers believed there were few or no linkages between mind and body. This group approached treatment from a "mechanistic systems" perspective. They believed problems in the cardiovascular system were due to failure of some part of the system. It was a *parts* problem.[5] If we could "fix" the problem with pills or surgery, it could be alleviated.

Others, however, picked up on the work of Walter Cannon (1932) who proposed the fight-flight response when describing how feelings of threat could stimulate the adrenal glands, and Selye (1936) who proposed the General Adaptation Syndrome (GAS) as the body's generalized response to stress. Some of these, grouped together, talked about Psychosomatic Medicine and provided additional data to support mind-body linkages (Alexander, 1950; Cohen, 1954; Engel, 1956; Funkenstein, King & Drolette, 1957; Janis, 1958). Each made significant contributions, paving the way for the next generation of scientists interested in mind-body relations. While seen as fringe scientists by many of their peers, they were actually creating an environment conducive to a paradigm shift.

However, most medical research carried out through the 1960's focused on communication between the neurological and various biophysical systems. The researcher's goal was to find evidence that there *are* brain-body linkages. They still didn't fully understand the importance of the emotions. For example, Choh Hao Li isolated an amino acid (beta-endorphin) from the pituitaries of camels, but not understanding the significance of his findings, failed to pursue that line of research.

> The science of Psychoneuroimmunology opened the door to the possibility of continuous, dynamic, interactive linkages among the multiple parts of the body.

Nevertheless, Solomon (1964) proposed relations among our emotions, immunity, and disease and coined the term *psychoimmunology*. The paradigm was shifting! And then, two landmark studies launched the explosion of research we now know as *Psychoneuroimmunology*. Pert, Pasternak, and Synder (1973) located and labeled the receptors in the brain for an opiate such as morphine, and two independent groups of investigators (Hughes Kosterlitz, & Leslie, 1975; Simantov, Childer, & Snyder, 1975) simultaneously discovered the opiod neuropeptides. Concurrently, Ader and Cohen (1975) reported the immune system could be behaviorally conditioned in a *bilateral direction*. This implied there were feedback loops, rather than linear processes.

The Paradigm Shift

The paradigm shift was in full motion! Pert completed her postdoctoral studies in Pharmacology at John Hopkins University in 1975 and went to the National Institute of Health where she held various research positions until 1987. After leaving NIH, Pert founded and directed a private biotech laboratory and continued her work linking mind and body. In 1981, Ader published a compilation of studies by renowned scientists providing clear evidence of the linkages between the brain, body, emotions, and the immune system. He labeled this psychoneuroimmunology (PNI).

PNI is common language today. A flood of research has shown all body systems are in communication, *a continuous feedback process with loops between and among multiple systems all at one time.* While we can study simple linkages, it is still impossible to be sure where something might start and where it might end. It is an ongoing process!

> *Your biochemical messengers act with intelligence by communicating information, orchestrating a vast complex of conscious and unconscious activities at any one moment. This information transfer takes place over a network lining all of your bodily systems and organs, engaging all of your molecules of emotion as a means of communication!...Your brain is actually a 'mobile brain' that moves throughout your entire body—since it is located in all places at once and not just in your head!* (Pert, 1997, pp. 8-9).

Now, for example, we know the cells of the immune system make hormones nearly identical to those made by the endocrine system allowing the immune system to communicate with all the glands of the endocrine system. This means the immune system can initiate the stress response because it makes ACTH. The immune system can also alter our moods by secreting endorphins that affect the brain (Blalock, Harbour-McMenamin & Rogers, 1985). Endorphins were once thought to be excreted *only* in the brain. We also know the brain can affect the immune and endocrine systems by secreting neuropeptides and hormones, which alter their functions. The body and mind are interconnected. No longer seen as a body and mind, they could be more appropriately thought of as holistic beings. But, some are not there yet; they call this relationship a bodymind.

The Bodymind

Diane Connely first proposed the term bodymind suggesting the body and mind can no longer be thought of as two entities. Pert uses this term when describing the effects of emotions on physiology, and vice versa. It was believed the mind, composed of thoughts and emotions, was located in the brain largely because we thought neurotransmitters and their receptors existed only in the brain. However, we now know neurotransmitters and their receptors are located in all systems of the body. For one of many examples, activity in the intestines releases messenger molecules that create emotion, and emotions release messenger molecules that affect the GI tract. *So, the mind (emotions and thoughts) exists throughout the body.*

> The body has a mind of its own; it is composed of neurotransmitters that circulate throughout the body, with continuous feedback loops.

The process of communication or flow of information throughout the organism is evidence that the body is the outward manifestation of the mind. Neuropeptides are the main biochemicals of emotion linking the major systems of the body into one unit—the bodymind, and emotions are involved in translating information into physical reality (Pert, 1997, p.27).

Pert concluded that our biophysical being has interacting networks with millions of cells, each with millions of receptor sites. Interestingly, the groups of neurons, which process emotion, pain, and input from the five senses, have the largest number of receptor sites where neuropeptides are received and released.

Clearly, communication between mind and body is very extensive and complex, but limited space prevents us from discussing numerous examples. We will describe a few, commonly encountered in health care, to illustrate the point.

The Brain. Although three areas of the brain (cortex, limbic system, and hypothalamus) have high concentrations of peptide receptor sites, the limbic system and the hypothalamus have the highest concentrations. The cortex, the seat of conscious awareness and attention, filters and processes information coming from the five senses. While the limbic system creates emotional states and coordinates memory, learning, and emotion, the hypothalamus controls homeostasis and all autonomic functions. Thoughts and feelings affect what we learn and remember and affect autonomic function.

The periaquaductal gray area of the brain influences pain perception and the placebo effect (how our expectations affect healing). Our thoughts and feelings can influence not only what we expect, but also the effects of those expectations.

The limbic system of the brain seems to be most closely associated with emotions as determined by Positron Emission Tomography (PET), which allows researchers to view the brain as it functions in a live individual. Using PET, Pert discovered that 85-95% of neuropeptides she had studied had receptors in the limbic system, indicating they may be the molecules associated with feelings (Pert, Ruff, Weber, & Herkenham, 1985; Pert, 1986). As these neruotransmitters travel through our bodies and attach in the brain, they cause us to feel emotions, and conversely, by feeling emotions, more neuropeptides are released, affecting the rest of the body.

> The opiate neuropeptides, similar to morphine in composition, exist throughout the body.

The Opiate Neuropeptides. One of the larger known groups of neuropeptides, the opiates (see Table 3.1), have a chemical composition similar to morphine. Various types of opiates reside in the cells of numerous body systems including the central nervous system, immune system, GI system, and others. These opiates, released in response to "good" stress (challenge), "bad" stress (threat), exercise, deep breathing, beauty, and laughter, are able to attach to cells all over the body and affect their function. Some kinds of opiate peptides decrease immune function, such as those released in response to chronic stress. Other types increase immune function (Kaye, Morton, Bowcutt, & Maupin, 2000) and create experiences of relaxation, happiness, and higher consciousness.

The GI and Endocrine Systems. The entire gastrointestinal system is full of peptide receptors, so thoughts and feelings can influence digestion, assimilation, and elimination. We have all experienced "gut feelings," or the effects of stressful emotions on some aspect of this system from "butterflies" to diarrhea and constipation. Every gland of the endocrine system contains receptors for peptides, so what we think and feel affect reproduction, thyroid function, sugar metabolism, and the stress response.

The Immune System. All cells in the immune system, from natural killer cells to T- and B-lymphocytes, have peptide receptors on their walls. On their cell walls, white blood cells have receptors for every peptide known, so they travel to peptides and bind with them. The peptides increase or decrease the activities of the white blood cells in that area of the body, including wound healing and destroying invaders. Since our thoughts and feelings can trigger and direct peptide travel, we may be able to influence healing in specific areas of the body.[6]

In the late 1980's, Candace Pert and colleagues isolated peptide T, a synthetic neuropeptide that seemed to block HIV from entering the cell. One study of 11 people infected up to 17 years with HIV, showed the administration of peptide T blocked chemokine receptors, greatly reducing the levels of HIV in the plasma, white blood cells, and monocytes (Polianova, et al., 2003). In an interview, Pert (2003) discussed her recent study with rats, stating that evidence suggests that peptide T, a chemokine[7] antagonist/agonist, may be beneficial in the treatment of Alzheimer's and other brain diseases, by delaying or eliminating neuronal degeneration.

> We have linkages between our brain and gastrointestinal system, our immune and our endocrine system, our musculoskeletal and immune, and on and on. Every part of our biophysical being can communicate with every other part. These are continuous, dynamic linkages among the multiple parts of our being. Communication occurs cell-to-cell and energy field to energy field. So, we can communicate biophysical energy fields to emotional and spiritual energy fields. This is what makes the biophysical-psychosocial being a *holistic being.*

Conclusions

The above section provided a brief overview of communication between mind and body. We said mind-body communication occurs because our thoughts and feelings influence the release and movement of many kinds of messenger molecules that travel throughout the body affecting all aspects of cellular function, negatively and positively. And conversely, all systems of the body release messenger molecules that travel to the brain affecting what we think and feel. The science of mind-body relations grows by the hour because we have the technology to "see" molecular structures and measure electrical charges. We also have a language we can use to describe and explain these relations.

We have a slightly different problem when it comes to talking about integration of spirit with mind and body. While we know electrical conduction (and, therefore, energy) is part of every living organism, we have trouble measuring some types of energy. The next section addresses some of these issues. Specifically, we will talk about the integration of spirit with mind and body.

INTEGRATING SPIRIT WITH BODY AND MIND

A major tenet of Modeling and Role-Modeling is that relations exist between mind, body and spirit. Erickson et al. state:

> *Human beings are holistic persons who have multiple interacting subsystems. Permeating all subsystems are the inherent bases. These include genetic makeup and spiritual drive. Body, mind, emotion and spirit are a total unit and they act together. They affect and control one another interactively. The interaction of the multiple subsystems and the inherent bases creates holism. Holism implies that the whole is greater than the sum of parts* (1983, pp. 44-45).

Connection as Energetic Exchange

We have an inherent need to be connected, spirit with mind and body. This need motivates us to find meaning in our existence, better understand who we are, and realize our reason for being. The model of holism (shown in Figure 1.3) indicates our spiritual drive helps integrate spirit, mind, and body. It draws from the Universal Field, and permeates our biophysical-psychosocial being bringing "Universal information" with it. We send energy back into the environment by way of spiritual energy although the nature of the energy sent back depends on how fully integrated we are as human beings.

This is where concepts of Needs, Attachment, Loss, and Developmental Residual enter. Each will be discussed in later chapters. For now, to simplify, we can say we have an inherent spiritual drive that draws energy from the environment and all that it contains, including Soul and Universal energy. This energy is transformed, used, and redistributed through multiple methods, including the charkas and meridians (Gerber, 2000, p.21) to enhance our holistic well-being. A growing body of evidence suggests that when we include spirituality in our lives, we have improved physical, mental, and emotional well-being in a variety of physical and emotional conditions (Matthews & Larson, 1995).

> *Healing involves the movement of energy. We are made of energy. We think with energy. We feel with energy. Health and vitality can manifest only when the energies are aligned, balanced, and working in harmony with the Soul (The Soul as Healer.* L. J. Nichols, 2000, p.13).

In this section, we will revisit and extrapolate some of the concepts presented in Chapters 1 and 2 as we explore how the spirit integrates with mind and body. How might the connections between Self and Universal Field occur? Since the Self and Universal Field are energetic in nature, we will explore these connections as an exchange of energy.

Subatomic Particles

As stated in Chapter 2, everything in the universe, including us, is made of atoms, which are made of subatomic particles (electrons, protons, neutrons, photons of light). Subatomic particles are made of even smaller particles called quanta. These tiny particles are in constant movement. Bohr (1961) stated that isolated material particles are abstractions, and that particles are interconnected, continually changing patterns in a "cosmic web." The "bootstrap" hypothesis of Chew (1968) suggested all things are made to exactly fit together as a whole, and all things follow this inherent pattern. All things are energy in various forms.

Energy Waves

The movement of subatomic particles generates vibrations[8] or waves of energy. These waves produce a vibrating field around the particle, which creates a force affecting other particles near it. Since moving particles create an energy field, there are multiple fields at the same time. We have energy fields within us and around us—all constantly moving, changing, interacting, and affecting one another.

Consciousness

Many different types of energy fields interact, and in doing so, affect the function of the body. This includes light energy or photons. Gerber (2001), a leader in Vibrational Medicine, stated:

We know that the cells of the body actually emit weak pulses of light. Those weak cellular light pulses seem to be part of a light-based communication system that helps to coordinate the actions of the cells within each organ. The pulses of light emitted...are just one of the many different informational codes the human body and its individual cells use to regulate the function of organs on a day-to-day and moment-to-moment basis. Our cells communicate through coded messages carried by hormones and biochemicals as well as through electrical signals...and through weak light signals. The cells of the body appear to have their own inherent intelligence... (p. 11).

Because all things are connected, these complex interactions within the body also interact with the environment. As a total, Universal Intelligence is created by a merging of all energy fields, human, and other. Gerber (2001) called this intelligence *Consciousness* and considered it the source of all information. According to him,

Consciousness is not merely a by product of electrical and chemical signal processing in the human brain. Consciousness is a kind of energy itself...Consciousness has ghostlike qualities that allow it to reside not only in the brain, but beyond the body itself (p. 10).

Pert (2003) also addressed this issue:

According to information theory, the movement and storage of information is intelligence. Information moves throughout the body in the form of peptides so that intelligence, or mind, is throughout the body. All areas of the body send and receive information to and from each other using the peptides as messengers to create one whole, coordinated, interconnected being. Information can infinitely continue to increase, and is beyond space and time. It belongs to its own "inforealm" that we experience as the mind, emotion, and spirit. Some call this the field of intelligence; some call it God (p. 310).

Deepak Chopra (2004) offered another way of thinking about such intelligence, defining it as "the potential for all creation" (p. 34). According to him, "The universe is a mirror of consciousness" and "The physical world mirrors a mind; it carries intention and intelligence in every atom" (p. 102). He argued that we have the potential to affect others in positive and negative ways because of Consciousness—Consciousness is much greater than we are, but it is in and around us.

In the one reality, consciousness creates itself, which is the same as saying that God is inside his creation. There is no place outside creation for divinity to stand—omnipresence means that if any place exists, God is there. But, whereas God can be attentive to an infinitude of worlds, human beings use attention selectively. We put it in one place and take it away from another. By paying attention we add the creative spark, and that part of our experience, either positive or negative, will grow. Violence begets violence, but so too does love beget love (Chopra, 2004, p. 103).

According to this way of thinking, Consciousness is an intelligence, which provides information about the structure of our Universe and all knowledge about our nature. It is Universal Intelligence. This idea relates back to the notion "we are energy first" presented in Chapter 2. Recall the idea of the "Kirlian phantom-leaf effect" (Gerber, 2001, pp. 26-27), which provides evidence that all living organisms have an invisible etheric body that guides cellular placement in the physical body—the etheric body guides the growth and development of the physical body. This "knowledge" contains all the codes needed for the growth of the organism. This holds true for all living creatures. *This is Consciousness.*

> *We are part of a psychosomatic network run by intelligence that has no bounds and is shared among all of us in a bigger network. We are all individual nodal points, each an access point into a larger intelligence. This shared connection gives us a profound sense of spirituality, making us feel connected and whole. When we think otherwise, we suffer the stress of separation from our source. What is it that flows between us all? The emotions! They are the connectors, flowing between individuals, moving us as love, sorrow, and compassion. Like information, the emotions travel between the two realms of mind and body, as peptides and their receptors in the physical realm, and as feelings in the nonmaterial realm* (Pert, 2003, p. 207).

Interestingly, thoughts of *Consciousness* as being *in us* and *around us* and as being *of God* are not new to Nursing. Florence Nightingale proposed something quite similar when she stated: *What is Spirituality? Feelings called forth by the consciousness of a presence of higher nature than human* (Calabria & Macrae, 1994, p.120).

> *In a two-year study of the brains of people who practiced Buddhist meditation, feelings of unity, calmness, and transcendence corresponded to increased activity in the frontal lobes of the brain* (d'Aquili and Newberg, 1998).

Distant Connections

In our discussion of connection as an energetic exchange, we briefly mentioned connecting with others. Since connecting with others plays a major part of a nurse's day, we will explore this a little further. We experience distant connections in every day life, but haven't always had a language to describe our experiences. Have you ever noticed someone keeps popping into your mind, and very shortly, they call you and say they have been thinking about you for days? Most of us have experienced this example of distant energy connection.

Have you ever felt "watched" and turned around to find your dog or cat, or a stranger, staring at you intently from across the room? This, too, is a distant energy connection. Have you ever wondered what it means to say, "I send you my love" or "I'll send you healing thoughts"? Research findings suggest we are able to affect others with our thoughts and feelings (Schlitz & Braud, 1997) through energy connections.

Nonlocality. John Bell's theory of interconnectedness indicated that once subatomic particles have established a connection, they remain connected energetically over distance, and can communicate with and affect each other. They establish a nonlocal connection. Traveling faster than light, and not using any known signals of communication between particles, their effect is instantaneous and the power does not diminish with distance. According to Bell, the world is full of nonlocal influences, not only in the subatomic world, but also in the events of everyday life (Aspect, Dalibard, & Roger, 1982; Herbert, 1985). In replicated research of nonlocal influences, when two people established an emotional closeness, their brains (EEG) exhibited this nonlocal phenomenon (Grinberg-Zylberbaum, Delaflor, Attie, & Goswami, 1994).

Gerber (2000) refers to L. Dossey's (1993) work when talking about nonlocal connections. He proposes:

> *There are also a number...who seek to understand healing in terms of something other than just an energy transfer. For example,...Dossey, author of* Prayer is Good Medicine, *believes that healing is due to the effects of Consciousness, or more specifically, our 'nonlocal mind'. This term, 'nonlocal' refers to various phenomena that demonstrate that our minds can observe and even influence individuals, objects, and events widely separated from the observer by distance and time* (pp. 382-383).

Distant Intentionality. Distant intentionality is the intent to have an effect on another from a distance and includes the effects of mental intention on "non-living" and living systems. Numerous research studies have provided evidence of distant intentionality.[9]

Jahn and Dunne (1987) have shown that with their minds some people can influence machines from a distance. Benor (1990, 1992a, 1992b) reviewed 131 published laboratory-controlled studies on distant intentionality and healing on a variety of living systems including enzymes, bacteria, cells in test tubes, animals, and humans. He found 56 studies reported statistically significant results in the desired directions. For example, conformation (winding or unwinding of the DNA helix) of human DNA in a test tube was influenced significantly by focused human intentionality (Rein, 1995). Schlitz and Braud (1997) evaluated 30 published studies and concluded that a significant desired effect could be demonstrated. Schmidt, Schneider, Utts and Walach (2004) concluded there was a small, but significant effect suggesting distant intentionality cannot be ruled out even though there is no known theoretical conception that can incorporate this finding.

Healing can be facilitated by communication of healing energy across time and space. This is known as distant intentionality and distant healing.

Distant Healing. Distant healing, under the larger umbrella of distant intentionality, attempts to benefit another, rather than to simply have an effect. Distant healing is defined as "a consciously dedicated act of purposeful thinking aimed at benefiting another person's physical or emotional well-being, at a distance" (Sicher, Targ, Moore, & Smith, 1998). It includes prayer, directed thoughts and feelings, and spiritual healing techniques. Distant healing also involves energy-based therapies like Therapeutic Touch, Reiki, and Healing Touch. Studies have provided considerable evidence that purposeful thought has a significant effect on the well-being of those on the receiving end of the connection.

H. Erickson recounts the following story to illustrate the concepts discussed above.

My husband (Lance Erickson) had undergone his second open-heart surgery in less than a month. He was thought to be septic, but no organism could be cultured. His white blood count fell to 2.0 or less. He had two cardiac arrests and was placed on the critical list. I had been advised he might not be able to "fight off the infection" and the family should be called. Our children were all notified, including our son and daughter-in-law who were teaching in Turkey. They asked if they should come home, and I told them he would either get better or worse before they could make arrangements, and it would be better if they stayed there and sent him love and healing energy.

Over the next several days, my husband occasionally said, "Oh, that is so nice, thank you." When asked what he was talking about, he would say I had been rubbing his feet. In reality, neither I, nor anyone else in that room had been rubbing his feet. This happened many times.

Later, after he was better and able to go home, his son and daughter in Turkey asked if he had received the energy they sent. When we inquired about it, they stated that they sat together, purposefully thought about him, and sent energy to his feet. I will always believe the energy sent across the ocean was very important in his ability to recover. He is now 4 years post operative, playing with his grandchildren, golfing with friends, and living a full, enriched life.

The Unified Field Theory

Einstein proposed that all fundamental forces (all energy fields) are just different manifestations of the same force. He called this the Unified Field Theory.[10] Brian Greene, author of *The Elegant Universe* (2003), presents a magnificent description of scientific work that helps us understand string theory, symmetry and super symmetry, and provides evidence that points in the direction of a Unified Field. McTaggart (2002), who has extrapolated from this work, says the Unified Field is the single source of all energy, including Zero Point Energy (p. 23).

We may, therefore, regard matter as being constituted by the regions of space in which the field is extremely intense. There is no place in this new kind of physics both for the field and matter, for the field is the only reality. (Albert Einstein [1961] quoted in Capek, p. 319).

Some describe the Unified Field as universal energy where all "knowing," all "intelligence" resides (Chopra, 1989, 2000, 2004; Dyer, 1989; McTaggart, 2002). According to these authors, the Unified Field—an energy field of pure intelligence—is thought to be the core of the universe, i.e., the core of life. *We believe Universal Energy gives rise to The Universal Force.* Some call this a Life Force (Gordon, 2002), others call it the Divine (Dossey, 1993), God (Lesser, 1999), and Consciousness (Chopra, 2000; Gerber, 2001).

A few physicists accept Zero Point Energy as real energy, which we cannot directly sense, since it is the same everywhere, even inside our bodies and measuring devices. From this perspective, the ordinary world of matter and energy is like foam atop the quantum vacuum sea. It does not matter to a ship how deep the ocean is below it. If the zero-point energy is real, there is the possibility that it can be tapped as a source of power or be harnessed to generate a propulsive force for space travel (http://www.calphysics.org/research).

Zero Point Field. At one time, space was described as a void, a vacuum. As physics advanced, subatomic particles were observed to suddenly appear, and disappear in space. Einstein's equation $E=mc^2$ means that energy (E) and matter (m) continually transform into each other at very high speeds (c^2). Subatomic particles constantly travel at very high speeds. It was concluded, based on this equation, that space must be a field of energy from which matter, or particles, could arise and into which they return. Is it possible they move into an energy field we haven't yet been able to study? Some think they do; they call this the Zero Point Field. Zero Point Energy is said to exist in an empty space, where subatomic particles can continue to move even at a temperature of absolute zero. It is also believed to reside within and outside us (www.calphysics.org/research).

The potential for understanding how the Soul connects with our mind and body may lie in understanding Zero Point Energy and its connection with other types of energy fields.

Integration

So, what do we think about the linkages among spirit, mind, and body? There is no separation between the spirit, mind, and body, of an individual, between two individuals, or between an individual and Higher Power. All we see and experience is composed of subatomic particles that are mostly space with some tiny particles moving in patterns, communicating with each other through photons of light. When packed densely, energy particles are transformed to create matter.

Within the body, we have multiple energy fields created by moving particles. Messenger molecules convey information through harmonious vibratory dances with receptors. Our thoughts and feelings are vibrating waves of energy. Our spiritual essence and the Universal Field of Intelligence are vibrating fields of energy. It seems likely that we can intentionally use thought and emotion to connect and communicate with others and a Universal Force, i.e., Higher Power or God.

We have the ability to receive energy from the Universe. We also have the ability to send energy into the Universe. We have to decide what kind of energy we want to send out to others.

Given that we are holistic beings, the energies created by the millions of transactions occurring at any given time within our "self" determine what is sent back into the Universe. Without awareness, we can, and do, send energy vibrating at many different levels. With awareness, we can *purposefully* send energy. If there is a Unified Field where all intelligence resides (and we think there is), this, too, would be where our spiritual energy interfaces with the mind-body energy. We think we draw from Zero-Point Energy (from the Unified Field) and give back to it. However, we are still open to new understandings, new science, that will help us better understand how the mind, body and spirit work together.

Suffice to say, we believe spiritual energy links us to our Soul and the Soul is the essence of our Self. Since spiritual energy is necessary to discover and explore Soul-work specific to this lifetime, it might be considered *the bridge between two energy fields: the Soul and the biophysical fields.* We cannot talk about the holistic person only in the context of mind-body relations; the spirit must also be integrated in order to achieve high-level wellness or eudemonistic health. We must discuss it as mind-body-spirit, all connecting, interacting and shaping the essence of who we are, for without spiritual energy integration, we are not really holistic beings. This is the dynamic process of Being. Our holistic well-being depends on healthy connections and interactions among mind, body and spirit.

As far as types of energy and energy fields are concerned, we suspect when all is said and done, we will find Einstein was correct: All fundamental forces are really the manifestation of one super force—the Universal Force, which is drawn from Zero Point energy field. If this can be accepted with faith, we need to remember this force resides in us as well as around us. This is important because "our intent" will determine the nature of energy sent into the environment, energy sent toward specific people and energy sent to the universe, in general. These capabilities are the bases for all types of communication including Presence, Distant Intentionality, Distant Healing, Prayer and other types of nonlocal messaging.

IMPLICATIONS

The implications are staggering: constantly moving fields of energy permeate, interact, and transform one another—and in doing so, dictate the nature of the universe; and we are part of this dynamic, never-ending process! Our thoughts and feelings influence these energy fields, too. We draw from the energy fields of others, both near and far, and we contribute to energy fields, both near and far. What we think about, what we hope for, our intent, and expectations influence the creation of not only our reality, but also the reality of others. As we learn to more fully connect within ourselves—mind, body and spirit—we are more able to fully connect with others. When this happens we will have a new and deeper understanding of what it means to be meaningfully connected with Self, Others[11] and a Universal Force.[12]

Earlier, we talked about synchrony cell-to-cell. Now, we can talk about synchrony between energy fields and between people. We know emotions stimulate the outpouring of neurotransmitters.   Neurotransmitters vibrate at different frequencies and so do receptors. When they synchronize, the message is received. When they don't, the message is denied. Matching and synchrony are crucial for cell-to-cell communication. The same holds true for the energy fields of people.

Different emotions cause the release of specific neurotransmitters, which affect the vibration of the receptor.   If they vibrate in "synch," they connect, vibrating in harmony with that emotion. "Extracorporeal peptide reaching" proposes that the vibrations of the receptors on our cell walls can cause the receptors on the cells of another person to vibrate in response to them creating emotional resonance and allowing us to feel what others feel (Pert, 1997). This may help to explain distant intentionality.

The Thinker and the Thought

We often allow ourselves to get caught in a river of thought, tossed around like a twig, never realizing the water is not over our heads; all we have to do is stand up and walk over to the bank. Our thoughts and feelings are part of who we are, but we can learn to control them. They were never meant to run the show.

Since we are people with free will, we can learn how we want to think and feel, and what we want to believe, moment-to-moment, day-to-day. And we can learn how to become more fully ourselves. Since our thoughts create feelings, if we learn to change what we think, we can change what we feel. Furthermore, since our feelings tend to drive our behavior (actions), we can change our actions by changing our thoughts.

Just as it is our free will to decide whether to eat eggplant or hamburger for lunch, it is our free will to decide to yell at the person who cuts in line in traffic, or let them in with a smile! Not only can we use our free will to influence our thoughts and actions, but our choices can also influence the reality we experience each day. What we believe and expect to happen influence what we perceive and experience in the world.

Beliefs and Healing

When we have a belief about an event or expect a particular outcome, the brain often begins making changes in the body 20-30 seconds before the event actually occurs. For example, when we are ill, our thoughts seem to be able to turn on the body's ability to heal itself, creating and releasing just the right chemicals to bring about what is expected (Benson, 1996). "Placebo" response refers to the phenomenon of people experiencing improved health outcomes from pills or procedures, which have no known medical benefit. They believe these interventions might help them because health care professionals told them so.

In one research project studying the effectiveness of knee surgery, none of the clients knew who was in the experimental group and who was in the control group (received the placebo). The experimental group received the real knee surgery, and the "placebo" group only had slits cut in the leg with no intervention. At two years post surgery, both groups had the same amount of relief (Benson and Friedman, 1996). "Placebos" have also been shown to have significant effects 70% of the time when treating coronary artery disease, bronchial asthma, duodenal ulcer, angina pectoris (chest pain), and herpes simplex (Benson and Friedman, 1996). Research with placebos demonstrates the power of the mind to stimulate healing in the body when we expect it will occur. When we have poor expectations, we can also create the *nocebo* effect, with decreases in health (Benson, 1996).

Expectation and Perception

What we believe and expect affects what we perceive. Due to the intimate connection between what we think and feel, our thoughts and feelings allow us to enter the communication of the bodymind through the movement of neurotransmitters. This means we have the potential to create change in the world we experience. Earlier in the chapter, we stated that the hypothalamus and limbic system have the highest concentrations of neuropeptide receptor sites. There is also a large concentration of peptide receptors in the cortex of the brain where we process input from all five senses. We cannot focus on the entire input coming in at once, so depending on our thoughts, feelings, beliefs, memories, and expectations,[13] the brain chooses what will be processed. When we have expectations about what the future holds, the brain will bring to our conscious awareness only that input which supports that belief (Pert, 1997; Walker & Walker, 2003).

There are several techniques we can use to enrich our lives and facilitate healing in our clients by choosing our thoughts and feelings. Heart Touch[14] is one of them. We have included this technique in Appendix A and invite you to use it to enjoy your work more fully. When nurses in a hospital setting practiced HeartTouch, they experienced less stress, and greater spiritual well-being and hardiness (Walker, 2006). Of course, since we are holistic beings, the type of energy we send is related to what we expect to happen!

I have found two easy tools that change what I am thinking and feeling wherever I am. You can try them yourself and teach them to clients.

First, change the speed and depth of your breathing. When stressed, we breathe fast and shallow. When we take deeper, slower breaths, our physiology changes from the stress response to the relaxation response. Our thoughts and feelings change. Awareness of the breath brings us to the present moment, so we can choose what we think.

Second, when the corners of the mouth turn up, endorphins are released, and thoughts and feelings change. So smile at yourself in windows, smile when you are headed into a challenging event, and smile waiting traffic, even if you don't feel like it (M. Walker, October 20, 2005).

Food for Thought

How would our lives be different if we believed that what we think and feel each moment, each day, plays a key role in creating the health of our bodies? What if we believed that our clients' feelings affect how well they cope with stress and their ability to heal? What if we really believed *what we think and feel* creates changes in *our clients' bodies*? How would these beliefs affect the way we practice nursing? How would they change our interactions with family members and others we meet along the way? These premises are basic to Modeling and Role-Modeling (1983). Ways for you to think about them and ideas for practice are provided in Chapters 9-13 of this book. But, there are other important considerations. Not only do we have the ability to help people, we also have the potential to harm.

Word to the Wise

In our discussion of how thoughts and feelings affect the body, we must also address several related issues:

    1) the individual's propensity to assign guilt and blame when things don't turn out as expected,
    2) the individual's vulnerability when in need, and
    3) the individual's need to control his or her life.

Since these are interwoven concepts, they will be addressed together.

The No-Fault Clause. If we become sick, we may decide to apply our knowledge of the mind-body connection to heal our bodies. But what happens if we aren't successful? What happens when we can't cure our sickness or disease? Some people have said they feel guilty, that they must not have "done it good enough." Or maybe they should have "tried harder." Others have even said they must not "deserve" to heal.

When our body or feelings do not respond to our efforts to apply mind-body techniques, or our clients are unable to use our well-intended advice, it is not *our fault and it is not their fault*! We need to be clear this is not about awarding credit or placing blame, or about being responsible for the cause of illness or disease. It is about learning to think about mind-body-spirit relations, so we can enhance growth.

While it is important to learn not to blame families, friends, or ourselves, it is to our greatest benefit to learn to think thoughts that help us better understand others. If we can remember that "needs drive behavior," then we might be able to think about which needs are being met by being sick, and whether there is another way to meet those needs. When we remember we are holistic beings, we might discover physical illness happens because we have the need to become more fully connected, spirit with mind and body.

Vulnerability. If our thoughts are powerful enough to have a healing effect, we must also address the possibility of their having a harmful effect (Dossey, L., 1997).   Luckily, we must have developed the ability to shield ourselves from the negative thoughts of others, or we would never have survived. For example, Schlitz and Braud (1997) found receivers could block the thoughts of senders. They reported that even if the receivers didn't know when they were being thought about, they weren't affected, if they didn't want to be. Dora Kunz says our energy field protects us from negative energy when we are healthy. However, when we are not well, physically or emotionally, we are more vulnerable to outside energy (1991). Since many of our clients are ill, they are more vulnerable, and so may be more affected by what we think and feel.

We're Doing our Best. And what happens when our clients choose not to follow our "advice," advice we are certain will help them heal? Without understanding that *people do the best they can*, given their circumstances, it is difficult to recognize they care, they *want to be healthy,* and they want to be loved. When we fail to understand this in our clients, we may never see or hear behavior suggesting they are human beings who need our help. Instead, we may fall into the "blaming trap." This then becomes a vicious cycle. We project our attitudes and beliefs, and our clients respond with a sense of helplessness and or hopelessness. They become what they expect, and we feel equally helpless because we have not found a way to "fix" them.

Remember, clients, too, have a need for affiliated-individuation and they sometimes think it is better to be sick than lose our affiliation. If confronted with such a situation, people will sometimes gain control by being sick. At least, when this happens, their need to be taken care of is minimally addressed. They should not be faulted for this, but helped to find other ways to be both affiliated and individuated. We will discuss this issue further in Chapters 9-14.

> It is important to bear in mind that sicknesses or situations can help us find new ways to view our world, interact with others, and live our lives. They are part of our life journey.

Finding Meaning. Sometimes we don't understand the *meaning* of the problem or the *purpose of the condition*. When this happens, it is important to remember many experiences in our life journey help us learn more about ourselves. We might be too focused on our mind and body to understand the importance of the spiritual journey. Sometimes we forget healing can occur even if the body dies. When this happens, families mend broken ties, individuals reconnect with a Higher Power they thought they had lost, and so forth. But, we can never know what healing is for another, or why events happen as they do. As we become more aware of what we are thinking and feeling, we can better look into our own hearts. Here we find true meaning.

> When we unconditionally accept another, we exchange energy that helps both of us grow and heal.

We believe deeper understanding of these ideas helps us embody the concept of unconditional acceptance—a prerequisite to knowing how to love and nurture the body, mind, and spirit, a prerequisite to helping our Self reach its greatest potential. When this happens, we can be aware of our thoughts, and change those that are not growth-producing. This includes valuing what our clients believe they need in order to heal, and knowing what they expect, they will likely experience. We will know Universal Energy is ever present, ready to help our clients and us, if we ask. This is Modeling and Role Modeling.

ENDNOTES

[1] For a more detailed account, I recommend referring to your favorite anatomy and physiology book, or to a website such as http://www.mcgill.ca

[2] Which breaks down to make dopamine and its derivatives.

[3] Which breaks down to make serotonin.

[4] Interestingly, the vibrating receptors are very sensitive and can be affected by other energy fields. Thus, fields created by other forms of energy (such as light and sound) can either interfere or enhance "binding" of the messenger molecule with the receptor site.

[5] For example, hypertension was due to something in the blood vessels that made them constrict—something in the cardiovascular system. Alternative views were accepted only after studies repeatedly demonstrated clinical evidence of mind-body relations. A nursing study done by Erickson and Swain (1982) was one such example. That study provided evidence that hypertension could be alleviated with interventions focused on the psychosocial aspects of the human being.

[6] If these ideas interest you, see Capra (1983) or Walker and Walker (2003) for a more detailed discussion.

[7] What are chemokines and what do they do? Arenzo-Seisodos F, et al. (*Nature*, October, 1996, October) say chemokines are soluble proteins that attract white blood cells to an inflamed area or site of infection within the body. They are made and secreted by various cells in the immune system. Each chemokine binds to a specific receptor on the surface of white blood cells such as monocytes, lymphocytes, basophils, and eosinophils. This interaction is extremely precise, meaning the chemokine will only dock to a chemokine receptor of a specific shape. This exact match-up of chemokine and receptor triggers a cascade of events within the cell leading to chemotaxis, the mobilization of immune cells to an area of the body where they are needed. HIV blocked by chemokine antagonist, *Nature* 3;383 (6599:400).

[8] As in all areas, experts disagree on some points. However, most agree that we are energy fields, with areas of different frequencies of vibration, all affected by different forms of vibration. For example, when you heat ice you get water, and if you heat the water, you get steam. All three are hydrogen and oxygen vibrating at faster speeds. Similarly, we are beings of one essence, with different aspects, each vibrating at different frequencies from slowest to highest, starting with the physical body followed by the emotional, mental, astral, spiritual, celestial, causal, cosmic, soul, integrative, eternal, and universal mind bodies.

[9] Recent research has indicated that prayer may not have a positive effect on those intended to receive healing energy from God. However, until the methods are carefully reviewed, we continue to hold that positive intent has the potential to send healing energy.

[10] While unable to prove his theory, scientists today are testing string theory (Greene, 2003), which takes Einstein's postulation to a new height. A better understanding of how all energy fields relate will help us explain how the spirit integrates with mind and body.

[11] In 1991 D.L. Childre founded the Institute of HeartMath to determine the role the heart plays in our health, and to measure the qualities he believes are associated with the heart, which include appreciation, care, compassion, and love. Their research suggests that when we focus our attention

on the area of the heart and intentionally cause ourselves to feel different emotions, the heart responds to these emotions in a variety of ways. The heart then affects the rest of the body. The rhythm of the heartbeat produces an electromagnetic field that can be detected 8-10 feet away from the body. The electrical patterns generated by the heart can be detected in our brain waves (Song, Schwartz, & Russek, 1998). By placing an electrode anywhere on the body, the electrical signal of the heart can be detected, indicating that it permeates every cell (Childre & Martin, 1999).

[12] In America, 90% of the people feel that God loves them and 77% believe that God can cure people who have a serious illness (Larson, 1998). The spiritual texts of most cultures including Hinduism, Judaism, Christianity, Buddhism, and Islam describe a relationship with the Divine that often includes omnipresence, healing, and oneness with all. Research in neuroscience suggests that our brains seem to be wired to experience the Divine (Benson, 1996). Here is a personal story about these connections as reported by M. Walker. *When we moved into our new house, we discovered a stray cat that lived under the house. We started feeding her and gradually she would let us pet her for a few minutes, now and then. We named her Lilly. One day she was sitting in the backyard in the heat of the Texas summer sun, barely moving. Usually, in the middle of the day, she was under the house. I walked up to her, and she still didn't move. I brought her some water, thinking maybe she had eaten something that didn't agree with her. I came back an hour later and her head was in the water bowl with her tongue hanging in the water.*

I took a deep breath and tried to make the decision whether to take her to the vet or let nature take its course. I called a friend and off to the vet we went. She purred all the way as I held her wrapped in a blanket.

In an instant, the vet said she had a bladder blockage, a simple surgery would fix it, and she would be out in a couple of days. Feeling very relieved, I left for a weekend out of town, planning to pick her up on Monday. When I returned, my husband said Lilly was not doing well and we immediately went to the hospital. She still had an IV and urinary catheter and was having little output. She had not eaten. The vet said her severe kidney failure meant she would never have a good quality of life. The vet asked if we wanted to euthanize her to prevent further suffering. We were shocked, expecting to be bringing her home. We asked if they would keep her overnight and run the lab tests again in the morning. If nothing had changed, we would do it at that time.

We went home and prayed and prayed. We thought about the fact that Lilly had not gone under the house to die, as cats often do, but stayed in the yard for hours in plain view. We told God that if Lilly was to live, we needed a very clear sign by morning. We went in first thing and the vet came in. She said she had run the lab tests three times, and could not explain the results; they were perfectly normal! We stayed with Lilly, doing energy-based healing on her for an hour. Over the next two days, she began to improve. Finally we brought her home. Lilly now lives inside, playing and purring all the time (November, 2005).

[13] *I want to share with you an experience I had about expectation that forever changed my life. I went to a conference on subtle energy medicine, and Marilyn Schlitz was speaking about the power of our expectations. She asked us to view the video of a basketball game she was about to show, and count the number of times the red team had their hand on the basketball. I watched carefully and counted 15. She asked whether anyone had seen anything unusual. Of 200 people only 25 raised their hands. She asked us to watch it again looking for anything unusual. To my amazement, I noticed that it was not even a basketball game and everyone had a basketball, each bouncing his own. We all proudly told her what we had seen and she asked whether anyone had seen anything else. This time only 2 people raised their hands. She told us to take a moment, focus, and ask our brains to allow us to see what we did not expect. After a few minutes, we watched the video a third time. I was shocked to see a gorilla among the people pounding its chest! I had not seen it, even when I was trying to see something unusual. It made me wonder what is happening all around me that I am not seeing. Who in my life is being kind and I don't see it because I expect something else?* (M. Walker, personal communication, October 15, 2005).

[14] This technique has been studied with a group of nurses in the hospital setting and reported in Walker (2006).

SECTION 2

SECTION II

MRM CONCEPTS RELATED TO THE HOLISTIC PERSON

We are poised on the brink of a revolution-a revolution as daring and profound as Einstein's discovery of relativity. At the very frontier of science new ideas are emerging that challenge everything we believe about how our world works and how we define ourselves. Discoveries are being made that prove what religion has always espoused, that human beings are far more extraordinary than an assemblage of flesh and bones. At its most fundamental, this new science answers questions that have perplexed scientists for hundreds of years. At its most profound, this is a science of the miraculous.

Lynn McTaggart (2003). *The Field: The Quest for the Secret Force of the Universe,* p. iixv.

This section includes five chapters designed to expand the conceptual understandings of the Modeling and Role-Modeling theory first presented in Erickson, Tomlin, and Swain, 1983, *Modeling and Role-Modeling: A Theory and Paradigm for Nursing.* Each chapter is written to clarify or expand on selected concepts, including Self-care, developmental processes, affiliated-individuation within the context of need satisfaction, attachment-loss-reattachment, and coping and adaptation. Appendices B-D includes taxonomies of developmental residual (B), needs (C), and selected considerations related to cognitive development (D). These are provided to enrich your understanding and enhance observation skills.

CHAPTER 4

SELF-CARE:
KNOWLEDGE, RESOURCES, AND ACTIONS

JUDITH E. HERTZ AND LINDA BAAS

Seventy-five-year-old Anna Martin smoked nearly two packs of cigarettes every day for almost 60 years. Now she is home, recovering from a myocardial infarct (MI) that occurred two weeks ago. While hospitalized, she quit smoking. The home health nurse visited to monitor her recovery and help her adapt to life after a myocardial infarct. During the first visit to Mrs. M.'s home, the nurse noted a pack of cigarettes on the table near her chair. Mrs. M. stated she no longer smoked, but "felt better" knowing they were "close by"; it made her less anxious. She had no intention of smoking again, she informed the nurse, and was upset because family, friends, and health care personnel (physical therapists, occupational therapists, and nurses) kept trying to take them away from her. From the MRM perspective, Mrs. M. had volunteered Self-care Knowledge, provided information about her Self-Care Resources, and was taking Self-care Action.

OVERVIEW

Self-care, a concept common to health care, is the core of the Modeling and Role-Modeling theory and paradigm. Erickson, Tomlin, and Swain (1983) described three components of Self-care: Knowledge, Resources and Actions (p. 48), and provided guidelines for considering these within the context of a human's world-view (p. 83, pp.116-220).

This chapter builds on these concepts. We start with a discussion of Self-care Knowledge, including a description of knowledge known, but not known! In the next section, we address Self-care Resources and describe external and internal resources including state and trait resources. A discussion on trait resources derived from developmental residual ensues, followed by Self-care

Actions, and the concept of Perceived Enactment of Autonomy. Finally, the relationships among this midrange theory of Self-care, the primary source of information, and other parts of MRM theory are explored as we discuss the case presented at the beginning of the chapter.

SELF-CARE KNOWLEDGE

Self-care, unique to each individual, starts at birth and runs the full spectrum of human life. The three components of Self-care, Self-care Knowledge (SCK), Self-care Resources (SCR), and Self-care Actions (SCA) (Erickson et al., 1983) are inextricably interconnected, as shown in Figure 4.1, yet each stands alone. Each is unique to the individual, but there are commonalities among people. While these concepts were presented in the first book on Modeling and Role-Modeling (Erickson et al., 1983), this chapter presents more detail, helping readers gain a deeper understanding of the uniqueness of each human being while also capturing a perspective of human commonalities. Each component is discussed individually; however, we encourage you to review Figure 4.1 and keep these relations in mind as you explore SCK, SCR, and SCA.

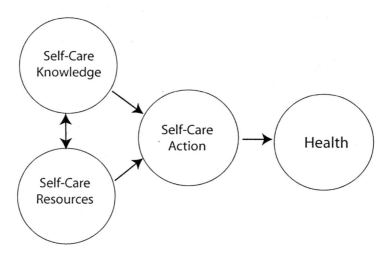

Figure 4.1 MRM Self-care concepts. Adapted from Hertz 1991.

SCK Defined

Self-care Knowledge (SCK) is the personal understanding of what is needed to help us grow, develop, or heal. It includes awareness of personal needs and goals, as well as strengths, capabilities, characteristics, values, and liabilities. It also includes recognition of what is not needed.

Our Self-care Knowledge not only includes awareness of psychosocial and emotional stressors, stress responses and resources, it also incorporates knowledge of the physical self. Many people, for example, know what makes their bodies feel good or strong. These may be psychosocial or biophysical factors. Many people can identify which foods, when consumed, make them more awake and alert, and which make them drowsy. Others recognize overeating makes them uncomfortable, even before having that extra dessert. Many know how their bodies respond to stress: some develop a stiff neck; others may have stomach pain. Regardless of the specifics, many people know how they will react physically because they have learned the response from repeated life experiences. They have developed Self-care Knowledge and are aware of it.

> *At some level a person knows what has made him or her sick, lessened his or her effectiveness, or interfered with his or her growth. The person also knows what will make him or her well, optimize his or her effectiveness or fulfillment (given circumstances), or promote his or her growth* (Erickson et al., 1983, p. 48).

Given that we are holistic beings, Self-care Knowledge is not always expressed logically. For example, we frequently hear someone say they are sick with the flu because they have too much work to do. While we all know a virus causes the flu, holistic people know sickness has a multi-factorial etiology. While we know influenza is caused by a virus, we also know our bodies are less able to contend with the virus when multiple psychosocial stressors occur at the same time. We have limited resources available to contend with stressors at any given time and we know it. This, too, is Self-care Knowledge.

At Some Level We Know

An interesting aspect of SCK is that we have knowledge which is not consciously known. We know things about ourselves that are forgotten or buried, things important for us as we grow or heal. This "knowing, but not knowing what we know" is not unique to nursing. Other disciplines label this phenomenon as emotional memory (Charles, Mather, & Carstensen, 2003; Witvliet, 1997) or state-dependent memory (Rossi, 1986; Rossi & Cheek, 1988) and describe how memories of events can arouse emotions and affect a person's current behavior and learning.

When memorable events occur, we experience them in many ways. We notice the action, physical location, sensations (smell, taste, feeling, emotional reaction, etc.), people involved and their demeanor or dress. We cognitively analyze the events and assign them social meaning; sometimes, think of them spiritually, and respond to them emotionally or biophysically.

They can be major historic events such as the September 11, 2001, attack on the United States, a natural disaster such as an earthquake or hurricane, or election of a favorite candidate (Levine & Bluck, 1997; Witvlet, 1997). They can also be more personal events such as a graduation, birthday, wedding, divorce, death of a family member, or a catastrophic injury. Our responses to these events are stored to be mobilized at a later time.

The memory of these events is stored in such a way that later, when we have experiences which even remotely remind us of the original event, or any part of it, we tend to have reactions very similar to those of the first experience.[1] Our heart may beat faster; we may breathe hard, become fearful or excited, and so forth. Since the type of "storage" depends on the meaning of the event to the individual, the type of response we have also depends on the meaning. However, the meaning of the event may stay buried until the individual is ready to address it, rework the experience, and use it as a resource.

H. Erickson provides the following example:

A number of years ago when our children were entering school, my husband and I decided to find a school that would meet our needs and then move into that neighborhood. It didn't take long to find the school, but it took nearly a year to find the "right place to move." We looked at many houses and none of them were "right."

We started looking at property. I got so good at "looking," we just had to drive by and I would know. That is, I'd know it wasn't the right one! Then, one day, I saw an ad that said, "Mysterious drive; wooded lot for sale." I thought we should explore it. Upon arriving at the site, we discovered the "mysterious drive" was a lane, filled with water that led about a quarter mile past a natural bog and ended with a basement on a wooded lot. We couldn't drive back, so we waded through the "lane," carrying four kids! When we rounded the curve, and saw the place, I immediately said, "This is it!" My husband was aghast, but had learned to pay attention to my intuition.

So, over the next few months we built a road, tore down the old basement, and designed and built our dream home. We loved it. Whenever people exclaimed, "How lovely!", I always responded with something like, "Well, it is a nice house, but it is really the land we like." Now, some people don't like looking out over a "swamp," they don't like getting stuck in snow filled roads, and they don't like having their home surrounded by trees, so I often watched their non-verbal language and noted they didn't seem to understand my response.

Over the next few years, we were each offered opportunities to move, but I could never imagine doing that. I usually used the excuse, "The kids are in school" which was, of course, true. But, periodically I wondered why I responded as I did. A friend suggested maybe I felt unworthy of such a lovely place. I thought about that, and decided that wasn't it, but I didn't know the real reason. I told myself, "When you are ready to know, you will!"

A couple of years later I was driving along "our road." The butterflies were flitting, birds were singing, water in the stream next to the road was gurgling, and the bog was filled with wild plants. Suddenly, I remembered my life as a young child (4-7 years of age). We had lived near such a place; I would go down to the bog and watch the rabbits, see the plants, and so forth. It was my haven! Now, I knew why this property was so important! And suddenly, I also knew I didn't have to live there; I could recreate that space wherever I went! We know what we need, but we don't always know what we know!"

We all have Self-care Knowledge. We are aware of some of it, and unaware of the rest. Nevertheless, at some level, we all know what interferes with our ability to grow, develop, and heal. We also know what we need to help us. These are Self-care Resources.

Learning to *Know* What We Know

Can we help people become more aware of their physical bodies? According to Modeling and Role Modeling Theory, the answer is yes. Often, in our busy lives, we ignore cues about taking better care of our physical self. We go to work knowing a day of rest will help us recover from a cold. In some cases, people have never learned to pay attention to these cues. Learning them takes time and training for some people. Others experience the cues, but do not know what to do with the information. However, people have the innate ability to become aware of physical cues, and we know nurses can help them learn.

Jean Johnson and her colleagues' (1970) early work showed people are able to separate physical pain from psychic pain, an important understanding in helping them learn to be comfortable. There are other examples, but for the sake of brevity, we will describe two (exercise physiology and stress reduction), each supported by an impressive quantity and quality of research.

Exercise Physiology. The first example is from the field of exercise physiology. More than three decades ago, Borg (1973) conducted initial studies of perceived exertion. In this situation, body awareness is focused on the perception of exertion associated with various levels of exercise intensity. This perception of exertion includes paying attention to physiological signals associated with increasing heart rate, respirations, and skin changes from increased perfusion and diaphoresis. He developed the Borg Rating of Perceived Exertion (RPE) Scale as a single measure of these complex physical sensations (Noble & Robertson, 1996). The original scale consisted of 15 points ranging from 6-20. The descriptors for the scale ranged from very, very light to very, very hard exertion. There was a strong relationship between RPE and heart rate. RPE has been used to self-monitor exercise intensity.

Use of the RPE scale is now recommended during exercise training and exercise testing by the American College of Sports Medicine (2005) and American Association of Cardiovascular and Pulmonary Rehabilitation (2004). Many exercise facilities post the Borg Scale and use it as a guide for exercise intensity when doing aerobic workouts. It is a simple way to monitor and increase exercise effort without the hassles of stopping exercise to check the pulse. It is also commonly used in cardiac and pulmonary rehabilitation to monitor effort.

At the other extreme, athletes learn to use perceived exertion to monitor effort during running, cycling, swimming, and many other competitive aerobic sports. The athlete stays within a certain range of effort during various stages of the competition to prevent depleting energy stores too early in an event. A mistake in interpreting the level of intensity may result in "hitting the wall" and having no aerobic metabolism left to finish the event.

Stress Reduction. The second example is found in the area of stress reduction. Becoming aware of body cues associated with stress is the foundation to reducing stress through various techniques (Dossey, Keegan, & Guzzetta, 2005). Biofeedback is a method in which the person focuses on a specific cue such as skin temperature. The goal is to increase warmth and blood flow to the extremities, a sign of relaxed vascular tone. Other techniques focus on breathing and breath control to slow the sympathetic nervous system.

Progressive muscle relaxation uses suggestions to contract and relax specific muscle groups, continuously contrasting the relaxed to the non-relaxed muscle group. Imagery and self-hypnosis provide other ways to reduce stress by placing the mind in a relaxed state, so the body can also become free of stress responses.

Body scans are used in conjunction with many stress reduction and self-regulation techniques (Kabot-Zinn, 1995). The body scan consists of systematic focused attention to specific parts of the body or physiologic processes. Thus, the person may focus on a head-to-toe check of muscle tension, skin warmth, or breathing patterns. When people perceive differences from their normal state, they can invoke actions aimed at directly reducing the stress on their physiologic functioning. Benson and Klipper's (1976) seminal research in body awareness led to the development of many types of programs aimed at reducing the stress response.

We can learn to use Self-care Knowledge proactively to help others and ourselves. When people learn to recognize they are in a stress state, they can learn they are likely to fatigue sooner and experience physical symptoms earlier than when in nonstress states. But, first, they have to learn the symptoms of "being in stress"!

According to Selye (1976) we can only tolerate a stress state for 72 hours without depleting our stress-response resources. If so, we have to find ways to relieve the stress by the third day (or sooner) or accept that we will deplete our stress-response resources.

We can use this knowledge to take Self-care Actions. We can become experienced at recognizing cues that help us understand our "whole self" better. When we learn to be proactive, we have created Self-care Actions. Simply stated, we can learn to use our Self-care Knowledge to mobilize Self-care Resources. When we do this, we are demonstrating Self-care Actions.

SELF-CARE RESOURCES

We use Self-care Resources in order to acquire optimum holistic well-being. Self-care Resources are needed to survive and thrive, and include everything we use to grow, develop, maintain or regain health, and promote healing.

Self-care Resources help us through difficult situations and provide foundations needed for growth. Often they create resources we can use at a later date under similar (and sometimes different) circumstances. These resources enable us to face challenges with confidence. When we perceive we have the resources, the perception itself becomes a resource. This perception of adequate resources helps us live to the fullest and look to the future.

> The drive to build resources exists within us, but their development is influenced by our past relationships. For example, personal traits, attitudes, or activities developed as a result of our experiences with family, friends, and acquaintances become Self-care Resources. Examples of activities that can be used as Self-care Resources include knowing how to slow our breathing, calm our minds, stimulate "happy neurotransmitters" and so forth.

Sometimes Self-care Resources seem in opposition to what another person would consider helpful. Take, for example, second day postoperative patients who need to walk, but think they require the nurses to help them get out of bed, walk, and simply move around the room. While nurses may perceive these patients are just fine and can get along without them, *if the clients perceive they need someone to be with them, then they probably do! They may be physically able, but need someone to help them feel safe, or valued. Their asking is a type of Self-care Resource.* Our challenge is to find alternative ways of helping clients meet their needs—ways that are better for both of us.

> Self-care Resources can be internal to the individual or derived from sources external to the person. Internal resources reside within us or are those we perceive to be part of our personal being. Internal resources can be *state* (temporary) or *trait* (stable, enduring) resources. External resources are all other people and things *perceived to be available for our actual or potential use.*

External Resources

Mixed Findings

Research findings on social support, often considered the primary external resource by health care providers, are mixed. While the concept was envisioned as the actual or perceived helpfulness of others who may be able to assist in some way during an acute or chronic problem, or help the person attain or maintain health (Stewart, 1993), it is often from the health care providers' perspective, rather than the clients'. Researchers and clinicians associate social support with improved outcomes, but that is not always the case. According to Norbeck (1998), social support is complex, with positive and negative potential outcomes needing further study. Again, we think this is because social support is very personal. The recipient of the support has to view it as helpful, or it will not have the effects we hope to see.

Early researchers equated a lack of social support with being unmarried or socially isolated. An increase in mortality and morbidity was found in several large epidemiological studies of people who had health problems and were also unmarried or socially isolated (Blazer, 1982; Stewart, 1989). While results were impressive, the way social support was defined in these studies was *not from the perspective of the people studied.*

Sometimes support was defined as marital status. It did not take into consideration what the person with a health problem perceived as a supportive relationship. Subsequent studies examined the number of people in the social network and found a positive relationship between outcomes and number of people in the network. While not really holistic in nature, these studies were the beginning of research that examined support from the perspective of the individual.

Social Networks

Not all studies of social network have had positive results. Tilden (1987) identified a "darker side" of social support, which was the result of the indebtedness one felt as the recipient of support from those in their network.[2] Reciprocity was found to be an important intervening variable in understanding the role of social support. If the person felt there was a way to reciprocate the kindness by giving something back to the supporter, it kept the giver and receiver of support on the same level. The ability to repay the person for their kindness could mediate a negative response. The payment need not be monetary, nor need it be proportional to the original gift or support. The meaning behind the repayment was most important. Work in this area led to evaluation of the quality, not necessarily the quantity, of support available.

However, studies have shown that repeated reliance on social support systems can lead to strained relationships with family or friends. Also, support is viewed as emotional, informational, and as an aid in performing tasks and activities. In a group of 292 older patients with heart failure, those with lower levels of social support had more recurrent cardiac events and higher mortality one year after the initial hospitalization (Krumholz et al., 1998). A special concern for the elderly is that the primary support person is often also old and has chronic health problems.

"Support groups," a type of social network, can become an external resource. Groups can provide a setting for sharing experiences, information, and a sense of belonging. The group may provide the opportunity to feel attached to others and remain socially integrated. Repeatedly, studies have found group participation is powerful in promoting self-care confidence and support (Kinney, Mannetter, & Carpenter, 1992). However, this is not true for all people. For example, men with prostate cancer benefited from support from only one other person rather than a support group (Weber, et al., 2004).

Health care providers can also be external resources for clients. They can provide emotional care and also referrals to other services. Nurses, physicians, dietitians, physical therapists and a myriad of other professionals can offer unique contributions to help people attain or maintain health. They can provide the teaching needed to facilitate Self-care. Sometimes, however, health care providers offer the support and teach what they think the client needs without ever asking the client. Under these circumstances, their "good intentions" may not have the hoped-for outcomes. Rather than feeling nurtured and cared for, clients may feel they have been "talked at" and "pawned off" to take care of themselves.

Systems as Social Networks

When individuals believe their needs are met, they acquire internal resources.[3] This is a basic premise of the Modeling and Role-Modeling theory (Erickson et al., 1983). However, need satisfaction often requires the efforts of others during one's time of need. For example, physiologic needs include food, water, oxygen, glucose, sleep, and medications for various health problems (see Chapter 6 and Appendix C). When someone helps with need satisfaction, they have served as an external resource. When they are *perceived to be available in the future*, they continue to be an external resource.

The physical environment can also be an external resource. For instance, if a community design provides for safety, more people will walk because it is healthy. Some work settings are now designed to improve the health of the workers. Vending machines offer food items with higher nutritional value. Elevators run slowly to encourage people to walk 1 or 2 flights of stairs. Communities are being built in ways that increase social contact. Front porches provide a place where people can sit, read, and greet their neighbors. Congregate housing for the elderly may be built more like homes, with a common dining room, kitchen, living room, but multiple bedrooms for "new families" of 6 to 10 people. In many of these examples, the environment actually helps meet growth needs, too. The settings provide the resources to help one flourish. However, no matter how lovely or well designed, if it is not perceived as a resource, *it is not*. As a result, what others might consider as external resources are not resources for everyone.

> External resources can be either animate objects (people, dogs, cats) or inanimate objects (a blanket, house, book, sunset). The primary purpose of external resources is to help build internal resources. Strong external resources help us build healthy affiliated-individuation.

Other External Resources

All other things, animate and inanimate, can be used as resources if the individual perceives them as such. Often people have a favorite nurse, pillow, breakfast cereal, book, or picture they need to have under certain conditions. Later in this book, you will read chapter 7 that describes these "things" as attachment objects. All attachment objects can be used as external resources. The possibilities of external resources are endless. Still, some people retain the perception of very limited external resources. This is because those external resources have not met their needs repeatedly.

Implications

External resources are extremely important because they are the primary source of need satisfaction from prebirth on. They are also the basis for healthy affiliation need satisfaction. Since the MRM theory (Erickson et al., 1983) argues that affiliated-individuation is necessary for normal growth and development (p. 68-70), the individual's well-being depends on strong external resources.

Internal Resources

Internal resources reside within us. They are derived from the growth and development of our *holistic being*, starting at conception and continuing through the life span. They include all biophysical resources (such as a healthy pancreas), and need assets (such as feeling loved), traits, strengths and virtues. Internal resources can be thought of as state (temporary) or trait (stable, enduring) resources.

State Resources

State resources are derived from need satisfaction, and we need them to live and grow. For example, Self-care Resources at the physiological level include stored neurotransmitters, healthy oxygen levels, free glucose, zinc and other chemicals to be used, as needed, for the functioning of our body, management of our developmental tasks, and so forth. We also need state resources to meet other types of needs such as security, belonging, and love needs at various times.

Although we use state resources to respond to stressors, contend with stress responses, and adapt to life, some of their characteristics limit our ability to mobilize them. For example, they are not stable; they develop in a short period of time and disappear just as fast. Since they are derived from getting our needs met, their development partially depends on our perceptions of our relationships with others. When we perceive our needs unmet or unsatisfied, minimal, if any, resources are produced.

On the other hand, when our needs are met repeatedly, we develop need assets, which have more stability than state resources. It is like having money in savings. They are available for our use at any time, and they will be "used up." But, if we have a little extra in savings, they last longer. Specific examples common to all nurses are those related to our biophysical functioning. We look at our laboratory reports to see if we have enough hemoglobin, white blood cells, oxygen saturation and so forth. These are assets used when we have stressors that call on the body to respond. Without adequate biophysical resources, we cannot respond to daily stressors without over taxing our body. Nevertheless, if not replaced, they can be used up.

Trait Resources

Sometimes the concepts of resources and residuals become confused. Resources can be used to help us grow and develop. They are needed to meet needs, deal with emergencies, work through developmental tasks, heal (when needed) and simply, survive. Residuals, on the other hand are products that develop as we have profound life experiences. Residual (trait resources) occurs when we develop as biophysical beings, when we have vivid life experiences, and as we develop as psychosocial beings. This means there are three types of trait residual that have the possibility of becoming Self-care Resources: Genetic Resources, Stored memories, and Psychosocial Development. The positive residual and some of the healthy negative residual can become Self-care Resources. However, excessive negative residual is not viewed as a resource; it has the potential to impede growth and well-being.

Genetic Resources. The first type of trait residual is derived genetically from biological parents. These genetic predispositions can help us grow, develop, and be healthy. They can also predispose us to limitations and illnesses. Nonetheless, how one views this type of residual determines whether or not it is a resource. Not all negative residual impedes our well-being; not all positive residual enhances it. It depends on the individual's Self-care Knowledge. Nevertheless, these resources can be used, when it is perceived they are available. They can also be used, without conscious awareness, to keep us healthy, to help us contend with stress and grow.

Stored Memories. The second type of trait resource is described above as "stored memories." This residual can also be either positive or negative and will carry neurotransmitters based on the stored memory. Resources derived from stored memories can be retrieved or mobilized when a similar experience or some aspect of the experience occurs. For example, *a father and child have been playing together and having a wonderful time in the backyard, when the father looks to the sky and sees a beautiful sunset. He points out the sunset to the child; both have a sense of contentment, beauty, safety for themselves, a sense of being loved, and belonging to the other. The memory is stored. Weeks later, the child looks at the sky, sees a lovely sunset and feels loved and connected to her father. Years later, she walks into a public garden, notices the smell of the grass and again, remembers at an unconscious level, the first experience. She feels happy, close to her father, and filled with love—although she does not know why!*

Psychosocial Development. The third type of trait resource is derived from psychosocial development. These processes were described in the first book (Erickson, Tomlin, & Swain, 1983) and will be expanded in Chapters 6 and 7 of this book, so we will not go into detail here. However, it is important to remember both positive and negative developmental residual can be produced as we go through the stages of life. Each needs to be considered when thinking about Self-care Resources. While positive residual and healthy negative residual can be mobilized as resources, excessive negative residual impedes health.

Erik Erikson (1963) described a series of developmental tasks one faces throughout the lifespan. As we work on the task, Erikson referred to the sequelae of these challenges as strengths and virtues. Strengths are the assets accumulated and saved as we work through developmental tasks. Virtues are the attitudes derived from the developmental task work.

Developmental residual strengths and virtues form the basis for some resources we use for Self-care Actions. Chapter 5 describes these in detail and Figure 5.1 provides a summary for easy review. Appendix B also provides a Taxonomy of Developmental Residual.

Upon examination of the list of strengths and virtues for the various stages, it appears they are internal in nature. Those related to the first few stages seem most important in terms of learning about external resources. These include Hope, Self-control, Direction, Competence, and Wisdom. While it might look like the remaining stages are more externally related, that is, the nature of the strength or virtue appears to involve relationships with others we cannot forget these are built on the first few stages. Therefore, all the strengths and virtues are internal resources, but *all of them depend on our relations with others while we work on a specific developmental task.*

H. Erickson stated:

> *People depend on others for survival during the first two stages of life, Integration and Trust. Therefore, we all need someone who will meet both affiliation and individuation needs repeatedly so we can acquire strengths and virtues needed throughout life. Without such relationships, we will have trouble with later life developmental tasks* (Personal communication, November 10, 2005).

Nevertheless, strengths and virtues derived from each stage of life provide resources needed to build relationships that enhance development of additional state and trait resources. When these resources are strong, the person can face challenges with determination and confidence that they can make the most of the situation. The following section provides information about several of these traits, derived from developmental work.

Specific Traits Derived from Selected Developmental Processes

Hope for the Future

Hope, a powerful internal resource that provides a positive expectation of future events, is the virtue of the first developmental stage. Optimism and Resilience are characteristics associated with hope.

Generalized and Particularized Hope. Two forms of hope have been described (Curl, 1992). Generalized hope entails an optimistic outlook on life and a positive outlook for the future. Particularized hope is the desire to see a specific outcome for an identified situation. Generalized and Particularized hope may be intertwined. Someone with a positive outlook may be more realistic and positive about specific outcomes.

On the other hand, a person with a low degree of Generalized hope may be less realistic about Particularized hope. This could contribute to feelings of hopelessness when the hoped for outcome does not occur. Eventually, hopelessness may lead to feelings of helplessness and morbid depression, or as defined in Modeling and Role-modeling, Morbid Grief (Erickson et al., 1983, p.69), which is described in Chapter 7 of this book.

When the hoped-for outcome does not materialize, it becomes another perceived loss for the individual. However, for a person with a high degree of developmental residual, this type of loss could be re-examined, perhaps seen as unrealistic, and viewed as a growth opportunity. The loss would be minimal, and the experience, perceived as a challenge rather than a threat, could be used to build resources.

In a study of healthy elders, Curl (1992) found a strong relationship between Generalized hope and Trust and Spirituality while Particularized hope was related to control. These findings support the information presented in Chapters 5 and 12 on the nature of developmental residual and how to facilitate it.

Using Hope. People who exhibit Hope often reframe[4] stressful situations in a positive way. They "see the glass as half-full rather than half-empty" and frequently find ways to make meaning of the experience—to make it work for them, rather than against them.

Hope was related to morale and social functioning, but not physical functioning in adults with heart failure (Rideout & Montemuro, 1986). Hope, as developmental residual, provides a positive orientation and foundation for other internal resources. This positive orientation enables some to see the good in others, be a rock in times of crisis, and have resilience during stressful times (O'Malley & Menke, 1988).

Control

Control, the strength derived from the second developmental stage, Autonomy versus Shame/doubt, can be actual or perceived. In a given situation, the person may have actual control to make a change or act in a specific way. However, in another situation, he may not have full control to do as desired. Instead, he perceives he has control over some aspect of the decision-making or implementation of a plan of care. Perceived control has been related to lower levels of anxiety, depression, and hostility in the six months after an acute myocardial infarction (Moser & Dracup, 1995).

In qualitative studies of recovery, control was found to be an integral part of the process (Baker, 1989; Johnson & Morse, 1990). Much research has been done on patient controlled analgesia. When the patient can control the delivery of pain medication, there are improved outcomes including better analgesia, early and increased amount of ambulation, decreased anxiety and stress, and shorter length of hospitalization. Many other examples can demonstrate that giving clients a sense of control improves their health.

Purpose and Competence

The third and fourth developmental stages include challenges of Initiative versus Guilt and Industry versus Inferiority. The strengths and virtues of these stages provide the person with Purpose and Competence. These virtues are similar to what is now referred to as self-efficacy.

Bandura (1982) popularized the concept of self-efficacy, the belief that one has both the knowledge and the skills to perform a specified behavior. Self-efficacy is pertinent to the person with a chronic or acute illness as well as the healthy individual who needs the knowledge and ability to perform Self-care behavior.

Many new skills are needed when one first learns of an actual or potential health problem. New medication or nutritional regimens may be complicated. For instance, to prevent hypoglycemia in a person with Type 1 diabetes mellitus, the schedule for insulin in relation to meals and exercise must be timed appropriately. Carbohydrate counting may be needed to provide more dietary control and variety. This degree of glucose management and personal control requires many skills. However, when people believe they can be successful, they are more likely to demonstrate the complex skills needed to take on this new Self-care Action.

As one develops a sense of self-efficacy, positive reinforcement increases the sense of control over the disease. Self-efficacy has been studied in various chronic illnesses. In a sample of 43 subjects with heart failure, scores were predictive of actual performance on cardiopulmonary exercise testing (Oka, Gortner, Stotts, & Haskell, 1996). It has likewise been studied in many types of recommended health promotion behavior, including smoking cessation, exercise, self-breast examination, and healthy diet. In each case, the belief that one has the knowledge and skill to do the activity is what is important.

Knowledge. Factual information, or knowledge, has been described as a component of self-efficacy, but it also has broader implications as an internal resource. "Knowledge is power" is a popular saying that exemplifies how people with health problems can gain control over their illness. Studies have delineated the specific information that clients request for various health problems. The area of patient education needs to focus on food and diet, activity, and medications; all are important aspects needed for Self-care. As people gain better understanding of their disease, there are increased Self-care activities (Roglieri, Futterman, & McDonough, 1997).

Providing patient education has long been a nursing role designed to build skills so an individual can take Self-care Actions. A specific teaching method, focused on concrete-objective information, may be most useful in helping a person gain Self-care skills.

Sensory Preparation. Jean Johnson performed much of the original research on this technique of helping people learn. She called it "sensory preparatory information" (Johnson, Babbs, & Leventhal, 1970; Johnson, 1999). This method personalizes the experience of living with the disorder and addresses common experiences along with the factual information needed for Self-care. It is so commonly practiced most nurses cannot imagine doing patient education any other way.

When using sensory preparation to help people stop smoking, the nurse provides factual information, but also includes what will be experienced during nicotine withdrawal. The increase in coughing and mucous production is also an important point to include in teaching. If this is included, people who try to stop smoking will be better prepared to handle the signs and symptoms. Considerable research has supported this method; it increases a feeling of control and, therefore, results in improved outcomes (Christman, Kirkhoff, & Oakley, 1992; Suls & Wan, 1989).

You may think this definition of knowledge, which builds upon cognitive and emotional aspects, sounds like Self-care Knowledge. Well, it is. Self-care Knowledge can become a resource. Later in the chapter, this will be discussed in more detail.

Wisdom

Wisdom is related to knowledge, but is higher level cognitive functioning. The last Eriksonian developmental challenge is Ego Integrity versus Despair with the virtue of Wisdom. As one ages, the accumulation of learning results in judgments and insights, which are the result of life-long challenges and learning situations.

Wisdom entails the ability to see beyond the immediate situation and think broadly with a future direction for the self, family, community, and even upcoming generations. The wise individual has almost intuitive instincts because of the ability to process a life's worth of learning into a decision made in minutes or seconds.

Several additional internal resources have been described in the literature. In a sample of elderly people with heart failure, Vigor, a perception of energy and inner strength, was associated with quality of life, but not related to the severity of the illness. Predictors of vigor in these older adults with chronic disease included general health perceptions, mental health, and energy expended in planned exercise (Fontana, 1996). These concepts are similar to those found by H. Erickson (1984), when she studied Self-care Knowledge.

Spirituality

Spirituality, or belief in the importance and meaning of life, is seen as the core of the holistic individual in Modeling and Role-Modeling Theory. This belief lays the foundation for a hopeful outlook or positive orientation. In one study of adults with heart failure, spirituality was found to have a stronger relationship with overall quality of life and health-related quality of life than with participation in religious activities (Beery, Baas, Fowler, & Allen, 2002).[5]

Past coping experiences help people develop skills to cope in the present. Some skills are cognitive while others are emotion-based. A cognitive coping style may be used to make a list of pros and cons to help make a decision. The person who uses laughter or anger when stressed is using an emotional form of coping. Past coping styles that were successful for the individual are often used again. These become another internal resource to be used in Self-care.

As stated above, it should be noted some coping styles are constructive, while others may appear to be destructive. Nursing interventions can be aimed at helping the person gradually replace less effective coping strategies with more effective ones (Suls & Wan, 1989).

SELF-CARE ACTIONS

Key to Health and Healing

Self-care Action is the mobilizing and use of resources required to meet our needs. The situation, described above, where clients ask nurses to walk with them, is an example of Self-care Action. People know what they need and they will act to get those needs met.

Personal Meaning

In MRM theory, Self-care Action is *based on personal meaning to the individual*. This is crucial to health and healing. Since individuals have different meanings for the same word, how they perceive the concept, "being healthy" determines which Self-care Actions they deem helpful in order to get healthy and maintain health. For example, health is defined broadly in terms of need satisfaction, including meeting self-actualizing needs (Smith's eudemonistic health, 1981), growth and development (Erickson et al., 1983), coping and adaptation, and a sense of well-being that is more than the absence of physical and mental health problems (World Health Organization, 1948).

Healing, a related concept, means to make whole and therefore, denotes holism and holistic health processes. All aspects of the individual, from genetic endowment, spiritual drive, to physical, social, and psychological functions, are part of this holistic health and healing. Health and healing and trying to become the best you can be are inherent drives common to all human beings (Frankl, 1985). So, Self-care Actions vary by the person's world-view, their health problem, and how they think of possible outcomes.

It is important to remember that *anything we do to take care of ourselves can be identified as a Self-care Action*. Therefore, learning to breathe deeply when anxious, imagining the sun on our back when cold, choosing to be dependent on another, and joining an exercise group, are all Self-care Actions. Each of these is aimed at satisfying a perceived unmet need.

We will do what we have to in order to survive; that means to have some degree of affiliated-individuation. Sometimes others do not perceive our Self-care Actions as "healthy behavior." Usually, this happens when others don't recognize our needs or don't understand our perceptions. Sometimes it happens because people have not learned or developed alternative ways of thinking about need satisfaction. For example, people are often accused of acting childishly or wanting to be taken care of when the observer thinks they are perfectly able to care for themselves. The truth is they *are taking care of themselves* by "asking" to be taken care of! The problem is, the one who needs to be taken care of hasn't learned how to ask for help in a way others perceive acceptable. Nevertheless, all people have an inherent need to grow and become the most they can be.

Perceived Enactment of Autonomy

Building on this idea that all people have an inherent drive to become the best they can be, Self-care Actions was expanded to include the concept of Perceived Enactment of Autonomy (PEA) (Hertz, 1991, 1996). PEA is the perception of doing what is best for oneself based on personal values, needs, goals, strengths, and resources, in order to influence health processes and healing. However, doing what is best for one does not mean one must always act independently; it is possible to rely on others (i.e., to be dependent) as a means of doing what is best for oneself.

In other words, people can meet their needs for affiliated-individuation (i.e., independence and self-esteem as well as dependence, love, and belonging) simultaneously. It involves using SCK and mobilizing SCR to care for oneself.

Perceived Enactment of Autonomy is a prerequisite to taking SCA. It precedes SCA and represents the potential for SCA (see Figure 4.2). Because Self-care Actions are unique to each individual, PEA helps nurses promote Self-care Action by supporting the client's sense of autonomy.

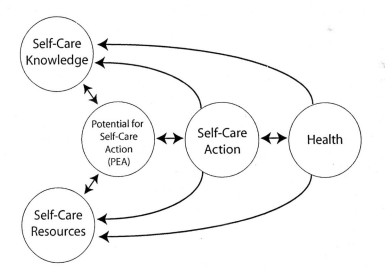

Figure 4.2 MRM SCK concepts, PEA and health. Adapted from Hertz, 1991.

Commonalities

Although SCA are unique for each individual, it is possible to identify common actions or Self-care activities employed by people. Recently, sixteen categories of Self-care activities emerged from interviews with older adults living independently in senior apartments (Hertz, Rossetti & Nelson, 2006).

These 16 categories of SCA were grouped into five larger themes:
(a) Adapting to life as an older adult;
(b) Meeting needs for affiliated-individuation;
(c) Using self-care knowledge to promote and strive for holistic health;
(d) Self-managing health problems and issues; and
(e) Preventing health problems and issues.

While these themes depict Self-care activities reported by older adults, they might also apply to younger people. For younger people, the first theme, i.e., adapting to life as an older adult, would probably be reworded to adapting to life as a teenager, young adult, and so forth.[6]

Although not framed by MRM theory, other researchers have identified similar types of Self-care activities used by older adults worldwide (Bickerstaff, Grasser & McCabe, 2003; Leenerts, Teel, & Pendleton, 2002; Maddox, 1999; Wang, Hsu & Want, 2001).

Overall, these reported SCA indicate that individuals act to meet their holistic health needs via the actions they take on their own behalf, and that relying on other people is part of caring for oneself. Furthermore, caring for oneself in order to influence health and healing is more than preventing or treating physical or mental health problems. It also includes coping with daily life, finding meaning in life through activities including, meeting spiritual needs and balancing independence with dependence. Rarely were activities of daily living, such as bathing, dressing, and grooming, identified as SCA despite their being viewed by nurses as important Self-care tasks (Singleton, 2000).

Implications

Do people incapacitated by an illness (e.g., comatose, mentally ill, people with dementia) or considered incapable of decision-making (e.g., infants and young children), carry out Self-care Actions? According to MRM theory, it is possible for them to have Self-care Knowledge at some level of consciousness and have access to Self-care Resources that could be mobilized for Self-care Actions. All living people have Self-care Knowledge, Resources, and can take some Action. Refer to the story of Mrs. Cook in Chapter 1 as an example of a comatose person drawing from an external resource, so she could mobilize her own resources at a time critical to her well-being.

From the MRM theory perspective, Self-care Actions involve using personal SCK to mobilize internal and external SCR needed to grow, heal, and be healthy. This means that Self-care Actions (SCA) will be unique for each individual. While we can enhance and promote Self-care Knowledge and Self-care Resources, it is always crucial to observe the client's response to determine whether we have achieved our goal. The "correctness" is determined by each individual's model of the world. Likewise, one person cannot prescribe Self-care Actions for another. They are determined by each person's unique model of the world!

<u>Recognizing Cues.</u> As stated above, we can only tolerate a stress state for 72 hours without depleting our stress-response resources. Therefore, we can learn that we need to find ways to relieve the stress on the third day (or sooner) or we will deplete our stress-response resources. We can use this knowledge to implement Self-care Actions. That is, we can become experienced at recognizing cues that help us understand our "whole self" better. When we learn to be proactive, we have created Self-care Resources that can be used when needed. Simply stated, we can learn to use our SCK to mobilize SCR. When we do this, we demonstrate SCA.

As with any other aspect of MRM theory, the challenge for nurses is to first understand the client's model of the world and then design interventions based on that model. For instance, persons unable to verbally express SCK and verbally recognize SCR, such as people in a coma, might be able to express their Knowledge via physical signs. For example, the person's respiratory rate might increase. While mobilization of resources might not be as clear, if oxygen is provided to that person, the respiratory rate might decrease; thus, the person mobilizes Self-care resources to care for oneself.

At the very least, when applying MRM theory, it is the nurse's obligation to seek and interpret various cues (from the client) regarding that client's SCK and SCR in order to promote SCA. Knowledge from biological, psychological and social sciences along with information from significant others and other health care providers can be used to supplement the client's unspoken communications and model and role-model with that client.

<u>Relations with Health.</u> SCA, SCK, SCR, and health and healing, all closely interrelated, are important to understand (see Figure 4.2). For example, as previously explained, one's perception of SCK can affect the recognition of SCR. Likewise, Self-care Knowledge and Resources both influence the prerequisite to Self-care Action i.e., Perceived Enactment of Autonomy, and subsequent actual Self-care Actions followed by health and healing outcomes. Perceived Enactment of Autonomy can also directly influence Self-care Knowledge and Resources.

Changes in health and healing outcomes can also directly influence Self-care Knowledge, Resources and future Actions. They can also influence Perceived Enactment of Autonomy. However, the meaning of health and healing will determine the outcomes. When such changes influence Perceived Enactment of Autonomy, it is probably because they have influenced changes in SCK and perceptions of available resources rather than through direct feedback relationships with health and healing. In a nutshell, because Self-care model concepts are closely interrelated, health and healing can only be important to the extent we take in new information in the process. We need to remember this information can be both positive and negative. For example, H. Erickson has repeatedly talked about people who learn that getting well means being cut off from their perceived support system. When this happens, getting well can be seen as something to avoid!

Finally, SCA are related to other aspects of MRM theory. For example, in caring for one's self, clients meet their basic and growth needs including affiliated-individuation, striving to grow and develop throughout their lifetime, adapting to perceived stressors including coping with losses, and maintaining holism as a human being. In fact, SCA is a key concept that unites and integrates all these other aspects of MRM theory!

SELF-CARE INTEGRATION

An interesting but challenging facet of SCK and SCR is that the two are intertwined. Although separate concepts, they are interdependent. For example, the acknowledgement of available resources can influence how and what a person says about their SCK. While there may be supportive family members available to the individual (from the nurse's perspective), if the person does not perceive or sense the presence of those supportive family members, then that person would likely verbalize a need for supportive family members. Conversely, if there appear to be unsupportive family members (from the nurse's perspective), but the individual perceives support, that person will probably indicate they receive adequate support.

Furthermore, if an individual's SCK is at a subconscious level, that person might not realize the existence of corresponding internal or external resources. If a client does not perceive that emotional and social support from other people can be used to influence their health processes, then the presence of those supportive individuals is meaningless (or worse) to that client.[7]

How can nurses use this information when caring for clients? First, it is important to assess what the client views as necessary for health and healing. Simple questions can uncover SCK from the client's perspective. The following questions can be asked:

> *What do you need to influence your health? What is most important to you at this time in your life? What are your goals? Why did you come to the hospital (clinic, nursing home, nurse, etc.)? What physical symptoms or body functions are of concern to you?*

Second, it is also important to identify what SCR the person perceives are available. Questions like the following, might help uncover this information.

> *What do you currently have available to influence your health (or relieve symptoms or improve functioning)? How do other people affect your ability to influence your health? What helps you meet your goals? What helps you get what you need to influence your health? How does your situation in life affect your health?*

In intervening with clients, nurses can build on the client's SCK. The first step is to acknowledge what the client considers important for health and healing.

Using that knowledge, the nurse can then plan health-directed goals with the client.

For clients who have difficulty stating their personal needs, goals and desires, a process such as values clarification (Wilberding, 1985) or a standardized assessment tool such as the Borg RPE Scale (Noble & Robertson, 1996) can be used to acquire secondary source of information. Sometimes these processes facilitate the client's identification of SCK. To build personal resources, nurses can also simply point out the internal and external resources. Verbal recognition of the client's personal strengths, such as the ability to cope with many demands in life, is one example.

Another way of building resources is by identifying and referring clients to health-related services such as respite care or financial support. The mere acknowledgement of resources by a trusted nurse is a first step to building those resources. Embedded commands (see Chapter 6) might also be effective. For example, a statement can be used to Role-Model and build resources: "Because you did this in the past, I am certain you will be able to do it when it becomes necessary in the future."

Case Analysis

At the beginning of this chapter, we presented Anna's story. The following analysis of that case provides an example of how the concepts of Self-care can be applied.

Anna Martin was taking Self-care Action by insisting she have a pack of cigarettes by her side at all times. How could that be SCA? First, she related her "need" to keep the pack in view; it made her feel better. She stated her personal knowledge, or SCK. She also used resources available to her (e.g., the cigarette pack) to meet that need and, thus, was caring for herself. What does this need really represent? That is a question the nurse needs to answer through probing, observation and analysis. More than likely, Anna was coping with the impending loss of her attachment to cigarettes as represented by the cigarette pack. They had been her "friend" for 60 years! She could depend on them; they made her feel safe.

So, it is important for the nurse to acknowledge that attachment and its impending loss. Common sense, knowledge of the difficulties people encounter when trying to quit smoking, and recidivism to smoking, should also assist this nurse in deciding how to intervene.

If this SCA represents coping with loss of an attachment object, one of the first interventions would be to explore a possible new attachment object. In addition to acknowledging the importance of this attachment to Anna the nurse could ask Anna about some of the potential future risks (e. g., temptation to smoke, recidivism) if this object (cigarette pack) is kept nearby. Nurses can also explore with Anna what she might do if these risks emerged? How would she handle them?

It is important to nurture Anna's strengths by recognizing her ability to stop smoking after 60 years along with her goal to stop smoking permanently. Goals could be established with Anna's input. However, it is risky on our part to negotiate upfront to permanently get rid of the cigarette pack. Until Anna has found other ways to get her needs met (including her physiological needs), she will be at risk.

When first intervening, be sure to set short term goals that can be met. For example, the nurse might ask Anna if she could get along without any cigarettes. If Anna is willing, it might be possible to gradually decrease the number of cigarettes in the pack each day. When the pack is empty, Anna may still choose to keep it close-by. Remember, until she has a replacement that will meet her needs, the cigarette package will still be important.

We can also use temporary transitional objects such as a business card to facilitate the process. The business card could represent the nurse's support even though she may not be physically present. A simple statement indicating that Anna will know the nurse supports her every time she looks at the card could be a first step to replacing the cigarette pack and promoting Self-care Actions.

You should remember some clients are too depleted to be able to use this type of input. Rather than seeing it as helpful, they see it as "being put aside again." They do not want to take care of themselves! Temporarily impoverished, they don't have the resources. To them, being referred is the same thing as being rejected or abandoned. For such individuals, more subtle approaches are needed. Such approaches will be discussed in Chapter 11.

The Primary Source of Information

When using Self-care Knowledge as the primary source of information (Erickson et al., 1983, p.183), you start by asking clients to describe their situation and organize your data around the four categories for data collection: Description of the situation, Expectations, Resource Potential, and Goals and Life Tasks.[8] After you have collected information from your client that is Self-care Knowledge, you may want to go on and collect additional information that is considered Secondary Source of Information. You do this by asking questions such as:

> *What symptoms do you experience? How do the symptoms appear? Is there a recognizable pattern? When and how do you know your health problem is worsening or improving? What are stressful situations? What signs and symptoms of stress do you experience? What do you do when these physical cues are recognized?*

These are important questions, and may at some point in time become your client's Self-care Knowledge, but until this information is offered, when you ask about the situation (in general terms and open-ended questions), it is not. However, you may want this information in order to better understand your client's view of the world, his expectations and ability to mobilize resources needed to contend with physical health problems.

However, when you ask broader, more open-ended questions, don't be surprised if your client tells you that physical symptoms are caused by psychosocial stressors such as, "My cat died," "My son moved," "I'm alone," and so forth. Just remember this information is important in order to manage physical symptoms.

Implications. This means many situations will arouse emotions and feelings in clients because of SCK. Nurses should closely observe their clients for reactions to various interventions, people, and objects in clinical settings. For example, if somebody was hospitalized for an injury after a motor vehicle accident, the nurse should try to discern the person's memory of that accident. If the person remembers driving in a white car or seeing a teddy bear or wearing "my favorite purple top," the nurse should recognize that white vehicles (such as an ambulance), a teddy bear gift from a friend, or the nurse's wearing a purple top might trigger an unpleasant memory and impede health and healing processes.[9] Additionally, avoiding discussion of "typical" memorable events when relating to and intervening with clients is warranted until the nurse clearly understands that person's model of the world. Likewise, maintaining a neutral appearance and demeanor might also be worthwhile until the client's SCK is brought to the surface. Chapter 10 provides some guidelines for creating a safe environment so that you can build a "caring field" (Watson, 1999).

In the case of a pleasant remembered event, the nurse can build on and utilize this aspect of SCK to facilitate Self-care Actions, holistic health, and healing. For example, when learning an elderly client has a pleasant recollection of being greeted by a beloved mother who always had a smile on her face and listened to tales of the day after the child returned from school, the nurse could purposefully smile and listen to the client during role-modeled interventions.[10] In fact, research findings indicate that for many people a smile, rather than a frown, facilitated learning on a variety of topics including health-related topics (Mather & Carstensen, 2003). This is one very simple example of the application of the concept of SCK in practice.

Conclusions

In the original work, Self-care Knowledge was described as the basis for one's personal model of the world. This model reflects the individual's interwoven perceptions that include all three components of Self-care: Knowledge, Resources and Actions. Self-care Knowledge takes many forms. It includes cognitive, biophysical, emotional, social, and spiritual aspects. The cognitive component is the factual information they have about health, disease, treatment, and themselves. The psychosocial aspect is related to past experiences that shape their reactions and needs in the present. The biophysical aspect focuses on body cues and perceptions of physiological changes. Some physical cues may be normal, while others are abnormal. Regardless of the person or situation, what the individual knows about their health and what they need to attain or maintain health, includes all three components of Self-care. Therefore, the nurse must include all aspects of Self-care when assessing a person.

The nurse should develop a framework for asking questions related to each component of Self-care Knowledge in order to build the personal model of the client's world. The original model, described by Erickson et al. is recommended because it offers clients the opportunity to express what is in their holistic self, not just what we want to hear.

As mentioned above, it is often up to us to collect Secondary Source information as well. That is, it is often useful to ask open-ended questions to get the specific information we want, but we need to remember this is not Self-care Knowledge unless offered first by the client. Based on this model, a mutually agreeable plan for Self-care can then be devised. As people grow, they can learn to recognize physical and emotional cues, and know what to do to feel better.

ENDNOTES

[1] Similar ideas were presented in Chapters 2 and 3 when we talked about neurotransmitters excreted during life events and then stored in the cells. The authors noted these "memories" are activated when the individual encounters a similar situation.

[2] This is what Erickson et al. (1983) described when they said it is important for us to determine if the social support persons(s) are invigorating or draining.

[3] This point will also be the focus of Chapter 6.

[4] Reframing will be further discussed in Chapter 12.

[5] This suggests spirituality is different from religion. For a detailed discussion on this, see Chapters 1 and 9.

[6] The general use of this scale has not been validated on younger groups, so it provides a fertile area for future research.

[7] When someone is expecting that another will provide help, and that person does not, the first experiences this as a loss and results in additional needs.

[8] See Erickson et al. (1983) for details.

[9] Assuming the hospital experience was tied to the motorcycle accident in the client's mind, and it was a negative experience!

[10] She could also encourage her client to bring her mother's picture with her.

CHAPTER 5

DEVELOPMENTAL PROCESSES

MARGARET E. ERICKSON

"One day he just decided to potty train himself." "He's come so far in the last several months." "She really matured over the summer." "I can tie my own shoes now." "When I was a teenager, I was trying to figure out who I was. Now, as a mother, I find myself trying to help my kids discover who they are!"

OVERVIEW

We have all heard such statements, usually made in a tone of surprise, nostalgia, or even awe. While we know people change over time, it is always interesting when it happens to us or our loved ones, especially when it seems to "happen overnight." Yet, we all go through developmental processes.

Some developmental theorists contend development is a gradual, continuous process that happens over time. They think we may go through stages, but they are not marked, or necessarily even sequential. Others say development is a predictable, continuous process throughout our lifetime (Schuster & Ashburn, 1986). Erik Erikson (1963) supported the latter view. He also claimed development is chronological and age-related; sequential and predictable; task focused and epigenetic.

Modeling and Role-Modeling theorists have adopted Erikson's position. The authors propose growth and development are inter-related, but not the same. Erickson, Tomlin and Swain (1983) state:

> *Growth is defined as the changes in body, mind, and spirit that occur over time....Growth implies ongoing integration of these various facets of a person. Growth facilitates development. Development is the holistic synthesis of the growth produced, increasing differentiations in a*

person's body, ideas, social relations, and so forth. Growth and development promote health (pp. 46-47).

They go on to say:

Erikson describes eight stages of psychosocial development through which we all progress. Each stage represents a developmental task or decisive encounters resulting in a turning point, a moment of decision between alternative basic attitudes (for example, trust versus mistrust or autonomy versus shame and doubt (p.61).

They also contend that development is an inherent process. By working through developmental stages, people aim for self-actualization.

Individuals are born with an inherent desire to fulfill their self-potential....Each human is also born with a capacity for growth and development over the entire life span. People are always and invariably in a continuous movement or changing state. If they are given accurate information, emotional support, and assistance for the changes they desire, they will make good decisions for themselves (p.46).

This chapter describes the Modeling and Role-Modeling perspective on human psycho-social-spiritual development. While I believe physical development occurs in a predictable manner, and is as important as the psycho-social-spiritual development, I assume the reader is informed regarding physical development.[1] I also believe cognitive development is important, but cognitive development parallels psychosocial developmental residual. Appendix D provides a few guidelines prepared by H. Erickson for those who wish to have more information in this area. In this chapter, I will focus on the psycho-social-spiritual development of the human.[2]

I begin the first section, Overview of Developmental Theory, by talking about growth as a prerequisite to development. This discussion will be followed by three other considerations: Chronological Development, Sequential Development, and Developmental Residual, respectively. In the original book (Erickson et al., 1983), the authors integrated these concepts adopted from Erikson's work with their own ideas. They are expanded in this chapter.

Although Erik Erikson provided the basis for understanding development as an eight-stage process, Modeling and Role-Modeling theorists proposed that our ability to negotiate the stages is determined by how our needs are met and by the attachment-loss-reattachment process. They also indicated we are holistic beings, which has an impact on our developmental processes. I will further build on these ideas as I discuss the linkages between resolution of the chronological stages and the epigenetic process.[3]

The next section of this chapter is devoted to a philosophical discussion about the stages of development, followed by a more specific discussion of each of the developmental stages and the related task. Developmental residual that emerges with task resolution will be presented along with a discussion of several related issues. These include Dimensions of Residual, Epigenesis, Balance, Strengths and Virtues, Negative Residual, and Prerequisites respectively. Again, the basic ideas are adopted from Erikson's work (1963), but have been further developed by the authors of Modeling and Role-Modeling. I will elaborate on these ideas.

This section will include the original eight stages presented in Erickson et al. (1983), and two new stages I am adding.[4] The first is pre-birth and the second is the final stage of existence as a human being. The first is called the Stage of Integration and the last is the Stage of Transformation. The addition of these stages is not intended to negate earlier work (Erickson et al, 1983) or to presume all readers will be comfortable with these ideas. You may wish to include these two stages in your understanding of development. It is also acceptable to use only the original eight stages as a way of thinking about Modeling and Role-Modeling. I invite you to read and make your own decisions.

DEVELOPMENTAL CONCEPTS IN MODELING AND ROLE-MODELING

Developmental Theory

It is always amazing to watch the ongoing, interrelated processes of growth and development. When babies are born, they are unable to hold up their heads, reach for a toy, hold a crayon, use the toilet, understand another person's point of view, hold a job, make choices regarding right and wrong, or understand the importance of values and ethics in our daily lives. Nevertheless, when they are loved and cared for, physical, cognitive, and psychosocial growth occurs, and soon they are able to accomplish and perform physical and social activities impossible at birth. By the time they are five or six years of age, they will have grown and changed so much it is hard to remember a time when they couldn't hold up their head. Development is a natural aspect of the human being. "Survival of the human being is dependent upon some growth. Without some growth, we cannot survive as human beings. Furthermore, growth is a prerequisite to healthy development. Interestingly, as we develop, we also grow. We grow, so we can develop and as we develop, we grow!"[5] (H. Erickson, personal communication, November 2, 2005).

Inherent Development

Basic assumptions in the Modeling and Role-Modeling theory are that we have an inherent desire and capacity for growth, growth occurs as our needs are met, and growth is needed for healthy development. These inherent tendencies exist throughout life. More specifically, growth includes the physical, psychosocial, cognitive, and spiritual changes people experience as their needs are met.

Growth precedes healthy development, comes from healthy development, and occurs in a predetermined, stage-related sequence, with a specific task at each stage.

Each of us will experience these stages and their related tasks in a sequence the same as everyone else. For some it is more difficult. I have heard people say their child jumped a stage and went on to the next one without ever working on the stage-related task. However, upon discussion of this observation, parents often acknowledge their child had proceeded through the stages as predicted, but because of their nature or life environment, they hadn't acted like other children in the same stage. They had experienced less difficulty with the task-work.

This is common in Autonomy, because parents look for the "terrible twos" often associated with this stage of development. Not all children express themselves in ways typical of the "terrible two syndrome." However, upon closer observation, it becomes obvious the task is not about saying "No," but about decision-making. When we think about stages of development in respect to the related task, it is easy to understand all children are alike; still each of us is unique. We each have our journey.

There is a pattern in which the tasks emerge; it is preordered, structured and a basic aspect of human nature (H. Erickson, personal communication, November 23, 2005).

Chronological Development.

Development is age-related. People go through stages at specific times in their life. However, there is some variation, because each of us is a unique human being with a personality and Life Purpose. While we will all be challenged with the same developmental task, at approximately the same time in life, each of us will approach it based on our previous experiences, our genetic makeup and our personality. Some of us will have more difficulty or take more time in one task and then speed through a task with which others struggle. While we all travel a similar path, we have our own journey to complete.

Sometimes developmental progression appears to be stalled and task resolution requires a long time. Many parents have experienced these feelings, waiting for their young child to work through the stage of Autonomy! At other times, changes seem to appear overnight. For example, shy children cling to their caregivers and are suddenly able to go to school or out to play with just a backward glance at them.

> *There is a predestined time in life when each task is the focus of our attention. However, there is a range in age for task-work. Some will achieve the task earlier and some will take longer. But, time is restricted. We seem to have a built in "clock" that says, "Time to move-on." All of us will experience the tug of moving to the next stage at the same time we experience hesitancy. Nevertheless, we will be confronted with the new task. It is inherent, it is time-related, and it will happen!* (H. Erickson, personal communication, November 23, 2005).

It is important to know the difference between these children and those who have had difficulty with need satisfaction. Many children (who seem to linger in a stage of development) are doing just fine. They are growing and developing a "healthy bank of resources"; they simply need to take the "next step" in their own time. They may surprise others because they appear to suddenly move on or change overnight. However, in hindsight, we can often see the gradual change in behavior (i.e., gradual growth).

Development is like that. It is as though the person has accumulated enough "resources" to change rather rapidly. We need to remember "resources" (which are stored as we grow) are acquired from repeated need satisfaction. This process can be compared to collecting enough quarters to trade for a ten-dollar bill. While they are similar in some ways, a stack of quarters, looks, feels, and is treated differently than a ten-dollar bill! Now consider putting the ten dollar bill in the bank. The ten dollars won't change, but interest will be made on the money, so if you wanted to draw on it, you would have ten dollars and something left over. Development is similar. Developmental residual has the potential of increasing or growing over time.

Another analogy might be watching a rose bush grow: stalks come out, leaves grow, buds appear, and petals unfold. While each phase demonstrates growth, when you stand back and see a bush covered with beautiful roses, you see something greater than the sum of the parts. You can remember the growth, but now you see the development.

Epigenesis. Although stages occur in a sequential, predictable process, with focused attention on a specific task at each stage, we rework each task within the context of each of the other stages (and tasks). This happens at every stage of life, throughout our lifetime. This is the epigenetic process. While it is crucial to address the task at the appointed time (or stage of life), it is also important to continue working on each task across the lifespan in order to have residual grow to its full potential.

> Epigenesis is the continuous growth process across a lifetime. While there is a critical time for initial growth, epigenesis is our ability to continue growing. For example, in the formation of a fetus, there is a specific time for the eye to start growing; however, our eyes continue to grow and change across our lifetime. This happens in all aspects of the holistic person.

Erikson (1963) draws an analogy between psychosocial development and the normal development of our organs. He states, "In this sequence of development, each organ has its time of origin. If the eye, for example, does not arise at the appointed time, it will never be able to express its self fully" (p. 65).

Sometimes our work appears similar to the original task-work; upon careful inspection, however, it is obvious the task is being reworked at a higher level. For example, an infant's primary task in the first year of life is to develop a strong trust of the caregivers and balance it with a healthy sense of discernment (i.e., mistrust or ability to discern whom to trust and whom not to). Nevertheless, the infant is simultaneously working on the other stages of life, trying to acquire a primitive sense of autonomy, initiative and so forth.

As adults, working on the developmental task of Intimacy, we are reworking earlier tasks, aiming for a deeper, greater resolution. We are also preparing for upcoming developmental tasks. For example, during the stage of Intimacy versus Isolation, our task work requires focus on the development and maintenance of a strong, satisfying relationship with another person. Simultaneously, it also requires reworking issues related to Trust, Autonomy, Identity, and other developmental tasks at a deeper and different level. Clearly, the type of Trust and Autonomy needed in the stage of Identity is different from that in Intimacy. Reworking the original task within the context of the current, chronologically-based task is the essence of developmental epigenesis.

> *If I say, for example, that a favorable ratio of basic trust over basic mistrust is the first step in psychosocial adaptation, a favorable ratio of autonomous will over shame and doubt...(there are) a number of fundamental relations that exist between the two steps, as well as some facts fundamental to each. Each comes to its ascendance, meets its crisis, and finds its lasting solution during the stage indicated. But, they all must exist from the beginning in some form, for every act calls for an integration of all* (Erikson, 1963, p. 271).

The beauty of an epigenetic model is that people always have the capability of growing, integrating, and becoming. There is always a possibility of reworking an earlier task and achieving a more favorable balance of residual as an outcome. A stronger, more positively balanced residual helps us be stronger and healthier. As human beings, we can always maximize our potential and be all we can be. It is never too late. That is the nature of epigenesis. Erickson et al. (1983) eloquently state this important philosophical belief. They assert:

> *...The utility of Erikson's theory is the freedom we may take to view aspects of people's problems as "uncompleted tasks." This perspective provides a hopeful expectation for the individual's future since it connotes something still in progress. Compare this to the perspective that one is*

"fixed" in a state of development, is schizophrenic, obsessive-compulsive, passive-aggressive, a denier, manipulator, and so forth (pp. 62-63).

Developmental Residual

Each of us will move from one developmental stage to the next. As we do, we will take the products of the task-work into the next stage. This is called developmental residual. Not only does residual help us as we are confronted with the task of the new stage, it also helps us rework each of the previous stages (see Table 5.1).

Developmental residual is like a bank account. There is a savings account where we have stored information from which we can draw and use as positive resources. There is also another account, sometimes seen as a deficit account, where we have stored other information. The two are not really separate, but intermixed, so we have a balance of stored information that determines the total residual or task-work product of each stage. This means there are two types of developmental residual: positive and negative.

Keep in mind, however, we can also enter any stage with minimal negative residual, and because of life events, develop excessive negative residual related to this specific stage. When this happens, we are more likely to see indications of negative residual at that particular stage, but not necessarily the earlier stages.

Erickson et al. (1983) talked about healthy residual and the strengths and virtues that come with it when they said: "As a maturing individual negotiates or resolves each age specific crisis or task, the individual gains enduring strengths and attitudes that contribute to the character and health of the individual's personality" (p.61).

In reality, no one ever achieves complete task resolution the first time he or she works on it. However, we can reach a threshold of achievement (growth), which will enable us to move to the next stage and tackle the next task with sufficient resources. When we work on a developmental task, we have the potential to grow. When growth accumulates, resources are built. When the accumulation reaches a saturation point, a threshold is met and positive residual occurs. And with the residual come strengths and virtues. Erickson et al. (1983) further described them as: "… internal resources that an individual can use to promote health and growth. These strengths can be defined in terms of attitudes, endurance, patterns, or whatever other way you (or your client) choose to define them" (p. 128).

Dimensions. Two types of residual or (task-work products) develop as we work on our stage-related, developmental tasks. Erik Erikson presented them as positive or negative residual and as one versus the other. Although he implied a balance or ratio between the two, he was never clear about this possibility.

TASK:			INTEGRATION OF SPIRIT	BUILDING TRUST	ACQUIRING AUTONOMY	TAKING INITIATIVE	INDUSTRY
TIME FRAME:			Pre-birth to shortly after birth	≈ birth to 12-15 mths.	12-36 mths	2 to 2.5 yrs – 5 to 7 yrs	5-6 to 10-13 yrs
Residual Continuum	Negative	High	Duality — Separateness	Mistrust	Shame	Guilty	Feelings of inferiority
		Low	Duality — Groundedness	Discrimination Ability — Stranger Awareness	Introspection — Self-evaluation	Responsibility — Accepts responsibility	Limitations — Recognizes limitations
	Positive	Low	Unity — Synchronicity	Trust — Insecure attachment	Autonomy — Need to make good decisions	Initiative — Interest in joining society	Competency — Self-competence
		High	Unity — Holism	Trust — Secure attachment	Autonomy — Ability to make a good decision	Initiative — Proactive joining	Competency — Competence as a team member
Resources	Virtue		Groundedness	Hope	Will-power	Purpose	Competence
	Strengths		Awareness	Drive towards the future	Self-control	Direction	Methodological approach to problem solving

IDENTITY	INTIMACY	GENERATIVITY	EGO INTEGRITY	TRANSFORMATION
11-12 to early 30's	Mid 20's to 40's-50's	Mid life to early 60's	Early 60's to Transformation	Post Ego Integrity
Role-Confusion Ability to define own roles. Total role confusion	Isolation Individuate from "we" to "me" Distantiation	Stagnation Recognizes life work Self-Absorption	Despair Awareness of mistakes Despondency about life	Disconnecting Letting go of human form Giving up on human form
Self Identity Sense of uniqueness Sense of Self influenced by others.	Intimacy Interconnectedness Sense of "you" and "Me"	Continuity Projection of life work Awareness of life purpose	Ego-Integrity Satisfaction with life Acceptance of life	Reconnecting Reuniting spiritual energy with soul Letting go of human form
Fidelity	Being in Love	Caring	Wisdom	Virtue
Devotion	Affiliation with Individuation	Production	Renunciation	Peace, Cosmic Understanding and Compassion

Table 5.1 Developmental residual by stage of development

H. Erickson said the following about this:

> *While Erikson suggests a healthy balance or favorable ratio, it is not clear he conceptualized developmental residual on more than one continuum. When I talked with him about this in the early 1980's, he said it was a methodological problem he didn't want to be bothered with. He had conceptualized the stages, he said, and really didn't want to be worried about embellishing or clarifying that model. When I suggested there are two dimensions, he agreed, saying he probably never should have used the word 'versus' when talking about the residual, although he wasn't sure.*
>
> *For example, Erikson talks about Trust versus Mistrust. This suggests that these two types of residual are really two ends of the same continuum. My observations, thoughts, and research convince me there are two dimensions. One is positive and one negative, although we need some of both to be healthy people.*
>
> *These residual dimensions range from low to high. It is a matter of degree or how much residual is left at the end of each developmental stage. The two types, positive and negative residual, interact to create a ratio or balance of the two. For example, the first stage described by Erikson was the stage of Trust. In this stage there is positive residual (i.e., a sense of trust) and negative residual (sense of mistrust). The amount of the residuals balanced with one another creates a ratio of the two. The more positive the ratio, the greater the resources, and vice versa. Since residual from one stage provides a foundation for residual at the next stage, the amount of residual changes across the lifespan and the ratio of positive to negative changes accordingly* (personal communication, December 11, 2005).

While Erikson (1963) didn't address the issue of healthy negative residual, H. Erickson states a small amount of "negative residual" is important. For example, it is important for children to learn whom they can and cannot trust. While this is a part of mistrust, it is also an important resource. We think a degree of negative residual is important for healthy growth and development. Another example would be the "negative residual" related to the stage of Initiative. This is Guilt. While Guilt can be a serious detriment if too extensive and not balanced with healthy initiative, we need to remember that people who grow and never learn their responsibilities to others fail to develop morally. Therefore, a healthy amount of responsibility probably precedes true guilt, as described by Erikson.

In each developmental stage, two types of residual are built as we work through the related task. When we emerge from one stage and move into another, we acquire characteristics, attributes, attitudes, strengths and virtues as a result of our 'work' during that stage. These are called developmental residual because they reside in us as a result of our task work at each stage. There are two types of residual: positive and negative. We need a healthy balance between the two if we are to continue to grow and become the most we can be (H. Erickson, personal communication, November, 24, 2005).

Trait Resources

I have mentioned developmental stages occur in a predictable sequence, and each stage has a specific task. I have also said task resolution determines the resources we have as we move onto the next stage. When people are able to take a healthy balance of developmental residual from one stage to the next, some of the resources create strengths or attributes that can be used throughout life. They become trait resources. They affect how we experience events in our lives, how we handle stress, and how we work on future developmental tasks.

According to Erickson et al. (1983), "...people who normally negotiate the critical step or turning point of each and all preceding stages in sequence have at their disposal strengths and resources essential for effective, age-appropriate functioning that includes observable behavior, introspective experiencing, and unconscious inner states" (p.62).

Let's go back to the "bank account" analogy for a moment. When we successfully resolve a task (as appropriate for the chronological stage), we build positive developmental residual that can be accessed and utilized when needed. If we equate positive developmental residual with money in the bank, it is easy to see individuals who have money (resources) are able to pay or manage bills and debts (losses or other stressors) when they occur. On the other hand, individuals who approach life with negative developmental residual (minimal savings or even debts) have limited resources to deal with life challenges. When they receive a bill, they have minimal or no money (resources) to pay it off (take care of losses or other stressors).

Developmental residual from past and current developmental stages continues to build as we proceed on our life journey. We build attitudes, life views, strengths and limitations. However, we always have the potential for continuous, healthy growth. This is because of the epigenetic process. The Modeling and Role-Modeling theorists adopted, expanded and integrated Erikson's theory with others (such as Maslow) to create the Modeling and Role-Modeling theory, which continues to grow. The following section describes how I have elaborated on Erikson's work to correspond with H. Erickson's current thinking about Modeling and Role-Modeling.

DEVELOPMENTAL STAGES EXPANDED

Philosophical Discussion

Psychosocial or Holistic Development?

Most people would agree human beings are holistic in nature. We are made of physical, mental, social, cognitive, and spiritual components which work together, interact, and when synthesized are greater than the sum of our parts. In question, however, is where and when do these parts first come together? At what point do we as human beings begin to grow and develop? There is no doubt physical growth of the infant begins in-utero. Extensive research has provided evidence of the moment the merged ova and sperm combine, then begin to separate, and differentiate, forming a new physical entity. We know a rudimentary circulatory system emerges sometime around the eighteenth day, initiating a heart beat—a symbol of life for many.

However, according to Erikson, the initial stage of development starts at birth and lasts through the first year of life, and the last stage of development takes place during our senior years as incarnate beings.

<u>Psychosocial Beings.</u> This is because his model of development focuses on psychosocial development. It does not include physical, cognitive or spiritual development. Nevertheless, if we asked the question, at what point does the human actually start to grow and develop, most would argue life starts some time before birth. That is, we at least have a biophysical body before birth. Montagu (1960), based on a review of the literature, suggested that even the psychosocial subsystems start developing before birth. (I suggest that in Chapter 7) Some parents talk or sing to their baby before birth, so it will be accustomed to their voices.[6] This suggests the baby begins its sojourn as a holistic being even before birth!

<u>Holistic Beings.</u> According to Erickson et al. (1983), "…human beings are holistic persons who have multiple interacting subsystems that are all permeated by a spiritual drive" (p.44). This statement has led me to ask these questions: "When does the infant become more than a physical being? At what point does the spirit of a person connect and integrate with the physical body? Does the connection occur at birth or in-utero? When does the human begin to grow and develop as a spiritual being?" H. Erickson describes the relationship between spirit and Soul in Chapter 1, but does not indicate when the spirit integrates with the human body. She simply implies it happens. In a personal conversation with her, she stated,

> *Life is about the integration of the two (spirit and the biophysical body), so we can fulfill our Life Purpose. We have an inherent spiritual drive that mandates integration before the Soul-Work (Life Purpose) can happen. I think there is a 'time for the beginning of integration' just as*

there is a time for physical development. Embryologists can predict when the biophysical formation of the human will occur. That is because we have an energy-based, physical template that drives our development. I think we have a spiritual template, too, and that dictates when our spirit will begin the journey of integrating with and permeating our physical being (H. Erickson, personal communication, 2005).

To expand on this train of thought, if we have a physical template that dictates how our body is formed during the embryonic stage of life (prebirth) and we have a spiritual drive that permeates and influences all subsystems of the biophysical, psychosocial being, then an obvious question follows: When does the spiritual drive influence integration of the spirit with the rest of the person?

Some of us believe we are spiritual beings, with a Soul before birth. If so, we can assume our spirit connects to and integrates with our biophysical psychosocial body at some point before birth. I support this notion. I think we have the potential to be holistic beings before we are born. We are not just biophysical beings, we are also psychosocial beings and spiritual beings, all integrated to create a holistic being. If that is the case, psycho-social-spiritual development in humans must begin before birth, continue through the lifespan, through the death process and after.

New Development Stages

Based on the assumption that psycho-social-spiritual development starts before birth, continues through the lifespan, and even after physical death, two new stages of development are proposed. The first is Integration, the stage in which the spirit connects to the biophysical-psychosocial body. The second is Transformation, the stage in which the spirit leaves the body. Both will be discussed as I review the stages, tasks, and related issues.

I know there are many philosophical concerns related to this proposal. For clarification of one such question, "What is the difference or relationship between the spirit and the Soul?" I turned to H. Erickson. When discussing her interpretation of how the spirit and Soul relate, she says:

Our spirit is derived from our Soul. It is our Essence of Self, our basic way of Being within this lifetime. Although it is who we are without the influence of others, it is defined by the context of this lifetime. It does not change in nature, but it does evolve in how it is expressed (Personal communication, November 12, 2005).

When asked to clarify the difference between the spirit and the Soul, she stated:

Some do not make a distinction. Maybe that is the best way to handle it, but I can't make it that simple. I think the Soul is more cosmic; it is probably a higher level of energy and it is closer to "understanding" the "knowledge of the Universe." The spirit comes from the Soul and goes back to be reabsorbed by the Soul, but it is more 'earth bound'. I think it is necessary for us to have a spirit that doesn't "know everything," so we can do our lifetime work. You may remember in Chapter 2 when we talked about energy, we stated all energy probably comes from a single source. We also talked about the ability of energy to be transformed from one type to another. Yet, in everyday life, when we talk about energy, we usually talk about different types of energy and rarely indicate they all come from the same source! There is electrical energy, sound energy, light energy, and so forth. The fact is they may all have come from the same source and they may all go back to the same source, but they have been transformed and differentiated, so they serve a specific purpose. This is necessary for two reasons: We need energy differentiated, so our multiple subsystems can function as required by the human body and, secondly, because the human mind is so limited and influenced by feelings we have difficulty understanding cosmic concepts when we live on a physical plane. To make it simpler, I think the spirit is energy drawn from the Soul and transformed, so it is compatible with a physical being.

You may also remember we said incompatible energy fields, energy fields that vibrate on different levels, have difficulty synchronizing. Our spirit (an energy field) has to be able to synchronize with the energy fields of our biophysical body in order for them to integrate. So, Soul-type energy has to be transformed and differentiated, so it can integrate with the rest of our human form. That way we can become holistic, integrated, incarnate beings.

When spiritual energy is transformed back into Soul-type energy (at the time of Transformation), it will vibrate at a higher level, add new information to the Soul's understanding and information. So, you could say they are the same thing just as some say lightning is the same as the electrical conduction of heart signals, but that is too simplistic for me. It doesn't help me understand what and how (Personal communication, November, 2005).

Both H. Erickson and myself know that some readers who identified with the original book will not accept this orientation. We hope those who wish to stay with the Eight Stages of Development, as discussed in the original book by Erickson et al. (1983), will continue to work with that model. This book is not intended to replace that work, but expand on it. We both firmly believe there is no right or wrong way to view the world; there are only views consistent with our individual philosophy and belief systems

GeroTranscendence: A New Stage or Not? Tornstam (1997) proposed another stage of development called GeroTranscendence. It has not been included in this chapter because I think it is inconsistent with the Modeling and Role-

Modeling philosophy for two reasons. First, GeroTranscendence is not a stage of development, but is, instead, healthy residual one would expect to see in the elder person who has worked through each of the tasks and achieved a strong ratio of positive residual over negative residual. That is, when a person reaches this stage of life with a ratio of high positive residual and low negative residual, we would see characteristics Tornstam attributed to the stage of Gerotranscendence[7] (see Table 5.2).

The second reason to not include the stage of Gerotranscendence is that both H. Erickson and I believe people with high levels of positive residual have the capability of transcending across the lifespan. It does not happen just when we get older. It happens when we are in touch with our spirit, when we feel fully integrated, and when we are one with the Universe. While those moments may be rare for some, enough people have described them, so we believe they happen throughout life. Therefore, the idea of GeroTranscendence is too limiting for us.

Table 5.2 Comparison of GeroTranscendence attributes and high positive residual in Ego Integrity.

Attributes of GeroTranscendence	High Positive Residual in Ego Integrity
Transcendence of time, e.g., experience presence of absent relatives.	Increased spiritual awareness and experiences.
Lack of fear of death; immortality in genetic chain.	Does not fear death, believes next step part of journey and Higher Being.
Acceptance of mysterious dimension of life.	Believes we are a part of a bigger picture, we do not control all things.
Enjoyment of subtle to grand experiences and a joy in nature.	Enjoyment in simple & grand life events, nature and natural wonder.
Recognition of "hidden aspects of self."	True to increased awareness of aware inner Self.
Diminished self-centeredness.	Focuses on others rather than self.
Egotism to altruism.	Focus on making world better place for others, sharing of self.
Discovery of the child within.	Playful, approaches life with child-like wonder.
Ego integrity.	Satisfied with own life, accepts choices, decisions and mistakes made in the journey.
Interest in meaningful relationships.	Need to share self; interest in growth of others.
Differentiates between self and role.	Strong sense of inner self. Perceives life mission has been accomplished, even if all goals have not been accomplished.

TEN STAGES OF HUMAN DEVELOPMENT

Background

This section provides details about each stage of development including the tasks, residual, and prerequisites. In some cases, I will also discuss epigenesis. Generally, I draw from Erikson's (1963) work and use his language,[8] but there are some deviations and expansions. For example, I present two dimensions of developmental residual and provide examples. While Erikson was clear we need a "favorable ratio" (p. 274), he continued to talk about residual as a single dimension. I do not; I clearly discriminate between positive and negative residual and discuss them as two separate dimensions. I have used the Developmental Taxonomy (Appendix B) developed by H. Erickson (1977), her other work (1988, 2000), my clinical experiences, and my views on development to guide my discussion of each of the developmental stages.

I also deviate from Erikson (1963) in the discussion of strengths and virtues. Apparently Erikson thought the words "basic virtues" were important, but somewhat troublesome. He stated,

> *While I cannot discuss here the methodological problems involved (and aggravated by my use of the words 'basic virtues'), I should append the list of these strengths because they are really the lasting outcome of the 'favorable ratios' mentioned at every step of the chapter on psychological stages....The italicized words are called basic virtues because without them, and their re-emergence from generation to generation, all other and more changeable systems of human values lose their spirit and their relevance* (p.274).

> *I think Erikson (1963), when distinguishing between strengths and virtues, may have been trying to differentiate human attributes that are a part of the personality from those that are a part of our moral fiber. However, he seemed to have had some difficulty with this distinction. I think holistic people cannot really be separated into "parts" in this way, so I call them resources. I will identify them as strengths and virtues in honor of Erikson, but I perceive them all as Self-care Resources* (H. Erickson, personal communication, November 22, 2005).

Integration

Task Work

H. Erickson, in Chapter 1, introduced the idea of Soul energy vibrating at a higher level than our body's energy. She also said spiritual energy, derived from the Soul, vibrates at a lower level in order to integrate with the body. Chapter 2 built on Einstein's theory to introduce the idea that energy can be converted to matter and vice versa. Brekke and Shultz went on to say we are energy first, our bodies are multiple energy systems, and an energy template guides the development of our bodies. In Chapter 3, Walker and Erickson built on this and stated that energy fields have to synchronize before they can be integrated.

Since spiritual energy (drawn from the Soul) might vibrate at a higher level than biophysical-psychosocial energy, the two energy fields have to merge in order for us to be holistic beings; to do this they have to synchronize their vibrations. I support these assumptions. Having witnessed the birth of many babies, it is clear that most babies can be thought of as mind-body-spirit beings at birth.[9]

Therefore, I think the initial stage of life starts prebirth and runs until birth or shortly after. During this time, I think the two energy fields synchronize—the first step toward integrating with one another—before they can connect and then integrate. This is the Stage of Integration. The work (or task) of this stage is to Synchronize Spiritual Energy with the incarnate body. While Spiritual Integration continues across the lifetime, I think it starts in the initial stage of life, prebirth. Because time starts at zero, and we are talking about development within one lifetime, I will call this Integration, the Zero Stage of Development.

Residual Dimensions

In the Stage of Integration the focus is on achieving a healthy balance between Unity and Duality. Unity is positive residual and Duality is negative. At the low end of the continuum of positive residual is a synchrony of the spiritual energy field with the biophysical-psychosocial energy field.[10] At the high end of the continuum is a sense of holism, which creates the incarnate form of the human being (i.e., to have the spirit embodied in human flesh). It is necessary to have more than a connection or synchrony of energy fields in order to do our Soul-Work for this lifetime; we have to achieve integration. *Without some degree of integration, we are in human form, but not incarnate form. Therefore, we are not fully holistic.*[11]

Duality, at the low end of the continuum (or healthy end of negative residual), is Groundedness and at the far end is Separateness. Healthy Groundedness helps us stay integrated as a holistic, body-mind-spirit human being. Without Groundedness, we might not attend to our physical needs. However, excessive Groundedness creates an inability to be aware of our spirituality. While I believe all humans have Souls, I think all humans do not recognize their Soul or complete their Soul-work in this lifetime. I think this is because they have an unhealthy separation of spirit and the biophysical-psychosocial body.

Implications. Since we carry our developmental residual from stage to stage, healthy integration of the spirit with the rest of our being is a prerequisite for working on the next stage, the task of building Trust. This makes perfect sense from two perspectives: first, how can we possibly learn to have trust in others and be confident we will be cared for if we are not connected with our own Self? We must have some sense of who we are as holistic beings before we can connect with others.

Second, why would we learn to trust humans, to connect with and attach to, if we weren't first grounded in the human form? Why not just stay in the spiritual form? If we are truly holistic beings, then there is more to us than just the psychosocial-biophysical being! We need a healthy ratio of integration of spirit and Groundedness in order to build healthy, secure attachments.

Facilitating Factors

The unborn baby's ability to successfully work through the Stage of Integration depends on the mother's ability to meet the baby's needs in-utero. A uterine environment that is experienced by the fetus as safe and well-nourished, facilitates healthy task resolution. These infants acquire and build healthy Integration-type internal resources that will be used as they move into the next stage of development, Building Trust. On the other hand, babies who are unable to get their needs met in-utero will have difficulty building these internal resources. When this happens, I think sometimes the mother will do her best to "take care of her intrauterine baby," but, for many reasons, the baby's needs are not met.[12] This does not make the mother responsible for the baby's inability to attain a sense of need satisfaction; it simply means there is incompatibility between the two. Sometimes external sources can help both adapt. A very specific example of this situation is when a mother has Rh negative blood and the baby has Rh positive blood. An incompatibility may interfere with the development of the physical being and this in turn might interfere with spiritual integration.

Impeding Factors

We have discussed healthy residual and the related resources that come from this dimension. But, what happens when we hit the threshold after which the balance begins to tip toward unhealthy residual? What does that look like in this stage of development? I think there is a continuous separation of the spirit from the rest of the human being. When this happens, we have more difficulty with all the next stages of life. After all, we have an inherent need to be holistic, but how can we if a major aspect of us (our spirit) is separated from the rest of us?

Epigenesis and Finding Balance

Our work is not done before birth. We have to rework the task of Integration at each of the next eight stages of life. That is, we have to continue learning to have unity in mind-body-spirit while learning to be grounded. Although the spirit and body must be connected and integrated for growth and development to occur, a healthy level of separation must also be present. While we begin our life journey as spiritual beings, incarnate beings must have some level of separateness if they are to stay "grounded" and focus on and accomplish daily routines, needs, and tasks.

Getting up in the morning, going to work, feeding the children, getting household chores done, preparing meals, and other routine tasks of daily life are required, since we are earthbound. While our Life Purpose may be about doing Soul-work, we have to stay grounded to do it. That is, in order to complete our Soul-work, we must pay attention to the biophysical psychosocial being that enables us to interact with others and learn our life lessons. If we were always completely unified with and focused on our Soul, it would be difficult to refocus our energy to accomplish mundane activities that provide a safe and functioning lodging for our Souls. As I have told my children many times, "Our body is the physical vessel that allows our Soul to do its work. We have to take care of our bodies, so we can do our Soul-work in this lifetime."

Resources

Strengths. The resources gained with the acquisition of a healthy balance between Unity and Duality are awareness of our Self as a unique, holistic being and an ability to be aware and grounded at the same time. More specifically, as a result of synchrony and early integration of spiritual energy with the biophysical form of the human, we develop an awareness of our Self as a holistic being. We can call this Awareness because we are not yet ready to actively work on our Life Purpose, but we are beginning to experience ourselves as unique individuals!

Virtue We also have to get used to being earth bound! We are no longer just "spiritual energy," so we have to establish ourselves on earth, in the human form. Our True Self (our spiritual energy) is now "seated in our biophysical body."[13] As we acquire this sense of being a holistic being living in human form, we acquire a sense of being grounded. I call this the virtue of Groundedness. These two, the strength of Awareness and the virtue of Groundedness serve as resources, which facilitate growth and prepare us to work on the next task, building a trusting relationship.

Integration is the Zero stage of development. It starts prebirth and continues until birth or shortly thereafter. The Task work of the stage is integration of the spirit with the biophysical-psychosocial body of the human being. The Developmental Residual Dimensions are Unity and Duality. Unity ranges from synchrony of the energy fields to a sense of holism. Duality ranges from Groundedness (in human form) to Separateness of spirit from the human body. The Strength is Awareness and the Virtue is Groundedness.

Building Trust

Task Work

The first stage of development, Building Trust, starts at birth and continues for the next 12-15 months. During this stage infants focus on acquiring a trusting relationship with their primary caregivers. Infants who come to this stage with positive residual from the stage of Integration have established the initial groundwork for a healthy trusting relationship. They are prepared to be aware of themselves as unique individuals and to develop relationships in this lifetime. They are also prepared to feel connected and safe, a prerequisite to learning that they are separate from their caregivers!

This is a difficult time for many babies. Their bodies are erratic, they haven't learned how to understand or communicate their needs, and they aren't used to being a separate unit from the mother.[14] During this stage, infants have to first learn to regulate their own bodies, and then communicate their needs in ways the caregiver can understand. This is a huge task! Then they have to learn they and the mother are separate beings, but that they can trust the mother (or the caregiver) to look out for them, to protect, nurture, stimulate, and value them. They also have to learn it is okay for them to extend their trust to some, but not all other people. When this happens, they have the foundation needed to build relationships based on mutual trust and respect. They have achieved their first post-birth developmental task. They have learned others love and value them; therefore, they are worthy of love and respect.

Residual Dimensions

The task of Building Trust has two dimensions of residual: a Sense of Trust, the positive residual, and Discrimination Ability, the negative residual. We must remember, however, all negative residual has a healthy component to it. As indicated above, it is a matter of "how much is healthy."

The dimension, Sense of Trust, has at the low end of the continuum (i.e., the least amount of positive residual) an insecure attachment with the care provider. While there is a connection, the infant has learned the affiliation is conditional. At the high end of the continuum is a strong, secure attachment that includes a sense of affiliation and individuation with unconditional acceptance. As the sense of trust grows, so does the child's sense of worth.

There is also a negative residual that emerges. Healthy (low end of the continuum) negative residual leaves the infant with the ability to discriminate those who can be trusted from those who cannot. It is important to have this information, so we can judge who is safe and who is not. At the other end of this continuum is a strong sense of mistrust of others. People who have strong mistrust tend to either never attach to others, or, if the attachment had started, tend to withdraw and detach.

Implications. Initially, infants do not have the cognitive ability to differentiate between themselves and others. Subsequently, when their needs are met, they perceive the world as a safe and trusting place. These infants develop a strong sense of trust. When they get older and develop cognitive skills, which allow them to recognize the difference between their primary care-provider(s) and others, they begin to have "stranger anxiety." This cognitive growth allows them the ability to develop a sense of healthy mistrust. Healthy mistrust is necessary, for it allows us to think about and discern between people and situations that might impact us positively or negatively. When infants acquire a high level of trust and a low level of healthy mistrust, they build positive residual which is taken to the next stage.

Facilitating Factors

As mentioned earlier, before we develop trusting relationships with others, we need to have a sense of our self as a holistic being. This process is initiated prebirth during the Stage of Integration. It is continued as babies build trust. To build trust, it is necessary to perceive need satisfaction, which is not always easy. During the first year of life, infants depend on others to help them meet their needs. They require assistance and support for food, hydration, clothing, elimination needs, safety and security, love and belonging, esteem and self-esteem need satisfaction. When their needs are met repeatedly and consistently during this stage, babies learn to "trust" that others will be there when needed, to care, protect, and love.

Impeding Factors

On the other hand, people who acquire excessive negative residual from this stage of life will not have acquired a sense of Hope. Pessimistic about the future, they may perceive many life experiences as threatening, scary, or overwhelming. They have difficulty relying on others. Past experience has taught them they cannot trust others to meet their needs and they may experience feelings of abandonment or anxious attachment to their primary care giver. At the minimum, they perceive they are not worthy. If they have high levels of mistrust, they may act aggressively or be detached from those around them. The worst scenario is they may detach completely and forever have difficulty with human relationships.

Resources

Strength. When infants reach a satisfactory level of task achievement in this stage, they acquire and internalize a motivation to move forward, to continue to grow and explore. This strength, Drive Toward the Future, enhanced by the strength Awareness (Stage of Integration) enables healthy people to move forward in their life search with minimal external resources and persevere when life is difficult.

Virtue. People who have successfully acquired a healthy balance between trust and mistrust have also developed the virtue of Hope. Hope enables us to approach problems from an optimistic perspective. We have heard the old adage, "Is the glass half empty or half full?" People who have a sense of hope are usually able to look at life events and experiences as a "glass that is half full." Life is generally perceived as a challenge rather than a threat. Approaching new experiences with a sense of confidence and optimism, they believe things will work out and they will be all right. They also believe other people will be available when and if needed. Even though there may be threats to getting their needs met, they have faith their needs will be satisfied.

Case Examples

Melanie is a happy, healthy, nine-month-old baby who prefers to be with her mother or father. She will also happily go to grandma or grandpa whom she knows well. However, when she is taken to a family reunion with many new people, she pulls away from "strangers" and refuses to be held by anyone she does not know. If someone new approaches, she shows signs of anxiety, hides her head in her mother's shoulder, and holds on tightly. When the stranger she perceives as threatening leaves, she happily resumes actively watching the people and room activities from the safety of her mother's arms.

Melanie's behavior demonstrates a sense of healthy trust and mistrust. Although she prefers to be with her parents, she "trusts" her grandparents will keep her safe and take care of her needs. Melanie also has a healthy sense of mistrust, shown by her pulling away from people she does not know. This ability to discern between individuals with whom she is safe and valued and individuals with whom she is not illustrates healthy task resolution in the stage of Building Trust.

Sara, who is also nine months old, does not appear to care who holds her. If her mother puts her down or passes her among strangers, she willingly goes to anyone who offers to take her or sits passively with little or no affect. She does not seem to prefer her parents, and she does not exhibit any signs of a healthy sense of mistrust.

Unlike Melanie, Sara's behavior demonstrates she has had difficulty developing a strong, secure attachment to her mother. Consequently, she does not seem to differentiate between a safe, trusting caregiver and one who may not be. This inability to discern between individuals who can meet her needs and those who may threaten them illustrates unhealthy task work in this stage of development.

The first stage of development is Building Trust. It starts at birth and continues until 12-15 months of age. The Task work of this stage is to learn there are people who will protect, love and respect you without conditions. Children also learn to discriminate those who are trustworthy from those who are not. The Developmental Residual Dimensions are Trust and Discrimination. Trust ranges from insecure attachment to secure attachment. Discrimination ranges from the ability to identify those who are unsafe to excessive mistrust with detachment from people. The Strength is Drive for the Future; the virtue is Hope (or a sense of Positive Orientation).

Autonomy

Task Work

During the second stage of development, we are confronted with learning to make decisions, so we can have control over our lives. Resolution of this task usually occurs sometime between 12 to 36 months of age. Increased and improved fine and gross motor skills allow us to physically explore and manipulate our environment. This helps us expand our horizons and redefine ourselves. As we explore, we are confronted with new experiences requiring problem solving and coping skills. But, as toddlers we are still very dependent on our caregivers. We have to learn to make decisions our caregivers will affirm and support! This is no easy task. Not only do we have to learn to exert our will, we have to learn to do it in acceptable ways!

Erik Erikson (1963) says this stage is about learning to hang-on and let-go (p. 231). There are various ways of thinking about this issue. For example, learning to use the potty is a matter of hanging on and letting go; so is learning to compromise about what we want and how to resolve our needs. Toddlers require lots of help learning to compromise, so they perceive they are in charge and making the "important decisions"! Their primary task during this stage is to learn to make decisions about their lives, but within the context of others.

Residual Dimensions

The two dimensions of developmental residual related to this stage are Autonomy and Introspection. Autonomy has, at the low end of the continuum, a need to make "good" decisions and at the high end an ability to make good decisions about our lives. They are not about directing the lives of others, only our own.

The counter side, the negative residual, is Introspection. This dimension is on a continuum from doubt to excessive doubt that becomes shame. While it is important to think about our decisions and consider their merit, too much doubt can result in shame. Now, not only is there a problem with our decision-making, but also with how we feel about ourselves because of those decisions. There is a difference between being introspective and thoughtful and feeling shameful.

Implications. Sometimes children working on this task appear to always want their way. For some people, this is perceived as letting toddlers have their way at someone else's expense. This is not healthy autonomy. This is the stage when children learn to control their lives by the decisions they make, while learning to respect the parameters set by their caregivers. People want to be connected to others, to have their approval and respect, but simultaneously, they also need to be able to run their own lives.

As children successfully learn to control different aspects of their lives such as the clothes they wear, the toys they play with and their bodily functions, they learn to make and carry out decisions and successfully problem solve. They develop confidence in their ability to control their own life and be self-directed.

They begin to learn responsibility for their choices and actions. Children who have a healthy level of autonomy and some ability for introspection have feelings of good will and take pride in their work. However, acknowledging their limitations, they realize their inability to control all aspects of life and learn to negotiate with others.

Epigenesis. During this stage, toddlers rework Integration and Trust within the context of Autonomy. They continue to discover themselves as holistic beings, and need others who will not only love and protect them, but also allow them control over their lives (within set parameters). They also learn to stay grounded and discriminate trustworthy people from others. Even though they learn to introspect and self evaluate, they still need to feel safe, loved and protected.

Facilitating Factors

Although parents need to support children as they learn to make decisions, limits and boundaries also have to be established and maintained in a firm loving manner. It is unhealthy and unrealistic for young children to make all the decisions. They do not have the cognitive or emotional capability or skills. However, encouraged to make some decisions and accept the natural consequences of those decisions, they learn their limitations. This helps them develop an ability to make good decisions and develop a sense of self-control. They learn what is acceptable and what is not; they learn where they have control over their lives and how that control affects their relationship with others.

As they grow, toddlers continue to emotionally and physically individuate from their caregivers, but they can only do this because they trust the caregivers will be there when they return. The work of Bowlby (1960), Fraiberg (1967, 1977), and Mahler (1975) has shown small children must be able to *refuel* or reconnect with their caregivers as they explore new terrain. Erickson et al. (1983) spoke about this phenomenon as "synonymous with *getting our battery recharged*. The child returns to a safe, secure attachment figure in order to rest and store up sufficient energy to venture into the world again" (p.72). They refer to the two year old who runs away from mama only to quickly return, grasp her leg and *refuel*. They say that the need to refuel is a lifelong need met through our affiliations with other people.

Impeding Factors

Sometimes caregivers perceive children demonstrating healthy autonomy as stubborn, or difficult. They think the child is trying to "spite" them. Since this age and stage is typically thought of as "potty-training time," some caregivers get into a power struggle with their children over toilet training. As parents, we are ready to get them out of diapers and into underwear. Nevertheless, this is one area where children ultimately make choices to control their bodies and their eliminative functions.

Caregivers who push children into toilet training or other life events instead of waiting for the child to be ready, often experience a battle of wills. Such a situation becomes a lose-lose situation for both the child and adult. Parents become frustrated and often more controlling, frequently becoming angry and disparaging with their child. The child may become obstinate or experience feelings of embarrassment, being small, or impotent. As a result, the child internalizes feelings of failure, shame, and doubt, and feels isolated or disconnected from the parent(s) rather than experiencing healthy feelings of affiliated–individuation.

When children repeatedly learn they are incompetent, unable to assume control, or make good decisions, they begin to feel other people control their lives. As a result, they learn to depend on other people or external controls to manage their behavior. They may have difficulty expressing their views and coping with problems. They may also be indecisive and lack confidence. Often, these children feel sad or angry believing nothing they do is right or good enough. Although appearing to be overly compliant and working hard to please, they may also exhibit impulsive, stubborn, aggressive, and angry behavior.

On the other hand, when parents are patient and allow the child to set the pace, the process will be smoother. Successful potty training results in a win-win situation for the both when parents positively support and encourage this new ability. Consequently, the child becomes more autonomous while simultaneously receiving positive feedback from the parents, which strengthens the child's feelings of affiliated-individuation.

Resources

Strength. Successful resolution of the task of decision-making results in the acquisition of self-control. Children learn to assert their will, problem solve and make safe and wise decisions. They also learn self-control is not control of others, but control of self.

Virtue. As children gain a sense of self-control, they also develop an attitude or virtue of will power. They learn to cope with problems and problem solve. They gain the ability to manage their lives, but not at the expense of losing their affiliations. Instead, they learn a new way of exerting their individuation. The strength of self-control and the virtue of willpower are needed as the child enters the next stage of growth and development.

Case Examples

John is a normal, healthy twenty-two-month-old. His mother and he attend a playgroup with other mothers and their children. John is happy to play by his mother and near the other children. He frequently moves around the room to look at a new toy or see what another child is doing. Occasionally, he sits down for a few minutes to play in an area away from his mother. However, he regularly goes back to refuel and reconnect with his mother. If a stranger should appear in the room or someone he doesn't know well comes close, he immediately returns to his mother where he feels safe and secure.

John shows evidence of having adequately resolved the task of Trust versus Mistrust. He is now working on the stage of Autonomy versus Doubt. He has positive developmental residual, which allows him to explore the world around him in a trusting manner. At the same time, he also has healthy mistrust, which helps him protect himself in situations, which he perceives might be threatening to his well-being. As he explores his world, he refuels when necessary and continues to become more comfortable and independent in his growing world.

Susan is also a physically healthy toddler who regularly attends a mother-child playgroup. All of her playtime time is spent clinging to her mother. She refuses to leave her mother's side. When her mother encourages her to play with other children she buries her face in her mother's hair. She will not venture out into the room away from her mother. If a stranger appears in the room she cries and holds on tighter.

Unlike John, Susan has a lot of negative residual from previous developmental stages. Her behavior indicates very little trust in her environment. She is afraid, feels threatened, and does not trust she will be safe. She has a deep sense of mistrust and inadequate feelings of trust. As a result, she has difficulty working on the stage of Autonomy. Since she feels unsafe and insecure in her environment, she is unable to explore the world around her.

As they become more confident in their explorations, children encounter opportunities which allow them to experience feelings of independence and control. All parents have struggled with the small child whose favorite word is "No." Overnight, your darling little boy, who has been sweet and agreeable, begins to say, "No" or "No do that" to everything asked of him. When told to follow a direction or instruction, he may throw a marvelous tantrum. Often the parent perceives the child's behavior as signs of disobedience or defiance.

The second stage of development is Acquiring Autonomy. It starts between 12-18 months and continues until 2 1/2 to 3 years of age. The Task work of the stage involves learning to make decisions and self-evaluate. The Developmental Residual Dimensions are Autonomy and Introspection. Autonomy ranges from the need to make decisions to the ability to make good decisions. Introspection ranges from healthy self-evaluation to excessive doubt resulting in shame. The Strength is Self-Control; the Virtue is Will-power.

Although children may not follow directions as asked, the intent on their part is not to be disagreeable or disobedient. They are simply trying to exert their self-will. As they learn to become more autonomous they need to separate both physically and emotionally from their parents. This process requires they make decisions and control experiences and events in their daily lives. This is not to say that their decisions are always in agreement with their parents' opinions.

Initiative

Task Work

During Initiative, the third stage of development, children start moving away from their immediate family or caregivers. It starts around 2 to 2 1/2 years and runs until 5-7 years of age, depending on the child. Moving into this stage, children have usually mastered their immediate environment. Since we have an inherent drive toward growth, they are now challenged with the task of expanding their social circle beyond the immediate family. This means learning to negotiate with people they have not known since birth; people who don't accept and love them just because they are family members. Usually it is people their own age, which is even more difficult. The need to expand their environment and social circles while simultaneously learning to internalize responsibility for their own actions is the essence of Initiative.

Residual Dimensions

The two dimensions of this stage are Taking Initiative and Assuming Responsibility. Erikson (1963) called these Initiative and Guilt. Initiative is our ability to act somewhat independently of the caregivers as we reach out to new people and experiences.[15] Children who develop minimal initiative may demonstrate interest in making friends and trying new activities, but show little independence in doing them without the parent's negotiations. On the other hand, those with high positive residual exhibit an ability to be assertive (not aggressive) in their actions; with minimal support from the caregivers, they are able to start negotiating new relationships and activities.

Negative residual derived from this stage ranges from feeling responsible to feeling guilty. Erikson called this Guilt. I have chosen to reframe it because it is important to have healthy negative residual. Children with a healthy "dose" of this residual have started to learn that behavior is contextual; their actions have consequences and they are responsible for those consequences. At the other end of the continuum is an excessive sense of responsibility, which creates feelings of guilt. The difference between assuming responsibility and feeling overwhelmed with our responsibility is huge. It is the difference between healthy introspection and learning from experiences, as opposed to experiencing so much guilt, we are afraid to take action or simply blame others for both the actions and consequences.

Implications. Although children need to learn to reach out, take risks, and make new acquaintances, they also have to learn responsibility for their actions. This is also the time in life when society begins to treat children differently. No longer viewed as toddlers, they are now preschool children. They are old enough "to know better," as many adults will say of the four-year-old who hits her two-year-old sibling. The challenge for these children is learning to negotiate with various people and assuming the responsibility for doing it!

Children who repeatedly experience positive outcomes when they take initiative learn to feel good about their decisions. They seek social interactions, enjoy competition and take pleasure in a contest and in winning. The pleasure is in being successful in their endeavors rather than "beating" someone else. They continue, during this period of development, to become more adept and competent with their fine and gross motor skills. Manipulation of tools such as a crayon, a pencil, or a mixing spoon, when baking with an adult, allow them to gain pleasure in their mastery of skills, which in turn allows them to seek out new experiences and activities. When primary caregivers support and encourage exploration, independent thinking, and decision-making, children are purposeful in their lives. Goal-directed, thoughtful, and purposeful choices are made.

A final word about residual in this stage of development. Because this stage is about learning to take initiative, which can be very stressful, some children have somatic responses to the stress (e.g., such as stomach aches, head aches, or sore throats). This is normal for children at this age. When this happens a few times, a coping mechanism is learned: when stressed by normal, everyday activities, if you "don't feel good," you don't have to continue the activities. Sometimes these last for several months and then disappear when the child becomes a proficient negotiator. However, for those who develop more negative residual this can become a lifetime pattern known as a somatic response syndrome.

Over time the individual may consciously forget the original events, and lose track of the relationship between stressor and stress response. Nevertheless, they have learned how to handle stress at an unconscious level and sometimes even at a cellular level. When confronted with similar situations later in life, they are likely to have similar responses without understanding where these were learned or why. Erikson called this malingering. We think of it as a learned response to stress, embedded in the developmental residual.

Epigenisis. Children who have internalized self-control and will-power have less trouble working through this task. Using self-control, they learn to influence the environment and people around them in ways that "work for them." They are persistent, and willing to try repeatedly, if necessary. They have learned rudimentary negotiation skills, which is very different from learning to manipulate people to get what they want. Manipulation of objects is fine; manipulation of people is not.

Facilitating Factors

Some children have a natural tendency to reach out to others, expand their horizons, and seek new experiences. These children simply need continued support and guidance from caregivers, a clear understanding of their parameters, and opportunities to do the work of this task. Some children who have had difficulty with the stage of Autonomy will discover this as their opportunity to exert their will and have control over what happens to them. Some will be in preschool or day care where they have multiple opportunities to interact with others. As they learn about themselves, they are better able to negotiate this stage. They are also able to rework earlier tasks and develop a more favorable balance of positive and negative residual. They simply need a consistent and supportive home environment, which affirms their worth and gives them the room to negotiate options.

Impeding Factors

Children who enter this stage with moderate to excessive negative residual, have another problem—they don't have the resources needed to move out of the family circle and they don't know how to negotiate relations with others without compromising themselves. Children who have minimal trust and autonomy and moderate to excessive mistrust or shame may have difficulty reaching out to people they don't know. They may be fearful of being unsafe or mistreated. They might also be too concerned about "being responsible for their actions" to take the risks needed to move away from a safe environment. As a result, they may choose safety over new opportunities, resulting in an inability to work through the task of this stage of development.

Manipulation of others is another example of behavior that may be seen in children who enter this stage with strong negative residual. These children have learned they have to control others in order to have control over their own lives. They treat peers as objects without feelings, often using them to get their own needs met, and learning little about their responsibility to others. They have not learned to compromise or recognize that healthy affiliated-individuation means both members of the dyad get their needs met!

A third outcome of strong negative residual is that these children might "lash out" or interact with others in aggressive, threatening ways, discouraging peers and adults from seeking their company. When this happens, peers will not want to play with such a child, and adults will often say such a child is a bully or worse. As a result, they often leave this stage with more negative residual.

Resources

Strength. The key strength derived from work on this task is a sense of direction. This strength helps us focus our lives.

Virtue. We also develop an attitude or virtue of purpose. Now not only can we focus on what we think is important, we also have an assigned purpose to our focus. We have a strong sense of holism (Integration), optimism for the future (Trust), will-power to carry out our decisions (Autonomy), and a purpose for our activities. We also have a healthy sense of being grounded (from Integration), an ability to discriminate those who are trustworthy from those who aren't (Trust), a healthy ability to self-evaluate decisions (Autonomy), and a capacity to take responsibility for our actions (Initiative). We have achieved a great deal in five short years!

Case Examples

Elijah attends preschool with his classmates. One Monday morning, he runs into his classroom and announces he had a birthday over the weekend and he is now 5 years old. He received a Spiderman costume as a gift and wants to play "Spiderman." He declares, "I am going to be Spiderman. Does anyone want to play with me?" His classmate Bobby replies, "I want to play, but I want to be Spiderman, too." Elijah answers, "I am going to be Spiderman first because it was my idea, then it will be your turn. Okay?" Bobby agrees with the plan and the two boys go off to play together.

Elijah is able to assert his wishes and negotiate with Bobby. He is straightforward about his intent, does not try to manipulate Bobby into playing with him and then leave him without a turn or a shortened turn. His ability to successfully achieve a win-win situation with Bobby positively reinforces his ability to take initiative, problem solve and negotiate. He has also learned he has responsibility to Bobby to "work it out," so Bobby is happy, too.

Anna is six years old and goes to kindergarten. She is rigid, uncompromising, and consequently, has difficulty playing with her classmates. She is unable to work with other children on projects as she believes there is only one way to do something. When confronted with a problem or new situation, she withdraws. Not initiating or participating in most games or classroom activities, she spends most of the day quietly playing alone.

The teacher has asked the students to make a picture of their family and home. Anna is having problems with her picture. Accidentally breaking a crayon, she begins to cry and is hard to console. Apologizing profusely, she says, "I know I shouldn't have pushed so hard on the paper. It was all my fault. I won't do it again. You can take my crayons away. I know I wasn't being careful with them." After settling down, she looks over to her classmate's picture and comments, "That's not the way to color a house or sky. Houses can't be purple, and the sky is never pink."

Unlike Elijah, Anna is having problems with the stage of Initiative. Her behavior indicates she is having trouble interacting with her social world. She does not show evidence of direction or purpose in her actions in her daily life. She also does not have the ability to work positively with other children. Unable to problem solve, she withdraws from new or challenging situations. Her worldview is rigid and she is unable to be flexible. Anna believes there is only one way to do things and everything needs to be perfect. When her crayon accidentally breaks, she feels guilty and deserving of punishment, exhibiting behavior and statements that provide little evidence of initiative and excessive feelings of guilt. Unless circumstances change, Anna will take negative residual (a low level of initiative and a high level of guilt) to her next developmental stage.

The third stage of development is Initiative. It starts around 2 1/2 years of age and runs until 5 to 7 years, depending on the child. The Task work of the stage is learning to be proactive and taking responsibility for our actions. The Developmental Residual Dimensions are Taking Initiative and Assuming Responsibility. Positive residual ranges from interest in moving into society to proactive initiations. Assuming Responsibility ranges from feeling responsible to excessive guilt. The Strength is Direction; the Virtue is Purpose.

Industry

Task Work

The fourth stage of development starts around the age of 5-7 years and continues until 10-13, depending on the child. During this stage, children learn to be industrious. During previous stages they learned to trust others, make decisions, and take initiative. Now they need to use the skills learned to set goals, prioritize them, and design purposeful strategies. The emphasis is on learning good problem-solving skills. This helps them learn they are competent, capable people.

This is also the age of learning to be a competent team member. Children are encouraged at home and at school to work as a team member. They join extracurricular groups where team activities are emphasized, and take on new responsibilities in the family. When they are able to achieve this type of social activity, they learn not only that they are competent individuals, but also that they can also be competent, capable team members. They are learning early skills needed to be an adult member of an industrious society.

Residual Dimensions

The two dimensions of developmental residual related to this stage are Competency and Limitations. Competency, a pleasure in "work completion," has competence as an individual at the low end of the continuum and competence as a team member at the high, positive end of the continuum. On the other hand, Limitations ranges from an ability to recognize our limitations on the healthy end of the continuum to feelings of inadequacy and incompetence on the opposite end of the continuum. A healthy sense of negative residual occurs as we learn that we need to occasionally re-evaluate our methods or goals. Sometimes we aim too high! It is important for us to acknowledge we have limitations, that we can't have expertise in all areas.

Implications

Children who have a sense of competence balanced with a healthy understanding of their limitations face minimal difficulty finding ways to direct their life experiences. Although they are influenced by peers, family members, teachers and other authorities, they are able to self-direct and self-evaluate. They learned to identify those who are trustworthy. Next, they learned to make good decisions, and take initiative. Now they are learning to incorporate all their previous "learning" into the task of goal-achievement. They are not only able to work independently, but are also learning to be a contributing member of society. They are ready for the next step, to learn about themselves as unique individuals living in a society with millions of other people.

While healthy inferiority helps us identify our strengths and limitations, an excess creates feelings of inadequacy and incompetence. When this happens, children are often overwhelmed by their limitations and unable to perceive their strengths, resulting in difficulties competing and/or working as a cooperative team member. They feel inferior to those who have the skills or knowledge needed to be successful in achieving their goals. They are unable to distinguish between limitations and weaknesses.[16]

Sometimes these people are simply unwilling to try to set goals and work toward them; it just seems futile. They live only for the moment. They may try to cover their feelings of inferiority by being unwilling to compromise or acting as if they know everything there is to know. They might say learning new ideas or skills is "dumb" or that they cannot learn from others.

Adults with little positive residual from the stage of Industry might want to set goals, but may demonstrate an inability to set and achieve long term goals. While they may try, they are often unsuccessful because they lack the strengths and virtues needed to follow through. Their failures only build on their sense of incompetence and inadequacy.

Sometimes these adults can set short-range (sometimes very short, insignificant) goals and be successful. That is because they are continuing to work on developmental work of the previous stages. For example, a person with minimum positive residual may want to start an exercise regime because his nurse suggested it was needed to protect his heart. He might say he plans to start walking a mile a day; he might even promise a significant other he would "stick with his plan this time." He might actually walk a full mile the next day, and even the second or third day, but we should not expect he will follow-through with his plan. Minimal residual will only provide sufficient resources to follow through with short-range goals. On the other hand, a person with strong positive residual from this stage is able to set goals, plan strategies, and find ways to achieve them. And they can do this with a team of peers.

Facilitating Factors
Children this age are enrolled in school, engaged in team activities, and involved with peer groups. All of these are natural settings where they can learn to be methodical and goal-directed. We might think it is easy to work through this stage of development because of the age group and associated activities, but this is not the case. It is true many people are able to focus on school activities or team

sports and work on this task. However, they also need sufficient residual from earlier stages of life in order to develop the capacity to set goals and plan strategies. Moreover, they need the physical and mental abilities to be successful, to have teachers, parents, and peers willing and able to facilitate their growth, guide them, and accept them as they are.

Impeding Factors

Needless to say, our ability to work through this stage successfully is influenced by our previously acquired balance of residual. When people enter this stage with mistrust, personal doubt, and/or excessive feelings of responsibility, they may have trouble taking the risks needed to work with a group, design strategies, and achieve goals. This seems obvious, but what about those who enter this stage with a fairly healthy residual, but still have difficulty?

According to Erikson (1963), numerous factors can impede growth at this age. He talks about the danger that threatens the individual and society when individuals feel the color of their skin, their background, or their clothes determine their worth (p.160). Although we can work on Industry individually, it should be remembered, as social beings, we have a need to be with people, to work and play with them, and the task of this stage depends on our ability to do this. When others remind us we are different because of who we are, or what we wear, or how we talk, walk or think, we have difficulty feeling included in the group. Keep in mind this is the time in life when many children seek a group of peers to accomplish their developmental task, for example, a softball, soccer, or swim team. They enjoy the teamwork, the camaraderie, and the success achieved by the team. When they are isolated and set apart from the group of peers for any reason they have no control over, they have difficulty working through this stage.

Balance. Erikson (1963) also discussed the potential for negative outcome of this stage and task. He stated:

> *But, there is another more fundamental danger. Namely, man's restriction of himself and constriction of his horizons to include only his work....If he accepts work as his only obligation, and 'that works' as his only criterion of worthwhileness, he only becomes the thoughtless slave of his technology and of those who are in a position to exploit it* (p.160-161).

We all know people who appear more dedicated to their work than their friends or family—people whose worth is defined by their status, income, or power base at work. These are probably individuals with a high sense of inferiority.

There are also people, perceived as excellent "workers," very competent and successful, who concede they are successful only because they work all the time and they are really fake. These people sometimes express fear of being discovered. While they may have developed sufficient Industry to be successful in a work environment, they may have also developed a strong sense of inferiority.

The balance between the two types of residual with more negative than positive residual could account for such attitudes. Unless we are able to develop a healthy balance of personal and group competence, we have difficulty learning about our strengths and limitations within the context of our peers. A healthy balance results in our learning to be competent as an individual, and being able to work with a group while learning about our strengths and limitations as a member of society.

Resources
Strength. Erikson labels the strength derived from this stage as Method. I would describe this as the ability to use a methodological approach to problem solving.

Virtue. The virtue or attitude acquired is a sense of competence. These resources are available, both as an individual and as a member of society.

Case Examples
Twelve-year-old Mark wanted an expensive, new bike, but knew his parents wouldn't buy it for him. He knew he was too young to work at a job in retail. His parents suggested he sit down and consider his options. He made a list of several jobs he felt he could do successfully. After thinking through his options, he narrowed his list down to the following ideas: washing cars, odd jobs at home, babysitting, or a paper route.

Upon reflection, he realized he didn't have much experience babysitting small children and wasn't always very patient. He thought about washing cars and doing odd jobs, but felt he would do better with a regular schedule and routine, clearly defined expectations, and a regular paycheck. He reviewed his ideas and thoughts with his parents and together they decided that although he had never had a regular job he could look into getting a paper route. Mark contacted the local paper and accepted a weekend paper route.

Although the hours required hard work as well as getting up early on his days off he always did his best. After a year of working and saving, he was able to purchase the bike of his dreams. Pleased with accomplishing his goal, he started thinking about his next project.

Mark shows evidence of successfully resolving the task of Industry. He uses logic to think through his possible job options. Knowing his strengths, limitations, and needs, he pursues a job he can accomplish. He is willing to learn a new job and commits to it. He has reached a high level of industry, but has also internalized a healthy amount of inferiority, which enables him to identify his strengths and limitations, as well as approach, learn, and complete new tasks.

Twelve-year-old Mary is an only child. Her parents have tried to provide for all her needs. She is used to having her way and doing as she pleases. She is bright, but does not apply herself at school, so her grades are mediocre at best. A class assignment requires she work in a group to develop a product that can be sold at the school business fair. She suggests hair adornments, but the other three students disagree with her and want to make balls with rubber bands. Angry, because they disagree, she pulls away from the group and turns her back on them.

Eventually, she rejoins the group. They are discussing how to make the balls so they will require minimal cost, time, and group resources. She is unable to contribute to the discussion in any meaningful way. When it is time to make the balls, she has problems completing one. She gets angry and refuses to continue with the task saying, "They are just stupid balls anyway, and I didn't want to do them!" She refuses to participate any further "with this dumb idea."

Mary's behavior demonstrates difficulty with task resolution in this developmental stage. Her comments and actions indicate high levels of inferiority and low levels of industry. She has trouble cooperating and working with her peers on the project, does not show any evidence of using logic or offer options to problem solve, and isolates herself when she does not get her way. Mary is not successful in undertaking a new task, setting a goal, showing good work habits, or being a responsible group member. She does not persevere in the task when she has difficulty, but gives up, experiencing a sense of failure, rather than achievement. She does not show any indication of the ability to use a methodological approach to solving problems and doesn't exhibit an internal sense of competence.

The fourth stage of development is Industry. It starts around 5-7 years of age and runs until 11-13 years of age. The Task work of this stage is learning to set goals and design problem-solving strategies. The Developmental Residual Dimensions are Competence and Limitations. Competence ranges from competence as an individual to competence as a team member. Limitation ranges from the ability to recognize one's limitations to feelings of inadequacy and inferiority. The Strength is a Methodological Approach to Problem-solving; the Virtue is Competence.

Identity

Task Work

Identity, the fifth stage of development, is a challenging time. The work of developing a personal Identity starts around the age of 10-13 and can continue until the early 30s. During the previous task, children had to learn about themselves as a group member. Now they have to decide who they are as unique members of society. They have to sort through how they are like those around them and how they are different.

It is also a time of idealism. While adolescents are sorting out who they are, they have to decide how they relate to their family, peers, and society at large.

They question the beliefs of each of these groups, including their values, religious teachings, norms, rituals, and other behavior. They have to decide what is "right and wrong" for them as an individual member of these groups.

Residual Dimensions

The two dimensions of residual related to this stage are Self-Identity and Role-Confusion. Self-Identity, the positive residual, has at the low end of the continuum, a sense-of-self, primarily influenced by the perspectives of others, and at the high end of the continuum, an understanding of one's unique role in society. People with strong positive residual have developed an understanding of their uniqueness as human beings and their role in society. They enjoy a healthy balance of affiliated-individuation with significant others and are ready to map out the next 20 years of their lives.

Role-confusion, i.e., not being clear about our worth, value, and role in society, is the negative residual from this stage. This dimension ranges from an ability to define our role as a unique individual to complete role confusion. When there is moderate to excessive role confusion, adolescents have difficulty identifying a direction for their future. They can't perceive themselves as having a worthy place in society. Instead, they feel alienated and without direction.

Implications. During adolescence, we explore who we are, where we are going, who we want to be, our attitudes and values, and different life paths and roles. It is a time of challenges, turbulence, tears, frustrations, joy, and much physical, psychological, emotional, and spiritual growth. Because this is a time of learning about ourselves within the context of others, we have to refocus on all earlier tasks within the context of not only who we are, but who we will become.

This means adolescence is also a time to rediscover our spiritual "Self" and to continue the work of spiritual integration. It is a time for spiritual questioning, reawakening, and reconnecting. Because adolescents have to rework each of these developmental tasks, they have an opportunity to reassess their "sense-of-self" and determine how it relates to their true Self.[17]

Given the opportunity to explore different facets of who they are and supported in that process, adolescents are able to integrate past experiences into a logical, coherent perception of Self. This understanding of one's "Self" is crucial for future relationships with others. If we do not know who we are, we are unable, as adults, to intimately connect with significant others. Instead, we might find our identity tied to what we do.

Erikson (1963), talks about the danger of this stage stating:

> *The sense of ego identity, then, is the accrued confidence that the inner sameness and continuity prepared in the past are matched by the sameness and continuity of one's meaning for others, as evidenced in the tangible promise of a 'career'. The danger of this stage is role-confusion. Where this is based on strong previous doubt as to one's sexual identity, delinquent and outright psychotic episodes are not uncommon. If*

diagnosed and treated correctly, these indicants do not have the same fatal significance, which they have at other ages. In most instances, however, it is the inability to settle on an occupational identity, which disturbs individual young people. To keep themselves together, they over identify, to the point of apparent complete loss of identity, with the heroes of cliques and crowds...Young people can also be remarkably clannish, and cruel in their exclusion of all those who are 'different' in skin color or cultural background, in tastes and gifts, and often in such petty aspects of dress and gesture as have been temporarily selected as the signs of an in-grouper or out-grouper. It is important to understand (which does not mean condone or participate in) such intolerance as a defense against a sense of identity confusion (p. 162).

This stage of development is one of the most difficult. It is, moreover, the most important because it involves reworking earlier stages and laying down residual for the rest of one's life. It is the time when people make decisions that will influence the rest of their lives, decisions, which can't easily be fixed or changed.

It is a time to rework the past and prepare for the future. For some it is comparable to reliving the stage of Autonomy. In reality, it is reliving Autonomy, but now we also have to deal with the residual accrued through the years. Sometimes that is very difficult. Parents and their adolescents need the support and understanding of immediate and extended families in order to negotiate this stage with healthy outcomes.

Facilitating Factors

Task resolution at this stage requires a healthy balance of positive and negative residual from earlier stages, plus support for the work of this stage. While the first is often easier for caregivers, the latter sometimes represents a challenge. Suddenly, children who had always accepted family values and family activities are no longer so accepting. They seem to find many flaws in the way parents think, act, and believe.[18] They are often more interested in another person than the family; they have "fallen in love"; they do things that are "embarrassing" or confusing for the caregivers who worry they are "getting in with the wrong crowd." They experiment, experiment, experiment!

While this is fairly normal behavior for the adolescent, it is important for the caregivers to continue providing clear guidelines about what is acceptable behavior and what is not. It is also important to respect the adolescent's need to explore, and to provide ample room for negotiation. While adolescents act like they are "all grown up," young adolescents still need help with parameters. They need to feel respected and valued, even when they make serious mistakes.

They also need to know caregivers believe and accept there is a difference between the person and the person's behavior. Sometimes people get confused and think "bad behavior" means a 'bad person." Adolescents need to know they are loved and valued, just because they are, but some of their behavior is not safe for them or respectful of others, and therefore, it is not acceptable, period. This stage of development is a time when each of the previous stages has to be reworked, so the "child" can move into "adulthood."

Caregivers should expect their adolescents to act like toddlers one moment and mature, responsible adults the next. It is the nature of the stage! Caregivers need to find time for themselves, so they will have time for the adolescents. They also need to make sure adolescents continue spending time with the family, and find ways to make the time enjoyable for everyone. They also have to respect the adolescent's need to move away from the family and find their own space. They have to make sure the adolescents know they are loved, valued and trusted, and that the parents expect they will be trustworthy. And then, the caregivers have to be prepared to discover their adolescents have used "adolescent type judgment" and made mistakes. When this happens, caregivers have to provide support, help the adolescents problem-solve their situation, and learn from the experiences. It is not a time to deride them, to remind them of their bad judgment, or tell them, "I told you so." Adolescents are filled with uncertainty; they need help rediscovering their worth, trying their wings, and finding their place in the world outside the family without losing the family.

Impeding Factors

Since adolescents often indicate they no longer need parental guidance, and in fact, sometimes fight fiercely against it, caregivers have to determine the balance between freedom and restrictions. Excessive restrictions or parameters are as dangerous as no restrictions. Excessive restrictions result in either overly submissive or rebellious reactions from the adolescents.

Adolescents need to know they are loved and respected even though they have decided to think differently, act differently, and live differently from how they were raised. When adolescents are rejected or degraded or fear they will be rejected or degraded, they have trouble sorting through their identity issues. They move toward role-confusion. They don't know what or who they want to become, and how they want to live the next 20 years of their lives. Sometimes, when this happens, rather than discovering themselves, they over identify with what they can do. They focus on how others see them, and what they think significant others want them to do with their lives. They lose the unique opportunity to discover the Essence of their Self.

Resources

Strength. Successful resolution of this task results in commitment to values, social norms and ideals. This strength is called Devotion. With Devotion comes the ability to be invested in a way of life and to adopt the ideals and values consistent with that pathway.

Virtue. The virtue or attitude derived from this stage is Fidelity. Fidelity is the commitment to be faithful and stay true to the values and ideals one has chosen.

Case Examples

Tom, a healthy 17-year-old boy, lives with his parents and two brothers. In the past he was clean and well-dressed, easy going, followed the house rules, did his homework, and had minimal problems with his younger brothers. Recently, he seems to be experiencing "growing pains." He complains all the time about rules regarding homework, socializing during the school week, curfew, his chores, etc. He refuses to go to church stating, "I am not sure I believe in that stuff anymore. I think I might try out Buddhism. I like some of their ideas. But, I'm not sure. I want to look into it."

Tom recently got a Mohawk haircut and dyed it purple. Yesterday, he came home with a pierced ear and a feather earring. His clothes are clean, but ragged, and he has a favorite t-shirt he wears all the time.

Recently, he has become actively involved in environmental issues. He has read a lot about the impact of toxic waste and pollutants on people, nature, and the environment. He is constantly talking about changes his family needs to make to create a positive difference, such as getting rid of their large vehicles and buying environmentally-friendly cars. Tom has also become politically active in organizations focusing on increasing awareness of global warming and the destruction of natural resources. He questions his parents' political allegiances to individuals who support big businesses and are unconcerned about the environment. Although his parents do not always agree, they encourage him to explore different ideas, paths, and roles and accept his comments and behavior without judgment.

Tom shows many signs of normal adolescence. He is working hard to figure out who he is and where he fits into his social world. He is experimenting with different ideas, i.e., learning about Buddhism, rather than continuing with his traditional religious upbringing. He has changed his physical appearance and is questioning the rules. As he steps out into the real world, he questions important issues regarding his values and beliefs, the environment, and political views. With support and acceptance, his life experiences integrate to create his personal identity.

Tom perceives a positive, holistic, and consistent internal sense of his role with his family, friends and society at large. He is comfortable with his perceptions of how he is like others, but different. At the same time, he has a healthy level of role "self-searching"; he is not sure about everything. He is open to new ideas, which allow room for change and growth.

Karen is a well-behaved, quiet, unassuming 18 year-old-girl. She comes from a very conservative, well-educated family. Her parents are both physicians. Karen is obedient and does as she is told. She is a straight A student and an excellent artist. Her parents decided when she was very little that she would also be a doctor. When she was younger, she told them she wanted to be a fashion designer when she grew up. They told her it was fine to draw and make up designs for fun, but she would need to have a 'serious' profession as an adult. Karen learned, over the years, to never question her parents' decisions. She attends church regularly and only associates with friends her parents have sanctioned. Although she gets angry at their controlling, domineering behavior, she never says anything, as she knows it will end in an argument.

Recently, Karen has chosen to do things against her parents' wishes. She is admitted to the hospital with depression.[19] Her parents became concerned when she started "acting funny." They stated that she refused to get out of bed, leave her room, do her homework, or participate in her daily activities. Upon admission, the mother answers all the questions directed towards Karen. Without being asked, she states Karen was "potty trained without a problem" and goes on to say they simply didn't accept an alternative, so Karen learned really fast that she had to use the potty. With tones of pride in her voice, her mother stated that Karen has been an ideal child since then, always doing what she is told. She said Karen keeps her grades up at school, does her chores at home, and keeps her room in perfect shape. Finally, the nurse turns to the mother and asks her to please let Karen talk for herself. Karen seems unsure about most questions requiring personal insight or opinions. When she does answer, her responses are subdued, hesitant, and fragmented. She frequently looks to her mother for the "correct" answers.

Karen is having a great deal of difficulty with the developmental task of Identity versus Role-confusion. She has tried to please her parents most of her life. While she shows a healthy sense of Trust, she had more difficulty with Autonomy. Rather than learning to trust her own ability to use good judgment and problem-solve, she learned she should follow her parents' direction, that her own decision-making was flawed. She showed little initiative, but seemed to find her "place" during the stage of Industry. She became a good student.

Over the years, she has learned it is not okay to develop or assume her own identity. She has not been encouraged or given the opportunity to think for herself, seek social peers, question ideas or beliefs she has been raised with, and, in general, discover who she is. She has been taught to do as she is told and be the "good daughter." Somewhere along the way she seems to have "lost herself."

Consequently, Karen is having trouble discovering and learning who she is and how she fits into the world around her. Her inability to answer personal questions or offer personal opinions suggests she is insecure and unsure of her self. She lacks confidence and doubts her capability to answer the nurse's questions correctly. Karen has a great deal of role-confusion and little sense of identity. Her short, fragmented answers are consistent with feelings of discontinuity; as a result, there is minimal, if any, evidence to suggest devotion to herself or any other object or cause. Karen will need help resolving the task of Identity versus Role-confusion before she is able to experience intimacy in the next developmental stage. We will talk more about this in Chapter 12, Facilitating Development.

For the time being, it is important to remember development is an epigenetic process. Therefore, Karen will need help with task resolution from Autonomy on. If we start with task work at Identity without addressing earlier tasks, we would be unsuccessful in our efforts. When we work from the bottom up (zero stage forward), we can help adolescents find a meaningful life pathway. While this may include a "career," it is not crucial to their growth and development. Sometimes a "career" should be thought of as a "way of life" rather than an "occupation for life." Since this stage extends over a long period of time, it might be better to think of it as early Identity work and later Identity work.

> The fifth stage of development is Identity. It starts between 10-13 years and continues until the early 30s. The Task work of the stage involves learning about oneself as a unique member of society. The Developmental Residual Dimensions are Self-Identity and Role-Confusion. Self-identity ranges from the a sense-of-self to a strong understanding of one's uniqueness, or Essence of Self. Role-confusion ranges from an ability to define our role in society to total role-confusion. The Strength is Devotion; the Virtue is Fidelity.

Intimacy

Task Work

Intimacy, the sixth stage of development, starts during the mid-twenties to early thirties and runs into the forties or fifties, depending on the person. It is the time for building a new kind of relationship with another human. Erikson (1963) described it as finding oneself yet losing oneself in another, or to "fuse (one's) identity with that of (another)" (p.263). It is a task requiring compromise and commitment from two individuals as they create a new entity—their relationship as a unit. They have to develop new ways of thinking, acting, and feeling that include mutual respect for one another as equal partners. While there continue to be two people with separate identities, there is a blending of the two that creates a new "Us." As with all other stages, retaining and maintaining a sense of affiliated-individuation is essential for task work.

Residual Dimensions

The positive dimension of developmental residual is Intimacy. At the low end of intimacy the couple recognizes 'you' and 'me', but are unable to create a 'sense of us'. At the high end of the continuum the couple experiences a feeling of being interconnected. A healthy balance of affiliated-individuation exists in both members of the couple.

Negative residual of this task is labeled Isolation by Erikson (1963) It is a matter of degree. At the healthy end of the continuum is the ability to individuate from the "us," to see oneself as an individual even though engaged in the relationship that creates the 'us." The other end of the dimension is the isolation of self from relationships. Erikson (1963) called this "distantiation" (p.264). He said, "The counterpart of intimacy is distantiation: the readiness to isolate and, if necessary, to destroy those forces and people whose essence seems dangerous to one's own, and whose 'territory' seems to encroach on the extent of one's intimate relations" (p. 264).

Implications. Intimacy doesn't happen overnight, or in a few weeks. It takes time. Intimacy is not love, as a couple often experiences during early relationship, nor is it just a commitment. Instead, it is a deep interconnectedness between two people that grows over time. It is strengthened by disagreements, followed by mutual respect, acceptance and compromise. Often people think it comes with a commitment to be together, but it isn't that simple. The development of intimacy takes time and perseverance.

When I was first married, it took me a while to think of our relationship as an "us" rather than a "me" or "you." Now I have learned the value of being a unit; together we are more than the two of us as individuals. Now, I know our relationship complements our individual uniqueness. The relationship has created strengths that stand on their own. Acceptance and validation as a unique individual affirms and strengthens our ability to be both affiliated and individuated.

People with negative residual are confronted with a different challenge. They have trouble being able to compromise without losing a sense of themselves as individuals. Most people who try to create intimate relationships do not demonstrate extreme negative residual. Instead, they tend to be somewhere in the middle. They often try to establish a relationship, might even marry, but have trouble compromising, or finding ways to think as a couple, rather than as individuals. They may choose to live together, raise a family, and appear to be a 'happy couple'. But, rather than living as a unit, they live parallel lives; they have not found a way to merge their paths without losing part of themselves. They often have difficulty compromising, so intimacy can develop. Sometimes they turn to competing, to struggling to establish who is right and who is wrong. Those who decide this is not productive often turn to simply living together, but living different lives. While this might seem like a healthy way to maintain the two identities, it should be noted that the *Us* is missing. They have not found much in common, they have not created a *togetherness* that is different from two individuals being together.

Distantiation or isolation from others is a lonely way to experience life. Weiss (1977, 1982) talked about different types of loneliness and distinguished between social loneliness and emotional loneliness. Social loneliness occurs when we are lonely just because there are few people in our environment with whom we can relate. When we have distantiation, we have an emotional loneliness. We push people away. We over individuate at the cost of our affiliations. By isolating ourselves, we lose our affiliates. We feel empty.

Strangely enough, others do not always recognize emotional loneliness. Instead, they see someone who pushes others away, someone who is self-absorbed, and often someone who lives a façade. People with negative residual are sometimes pretentious, and unaware of how they affect others. They lack the ability to love others in meaningful ways. They are so isolated they are unable to understand how anyone else feels or views life.

Facilitating Factors

People working on Intimacy seek an emotional connectedness where they can safely share their deepest thoughts and feelings. They want to share themselves in ways they have never done before. Strong, healthy Intimacy is a connecting of more than bodies; it is a connecting of spirits. With this type of relationship comes a responsibility from the partners to be receptive, patient, loving, kind, and accepting of one another. As partners in a spiritual partnership, we must enact what we wish to receive.[20] Factors that facilitate such attitudes and behavior include positive residual from previous stages as well as getting our needs met during the work of this stage. It might seem obvious that some of those needs are met by being in an intimate relationship with someone. However, we need to remember healthy intimacy also includes a sense of individuation on the part of the two people. This means the members of the dyad need to live lives separate from the relationship. They need to find friends, family, work, and other experiences outside the relationship that will help them meet their needs for individuation. At the same time, the two people in the relationship need to be comfortable with their partner's seeking experiences outside the relationship for need satisfaction.

Impeding Factors

Needless to say, healthy resolution of this task requires satisfactory resolution of earlier tasks. As we go through life, we continue to accrue development residual. What we have to build on determines how we experience our relationships with others at each stage of life. For example, it is impossible to have healthy intimacy without healthy trust! How can we trust someone will love us if we don't know whether we can depend on them? It also requires a healthy "dose" of autonomy. How can we create an 'Us' if we are afraid doing so would mean we can't make decisions that meet our needs? Healthy Intimacy also requires a healthy sense of Identity. We have to have a sense of who we are, with a glimmering of our True Self before we can enter a relationship of Intimacy. Without a basic understanding of who we are as individuals (Identity), we risk the loss of our self in the relationship.

While someone can enter this stage of life with healthy residual, unless they connect with someone else who has healthy residual, they are at risk for difficulty with the task. An intimate relationship has reciprocity. Both members have sufficient positive residual to interact in ways that will meet the needs of both members. Otherwise, one member is more likely to get their needs met at the expense of the other. When someone with healthy residual connects with another who is unwilling or unable to create intimacy, the first feels lonely and isolated rather than connected and valued. They may have opportunities for individuation, but at the expense of unmet affiliation needs.

Resources

Strength. As we work through the task of Intimacy, we develop the strength of Affiliation; we learn to be connected to another in a deep and enduring way.

Virtue. We also develop an attitude or virtue, described by Erikson (1963, p. 274) as Love. We think the type of love implied in Erikson's work is "Being Love" as described by Maslow and discussed in Chapter 6. Members of the dyad who have Being Love respect and value their partners for who they are, as opposed to what they can do for them. It is a type of love where we not only get our needs met by the relationship, but we are interested in the other member getting their needs met, too. This type of love extends to society as we move into the next stage of life and becomes compassion for mankind.

Case Examples

Steve, a successful graphics designer in Hollywood, has everything money can buy. He is handsome and popular and dates as often as he wants. He has a long history of relationships, but has not found the right person. Living in an expensive home with beautiful trappings, he appears to have everything.

Recently, he attended his 10-year high school reunion. He spent the evening talking about his "wonderful" life and shared expansive stories about his experiences and friendships with famous people. Everyone was impressed.

One of his old friends revealed it sounded like he had the ideal life. Steve replied, "I am thinking about giving it up. I feel like my life is empty. What I really want is to find someone I can settle down with and have kids. Someone who cares about me because of who I am, not because of my money or my job. I look around here and I want what everyone else seems to have—someone special who loves me, with whom I can share my life. I'm lonely and feel like there isn't anyone who really cares about Me. While I have a lot of independence, I'm lonely.

Although Steve has all the trappings of a successful life, he is missing the most important thing—an intimate relationship with someone else. Although he has had a succession of relationships he expresses feelings of loneliness. His life has little meaning without an intimate and meaningful relationship. As he works through this developmental task he will achieve intimacy. Steve is headed in the right direction.

> *Justine is 26 years old and has an 8-month-old daughter. She attends a support group for first-time mothers. She has had multiple relationships and is currently seeing someone new. When asked how things are going for her she replied, "The same old thing. I started going out with Tyrone and it's always about him. He thinks he's the hottest thing around. He wants to go out with his friends Friday night, but doesn't want me to go out with my friends—says he doesn't trust me. When I told him I was going out anyway, he got nasty. The funny thing is he's probably fooling around on me. I don't seem to do a very good job of picking them. He doesn't seem to respect me much. He says he loves me and pushes me for sex, but refuses to use condoms. When we are together, things are pretty good, so I don't want to cause any trouble. It's not like I can do much better."*

Justine is having problems getting her needs met in this relationship. Tyrone is not receptive to her thoughts and feelings. He does not respect her needs or requests. Although seeking an intimate relationship, she is involved with someone who has inadequate positive residual from earlier stages to develop an intimate relationship. His lack of responsibility for birth control, uncaring and hostile attitudes, and self-absorption demonstrate earlier developmental problems. His relationship with Justine is not mutually satisfying, but focused wholly on getting his own needs met.

Justine has low levels of intimacy and high levels of isolation. She realizes she is not in a positive relationship, but believes she doesn't deserve better. She is pessimistic and distrustful. Her history indicates she has been in many relationships, none of them satisfactory. There is little trust or sharing of feelings in her current interactions with Tyrone.

In both cases the individuals are confronted with the task of Intimacy. Steve seems to have a healthy balance of positive and negative residual. Now he is ready to focus on finding a partner and developing an intimate relationship. In all likelihood, he will be successful in his endeavors. Justine, however, is having difficulty in her relationship. She seems to have considerable negative residual from previous stages, which will have to be reworked before she is successful in her endeavors.

When people bring excessive negative residual into the stage of Intimacy, they bring mistrust, doubt or shame, guilt, and inferiority with them. None of these are attributes healthy, intimate relationships can be built upon. Her best chance for a good relationship is to find someone with healthy residual who is able to see her strengths and nurture her growth and reworking of Integration through Identity. With this relationship, she may be able to change her ratio of positive and negative residual and develop the resources needed to work on an intimate relationship.

> The sixth stage of development is Intimacy. It starts between 25-30 years and continues until the 50s. The Task work of the stage involves the blending of two people into a unit. The Developmental Residual Dimensions are Intimacy and Isolation. Intimacy ranges from two people as a couple to two interconnected people as a unit. Isolation ranges from an ability to define oneself as a separate person in a relationship to isolation of self from relationships, i.e., distantiation. The Strength is Affiliation; the Virtue is Love.

Generativity

Task Work

The seventh stage of development emerges sometime in the mid 40s to the early 50s and continues until the mid 60s, depending on the person.[21] The task for this stage is to evaluate our contributions to the well being of society. We become acutely aware that time on earth is limited, and want to ensure we "leave a mark"—that our "product" will continue on across time (even after we are physically gone). We search for understanding of our Life Purpose and become driven to fulfill it. We want to pass on how we think, what we value, and any special knowledge or talents we enjoy. People with a healthy balance of positive and negative residual leave this stage of life knowing how to balance "doing their life work" with simply living their lives. They understand it is not necessary to be industrious all the time to make a contribution to society; instead, it is better to balance our lives with productive work and healthy play.

Residual Dimensions

The two dimensions of developmental residual related to this stage are Continuity of Life and Stagnation. Continuity of Life has, at the low end of the continuum, an awareness of our Life Purpose and at the high end, confidence that the product of our life will go on beyond us, that we are fulfilling our Life Purpose.

The counter side, Stagnation, is on a continuum from perceived productivity to self-absorption. People with a healthy sense of negative residual recognize they have been a member of society and have made contributions. On the other hand, those who acquire a high level of negative residual leave this stage being self-absorbed. They have lost interest in the well-being of society, which often includes their own family and are only concerned with their own state of affairs. Disappointed that life isn't fulfilling, they do not seek ways to be productive or create change. And unable to adapt with the social changes, they often feel left behind, unimportant, and insignificant.

Implications. Generativity is often accomplished by facilitating healthy growth and development in one's significant others and helping them become productive members of society. Some do this through relationships with their families; others do it through work or social causes. They perceive the product of their work will make a difference in the future. It doesn't matter if it is the "way our children turn out," "what the students learn," or "how the Red Cross grows." What matters is the perception that others will be better off because of what they have done and are doing.

While a common way to work on Generativity is through family, there are other ways. Take, for example, a teacher who has influenced many lives, a scientist who has discovered a cure, and a doctor who has saved lives. Although the people in these examples are not focused on their children and their lives, they may be able to work through Generativity without difficulty. They are invested in the future and will be remembered and "live on" after their physical bodies are gone.

Individuals who successfully resolve this task are able to connect with their True Self; they are aware of their Life Purpose. They know the product of their life work lives on in others, not themselves. Yet, they know how to get their own needs met. While it may seem they make sacrifices for the well-being of others, they do not. They are just fulfilling their own needs by giving to the next generation. Approaching life with perseverance and steadfastness, they are not deterred from their path of intention. They are altruistic and give willingly and happily from their hearts. Giving is part of who they are rather than a requirement they need to meet. Their gratification in life comes from knowing the next generation will benefit because they lived industrious lives. They work well with others and are accepting of their own and others' human frailties. Here is an example:

> *Clare, the mother of several children, holds a prestigious position in the community. Her first priority, however, has always been her family. During the children's formative years, she actively participated in their school and extra curricular activities. She made cookies for class parties, took on the unending job of Scout leader, assisted with class assignments; the list goes on and on. She was always available for them. All four of her children are now married, settled, and doing well. She feels good about raising her children as well as the many students she has mentored and facilitated through the years. Her emotional and physical investments in her family and work are now paying off.*
>
> *Clare has now turned her energy and focus towards her life work. She is often absorbed in directing her time and energy into completing her scholarly work. Well known internationally for her contributions to her field, she realizes she needs to publish her ideas, so they will be available to those following in her footsteps. Her knowledge, expertise, and wisdom will live on through her words. Having spent her adult years nurturing the*

growth and development of her family and students, she feels positive about the outcome of her personal and professional life. She knows her spirit and work will live on through the lives she has shaped.

Clare has a reached a high level of Generativity, but is able to self-focus, so she continues to get her personal needs met—needs that relate to continued work on all tasks of life. That is, she continues to work on tasks of Integration, Trust, Autonomy, Initiative, Industry, Identity, Intimacy, Ego Integrity and Transformation. Specifically, as she reworks the tasks of these stages, she continues to develop positive residual related to each task. She is able to continue this work and move forward because she brings healthy developmental residual with her.

On the contrary, those who are unable to achieve a healthy balance of positive and negative residual experience a much different aging process. They become self-absorbed. Every physical ailment is a new sign of their decline. Unable to adapt to social changes, they feel isolated from society and often mourn for "the good old days." They fear the world around them is morally declining and nothing can be done about it. New discoveries are seen as a threat rather than an opportunity. They are in constant disagreement with others around them, furthering their isolation. Others perceive them as "old and crotchety." They often appear older than their age, frailer than their peers, and less able to care for themselves. This latter situation is a problem since they have often alienated many of their significant others, so few people have the desire to help them maintain independence. As a result, they become more dependent, more despondent, and decline physically faster than their peers.

Facilitating Factors

It is important to remember what has been stated before—that achieving healthy task resolution depends on the residual we bring into the stage. For example, healthy resolution of the task of Intimacy will certainly impact resolution of this stage. We have a need for affiliated-individuation; the stage of Intimacy helps us meet this need, so we are ready to refocus on our life-work. When our needs are met, we are better able to take initiative, create, and pass our "products" to others. When we have healthy intimacy, we are free to learn that our "life product" is more about how we think and feel than about what we have accumulated, acquired, or been awarded.

People often think life is about collecting objects, acquiring things, becoming powerful and being "respected" by employees or family members, and so forth. These are all "things of the physical world." When we enter this stage of life, we have to revisit who we are, what is important in life, and the question of our Life Purpose begins to nag us. While we may have had an awareness of our Life Purpose before, now it seems to pop into our consciousness more often. We think about all the things we have collected, or acquired, and become increasingly aware of the fact that our Life Purpose may be eluding us! Sometimes, this is because it is so obvious we can't see it. Often, we need to listen to others to learn about what we have "produced," what we have "cared" about. And usually, when we do that, we are surprised at what we find. As nurses, it is important to help people working on Generativity evaluate their lives from the perspective of what they gave to others of themselves, and to put aside how much they accumulated, and how much power they acquired. This is how we can help people "discover" their product and learn what is important in their lives.

Impeding Factors

Individuals who feel they have made no difference in or contributions to future generations experience self-absorption and stagnation. Their behavior often seems inappropriate in relation to their chronological age. They may overtly dislike their body or spend a tremendous amount of time and energy in personal upkeep. They are inept at personal interactions and relationships. They are unable to be other-oriented as they are too absorbed in their own life.

> *Trim and athletic, Justin, a financially successful 44 year-old stockbroker, takes tremendous care with his appearance, and loves his designer clothes. The other love in his life is his beautiful, shiny, cherry-red corvette. He has never married or had children as he doesn't want to be tied down and "likes to live his life without any hassles."*
>
> *Justin always dates women who make him look good. He has problems at work as he doesn't like to collaborate with colleagues and wants to do everything his way. He is often inappropriate in his interactions with others. Female colleagues have written him up twice for sexual harassment. Most of his colleagues think he's a jerk. When Christmas time comes, he refuses to participate in the charitable money and food drives saying, "People make their beds and now they have to lay in them." His actions are always oriented towards getting his own needs met.*

Justin and Clare represent different ratios of positive and negative residual. Justin demonstrates inappropriate behavior in his self-absorption with his appearance and car. He has problems in his personal interactions and professional relationships with others. His life decisions and choices revolve around his needs and wants. Not only is he unable to view the world through the eyes of other people, he does not care that he is self-oriented and has made no contributions to the world or future generations. He is disconnected spiritual, physically, emotionally, and psychologically from the world he lives in.

Resources

Strength. The strength derived from this stage of life is Production—the belief that we are "producing" that which we came to do. Production is related to our Life Purpose and our Reason for Being. Therefore, the "product" of our work may only be seen by how we affect others. It isn't always a material object, which can be viewed, measured or evaluated. Production may be as simple as "knowing" that because we have cared about other people, they are growing and becoming what they have the potential to be.

Virtue. The virtue or attitude derived from this stage of life is Caring. That is, caring about our work and the product of our work. H. Erickson gives the following example of the virtue of caring:

> *Many years ago I met Carl Rogers at a conference where he was a key presenter. I stopped him and told him how much I loved his work, how much it had meant to me in my own development, and how much I admired his courage for writing and talking about ideas of positive regard. I knew he was busy and, probably, had been stopped by dozens of people that day. He was an elderly gentleman, so he was possibly physically tired. I really didn't expect a response. You can imagine my surprise when he stopped, took my hand, and looked me in the eyes. But, you will never be able to fully understand how touched I was by what he said. While I can't remember his exact words, he first thanked me for my "kind words." Then he said he was a bit confused when people said such things, because he hadn't done anything exceptional. He said all he had done was to do what came naturally to him and because he cared about it, he did it a lot!*
>
> *Later, I sat in a session where he presented. After talking for about 40 minutes, he invited questions from the audience. For the next 30 minutes he responded with patience and respect for each and every participant. He was clearly "producing," teaching, sharing in a way that demonstrated tremendous care about his work and the people with whom he was interacting. I learned that day about generativity, production and caring. When generativity residual exists, respect for others also exists. One's work is done within that context* (Personal communication, 2005).

The seventh stage of development is Generativity. It starts between 45-55 years and continues until the 70s. The Task work of the stage is evaluating our contributions to society. The Developmental Residual Dimensions are Continuity of Life and Stagnation. Continuity of Life ranges from an awareness of our 'product' to confidence in our product. Stagnation ranges from a perceived product potential to self-absorption. The Strength is Production; the Virtue is Caring.

Ego Integrity

Task Work

Ego Integrity is the last stage of development as described by Erikson (1963) but next to last from my perspective. It emerges at the end of Generativity and continues until physical death. The task of Ego Integrity is to analyze the merit of our life. In the previous stage we had to assess the value of what we had produced in a life-time, now we have to decide if we have lived our lives well, which includes not only the product of our lives, but also the way in which we have lived. While we work on ego integrity throughout the life-span, this is the first time ego integrity is the focus of our work. It is the time to consider our Reason for Being.

During ego integrity, we have the opportunity to complete a life review, to think about what we have produced, and the way we have interacted with people in the process.   We ask ourselves questions such as, "Have I lived my life well? Have I made meaningful, loving relationships? Has my life made a difference? And, if so, was it positive? Have I accomplished what I came to do? Can I move on, knowing I have made a difference, that my life has had meaning?" Erikson (1963), describes it as follows:

> *It is the acceptance of one's one and only life cycle as something that had to be and that, by necessity, permitted of no substitutions;....For he knows that an individual life is the accidental coincidence of but one life cycle with but one segment of history; and that for him, all human integrity stands or falls with the one style of integrity of which he partakes. The style of integrity developed by his culture or civilization thus becomes the 'patrimony of his soul,' the seal of his moral paternity of himself. In such final consolidation, death loses its sting* (p. 268).

H. Erickson presented it this way:

> *During this stage of life, people often seem to become less interested in their belongings and their current way of being. This is not a form of detachment. It is, instead, a type of transcendence—a type of preparatory work, wherein the spirit reconnects fully with the Soul more frequently than it has in the past. It is not a pulling away, but a moving forward. As we move forward, we learn new things about our True Self, we discover and rediscover what we came here for in the beginning* (Personal communication, November 20, 2005).

This view is a little different from Erik Erikson's, quoted above. While Erikson states this life we are living is the *accidental coincidence of but one life cycle* we[22] think it is not accidental. We believe we are here to fulfill our Soul-work, determined before we took on a physical form. We do agree that this is "...but one segment of history..."; the rest came before and is yet to come.

Residual Dimensions
The two dimensions of residual found in this stage are Ego Integrity, the positive residual, and Despair, the negative residual.   Low to high positive residual ranges from acceptance of our life to satisfaction with how we've lived

our life. Low to high negative residual ranges from an awareness of our mistakes to profound despondency about our lives.

<u>Implications.</u> A healthy balance of residual from this stage results in satisfaction with how we've lived our lives, awareness of our mistakes, and acceptance of ourselves as human beings who make mistakes. This is different from being satisfied with what we produced in our lives. People who have a healthy resolution of Ego Integrity accept their life as they have lived it, product (stage of Generativity) and process (stage of Ego Integrity), and perceive they have accomplished their Life Purpose. They are in touch with their True Self and have a sense of dignity and self-worth. While they find pleasure in what they have done and how they have done it, they welcome the next stage of life accepting it will come when the time is right. For some, this is the same as knowing they are moving toward a Being One with the Universe; for others it is satisfaction that they have done a good job overall.

Those who have excessive negative residual conclude with Despair. They believe they were cheated; life didn't treat them well; others had opportunities they didn't have, and that is why they weren't successful. They view the next stage of life as "the end" and are often bitter and hostile, because they have not had a chance to live the way they wanted. They give up on the possibility of a "good life" but are afraid of the future, so they often hang on to a miserable existence. They are usually isolated and alone.

Facilitating Factors

The irony of each of the developmental stages is that people need others to help them work through the tasks. Some people enter the stage of Ego Integrity with healthy developmental residual, but, suddenly, find them selves alone, and with their aloneness comes loneliness.[23] Significant others who affirmed them in the past have moved on or moved away. While these seniors are managing physically, they are getting older and it is harder for them to move around, to do things that made them feel useful in the past. And it is harder for them to socialize and be with other people. Nevertheless, they need people who can tell them their lives are different just because they have known or been with the senior going through the stage of Ego Integrity. They need others to confirm the worth of their lives.

This is an important life lesson for everyone. While we have to choose our own pathway and take our own journey, we all need others to help us along the way. We have an inherent need for affiliated-individuation across the lifetime. Without it, we often have difficulty moving on to the next stage.

Impeding Factors

The most obvious impeding factor for satisfactory work on all stage-related tasks is negative residual. However, as we age, negative residual has a greater impact because it accrues and it is closer to the end of our physical lives. People who enter this stage of life perceiving their lives have not had meaning have difficulty finding pleasure in how they have lived their lives. Instead, they usually continue down the same path, become more isolated and with it, more despondent. However, there are many who enter this stage of life with a healthy balance of residual, and still have trouble. If you were to extrapolate from the section on Facilitating Factors, it would be obvious the major Impeding Factors such people experience are: multiple losses (or a pile up of losses) of significant others and social isolation.

Social Isolation has been discussed before, but warrants a few additional comments. While it can be due to excessive negative residual, social isolation can also be due to simply not having enough people available to us. It can also be due to numerous other factors such as physical frailty that interferes with our ability to reach out, lack of financial resources needed to help oneself be independent, and physical ability necessary to continue active social roles.

Resources

Strength. According to Erikson (1963), the strength derived from this stage of life is Renunciation. People who have successfully resolved earlier developmental stages acquire a positive outlook or perspective on life. They feel they have lived their life well and made good choices. Their lives have meaning and they experience feelings of dignity and worth. Although they may have made mistakes during their life journey, overall, they accept the life they have lived and own it. They feel as if they have been true and connected to their "Self" and are ready to take the next step, to move on.

Virtue. They have acquired the virtue of Wisdom and are ready and able to take the next step in life's journey. Erikson (1964) said that wisdom "...maintains and conveys the integrity of experience in spite of the bodily and mental functions. It responds to the need of the on-coming generation for an integrated heritage and yet remains aware of the relativity of all knowledge" (p.133).

> *Grace is an 89 year-old woman whose body has slowed down, but whose spirit is strong. She lives with her daughter and her family. The children stop by regularly throughout the day. She is an active part of their daily lives. They frequently discuss school projects and other ideas with her. Although life challenges her physically she feels good about her life. She knows she has made a difference in the world and to those around her. She may have an occasional regret, but states, "Overall, I would do it all again. I did the best I could at the time and I feel good about how I have lived my life."*

Grace has lived a meaningful life. She has a positive outlook and through retrospection can say her life was well spent. She enjoys being able to make suggestions about things important to her family. Satisfied with the choices and decisions she has made, she experiences ego integrity.

George is an unpleasant, crotchety, 85 year-old man. He lives alone in an assisted-living apartment. He is twice-divorced and has no children. He worries about the future, wishing he had lived his life differently. Most days he is alone in his apartment. Occasionally, he ventures to the common room to see what is going on and what other people are up to. But, he never stays long. His demeanor and attitude prevent other people from wanting to be with him and it just makes him feel more isolated and angry. Occasionally, he tells the visiting nurse, "When I am gone no one will miss me and my life won't have mattered."

Unlike Grace, who has achieved ego integrity, George experiences feelings of despair. He is unhappy with himself and his life. He does not feel that his life has value or that he is valued. He is disconnected from his spiritual "Self" and feels doubtful and gloomy about what the future will bring.

The eighth stage of development is Ego Integrity. It starts at the end of Generativity and continues until physical death. The Task work of the stage is determining how well we have lived our lives. The Developmental Residual Dimensions are Ego Integrity and Despair. Ego Integrity ranges from acceptance of our life to satisfaction with how we've lived our life. Despair ranges from awareness of our mistakes to despondency about our lives. The Strength is Renunciation; the Virtue is Wisdom.

Transformation

The ninth and final stage of life as a holistic human being starts shortly before or at the end of physical lifetime. While some call it the time of death, I do not. We do not believe the 'person' dies, only the human form dies. We prefer to call it "passing on," "moving on," or "transforming." We think this stage of life is yet one more type of attachment-loss-reattachment as described in Chapter 7. Rather than thinking about death and dying, we choose to think about transforming. The first implies the end while the other implies a new beginning.

Task Work

The task of transformation involves our ability to separate our spiritual energy (our spiritual self) from our physical body and transform to Soul energy. When we make this transformation, we leave behind all the trappings of our human body, but take with us the Essence of our Self. We reconnect with our Soul and the Essence of our Self is incorporated. To say this another way, as our spirit leaves our physical body it rejoins our Soul, and transforms as part of our Soul. As such, it becomes part of the Universal Field–that from which it came. During this process, the journey of life comes full cycle to where it began, only now the Soul has new understandings. We are energy again, connected with the Universe, or, as some would say, with God.

For some individuals, transformation occurs over a few moments; for others it requires more time. When individuals are not able to smoothly separate spiritually from their body and reconnect to their original source, they sometimes linger until they have 'finished their business'. Most of us have witnessed this happening, but we don't recognize it.

However, if people are not well integrated before they enter this stage, they may come to this stage with a high negative residual, i.e., Duality, and have a disconnection of spirit from incarnate body. Under these circumstances it may be harder for transformation to occur smoothly. They have not "finished" their business, their Soul-work planned for this lifetime. They came with a Life Purpose and it hasn't been accomplished, so their spirit is hesitant to leave the physical world.

Developmental Residual

This stage of development has two dimensions similar to those of the first stage, Integration. They are the reversal of Unity and Duality. So the positive residual is Reconnection and the negative residual is Disconnection. Healthy reconnecting in this stage is the opposite of what it was in Integration. Instead of connecting with the physical body, it is now time for the spirit to move on, reunite with the Soul, transform the energy, and reconnect with Universal Energy. This requires spiritual energy to vibrate at a higher level than the biophysical psychosocial body and gradually increase vibrations until it synchronizes with the Soul.

This can happen in a split second or take considerable time. When we go into this stage with a highly integrated spirit, we have to "unzip" it from our physical being. This does not require much work, but it does require 'letting-go'. That is, we have to "let go" of our groundedness! (Remember that groundedness comes from a healthy resolution of the stage of Integration).

Many of us have heard stories (or witnessed the experience) where the spirit separates from the body and lingers for a period of time. For whatever reason, the spirit "unzipped," the residual of Unity, but not the residual of Duality. When both are accomplished, the spirit is able to move on and transform.

> Disconnecting, the negative residual related to this stage, ranges from letting go of being grounded to giving-up on Transformation.

Facilitating Factors

Clearly, the most important prerequisite to complete Transformation is a healthy residual from earlier stages. When we have had the opportunity to review our life and decide we have "completed our work," we are already on the road to letting go of the incarnate form. Many of us have had the experience of working with someone who was sick, but not considered terminal. Yet, that person said good-bye, and within hours, passed on. When this happens, everyone is surprised. We often hear colleagues or family members say, "But they didn't seem that sick!" People who seem to let go with such ease tend to understand where they are going (spiritually), have permission to let go, and embrace the future.

Impeding Factors

Still, for even the healthiest person, letting go is not always easy. Sometimes we don't feel satisfied; we haven't had "time" or "opportunity" to finish our work. Sometimes it is painful to leave those we love and sometimes people don't have permission, from loved ones, to move on. Each of these is an important factor to consider as we work with those who are at this stage of life.

One of the more important things to remember with healthy people is they too need reassurance that they have left "themselves" behind, and everyone who came in contact with that spirit has benefited and will continue to benefit. H. Erickson states she has been with a number of people who quietly passed on only moments after hearing her say they would always be with their loved ones and would always be a part of her heart. The spirit, when integrated with the human form, sometimes needs reassurance that it has loved and been loved, that love continues, and that it leaves permanent residual in us.

Sometimes, people are hesitant to let go of the incarnate form, to leave their human body, because they don't want to pain those they love. When this happens, loved ones have to give them permission to let go and to move on. Without permission, some people will linger for days.

Finally, there are those who linger because they are afraid. They haven't been able to work through their developmental tasks and come through with healthy residual. They haven't been able to integrate spirit with body, and know the Meaning of their lives, to understand that the challenge is living in the incarnate form, not being in spiritual form! So, they linger. Yet, with a little kindness, a little love and understanding, they are able to let go and move on.

Resources

<u>Strength.</u> The strengths derived from satisfactory work in this stage are peace and freedom, combined with cosmic understanding and compassion. Cosmic understanding and compassion involve a Knowing and Loving that extends beyond our physical life. Soul Knowledge is knowledge shared with others in the Universal Field and Loving is that which goes beyond the physical and emotional parts of an incarnate life. It is the basis for compassion in human form and the essence of Soul fulfillment in spiritual form.

<u>Virtue.</u> The virtue acquired is a sense of Oneness, an interconnectedness with our Soul and the Universal Energy Field. When we achieve a sense of Oneness, we are free to evaluate our Soul work, share our wisdom, and send our loving energy into the Universe. We are able to become *One with All*.

H. Erickson tells the following story as an example of several of these issues.

My brother had lung cancer. He had struggled with it for over a year. During that time he addressed several of his developmental issues, reworked his tasks, but still, he was not ready to move on. He had a number of surgeries, went through chemotherapy, and finally when it seemed like there weren't many options left, he was turned over to hospice for terminal care. He had spent the last several months at home with his loving wife. His children all came to visit, each showing him how much they loved him. His sisters, mother, and other friends did the same.

As fall approached, it became clear he was getting worse. He lived in Michigan and I in Texas. I called him regularly. He went through the holidays, enjoying his family, but experiencing considerable pain. One day, when I called him his wife told me he was in so much pain and the medication simply wasn't helping. I asked to talk with him. When he came on the phone I asked about his pain and he said that he just couldn't get rid of it, yet taking medication made him hallucinate, he hated to take it, but also hated to not take it. First, I told him that there are many kinds of pain, and often our "other" kind is the major problem, saying, "You know, not physical, but the other kind" is the worst. I also said that pain medicine wouldn't do much for that, but understanding he had been a good man, a good brother, a good father and that many people loved him was important. I said it several times, reassuring him as he quietly listened. I talked about his many kindnesses, how he could know he was loved and had loved and then was quiet. He was crying. I asked if he understood what I was saying. He said yes, and it had helped a lot. Then he said the medications had made him hallucinate, so he didn't like them. I asked him to tell me about it and he said for the past several days, he had imagined Dad was there talking to him, and he knew he wasn't, because he had died several years before. I told him Dad probably was there, that often those who had passed on before us, those who loved us would come back to help us on our journey. He was very quiet, so I asked him if he knew what the journey would be like. When he said no, but he wanted to know, I talked about the separation of spirit from body, movement toward the light, the tunnel and so forth. I also told him Dad would probably be there to help him along.

The next day, I went north to be with him. He seemed to be comatose, but would rouse up when talked to. Within a few hours he had the "death gurgle." The hospice nurse told everyone he would soon pass on. His children and our Mother came to say goodbye. But, he didn't let go. The following day, I asked his wife if she had given him permission to go on. She said no, she didn't want to. We talked and then she decided she wanted to say good-bye in private. After that, his respirations changed, his blood pressure dropped and within minutes, I was unable to get a pulse. It appeared he had passed on. I could feel his spirit in the room. But, then, several of his children gathered around him, crying hysterically, telling him they loved him that they didn't know how they would be able to go on. Suddenly his pulse came back, he started breathing again, and everyone calmed down. That happened around one p.m. For the next several hours, the children took turns going to him, stroking him, telling him they loved him, and then one by one they left his side. They started playing his movies, one after the other, movies he had loved in his lifetime. Throughout this time his body felt empty although he continued to breathe, have a strong pulse and even put out urine. Throughout this time, I could feel his spirit in the room. It was there, but it wasn't in his body!

Finally, about 7 in the evening, all of the family seemed to settle down. Some decided they needed to go home and see their children. Others made arrangements to go eat, and so forth. I decided to go rest; I told him I was going to rest, all the children were fine now, and that it would be okay for him to go on. I also assured him Dad would soon be near him to help him on his way. I left the room, headed for the bedroom, but didn't make it. Within less than a minute from the time I talked to him, one of his sons called me back and said he had just simply stopped breathing. Nothing else happened, he just stopped! I said he had let go, and advised them to notice how peaceful he looked. They agreed. A few minutes later, one of the daughters said she thought he was really gone now, and mentioned that the room felt different! I agreed; he had really moved on. It was one of the few times where I have experienced the spirit hanging around for such a long time; usually it just seems to move on. But, it didn't in this case; I think he had to stay and be sure his children and wife were ok.

Letting go and moving-on need not be painful or hard. It need not be a difficult time. What is difficult is maneuvering our way through life, trying to 'remember' why we came, to be true to our Soul commitment, to learn our lessons, and to come to grips with the idea that our lifetime is an opportunity that we have used well or not. What is not hard is separating spirit from body or letting go of our body. To alleviate this difficulty we need to remember that we can always be with those we love and they will always be with us. Remember, we are spirit first; this holds true for all of us. We can always be together in spirit if we choose (Personal communication, November 20, 2005).

The last stage of development is Transformation. It starts at the end of Ego Integrity and continues until our spiritual energy rejoins Universal Energy. The Task work of the stage is letting go of the physical body and human life. The Developmental Residual Dimensions are Reconnection and Disconnection. Reconnection ranges from letting go of the human form and physical life to reconnecting with Universal Energy. Disconnection ranges from separation of spiritual energy from human form (letting-go of being grounded) to giving up on ability to reconnect to Universal Energy (transformation of spiritual energy).

ENDNOTES

[1] If you wish to brush up on physical development, there are many excellent books that will help you revisit those processes.

[2] Cognitive development is also not addressed, although it is also an important aspect of human development. The original book (Erickson et al., 1983) includes a discussion regarding the role of cognitive development.

[3] C. Gilligan (1993) suggested that women and men go through developmental stages in a different order. She believes that men must resolve the developmental stage of Identity before they can experience an intimate relationship. On the other hand, she states that women must experience and resolve the developmental task of Intimacy before they are able to resolve the task of Identity. This suggestion is refuted by the Modeling and Role-Modeling theory, which recognizes the order of the developmental stages as, identified by E. Erikson. Throughout life, individuals (male and female) work on being both affiliated and individuated in their relationships with others. Before one is able to connect with another person in an intimate way they must first know themselves. This requires that they have achieved some awareness and insight into who they are and have worked through the developmental task of Identity. Before we are able to be connected, we much first be secure in a sense of our own "self." In order to be affiliated we must also be individuated (for more information on Affiliated-Individuation refer to Chapters 6-7).

[4] While I include these two new stages of development in this chapter, I think it important to share with you how I came to this "knowing." Probably the seeds have been growing in my head for some time. I will never know. What I do know is that H. Erickson has been commenting for some time that there has to be another stage after the stage of ego-integrity and it has to be Transformation, not Transcendence. When I thought about this, I commented that if there was a stage of Transformation, then there had to be something that happened before the stage of Trust. I thought about this for some time. Then, in May 2005 the Society for The Advancement of Modeling and Role-modeling called a Writing Retreat for people interested in working on this book. Eileen Curl and I worked together in a small subgroup to discuss this chapter and plan for the layout, etc. We discussed these issues at some length and concluded that there were two stages, the first was Integration and the second Transformation. When we reconvened with the entire group that had gathered to work on this book, we shared our ideas. The group supported our thinking, challenged us to clarify a few points, and blessed our plan! With that, the two stages of development were added as part of the developmental process. So, while I use the word 'I,' the thinking, soul-searching, and clarifying has been a process that could not have happened without the input of several others, including Eileen Curl.

[5] *Some are confused by this statement; let me clarify. Just as an acorn has to grow before it can develop into an oak tree— something that looks different, functions differently, has a different size and shape, and so forth—so does the human have to grow before development can occur. At the same time, once the acorn has changed into an oak tree, now the oak tree can grow and make new acorns. Humans can to!, Developmental residual produces new resources, which can grow and grow. The cycle can go on and on across time. Such is the nature of human growth and development; such is the nature of the Soul* (H. Erickson, personal communication, January 22, 2006.)

[6] We would say that this initiates the bonding process between parent and child, bonding on the part of the parent and on the part of the child.

[7] It reminds me of the movie made a number of years ago, *Everybody Rides the Merry-Go-Round* in which both positive and negative residual was illustrated across the lifespan. In addition, the accruement of residual was illustrated. The healthy senior at the stage of Ego Integrity in that movie is very much like Tornstam's version of GeroTranscendence.

[8] For example, Erikson (1963) labeled the 8 basic stages of development, the nature of the task, and the strengths and virtues.

---

[9] When my youngest son was about 3 minutes old, my mother walked over to him to say hello. He focused his eyes on her eyes, looked into them with a piercing gaze. She said she knew right then his spirit was saying hello. While this doesn't happen with all newborns, it does with some. Furthermore, most newborn babies make eye contact when given the opportunity. While you might say this indicates their cognitive or social curiosity, the recipients of this experience know it is more than an "earthly experience."

[10] This could also be thought of as a connection of the body-mind and spirit.

[11] See Glossary for definition of *human being* and *being.*

[12] Infants, such as babies with Fetal Alcohol Syndrome or those suffering prenatal cocaine addiction who have experienced traumatic in-utero environments or have difficult maternal-infant relationships, have been shown to exhibit behavior that indicates insecure attachment or complete detachment from their caregivers.

[13] *They are the precursors to healthy affiliated-individuation as it relates to mutuality. The virtue that emerges secondary to these strengths is the ability to be aware of one's spirituality. As we proceed through the life cycle, this virtue becomes more sophisticated and we begin to search for our Life Purpose and Reason for Being* (H. Erickson, personal communication, November, 2005).

[14] Remember that a newborn baby is suddenly separated from its shell, its wrapping, its home. Often this is a traumatic experience. It hurts to be born. In addition, once delivered, the baby is suddenly responsible for actively acquiring its own oxygen! It has to circulate its own blood without any help from mom, it has to *be* an entity separate from its "other half," i.e., the mother's intrauterine environment.

[15] Remember children cannot act independently (or demonstrate individuation) unless they have a sense of affiliation. They have to have a backup plan.

[16] I think limitations means we are limited in knowledge or skills needed to accomplish the goal. Weaknesses imply we don't have the capability to learn the skills or acquire the knowledge needed to achieve the goal.

[17] For a review on the difference between a sense-of-self and True Self, see Chapter 1.

[18] Family values are often reviewed only to discover they were accepted for the wrong reasons. After all, parents are people too—people who also went through the stages of development and had to determine where they fit in and where they didn't. Couple that with changes in society over time, and this stage proves to be one of the most difficult for everyone involved.

[19] Keep in mind depression can be trait or state. When it is trait, it is due to morbid grief. We need to look for the first loss. In this case, it would most likely be related to the stage of Autonomy.

[20] As a small child I remember a favorite Christmas story, "The Gift of the Magi," shared with me by my parents. The author, O'Henry, tells a wonderful tale about a poor young couple, Jim and Della, who are very much in love. Although they own very little, they have two objects they both greatly treasure. Jim has a gold watch that is a family heirloom and Della has beautiful hair that "fell about her rippling and shining like a cascade of brown waters" (p. 2). Christmas time arrives and neither of them have money to buy a gift for the other. Driven by a need to get their partner a gift they decide, on Christmas Eve, to sell their most cherished possessions for money. Jim sells his watch for a set of beautiful hair combs for Della. In turn, Della sells her beautiful tresses for a magnificent chain for Jim's watch. The wonder of this story is that although Jim and Della both loved their treasures, they loved each other more. This story provides an excellent example of a positive intimate, loving relationship. Both individuals have their needs met and are focused on the needs of their partner. They have a relationship that unites them but they are still able to make independent decisions (i.e., making a decision to sell their items). They are loving and supportive despite financial hardship. Their behavior indicates they have satisfactorily resolved the task of Intimacy.

[21] The onset of this stage of life has changed, i.e., increased, as the average life span has increased. Thirty years ago most people were middle-aged by the time they were in their late forties. At that time, the average life span would have been somewhere in the seventies. Today, a comparable cohort would be middle-aged in their fifties and have an expected life span in the eighties. Today,

some people will enter this stage earlier and move on to the next stage earlier than indicated here. This is because they also moved through Identity and Intimacy at an earlier age.

[22] When I use the word *we* I am referring to a group of people discussed above, Endnote 5.

[23] This is a type of social loneliness.

CHAPTER 6

AFFILIATED-INDIVIDUATION AND SELF-ACTUALIZATION: NEED SATISFACTION AS PREREQUISITE

MARGARET E. ERICKSON, HELEN L. ERICKSON, AND BETTY JENSEN

They were thrilled with the news; they were going to have a baby! Together they planned to make sure she got enough sleep, a healthy diet, exercise, and support she needed to feel positive about herself and her life. They frequently sang and spoke to their baby as they waited. They didn't know if the baby was male or female and didn't care. They just wanted a baby. At his birth, they were delighted to get to see their son for the first time. They named him Adam and took turns holding him close to their chests as they, gently and quietly welcomed him to the world. For the next several weeks, Adam's parents worked hard to get to know him, trying to meet his emotional and physical needs. As he grew, he seemed to settle into his new life.

When Adam was a month old, he turned toward his mother's voice and listened to her quietly talk to him. After a few minutes, he looked away from her, resting his head on her shoulder. As an active two-year-old, he enjoyed playing in the room near his mother. He frequently stopped what he was doing and ran to hug her, touch her, or tell her something, and then returned to his play. In pre-school, he enjoyed being with friends for a few hours, and was ready to reconnect with mom. Some days, it was difficult to be away from her.

When in third grade, Adam returned from school, one day, and said he needed help making a model for science class. He asked for suggestions and then commented, "Those are good ideas, but I think my model will be a volcano." When his mom stood up to leave the room, he said, "I need your help. This is going to be hard." He then proceeded to make the model with minimal assistance, but enjoyed having her hand him the glue, scissors, etc., as he completed his work.

At 15, Adam played football with his high school team. He loved the game and enjoyed being the extra point kicker for the team. When one of his teammates questioned why he didn't want to get "out there" and "play ball," he responded,

"I have the best of football. I get to be part of the team, and I also get to do what I like. I know when I make a really good kick and get the points."

On his wedding day, his best friend asked him why he wanted to marry Elizabeth. Adam replied, "We have a great time together and I know Elizabeth is my Soul mate, but she also respects my need to hang out with friends, play a round of golf, or work late some nights. Many women I dated never gave me space or understood my need to be 'me' as well as a 'partner'. We both love being together, but we also love our time apart."

Adam and Elizabeth were looking forward to seeing old college friends at their 30th class reunion. They had dinner together and spent the remainder of the evening apart, visiting with other people. Later, on the way home, they had a great time sharing their evening experiences with one another.

As time passed, they become grandparents. They enjoyed the time with their grandchildren sharing stories and events of their lives and helping the children learn and grow. They also enjoyed time independently working on interesting projects, events, or activities. Looking back, they decided their lives had been meaningful. They felt good about the decisions and choices they had made. As Adam aged and his physical body began to slow down, he spent more time quietly being with his loved ones and less physically involved in life around him. He contemplated the next step in his journey. One day, when he was approaching his 80th birthday, he slid on the ice and hit his head. He was rushed to the hospital, still conscious, with his wife at his side. He turned to her, told her he loved her and that he would be waiting for her. Then with a twinkle in his eye he added, "I'm fine and you're not to worry and not to hurry, I'll wait as long as I need to." With that, he took a breath, slowly released it, closed his eyes, and passed on.

OVERVIEW

As human beings, we have an inherent drive to be independent, to discover our Self, and be the best we can be. At the same time, we have an inherent need to develop relationships, interact with others in meaningful ways, and experience a healthy sense of connectedness. These needs interface to create an inherent need for affiliation and individuation, which can be satisfied when our needs are met repeatedly and consistently across the lifespan. When affiliation and individuation are in balance, we are able to find meaning in our life, work on our Life Purpose, and self-actualize.

When it comes to need satisfaction, no two people are alike because there are many ways in which needs can be met. Many people with a lifetime of unmet needs don't thrive; others learn to get needs met in unhealthy ways, and still others somehow manage to get by. However, of this latter group, most are never able to develop close loving relationships. They often appear to be "pulling themselves up by the bootstraps," but are unable to maintain the momentum. They just don't have the internal resources needed for healthy affiliated-individuation, a prerequisite for Self-actualization.

This chapter is about human needs. It describes Maslow's (1968) Motivational Theory as well as concepts of inherent needs and types of needs, and discusses how needs drive behavior, including three factors that influence the perception of unmet needs: meaning, past experience with need satisfaction, and availability of resources. Next, we discuss the relationship between holism and need satisfaction, types of relationships based on need satisfaction, and Maslow's conflict theory. The chapter closes with a discussion on the Being Process, the process of self-actualizing.

HUMAN MOTIVATION

Affiliated-Individuation, Precursor to Self-actualization

We have an inherent need to be connected and to belong from prebirth until Transformation. Being connected meets our need for safety, security, being loved and loving. We also have a need to be individuals and maintain a sense of independence and self-esteem. Healthy separation meets our needs for competence, mastery, worthiness, and acceptance by others. Our need to simultaneously feel both connected to and independent from significant others was labeled Affiliated-Individuation (Erickson, Tomlin, & Swain, 1983). They state,

> *Individuals have an instinctual need for affiliated-individuation. They need to be able to be dependent on support systems while simultaneously maintaining independence from these support systems. They need to feel a deep sense of both the 'I' and the 'we' states of being and to perceive freedom and acceptance in both states* (p. 47).

They further described this need saying,

> *The infant needs its mother, the mother 'needs' the infant; the husband 'needs' his wife; the teenager 'needs' his friends...But, an equally important component of these human relationships is the need for each member to be simultaneously independent of the other person* (p.68).

H. Erickson recently stated:

> *I think affiliation and individuation are two different dimensions, just like developmental residual has two different dimensions. The trick is in finding a healthy balance between the two. When people are over affiliated, their individuation is at risk. Sometimes, they will sacrifice affiliation in order to acquire a sense of individuation. There are two*

times in life when people are most vulnerable for this: the stages of Autonomy and Identity. For example, the young adult, threatened with rejection by the family if he takes "the wrong position" on lifestyles, religious or political views, may choose rejection by the family in order to establish his own Identity. But, work on Identity requires that all Basic Needs are met to some degree, which means safety, security, love and belonging needs, as well as self-esteem needs have to be considered. So, such a young man would lose some of his affiliation in order to feel individuated. Such an experience would affect his task work, and could impact his ability to build an intimate relationship in the next stage of life, unless he is able to find a new attachment object that would encourage both affiliation and individuation.

When there is a conflict between affiliation and individuation, people usually choose affiliation over individuation. Of course, this depends on the life stage, type of developmental residual laid down during the various stages, and availability of an object to meet their needs at the time. While it sounds complex, it really isn't. Simply stated, we need a healthy balance of affiliated-individuation—all of us, from the inutero baby to the person in the stage of Transformation. While it might be tempting to say Affiliated-Individuation is similar to Belongingness-Self Esteem, it is not. Affiliated-Individuation is more than that. It is the overall sense of being connected while maintaining a strong, healthy sense of Self (Personal communication, November 21, 2005).

This suggests the nature of affiliated-individuation is the same across the lifespan, but is demonstrated differently depending on the developmental stage. In fact, since affiliated-individuation depends on the way our needs are met, there is an interaction between the behavior demonstrated by an individual and the behavior of the significant other in the relationship: and these vary by developmental stage.

Variance in Affiliated-Individuation

Adam's story describes the behavior of someone who has had a life-time of healthy affiliated-individuation (Erickson et al., 1983, p. 47). Because of his secure relationship with his parents, he successfully maneuvered developmental tasks, accruing strengths and virtues along the way. Approaching his final stage, he knew he had lived his life well, and would go on to reunite with others he loved. Adam's story is the ideal, but not everyone shares similar life experiences.

Others have their needs met across the lifespan, but not as consistently as Adam. As a result, they have more difficulty establishing secure relationships. Some feel more affiliation and others more individuation. Although they grow and develop in a quasi-healthy manner, they aren't able to self-actualize as Adam. They approach their senior years resigned that their lives have been satisfactory, but not fully satisfying.

Still others, their needs met minimally, have difficulty with affiliated-individuation throughout their life span. Some, over-affiliated, are unable to find their way. They cling to significant others, constantly searching for evidence of their worth in what others say or how others treat them. On the other hand, those who over-individuate live on the fringe of society; sometimes "invisible" to the usual observer and, at other times, more obvious.

There are many variations of these prototypes of affiliated-individuation; no two people are exactly alike. Nevertheless, a healthy balance of affiliated-individuation is necessary for us to self-actualize, and need satisfaction affects both. Therefore, an in-depth understanding of needs theory is important. The following pages provide a discussion on several related topics: inherent needs, types of needs, behavior driven by needs, and conflicts created by unmet needs.

Needs are Inherent

Need satisfaction is necessary for life and a prerequisite for growth. Maslow believed that prolonged unmet needs cause people to become ill. On the other hand, need satisfaction prevents illness and restores health. Our drive for need satisfaction can be inactive, at a low ebb, or functionally absent in the healthy adult because Basic Needs have been repeatedly met in the past (Maslow, 1968, p. 22).

Need satisfaction is a crucial part of life. It determines what happens to us every day and in every phase of our lives. Yet, we often discount the importance of our needs. We have all heard children being told, "You don't need that, you just ate!" or adults who discount their own needs saying, "I don't need that, I just want it!" Sometimes, both these statements are true reflections of what the individual is feeling, but not always. Sometimes, we use the word need when we really mean want or desire. Other times, the word appropriately expresses what the person is experiencing. The difference is the mandate for a response. While needs mandate a response, wants and desires do not. People will not become deprived if wants and desires are not attended to, but they will if needs are not addressed. This is because needs are part of our basic nature; they drive our behavior.

Most nurses are familiar with Abraham Maslow's basic need theory, described as the Psychology of Being (Maslow, 1968). Maslow believed all people strive to be the best they can be. He argued that our inherent aim is to become self-actualized, but lack of need satisfaction sometimes interferes. He stated growth occurs when our needs are met repeatedly, and that unmet needs interfere with our ability to grow and adapt.

> *We have, each of us, an essential biologically based inner nature, which is to some degree 'natural', intrinsic, given, and in a certain limited sense, unchangeable, or, at least, unchanging. Each person's inner nature is in part unique to himself and in part species-wide....this inner nature, as*

much as we know of it...seems not ...evil....The Basic Needs (for life, for safety and security, for belongingness and affection, for respect and self-respect, and for self-actualization), the basic human emotions and the basic human capacities are on their face either neutral, premoral or positively 'good' (Maslow, 1968, p. 3).

Universality

Maslow contends (and we agree) that human needs are universal—they cross cultural and ethnic lines. Everyone has the same physiologic needs as well as safety, security, love, esteem, self-esteem and self-actualization needs. However, one's culture affects the expression and the ways people seek to get them met. Teenagers in one culture may seek esteem from their peers by wearing brand label jeans; in another culture, this behavior might be meaningless or even inappropriate. While we all have a drive for need satisfaction, we are different, so need satisfaction varies. Nevertheless, all people have basic and growth needs that drive behavior. Repeated need satisfaction also influences behavior. This is because need satisfaction produces developmental residual, and developmental residual affects our perceptions, attitudes, and general approach to life.

Types of Needs

Maslow also said we have multiple types of needs that can be categorized as Basic and Growth Needs, which are similar, but also different. Basic Needs satisfaction is necessary for survival. Therefore, unmet Basic Needs create tension, while satisfaction reduces tension. On the other hand, Growth Needs satisfaction creates tension and additional need for the experience. The tension is not resolved until we are saturated with the experience. Unmet Basic Needs create distress while unmet Growth Needs create eustress. Growth Need satisfaction is necessary for us to thrive, grow, create healthy developmental residual, and self-actualize.

Basic Needs.

Basic Needs exist in a four-level hierarchy with biophysical needs at the first level, followed by safety and security, love and belongingness, esteem and self-esteem needs respectively All four levels of Basic Needs must be satisfied to some degree before we seek Growth Needs satisfaction. Interestingly, while Basic Needs are hierarchical, it is possible to work on satisfaction of several levels simultaneously. For example, when babies are happy with what they are eating, how they are handled, voice tones and eye contact they experience, their physiological, security, love and belonging needs are all being met at the same time.[1]

Goble (1974), describing Maslow's basic need theory says:

The human being is motivated by a number of Basic Needs which are species wide, apparently unchanging, and genetic or instinctual in origin...The most basic, the most powerful, the most obvious of all man's need are his needs for physical survival;...Once the physiological needs are sufficiently satisfied, what Maslow describes as safety needs emerge...When physiological and safety needs are met, needs for love, affection, and belongingness emerge...(and, finally), two categories of esteem needs, self-respect and esteem from other people. Self-esteem includes such needs as desire for confidence, competence, mastery, adequacy, achievement, independence, and freedom. Respect from others includes such concepts as prestige, recognition, acceptance, attention, status, reputation, and appreciation (pp. 38-42).

Simply stated, we seek Basic Need satisfaction in somewhat of a hierarchy. If people are starving or unable to breathe they will do what is necessary to get those unmet physiological needs satisfied. They are not focused on higher Basic Needs such as love and belonging or esteem needs until they are able to get enough oxygen in their lungs or until the hunger has been at least partially satiated. Similarly, when physiological needs are met, safety needs emerge, and so on. At the same time, unmet needs from any level of the hierarchy can emerge. When one of the lower needs is threatened, that becomes our focus, and motivates our behavior—all other issues are put aside.

The following story illustrates this point:

Mr. Jones, raised in the ghettos of Chicago, talked about his earlier life. He said he had been a gang member as a young man. His mother worked two jobs, so there was usually enough food to eat, but as he grew, that was not sufficient. He sought companionship from those available. When asked which needs he had met through the gang, he commented that participation in the gang helped meet his safety, security, love, belonging, esteem and self- esteem needs. However, "when we were in a rumble (fight), the most important need was making sure we were safe. You don't care about anything else when you are worried about having a gun or knife at your back. Your whole focus is watching your back!

This story also illustrates another point. While we might find ways to meet our needs consistently, sometimes our resources are inadequate for building need assets or facilitating long-term growth. In fact, they might even result in unmet needs at another level.

When asked about this, H. Erickson stated:

Sometimes when Basic Needs are unmet over time, people resort to getting them met in whatever way possible. As some have said, 'It is better to have a mother (or significant other) who only meets a few of my needs now and then, than to have no one at all.' Some people have few resources to help them in healthy ways; they have few alternatives. As a result, they choose to get some needs met at the expense of many unmet needs. Often, their needs are met through negative or abusive attention, rather than growth-producing care. While they may get some needs met, the way it happens has negative consequences. In actuality, they sometimes risk their physical health in order to get belonging needs met. Of course, this will impede their overall well-being. Maslow talks about this when he talks about our struggle between need for safety and need for growth (Personal communication, November 18, 2005).

Every human being has both sets of forces within him. One set clings to safety and defensiveness out of fear, tending to regress backward, hanging on to the past, afraid to grow away...,afraid to take chances, afraid to jeopardize what he already has, afraid of independence, freedom and separateness. The other set of forces impels him forward toward wholeness of Self and uniqueness of Self, toward full functioning of all his capacities, toward confidence in the face of the external world at the same time that he can accept his deepest, real, unconscious Self...Safety has both anxieties and delights; growth has both anxieties and delights. We grow forward when the delights of growth and the anxieties of safety are greater than the anxieties of growth and the delights of safety....Assured safety permits higher needs and impulses to emerge and to grow towards mastery. To endanger safety, means regression backward to the more basic foundation. What this means is that in the choice between giving up safety or giving up growth, safety will ordinarily win out (Maslow,1968, pp. 46- 49*).*

We will discuss this issue further when we talk about Holism and Need Satisfaction.

Need Status. Need satisfaction is necessary for survival, but ironically, it is also temporary. While we may feel fully satiated at one moment in time, it is always possible those same needs are unmet a few minutes later. H. Erickson, (1996) proposed that we might think about needs satisfaction as an ongoing process and need status as a dimension (or as a scale) from need deprivation to need assets. Since unmet Basic Needs create tension, we have a drive to decrease the tension: the greater the deficit, the greater the tension. She proposed that as the tension reaches a threshold (probably at point 2 on a 0-5 point scale as shown in (Figure 6.1), we typically initiate behavior to decrease the tension related to the unmet Basic Need(s).

Deprivation	Deficit	Unmet	Met	Satisfied	Assets
0	1	2	3	4	5

Figure 6.1 Variance in Basic Need Status as proposed by H. Erickson.

For example, when we are hungry (that is move toward unmet need status, perhaps a 2.5 on the scale), we start to think about finding food to meet this need. When we reach unmet status (2 on the scale), we probably start acting on our thoughts; we may actively seek food. If we are unable to fulfill our need, we continue to move toward need deficit, become more focused, and finally reach need deprivation (0 on the scale).

However, what we have learned about our ability to satisfy our needs in the past will determine our ability to continue actions aimed at need satisfaction. If we learn, early in life, that our actions are futile, we may simultaneously learn we can't achieve need satisfaction. The tension continues to mount, but with it comes a sense of helplessness and ultimately, hopelessness. (We will discuss this issue in more detail later)

Alternatively, when Basic Needs are satisfied (to some degree), the tension begins to dissipate. When a threshold of basic need satisfaction is met (3 on the scale), it is no longer perceived as an unmet need, and behavior aimed toward need satisfaction diminishes.

> The aim is to eliminate the tension caused by unmet basic needs. The more the needs are met, the less tension we experience, the less we focus on need satisfaction. Ultimately, the drive simply fades away for the time being.

We should remember, however, the nature of the resources used to meet the needs has implications. We will discuss this when we talk about Needs and Holism.

Growth Needs

Growth Needs emerge when Basic Needs have been met to some degree. Because we have an inherent drive to explore, be creative, and expand our horizons, Growth Needs emerge when we feel safe, connected, and somewhat self-sufficient. Growth needs are related to Being Values (Maslow, 1968). This means that satisfaction of Growth Needs is necessary for us to work toward self-actualization. They are the feelings we experience as we Become more fully who we are by nature. Although there are many types of Growth Needs (see Figure 6.2), they are not organized hierarchically. Maslow (1968) stated the following:

> *The single holistic principle that binds together the multiplicity of human motives is the tendency for a new and higher need to emerge as the lower need fulfills itself by being sufficiently gratified. The child who is fortunate enough to grow normally and well gets satiated and bored with the delights that he has savored sufficiently, and eagerly (without pushing) goes on to higher more complex, delights as they become available to him without danger or threat"* (pp. 55-56).

All of us have an inherent drive toward satisfaction of some Growth Needs, such as wholeness and beauty. However, the degree to which we seek satisfaction of other types of Growth Needs depends on who we are, our interests, likes and dislikes, what we perceive as our life work, and where we are in our Life Journey. Some Growth Needs are more important at earlier stages, while others are more important at later stages. For example, it is important for people to learn how to be playful and experience justice in childhood. On the other hand, older adults have a greater need for beauty and self-sufficiency. Nevertheless, all Growth Needs are important for all human beings at all ages. Growth Need satisfaction is necessary for us to move toward self-actualization. Goble (1974), describing our inherent drive toward Growth Need satisfaction, quoted Maslow saying, "What a man can be, he must be and man has the desire to become more and more what one is, to become everything that one is capable of becoming" (p.42).

Need	Being-Value
Wholeness	Unity, integration, tendency toward interconnectedness.
Completion	Ending, finish, fulfillment.
Justice	Fairness, lawfulness, orderliness.
Aliveness	Spontaneity, full-functioning.
Beauty	Aliveness, richness.
Uniqueness	Individuality.
Playfulness	Fun, joy, amusement, humor, exuberance.

Figure 6.2 Examples of growth needs and related Being-values.
Adapted from materials drawn from Goble, 1973, pp.47-48, and Maslow, 1962.

Need Satisfaction Creates Tension. Growth Need status differs from Basic Need status in many ways. While Basic Needs satisfaction is necessary for survival and early development, Growth Needs satisfaction is necessary for self-actualization. Growth Needs satisfaction encourages continued interest in the object (which meets those needs) and the tension grows. Compare this to Basic Needs where the tension dissipates with need satisfaction. With Growth Needs we become more interested, more focused on the object or experience that meets these needs; therefore, tension increases. Take for example, the need for beauty, an inherent Growth Need shared by all humans. As we discover the feeling of Growth Needs satisfaction when viewing a beautiful sunset, we realize we are different during and after the viewing from what we were before. That is because Growth Needs satisfaction precedes transcendence. The experience of beauty helps us meet Growth Needs and transcend. H. Erickson states:

The more our Growth Needs are met, the more we experience transcendence, and the more we get in touch with our 'Self'. Through this process we come closer to understanding our Reason for Being; we come closer to discovering our Soul-Work. While there comes a point when Growth Needs Satisfaction may move from one type of need to another, there is never a time when we aren't driven toward some type of Growth Need satisfaction, if our Basic Needs are met to some degree (Personal communication, November 20, 2005).

The drive for Basic Needs Satisfaction diminishes with gratification, while Growth Needs Satisfaction leads us to seek additional experiences to further satisfy our Growth Needs. Growth Needs satisfaction is a prerequisite for transcendence and self-actualization.

Need for Information

Maslow also talks about our need for information (1968, pp. 60-67). While attaining information sometimes meets our needs, it can also have the opposite effect at times. Maslow calls this The Need to Know and The Fear of Knowing. For example, there are many times when we need to know something in order to feel safe and secure, loved and connected. Such 'knowing' may also meet our esteem needs. At other times, we dread learning something; we have a fear of knowing. For example, people who have had cancer and then find a recurrent mass are fearful of the report.

When we are fearful of information, it is because there is an anticipated loss with it. The difference, whether it is fear of knowing or need to know is very personal. We can make that determination only by asking our clients. For example, some people going to surgery will want all the details, others will not. I have found it helpful to tell them what I can about the procedure and how I can help them, and then ask what they want to know. Usually, those who have a fear of knowing will ask questions that address their safety and security status before they ask about the operative experience. Some will say they do not want to know anything. Under those circumstances, it is helpful to teach them techniques they can use after surgery. Such techniques include ways to cough without excessive discomfort, ways to be more comfortable such as deep breathing, relaxing, and so forth. It is also important to remind them that they will not be alone, that their nurse will be there to help them be as comfortable as possible. In Chapter 11, I describe a situation in which Jimmy first had a fear of knowing and then a need to know (H. Erickson, personal communication, November 22, 2005).

<u>Implications for the Teaching-Learning Process</u>. Healthcare providers frequently make the mistake of assuming they understand or know the client's needs. This is particularly true when it comes to teaching people what they should do to take care of themselves! Usually, this happens when people are labeled as a

medical disease or a health problem, such as a diabetic or a hypertensive. Such an approach often leads to frustration on our part and a lack of learning on theirs.

When we have our own agenda and presume to know what is needed without first asking our clients, we miss the opportunities to connect with them. We may assume our clients have a need to know, and therefore, we will teach them. It is like two ships passing in the night. Neither is affected, even though the potential was great.

The following story provides an example of the discrepancy that often exists between what nurses think someone needs to know and what they think they need to know.

> *An elderly Native American gentleman who had diabetes was getting ready to go home. Prior to discharge, the nurse taught him what she thought he needed to know. He patiently listened as the nurse taught him how to take care of his diabetes and manage his diet. She discussed routine information on diet, insulin administration, and self-care. After a lengthy discussion, she finally asked him if he had any questions. At first, he responded no, he understood. When she invited him to comment about anything in his life that seemed important, He proceeded to say, "Well, we only get fresh fruit on the reservation once a month and if we aren't there when it comes in, we can't get it. Also, I don't have a refrigerator, so how can I keep my insulin cold?"*

This is a classic example of what happens when we forget to ask the client to share their Self-care Knowledge. When we begin by asking how we can help them, we are able to address their needs before we initiate "patient education." In fact, when we think about it, we know those who practice Modeling and Role-Modeling do not advocate the concept of patient education. Instead, we attend to helping our client's learn what they need to know, so they can be healthy, grow, and be happy.

If we focus on helping our clients learn, then we have to start with Self-care Knowledge. We have to start with what they know about themselves, what they think has caused their problem, and what they think will help them. Without this information, we often start "blaming" our clients for not following our advice, not doing what they should do, and for causing their own problems.

As nurses, it is our job to understand what motivates or drives our clients' behavior. Frequently, we label a person as demanding, controlling, irresponsible, manipulative, difficult, or troublesome. Sadly, when we do this an understanding of the motivation behind the behavior is lost. Consequently, the client experiences more losses and a greater sense of unmet needs. This, in turn, triggers more behavior to get those needs met. Often, an ineffective cycle of behavior and response between the client and healthcare providers ensues. When we recognize clients have Self-care Knowledge and remember behavior has meaning, we can interrupt and change this cycle. We do this by remembering motivation drives our behavior and although needs are met or unmet only from within the context of the individual's world-view, unmet needs motivate us.

NEEDS DRIVE BEHAVIOR

Given that behavior is motivated or driven by unmet needs and that we have an inherent drive toward need satisfaction, what we will do to get our needs met at any given time is affected by several co-existing factors: the meaning of the unmet need, past experiences with need satisfaction, and availability of resources.[2]

Meaning

In the first Modeling and Role-Modeling Book (1983), and in the next chapter M. Erickson talks about the relationship between need satisfaction and attachment objects. When an unmet need, associated with an object to which we have bonded or attached, emerges, it is possible for us to experience a threatened loss. For example, 26 month-old Sally has a tattered, old blanket she has carried since she was tiny. It has repeatedly met her security needs in the past, so she now associates feelings of security with it. Her mother has decided to take her to play-group, thinking it will be good for her, but Sally feels insecure when she sees so many people she doesn't know. She wants her blanket, but it is not available. The feelings of insecurity mount. Now, not only does she feel insecure because she is going to play-group she also has the sense of loss of her blanket, the object that made her feel secure in the past.

A contrasting example would be to consider the toddler who loves grapes, bananas, oranges, and cantaloupe. When hunger strikes, any one of those objects will meet his needs. In fact, most toddlers would even settle for an animal cracker, or some other substitute, without feeling deprived. There is no significant meaning attached to the unmet need other than it creates tension. Many possible resources can alleviate that problem.

Past Experiences

Past experiences with need satisfaction also influence how we respond to unmet needs. People who are accustomed to getting their needs met respond as though they expect to get them met. Furthermore, if they trust others care about them and will look out for their welfare, not only do they respond with behavior that indicates trust and positive expectations, they also demonstrate willingness to compromise. Again, take Sally, the 26 month old who has lost her blanket. Even though she will experience an immediate loss of the blanket, if she trusts her caregiver, she will be able to accept reassurance (security needs) from her caregiver that will help her through the transition. Rather than sinking into intense feelings of loss, she will be able to draw from her external resource (caregiver) to allay her feelings of insecurity. If, on the other hand, her blanket has become her primary source of security, she will have increasing difficulty with Initiative activities, even with her caregiver's support.

Resource Availability

A final factor that influences our behavior, motivated by unmet needs, is the perceived availability of resources. Past experiences determine the nature of our developmental residual. People who come out of the stage of Trust with Hope have a positive attitude about the future. Although they, too, will have moments of impoverishment with despair, it takes less for them to mobilize internal resources and be future-oriented. Although they may have temporary feelings of helplessness, and act accordingly, they don't sink into hopelessness, even in dire situations. Instead, they perceive that somehow resources will materialize.

Some small children show enormous fortitude, positive expectations, and hope even when they experience multiple unmet needs. Nurses often talk about the premature baby who is a "fighter"; it is as though they have a will to live that supersedes their unmet needs. On the other hand, people of all ages, have demonstrated the opposite attitude. Some early studies undertaken by Harlow (1960) showed that baby monkeys who had sufficient food, but had not been comforted or loved, tended to respond to stress by giving up. The same has been found in human infants (Spitz, 1960). Interestingly, the extent of a human's social network does not make a major difference in these responses. While we can be surrounded by people who might help if called upon, if the person experiencing the unmet need does not perceive that the resources exist, they will act accordingly.

Sometimes, people who don't perceive they have resources actually have them, they just don't know it. They need help in discovering their abilities and learning that they can use past learning in new situations. They just don't know what they know! Here's an example:

> *Jane is in the third grade, so it is time for her to learn the multiplication tables. She informs her mother that she is dumb, can't learn, hates school, and begs to quit. Her mother asks why she feels that way and Jane explains that her teacher wants her to learn all the "times tables" and she just can't do that. Her mother responds by asking her how she learned to walk; Jane thinks that's a really dumb question, and has nothing to do with learning the times tables. Her mother disagrees, saying that when Jane was a baby, she had to work hard to learn to walk, and that when she was really little she couldn't even hold up her head! She goes on to explain that Jane was able to learn because she took one step at a time, first the head, then the chest, etc. and now she can run, ride a bike, etc. Finally, she reminds Jane that her only problem is she has*

forgotten how to learn, and that she has to break things into small parts to learn it well. Jane, surprised to know she was such a good learner, then declares she is going to take 10 days to learn her multiplication tables, 1 day for each set, 1-10. Her mother tells her that is a very good idea, and reassures her that she is a fast learner; she just needs to remember what she already knows.

Although some people are resource deprived, resource availability is not an all-or-none situation for most of us. Maslow states that "...most members of our society who are normal are partially satisfied in all their basic needs and partially unsatisfied in all their basic needs at the same time" (1970, p. 27-28).

This statement implies all of us have some needs that are met and some that are unmet at the same time. While some might think satisfaction of some needs could blunt our motivation to get others met, they forget we all have an inherent drive. Our behavior is a result of our inherent drive toward affiliated-individuation and self-actualization. We will seek need satisfaction one way or another. After all, we are holistic beings, and as such, very creative!

HOLISM AND NEED SATISFACTION

Any discussion of needs must take into consideration the holistic nature of humans. Although we agree needs are hierarchical, we also realize needs overlap and interconnect—they don't stand alone as discrete categories. Meeting needs in one subsystem may result in simultaneous need satisfaction in others. For example, feeling loved by a parent or spouse can produce a sense of emotional security. The toddler who feels unconditional love from a parent will also feel emotional security if the parent is clear about parameters.

On the other hand, need satisfaction in one subsystem may have a negative effect on need status in another subsystem. For example, adolescents who feel filial love may also experience feelings of inadequacy because the task of adolescence mandates they learn how to direct their own lives. What happens depends entirely on how the love is expressed, what conditions are associated with it, and to what degree the love allows both affiliation and individuation.

Maslow (1968) talks about the holistic nature of need satisfaction. He uses the need for food as an example, explaining it is more than a physiologic need, and in fact, achieving satisfaction of the need for food involves emotional and cognitive changes and approaches. In addition, eating may have many social, security, and love/belonging issues surrounding the ingestion of food. This means, satisfaction of one type of need might simultaneously meet others. As an example, enjoying dinner with a friend has the potential to meet many needs at once, or as indicated above, to meet some needs while simultaneously creating need deficits. Two case scenarios demonstrating the difference are presented below. Jay experiences healthy affiliated-individuation with his parents, enabling him to continue his work on Identity. Bill's parents demonstrate conditional acceptance, creating feelings of insecurity. He will have more difficulty with affiliated-individuation and the task work of Identity.

> *Jay, a 17-year-old, discussed his desire to take his girlfriend out to dinner with his parents. He explained it was her birthday and he wanted to make it special for her. His parents complimented him on his thoughtfulness and asked if he needed any help. When he asked for the family car, they agreed. Three days later, Jay and his girlfriend had a fun evening together. She told him it was one of the best surprises she had ever had. Later that night, Jay thought about the evening, and decided it had been just great. Although he had spent a lot of money, he was comfortable knowing he could earn more and that it is important to do "special things" once in a while. He fell sleep with a smile on his face.*
>
> *Bill, Jay's friend, decided this was a great idea. He approached his parents with the same plan. His parents asked him from where he would get the money; he said he had earned it mowing lawns. His parents thought it was money he was saving for college. Bill response was, "Yeah, I guess so, but I want to take Mary out for her birthday." His parents conceded it was his money, but reminded him that he didn't always use good judgment and he'd be sorry when it was time to go to college. Bill asked if he could have the car for the evening; his parents grudgingly gave him the keys. Although Bill and Mary had a nice dinner together, Bill wondered if he had made a good decision. He felt unsure about spending the money, so he decided to skip dessert and gave a small tip. Mary thanked him and said she had a good time, but when he got home that night, he felt confused. He'd had fun with Mary, but having spent so much money he decided he had made a big mistake. He felt unsure of himself, wondered if he'd ever learn to be a "man," and worried a little about his future.*

We are holistic beings, so needs met in one subsystem might meet needs in other subsystems or create unmet needs in other subsystems.

Exchange of Resources

As holistic beings, we can also learn to meet needs in one subsystem by drawing resources from another. For example, some people reduce anxiety by eating, while some stifle physical hunger (physical need) by telling themselves they aren't really hungry, they are bored! Unmet needs (which are stressors) create a drive toward need satisfaction. Sometimes resources in the same subsystem are not readily available, so we draw from an alternative subsystem or from external resources. However, alternative resources are often less helpful in satisfying the need, and over time, can create an unhealthy affiliated-individuation.

Failure-to-thrive babies is an example of this situation. These babies seem to draw from the biophysical and safety need assets in order to survive, but at a cost. The literature (Krugman & Dubowitz, 2003; Merck Manual: Diagnosis and Therapy, 2002) reports that failure-to-thrive babies have physiological and safety (physical) needs met, but not their love/belonging and emotional safety needs. On the other hand, let us consider refugee babies who have minimal food, but are alive despite formidable odds. When we see pictures of these emaciated, swollen-bellied babies clinging to their mothers, it is nearly inconceivable that they survive. Yet, they are able to draw from one subsystem (the psychosocial) in order to maintain another (the biophysical). And they seem to do this for some time. These babies, starved for food, are able to survive because they are deeply loved, but there is a cost for their general well-being. The same holds true for failure-to-thrive children. They can survive, but not thrive.

One final way to think about need satisfaction of the holistic person is to consider what happens when we ignore needs in one subsystem because we are building assets in other parts of our being. This is different from any situation in which we meet needs in one subsystem at the disadvantage of another, or draw resources from one subsystem to meet needs in another. In this case, we are not just meeting needs, we are building need assets in one subsystem. But, sometimes when we do this, we are so involved or care so much about what we are doing, we either ignore the alternative subsystem, or purposefully choose to focus on one subsystem, even though it might have a negative effect on another.

For example, we routinely hear people talk about getting so fully involved in a work project, they forgot to eat anything the entire day. While they may have unmet needs in one area, their need assets in another offset the unmet needs. This is different from those who work so long they don't have time to eat. The first is a self-actualized person building self-esteem and growth need assets at the expense of his physiological needs. The latter is someone who has had difficulty in the task of Industry, and as a result, perceives he must work long hours to be acceptable, to be respectable. This is a typical "work-a-holic." This is also different from the person who chooses to meet their love needs over their physiological needs. Perhaps, this is what happens with some mothers of emaciated babies. Instead of eating the food their bodies need, they might offer it to their children, because of their love. H. Erickson (1976), and Erickson et al. (1983), called this maladaptive equilibrium (see Chapter 8). H. Erickson stated:

> *Remember, maladaptive resources are not as powerful as adaptive resources. They do not help reduce need-related tensions or those that are specific to the type of needs. The potential outcome (need assets and developmental residual) provides fewer resources. It is like taking a piece from puzzle A and making it work in puzzle B. Although it may work, it really doesn't fit, it doesn't align with the other parts, it doesn't create the overall strength a matched puzzle piece would. You might want to refer back to our discussion in Chapters 2 and 3 for more detail about*

"matching," "being in synchrony," and "creating resources" (Personal communication, November 28, 2005).

These exchanges among the subsystems exist because we are holistic persons with continuous, dynamic interaction among the parts. It works for us and against us. It helps us survive serious deprivations, and it also helps us accomplish life goals. The implications are interesting. That is, while one person may get a physiological need for food met by eating, another might do it by visualizing himself eating food, metabolizing it, and getting energy from it.[3] If he has resources available in some part of his holistic being, this type of action might temporarily meet his need for hunger.[4]

> *We are holistic beings, so we can draw resources from one subsystem in order to maintain another, and we can build assets in one subsystem while ignoring needs in another. Need assets are "stored memories."*

Implications

As nurses, we often use Maslow's hierarchy to prioritize nursing care. We make certain our clients have oxygen, food, water, warmth, stimulation, and all the basic physical needs required for physiological and safety maintenance. Unfortunately, we do not always remember the importance of facilitating satisfaction of the other Basic Needs. Thus, physiologic issues often take priority over love/belonging, esteem and self-esteem needs.

While at first glance, this may be appropriate in today's society of high turn-over, acute care demands, and inadequate nurse-client ratios, reconsideration of the above discussion demonstrates the need to consider the client's perspective before we prioritize our care.

Unmet needs in one subsystem of the holistic person have the potential to create greater need deprivation than unmet needs in another, depending upon the client's perceptions of what is needed, what will help, and how to get help. We realize, of course there are times when physical needs take priority, and, usually, these are the times when physical life is threatened. However, even in those circumstances, the needs of the holistic person should be considered. The following case provides an example:

> *An older man was admitted for chest pain and acute respiratory distress. He was started on oxygen, and received several medications. However, he continued to have angina and became more agitated. His case manager heard he had been admitted and came to visit. Holding his hand, she asked him what she could do for him. He replied, "It is really cold outside today and when it gets darker it will only get worse. My little dog is outside without food and water and I am afraid he won't make it if someone doesn't take care of him. He's my best friend and he is all I*

have." The nurse proceeded to contact a neighbor who was willing to take care of the dog. Upon hearing the dog was safe and sound, his agitation and chest pain disappeared.

In this case, the anxiety caused by concern over his dog (his belonging and love needs) had the potential to increase his physical distress. Once these needs were met, the gentleman was able to benefit from the care designed to decrease his physiological and safety distress. As the nurse acted upon her client's Self-care Knowledge, her client was able to utilize external resources to help himself.

This discussion of need status and the holistic nature of the human being brings up another topic: How need satisfaction affects our relationships with others. This will be discussed next.

BEING OR DEFICIT RELATIONSHIPS

Being Orientation

How our needs are met across our life span influences our relationships with others. When we have our needs met repeatedly, we build need assets. These assets affect how we think about others, how we relate to them, and what meaning they have for us. A person with healthy positive residual is able to withstand the loss of Basic Needs satisfaction for periods of time.

Maslow postulates that self-actualizing needs (or Growth Needs) are dominant in people who have acquired a solid foundation of Basic Needs satisfaction. While all people have Growth Needs, they are suppressed if Basic Needs are not met. People who have such a foundation of need satisfaction develop a way of thinking about others and relating to them. It is called Being Motivation. Their behavior is motivated by Being values and characteristics (See Figure 6.2).

People with Being Motivation exhibit a drive to learn and grow, find meaning in their lives, and relate to others with true reciprocity. They are not concerned with safety issues and do not seek relationships to meet safety needs. They have the ability to focus on others rather than themselves. Their Growth Needs can be met when they are able to facilitate growth in others. However, they don't focus on others or facilitate others at their own expense! They actually gain a deep sense of enjoyment when they observe growth in others; they do not perceive that another person's growth is their loss.

They enjoy receiving, but also have their needs met when giving to others. Although needs gratification seems to be very egocentric, the healthy self-actualized individual is, typically, both self-confident and altruistic. They can satisfy their own needs without being driven by what others think or say, and are far more likely to be concerned about the welfare of others than those who have Deficit-Type Motivation. They have a healthy ratio of affiliated-individuation.

Persons with Being Motivation often transcend the physical plane; they are able to see potential good in others and in the world. They simply seem to have a storehouse full of need assets, so it takes little to get unmet needs satisfied. It takes little for them to change a negative experience into a positive one, and little to find the strengths in their significant others. They are happy people with a high level of well-being. Take for example, Faith.

> *Faith, a 67-year-old retired school teacher has osteoarthritis as well as mild hypertension. Despite these chronic health problems, she is physically active and has minimal complaints. Faith teaches an art class and chair yoga three times a week at the local senior citizen group, and at the local elementary school, she participates in a reading program teaching children to read. In addition, she volunteers, through her church, helping people who are housebound. She also takes classes at the local community college. Her last class was on Art History during the Renaissance period. She plans to take an anthropology course next.*
>
> *Her children have asked her to slow down, to alter her busy schedule and move closer to them. She comments "I would love to be closer to you, but I get so much pleasure out of my life and the work I do here. I know I make a difference in the lives I touch and I get so much out of the time I spend with them. I always get more from them than I ever give."*

Faith exemplifies someone whose needs are motivated by a being-orientation. She has physical needs, which she addresses, but they do not monopolize her thinking. She is able to meet her Basic Needs without much trouble. Her lifestyle and choices indicate she is oriented towards Growth Needs satisfaction. She enjoys sharing herself with others and derives pleasure from giving from her heart and herself. She seeks out knowledge and understanding and is focused on learning and personal growth. She has a good grasp on her Self. Transcendence is a way of life for her.

Deficit Orientation

People who experience prolonged difficulty with need satisfaction often end up with deficit or deprivation need status. When this happens, they develop a way of relating to others known as a deficit orientation. Their motivation for relationships is based on this orientation.

Maslow (1968) stated that deficit-oriented people have difficulty finding ways to meet their own needs in a healthy way. As a result, they often seek others as a resource for their own need satisfaction. Instead of relationships based on mutual needs, they build relationships hoping to get their own needs met. Self-oriented and unable to perceive the world through other people's eyes, their behavior and interactions with others are driven by their unmet needs. They have an imbalance of affiliated-individuation. Some overly affiliate, others overly individuate.

Deficit oriented people can be easily threatened when they perceive the actions of their significant others are not aimed at meeting their needs. For example, Janice, who has a deficit-type orientation toward relationships, is married to Tim. When Tim decides to return to school to seek a BS degree and find a better job, Janice may see this as a rejection, a threat to her personal need status. While Tim may try to explain this decision will make it better for both of them, Janice can only imagine Tim is "moving away," finding new friends, changing, and developing new personality characteristics. These perceptions result in more unmet needs, and possibly a feeling of deprivation.

Relations built on deficit-type motivation are rarely healthy. The partners have difficulty merging together to create a "unit" and concurrently accepting their partner's differences. Rather than relating to one another as the other half of a working unit, and a unique human being with differing views, likes and dislikes, deficit-oriented people want their partner to "view life through their eyes." People with deficit-orientation are attracted to the other person as a source for need satisfaction, not as a unique human being with unlimited growth potential.

This is not to say all people who seek a relationship to get their needs met are deficit-oriented. To the contrary, we all enter relationships with others to get our needs met. We all have an inherent drive toward safety and belonging, all of us will seek satisfaction of those needs through our relationships; that is the nature of a relationship. However, those with a deficit-orientation will seek need satisfaction even when the relationship is unsatisfying in many ways. For example, someone might enter a relationship to get safety needs met, but because of the relationship, they end up with loving and/or self-esteem need deficits.

Unfortunately, some people will stay in such relationships, and because of their deficit-orientation, they will chose one Basic Need over another. While they (and others) may perceive the behavior unhealthy, inappropriate, or even destructive, if they perceive no other choice, they may continue to repeat the behavior. This holds true for adults and children. For example, children who learn they can get attention (belonging) if they misbehave. Although they may be disciplined or even punished for their behavior, they will continue to act-out if they are getting their belonging needs met through negative attention. Each time the behavior results in the need being met, it reinforces the behavior, even though it may result in unmet love needs.

How we relate to others is determined by how well our needs have been met over time. We learn how to relate with others through past relationships with others; the cycle continues. We are motivated by what we have experienced.

CONFLICT THEORY

Another important factor in human motivation is the nature of conflict. Conflict is part of every day life, and conflicts occur because we have an inherent drive to survive and protect ourselves, as well as an inherent need to grow. Confronted with situations that require choosing between two or more outcomes, and faced with a conflict, we don't always find ourselves in a win-win situation. However, how we perceive a situation, our past influences, and our current perceptions, determine the kind of conflict we experience. A simple conflict for one person may be seen as a major catastrophic conflict for another. While conflicts create unmet needs and interfere with our ability to mobilize resources, they also offer opportunities for need satisfaction. It all depends on how we perceive the situation.

Types of Conflict

Maslow (1943) discusses four types of conflict people experience shown in Table 6.1. Each is described below.

Table 6.1 Maslow's conflict theory	
Type of Conflict	**Nature of Conflict**
Approach-Approach	Person is caught between two equally attractive options
Approach-Avoidance	Person is simultaneously attracted and repelled by a single event.
Multiple approach-Avoidance	Person must choose among several options, all of which are both attractive and repellent.
Avoidance-Avoidance	Person is caught between two equally unattractive alternatives; two events or needs that are equally threatening; two options that have the potential for catastrophic outcomes.

Approach-Approach. This type of conflict is usually non-threatening although resolution requires the use of resources. With an Approach-Approach type of conflict, we usually get some of our needs met. We simply have to choose between two options. For example, you decide to have an ice cream cone. Now, you have to choose either Butter Pecan or Vanilla Cherry. You love both kinds, and either of the two options will meet your needs. You just have to choose which one will be best today! While this is a win-win situation, one option may result in more need satisfaction. Therefore, one option will build more resources than the other.

Approach-Avoidance. Approach-Avoidance conflict often relates to the tension caused by having to choose between safety-type needs and Growth Needs. Consider as an example, four year old Stacie who has security needs along with the need to make friends and explore beyond her family circle. When offered the option of going twice a week to a play-group where her friend Emily will be, she is excited and wants to go. But, when confronted with a choice of going to a play-group without mama or staying home, she has a typical Approach-Avoidance conflict. She wants to go, but not without mama. At the same time, staying at home with mama means she cannot go to the play-group and be with Emily, or try something new. She is both drawn toward and repelled from the choice of going and the choice of not going.

Multiple Approach-Avoidance. Multiple Approach-Avoidance conflict is Approach-Avoidance conflict with multiple options. In each case, there are both attracting and repelling factors. We can use the same example, only add another option: Stacie now has the options of going to the park with Mary (another friend) and her mother, going to play group with Emily, or staying home with mama. Which to choose? Again, the healthiest conflict resolution is for her to choose the option that will meet more needs than it will leave unsatisfied.

Avoidance-Avoidance. The Avoidance-Avoidance type of conflict differs considerably from the others. In this case, there is no positive outcome; both are perceived as threatening experiences, and both will result in unmet needs. Let's use the example of the person who has worked in a factory for the past 28 years and now learns that the factory will close. He is confronted with losing his job before he is eligible for retirement or moving across the country to work in another state at a lower income. He has to struggle between two options: one in which he will not be working and not be eligible for retirement; the other in which he has to leave his family and friends, assume the expenses of a move, and begin afresh with other people. Both are perceived as threatening; both have implied losses. This type of Avoidance-Avoidance conflict is not uncommon. The range in unmet needs that results from such a conflict can be from minimal to life threatening.

It is important for us to think about the choices we make, consider the conflicts involved, if any, and, if so, the type of conflict. As you will see in Chapter 11, we can learn to reframe threatening experiences so they are perceived as challenges, instead. When we do this, we can change almost any conflict into an Approach-Approach situation.

Learning to reframe our experiences helps us change our need status from a deficit to a satisfaction state. Over time, this affects how we live our lives and how we relate to others. Repeated need status influences our motivations and drives our behavior. It influences how we build relationships, alters how we experience conflict, and impacts our ability to become the most we can be, to self-actualize.

THE BEING PROCESS

We have an inherent drive to be all we can be, to self-actualize. This lifelong need motivates us to accomplish our life missions, and in the completion of that task gain a sense of self-fulfillment. In his book, The Farthest Reaches of Human Nature (1982), Maslow talked about the Psychology of Being, and addressed several of its attributes (pp.121-126) stating that self-actualizing is a process that includes "Transcending of time and space" (p. 123) and contains "states tending toward ultimate holism" (p. 124). These are moments when we become more fully connected to our Self, more holistic with mind-body-spirit integration. Earlier he had said:

> *We may define it as an episode, or a spurt in which the powers of the person come together in a particularly efficient and intensely enjoyable way, and in which he is more integrated and less split, more open for experience, more idiosyncratic, more perfectly expressive or spontaneous, or fully functioning, more creative, more humorous, more ego-transcending, more independent of his lower needs, etc. He becomes in these episodes more truly himself, more perfectly actualizing his potentialities, closer to the core of his Being, more fully human* (Maslow, 1968, p. 97).

Maslow (1982) provides 35 ways to think of Transcendence, a major characteristic of self-actualizing. Two of them are presented below.

> *•Transcendence in the sense of loss of self-consciousness, of self-awareness, and of self-observing...It is the same kind of self-forgetfulness which comes from getting absorbed, fascinated, concentrated. In this sense, meditation or concentration on something outside one's own psyche can produce self-forgetfulness and therefore loss of self-consciousness, and in this particular sense of transcendence of the ego or of the conscious self.*

> *•Transcendence in the metaphysical sense of transcending one's own skin and body and bloodstream, as in identification with the Being Values so that they become intrinsic to the Self itself (p. 259).*

Transcendence happens across the lifespan. It is the outcome of Peak Experiences: those seconds or moments in our life when everything seems to come together and take us to a higher place. According to Maslow (1968), when we are having a Peak Experience, we feel more integrated, more holistic, than at other times (pp.104-106). Clearly, Transcendence is self-actualizing and Peak Experiences are precursors to Transcendence. What then interferes with our natural propensity to self-actualize?

Maslow (1968, p. 46) stated that we all have two sets of forces, those that drive us forward and those that hold us back. How we experience conflict between these two forces determines our ability to have Peak Experiences and transcend. As we learn to accept ourselves as we are, we learn to become more of what we are meant to be; we learn how to Be and to Become. But, we are social beings; we need help learning to accept ourselves, love ourselves, and become the most we can be. We need help learning to self-actualize.

> *Being can mean 'expressing one's nature,' rather than coping, striving, straining, willing, controlling, interfering, commanding....It refers to effortless spontaneity which permits the deepest, innermost nature to be seen in behavior* (Maslow, 1982, p. 126).

Case Analysis

The drive for Affiliated-Individuation (AI) exists throughout our lifetime, but the nature of AI varies based on the age and stage of the person. AI is expressed differently in the infant than in the older child, the adult, or even the senior. In addition, what people need at each stage varies. Adam's story, presented at the beginning of this chapter, provides examples of healthy AI across the lifespan.

Throughout his life, Adam's choices, and words clearly indicate his strong healthy sense of both affiliation and individuation. As a baby, he is connected to his mother as he listens to her talk. He also separates or individuates when he turns his head away from her. As a toddler, he is able to physically remove himself from his mother while he plays, but he continues to need to be attached to her as evidenced by his frequent need to check in or refuel (Mahler, 1975). Refueling is essential at this age, since children have not yet built sufficient resources to be able to individuate for long periods of time.

As time passes, Adam continues to seek healthy affiliation as demonstrated by his request for his mother's help on the school project. He also demonstrates individuation in his choice to play a team sport in high school, the choice to be married, and attend the reunion with his wife.

It is important to note that Adam was able to fulfill his inherent need for affiliated-individuation because his caregivers gave him permission. They didn't force him to become something he didn't have a natural propensity to be. They reinforced his natural strengths and characteristics, and loved him for who he was. They created an environment where healthy affiliation could develop; Adam had a natural tendency to complement his affiliation with a sense of individuation. He was facilitated in simultaneously achieving a healthy balance between the two.

As Adam aged, he focused his attention first on his life work and then the value of his life. Adam was comfortable with who he was and why he was here on earth. When he approached death he was comfortable moving on; he knew that he had lived his life well and that his spirit would transcend physical life. It was not a difficult time for him; it was simply a time of transformation.

We all have needs that exist across our lifetime. We need to be affiliated and individuated. With our affiliation, we need to know we are loved and that we have loved, that the Essence of our Self is safe with those who love us, and that we can grow and become the most that we have the potential to be without threat of loss of love and acceptance. With our individuation, we need to know that we are accepted for who we are without façade, pretense, or conditions. We also need to be able to pursue our Life Purpose, to discover our Reason for Being.

> *As humans, we have these needs throughout our life; as health care providers we have an obligation to help people satisfy these needs to the best of our ability. We know we cannot live another person's life, so we have to learn that the best way for us to meet our obligation to others is to become the most we have the potential to be, to help ourselves self-actualize as much as possible. As we learn our own lessons, travel our own pathway, trust in ourselves, and learn from our mistakes, we pursue the Being Process. When this happens, we are able to put loving, unconditional energy into the environment that will help others. We do not have to do; we only need to Become* (H. Erickson, personal communication, February 28, 2006).

ENDNOTES

[1] We may also be addressing the need for information, beauty, and order; we never know for certain, since it is more difficult to know when another person is experiencing Growth Need satisfaction than it is to assess Basic Need satisfaction.

[2] Keep in mind that people with multiple unmet needs have limited resources. Those with multiple need deficits or need deprivation are at a greater risk. They simply don't have the resources to mobilize, plus, they have learned there are no resources that can be mobilized.

[3] For some this may seem far-fetched, but we need to remember that we are holistic people. Recent studies have shown that a neuropeptide, Ghrelin, triggers hunger sensations. Since we know we can effect changes in neuropeptides by what we feel and think (see Chapter 3), it is not a far reach to think we could learn to allay Ghrelin by visualizing the eating, digesting and metabolizing of food!

CHAPTER 7

ATTACHMENT, LOSS, AND REATTACHMENT

MARGARET E. ERICKSON

As an eleven-year-old, I was an avid reader. One Christmas, I received a box of Harlequin Romance books my younger sister had picked up at a library book sale. They were used and a bit ragged. On Christmas morning, none of that mattered. I was delighted with my gift. My sister had understood me, had stepped into my world, knew what I enjoyed, and had given it to me. This gift had several meanings: first, it met my needs to be accepted (esteem needs). Because it came from someone who was important to me, it also met my belonging needs. I felt connected to her and assumed she was to me since she knew what I wanted.

I also knew the box of books had exceeded her Christmas budget. This unselfish act on her part indicated her love for me. Thus, this box of books also met my need to be loved. I felt happy. This magnificent box of ragged books helped me feel secure in our relationship. To this day, my favorite one sits on my bookshelf. Although it is taped together and the pages are brittle, it still evokes memories of one of the best Christmas presents I ever received.

OVERVIEW

What do we mean when we say things like, "I need to see my friend," "That is my favorite book," "I just love that shirt!," "I feel uneasy until I've had time to think about what I want to say in that paper," "I don't think I can get along without my cat," "I've felt lousy ever since I said that to my friend," "I've been lost since my wife died"? Is this frivolous talk or do these common phrases carry important meaning? Helen Erickson (1997), said cues are embedded in ordinary language, which nurses need to interpret in order to grasp what is important to their clients. Embedded cues are often difficult to interpret, unless you have a theory to use. However, interpretation helps nurses understand the significance of every day comments, and this understanding is necessary before purposeful interventions can be designed.

According to H. Erickson (1976) and Erickson, Tomlin and Swain (1983), any object which meets our needs repeatedly becomes an attachment object (pp. 88-92). People may attach to animate objects such as a person or pet, inanimate objects like a book, a bicycle, or abstractions such as an idea, a bright blue sky with lazy clouds floating overhead, or even a life goal. Loss occurs whenever there is a real, threatened, or perceived loss of the attachment object. While a person's ability to contend with the loss is determined by their ability to mobilize resources, loss resolution is necessary to move on with life, heal, grow, and develop.

This chapter expands on the mid-range theories of Attachment-Loss-Reattachment and Needs-Attachment-Developmental Residual previously presented by H. Erickson (1983, 1990b) and Erickson et al. (1983).

BACKGROUND

Needs are innate instincts that give rise to an internal drive when imbalanced....Needs must be met repeatedly for object attachment to occur. Object attachment facilitates achievement of developmental tasks, which produces growth to a higher level of development...Transference occurs when an individual has outgrown an object or when there's been a resolved loss (H. Erickson, 1976, pp. 1-3).

The idea of attachment objects is not new. It was first presented by Freud (1920), but did not become a key aspect of psychoanalytic thinking until Fairbairn (1952); Klein (1952); Winnicott (1953); Bowlby (1958, 1969, 1973, 1982); Ainsworth (1968), Fraiberg (1967); and Robertson and Robertson (1969) presented their ideas about object phenomena. Each of these made a major contribution to the Object Relations theory; each discussed it within the context of their discipline.

Bowlby's Contributions

Perhaps the work that has the most importance for Modeling and Role-Modeling theory was presented in Bowlby's trilogy: Attachment (1969), Separation (1973), and Loss (1982). These books set standards for the attachment-separation-loss process. Two case studies videotaped by Robertson and Robertson (1968, 1969), Bowlby's colleagues, illustrate young John and Jane's responses when separated from primary caregivers over a period of time. These films demonstrated that separation produces feelings of loss, and without alternative attachment objects, the grieving process results. The Robertsons noted that unresolved grief had long-term effects on the child's relationship with its caregiver.

Through their seminal work connecting attachment with loss and grief, Bowlby and colleagues helped health care providers understand the consequences of separating parents and children during hospital stays. As a result of their work, most pediatric units now have open visiting hours with sleeping accommodations for parents. Their contributions will be described in more detail below.

Attachment theory and Modeling and Role-Modeling

While early work on attachment is extensive and convincing, the authors focused primarily on objects as phenomena and on linkages between attachment objects and loss. Their goal was to address what happened when loss was unresolved. They did not address how to facilitate healthy growth and development, healthy ways to resolve losses, and the implications of morbid grief. Nor did they connect attachment phenomena with needs theories and developmental processes. This was the contribution of the Modeling and Role-Modeling theory (1983).

Preliminaries: H. Erickson Postulations

Attachment, Loss, and Grief. Since the mid 1970's H. Erickson has talked about attachment phenomena and their importance in nursing. She postulated relationships among attachment, loss, grief, and prolonged morbid grief; and proposed linkages among attachment status, needs satisfaction, and developmental processes in 1976. She stated:

> *An object that repeatedly meets one's needs becomes an attachment object. When that object is lost, grief results. Loss occurs whenever the individual perceives that loss has occurred. Loss can be real, threatened or perceived. It cannot occur until attachment (to the object) has been established. Loss always results in a grieving process. Morbid grieving occurs when there's an unresolved conflict, ambivalence or guilt associated with the loss and or there is inadequate transference (of attachment to another object). Morbid grieving interferes with resolution of developmental tasks* (Personal communication, September 19, 1976).

She went on to say that attachment can be either secure or insecure, and that insecure attachment takes two forms, clinging or push-away behavior. In either case, insecure attachment can interfere with our ability to produce healthy developmental residual as we work thought developmental tasks. On the other hand, secure attachment (the basis for feeling safe and secure), helps us produce healthy residual.

H. Erickson credits three key authors as her source for understanding how attachment phenomena relate to loss, normal grief, and morbid grief. These are: Engel (1964, 1968), Kuebler-Ross (1969), and Bowlby (1958, 1969, 1973, 1982). Each will be discussed briefly in the next section, but first the contributions made by H. Erickson, C. Kinney, and I will be presented.

The Old You, Now You, and New You. Helen Erickson proposed a model that can be used in practice based on the attachment-loss-grief mid-range theory. She called this model "The Old You, Now You, and New You" (1983). This model, developed to help RN students discover what interferes with their ability to grow and develop, is based on her ideas about attachment objects, need satisfaction, loss, and grief. She emphasized the necessity of letting go of the lost object in order to move on and continue to grow. She argued that giving-up on a lost object results in prolonged grief and can evolve into morbid grief.

H. Erickson's early work provided the base for the first publication, *Modeling and Role-Modeling: A Theory and Paradigm for Nursing* (1983), which she co-authored with Evelyn Tomlin and Mary Ann Swain.

Later, when discussing how to work with adults on Generativity (2002), H. Erickson stated there are soul-related needs which differ from biophysical needs. She proposed that loss of soul-related needs might be more devastating than other types of losses. These ideas were not expressed in the original Modeling and Role-Modeling publication (Erickson et al., 1983) although they might have been implied in the holistic person model proposed in that work (p.45), and reproduced in this book in Chapter 1 in which she talks about the Soul and spirit of the holistic human being.

C. Kinney's Contribution

C. Kinney, a colleague of H. Erickson's, adopted Modeling and Role-Modeling for her professional practice. Early on, she focused on linkages among attachment-loss-reattachment and life span development. She developed a model labeled the Attachment-Loss-Reattachment Life-Span Development Model (1990a) (see Figure 7.1) to show linkages that included types of attachment with developmental processes and health outcomes. Applying these concepts in her private practice, she presented an elegant case study (Kinney, 1990b) describing a client's process of growth, healing, and development. This case study illustrates how early life relationships affected her client's world-view and how she, as a practitioner, interpreted her client's data and used it to plan interventions. Kinney builds on this case study in Chapter 9 of this book as she describes the importance of a trusting and functional nurse-client relationship, built on heart-to-heart connections.[1]

M. Erickson's Contributions

Using the Modeling and Role-Modeling theory and paradigm as a context, I focused on teenage mothers and their ability to attach to their infants. I believed that the mothers' need status has been overlooked as a predictor for how well they attach with their babies. Although the literature provides ample evidence that infant attachment is important, maternal attachment is often neglected.

I proposed that a process occurs; attachment doesn't just happen. It is the result of healthy bonding. I believe bonding starts when needs are first met by a maternal-infant connection. After repeated need satisfaction, bonding occurs and attachment follows. I labeled this the Bonding-Attachment Process (1994). Later, I developed the Erickson Maternal Bonding-Attachment Tool (EMBAT) (1994) to test my hypothesis that the mother's type of orientation, i.e., Deficit versus Being orientation, affects maternal bonding and attachment. Initial results provided reliability and validity for the EMBAT.

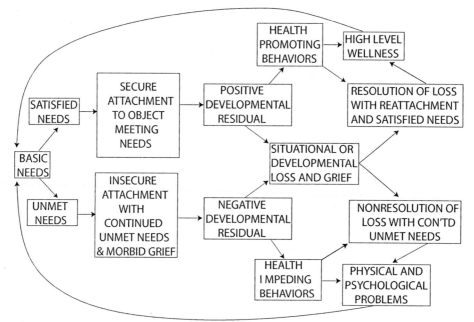

Figure 7.1 The Kinney Attachment-Loss Model. Produced here with permission of C. Kinney, 2/22/2006

While several instruments that measured either maternal bonding or maternal attachment (Avant, 1981; Cranley, 1981; Leifer, 1977; Muller, 1993) existed, none were designed to measure either phenomena as sequential or contextual. That is, there were no instruments designed to assess attachment as an outcome of bonding and there were no instruments that measured attachment within the context of the mother's underlying motivation for her relationship with her infant. A follow-up study was designed to further test the Erickson Maternal-Infant Bonding-Attachment Instrument (EMIBAI), developed in an earlier study (Erickson, 1996b), as a sequential and contextual instrument.

Results provided evidence that Bonding is a precursor to Attachment and there is a Bonding-Attachment Process (1996). This work will be presented in an upcoming book, *Modeling and Role-Modeling: Research Findings and Measurement Issues* (Erickson, H. (Ed.), 2007). While this tool was specifically developed for teenage mothers, the Bonding and Attachment mid-range theory can be applied to all age groups. Implications for other relationships will be discussed later in this chapter.

Conclusions

The ideas of attachment phenomena, loss and grief are not new. They have been proposed and studied by members of various disciplines. Nevertheless, linkages proposed in Modeling and Role-Modeling offer new ways to connect old ideas and add new dimensions. While previous authors discussed various relationships among attachment, loss, grief, and reattachment, these were not described in detail. Furthermore, secure and insecure attachment, the Bonding-Attachment Process, and implications for morbid grief have been glossed over. I hope to add to your understanding of these concepts in the following sections.

ATTACHMENT: PREREQUISITE FOR GROWTH

Attachment Phenomena

Attachment objects are essential

Attachment objects are a necessary part of life. They serve as a vehicle for need satisfaction, a precursor for growth. Usually, discussions focus on attachment objects that satisfy biophysical-psychosocial needs. That is, we discuss how these objects meet needs deemed important in the Modeling and Role-Modeling theory: physiological, safety and security, love and belonging, esteem, self-esteem, affiliated-individuation, information, and various types of growth needs. The holism model (Figure 1.3 in Chapter 1) indicates we have several subsystems, all of which interact continuously. Assuming this model reflects reality, we can think of the human as multiple dynamic subsystems, continuously interacting (Erickson et al., 1983, pp.47-48). This means that something which meets one's needs in one subsystem will impact another. The importance of attachment objects is obvious; what might seem to be a social attachment object (such as perceptions of one as a nurse) has the potential to affect the well-being of the entire person. Attachment to the object can result in chemical changes in other subsystems. On the other hand, so can loss of the object.

Attachment objects are unique to the person

Attachment objects are as varied as human beings. The same object may be important to several people, but for different reasons—it may meet different needs for each individual. Or, an object might be very important to one person, but viewed as junk by another. The story I presented at the beginning of this chapter provides an example. While those books were special to me, my younger brothers looked at my treasured box of books and said, "Yuk! Who would want that old box of dirty books about hugging and kissing?" Clearly, what meets the needs of one person may be seen as repulsive by another.

Attachment objects are very personal and related to specific developmental tasks. That is, at each stage of life we have specific tasks to work through. Therefore, needs are met in specific ways depending on the stage-related task. What meets our needs becomes an attachment object, so attachment objects are both personal and age-related. What works at one stage is not usually helpful at another.[2] World-views determine what is meaningful to individuals and, therefore, what meaning an object has for them.

Attachments and Stored Memories

Sometimes our first encounter with an object affects us profoundly. It meets many needs at one time. Multiple chemicals are produced in response, and when the experience is intense, multiple chemicals, neurotransmitters, and hormones are excreted. As discussed in Chapters 2, 3 and 4, the memories are stored in our cells as chemicals and energy.

Recall of the experience depends on reconnecting with the object or something associated with the object that initiated the response. When we reconnect with the same experience either through the object, by thinking of it, or associating with it, we stimulate a similar cellular response. For example, whenever I think of the moment I opened that marvelous box of books, I can feel the excitement, joy, and connectedness. My cells are flooded with the chemicals and neurotransmitters related to these feelings, which are almost as strong as they were the first time I had them. These feelings are emotionally experienced, stored and can be remembered at the cellular level. Re-experiencing these feelings (or stored memories) is part of what we call Self-care Knowledge. See Chapters 3 and 4 for more information on this topic.

> Attachment objects are unique to the individual and depend on one's world-view. We cannot understand the importance of any object for any other person without first modeling their world.

Transitional Objects

H. Erickson (1976) and Erickson et al. (1983), discussed transitional objects as objects that represent an important attachment object and are usually age-specific (pp. 68-69, p.177). Examples of transitional objects include the blanket often favored by the infant—a blanket that represents the care provider's comfort; a picture of the mother taken to day care—a picture that helps the child remember the mother; the favorite baseball cap of the middle-aged child—a cap that reminds him of his friends, and so forth.

The purpose of transitional objects is twofold: first, they meet needs in lieu of the attachment object, which they represent or symbolize, and second, they facilitate normal, healthy developmental processes. That is, they help people let go of attachment objects acquired in one stage of life,[3] so they can move on to the next stage. They enhance transitions!

> Transitional objects are specific to the person, symbolize an attachment object, are inanimate or nonhuman, and are frequently experienced through one or more of the five senses: touch, sight, smell, sound, and hearing. Items such as a warm fuzzy blanket, a photograph, a letter or a business card are common transitional objects.

Transitional objects are extremely important as they help people feel connected to significant attachment objects when separated from them. Erickson et al. (1983), illustrating the importance of transitional objects, offered the following example:

> *...the small child who is experiencing separation-individuation anxiety when mommy goes off to work. When asked what will make him feel better, he might say, "To have mommy with me." Why not give him mommy, then? That is, why not give him mommy in a symbolic yet concrete way? A picture of mom, tucked or pinned to his undershirt, somewhere he can feel it, will often relieve such anxiety and facilitate this small child's march out into the big, scary world* (p.122).

"This example has been recommended to many mothers who sought help with children reluctant to go to day care or nursery school. Interestingly, many reported that their children coped very well with such a simple intervention" (H. Erickson, personal communication, October 11, 2005).

Stage-Related Transitional Objects. As stated above, transitional objects not only meet needs during daily situations, they are also important during times of change. In other words, transitional objects help us move from one stage of development to another, for example, the toddler's blanket, teddy bear, or other inanimate object that helps him be safe at night while he learns to sleep on his own, to be autonomous. His blanket symbolizes his attachment to his mother or caregiver; it meets his need to have a consistent caregiver. It helps him to continue building a sense of Trust even as he moves into Autonomy.

Consider other examples commonly experienced across the life-span: the new college student hauling his favorite pillow off to school, because it makes him feel better; the tradition that a new bride wear "something old"—something old that is usually kept as a memento of the wedding; and so forth (see Table 7.1). Each of these objects are transitional objects—objects that help us move from one stage of life to another. Each meets our needs, gives us the courage to move forward, gain a deeper understanding of who we are, and achieve our potential.

Table 7.1 Examples: Needs, Attachment Phenomena, and Transitional Objects by Stage

Stage	Needs	Attachment Object	Transitional Object
Trust	Belonging	Primary caregiver	Blanket, pacifier.
Autonomy	Safety	Caregivers	Blanket, pillow, favorite toy.
Initiative	Self-esteem	Caregivers, significant others	Toy, doll, clothing.
Industry	Esteem	Caregivers, friends	School binder, homework project.
Identity	Belonging	Peers	School jacket, group pictures.
Intimacy	To love	Significant other	Note from significant other, picture, wedding ring.
Generativity	Self-esteem	Significant other, colleagues	Awards, recognition of Productivity.
Ego Integrity	Being loved	Family members	Memorabilia.

Table 7.1, above, provides examples of various needs and common attachment phenomena. It should be noted these are not inclusive. Some people have very different attachment objects and never experience any of those shown in this table. Many factors play into such variance in the population. Things such as culture, religion, ethnicity, and geographic location have an important influence on the type of object that would meet a person's needs.

Transitional Objects and Affiliated-Individuation. As time passes, most attachment and transitional objects are relegated to the past and are no longer needed, like the frayed teddy bear needed when we were first learning to sleep on our own. As we change over a life-time and find new "security objects," most of us come to recognize the "bear" as an old, ragged bear we needed once, but no longer meets our needs. When this happens, it is tossed aside without further thought.

There are times when we never seem to outgrow the memory of an attachment object because it represents a significant person or time in our life. Under such circumstances, the memory of the object evokes feelings first created by the object.

Years ago Dolly Parton wrote the song " A Coat of Many Colors." In it she describes her early years as a child and how her mother sewed her clothes to save money. One winter, her mother made her a coat from scraps of material, rags, and clothes that no longer fit. Dolly loved the different colors and patterns; she didn't care it was different from those worn by other children. She didn't see it as a coat she had to wear because they didn't have money to buy one, or as an object of derision, embarrassment, or shame. Instead, it was perceived as a wonderful gift from her mother. It evoked feelings of love, comfort and well-being; it also kept her warm.

Years later, her attachment to this coat was demonstrated when she wrote about it and the experience of receiving it. This object—her beloved coat—met her need for affiliated-individuation. It helped her feel a sense of security, love and belonging, and esteem, so she could continue her work on the task of Initiative, and make her way in the world outside her immediate family. Nevertheless, she would always carry with her the stored memories of her affiliation with her mother.

Here is another example of a transitional object, one that we all can carry with us without difficulty.

> *Tom, an elderly patient with COPD, was anxious about going home from the hospital. I asked him what he was most concerned about. He stated, "When I am here, I can reach you whenever I need you. When I go home, you won't be there. When I have trouble, I'll be alone." With his concern in mind, I gave Tom my business card with my telephone number on it. He looked at it, put it in his wallet and said, "Thanks. I feel a lot better now. Although you won't be physically with me, I'll always feel like you are here (pats his chest) with me."*

Sometimes transitional objects that meet affiliated-individuation needs are less obvious, but still important. The following story illustrates this point.

> *My brother owned a beloved pair of tennis shoes. He and his shoes were inseparable. They were with him through high school, on the night of his high school graduation, and on his first day of college. They had camped with him, run with him through the dorm hallways, played tennis, worked with him on hot roofs when he worked in construction, and were present for many of his other life events, experiences, and adventures. These shoes were highly valued; they ranked very high among his personal items. It didn't matter that they were filthy, had more holes than cloth, and were held together by duct tape.*
>
> *Although he treasured them, our mother was appalled he had been wearing them long past their natural demise. She suggested, over the*

years, he get rid of them and buy some decent shoes. She offered to pay for new ones, but he was not ready to part with them.

After college graduation, he prepared for an adventure; he had joined the Peace Corps. The night before he left, he told our mother she could throw out his shoes—he was now ready to let go of them. They had served their purpose. He no longer needed them to get his needs met. He had moved into another developmental stage where the old shoes no longer had meaning. He was ready to find new attachment objects. The beloved old, ragged shoes were now just that—old, ragged shoes that would always be remembered by many of us, but would no longer be needed in the material form.

In this example, the shoes probably were unimportant when first purchased, but as time went by, they took on new significance. They were comfortable, easy to put on, and different from what most kids wore in a cold, wet climate. His family and friends often asked him why he didn't wear boots or "decent shoes" that would keep his feet warm and dry as he trudged through the cold wet snow. He enjoyed "being himself"; he wore what he wanted. The familiarity was more important than the physical comfort.

Since he wore these shoes during the stage of Identity, a time in life when we sort through how we are like our significant others and also different from them, they were important symbolically. They met his needs through most of his adolescence and into young adulthood. When he came home from college, he had worked through the first few years of Identity and was ready to move on. His shoes were no longer important or useful to him at this point, he tossed them out.

Interestingly, when he decided to throw them away, our mother decided to retrieve them! Because they represented his adolescence, search for independence, and his successful achievement of personal Identity, they helped her feel connected to him as he left home. They helped her remember the child, even as the man stepped forward. The old, ragged shoes became her transitional object, which she kept until he returned home several years later. Upon his return, they once again became "old, ragged shoes" and were sent to the trash bin. They are gone, but the memories live on.

Many of us have had similar experiences. A favorite book, shirt, toy, etc., is no longer used in the traditional way, but evokes such strong feelings and memories that we continue to keep it long after it can be used for its original intent. I was only eleven years old when I received my "box of books." Nevertheless, when I think of that one book still sitting on my shelf, I re-experience the feelings I had when I received the entire box. While I no longer need the entire box to initiate the memory, a single book (and even the memory of the book) serves to recover those feelings of security and belonging, and of being loved.

Soul-related Objects

Although we typically talk about attachment and transitional objects that meet our biophysical, psychosocial or cognitive needs, H. Erickson suggested (2002) there are also objects that meet our Soul needs. She proposed that some objects may be more important because they represent factors that support the Self. In a personal conversation she expanded on this stating,

> *According to philosophers like Zukav (1989), the Soul is the seat of the Self. Needs related to our Self help us discover and fulfill our Life Purpose because we connect our human body with the Soul through our spirit. Needs related to our biophysical-psychosocial being support our mind and body as we take our life journey. These are body-emotion-mind needs. Attachment objects that meet these needs nurture our biophysical, social, emotional, and cognitive needs. Satisfaction of spiritual needs (which connect us with our Soul) helps us find meaning in our lives. While satisfaction of all types of needs is important and must be repeatedly achieved across a lifespan for maximum health and well-being, needs that help us connect with our Soul are probably much more important.*
>
> *Objects that help us meet our Soul-related needs (or spiritual needs) are very different from those that help us meet our biophysical-psychosocial type needs. Our attachment to objects that meet our spiritual needs might take on more meaning than we had ever imagined. While it might seem that Soul-related needs emerge more in the later stages of development, I have seen many children who exhibit signs of spirituality.*
>
> *I'm convinced spiritual needs exist across the lifespan. When they are satisfied, we experience transcendence. If this is the case, an object that helps us meet these needs would be important at any stage of life. For example, I decided to be a nurse when I was around five years old and never deviated from that decision. I think nursing is my "calling," it is an attachment object for me; it is a way of thinking and a way of being. 'Nursing' helps me find and define meaning and purpose in my life, and has helped me define my relationship with my family, an important part of discovering my Life Purpose* (Personal communication, October 20, 2005).

Spiritual attachment objects are extremely important. A friend of mine, Bala Jassen, said life is about learning how to align our biophysical, social and emotion spheres in our lives with our Soul's purpose. I think my family and Nursing has helped me do that (H. Erickson, personal communication, October 20, 2005).

THE BONDING-ATTACHMENT PROCESS

I have already mentioned that human beings have a need to be attached to people, things, and ideas throughout the lifespan. This is a part of our nature. I've also reiterated that attachment occurs when needs are met. This leads to a discussion about the bonding-attachment process. Bonding can occur without attachment, but attachment cannot occur without bonding. Bonding starts with the first sensation of being connected (because our needs are met), and continues until attachment occurs. It is a part of the attachment process, so I call it the Bonding-Attachment Process (Erickson, M. 1994).

> Attachment is not something that happens instantaneously; it is an outcome of bonding. When we begin to feel connected, bonding starts. When we acquire a sense of connectedness, we experience attachment.

The relationship between bonding and attachment is comparable to the relationship between growth and positive residual. Growth always precedes developmental residual, but growth can happen without creating residual. Furthermore, developmental residual can be enhanced throughout the life-time as we grow. Likewise, bonding continues even after attachment occurs because the object repeatedly meets the same needs, meets new needs, or because the object meets needs from a different developmental perspective. As bonding continues, the strength of the attachment increases.

But, time does not stand still. When an object no longer meets our needs, the bonding "becomes unglued," attachment diminishes, and the object loses significance and we let-go of the object. As we do this, we concurrently initiate the bonding-attachment process with a new object. This pattern of bonding, attaching, letting-go and reattaching occurs repeatedly across the life span in the healthy person. It is part of the final phase of life, Transformation, when the spirit separates from the body. But, where does it start? Here are my thoughts and the implications.

In the Beginning

Our biophysical lives begin when two cells connect, work together in a synergistic relationship, and begin to grow together to create a new life. We know this from our understanding of embryological growth. We might say this is the first type of bonding in human life.

But, what about the spirit?

In Chapter 1 H. Erickson posed the question, "Which comes first: body or Soul?" What if the Soul comes first? She posed that the Soul comes first. She went on to say that the spirit is energy derived from the Soul, vibrating at a lower level, so it can integrate with the human form. I built on this idea in Chapter 5 when I described the stage of Integration, saying that our spirit integrates with our body before or shortly after birth. If these ideas resonate with you, then it is possible to believe that the first incidence of bonding is the integration of spirit with biophysical body. The implications for such a consideration are immense. But, let me start with the idea of attachment of the spirit with the biophysical-psychosocial being.

Connecting Body with Soul

In Chapter 1, H. Erickson proposed that the Self is the purest form of who we are within this lifetime and that being in touch with our Self is how we can uncover our Life Purpose, better understand the implications of our life journey, and find meaning in our life. She also proposed that people often have difficulty uncovering the purpose for their existence, so they have difficulty finding meaning in their lives. This is because they have not fully integrated spirit with human form. H. Erickson states that the greater our connection to our Soul, the clearer our Life Purpose and the easier it is to discover our Reason for Being. Perhaps the problem is not connecting with the Soul, but the spirit connecting with the body! Unless the spirit is well integrated with the body, it would be impossible to connect with the Soul, an energy that vibrates at a much higher level than that of the holistic being.

I think bonding of spirit with body comes before integration of spirit and body. Integration is a type of attachment, spirit to human form and vice versa. Although the spirit might bond with the body prior to or at the time of birth, bonding doesn't assure Integration. Integration is a two-way process: spiritual energy has to synchronize with the body-mind energy field and the body-mind has to synchronize with the spiritual field before integration can occur. It is a complementary process. When the two synchronize, we can assume bonding has occurred, and integration of body-mind-spirit has been initiated.

While this discussion may seem more conceptual than practical, the implications are important. It suggests our first attachment is of spirit with human form and human form with our spirit! The possibilities of secure and insecure attachment warrant further consideration.

> We can understand our Life Purpose, the implications of our life journey, and find meaning, only after we are well-attached, spirit with human form and vice versa.

Maternal-Infant Well-being

I believe the maternal bonding-attachment process starts during the developmental stage of Integration and provides us with a foundation. Perhaps the integration of spirit with the human form lays the foundation for building a maternal-infant relationship. As I've said in Chapter 5, the stronger the foundation, the more developmental residual we carry to the next stage of development. But, I also said in Chapter 5, prebirth development depends on the mother's well-being and the receptivity of the uterine environment.

Mother as a Reservoir of Resources

Throughout this discussion, I will use the word baby even though I am talking about the biophysical-psychosocial being others would define as an embryo, fetus, prenatal infant, and postpartum infant. While they distinguish among these four stages in order to define the developmental stage of the baby, this is not the point of this discussion. Therefore, the word baby refers to the embryo, fetus, prenatal infant, and finally, the postpartum baby.

Most healthy, happy women begin to feel connected to their unborn baby soon after they learn they are pregnant. They are excited about their pregnancy, eagerly anticipate the upcoming birth, and anticipate joy in motherhood. Over time, their feelings of connectedness evolve into an emotional attachment with their unborn infants (Erickson, M., 1996). This is because the pregnancy, the idea of being pregnant, being a mother, or some other aspect of the pregnancy meets their needs. These women have little trouble bonding and attaching with their unborn baby.

The opposite also exists. Some women are not excited about being pregnant; they do not want to be a mother and do not want their babies. They perceive the pregnancy and the idea of motherhood as a burden. Some lack support and feel overwhelmed. Clearly the pregnancy, the idea of being pregnant, being a mother, or any other aspect of the pregnancy do not meet the needs of these women. While they may get some needs met by the idea of having a baby, the connection is not strong enough to result in attachment.

> The maternal intrauterine environment serves as a reservoir of resources for the growing baby. The well-being of that environment impacts the baby's well-being.

Every woman creates a different environment for the baby's growth, embryo to full-term baby. Happy women secrete happy-type neurotransmitters such as serotonin and endorphins. They also have lower levels of free-floating cortisol and other stress hormones. They generally eat well, nourish their bodies with healthy foods and take care of the "baby's home before birth." While some may have difficulties with their pregnancy, they are able to overcome these and create a growth-producing environment for their babies.

On the other hand, mothers who are disconnected from their growing babies are less concerned about their prenatal babies' well-being. Although they may take care of themselves, they are not as concerned about providing resources for the baby. When they perceive the baby negatively, they also secrete neurotransmitters and other chemicals that have the potential to interfere with the baby's growth. Sometimes they take in foods or drugs that actually alter the baby's growth and impede healthy development.

Of course, life isn't this simple. There are many mixtures of feelings and each person is unique. Some are ambivalent: one day they are excited and the next day they are not. Their babies experience inconsistency between a healthy, peaceful growth environment and an unhealthy one. Most babies are able to adapt to the environment, but it might still have an impact on their overall well-being.

Maternal Orientation

As stated in Chapter 6, people whose needs are met repeatedly develop a Being Orientation while those, whose needs are met inconsistently or inadequately, develop a Deficit Orientation. Being Oriented people are concerned with the growth and uniqueness of the other member of the dyad, while Deficit Oriented people seek personal need satisfaction from the relationship. The two types of orientation have the potential to impact the maternal-infant bonding-attachment process.

Being Oriented mothers are more likely to connect with the baby since the anticipated relationship meets their belonging and growth needs, while Deficit Oriented mothers tend to connect with the baby because they hope the baby will meet their love and self-esteem needs. Imagine how disappointing it is for Deficit Oriented women when they are nauseated during the pregnancy, gain weight, lose physical agility, or are unable to go out with friends; these do not meet the need to be loved or feel good about one's self. Unless the mother is future oriented and can imagine the relationship several years down the road, she might have trouble bonding with her baby. As indicated above, this would affect the maternal environment.

> The mother's orientation to her baby has the potential to affect her bonding with the baby. Maternal bonding affects the baby's biochemical, neurotransmitter environment. This, in turn, affects the baby's ability to grow and develop, embryo to full-term baby.

Baby as a receptor

Babies will thrive when the environment is receptive and their needs are optimally satisfied. That is, when the mother is able to meet the baby's basic physiological needs as well as the need for a safe, secure, and loving environment, the unborn infant will not only survive, but also thrive.[4] The baby follows the predetermined growth pattern laid down by nature. On the other hand, inutero babies have more difficulty finding the resources they need when they experience an environment filled with stress-related neurotransmitters and chemicals. Some of these infants develop biophysical systems with slightly different chemical combinations from those who live in a low stress environment. The implications are significant.

Research shows teenage mothers, typically high-stressed, may experience less satisfaction with parenting, expend less time commitment to the parental role, and have less optional maternal-infant interactions than older mothers (Panzarine,

1989; Ragozin, Basham, Crnic, Greenberg, & Robinson, 1982; Seymore, Frothingham, Macmillan, & Durant, 1990). These mothers may also be less accepting, accessible, and sensitive to their children's needs (McAnarney, Lawrence, Ricciuti, Polley, & Szillagyi, 1986) as well as have inadequate knowledge regarding normal child health and development (Baranowski, Schilmoeller, & Higgins, 1990; Elster, McAnarney, & Lamb, 1983; Klein & Cordell, 1987; Parks & Arndt, 1990; Reis & Herz, 1987; Showers & Johnson, 1985; vonWindeguth & Urbano, 1983). Each of these can affect the maternal-infant bonding-attachment process.

Montagu (1960) described another postpartum factor that resulted from a high-stress intrauterine environment. According to him, these babies were often non-cuddler babies at birth and soon after birth demonstrated push-away behavior. The mothers often had difficultly comforting them, because they didn't respond to the usual maternal comforting strategies, such as cuddling, close contact, soft voice tones, and so forth.

Each of these factors can significantly impact the maternal-infant relationship. But, when compounded with a mother with Deficit Orientation, the impact can be much greater. Newborn infants, in the best of circumstances, need help as they struggle to achieve biophysical stability. When this problem is compounded by a mother who thinks her baby doesn't love her because she cries too much, doesn't respond to breast feeding, and so forth, she may feel her baby doesn't like her or is detached from her. She is likely to respond accordingly and disconnect from her baby. The relationship is reciprocal; the well-being of one determines the well-being of the other.

> Developmental residual laid down in each stage of life serves as a resource for future stages. The nature of the Maternal-infant Bonding-Attachment Process during the stages of Integration and Trust has the potential to affect the child's entire life. As care providers, we have the unique opportunity to facilitate mothers and their infants in developing and maintaining healthy, interactive, mutually satisfying relationships. This can be accomplished by respecting and unconditionally accepting clients and facilitating maternal and infant need satisfaction through healthy attachment objects.[5]

LOSS AND NEW ATTACHMENT OBJECTS

In the original book, H. Erickson and her colleagues (1983) described the relationships among attachment, loss, grief and attachment to new objects (pp. 88-92). Earlier in this chapter, I talked about attachment phenomena, the bonding-attachment process, and maternal-infant well-being as it relates to these concepts. This section is dedicated to three concepts: loss, grief, and resolution. Two types of losses are presented: Situational and Developmental. Normal and morbid grief will also be discussed. Attachment to new objects is the focus of loss resolution.

Attachment is necessary for us to grow and develop; so is loss! We have to learn to let go of objects in order to move on and tackle the next challenge coming our way.

Situational Losses

Life and Loss

Connecting to people, things, and ideas is part of every day life for most of us. When these "objects" repeatedly meet our needs, they take on a significance that is personal, unique to our world-view, and necessary for our growth and healthy development. Sometimes we attach to them.

Unfortunately, people often experience the loss of the object when least prepared. The more needs the object meets, the more intense the resulting loss. Sometimes we are facilitated in finding new attachment objects. This helps us work through the grief which results from the loss. But, sometimes it isn't so simple.

The loss of an object that meets our basic needs for safety, love and belonging is often the most difficult to resolve. For example, the loss of a parent during infancy can have a life-long effect. This is not a loss due to normal developmental processes; it is a situational loss humans are not prepared to cope with, even with help. Situational losses are very different from developmental losses, since usually, there is no opportunity for growth prior to the loss.

> Losses are situational and developmental. They can be real, threatened or perceived. Loss is always preceded by attachment and always produces a grief response. The intensity of the grief response depends on the nature of the attachment. When an attachment object meets multiple needs, and we perceive inadequate or unavailable new object(s) to meet those needs, loss resolution is more difficult. Sometimes people are unable to completely resolve the loss, but give-up trying. The result is Morbid grief.

We all experience multiple situational losses.[6] Some are obvious and some are more obscure. Many are perceptions unique to the individual. We lose our health, time, opportunities, treasured belongings, relationships, beliefs, control, physical objects, and so forth. The list goes on and on. In any case, the loss is real and very personal.

Loss is Personal

Many parents have made the mistake of trying to replace a child's old or missing toy or worn, filthy blanket, with a new one. From our perspective, the teddy bear is dirty, only has one eye, has been sewn several times, and is a "must go." From the child's perspective, it is a treasure. The new blanket or toy may be similar in appearance or even have identical physical properties, but it will never replace the loved and trusted one. When a loved or valued attachment object is taken from the owner, a loss is experienced. The type of reaction depends entirely on the value of the object to the owner and their perception of control over the loss.

Anticipatory Losses

If the person perceives the object no longer meets his needs, only minimally meets them, or the person feels in control of the situation, feelings of loss will be minimized and loss resolution will be much easier. Sometimes this happens with anticipatory loss. Take for example, Anne[7]:

> *Anne, who had been suffering from anxiety attacks and depression, arrived for her latest counseling session in high spirits. Her face was glowing, there was energy in her walk, and she was smiling. When asked what had brought about the change, she replied, "I finally left my husband and applied for a divorce. I feel freer than I have in years. I moved out of our house and found a new place I have been getting settled into. It's comfortable, cozy, and all mine."*

Anne had made the decision to leave her husband and perceived the experience in a positive, growth-oriented way. She had a new home she was excited about and felt like she had gotten rid of a burden, rather than experienced a major loss. This didn't happen overnight. Anne had been working on this decision for several months; she had been doing anticipatory grieving as she worked through her choices. By the time she realized the relationship was a burden and it stilted her growth, she had already worked through the loss, resulting grief, and moved on to another perception of herself, a new attachment object. In contrast, if Anne's husband had decided to get a divorce before she had the opportunity to work through these processes, we would have seen a different outcome. Anne would have felt a major loss and would have taken considerable time to work through her grief response.

Situational losses don't always offer such opportunities; many of them come when least expected and take their toll. Some losses are not anticipated. That is, sometimes we experience losses when planning for the future. These are challenging losses.

Challenging Losses

Feelings of loss may be experienced because of choices we make. For example, when we accept a new job away from the present location, which we perceive as an opportunity, we will have to leave our current home, support systems, and other attachment objects. In this situation, we would have less difficulty with the losses, since we have chosen to move. By the time the decision is made, we have already begun to bond with new objects. We have moved toward a new way of thinking about our work and ourselves in the work-related role. We may have decided how we can keep old support systems in new ways, and we may have already begun to bond with new support systems. The difficult part was the "deciding part"; once that is done, we have already moved through some of the grieving necessary for loss resolution. When we choose to make a change, we perceive control over our lives. It is easier to let go things we are leaving behind. The loss still exists, but the grieving process is much less significant. For some, it may not even seem to exist. But, it does. It is just perceived as an opportunity and/or a challenge. When we experience losses as opportunities or challenges, we move through the stages of grief more rapidly, with more positive anticipation, and less conflict.

Threatening Losses

On the other hand, when we experience losses that are outside our control, we feel threatened and have a different experience. From the observer's perspective, these may be real or not. That is, threatening losses can actually happen or can be perceived as possibly happening.

Threatening losses are more difficult to resolve. Let's use an example of what happens when we have to move, because we lost our job. This is a real loss, which can be perceived as threatening. Instead of anticipating our self in a new role, feeling good (self-esteem) about the change, and being excited about the opportunities, we have lost our image of ourselves as a productive, valued worker, to that of one without value. The loss of the job is not only a real loss of employment that can create unmet safety needs, but it also has, embedded in it, numerous other losses that can result in unmet needs at other levels such as feelings of belonging, esteem and self-esteem. These are real experiences and can have serious implications.

Other types of threatening losses range from things as abstract as the child's perception that the parent will detach[8] if they aren't good, to our perception that we will lose our job with the next group of pink-slipped employees. Again, loss is personal, so what may seem threatening to one person is not to another. We should never assume we know what is important to another person.

Threatening to Challenging. Sometimes when we anticipate a threatening loss, we are able to cope with the experience by mobilizing resources. Often we do this by "bargaining" with ourselves. This reframes the experience, making it a challenge. During these times, we consider the various options, weigh the positive and the negative aspects, and conclude that the benefits from the changes outweigh the disadvantages. When this happens, we have a "sense of control"; we are able to work through the loss and move on. People often need help with this process. Anne, described above, is just such a case. When she first arrived for counseling, she was threatened with loss. By the time she arrived for the session described above, she had reframed her perspective on the attachment object (i.e., her marriage), perceived the loss as an opportunity, and was ready to move on.

Developmental Losses

Along with situational losses there are also developmental losses related to our stages of development. As our needs change and we work through different developmental tasks, our attachment objects change. "For example, small children derive comfort and love from very concrete objects, while healthy, older people tend to attach to more abstract, symbolic objects (such as a role, identity, a place, a thought, a relationship or an ideal.)..." (Erickson et al., 1983, p. 91). Because we have an inherent drive to "develop," we cannot avoid the developmental tasks associated with our chronological age. For example, during early life we have to build Trust, Autonomy, and Initiative; these are our developmental tasks. We will be confronted with them and we will have to deal with them like every other human on earth. Objects that help us work through our tasks at each stage are important at the time, but as the work of the tasks varies, so must the attachment object. As we emerge into a new stage of development, we will experience real, threatened, or perceived losses of attachment objects that met our needs in the previous stage.

These losses are a normal part of life; they must happen for us to be able to move on and work on the next task. Nevertheless, we experience a sense of loss and grief. Our ability to resolve the loss is the same as in situational losses. The more resources we have, the easier it is to find new objects that will meet our needs. Table 7.1, above, provides some examples of attachment objects across the life span, objects that are related to specific tasks. Table 7.2 provides examples of normal developmental losses by age.

For more information on the relationships between need satisfaction, attachment, and developmental processes, refer to previous work by H.Erickson, (1990a); M. Erickson, (1996); Erickson et al., (1983); Kinney, (1990b); Kinney and Erickson (1990). Also, see Chapters 11, 12, and 14 in this book.

Table 7.2 Examples of Normal Developmental Losses	
Age	Developmental Loss
Infant	Weaning from bottle or breast
Child	Going to kindergarten/leaving home
Adolescent	Graduating from high school/ leaving behind old friends
Adult	Moving from single to married status Changes in jobs or job roles

Loss Produces Grief

A loss can only occur after an attachment has been established and all losses produce a grief response. As indicated above, a loss is sometimes minimal; we may have an opportunity to anticipate it, it is seen as an opportunity or a challenge, so the grieving process is completed fairly rapidly. Rather than feelings of sadness, we might express nostalgia. Nostalgia is a "tug to the past" and often precedes letting-go of the lost object.

A number of authors have written about mourning and grief, but as indicated above, three have influenced the authors of Modeling and Role-Modeling: Bowlby (1982), Engel (1968), and Kuebler-Ross (1969). Table 7.3 shows the stages of the grieving process as described by these authors. Interestingly, each of the authors included stages that symbolize healthy loss resolution and unhealthy resolution

Table 7.3. Stages of grief according to contributing authors

Engel	Kuebler-Ross	Bowlby
Shock/disbelief	Denial/shock	
Awareness	Anger/hostility	Protest
Resolution	Bargaining	
Loss Resolution	Depression	*Despair*
Idealization	Acceptance	*Detachment*

(Key: Healthy resolution; *unhealthy resolution*)

George Engel

Engel (1964) describes four healthy stages of grief as shown in Table 7.3. Losses are resolved by working through these processes. He also describes the stage of Idealization. This is the stage in which the individual is unable to resolve the loss, so the object becomes "bigger than life." When idealization occurs, the individual is unable to weigh positive and negative aspects of the lost object. It is idealized, remembered as "perfect," and the individual perceives that no other object is able to serve as a new attachment phenomenon. Since Engel discussed grieving as the process that happens when we lose someone or something important to us, the implications are extensive. For example, a person might spend a lifetime searching for the idealized lost mother. When idealization occurs, not only is the lost object remembered as perfect, but is sometimes "absorbed" by the grieving person. That is, the characteristics, behavior, attitudes, likes and dislikes of the lost object are adopted by the grieving person. In some cases, physical symptoms emerge as well. All of this is seen in morbid grief, which will be discussed below.

> Engel stated that idealization occurs most frequently when there is an unresolved conflict in respect to the lost object.

Kuebler-Ross

Kuebler-Ross (1969) also provided a way to think about the grieving process. Her initial work focused on the stages of death and dying. During that period, she identified a five-stage process we experience when we learn our time on earth is limited. She stated that people first enter a period of Shock, asking how this could be happening, sometimes stating it isn't really happening; it must be a dream. Observers might think the person confronted with the loss is denying it will happen, but Kuebler-Ross says they are only coping, in their own way, and they soon move into a stage of Anger.

When we enter this stage, our behavior is often focused on every thing and every one that has anything to do with our life. Nothing seems to be right! For example, we might be angry health care providers can't "fix" things, angry significant others don't know how to "make it right," angry we have "created this situation," and/or simply angry at the situation. Kuebler-Ross also talked about hostility as a possibility at this stage. I believe hostility is a sign of morbid grief and not a healthy response to the threatened loss of "the object," i.e., loss of biophysical life.

Kuebler-Ross's other stages, Bargaining, Depression and Acceptance, all seem to be consistent with a healthy grief response. During bargaining, the dying person tries to negotiate with others for a different outcome. For example, "What if I quit smoking?" or "What if I eat differently, or quit other unhealthy behavior?" When it appears bargaining isn't going to change the outcome, sadness emerges. While Kuebler-Ross labeled this stage depression, it should be noted there is a difference between clinical depression (that is a morbid response to loss) and a sense of depression that is temporary and directly related to the loss of an attachment object. I will call this deep sadness.

Finally, Kuebler-Ross talks about Acceptance. During this stage, the individual begins to accept the loss is real and initiates a letting-go process. In her later work, she stated those who were able to do this, to accept the loss of attachment to the physical body, were those who were able to envision spiritual life after physical death. This is comparable to the task work of the stage of Transformation, described in Chapter 5.

John Bowlby

Bowlby (1982) focused on the loss of the mother/caregiver figure, offered the stage of protest, and described it as a healthy response to the loss of the attachment object. During the stage of protest, the child cries and demonstrates anger that the object is gone. Bowlby also offers the stage of despair, which occurs when the child perceives the object is not going to return. During despair, the child may discontinue crying and simply withdraw. Minimal physical activity is noted when in despair and the child (or person) is vulnerable for physical illness. If the lost object is not recovered, detachment occurs. When detachment occurs, the child no longer tries to recruit people to bond with; in fact, they often push them away. Detachment in childhood is a precursor to a lifetime of detachment. Take for example the story of Teddy:

> *Teddy, a sweet, happy, and loving 18 month-old was admitted to hospital for pneumonia. Hospital rules prohibited his mother from visiting him. Initially, he was grief-stricken, crying for her all the time. Staff were busy attending to other children, and he was left to himself. As time passed, he became quieter and more withdrawn. After weeks of hospitalization, he was able to go home. His mother recognized he was much quieter, unsociable, unempathetic, and no longer the loving child she had admitted to the hospital.*
>
> *As years passed, Teddy continued to have problematic social relationships. He was unable to feel close to or develop any meaningful relationships with others. Decades later, he was arrested for his horrific crimes committed as the "Unabomber." At the time of his arrest, his mother said he had never been the same after his hospitalization. She stated that upon admission he had been such a wonderful little boy, but when he came home he had been disengaged and detached.*

Normal Grief

The normal Grief Process (Engel, 1968) should last no more than 12-14 months. Some resolve the loss sooner; others take a bit longer. It all depends on the significance of the loss and the individual's ability to replace the lost object with new objects. When the loss is significant, there is usually an acute phase of grief that lasts 1-4 months.

Initially, the grieving person demonstrates some or all the signs and symptoms shown in Table 7.4 (see below). It is not uncommon to see overt signs of stress that include altered physiological responses. Chapter 2 Mind-Body Relations and Chapter 8 Stress Theory discuss some of these normal biophysical changes. The immune system is often less effective, illness is observed, and so forth. This is common and should be considered a normal response. I've often heard students say they are sick, or they have a cold. When asked why they think they have a cold, they often respond with statements such as, "Things are really going lousy at home," "I've got two tests next week" or "My baby has been sick."

These are often normal life events with situational losses that have produced a grief process (Lindemann, 1952). Because they are holistic people, their bodies are vulnerable. Unable to mobilize necessary resources, they get physically ill. If I ask them when they think they will be well, most of them can put a time line on their illness. Normal grieving is time limited.

Common feelings described during the early phase of acute grieving include: lethargy or fatigue unrelated to physical activity; a "choked feeling," restlessness or inability to relax or sleep, tearfulness or on the verge of crying all the time, trouble sleeping, feelings of anger, tension, emptiness, sadness, being afraid, unusual somatic responses, and lowered self-esteem or uselessness. Other feelings can also be expressed, since each person has their own way of expressing grief.

The normal grief response diminishes with time. Signs of loss resolution (reversal of signs of loss as shown in Table 7.4) should be seen by six months. Generally, as the loss is resolved, new attachment objects emerge. Sometimes these are the same objects the person was attached to before, but they are perceived differently. That is, it is not uncommon for the person who has reattached to describe the object differently and identify how it meets his/her needs differently.

Table 7.4 Common signs and symptoms observed with acute grief

Signs	Observable Symptoms
Diminished productivity	Breathlessness
Forgetfulness	Strained facial expressions
Decreased ability to concentrate	Altered skin coloring
Preoccupation with lost objects	Wrinkled brow and base of nose
Decreased creativity	Mouth drawn down
Increased use of drugs	Decreased communication
Altered biophysiology	Increased illnesses
Accident proneness	Change in physical movement
Social withdrawal	Distancing
Sleeping difficulty	

Anniversaries

Often, people who have not resolved the loss of an object revisit the experience on the anniversary of the loss. This can happen for many years. Each year, the memories are re-experienced and grieving occurs again. Because state-dependent memory is so much a part of the holistic person, cellular response occurs with the memory and all the feelings are re-experienced. People often get physically sick on or around anniversaries (of a loss); some even take on the illness of the lost object. I remember a story told by H. Erickson that demonstrates this point.

Years ago, when I worked as a staff nurse at The University of Michigan Medical Center, we had a wonderful elderly couple who came to

us for their care. Survivors of a World War II German concentration camp, they came to the United States in the '50s to start over. They had three children, all grown and away from home. Whenever one of them came into the hospital, the other would spend most of his/her time there as well. They were fully devoted to one another. They told me they were able to get through the horrific experiences in the concentration camp because they knew they had each other.

One Fall, Mr. M, the husband, was admitted for a work-up to determine why he wasn't feeling well and to see what could be done. After several days of tests, he was diagnosed with a very rare case of leukemia. The interns and residents were excited because it was the first case ever seen at U of M Hospital. They didn't expect to ever see another case, so they hovered over Mr. M.

After several months of being admitted, discharged, and readmitted, Mr. M. presented himself for his final visit. His wife sat next to his bed the entire week. She was there when he died. When we finally convinced her to go home with her daughter, we were shocked to note her voice had changed. She sounded just like her husband! She walked like him, and had even taken on some of his mannerisms. All of this had happened in just a couple of hours. Exactly one year later, on the anniversary of his death, she was admitted to the hospital. We were once again shocked to see that she had not only taken on more of his mannerisms, but now she also exhibited the same signs and symptoms he had! Blood work showed that she, too, had a type of leukemia, but before it could be diagnosed fully, she died. She took her last breath on the anniversary of his death. As she took that breath, she looked toward the ceiling, smiled and called his name, then said, "Here I come." With that she left her biophysical body and moved on.

I often thought about this couple. I suspect the losses they had experienced as young people living in Germany, captured, imprisoned, and tortured were enough to result in morbid grief. However, they had each other. Such strong attachment helped them go on with life. The loss of such an attachment would be nearly impossible to replace at their ages. The grief was so acute Mrs. M lost her will to go on physically. I am convinced, however, that she moved on spiritually! I saw it happen! I don't really think this is morbid grief. It is knowing when to let go (Personal communication, 1976).

Morbid Grief

When the symptoms of grieving are as acute 12-14 months after the loss as they were the first few months, we should consider the possibility of morbid grief.[9] Morbid grief interferes with our ability to work on developmental tasks, rework earlier life tasks in healthy ways, and move on with our lives. Remember

Teddy, discussed above—Teddy who became the UnaBomber. As an infant, Teddy experienced abandonment. While the nurses and doctors probably gave him excellent care, his mother was not there. Unable to find a new object that would meet his needs repeatedly, he was unable to reattach. His sense of trust in his care-providers was not strong enough to compensate. He detached from the world around him. Incapable of trusting others to meet his needs, he lacked the resources needed to move into the next stage with healthy residual. Each task thereafter was approached from the negative side of the stage.

Although this is an extreme example of the consequences that occur when a person experiences a major loss and is unable to replace an attachment object, it clearly illuminates the devastating impact it had on Ted's ability to heal and move on in his life. Morbid grief results in an inability to move forward in the developmental process in a healthy way.

Prolonged Morbid Grief

Sometimes health care providers are fooled by the signs and symptoms presented by clients. They think these are related to recent events, and that nursing care should address the current medical problem. The MRM theory says people in morbid grief will only develop other problems if the original loss is not addressed. Take, for example, the following story told by H. Erickson.

Donna, a colleague who worked as a home health nurse, contacted me for help. She described her client, Mrs. B., as a difficult lady to work with; she said she had numerous medical problems. Although Mrs. B., seemed to understand what she was told to do to take care of herself, she never complied. The nurses who worked for the home care agency, believing they might be giving her too many instructions, decided to focus on one thing: a low salt diet. They theorized this might bring her blood pressure down, improve her cardiac and renal condition, and maybe help her lose fluid. Donna wanted to know how to get Mrs. B. to stay on the low-salt diet. I told her a low-salt diet was not the issue, and that she would never understand the problem unless she asked her client what was going on. Nevertheless, Donna decided she needed to teach Mrs. B. to comply with the doctor's orders: a low salt diet.

With this goal in mind, Donna proceeded to her client's home for a visit. Mrs. B. immediately answered her knock on the door and was delighted to see Donna. She invited her in, offered her a drink, and then sat down to "listen" to her instructions. Throughout Donna's "teaching," Mrs. B. smiled, nodded, and agreed with everything being said. At first Donna thought she was making great headway, then, suddenly, she looked into Mrs. B.'s eyes and, as she later said, "I knew immediately she wasn't paying one bit of attention to what I was saying. So, I stopped and said to her, 'You know, I bet you have a better idea than I about what you need. Can you tell me what is the problem?' Mrs. B. nodded and said, 'Yes, my problem really is that I'm lonely.' The rest of the conversation went like this:

> *'Wow, you're lonely! Why is that?'*
> *'Well, I've been lonely since my husband died!' 'Wow, since your husband died! When was that?'*
> *'About 25 years ago.'*
> *'Wow! I never thought of that. When did you start getting sick and having all these troubles?'*
> *'Oh, they started about a year after my husband died.'*
> *'Wow!'"*

Donna contacted me and told me the story. I told her Mrs. B. was in morbid grief, and that she would need to find out the rest of the story. Why was she unable to find new attachment objects? My guess was she had multiple unresolved losses in the past. The loss of her husband simply brought back the memory of earlier losses. I also told Donna she had probably experienced a major loss of caregiver, and her husband had replaced that person. Now the nurse was replacing the husband. Mrs. B. had found attachment objects—that is, she had found objects to which she could affiliate, but was unable to experience true affiliated-individuation. This would suggest losses in the first 5-6 years of life.

Donna later told me Mrs. B. revealed her mother had died when she was 4 and 1/2, that she had gone to live with her aunt, and had never really felt loved or safe until she married her husband (Personal communication, 1990).

Mrs. B. had, during the stage of Initiative, suffered a loss she was never able to fully work through. She had carried morbid grief with her the rest of her life. This had interfered with her ability to work through the developmental tasks and produce healthy residual. She continued to seek people to take care of her, love her, and protect her. Since her loss was not in her first year, she had been able to get along. She had managed until she lost her husband who had replaced her mother. That loss had been more than she was able to handle because she was unable to find another suitable attachment object.

I saw similar things when I worked as a nurse at a Veteran's Medical Center that treated a large population of Vietnam Veterans. Most of them were diagnosed as suffering from PTSD. They had multiple physical and emotional health problems requiring frequent admissions and treatment. At the core of the physical and emotional problems there were grief stricken souls struggling with the multiple losses they had experienced during combat duty. I remembered one man, Jeff, telling me:

> *I came from a small town and had just graduated from high school when I enlisted. I was excited to serve my country, do the right thing. What does a seventeen-year-old know? I ended up overseas, and our job was to*

make sure our men were safe. We cleared the way. In the process, I know we killed a lot of innocent children, men, and women. And for what? It wasn't what I signed on for. I was going to be a brave, decent, and honorable man and serve my country. But, instead I ended up killing innocent people. In the process I lost myself and my humanity. Now, here I am almost 20 years later, and I still haven't found myself.

Jeff experienced major losses during the stage of Identity and, as a result, did not develop a strong, positive sense of self. Unable to work through his war experiences, he developed morbid grief. He spent the next two decades trying to "find himself." He had difficulty holding jobs, became a drug and alcohol abuser, and had many unsuccessful relationships. Like Ms. B., Jeff had been unable to deal with his losses, and move on to develop new, healthy attachment objects.

> We need to remember prolonged morbid grief can exist, even when others don't recognize the original trauma. Trauma, as with all other things is personal; it depends on the individual's perspective.

Loss Resolution

Nursing interventions can help people move from morbid grief to loss resolution. Take the example of Mrs. Jones as reported by H. Erickson (1990a, pp. 19-20). In this case, Mrs. Jones was in morbid grief when the student began to work with her. Admitted to the hospital for terminal care, she knew she was dying from cancer and had given up. She no longer looked for objects that would meet her needs, and expressed feelings of hopelessness, fatigue, and inability to go on. After assessing the situation, the student planned purposeful interventions that helped Mrs. Jones return home and live her life fully until she took her last breath. To quote,

The visits over the next two weeks were quiet, peaceful times of sharing. Mrs. Jones would be out of bed, dressed, hair combed and smiling when the student arrived. The two would discuss the beauty of the day, the wonders of life, and the possibility of a here-after. Mrs. Jones commented that she was no longer sad or angry, that she felt very contented and at peace. One week after the student's last visit the daughters called to inform the student that their mother had died quietly in her sleep. They commented that she 'almost looked like she had a smile on her face' (Erickson, 1990a, p. 25).

As nurses, we frequently work with patients who are dying physically, as well as others who feel they are dying spiritually. Often, nurses are caught up in the idea that fixing someone's physical condition and preventing their death is our end goal when we plan and implement care. In reality biophysical death is but another stage in life's journey. It is not the end; it is just another stage. How we facilitate that journey determines whether or not we are able to play out our role as spiritual healers and guides.

> *Ginger, a sweet, southern born and bred 89-year-old woman was dying of cancer. Her loving family was having a hard time with her illness. Ginger, however, seemed to be at peace with the situation. When asked what we could do for her, she requested we get her pain medications in "a timely manner," allow open visiting for her family, and help her children as "they are having a really hard time with this." Being new to the Oncology Unit I, asked her how she could be so calm when life was so difficult. She said, "I have had a good life and soon it will be time for me to leave. My body can no longer do what it needs to do. I know where I am going and look forward to being with loved ones who have passed before me." When asked how she felt about leaving her family, she replied, "It is hard to see them so sad, but I know we will be together again when it is the right time." A few days later she passed on quietly, and at peace, with her family by her bedside.*

Although Ginger was dying, it is evident by her statements that she perceived an important difference between her body and her Soul. Although her body was no longer healthy and able to maintain a physical existence, her Soul was strong and healthy. She explained that who she is, her essence, would be moving on soon. Unlike Ted, who suffered a major loss and was unable to form a new attachment, Ginger who was "dying" was able to form a new attachment. Although she would have to let go of her physical world, she was reattaching to her "self" at a higher level–she was reconnecting with her "self" as a spiritual being. She looked forward to her transformation; she was able to take her last breath with peace and dignity.

IMPLICATIONS FOR PRACTICE

Interestingly, in their original work, Erickson et al. (1983) were adamant that Self-care Knowledge is the key to understanding the significance of an object, the individual's attachment to that object, and the significance of the loss of that object. Self-care Knowledge, threaded throughout the original text (pp. 148-168), is the primary source of information needed by nurses interested in using this theory. The authors provided extensive guidelines for data collection and interpretation.

More recently, H. Erickson made the following statement:

There is a significant difference between loss of an object that represents loss of self and loss of objects that represent factors-that-support-the-self.

> *The difference is the loss of Soul-related-needs and loss of biopsychosocial-related-needs. The first is connected with our Soul and the second is related to our biophysical being that houses our Soul* (2002, p. 288).

MRM theory suggested that the "self" is the emphasis of nursing care, but prior to this statement the significance of the loss of spiritual attachment objects was not discussed. The above statement suggests that the grieving process varies with the significance of the lost object.

If we want to know what is important to others, what has the potential to meet their needs, we have to observe their attachment behavior. That is, we have to observe how they respond in the presence and loss of that object. Whenever possible, our observations should include simple questions that help us understand how another person feels and thinks about the object. This is part of their Self-care Knowledge.

As health-care providers we have opportunities to share in the most private, intimate moments of peoples' lives. Frequently our nurse-client interactions are related to current or past losses experienced by our clients. Sometimes they are suffering grievous physical injuries or are dying. Physical cures or "fixing it" for them is not a possibility. However, during our time together, we do have the chance to facilitate them in the healing process, to help them achieve higher states of well-being. This requires that we model their world, protect their current support systems, unconditionally accept them as well as their attachment objects, and help them recognize, deal with, and accept feelings related to present or past losses.

Only then are we able to help people learn to let go of things meaningful to them and reattach to people, objects, or ideas that will meet their needs. As nurses, we are able to intentionally act as spiritual bridges, allowing people to connect their past with their future, in a positive, growth-oriented manner. It is our duty as well as our privilege to be part of this lifetime process and journey.

ENDNOTES

[1] This is the first Aim of Intervention in the Modeling and Role-Modeling theory and paradigm. (Erickson et al., 1983, p. 170).

[2] See footnote #3 for detail.

[3] A fuzzy blanket is considered an appropriate transitional object for an infant, toddler, or even young child. However, we would not expect to see a high school student packing his baby blanket into his backpack as he heads to school. For an adolescent working on Identity issues, a "cool" jacket or pair of jeans would be considered more appropriate for his age and developmental stage.

[4] This statement is made with the assumption that there is nothing wrong with the baby itself. Sometimes there are genetic or other defects in the embryo that interfere with the baby's growth. The mother may or may not have anything to do with these alterations.

[5] Unhealthy objects would be something that impedes normal growth and development. For example, people who feel comforted when they smoke would not be encouraged to continue getting their needs met through the use of cigarettes.

[6] Situational losses are all losses that are not related to normal development. A student leaving elementary school will experience a normal developmental loss as he leaves behind his younger childhood and moves up to middle school. This loss is normal and is required for his growth and development. On the other hand, if this child falls, breaks his leg, and as a result is unable to play in his team's baseball championship he would experience a situational loss. The loss occurs because of a situation or life event not because of normal development. As human beings we experience both developmental and situational losses through out our lifetime.

[7] This story and analysis was reported by H. Erickson, December 11, 2005.

[8] It might be interesting to recall that Bowlby described detachment as a behavior that occurs after prolonged absence of an attachment object. This behavior is considered a symptom that predicts morbid grief. Detachment is comparable to Engel's giving-up given-up behavior where the individual simply gives up on trying to resolve the situation. Harlow's monkey studies (1960) showed that infants that gave up tended to develop unhealthy responses to stress; they were more vulnerable to disease and more likely to succumb when getting sick.

[9] Before you determine that morbid grief exists, explore to determine whether additional losses have occurred that could be the cause of the grieving process.

CHAPTER 8

ADAPTATION:
COPING WITH STRESS

DIANE BENSON

Harvey, a successful attorney in a San Francisco law firm, lives just south of the city, and commutes to work by public transit. Approaching his 50th birthday, he sees this event as a milestone. His son, Harvey Jr., just started high school and seems to be adjusting. His wife, Brenda, recently started another "home business," this one in interior design consulting. During the weekends, Harvey works in the yard or attends sporting events. He doesn't pay much attention to his health. He knows he ought to get more exercise, but rationalizes, saying he is "pretty active" and has a "healthy diet." Besides, he is doing better than his father who had heart problems at an early age. Right now, he is not really stressed, and life is sailing along at an even keel. Life is good.

OVERVIEW

"I'm so stressed!" "You're stressing me out!" "I can't handle this any longer!" "I'm burned out." We frequently hear statements like these. We live with stress. It is part of everyday speech, and adapting to stress is part of everyday life. Comments, like the ones above, not only verbalize the presence of stress, but also imply the speaker is having trouble coping. On the other hand, when we hear the four-year-old, dressed up for her first ballet class exclaim, "I'm excited!" or the teen leaving for her first date say, "This should really be fun!" or the fifty-year-old heading off to the super bowl declare, "Should be a great game!" few people would recognize these as statements of stress. Nevertheless, both negative and positive comments indicate a state of stress. The difference is the first set of comments expresses bad stress, i.e., distress while the latter expresses good stress, i.e., eustress. Both types of stress are in response to stressors; both initiate mobilization of resources.

A major premise of the Modeling and Role-Modeling theory is that there are mind-body-spirit linkages. Stressors in one subsystem have the potential to create a stress response in another. This was discussed in the original book; this chapter is written within that context. However, this chapter will not focus on the mind-body-spirit linkages, but provide details about the coping process per se.

The first section of the Chapter will provide a minimal history of Selye's theory of biophysical aspects of stress. The second section will emphasize the individual's perception of the stressor; the third section will focus on the individual's ability to mobilize resources, followed by the nature of resources. The last section will present the G-APAM, an adaptation and expansion of the APAM, designed to assess a group's ability to cope with stress.

BACKGROUND

Adaptation, stressors, stress, adaptive ability, and adaptive outcomes are threaded through the Modeling and Role-Modeling theory and an understanding of these relationships is necessary in order to use the Modeling and Role-Modeling paradigm. Without a basic understanding of the stressor-stress-coping process, we cannot understand another person's worldview. For example, when someone who has had numerous health problems concedes that it seems like they have had one problem after another since they lost their job, it is important to link these two pieces of information and understand their significance.

Erickson, Tomlin, and Swain, (1983) defined stress as "The nonspecific response of the holistic person to any demand," a stressor as "A stimulus that precedes and elicits stress" (p. 255), coping as "The process of contending with stressors" (p. 253), and adaptation as "The process by which an individual responds to external and internal stressors in a health and growth-directed manner" (p. 252). Sometimes the demands (or stressors) are easy to contend with; sometimes they are not.

These demands can be stressors in any of the subsystems proposed by the Modeling and Role-Modeling theory: physical, social, psychological, cognitive or spiritual. They can be experienced as part of everyday life, or they can be situational or unexpected. Factors that influence our ability to cope include the individual's perception of the stressor, the nature of the stress response, and our ability to mobilize resources.

Several issues related to our ability to cope and adapt have been presented in previous chapters. H. Erickson proposed that we need to grow, to discover the Essence of our Self, and we can do this if we can cope and adapt across the lifespan (Chapter 1). Brekke and Schultz proposed that our feelings and thinking are translated into stored energy, and Walker and Erickson described how mind-body-spirit dynamically interact with one another. The authors explained linkages among perceptions, feelings, and the body's response. Clearly, the responses when we adapt easily differ from those when we have difficulty.

Hertz and Baas expanded the discussion and proposed that our perceptions affect our responses, and Self-care Resources are needed to contend with the stressors and stress. The concept of "stored memories" was reviewed in this chapter. M. Erickson; M. Erickson, H. Erickson and Jensen; and M. Erickson presented theories of developmental processes, needs and the attachment, loss, and grieving processes, respectively. Each of these also relates to our ability to cope and adapt. Unmet needs are stressors; they influence the residual that comes out of the developmental process. Attachment objects meet our needs, but their loss (stressor) causes a grieving process (stress response).

> Coping is the process of contending with stressors. It includes recognition of the stressor, the holistic stress response, mobilization of resources, and outcomes. Factors that influence coping include our perceptions of the stressor, the nature of the stress response, and our ability to mobilize resources. When we are able to cope in growth-directed ways, we adapt.

STRESS PHENOMENA

Biophysical Stress Response

Hans Selye, father of stress research, first recognized the effect of stress on the body when he was a medical student in the mid 30's, but put it aside when faculty told him it wasn't worthy of consideration. It was obvious there were similarities among sick people; good medicine was based on differential diagnoses. He didn't pursue his observations for more than 10 years, but then returned to what seemed obvious, arguing that medicine tended to treat symptoms rather than their cause. He was eager to discover the cause.

> *It is not to see something first, but to establish solid connections between the previously known and the hitherto unknown that constitutes the essence of discovery* (Selye, 1976, p. 6).

His original work focused on uncovering the nature of the obvious—why all people look alike when they first get sick. He identified a process, the General Adaptation Syndrome (GAS) (1976), which includes the three stages: alarm, resistance and exhaustion. The stage of alarm starts when we experience a stimulus or stimuli that mandate biophysical response and can last up to 24 hours.[1] During this stage, the body tries to mobilize adaptive energy needed to contend with the stimuli. When able to mobilize adaptive energy, the body moves to a stage of resistance where the stimuli are fought or neutralized.[2] When unable to mobilize sufficient adaptive energy, the body moves directly to the stage of exhaustion.[3] The GAS is the nonspecific biophysical response to stress, whether eustress or distress.

Selye spent years studying the GAS and drew four conclusions (1980): the stress response is a nonspecific response; a stressor is whatever produces stress; a stressor can act only if it is sensed as a stressor; and there is eustress and distress.

We experience eustress when we enjoy, seek, or welcome the stimuli (events or experiences). We experience Distress when the stimuli are unwelcome, threatening, or overwhelm the individual's ability to cope. Both types of stress use resources, so both are important in managing our lives. Sometimes what starts as eustress becomes distress. According to Erickson et al. (1983), "a stressor becomes distressful when it is prolonged or exceeds the individual's ability to mobilize adaptation energy. The result, from Selye's perspective, is a disease of distress" (p. 83). This non-specific pattern of symptoms that emerges with prolonged distress is the precursor to inflammatory diseases, immune system problems, and many diseases of the kidney, heart, blood vessels, which Selye called diseases of adaptation. He theorized this as the result of depletion of adaptive energy (1976, p.114).

According to Selye,

Adaptation energy seems to be something of which everybody has a given amount at birth, an inherited capital to which we cannot add, but which we can use, more or less thriftily in fighting the stress of life. Still, we have not fully excluded the possibility that adaptation energy could be regenerated to some extent, and perhaps even transmitted from one living being to another (p. 458).

Stress is the state manifested by a specific syndrome, which consists of all the non-specifically-induced changes within a biological system (Selye, 1976, p. 64).

Non-specific Response

Selye proposed the GAS as a series of responses involving the hypothalamus, pituitary, thymus, spleen, lymphatic structures and adrenal cortex. Early on, he argued hormones sent from the hypothalamus to the adrenal cortex stimulated corticoids that produced effects in the thymus, spleen, lymph nodes and lymphatic structures, ultimately producing bleeding ulcers in the duodenum. He called this a triad, or a "syndrome consisting of three manifestations." These are described in the original Modeling and Role-Modeling book (pp. 77-81) with a table of phenomena seen in each stage, created by H. Erickson when she compiled Selye's work (p. 79). However, for the benefit of the reader, I will repeat some of that work and add as needed to clarify.[4] It works something like this:

The initial alarm reaction has seemingly contradictory shock and counter-shock phases. The shock phase triggers, then suppresses the sympathetic nervous system; countershock follows and initiates the "fight or flight" response with sympathetic nervous system and adrenal hormone activation. In the resistance phase, the body maintains a hormonal response without sympathetic arousal. If the body is not able to return to prealarm homeostasis, the final exhaustion phase follows. Here, prolonged stress damages body systems, depletes the body's adaptive energy, and can result in eventual death.

The alarm phase (counter-shock) includes two stress-response cascades (See Figure 8.1): the hypothalamus-sympathetic stimulation cascade producing elevated blood pressure, heart rate, and respiratory rate, as well as other effects of sympathetic stimulation; and stimulation of the hypothalamus-pituitary-adrenal axis, resulting in the secretion of epinephrine and cortisol (Porth, 2002). These two axes interact through ultra short feedback loops. Cortical perception of stressors sends signals to the limbic system, a cluster of brain structures which includes the thalamus, hypothalamus, hippocampus, amygdala, and the locus coeruleus (Porth, 2002; Zautra, 2003). The locus coeruleus releases the neurotransmitter, norepinephrine, which then excites the hypothalamus (LC/sympathetic axis). The hypothalamus stimulates both the sympathetic nervous system, and the adrenal medulla producing epinephrine release.

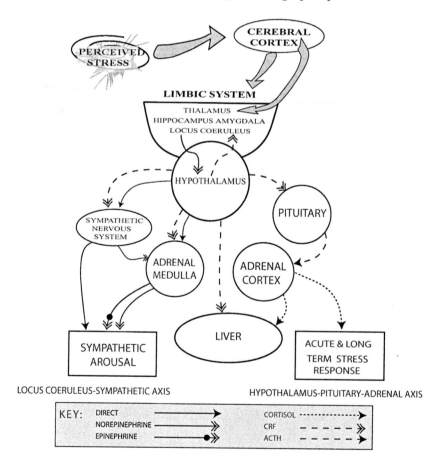

Figure 8.1 Multiple stress response cascades, compiled from various sources.

The hypothalamus releases corticotrophin-releasing hormone (CRH) which then produces pituitary secretion of adrenocorticotropic hormone (ACTH); ACTH stimulates cortisol production by the adrenal glands–a sequence termed the HPA axis. CRH is both an endocrine regulator, as described, and a neurotransmitter (Porth, 2002), with receptors throughout the brain and a number of peripheral sites (See Table 8.1). CRH has been found to have a broader role in the stress response than previously thought. Overall, the physiologic stress response has been extensively studied and is much more complex than is presented here, involving vasopressin and fluid balance, endogenous endorphins and pain perception, and growth hormone, for example.

Table 8.1: CRH Receptor Locations

Brain	Peripheral
Neocortex	Adrenal Medula
Cerebellum	Prostate
Limbic system	Gut
Pituitary	Spleen
Locus Coeruleus/sympathetic axis	Liver
Brain stem	Kidney
Spinal cord	Testes

Adapted from Tsigos, Kyrou, and Chrousos (2005).

In the short-term alarm phase, cortisol promotes elevation of the blood glucose via mechanisms in the liver such as gluconeogenesis and glycogenolysis. During the resistance phase, autonomic arousal diminishes while cortisol production continues. Continued cortisol secretion produces multiple adverse effects including suppression of the immune system, leading to decreased resistance to infection. If the stressor continues into the exhaustion phase, body resources of adaptive energy are depleted and systemic damage appears (Selye, 1985).

Of primary importance in terms of stress is the fact that the hypothalamus clearly seems to respond to emotional/psychological stimuli from the limbic system and to intellectually perceived stress stimuli from the cortex. Since it in turn activates the body's principal adaptive systems, the autonomic nervous and endocrine systems, it appears to be a critical link in the chain of events through which psychological stress produces a physical reaction (Pellitier, 1977, p. 53).

Biophysical Effects of Prolonged Stress

Consistent with the GAS, the acute stress response "shuts off" as the stressor is handled or neutralized. This produces a recovery phase, which includes numerous feed-back loops necessary to return the body to pre-stress homeostasis.[5]

However, "Failure to turn off the stress response can have rather devastating consequences" (Zautra, 2003, p. 48).

Today, we know many ways in which stress affects the body. For example, secretion of cortisol during the stress response interferes with the mucous production in the stomach, allowing gastric acid contact with the stomach lining, leading to gastric ulcers. Immune suppression and cardiovascular effects are also widely documented long-term physiologic effects of the stress response.

Long term stress responses impact many body systems producing a form of premature aging (See Table 8.2). Particularly noteworthy are the effects on the cardiovascular system, immune system, and cognitive capability, three systems that are often the base of many common health problems encountered in today's society. Each of these will be discussed below.

Table 8.2 Long-term Stress Effects Related to Premature Aging

Cardiovascular System
    Elevated blood pressure & hypertension
    Coronary artery damage
    Increased reactivity of platelets & fibrinogen
    Hypercoagulability
    Increased risk of coronary atherosclerosis & myocardial infarction
Metabolic System
    Decreased lean body mass (protein catabolism); Abdominal fat deposits
    Insulin resistance and increased risk of Type 2 diabetes
Immune System
    Decreased T-lymphocytes, phagocytosis & cytotoxic function
    Decreased B-lymphocytes & antibody formation
    Decreased production of cytokines,[6]
Cognitive System
    Suppression of short-term & contextual memory
    Atrophy of hippocampus
Other
    Decreased gastric emptying; Increased colon motility
    GI ulceration from increased gastrointestinal permeability
    Osteoblast suppression & decreased bone density
    Suppression of growth hormone

Compiled from a variety of sources.

Cardiovascular

Repeated release of catecholamine elevates blood pressure leading to hypertension and damage of coronary arteries (McEwen & Lasley, 2003). Through its effects on growth hormone and sex hormones, cortisol increases abdominal fat accumulation, decreases lean body mass (protein catabolism), and causes insulin resistance and hypercoagulability (Tsigos, Kyrou, & Chrousos, 2005). Combined with the increased reactivity of platelets and fibrinogen, these effects increase the risk of atherosclerosis and myocardial infarction. Increased cortisol levels, linked with abdominal fat deposition and insulin resistance, increase the risk of type 2 diabetes (McEwen, 1998).

Immune System

CRH and activation of the HPA axis profoundly inhibit the inflammatory response because "virtually all the components of the immune response are inhibited by cortisol" (Tsigos et al., 2005). These effects include alterations of leukocyte movement and function, decreased production of inflammatory cytokines, and inhibited function of those cytokines on their target tissue. Tsigos et al. emphasize that "the effects of stress on the immune system are better characterized as immunomodulating,[7] rather than immunosuppressing" (p.116). Acute stress increases nonspecific immunity (natural killer cell cytoxicity and production of cytokines such as IL-6) and decreases specific or humoral immunity (Stetler, Murali, Chen, & Miller, 2005).

These effects are meant to be short-term; however, prolonged CRH production in chronic stress response is a different matter. Chronic, unrelenting stress is associated with declines in both nonspecific and specific immune responses: T-lymphocytes and cytotoxic function, and B-lymphocytes and antibody formation, especially immunoglobulin A (Stetler et al., 2005).

Other Biophysical Responses

During acute stress, CRH, by way of neuromodulation, decreases gastric emptying and stimulates colon motility. Activation of the CRH receptors and cortisol increase gastrointestinal permeability and create a dysfunctional gastrointestinal barrier (Tsigos et al., 2005) leading to the GI ulceration Selye noticed in his early research. Cortisol suppresses osteoblasts leading to decreased bone density (McEwen & Lasley, 2003). Lastly, both CRH and cortisol suppress the growth hormone with resultant failure to thrive in children (Porth, 2003).

> According to Selye, a stressor is an event that challenges biophysical homeostasis; disease is a consequence of our inability to mobilize sufficient adaptive energy (1976).

Effects of Stress on Other Subsystems

The above section addressed stress and its effects (regardless of which subsystem the stressor came from) on biophysical well-being. This is not to say that stressors arise in the biophysical subsystem, but that the stress response occurs there. We know stress is exhibited in all subsystems. We have attempted to discuss related issues in previous chapters, using slightly different language. For example, M. Erickson in Chapter 5, presented a discussion on developmental residual, primarily built in the psychological subsystem. Eustress helps build positive residual while distress produces negative residual. In Chapter 6, she discussed need satisfaction including our inherent need for affiliated-individuation. Needs are met within the context of our relationships with others; thus, needs are related to our social subsystem.

We have not presented a discussion on the effects of stress on the cognitive subsystem or the spiritual drive although H. Erickson, in Chapter 1, referred to spiritual growth and our inherent drive to discover our Life Purpose. She proposed that unmet needs (i.e., stressors) will interfere with that process. She also briefly discusses cognitive development in Chapters 11 and 12.

Ideally, we would have a discussion of the effects of stress in each of the subsystems, but space doesn't permit it. Nevertheless, I will include a brief discussion of two areas of importance. The first is the effects of stressors on cognitive processes. I suspect we would find that most stressors that cause cognitive effects start in the psychosocial subsystem and effect changes in the physiological subsystem, which effect changes in the cognitive subsystem. The second is burnout, a phenomenon reported in the literature that results from interaction among the social, psychological, and when prolonged, the physiological subsystems.

Cognitive Effects

While short-term stress response increases levels of cognitive function through stimulation of the sympathetic response and the reticular activating system, repeated stress affects the limbic system, particularly the hippocampus, which has high concentrations of cortisol receptors (McEwen, 1998). In the short term stress response, the hippocampus helps turn off the HPA axis, bringing the body back to homeostasis. The hippocampus also participates in short-term and contextual memory. Contextual memory provides the time and place for remembered events, particularly those with strong emotional significance (especially fear). In the long term stress response, cortisol and excitatory neurotransmitters suppress the mechanisms used in short-term memory, and eventually produces atrophy of the dendrites of neurons in the CA3 region of the hippocampus (McEwen, 1998). Thus short term memory and cognitive function are impaired.

Burnout

Burnout, studied in relation to job stress, is a syndrome that results from prolonged response to chronic interpersonal job stressors. Three dimensions: exhaustion with overwhelming fatigue, cynicism with negativity and detachment from clients and job, and inefficacy with reduced productivity and low morale were identified (Maslach & Leiter, 2005, p. 157). Factors associated with burnout are: impaired job performance, increased absenteeism and sick leave, physical health problems (especially cardiovascular), and strained family relationships.

Table 8.3: Burnout criteria according to Maslach and Leiter, 2005.

Mood symptoms: mental exhaustion, fatigue, depression
Psychological and behavioral symptoms, more than physical
Occurs in otherwise emotionally healthy people
Decreased work performance due to negative attitudes
Work-related due to origins in occupational psychology literature

Burnout does not happen overnight; feelings accumulate and create a sense of being worn out (see Table 8.3). The observed results are primarily psychological and social, but there are underlying physical repercussions. (Maslach and Leiter, 2005).

Considerable research has been done on burnout in the caring professions. For example, studies on the effects of staffing ratios have shown significant relations between emotional exhaustion and burnout in hospital nurses. These studies have also shown significant relations between burnout and nurses' job satisfaction, nurse turnover and patient mortality (Aiken, Clarke, Sloane, Sochalski, & Silber, 2002; Halm et al., 2005).

Conclusions

Selye (1985) compared adaptive energy to "an inherited bank account from which we can make withdrawals but to which we apparently cannot make deposits" (p. 21), although rest can restore resistance to close to previous levels. However, repeated triggering of the stress response can diminish adaptability, so biophysical depletion can occur. Disease results when the body reacts to excessive defensive demands, or demands that exceed our ability to mobilize adaptive energy (Selye, 1976).

The Modeling and Role-Modeling (MRM) theory, based on the premise that people are holistic, that there are ongoing, dynamic interactions within and among the subsystems, argues that stressors in one subsystem have the potential to effect stress in another. So, stressors produce stress, and our ability to mobilize resources determines the outcome.

While Selye's work provides clear understanding of the stress response in the biophysical subsystem, it does not address the dynamic interaction among subsystems. Furthermore, Selye proposed that we cannot "make deposits." This belief is not consistent with MRM, which maintains that resources are added with growth and positive developmental residual. The key difference between the two views is that Selye was talking about the biophysical body, while MRM is talking about the holistic person. H. Erickson acknowledges the biophysical subsystem has limited resources within itself, but it can borrow from other subsystems when needed. Moreover, humans have the potential to transform energy, which happens as they build developmental residual. She used, as an example, people who will themselves to live, even in the face of physical deterioration. (H. Erickson, personal communication, February 8, 2006).

This is the crux of it. Stress is part of life, and the ability to mobilize resources determines what happens next (H. Erickson, personal communication, October 13, 2005).

THE INDIVIDUAL'S PERCEPTION OF STRESSORS

A basic premise of Modeling and Role-Modeling is that our perceptions of stressors impact the outcome of the stress response (Erickson et al., 1983). Perceptions are a part of Self-care Knowledge in this theory. The authors stated,

> *Lazarus (1966) has given us another way to consider the problem of stressful versus distressful stimuli. While not using the exact words stressor or distressor, Lazarus has stated that the way an individual responds to an event or occurrence depends on whether the individual perceives it challenging or threatening. Within this context, we can assume that a psychological stressor could be conceptualized as an event or occurrence that is perceived as a challenge and that a distressor is an event or occurrence that is perceived as a threat (p.83).*

The Appraisal Process

Lazarus (1995) conceptualized stress and coping as a series of transactions between people and their environments.[8] He focused his life work on these processes and their effects. Early on, Lazarus and Folkman (1984) described an appraisal process with three phases: primary, secondary, and reappraisal (See Table 8.4). Primary appraisal determines whether coping is required, because harm or loss (actual damage), threat (potential damage), or challenge (opportunity for growth, mastery or gain) exists (Lazarus, 1999, p. 76). Primary appraisal is followed by secondary appraisal, a two-step operation, in which resources and coping options are evaluated and coping action(s) selected. The third phase, Reappraisal, or tertiary appraisal, is the continual process of revisiting primary and secondary appraisals as the situation evolves. This phase is a blend of appraising, choosing, coping and reappraising.

Table 8.4: Stress Appraisal as Described by Lazarus	
Primary	Is this stress? If so, is it harm or loss? Threat? Challenge? Benefit?
Secondary	Do I have the resources to cope with this stressor?
Reappraisal	Has the situation changed?

According to Lazarus, stress becomes distress when a person appraises the stimulus to be a stressor and the available coping resources are not equal to the demand. Otherwise, stress does not exist. Later, he acknowledged appraisal can be an unconscious process, based on learning from past experience (2000, p. 208).

He also identified "benefit," "goal relevance," and "perceived control" as factors in how things are appraised. He noted people are less likely to perceive the object as harmful or threatening when they have positive feelings about the object being appraised. This is considered the "benefit" factor. He also argued the meaning of the goal (of the coping) will influence the emotions experienced, and thus, the outcome of the coping process. This is "goal relevance." Finally, he said our perceptions of control influence the secondary appraisal. When we perceive we have control, we are able to identify and select coping strategies we are comfortable using. Without perceived control, people feel less able to identify and select coping options that will help them.

Stress and Emotions

Lazarus recently resynthesized his theory, based on his "...increasing recognition that stress and emotion are two interdependent themes that should be combined as one" (Lazarus, 2000, p. 195). He identified fifteen emotions associated with stress, including anxiety, fear, anger, hope, and sadness (Lazarus, 1999).[9] Cooper and Dewe (2004) agreed with Lazarus's premise that stress and emotions should be considered as a single, unified dimension, and argued that the stress response is secondary to emotions.[10] This is consistent with Zautra's (2003) view: stress and emotions are intertwined, but stress emerges because of emotions.

Zautra (2003) stated, "Stress represents an increase in the degree of uncertainty experienced over an important aspect of life" (p. 38). Zautra called emotions the "rhythms of the mind" (p.40); stress arises when those rhythms are disrupted.[11] In his model, uncertainty produces emotions, which in turn lead to stress. This is another way of saying perceived control decreases the perception of stress, consistent with Lazarus's secondary appraisal.

> *Those events for which the person does not have an effective coping response are the most stressful* (Zautra, 2003, p. 41).

Conclusions

Lazarus's model of coping states that how we appraise the stimuli affects our perceptions of them and our perceptions of whether we can or cannot mobilize needed resources. Our emotions affect our appraisal and our appraisal effects more emotions. All-in-all, how we perceive the stimuli will determine the nature of the stress response, which affects our ability to cope. The significance of the relationship between stress and emotions is discussed in Chapters 3 and 4 and provides support for the Modeling and Role-Modeling concept of holism.

Modeling and Role-Modeling theorists have incorporated Lazarus's work in several ways. First, they state individuals' ability to cope and adapt depends on their ability to mobilize Self-care Resources. They also consider it necessary to understand the individuals world-view and perceptions, including whether stressors are challenging or threatening, what they think about their lives and life events. They call this their Self-care Knowledge and say people take Self-care Actions to contend with stressors and stress. Sometimes these are conscious, purposeful actions and sometimes they are unconscious. Finally, the Five Aims of

Interventions (p. 170), designed to help nurses have intent in their care, includes concepts such as perceived control, need satisfaction (or benefit), and mutual goal-setting (or goal relevance), each of which relates to how stressors are appraised. The main difference in the two views (MRM and Lazarus) is that Modeling and Role-Modeling makes a clear distinction between stressor and stress while Lazarus does not. Therefore, it is not always clear when Lazarus's Appraisal Process refers to the stressor and when it refers to the stress response.

> *When we consider the stress response without looking for the stressor, we may understand the problem, but fail to understand the root of the problem* (H. Erickson, personal communication, February 8, 2006).

COPING RESOURCES

Selye (1985) defined coping as adapting to stress situations by removing stressors from our lives, not allowing neutral events to become stressors, developing proficiencies for handling potential stressors, and/or seeking diversion or learning to relax. Coping and coping strategies are integral to Lazarus's transaction model. His secondary appraisal focuses on one's ability to cope with demands that exceed the resources of the person. Lazarus identified three principles of coping as a transactional process: (1) coping constantly changes, (2) coping must be assessed independent of its outcomes, and (3) coping consists of what an individual thinks and does in an effort to deal with the demands that tax or exceed resources (Lazarus, 2000, p. 201).

Lazarus and Folkman (1984) differentiated two types of coping: problem-focused and emotion-focused. Individuals use both types of coping, often simultaneously. In fact, Lazarus pointed out that a coping action could have both functions (Lazarus, 2000, p. 205). Problem-focused coping is similar to problem solving strategies and is cognitive in nature. Coping actions may be directed at "the self or the environment" (p. 204). Emotion-focused coping aims at decreasing emotional distress. This type of coping could include reappraising the situation to change its personal meaning without denying its reality, a form of cognitive reframing.

While both types provide ways to think about coping and resource mobilization, it is important to remember that the Modeling and Role-Modeling theory conceptualizes stressors and stress in much broader terms. For example, a stressor (any demand) can be as basic as altered blood chemistry (such as inadequate oxygen saturation) to something as complex as a deer darting in front of the car as you speed down the road. Furthermore, the stress response incorporates past "learning" related to similar or associated stressors (see Chapters 3 and 4). Therefore, the potential coping resources are as varied as potential stressors.

Resource Consideration

Adaptation requires coping, the ability to mobilize available Self-care Resources (Erickson et al., 1983). To quote:

> *We use self-care resources in our aim to acquire optimum holistic well-being. Self-care resources are needed to survive and thrive. They include everything that we use to grow, develop, maintain or regain health, and to promote healing.*
>
> *Self-care Resources help us provide foundations needed for growth and help us through difficult situations. Often, they create new resources that we can use at a later date under similar (and sometimes different) circumstances. These resources enable us to face challenges in life with confidence and ability. When we perceive that we have the resources, the perception itself becomes a resource. This perception of adequate resources helps us live to the fullest and look forward to the future* (p. 48).

Internal and External Resources

Coping resources are both internal and external, according to Modeling and Role-Modeling theorists (1983, p. 48). Internal resources include our reserve of biophysical stores, growth assets, stored memories, and developmental residual with embedded skills and abilities we develop over time. External resources are outside the individual, within the larger system, such as perceived social support, tangible resources like money, environmental energy, nature, as we value it, and any other object or thing outside our personal domain.

Coping resources can be depleted by repeated stress (Frisch & Bowman, 2002), or inappropriate for a particular stressor, a situational mismatch (Lazarus, 2000). When "mismatched" resources are used repeatedly to contend with stressors, maladaptive equilibrium can occur (Erickson, 1976; Erickson et al., 1983). So, while Erickson et al. indicate internal and external resources, they also categorize them according to the types of needs they meet as perceived by the client.

Supply and Demand

Others propose alternative perspectives on resource availability. For example, Hobfoll (1998) says stress is a state where demands outstrip coping resources, but most stressful events "never approach the state at which they outstrip resources" (p. 54). He denies positive events can cause stress (eustress). In his theory, stress occurs when resources are lost, threatened, or do not grow following investment. According to him, the most common and simplest method to categorize resources, internal versus external resources, is the least helpful. His rationale is that "it is too broad to be helpful in understanding important differences with categories, and it has no theoretical basis" (Hobfoll, 1998, p. 57). Instead, he identified four categories of resources: objects such as possessions including shelter and food, conditions such as employment or family membership, personal characteristics such as self-esteem, and energies such as money or time. His theory is based on three principles: resource loss has much greater impact than resource gain; resources must be invested to protect against loss; and we need to build resource reservoirs (Hobfoll, p. 73). His theory suggests resource reservoirs are built during non-stressful times.

Ease and Dis-ease

Antonovsky (1979, 1987) studied coping resources in connection to health. His salutogenesis model described how some people stay healthy despite stress. He viewed health and illness on a continuum, the "health ease/dis-ease" continuum (Antonovsky, 1979, p. 55). He termed the movement toward the dis-ease end of the continuum as "breakdown."

His model deals with positive and negative stress by differentiating two responses to stressors: tension and stress. Tension is the first level of response, and stress is the second. If tension is managed effectively, no harm is done and the effects can be positive or salutogenic. However if tension is not managed effectively, stress occurs. Tension can be a type of eustress, while stress is distress. Antonovsky viewed stress as pathologic, leading to dis-ease. The ability to "manage tension, and avoid or manage stress or both, is influenced by factors known as generalized resistance resources" (Horsburgh, 2000).

Generalized resistance resources are "...phenomena that provide one with sets of life experiences characterized by consistency, participation in shaping outcome, and underload-overload balance" (Antonovsky, 1987, p.19). These resources include: knowledge, intelligence, and skills; ego identity (an integrated flexible sense-of-self); coping strategies; social support; cultural stability and ritual; value system such as religion; preventive health orientation; and genetic and constitutional health factors. He visualized each generalized resistance resource on a continuum with the low end representing a resistance deficit, increasing the potential for dis-ease, and the high end of the continuum representing the increasing resistance to dis-ease. Life experiences with consistency, participation in outcome, and balance help develop coherence, a central concept of his model. A sense of coherence is a global orientation consisting of comprehensibility, manageability, and meaningfulness (Antonovsky, 1987). A person with a strong sense of coherence is able to mobilize resistance resources in order to manage tension and/or stress.

Most of Antonovsky's generalized resistance resources would be categorized as internal coping resources. According to this orientation, internal resources are those the individual has developed over time, so they are available for use when needed, such as self-confidence, performance skills, history of coping success, religious faith (Kaba, Thompson, & Burnard, 2000), and various personality characteristics.

Traits and Developmental Residual

Many stress and coping theorists including Holahan, Moos, and Schaefer (1996) identified personality factors as internal coping resources that serve as mediators between stressor and stress response. These include optimism, perceived control, hardiness, self-efficacy, and a sense of coherence. While some of these have been mentioned before, they have not been discussed within the context of the ability to cope with stress. Each of these is related to positive developmental residual (Erikson, 1964; Erickson et al, 1983) and is discussed within that context.

Trust Residual

Optimism and Hope. "Fascination with the phenomenon of hope dates back to the Bible" (Raleigh, 2000) and is common to many belief systems. Scientific literature has an equal fascination with the study of hope; however, agreement on what hope is and how to study it is a problem (Campbell & Kwon, 2001; Kylma & Vehvilainen-Julkunen, 1997; Raleigh, 2000). Stotland (1969) published the first and most widely used operationalized model of hope. He stated that hope, an expectation of future goal attainment, is mediated by goal importance for the individual and motivates action to achieve that goal (Stotland). He believed hope is a component of adaptive coping in a difficult situation, and hopelessness is a factor in maladaptive behavior. His model of hope became the framework for much of the research on the concept, as well as the basis for many instruments used to measure hope.

In her review of the literature on hope and coping, Raleigh (2000) found hope described as a coping precursor, strategy, or outcome. She postulated hope may have a role in all three aspects of coping, citing examples of hope as a positive influence in the appraisal of a situation, hope as a strategy (such as prayer), and hope as an outcome of the process (p. 452).

Hope as an outcome has been found in studies of the elderly (Westburg, 2001). Herth (1989, 1990) found significant positive relationships between hope and coping in the terminally ill, and used hope as a coping resource in her model, Perceived Enactment of Autonomy, presented in Chapter 4. Hope has also been found to be a mediating factor between personal style predisposition and the development of depression, and as a direct mediator in depression (Campbell & Kwon, 2001).

Studies on optimism often define it similarly to hope. Boyers (2000) described dispositional optimism as a generalized positive expectancy about the future resulting in behavior which will make those positive outcomes occur, and found that optimism had a positive influence on coping with breast cancer. Brissette, Scheier, and Carver (2002) found optimism positively influenced coping during the life transition of first year at college.

Irvin (Irvin, 1993; Irvin & Acton, 1997) studied the relationship between stress and hope, using hope as an internal coping resource for caregivers of Alzheimer's patients. In her first study, she found positive relationships among the

Self-care variables: hope, perceived social support, and self-worth, with both hope and social support having a positive effect on stress (Irvin, 1993). In a later study, Irvin and Acton (1997) found hope to mediate the relationship between stress and well-being. Studies involving hope as a variable in the development of APAM are discussed later in this chapter (Barnfather, 1987, 1990; Erickson, 1984; Klienbeck, 1977).

Autonomy Residual

Perceived Control. Perceived control, locus of control, and learned helplessness are related constructs (Ruiz-Bueno, 2000). Perceived control, or a person's perception of the ability to influence outcomes, impacts "almost every facet of life" (Ruiz-Bueno, 2000, p. 461), especially, coping with stressful situations. Perceived control is a state phenomenon. It can occur in any human, depending upon one's ability to mobilize resources. Perceived control and locus of control are similar, but different concepts.

Rotter (1966) originally proposed locus of control as the primary source of motivation and reward for our actions. He distinguished internal from external locus of control, with the first coming from within the person and the second from outside the person. More recently, Skinner (1995) stated that locus of control is the same as perceived control.[12] Ruiz-Bueno (2000) compiled several studies linking perceived control and coping and found a positive relationship between the two variables.

> Internal control refers to the belief that forces within oneself are responsible for outcomes, while external control refers to the belief that an event is under the control of external forces such as fate, chance, or powerful others. Locus of control is on a continuum with a more internal locus being related to perceived control, and an external locus being related to learned helplessness.

Learned helplessness, identified by Seligman (1974), is a distress-prone personality pattern. More specifically, in this trait the individual is prone to experience feelings of helplessness when confronted by an event or experience they don't have immediate ability to manage. This does not mean these individuals never have perceived control, but that they are less able to mobilize resources needed for problem solving. They often attribute their situation to their own failures or lack of competency. As a result, they tend to feel helpless when confronted with an experience they can't immediately control.

Seligman and others (Garber & Seligman, 1980; Peterson, Maier, & Seligman, 1993) have shown relationships between learned helplessness and depression (Seligman, 1975), other stress symptoms, and mood disturbances, such as anxiety (Ruiz-Bueno, 2000). Seligman and colleagues (1993) also proposed an alternative, learned optimism, which would be a distress-resistant personality pattern. It should be noted these two traits are similar to those identified as developmental residual produced during the stage of Trust and Autonomy.

Learned helplessness is negative residual related to the stage of Autonomy and learned optimism is positive residual related to the stage of Trust.

H. Erickson makes the point that learned hopelessness would be the negative residual that emerges from the stage of Trust. This is different and has implications different from learned helplessness. (Personal communication, February 8, 2006).

Initiative Residual

Self-efficacy. The concept of self-efficacy, derived from Bandura's social cognitive theory (Bandura, 1997), refers to the belief in one's ability to exercise control over external events which affect one's life (Bandura, 1997; Siela & Wieseke, 2000). This belief seems similar to perceived control and the control component of hardiness. Perceived self-efficacy promotes active effort in challenging situations, reflecting resilience. Through self-reflection and active cognition, people create mental models that act as behavior guides when interacting with the environment. Then, through continued reflection and appraisal, people self-regulate behavior and emotions in response to environmental events.

While self-efficacy has been used in various research settings, the cognitive and behavioral self-management skills, which promote active collaboration, have been a factor in many health care studies (Siela & Wieseke, 2000). An online search of the social sciences literature for the last ten years resulted in 142 articles relating self-efficacy to topics as diverse as HIV prevention or fear of falling in the elderly. A similar search of the medical and health care literature found 838 articles. Two meta-analysis studies were found in the health care literature; both found that self-ratings of self-efficacy consistently predicted healthy lifestyle behavior (Gillis, 1993; Holden, 1991).

Industry Residual

Hardiness. Hardiness, the ability to endure hardship related to stress, helps us deal with otherwise stressful situations without suffering illness (Beehr & Bowling, 2005). Noting that many stressors of modern life carry the potential for increased material resources, such as increased salary and what money can buy, Kobasa (1979, 1985) investigated personality characteristics that helped some people in high stress occupations remain healthy while others became ill. She called this personality difference "hardiness," a constellation of three characteristics: control, commitment, and challenge (Kobasa, 1979, 1985; Maddi & Kobasa, 1984). Control is the belief that the person can influence or manage life events; the opposite of control is powerlessness (Ford-Gilboe & Cohen, 2000). This component reflects an internal versus external locus of control.

Commitment refers to active involvement in daily living; the opposite is alienation. Kobasa (1985) stressed commitment to self was most important for staying healthy under stress. Challenge reflects the belief that change provides opportunities for growth and development and is part of normal living; challenge is the opposite of threat (Maddi & Kobasa, 1991). This latter interpretation is the same as Lazarus's challenge versus threat appraisal and these three components are the same as those described in Chapter 5 as developmental residual that emerges with the stage of Industry.

Beehr and Bowling (2005) tested and critiqued Kobasa's work, and concluded that hardiness may be a construct with three distinct concepts and might include other personality characteristics such as self-efficacy, sense of humor, and low negative affectivity, a personal trait characterized by the tendency to experience negative emotions.

Identity Residual

<u>Coherence</u>. Antonovsky (1987) introduced the concept of coherence, stating we perceive the world to be more coherent when it contains comprehensibility, manageability, and meaningfulness. Comprehensibility refers to the extent to which stimuli make cognitive sense with information being ordered, consistent, structured, and clear (p. 16-17). Manageability is the perception that resources are available and adequate to meet demands posed by stressors (p. 17), while meaningfulness refers to the extent one feels life makes sense emotionally (p. 18). While the three components are dynamically interrelated, Antonovsky viewed meaningfulness as the most important for a sense of coherence (Horsburgh, 2000, p.180).

> *A sense of coherence is 'a global orientation that expresses the extent to which one has a pervasive, enduring though dynamic feeling of confidence that (1) the stimuli deriving from one's internal and external environments in the course of living are structured, predictable, and explicable; (2) the resources are available to one to meet the demands posed by these stimuli; and (3) these demands are challenges, worthy of investment and engagement'* (Antonovsky, 1987, p. 19).

Later, Antonovsky described positive relationships between coherence and health, assessed on a continuum from health to dis-ease. A strong sense of coherence enables one to mobilize "general resistance resources" needed to avoid and manage stress, and at the same time these resources help build the sense of coherence, a reciprocal relationship (Horsburgh, 2000). Finally, coherence has been theorized to influence both the primary and secondary appraisal processes as described by Lazarus.

Other Resources

While external resources are equally important to an individual's ability to mobilize resources, this topic was discussed extensively in Chapter 4 under Self-Care Resources, so will not be repeated here. Suffice to say, there is a significant difference between perceived external resources, and social networks (Erickson et al., pp. 125-26, 130, 138, 158-59, 162) and should not be confused. Social support is the external coping resource which has been studied most extensively. Social support as a coping resource is mentioned by many theorists, including Lazarus (2000) as part of secondary and reappraisal, Hobfoll (1998) as both a condition and energy resource, Antonovsky (1979) as a generalized resistance resource, and Selye (1976) as central to altruistic egoism. Social support was discussed in Chapter 4 as a Self-care Resource and is also discussed again in Chapter 11.

THE INDIVIDUAL'S ABILITY TO COPE

I have discussed the individual's perception of stressors, the phenomena of the stress response, and coping resources. What I have not discussed is the individual's ability to mobilize resources. While it is important for health-care providers to understand the coping process and factors that affect the outcomes, it is also important to understand how we can determine a person's ability to mobilize resources at any given time. This section addresses this issue.

Conceptualization of the Adaptive Potential Assessment Model

Engel (1962) proposed two types of responses to psychosocial stressors: fight-flight and conservative-withdrawal. Fight-flight is the psychological corollary to Selye's alarm phase; the conservative-withdrawal state is psychological giving-up, including depression. H. Erickson combined these two models to create The Adaptive Potential Assessment Model, APAM, a model with a holistic orientation, designed to assess an individual's ability to cope with stress. This model represents states, not stages, since she perceived people can go from one to the other directly, depending on their ability to cope. Her work (Erickson, 1976), was replicated by Klienbeck, (1977), incorporated in the theory, Modeling and Role-Modeling (1983), and further validated by Barnfather (1987), Barnfather, Swain and Erickson (1989a). The three states of coping according to the APAM are: Arousal, Impoverishment, and Equilibrium (Erickson & Swain, 1982, p. 94; Erickson et al., p. 80). Each state represents one's ability to mobilize resources, and has specific parameters (see Table 8.5) that depict the state (Erickson, 1976; Erickson et al., 1983).

Table 8.5: Parameters of the APAM by State			
Factor	Arousal	Equilibrium	Impoverishment
Hope	Moderate to high	High	Low
Tenseness/ Anxiety	Moderate to high	Low	High to low
Fatigue	Low	Low	High
Sadness/ Depression	Low	Low	High
Autonomic	Elevated	Normal	Elevated to normal
Motor/ Sensory Behaviors	Elevated	Normal	Depressed

Compiled from Barnfather, 1987; Erickson, 1976.

The Adaptive Potential Assessment Model represents dynamic movement among the states, depending on the individual's ability to mobilize resources when confronted with new stressors or coping with ongoing stress. For example, when in Equilibrium, new stressors will move one into Arousal, unless the stressors are so overwhelming it is impossible to mobilize resources. This latter situation would occur with massive trauma, or devastating loss. When in Arousal, additional stressors and/or ongoing stress would move one into Impoverishment. When in Impoverishment, new stressors might move one into Arousal, assuming sufficient resources were available, but could also move one further into Impoverishment. On the other hand, when in either of the stress states (Arousal or Impoverishment), if sufficient resources are available, people can move back into Equilibrium, a low stress or nonstress state.

Movement among the APAM states is fluid, based on an ever-changing context of stressors and coping potential. I am not going to revisit these states or their parameters, since they are discussed in earlier manuscripts (Erickson, 1976, 1982, 1983). Instead, I wish to provide additional information to enhance your understanding of the concepts.

Mind-Body Interactions

Impoverishment

Impoverishment (Erickson, 1976; Erickson et al., 1983) is a state of feeling depressed and anxious, two feelings associated with increased CRH and cortisol secretion (Tsigos et al., 2005). Wallenstein (2003) reported a series of studies showing depressed patients have "elevated blood serum levels of macrophages (or immune cells that secrete cytokines, interleukin-1, interleukin-6, and interferon-alpha). So, in other words, many depressed patients exhibit several classic signs of immune system activation" (p.136). The question is, as always, which comes first: the feelings or the chemical responses. Since cytokines may "actually cause depressed mood" (Wallenstein, 2003), it would seem there is an interactive relationship.

> *Without research that controls for appraisal of the stressor, we can't be sure which comes first, although we know from Chapter 3 it is a dynamic process with continuous feedback loops. In any case, it is clear our feelings are related to the production of chemicals, and those in turn create new feelings. From this perspective, people in a state of Impoverishment will continually lose resources, unless something is proactively done to counteract the process. These people feel out of control and cannot mobilize their own resources without help* (H. Erickson, personal communication, February 8, 2005).

To complicate the problem, interleukin and interferon type drugs are often prescribed as treatment for various diseases such as hepatitis and cancer; people who receive these drugs often report depressed mood, lack of appetite, sleep disturbance, and lack of interest in daily activities. Since these symptoms go away when the drug is discontinued, we might conclude the drug comes first, and the feelings (from the chemicals and their reactions) follow. But, what about the fact that the drugs were given because the person has cancer or liver disease? It is possible feelings of despair and fatigue are exacerbated by the chemicals, and are diminished when they are discontinued, because discontinuance of the drug means one is getting better!

Psychoneuroimmunology Revisited

PNI, discussed in Chapter 3, warrants a revisit in this chapter because of its connection with the coping process. PNI research, the study of linkages among the brain, neuroendocrine and immune systems, has shown that hormones and neurotransmitters can alter the function of the immune system, and its products, such as cytokines, can affect neuroendocrine function (Porth, 2003). For example, lymphocytes have receptor site chemicals produced by the HPA, such as cortisol, insulin, sex hormones, and catecholamines, and the HPA axis is activated by interleukins and other cytokines released by immune cells. The endocrine and immune systems communicate at many levels, both directly and indirectly through their mutual connections with the central nervous system (Wallenstein, 2003). Some of these connections are hormonal with feedback loops, and some are via neurotransmitters. (See Chapter 3 *Neurotransmission* and *Neuromodulation.*)

While the role of the stress response in immune suppression was discussed earlier, the reverse also occurs; "emotional and psychological manifestations of the stress response may be a reflection of alterations in the CNS resulting from the immune response" (Porth, 2003, p.186). Lymphocytes secrete cytokines that influence the stress response; the cytokines can stimulate the HPA axis. Amazingly, CRH is secreted by cells of the immune system (immune CRH). Immune CRH can activate mast cells, which leads to histamine release (Tsigos et al., 2005, p. 115). While it is rather complex, the bottom line is clear: mind-body relationships include continuous feedback loops that influence how the body responds at any given time. Our feelings and how we perceive stressors are integral to the stress response and stress responses can influence how we feel. How we interpret our life events and resources determines our perceptions of real, threatened or potential stressors and our ability to mobilize resources needed to cope with them. It is all interconnected, a situation Capra (1996) calls the "Web of Life."

Factors Influencing Stressor Appraisal

Attitudes, beliefs, values, and culture, all factors that influence our response to stressors (Cohen & Welch, 2000), can be conceptualized in many ways. Cohen and Welch describe three ways to think about attitudes: they can be implicit anticipatory responses learned from experience, filters, which affect how we perceive reality, or the outcome of behavior. That means individuals can hold different attitudes on different levels about a person or concept. In other words, cognitive attitudes and affective attitudes can be different about the same thing.

When we consider people have multiple subsystems, it is possible all three definitions apply, depending on how we contextualize the concept. For example, Modeling and Role-Modeling theory poses there are cognitive, social and psychological subsystems; therefore, all three definitions are important. Furthermore, appraisal of a stressor from one subsystem can be very different from appraisal from another.

Cohen and Welch (2000) said, "When there is agreement between the cognitive and affective elements, there is a stronger relationship between attitudes and behavior" (p. 336). This is because people are holistic, their subsystems interact; how they feel influences how they think and, therefore, how they act. When there is dissonance between our thinking and feeling subsystems, there will also be dissonance between our attitudes and our behavior. Beliefs and values are also important in the appraisal process. However, since social and psychological attitudes are formed by our beliefs and values, those values and beliefs are generally reflected in our attitudes (Cohen & Welch). Still, each influences how we perceive our life experiences and how we cope with them.

Coping Outcomes: Adaptive and Maladaptive

Coping outcomes have been described by some as adaptive or maladaptive. Zeidner and Saklofske (1996) reviewed the literature related to coping and found that the notion of coping effectiveness has been implicit. Interested in this topic, I did an online search in the social science, psychology, and medical literature and found 292 articles related to adaptive or maladaptive coping published over the past ten years. The majority of these articles addressed maladaptive coping (Densten, 2001), prescribed more effective coping techniques (Folkman, 1997), or demonstrated correlations between coping and health, physical, or emotional outcomes (Kaba, Thompson, & Burnard, 2000; Landrum, 1999; Leidy, 1989; Leidy, 1990, 1999; Leidy & Darling-Fisher, 1995; Leidy, Ozbolt, & Swain, 1990; Leidy & Traver, 1995; Welch & Austin, 2001).

According to Zeidner and Saklofske (1996), coping strategies should not be prejudged and we need to consider the context to determine if coping strategies are adaptive or not. They stated the context includes situational factors such as the nature and frequency of the stressor; personal factors such as personality traits and coping history; cultural and social factors; and the interaction between the person and the situation (p. 506). Their criteria for assessing coping effectiveness are shown in Table 8.6.

As described above, the Adaptive Potential Assessment Model proposed by Erickson (1976) and Erickson et al. (1983) refers to adaptive and maladaptive states as alternative states of equilibrium, rather than coping effectiveness. Erickson et al. (1983), defined adaptation as "The process by which an individual responds to external and internal stressors in a health and growth-directed manner" (p. 252), and maladaptation as "(t)he process an individual uses to cope with a stressor within one subsystem by taxing energies from another" (p. 254). They also stated, "...a stressor is a stimulus that is experienced as challenging or one that mounts an adaptive response; a distressor is a stimulus that is experienced as threatening or one that mounts (either directly or indirectly) a maladaptive response" (p. 83).

Table 8.6: Criteria for Effective Coping

•Resolution of the conflict or stressful situation
•Reduction of physiological reaction
•Reduction of psychological distress
•Normative social functioning (Deviation of behavior from socially acceptable norms is taken to be a sign of maladaptive coping)
•Return to prestress activities (substantial life change may be a sign of successful coping, particularly if the prior living situation was not ideal.)
•Well-being of self and others affected by the situation
•Maintaining positive self-esteem
•Perceived effectiveness.

Zeidner and Saklofske, 1996, p. 508

When these definitions and comments are placed within the context of the Modeling and Role-Modeling theory, the underlying implication is that people in a state of maladaptation have fewer resources available for coping with new or ongoing stress. Yet, the authors have not identified parameters that would distinguish these two alternative states of Equilibrium. Barnfather et al. (1989a) recommended that further work was needed to make these distinctions.

Adaptive Potential Assessment Tool

Background

The measures used in the construct validity studies of the APAM involved coding a recorded and transcribed life experience statement for anxiety and hope, plus a 72-item checklist that required subjects to understand complex instructions and reveal their feelings. This is time-consuming and not practical in clinical practice. While the criteria for categorizing people into states can be used in the clinical setting, nothing had been designed to incorporate all the criteria in one measurement tool. Hopkins (1994) took this as a challenge, and initiated the development of the Adaptive Potential Assessment Tool (APAT). She used anxiety, hope, sadness, and fatigue to differentiate the three APAM states. Her analysis of the construct validity studies supported the omission of autonomic responses and motor-sensory behavior, since these were nonverbal indicators of anxiety.

Findings

Hopkins's work used the coding and clinical judgment of Helen Erickson, developer of APAM, as criteria to determine sub-scale validity. H. Erickson's sub-scale scores correlated significantly with her APAM classification although the sub-scale for fatigue did not meet criterion. Hopkins concluded the APAT needed continued development in the fatigue sub-scale, speculating that the absence of nonverbal cues in the APAT design contributed to the difficulty. The advantage of a single tool for clinical research is obvious, and warrants additional study.

Clinical Assessment Model

The APAM, originally extrapolated from Erickson's (1976) clinical practice, has been taught to hundreds of nurses around the country and is used widely in clinical settings to assess client's potential to mobilize resources. The parameters are the same as described above. People in stress states have varying degrees of ability to mobilize resources; some are more able than others. So, the decision making process involves simple steps as shown in Figure 8.2. Staff nurses can make these judgments without using cumbersome research tools. Nurses do it all the time. However, they have a clearer direction of what to do with their findings, when they have a theory to back up their decision-making.

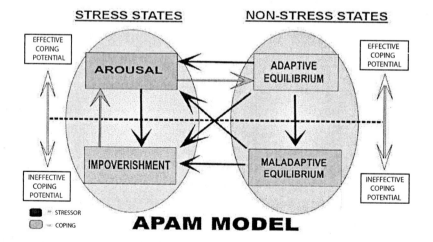

Figure 8.2: The Adaptive Potential Assessment Model.

H. Erickson made the following comments about this issue:

As I have stated in writing (Erickson et al., 1983, pp. 169-222), in classes, and presentations, as we prioritize time to be spent with clients and determine the type of care they need, we have to know if they are in stress or not. You can watch them, listen to what they say, and how they say it, to make such a decision. When they exhibit minimal tension, minimal anxiety, a sense of the future, and their motor-sensory behaviors are fairly calm, you can perceive they are in Equilibrium.

When they seem to be very tense and anxious, have high motor-sensory behaviors, seem to be thinking in short-term time periods, but have a sense things will work out, they are probably in Arousal. When they seem to be withdrawn, quiet, fatigued, and have diminished hope and projection into the future, they are Impoverished. Remember, people in Impoverishment may or may not exhibit tension and anxiety. Those with the fewest resources are most apt to have "used up" their tension; they just don't have the energy needed to be visibly anxious anymore.

Those in Equilibrium need us to help clarify, inform, and assist them in getting their needs met. You will recognize Maladaptive Equilibrium because they usually plan to meet their needs in ways that aren't consistent with their identification of the problem. For example, people with hypertension where the problem is in physical subsystem, may say their blood pressure will return to normal when their spouse (stressor in social subsystem) starts showing some appreciation for what they do. While this may seem strange, and nurses often think the two have nothing to do with one another, this is a classic example of someone in Maladaptive Equilibrium.

People in Equilibrium are very different from those in a stress state. They usually need someone with a friendly face who will listen to their concerns, help them problem solve, and not try to fix them. People in Arousal require a different type of care from those in Impoverishment. They usually want help similar to those in Equilibrium, although they are more intense and have more unmet needs. Nurses can respond to them by listening to their questions and providing information and support.

Those in Impoverishment are a different story. Often nurses fail to recognize these people as the most vulnerable, and in the greatest jeopardy. Yet, nurses need to provide them with direct assistance. These people often don't know where to start, how to ask for help; they are too "worn out." Nurses can start with them by centering themselves, so that they are better able to understand the person's situation and work from there. The opening story in Chapter 11 is about a man who was Impoverished. The story in Chapter 12 is about a man who, when in a nonstress state, had been in Maladaptive Equilibrium for a few years before I met him and who was in Arousal at the time of our first meeting. I hope you enjoy reading them (H. Erickson, Personal communication, February 7, 2006).

APPLICATION OF THE APAM

Remember Harvey, introduced on the first page of this chapter? He wasn't forgotten; you only heard part of the story. Let's follow the rest and see how it relates to the APAM.

As described earlier, Harvey is not really experiencing stress; he is in Adaptive Equilibrium, since his life is on an even keel. However, the situation gradually changes. During the next couple of years, several things happen. A major partner in his law firm moves, leaving Harvey with a larger work load, which requires him to work on most Saturdays. As a result, his exercise disappears; combined with increased consumption of fast food at his desk for lunch (and often dinner), his weight increases. At his next physical, Harvey's cholesterol, weight, and blood pressure are elevated. Harvey is managing, but with an unhealthy balance. He is in Maladaptive Equilibrium.

Since his father is not around much on Saturdays, these days, Harvey Jr. starts hanging out with a rougher crowd in school (who call him Hank). One day his mother, Jane, receives a call from school asking why Hank has not been in school for the last three days. As soon as Jane hangs up the phone, it rings again; this time the San Mateo Police are calling to say her son has been arrested and charged with drug possession and resisting arrest.

Harvey leaves work and meets Jane at the police station. He rushes in, face flushed, and out of breath. He is certainly stressed and is in Arousal. While talking with the arresting officer, he slumps in a chair, experiencing chest pain. Harvey is taken to the hospital and admitted to the coronary unit with Acute Coronary Syndrome. Harvey has elevated heart rate and blood pressure, but luckily, no evidence of permanent heart damage. Arousal continues.

A month later, while representing his son during a court appearance, he is not so lucky. His chest pain returns, only much worse. This time his diagnosis is myocardial infarction. Interventions are successful in limiting the size of the heart attack. However, when the night nurse, Dan, enters the room, he finds Harvey curled up in bed, choking back tears. As he opens up to Dan (who studied MRM in nursing school), Harvey says "I just can't take it any more. I've got to cut back my law practice, which is going to devastate my income. I don't know what is happening with my son, he won't talk to me any more. I'm supposed to take it easy at home, but my wife drives me crazy. I might as well have died with this heart attack; I'm just so tired of it all." Dan realizes Harvey is Impoverished; he needs help now to prevent further deterioration. Dan will have to apply the steps suggested in Chapter 9, and then facilitate Harvey in building and mobilizing resources as described in the original text (Erickson, et al, 1983), and in Chapter 10, in this book.

CONSTRUCT EXPANSION OF APAM

Benson's Group APAM

The APAM, designed to categorize individuals into states according to their ability to mobilize resources, has demonstrated reliability and validity. This raised the question in my mind, "Can groups also be categorized into adaptive potential states?" If so, assessment of these states could form the basis for framing leadership interventions with groups. Leaders could channel and direct the group to improve coping and effectiveness of the group task function.

As I considered this question, I revisited the three states and determined that a model designed to predict the type of group intervention needed to differentiate Adaptive Equilibrium from Maladaptive Equilibrium. I believed a group in Adaptive Equilibrium would be stable and functioning, whereas, a group in Maladaptive Equilibrium would need to be moved into Arousal in order to improve its effectiveness. An Impoverished group would need to be supported until it was able to function on its own and become effective. While the APAM model has been applied to work groups (Frisch & Bowman, 2002; Frisch & Kelly, 1996), no research had been undertaken to develop a model specifically for groups. The Group Adaptive Potential Assessment Model (G-APAM), designed to meet this need, is the product of a Delphi study looking at the assessment of adaptive potential in groups (Benson, 2003). Figure 8.3 depicts this model.

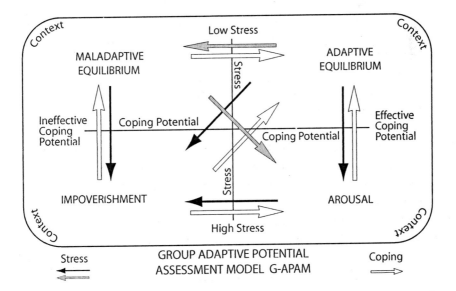

Figure 8.3 The Group Adaptive Potential Assessment Model. Reproduced with permission of Diane Benson, 2/28/2006.

Conceptual Background

Like individuals, groups must adapt in order to survive. However, groups are more complex; thus, adaptation becomes more complex. Moreover, context is central to understanding the dynamics of group function and context includes many factors essential to the group's ability to cope. A description of context, taken from various sources, but primarily adapted from Small Groups as Complex Systems by Arrow, McGrath, and Berdahl (2000) follows.

Context in G-APAM. All groups exist in multiple, inter-related, and overlapping contexts. These include the external environment, influence of and interaction with other groups, and characteristics of the group itself. Characteristics of the group include the group's ability to make decisions and manage conflict, collective information processing, the type of the group, stability of membership, social network of members, and its temporal dynamics.[13] Context also includes resources, internal and external, available for mobilization, such as energy, information, material resources and tools, and social support. Resource availability refers to resources from group members, the group as a unit, and from the environment. For example, group members bring knowledge, skills, energy, personal characteristics, and the ability to form an interaction network. All factors continuously interact to form the dynamic context of the group. Thus, the group context and the group members provide the resources and knowledge analogous to Self-care Resources and Self-care Knowledge as described in MRM theory.

Dimensions of G-APAM. Given that the group exists in context, the G-APAM is organized around two axes. The x axis represents coping potential which ranges along a continuum from effective to ineffective; effective coping potential facilitates adaptation, while ineffective coping potential does not. The y axis represents the level of stress ranging from low to high. These two axes form four quadrants. A group is in any one of the quadrants, at any given point in time, based on stress level and the effectiveness of its coping potential. Stress/stressors and coping produce movement within the G-APAM. Coping moves the group up toward lower stress, or to the right as coping potential increases or becomes more effective, as represented by white arrows. Stress, depicted by black or gray arrows, moves the group down, toward high stress, or to the left, as coping resources are depleted (see Figure 8.3).

G-APAM Descriptors. A Delphi panel was used to identify the descriptors of each of the four states in the G-APAM: Arousal, Impoverishment, Adaptive Equilibrium and Maladaptive Equilibrium. These group behaviors are supported by the small group literature for potential variables in group adaptive potential. Behavior representing effective coping potential is virtually identical for both stress and low stress. In addition, descriptors for ineffective coping potential in stress (impoverishment) appeared to be the opposite of behavior under effective coping potential in low stress (adaptive equilibrium); see Table 8.6. This finding supports the view that coping potential may be more important in group APAM than stress state.

The descriptors, hope and optimism, (effective coping potential), depression and burnout (ineffective coping potential) deal with collective affect, and represent the behavior closest to the original APAM predictors. Other descriptors for group adaptive potential included: Group cohesion, support within the group, commitment and attention to task, collective efficacy, communication characteristics, group decision-making, and conflict resolution (see Table 8.7). A full description of these factors, related research, publications, and the process used to develop this model can be found in D. Benson (2003) and will be reported in *Modeling and Role-Modeling: Research Findings and Measurement Issues* (Erickson, H. Ed., 2007).

Table 8.7 Group Coping Potential Behavior	
Effective Coping Potential	Ineffective Coping Potential
Hope & optimism	Depression, boredom & burnout
Increased cohesion	Decreased cohesion
Social support, helping each other	Scapegoating & blaming others
Attention to task	Non-productivity
Collective efficacy	Negativity without action
Open communication & active listening	Lack of meaningful communication
Effective decision-making	Poor or absent decision-making
Conflict management	Open or covert conflict

G-APAM Summary

G-APAM uses coping potential and stress level to create quadrants of group behavior within an encompassing context. Each quadrant contains a constellation of behavior since both axes are continua. Stress and coping produce group movement as context, stressors, and coping resources change. Stress tends to produce movement toward higher stress and less effective coping potential (down and left); and coping tends to produce movement toward lower stress and more effective coping potential (up and right). Panel member comments include the possibility of additional Group APAM states when groups are viewed as complex adaptive systems.

The descriptors illustrated differences between effective and ineffective coping potential, with some differentiation of the four quadrants of the model. Many factors cited in the literature as potential influences in group adaptive potential were reflected in the descriptors. These include group cohesion, hope and optimism versus depression, social support, task orientation, collective efficacy, communication and culture, decision making, and conflict management. Fatigue was indirectly indicated, while anxiety was not included. More work is needed to expand and refine descriptors.

CONCLUSIONS

Stress is part of life and has been the subject of much research during the last fifty years. Initially, Selye was interested in the physiologic response to stress. Eventually he and others, most notably Lazarus, came to see the body and the mind were linked and the response to stress was more of a process than a reaction. This process is based on perception, "Stress is in the eye of the beholder" (Cooper, 2005). There is good stress, i.e., eustress, and bad stress, i.e. distress, depending on whether the situation presents a challenge or a threat to the individual.

The mind-body connection is central to the stress response. The mind, with thoughts and emotions, is connected via the central nervous system to the rest of the body, especially the endocrine and immune systems. This connection has led to an entire field of study, called psychoneuroimmunology.

Coping consists of what an individual thinks and does in an effort to deal with stressors, or the demands that tax or exceed resources (Lazarus, 2000, p. 201). In the Adaptive Potential Assessment Model, coping is the process of mobilizing resources. Individuals differ in their ability to adapt to stress based on their capacity to mobilize available coping resources. Factors which influence individual stress adaptation include attitudes, beliefs, values, and culture; internal personality resources such as a sense of coherence, hardiness, hope and optimism, perceived control, and self-efficacy; and external resources, most notably social support. The effect of coping can be adaptive or maladaptive.

One model for assessing and categorizing an individual's ability to mobilize coping resources is the Adaptive Potential Assessment Model, which is a construct in the nursing theory, Modeling and Role-Modeling. APAM uses indicators derived from physiological and psychological stress research to classify an individual's potential for adaptation (mobilization of coping resources in response to stressors) into three different stress and non-stress states. These are the stress states of Arousal and Impoverishment that reflect different adaptive potential, and the non-stress state, Equilibrium, that can be adaptive or maladaptive. Adaptive potential is dynamic, with movement from one state to another depending on the ability to mobilize resources in response to current stressors. Recent research has depicted a four state Adaptive Potential Assessment Model, differentiating adaptive and maladaptive equilibrium, and expanded the application of the model from individuals to groups.

The Adaptive Potential Assessment Model is based on the premise that stress is part of life; Selye, Antonovsky, and other theorists clearly agree. How we perceive or appraise the potential stressors determines what is perceived as stressful. Stress happens when our appraisal tells us we need to do something to adapt to the situation. This need to cope can, in fact, create more stressors, requiring continual reappraisal. The answer to the question, "What is stress?" depends on our perceptions, coping resources at the time and our ability to use them in the situation and what happens next. As caring professionals with the goal of facilitating adaptation and growth, nurses need a way to assess the coping potential of our clients. The Adaptive Potential Assessment Model (Erickson, 1976; Erickson & Swain, 1982; Erickson et al., 1983) gives us a tool to do just that.

The Modeling and Role-Modeling (MRM) theory facilitates adaptation for individuals by Modeling their world and Role-modeling interventions to fit that world. In the context of MRM, modeling is the process the nurse uses to develop an understanding of the client's unique perspective or world, and role-modeling is the process of "facilitating growth and development at the person's own pace and within the person's own model" (Erickson et al., 1983, p. 95). Personal growth and development include the need to adapt to stress. In MRM, the Adaptive Potential Assessment Model (APAM) is the method used to assess the state of an individual's ability to mobilize resources to cope with stressors. The G-APAM is the method that can be used for groups.

ENDNOTES

[1] Remember, the entire process from stimuli to impoverishment lasts only 72 hours.

[2] An example from everyday life is vaccinations given to children to protect them from diseases. The body has to build antibodies to be able to provide such protection. Antibodies are developed during the stage of resistance.

[3] An example from everyday life is when we come down with influenza, caused by a virus, and end up with a secondary infection caused by bacteria.

[4] The novice may want to bypass this information and go to the next section, Effects of Long Term Responses.

[5] Review Chapter 3, in which the authors discuss the cavalcade of chemical responses that occur during these processes.

[6] Especially, tumor necrosis factor alpha, interleukin-1 (IL-1), and interleukin-6 (IL-6).

[7] Review Chapter 3 to understand the importance of this concept. This is neuromodulation specifically focused on the immune system. This means chemicals are released, but (only) those that are consistent with healthy, normal functioning of the immune system.

[8] The Modeling and Role-Modeling theory would call this a stressor rather than a stress response.

[9] It is interesting to note these are some of the same feelings described by Erickson (1976) in her work on the APAM.

[10] Interestingly, this is like Selye's observation that we need to consider the source before we consider the outcome, but the two are inextricably related.

[11] Note that the word rhythms might be thought of as energy fields.

[12] H. Erickson made the following comment in respect to this definition of perceived control: *I think the two concepts are very different. People can have either internal or external locus of control and perceive control over their lives, or, these same people can perceive they don't have control. While I suspect internal locus of control folks perceive control more often than the others, I think these are different concepts and shouldn't be mixed up. Both are important for application of Modeling and Role-Modeling; we need to understand an individual's orientation (internal or external) and we need to understand their sense of control (perceived control) at the same time* (Personal communication, February 6, 2006).

[13] The temporal state of the group includes its history and its anticipated future as they influence the present.

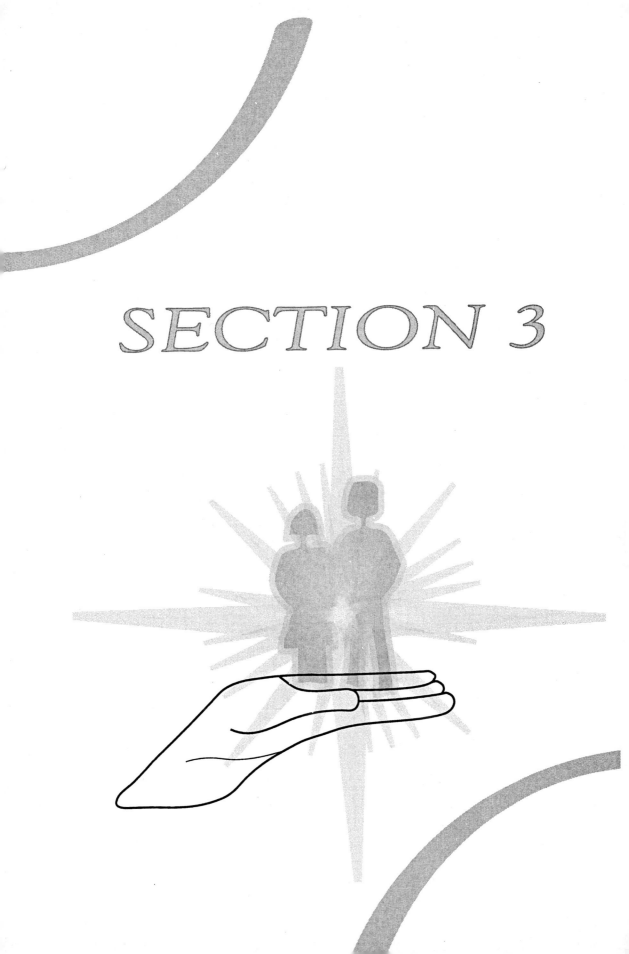

SECTION 3

SECTION III

THE HEALING PROCESS

The heart is more than just a living engine that pumps blood throughout the body. In fact, some thinkers and philosophers suggest that the heart is the seat of the human soul. Perhaps the soul doesn't exist within our hearts, but our hearts may contain the 'path' leading to the discovery of our souls. More than just an engine of flesh that beats unceasingly from the electrical stimulations of its pacemaker cells, the heart is also driven by a spark of spiritual energy or life force that would seem to leave the body at the time of death. ....(I)n the vibrational or energetic model, spirit is seen as the motivating force that animates the physical form. That is, our spirit, like a vaporous ghost, inhabits the mechanical vehicle we call the physical body. At the time of death, our spirit moves on, leaving behind only a lifeless shell. ....(I)t is the beingness of our spirit and its experiential journey through the physical world that creates the real adventure and mystery of a person's life.

Richard Gerber (2001). *A Practical Guide to Vibrational Medicine: Energy Healing and Spiritual Transformation* (p. 12).

The first section of this book was designed to expand the reader's understanding of how mind, body, and spirit interact to create holistic beings, a basic premise of the Modeling and Role-Modeling theory and paradigm. (Erickson, Tomlin & Swain, 1983). The second section built on this information and expanded on constructs embedded in MRM. This section presents application issues. Each chapter clarifies selected constructs including heart-to-heart connections, factors that enhance or impede connecting, nurturing growth, and facilitating development. The last two chapters address issues related to more difficult or traumatic experiences and the need for healing.

CHAPTER 9

HEART-TO-HEART:
NURSE-CLIENT RELATIONSHIPS

CAROLYN K. KINNEY

Our Greatest Fear

Our greatest fear is not that we are inadequate,
but that we are powerful beyond measure.
It is our light, not our darkness that frightens us.
We ask ourselves, Who am I to be brilliant,
gorgeous, handsome, talented and fabulous?
Actually, who are you not to be?
You are a child of God.
Your playing small does not serve the world.
There is nothing enlightened about shrinking
so that other people won't feel insecure around you.
We were born to make manifest the glory of God within us.
It is not just in some; it is in everyone.
And, as we let our own light shine, we consciously give
other people permission to do the same.
As we are liberated from our fear,
our presence automatically liberates others.

Marianne Williamson (1992). *A Return to Love* (pp. 190-191). New York: Harper
Collins.

OVERVIEW

Through the years, I have come to believe that when nurses and clients share deeply meaningful relationships, they connect *heart-to-heart*. These interactive, interpersonal relationships take on what Martin Buber, philosopher-theologian, called an "I-Thou" (Buber, 1970) or sacred nature. They facilitate growth in mind, body, *spirit*, and *Soul* in client and nurse alike. The more *conscious* we are in our intent to create heart-to-heart relationships, the more effectively we connect spirit-to-spirit with our clients, facilitate their ability to connect with their Soul, and experience holistic growth and healing. However, this requires that we embrace our spiritual nature, recognize we are spiritual beings first, and be fearless in sharing our spirit with others. I began this chapter with Williamson's inspiring prose-poem as a reminder that when we "...let our own light shine we consciously give other people permission to do the same. As we are liberated from our fear, our presence automatically liberates others."

This chapter revisits the concept of the interactive, interpersonal nurse-client relationship proposed by the Modeling and Role-Modeling (MRM) Theory (Erickson et al., 1983) with the intent of expanding our understanding of the potentially growth-producing and life-changing relationships that can occur between nurses and clients. It is organized into three sections. First, a discussion of the primacy of the nurse-client relationship is presented. Second, Heart-to-Heart relationships and spirit and Soul Connections are explored and explained. The chapter concludes with a case study, applying the perspectives of heart-to-heart Relationships and spirit and Soul Connections to the nurse-client relationship, and its outcomes.

PRIMACY OF NURSE-CLIENT RELATIONSHIP

Background

When I was introduced to Modeling and Role-Modeling in the 1980s, its emphasis on modeling the client's world as a prerequisite to providing competent nursing care appealed to me in ways no other nursing theory had. Prior to MRM, I explored various nursing theories and found I could not fully embrace them, primarily because they tended to objectify the client (often using the term 'patient'), and their nursing care approaches were typically from the nurse's perspective rather than the client's. While the importance of clients' needs was given lip service, the clients' perspective received little attention. Moreover, rarely did a nursing theory acknowledge the significance of the *relationship* between the nurse and client.

The MRM Theory (1983) authors posit that the fundamental nature of the nursing process is "the ongoing, interactive exchange that occurs when a caring, competent nurse relates to a client to nurture and support the client's growth and development toward health" (p. 104). This relationship begins at the moment of initial contact between nurse and client with recognition that the relationship itself is integral to the nurse's ability to model the client's world. As I gained understanding of MRM, I realized the nurse-client relationship must be cultivated through care and attention.

What I learned from others

Numerous client experiences over the years have helped clarify my thoughts regarding the nature and importance of the nurse-client relationship. One relationship that stands out was discussed in a publication several years ago (Kinney, 1990). The major purpose of the article was to provide a step-by-step description of five phases of the nurse-client relationship and the beneficial outcomes for the client (shown in Table 9.1) that evolved in concert with her developmental progression. These phases have been validated over the years in my work with several other clients.

Table 9.1 Phases of Nurse-Client Relationship and Client Outcomes

Phase	Description	Outcome
One	Working on Trust	Client attaches to nurse
Two	Working on Autonomy	Attachment to nurse maintained through use of transitional object
Three	Moving into Initiative	Client able to experience more control over situation
Four	Reworking Trust, Autonomy, and Initiative.	Client able to take more responsibility for own health.
Five	Reworking Trust, Autonomy, Initiative and Industry in stage of Identity.	Client integrates life experiences into holistic sense of self.

I have also had the privilege of guiding many undergraduate and graduate students through the process of inductively exploring their own philosophy and how they interface with the nurse-client relationship. Repeatedly, they have concluded there are key components of the relationship that affect client outcomes. These are shown in Table 9.2.

Table 9.2 Examples of Relationship Components and Client Outcomes

Relationship Components	Client Outcomes
Synchronous movement	Transformation of energy
Development of healthy Affiliated-Individuation	Spiritual awakening
Connecting with heart	Increased holistic well-being
Nurse, family, client bond	Stronger self-awareness
Mutual respect	Trust in self and others
Acceptance of client's beliefs	Increased sense of self
Compassionate care	Shows acceptance of Self

I have also learned that nurses benefit from deeply meaningful relationships with their clients; by giving of our heart, we also grow. Table 9.3 provides examples of these benefits.

Table 9.3 Nurses' expressed benefits from heartfelt experiences.

Renewed sense of Life Purpose
Transformation of self
Peak experience
Pieces of my heart
Changed perception of self
Higher sense of well-being
Heartfelt spiritual connection

Conclusions

It has become increasingly evident to me that there is more to the nurse-client relationship than we have acknowledged, comprehended, or communicated. When nurses use terms like "pieces of my heart," and "synchronous movement," and clients tell us verbally, in their demeanor, and in their actions that we have been instrumental in facilitating their growth and development, we understand, on some level, what is meant. I believe there is more to be understood about these linkages and their impact on the well-being of both clients and nurses. I propose that there is a need for a deeper understanding of the nature of heart-to-heart relationships that potentially lead to spiritual connections with our clients and facilitate them in connecting with their Soul. These connections facilitate their holistic growth, healing, and movement toward self-actualization.

HEART-TO-HEART RELATIONSHIPS

The Science of Heart-to-Heart Relationships

The term *heart* is defined as "a hollow, muscular organ of vertebrate animals that by its rhythmic contraction acts as a force pump maintaining the circulation of the blood" (Merriam-Webster's Collegiate Dictionary, 2001). However, in everyday language the word *heart* has broader connotations. Many idioms and commonly used phrases, such as *after one's own heart; from one's heart; get to the heart of; heart and soul; in one's heart of hearts; heart-to-heart,* reflect an intuitive knowledge of the heart as the source of meaningful ways of thinking and being. Poets and philosophers often describe the heart as providing subtle, yet essential knowledge and information. For example, the philosopher Saint-Exupèry (1943) stated, "...and now here is my secret, a very simple secret: it is only with the heart that one can see rightly, what is essential is invisible to the eye" (p. 70). Thus, the heart's role and function is far more complex than simply pumping blood through the physical body. Now, we know it serves as a key organizer of the whole person.

The Heart as a Reactor

We've known for years that the heart reacts to messages sent from other parts of the body. For example, the work of Friedman and Rosenman (1964) showed how emotions impacted the well-being of the heart. Following that line of thought, Ornish, Gotto, and Miller (1979), showed hostility plays a major part in cardiac well-being. More recently, Barrios-Choplin, McCraty, and Cryer, (1997), researchers at the Institute for HeartMath, identified how this happens. They found that *heart rate variability* (HRV*)*, a measurement of beat-to-beat changes in the heart rate, is a dynamic reflection of "our inner emotional states" (p. 35). They report that "By measuring people's HRV, the research team was able to see how the heart and nervous system respond to stress and different emotions as we experience them" (Barrios-Choplin et al., 1997, pp. 193-201). Their work further supported the notion that the heart reacted to messages sent from other parts of the body, but it added a new dimension. They also noted how these changes affected the body in return.

Their research revealed that disharmonious heart rhythms are inefficient and lead to increased stress on the heart, and this in turn affects other body systems. A typical HRV pattern of someone feeling angry or frustrated is irregular and disordered because the two branches of the autonomic nervous (sympathetic and parasympathetic) system fail to work in synchrony. In contrast, when the person has feelings of caring, appreciation, love, and compassion, the opposite is created. "These heart-based feelings generate the smooth and harmonious HRV rhythms that are considered to be indicators of cardiovascular efficiency and nervous system balance" (Childre & Martin, 1999, p. 37).[1]

While this was of interest, it wasn't until researchers discovered the heart produced a hormone called atrial natriuetic factor (ANF) that affects the blood vessels, kidneys, adrenal glands, and regulatory regions in the brain (McCraty, Atkinson, & Tomasino, 2001), that the heart was reclassified as an endocrine or hormonal organ. It was no longer thought to be just a pump. Prior to this, John and Beatrice Lacey (1978) had argued that regulatory systems of the body affected the brain, suggesting there are more feedback loops in the regulation of the body than previously known. This led to additional research of the heart-brain connections.

The Heart Brain

Researchers at the Institute of HeartMath concluded the heart has a mind of its own. According to Childre and Martin (1999), "it directs and aligns many systems in the body so that they can function in harmony with one another" (p. 4). Using the term *heart brain* to describe this heart *intelligence*, Armour (1991, 1999) reported that with each heartbeat neural information is sent from the *heart brain* to the brain in the head, as follows: the *heart brain* senses hormonal levels, rate of heartbeat, and pressure information, internally processes this information, translates it into neurological impulses, and then communicates with the brain in the head via the vagus nerve and spinal column nerves. In turn, these neurological signals have a regulatory influence on the autonomic nervous system impulses sent from the brain back to the heart, the blood vessels, other glands and organs, as well as the cerebral cortex, "...that part of the brain that governs our higher thought and reasoning capacities" (p. 30).

The heart also influences neural activity in the amygdala, the area of the brain related to emotional experiences. Thus, the neural activity of the heart has a continuous effect on our perceptions and emotions. As Armour (1991) maintains, "The existence of communication pathways linking the heart with our higher brain centers helps explain how information from the heart can modify these mental and feeling states, as well as performance" (p. 30).

Today, we know "The heart and brain maintain a continuous, two-way dialogue, with each influencing the other's functioning. It is also known that the signals the heart sends the brain can influence perception, emotional processing, and higher cognitive functions" (McCraty et al., 2001). While the heart is a pump, it is also a vital communication organ. It interacts with the entire body not only by way of pumping blood, but also by way of chemical communications that affect the neurological system throughout the body.

...the heart communicates with the brain and the rest of the body in three ways: neurologically (through transmission of nerve impulses), biochemically (through hormones and neurotransmitters), and biophysically (through pressure waves (Armour, 1991, p. 28).

The Heart's Electromagnetic Field

Not only does the heart communicate with the body through neurotransmission and neuromodulation[2] as discussed above, there is growing evidence it communicates through its energy field as well (Armour, 1991, p. 28). In fact, the pattern and quality of the energy emitted by the heart and transmitted throughout the body is the most powerful in the body. According to Armour (1991), "The heart's electromagnetic field is...approximately five thousand times greater in strength than the field produced by the brain... (It) not only permeates every cell in the body but also radiates outside of us; it can be measured up to eight to ten feet away..." (p. 33).[3] Furthermore, research (McCraty et al., 2001) has shown that the heart's energy field changes with our emotions and is registered by the brains of people around us. They propose that *energetic exchanges* may be the bases for intuition and even aspects of human consciousness (see Chapter 3).

Based on the findings of the HeartMath research, they theorize that "the heart is a major conduit through which spirit enters the human system" (p. 261) and the spiritual qualities of love, compassion, and appreciation increase the coherence and order of the heart rhythm patterns. Finally, Childre and Martin (1999) propose that, "coherence manifests when spirit merges with humanness" (p. 261).[4]

THE PHILOSOPHY LINKED TO THE SCIENCE

For centuries, healers, philosophers, and others have assumed the heart is the seat of our emotion, the center of our being. Common language reflected such thought. For example, people who are perceived as uncaring are often talked about as having a *cold heart* while those who show compassion are considered to have a *warm heart.* Nevertheless, until recently, most scientists argued that our heart is only a reactor to our feelings and thoughts. Still, science didn't curtail holistic practitioners who continued to view the heart as a major affecter of our overall well-being. Many pursued energy therapies that were primarily based in ancient philosophy or belief systems.

Today, the science produced by the Institute of HeartMath provides opportunities for us to revisit ancient knowledge and consider the wisdom passed down through the years. Brekke and Schultz proposed, in Chapter 2, that the human energy system is composed of meridians, chakras, and the auric field. Key to our discussion in this chapter is the concept of chakras, and specifically, the fourth chakra or heart chakra. Figure 2.1 provides an illustration of the relative location of the seven inbody and 3 out of body chakras related to the following discussion. Figure 2.3 provides an illustration of the energy fields of two people whose energy fields are synchronized and Figure 2.4 provides an illustration of two people in the same location, whose energy fields are not synchronized. All three figures are relevant to the focus of this chapter, heart-to-heart connections.

The Energy of the Heart

The Heart chakra or energy vortex in the upper chest is viewed, metaphysically and energetically, as the place in the body where the earth energies of the three lower chakras meet the spiritual energies of the three upper ones. It is believed to be strategically located to serve as a link between our physical, emotional, social, and spiritual selves and provides us with the ability to feel and experience our connection to everyone and everything (Dale, 2003).

Unconditional Love and Compassion.

The heart chakra is viewed as the seat of unconditional love and compassion. Its energetic influence affects our ability to consider the needs of self and others, to be gentle in our expectations of self and others, and to be fully engaged in the challenges and joys of life (Dale, 2003; Judith, 1996).

The ability to have unconditional love and compassion for others comes from experiencing the same for our self. Being with, knowing, and experiencing our own longings, suffering, and pain opens us to the potential of having a deeper understanding of others. Learning from our life challenges can provide us wisdom and understanding, which we can share with others.

Learning to love self and others is described repeatedly as the major expression of the heart chakra. As Gerber (2001) emphasizes:

> *The expression of love is perhaps one of the most important lessons that humans have incarnated upon the physical plane to learn. Without love, existence can be dry and meaningless. It is necessary that we learn to love not only those around us, but also ourselves* (p. 470).

Heart and Soul. Dale (2003) explains that while "most references to the human energy system concentrate on the front side of the chakras" (p. 113), there are important differences between the contributions of the front side and the back side of the chakras. The front side relates more to the conscious day-to-day reality, the back side pertains to the unconscious reality; it contains information stored in our unconscious mind. The back side is usually experienced through dreams, mystical experiences, intuition, or unexplainable physical sensations.

Additional ideas provided by Dale (2004) are related to the Heart Chakra's relationship with the soul. The back side connects us with our soul's playful aspects. Regardless of our chronological age, our soul has an ageless youthful quality; we are all "children of the Divine Source" (Dale, p. 120). The child's work is to play, learn, develop, explore, have fun, and grow. When the back side of the Heart Chakra is open and unblocked, we are more likely to be open to true desires of our soul and merge with spirit or the "divine light of the universe" (Dale, p. 120).

Conclusions

The heart plays many important roles in our lives and is highly significant to us—physically, emotionally, socially, spiritually, and energetically. It has its own intelligence and interactively communicates neurologically, biochemically, and biophysically with the brain and the rest of the body. It links our physical, social, and emotional subsystems with our spirit, and serves as a bridge between us, in human form, and the Universal energy field. From this latter perspective, it also serves to connect us with our Soul. This brings us to a discussion of the relationship between the spirit and Soul. H. Erickson states the following:

> *We know the heart is more than a pumping machine; it is an endocrine gland that sends and receives messages throughout the body. Since it creates the strongest energy field within the human body, it has the potential to affect the energy fields of our entire being as well as those of others. Science has affirmed these hypotheses, providing some validity to the beliefs of ancient philosophers and healers who perceived that the heart is the seat of our emotions, the center of our being. As we reevaluate their beliefs within the context of known science, some of their 'truths' become more plausible.*
>
> *If the heart has the strongest electromagnetic field, it has the potential to affect energy in other parts of our own body as well as those of others; the heart can send and receive chemical messages which impact how we view the world and experience relationships; and if the heart is our primary link to Universal energy, then it is possible the heart is the center of our holistic being. This would mean the heart serves as a coordinator for the mind and body and as a bridge, mind and body with Soul* (H. Erickson, personal communication, March 5, 2006).

SPIRIT AND SOUL RELATIONSHIP

Spirit and the Soul

The concepts of spirit and Soul are ubiquitous, yet mysterious in our modern, materialistic, and scientific culture. The words are used casually and frequently, yet they have multiple meanings. Often, soul and spirit are used interchangeably and distinguishing between the two may seem unnecessary. For the purposes of what I am proposing, I believe there is value in using Soul and spirit as two separate, but closely related concepts. Schwartz (1997) provides a simple yet instructive way to think about the differences. According to him, spirit can be seen as analogous to energy and soul analogous to information; spirit is love and soul is wisdom; "...spirit provides the force to do the work of the soul" (p. 76).

Spirit

In many languages the words for spirit and breath are the same. In Sanskrit, the word for breath is *prana*; in Greek, *pneuma*; in Hebrew, *ruach*; and in Latin, *spritus*. When we inspire, we bring the spirit into the body. Weil (1995) writes:

> *At the very center of our being is rhythmic movement, a cyclic expansion and contraction that is both in our body and outside it, that is both in our mind and in our body, that is both in our consciousness and not in it. Breath is the essence of being, and in all aspects of the universe we can see the same rhythmic pattern of expansion and contraction, whether in the cycles of day and night, waking and sleeping, high and low tides, or seasonal growth and decay"* (pp. 203-204).

Spirit, then, comes to energize and bring rhythmical expanding and contracting life into the physical body. As Dale (2003) states:

> *...the word 'spiritual' means just that—spirit-filled. The bravest and most worthy desire we can have as a human being is to be filled with the spirit, the true essence, of ourselves. As this self is really an aspect of the Divine Source, I believe that life is about learning how to accept that we are of the Divine Source (the All, the Great Spirit) and that we deserve to fully express this truth. Living on purpose is about expressing this spirit self* (p. 92).[5]

In the MRM theory, the spiritual drive is shown "permeating all aspects of the human being." H. Erickson (Chapter 1, Figure 1.3) asserts that the spirit or spiritual drive has more influence on our total well-being than any of the biophysical, psychological, cognitive, or social subsystems. It draws from and returns to the Universe, and "pulls us toward integration of body, mind, and Soul." To this notion of an integrating force, I add that spirit is that aspect of our selves which connects us to the Source of Life; it is the Life Force that energizes our holistic being. From the very moment we take our first breath, our spirit infuses within us our *Reason for Being*. Living with awareness of our spiritual nature is living *on purpose* and living *with purpose*.

Spiritual awareness involves subtle sensations—what might be called intuition or listening to an inner voice. When this inner voice is recognized, listened to, and heeded, our life and experiences are infused with meaning, clarity, and focus. Integrating our experiences with the meaning they hold for us can result in growth-producing and/or healing processes. There is a sense of calmness and peaceful awareness that comes from being connected with and attuned to our spiritual nature. This expanded awareness creates in us a sense of transcendence that contributes to fulfilling our life's purpose and connects us to our soul and our soul's purpose (Kinney, 1996).

Soul

Our soul can be conceptualized as a vast, eternal entity—the container of all containers. Its mission is to gather and unify. Its purpose is to show us there is "…something larger, more beautiful than the individual and to invite us, in radiance, to become a part of it. The agenda of the Soul then is to move us from focused individual awareness to a melting diffused awareness of our truly unified state" (Kingman, 1998, p. 89).

In *Modern Man in Search of a Soul* (1993), Jung explains that the deepest part of the mind is transpersonal and extends beyond the bounds of one individual. Jung coined the term 'collective unconscious' for his notion of the transpersonal mind explaining that it was a common possession of all humanity. Within the deepest layers of the mind there are universal patterns that shape who we are and provide direction for the development of our lives. He called these patterns 'archetypes' the most important of which was the Self. According to Jung, there is a universal pattern of wholeness, the Self that continually lives within each one of us whether or not we are consciously aware of it. As Thurston (1989) explains "…we might be tempted to say that it is sleeping inside us, but perhaps it is we who are asleep in our daily familiar consciousness" (p. 4).

That Which is in Charge. The soul could also be considered *that which is in charge* because it is the aspect of our self that "carries our purpose from the Divine Source—God, Buddha, Spirit, Creator, Christ, or other Higher Power" (Dale, 2001, p. 14). Our soul is the storehouse for "everything we experience from life to life, from chakra to chakra, from cell to cell" (Dale, 2001, p. 93).

From this perspective, it could be reasoned that the soul is the *source of our inner knowing* and *inner wisdom*. The soul knows what is needed, when it is needed, and knows when it is received in order to fulfill our life's purpose. Our life's purpose is to live our soul's purpose, learn what we are to learn, and grow as we were meant to grow, so we can contribute that which is ours to contribute.

Soul Needs and Being Needs. Maslow's (1996) distinction between basic needs and higher-level needs (i.e., being needs or self-actualization needs) is beneficial in understanding the soul's needs: *basic needs* come from feelings of lack and deficiency while *being needs* arise out of an awareness of abundance. Inherent in all humans is the potential for and striving to addressing being needs and moving toward self-actualization. As Wilber (2005) explains, based on Maslow's work, the human potential movement discovered that:

...in the farther reaches of human nature, in the realms of self-transcendence needs, in the deepest reaches of your very own Self and your ever-present I AMness, people reported being one with a Ground of Being, one with Spirit, one with infinity, a radiant riot of the all-encompassing, call it what you will...And not just as a passing state, but as a permanent trait—a permanent stage of competence acquisition. Not that you always live up to it, but that you always have access to it" (p xvii).

Wilber adds that competence acquisition in this higher sense of being is similar to learning a language. Once it is learned, it is permanently accessible whether or not it is used all the time. However, the more it is dipped into it or accessed the more it will be available and contribute to one's growth toward self-actualization. Maslow (1996) identified spiritual experiences or what he called *peak experiences* as one way to access self-actualization states. People at all stages of development and in all levels of basic needs satisfaction can have peak experiences. These experiences provide connections to the soul, address the soul's needs, and facilitate movement toward self-actualization.[6]

The Soul's Purpose. The use of metaphors and images is helpful in understanding complex concepts. In Chapter 1, H. Erickson uses the image of a string of pearls as a metaphor for how our life experiences accumulate, provide the basis for who we are, and build toward knowing our "...Essence of Self or our Soul-Work for this lifetime." Jung (1933) provides another illustrative metaphor for the nature of our soul's purpose..."...life is the unfolding of our tent of wisdom... each of us is born with our own unique tent" (p. 95).

This ancient image provides an archetypal metaphor for the human soul. While those of us living in modern times do not commonly use tents as our place of residence, we can still appreciate the process of unfolding our tent as a way of discovering and manifesting the potential wisdom that is within us. Whether we are aware of it or not, our tent is always with us; it provides an innate sense of purpose; it is our *place in the universe,* and what we can call our *Eternal Home.*

Conclusions

Heart, spirit, and soul are literally, energetically, and metaphorically linked in a cyclical, reciprocal way. Awareness through our heart facilitates our ability to relate heart-to-heart and, in turn, enables us to experience spirit-to-spirit connections. These linkages can occur simultaneously and automatically whether or not we consciously label them as such. Table 9.4 summarizes the material covered in this section. The key components of soul, spirit, and heart are aligned to show how the concepts interrelate.

	Table 9.4 Aligning Key Components of Soul, Spirit, and Heart	
Soul	Spirit	Heart
Vast entity Container of containers String of Pearls Tent of Wisdom	Source of energy Connects us to Life Force Spiritual awareness brings peace and calmness	Awakes to spirit A key organizer for connecting spirit with body
That which is in charge Contains Reason for Being or Soul's purpose in this lifetime Source of 'Inner Voice' Source of Being Needs	Connects to Soul and Soul's purpose for this life-time Listens to 'inner voice' Attends to being needs	Strongest energy-field in body Directs and aligns body systems Functions as "little brain"
Unified state Transpersonal Collective unconscious	Living on purpose and living with purpose Link to Divine Source	Continuous effect on perceptions and emotions
Eternal Home Our place in the Universe Sense of Abundance I AMness	Draws from and returns to universe Pulls us toward integration of mind, body, and soul Sense of transcendence	Connects to self and others through heart-based feelings: caring, unconditional acceptance, and compassion

INTEGRATING CONCEPTS

Connecting Heart-to-Heart

Nurses can and do form heart-to-heart connections, sometimes consciously, sometimes not. Applying the findings of the Institute of HeartMath, presented above, when we have feelings of compassion and love for our clients and ourselves, and our thoughts are directed at providing care based on unconditional acceptance of self and clients, we generate smooth and harmonious heart rhythms in our own hearts, and establish coherence in the rhythms throughout our bodies. When these attitudes, feelings, and thoughts are conveyed to clients by words, actions, we radiate electromagnetic heart signals and create an environment conducive to synchronized energy fields between the two. When our clients experience the synchrony between the two energy fields, we have created a heart-to-heart connection.

Spirit and Soul Connections.
Heart-to-heart connections create the context necessary for us to build a meaningful relationship, or a heart-to-heart relationship. This type of relationship makes it possible for nurses to connect, spirit-to-spirit.

Nurses can and do connect spirit-to-spirit whether or not they are consciously aware of doing so. When we experience acceptance and compassion in our heart for our clients, we send verbal and nonverbal *messages transformed into energy* that tell them we can be trusted. If we build on this and support them to trust themselves and listen to their inner voices, we increase their potential for spirit-to-spirit connections.

H. Erickson states,

> *When we create a context for building meaningful relationships, we can relate at the heart-to-heart level of connection or we can go deeper and build a spiritual relationship. To go deeper, to build a spiritual relationship with another person requires that we step into their world, understand it from their perspective, and build within that context. Otherwise, our good intentions, our love and compassion may be appreciated and may facilitate growth, but is unlikely to reach the depth necessary to have a spirit-to-spirit relationship. When we attain a spiritual relationship with another person, we are interfacing, Self (of client)-to-Self (of nurse). This is different from interfacing at the sense-of-self of one person to the sense-of-self of another* (Personal communication, March 7, 2006).

Spiritual relationships between two people help both persons experience satisfaction of higher level needs, such as beauty and creativity. Spiritual relationships also provide the context necessary for either or both people to recognize and address soul-related needs such as understanding the meaning of their experiences and realizing their life purpose.

H. Erickson goes on to say,

> *When we learn to connect heart-to-heart, we have taken the first step necessary to build relationships that have lasting impact on both persons in the relationship. We have created a Caring Field (Watson, 2005), the precursor to in depth work necessary to helping people heal. While we can facilitate growth without a spiritual relationship, we cannot facilitate extensive healing without one. This issue will be further addressed in Chapter 14.*
>
> *It is important to point out that all nurses can connect heart-to-heart. This is not something that requires a lot of time or extensive interactions, but it is something that is done purposefully. Nurses who work in intensive care units have told me they notice the difference in their clients' heart patterns when they are purposeful about connecting as compared to those times when they simply approach their clients with the intent of emptying vacupak bags, checking IV's and so forth. Heart-to-heart connections are a way of being. I've said previously, doing without being is empty. Now I'm adding to that statement and saying that doing*

without being may be worse than empty, it may have negative effects on others. Since we cannot not communicate, the nonverbal (and, therefore, energetic) messages we send when we don't establish an intentional mindset before and during our interaction can have a negative impact on our clients.

Some of you may say you don't have time, that spirit-to-spirit relationships take too much effort, too much time, and too much thinking about something other than what you have to do. My response to you is you have forgotten that the most important thing you can ever do to help another person is to believe in their worth and their inherent need to be valued and loved. This doesn't take time or thinking; it requires that you believe you are here for a purpose, and it has something to do with the work you have chosen. It has something to do with why you decided to help other people grow and heal. You simply have to believe in yourself first, and then you can more easily believe in the value of other human beings.

You also need to remember that a connection is the prerequisite to a relationship. The type of connection you create will influence the type of relationship you are able to build. When you have a heart-to-heart connection, you can build on that and create a heart-to-heart relationship, which provides the context for spirit-to-spirit connections. Perhaps some of us will go further and build spirit-to-spirit relationships as well, but from my experience, these relationships are less common. Nevertheless, they can happen (Personal communication, March 7, 2006).

Connecting, Spirit-to-Spirit

Our intention influences the nature of the relationship we build with others. *Relationships can be built at the spirit-to-spirit level when it is our intent to do so!* When we build such relationships, we can help people connect with their Soul and initiate understanding of their Soul-work. We can do this by having the *intent to create heart-to-heart relationships* with our clients and connect spirit-to-spirit with them. When we incorporate into our *Way of Being* an *intent* to make heart-to-heart connections and build a relationship within the context of the client's world-view, we create a Caring Field.

When we deepen the relationship, we connect spirit-to-spirit, enhancing the ability of both members to connect with their Souls. For example, when we affirm our clients' worth, facilitate their sense of control, help them recognize and build on their strengths and set mutual goals (for growth), we are using the Five Aims of Interventions.[7] As people grow and build basic need assets, they automatically have a drive toward higher need satisfaction. As we expand our work, help them experience the beauty, love, playfulness, and joy in *their world*, our clients experience being need satisfaction. As their experiences increase, they accumulate higher-level need assets, have transcendent experiences, and move closer to self-actualizing. As they do, they move closer to fully connecting with their Soul and understanding their Life Purpose.

> When we intentionally create heart-to-heart relationships, and address our clients' basic needs as well as their higher-level needs, we build mutual trust, facilitate secure attachment, and create healthy affiliated-individuation with them. As we do this, we create spirit-to-spirit connections. The outcome is that both nurse and client benefit in ways that enhance their own growth toward self-actualization.

REVISITING REBECCA

Rebecca's story, initially told several years ago in the article (Kinney, 1990) mentioned above, provides an example of how heart-to-heart connections can be enhanced to create heart-to-heart relationships, spirit-to-spirit connections and relationships, and Soul-to-Soul connections.

I will start with a diagram (Figure 9.1) that Rebecca gave me some time into our relationship. As she handed it to me, she explained that drawing it had helped her visualize and understand what she was experiencing. It was titled: *Phases of Dependency.* I was immediately struck by how the diagram visually captured the progressive phases of *Affiliated-Individuation (AI)*[8] and paralleled the progression of our relationship. Since Rebecca was a nurse and interested in learning about MRM, we had occasionally discussed how she could apply aspects of the theory to her nursing practice. I shared with her how her diagram could be interpreted within the context of AI and explained what this meant. She welcomed this alternative interpretation as being much more positive than her previous perspectives. She re-titled her diagram accordingly.

I see the progression of healthy AI represented by the diagram as being instrumental in the creation of a trusting, interactive, and interpersonal relationship or what I call a *heart-to-heart relationship.* This healthy AI also facilitated our ability to connect spirit-to-spirit and address some of her soul needs.

> When we have the intent of creating a heart-to-heart relationship many heart-based messages need to be conveyed. Messages such as: (1) I accept you as you are (unconditional acceptance), (2) I want to understand, and I care (compassion), and (3) all your needs are worthy of my attention (nurturance) are staples in the development of a trusting, functional nurse-client relationships within the MRM theory.

Creating a Heart-to-Heart Relationship

When we aim to connect heart-to-heart, we need to consider our own readiness for such a connection. While I learned to prepare myself using different approaches, two techniques, *Listening with Heart* and *Connecting with Breath* (See Appendix E), are meditations I routinely used, so I could be fully present, attuned to messages from within myself, and receptive to universal wisdom. They are also important techniques to help us stay connected to our clients and deepen the relationship.[9]

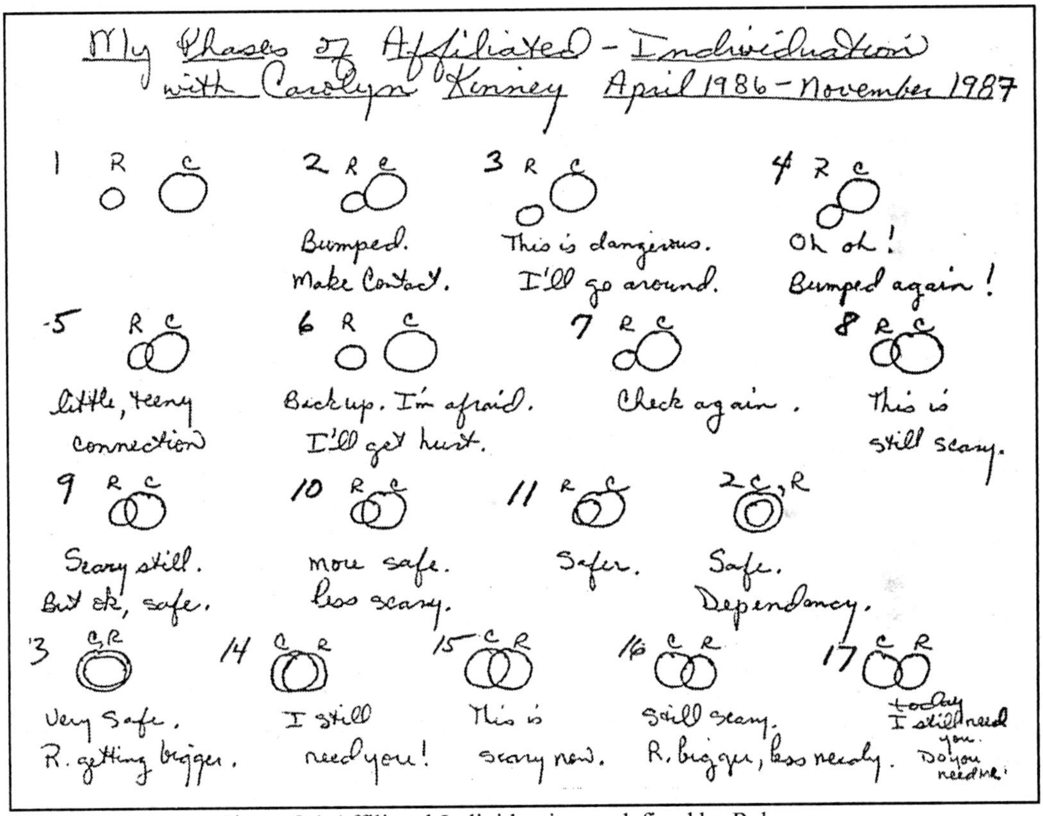

Figure 9.1 Affiliated-Individuation as defined by Rebecca.

One example that illustrates the importance of being prepared and staying connected follows.

One day during our meeting, Rebecca was visibly upset and crying. I realized she needed to be comforted, so she could calm herself and tell me what was happening with her. I reached over and touched her gently. In response to cues that she was receptive to my touch I reached out, moved closer to her, and held her. I quietly focused on my heart and breath, and then synchronized my breathing with hers. After about five minutes her breathing slowed, she had calmed, and said, "How do you do that?" I responded, "How do I do what?" She replied, "Make me feel safe and know deep inside that you really care." She was then able to tell me about the experience that had upset her.[10]

This story illustrates our relationship as shown in Phase 5, Figure 9.1. If you refer back to Rebecca's drawing, you will note that Phase 1 represents our relationship as being distant, or in isolation one from the other. Phase 2 represents a heart-to-heart connection, followed by the scare (Phase 3) it precipitated in Rebecca. Notice that Rebecca *never* moved back as far as shown in Phase 1; the heart-to-heart connection continued.

Phases 4-8 demonstrate a deepening of our heart-to-heart relationship. During this period we had our ups and downs, but each time Rebecca continued to draw closer, to try to merge. Phase 9 depicts the beginning of our sprit-to-spirit connection. You will notice that as this happens, Rebecca merges her Self with my Self; we connect sprit-to-spirit. As this happens, Rebecca visibly grows (see Phases 11-13). As she starts to emerge on the *other side,* she clearly states that she continues to need the relationship, but she is now different from what she was before we started. By the time she reaches Phase 17, she is nearly the same size as I am, and ready to *try her own wings.*

You may ask how this happened. It didn't happen in a few moments or even a few days. It took time. The following describes the process in more detail.

Deepening the Relationship

As Rebecca grew, our relationship grew; sometimes we made spirit-to-spirit connections. As a result, Rebecca became more comfortable sharing difficult experiences and beliefs. As she grew, she was confronted with past learning and memories and with discrepancies between her previous view of the world and her current knowledge. The conflicts, which resulted from the discrepancy between the two world-views provided me with opportunities to help her 'reframe' her thinking and 'remodel' her worldview.

One such opportunity occurred when Rebecca was considering the possibility that a longstanding problem with her leg might improve. Here is how I described this situation previously (Kinney, 1990):

...Rebecca started wondering what it would be like not to have the pain in her leg. We talked about what it meant for her to finally have a definite diagnosis and have the sense that she might be able to do something about controlling her pain and improving her ability to walk. She responded that she felt ambivalent about this possibility. The pain had been with her for a long time and in some respects was an indicator that she was alive, that she existed. I responded to this realization with 'So you don't know if you want to give it up?' 'Right,' she said, 'Maybe I'm not ready, maybe it means something to me that I can't explain in words.'

I supported her in this idea and said that things sometimes happen to people before they have the cognitive ability, the language and words, to label these experiences and the feelings associated with them. I fully understood and realized the pain indeed served a purpose. However, I emphasized, 'There are a lot of other ways of knowing we are alive, of knowing we exist, such as the joy, happiness, and pleasures of life. These pleasures are ours and no one can take them away from us. Pain is one type of sensory message, but other sensory messages are much more pleasant and meaningful. Having fun and enjoying pleasurable sensations are our rights, and we all deserve to have these joyful experiences.' She agreed to think about these ideas before our next appointment (p. 388).

At our next appointment, she said a friend had suggested she talk to her leg to see if she could discover why she was still having problems. She said she'd tried, but nothing happened, so wondered what I thought about it. I supported the idea and suggested it might take a while before she would be able to get a response; and it might work better if she did it while in a relaxed state.[11] I then suggested she ask her leg *what it needed* rather than being confrontational. "Oh," she said, "You mean be nice to it!" (Kinney, 1990, p. 389).

At the following appointment she announced that she had asked her leg, 'What's the matter, what do you need?' She had gotten a rather surprising response and was not sure what it meant....Proceeding cautiously, she said, 'It said, This is my body and you can't touch it. It just shouted at me!' I held her closer and comforted her by saying, That's right, it is your body, you are in charge of it and nobody can touch it without your permission. After several minutes she regained her composure and indicated she had not thought of her body in that way before—that it indeed belonged to her, that she owned it, and that she could take care of it however she wanted (p. 389).

This experience proved to be a turning point for Rebecca. It introduced the idea that by developing her ability to relax and being open to her inner voice, she could learn important information about herself. As a result, she began embracing the idea that she could have more control over the way she felt and thought, and she began incorporating more happy and joyful experiences into her daily life. She told me these positive experiences made her feel more alive and she realized she had much to live for and give others.

Connecting with Soul

As Rebecca became more comfortable with the idea that life could be full of joyful experiences, she began addressing her 'being needs,' her soul needs. She saw the value of having time to 'just be.' She spent more time outside, listening to birds sing, and enjoying the sun and breeze. She began looking at life more from the perspective of her life's purpose. She also began looking for opportunities to address her clients' being needs. She explained one day, "I don't think we pay enough attention to our clients' being needs. I was caring for a man recently and realized the ICU environment is so sterile and impersonal. I asked the man's family what kind of music he liked, brought in a tape I thought he'd like, and played it on my tape player. He really seemed to be both calmer and more alert after that."

Connecting with her soul provided Rebecca with the resources and desire to reach out and help her clients connect with their souls. As reflected in her AI diagram, the gentle dance between the two circles graphically reflects Rebecca's changing perceptions of her expanding sense of Self within the context of our relationship. Inherent in this growing awareness of her own worth and potential is movement toward self-actualization, a discovery of her true Self.

Reflecting on the many times during our work together when we talked about how much I was learning from her and that what she was teaching me would be passed on to others, I realize how far-reaching the impact of such a relationship can be. Knowing she is better able to help others because of her willingness to work hard on herself means that our work together has had a profound ripple-out effect. Seeing Rebecca become increasingly confident in her contributions as a nurse, wife, and mother, and her willingness to share her wisdom with others, has contributed to my sense of achieving my own life's purpose. I have benefited from many 'peak experiences' through my relationship with Rebecca and subsequently writing about it. Expanding my view of what our relationship means has given me a renewed sense of my life's purpose and has contributed to the progressive and never-ending realization of my own Essence of Self. I know I am enriched by enriching the lives of others.

Rebecca wrote a poem, specifically to be included at the end of the 1990 article. I offer it here because her own words provide the best evidence that through our relationship Rebecca addressed many of her basic, spiritual, and soul-related needs. I see her poem reflecting a timeless universal awakening and her opening to a transcendent window of possibilities.

Rebecca's Poem

My colors were purple and black,
My nurse helped me add red, orange, yellow, green, and blue.
Now I am a vibrant picture.

My pieces were scattered all about.
My nurse helped me gather them up and pull them together.
Now I am peacefully intact.

My garden was untended — full of thistle and weeds.
My nurse helped me clear it and plant my handful of seeds.
Now I flower with happiness.

A Path of unknown wonders lies before me.
I have my pictures, my self, my flowers.
I feel strong and alive!
My nurse can be so proud.
Now I am ready to set forth toward many more discoveries
(Kinney, 1990, p. 393).

APPLICATION TO CLIENTS IN MOMENT TO MOMENT INTERACTIONS

Rebecca's story is an example of working with a person who needed help healing. Healing takes time. Chapter 14 will address some issues related to this issue. We recognize this is a different type of practice than that of the hospital-based nurse or home-health nurse. For the time being, suffice to say, heart-to-heart connections can happen in split seconds, and they are the bases for developing trusting, functional relationships. You have heard or read many of my stories derived from acute, home health, and other settings. What has been written above about making connections pertains to all those as well. I learned years ago the way to be most efficient and achieve my goals, was to aim at building a relationship that connects person to person. I also learned this type of connection has to be within the context of the other person's world-view.[12] This type of connection is what I describe as a heart-to-heart relationship with spiritual connections (H. Erickson, personal communication, March 20, 2006).

IMPLICATIONS

While there are many implications that warrant discussion, I will focus on five. These are not necessarily listed in order of priority though I see them building progressively from one to the next.

1. At the beginning of this chapter, I indicated that relating heart-to-heart with our clients requires that we embrace our own spiritual nature, recognize we are all spiritual beings first and foremost, and be fearless in sharing our spirit with others. You may ask: Why is this important? How can I do this?

When we encourage and support others in addressing their being needs, we must prepare ourselves by first addressing our own being needs. The more comfort and confidence we have in our awareness that we are spiritual beings, and the more we are in tune with our purpose in life, the less fear we will have in sharing this way of thinking and being with our clients.

Increasing our ability to connect with our spiritual nature can be viewed in the same way as increasing our competence in any other knowledge and skill. The more we access and develop our skills the more competent and comfortable we will be in using and sharing them. Here are some suggestions for doing this.

a) Various HeartMath techniques can be used in preparation for creating heart-to-heart relationships. Specifically, practicing a technique called the Heart Lock-in for five minutes or more a couple of times a day has been found to help increase the practitioner's energy level and feelings of emotional and physical balance. (Additional information can be obtained from http://HeartMath.org)

b) Engaging in some form of regular meditation, contemplative prayer, breathing or relaxation exercises provides us the opportunity to be open to our spiritual nature and develop our ability to draw upon our inner wisdom and knowledge.

c) Also, the two exercises outlined in the Appendix E are helpful in focusing your attention as you prepare to work with your clients just prior to and during your contact with them.

2. We need to take care of our physical, emotional, as well as, spiritual needs in order to replenish ourselves and have the resources to draw from as we create meaningful relationships with others. Nurses tend to focus on everyone else's needs first, and then, if there is any time left, we attend to our own needs. It is helpful to be reminded that our relationship with ourselves provides the basis for our relationship with everyone else. How can we approach others with love and compassion if we do not do the same for ourselves?

3. It is important to be cognizant that when we approach clients with the intent of creating heart-to-heart relationships and addressing spirit and soul needs, we often are making a commitment to see them through difficult experiences and situations--to stay with them through what is commonly referred to as the dark night of the soul. This type of commitment comes very naturally to most nurses, in part because we are involved in the most intimate of care and are with clients during their most vulnerable times. Yet, there is more to being able to create heart-to-heart relationships than being at the right place at the right time. A sincere and genuine attitude and demeanor is critical to conveying that we are able and willing to be in this type of relationship with our clients.

4. We also need to acknowledge there may be situations and times we do not have the necessary knowledge, skills, and resources needed for a given client. We are wise to be aware when this happens and consult with colleagues or other sources and, when appropriate, help clients connect with whoever can offer the type of relationship they need.

5. Finally, it is important to recognize the rewards and benefits of heart-to-heart relationships are many-fold. Our own spiritual growth is enhanced by the heart-based service we provide to others. By giving, we receive. Healthy growth toward self-actualization includes dedication to helping others along the way. We are all striving for the same result of being the best we can be and reaching our fullest potential. When we form relationships with others for the purpose of helping them grow holistically, we all grow in mutually beneficial and reciprocal ways.

ENDNOTES

[1] They also learned the heart has a nervous system of its own that is extremely complex and able to function independent of its connection with the central nervous system. They explained this is how transplanted hearts are able to function when the vagus nerve has been severed, and not yet fully healed.

[2] See Chapter 3 for clarification of these concepts.

[3] This is done with magnetometers, very sensitive detectors of energy fields.

[4] This relates to the discussion in Chapter 5 about Integration, the merging of our spirit with the human form.

[5] *This quote implies we are body first and desire integration of our spirit. As stated in Chapters 1, 2, & 3, we are energy first, or spiritual energy first. However, most people think of themselves as body first. Thus, Dale's comment applies to their way of thinking. However, I would suggest we are in human form, but until our spirit is at least partially integrated, we are not human beings. The very word,* beings, *suggests we are more than a psycho-social-physical phenomenon.* (H. Erickson, personal communication, March 7, 2006).

[6] See Chapter 6 for more information on this topic.

[7] See the original MRM Book, pp.170-175, and Table 2.2 of this book for a review of the Five Aims of Intervention and their relationship with the Goals of MRM.

[8] Chapter 6 provides an in-depth discussion of A-I.

[9] These strategies promote the same type of heart-based communication developed and researched by the HeartMath Institute as described above.

[10] *This is a classic example of pacing before leading. If Carolyn had not synchronized her breathing with Rebecca's, stayed connected, and waited for Rebecca to take the lead, it is most likely Rebecca would have dried her tears, pulled away, and resumed her "I'm strong" attitude. Instead, she was able to experience healthy affiliation, resume the lead when she had mobilized sufficient resources, and move on. She grew considerably during this single interaction* (H. Erickson, personal communication, March 7, 2006).

[11] I had previously introduced Rebecca to the benefits of relaxation exercises, which we had practiced during our appointments.

[12] *As I've said previously, I was taught this in my basic program, but didn't learn it until I met my father-in-law, Milton Erickson, master in creating relationships that helped people grow and heal. For your enjoyment, I offer the website of the Erickson Foundation where you can find hundreds of wonderful readings about his work:* www. Erickson-foundation.org (H. Erickson, personal communication, March 7, 2006).

CHAPTER 10

CONNECTING

HELEN L. ERICKSON

One cold winter night, Mr. Brown rode his bike down a slippery hill, ran into a tree, and broke his hip. He was admitted to our unit for surgery and recovery. Little more was known about him other than he "seemed to live on the streets." The doctors reported his surgery as successful. By the time my "life-changing-experience" occurred, the doctors only visited him once a week. They had charted he could go "home"[1] as soon as he was able to walk with minimal assistance.

It was the nurse's responsibility to get him up, help him walk, and prepare him for discharge. But, it was impossible. He not only wouldn't get up and help himself; he repeatedly did things that alienated the nurses. He smoked in bed, which was definitely against the rules. He'd burned two mattresses by dropping cigarette ashes. Some nurses said it was on purpose, to get attention. He was constantly turning on his light to ask for something that seemed unnecessary from the nurse's perspective. He used mouthwash to give himself an enema and then got feces all over himself and his bed linen. He refused to get out of bed to eat, so food got all over the linen. The nurses complained bitterly that they had to change his bed more often than they did the acutely ill patients next door. He used his telephone to call the nurse's desk and then just breathed deeply and uttered unintelligible grunts; the nurses thought they had a perverse caller. When they discovered it was he, they were furious.

Over a period of weeks, the nurses responded to him by withdrawing. He would turn on his call light, and they would take a long time to answer. They kept the door to his room closed, so they didn't have to look at him or his mess. This of course, isolated him even more. Whenever the doctors suggested he be discharged, his temperature would spike and he would develop a "cough." Everyone was frustrated with him and his lack of interest in getting out of the hospital or taking care of himself.

I remember the night I looked up from the nurses' station to see two policemen entering our unit. They seemed "all business." They wanted to know who was taking care of Mr. Brown. Of course, I was! They said Mr. Brown had called the police and stated he was being misused! I was immediately flooded with feelings and thoughts. The situation was preposterous; the nurses were the ones being misused! Mr. Brown, all his antics, and the doctors yelling at the nurses to get him ready for discharge! And all because of Mr. Brown. What nerve to call the police and report misuse!

Nevertheless, the police report mandated an investigation. I tried to collect myself and act "professional" as my heart raced and head swirled! The police officers listened closely to what I had to say, and then headed off to talk with him. Upon returning from his room, they simply walked off the unit. Clearly, they were not pressing charges; but it made me stop and think. Actually, it changed my life!

OVERVIEW

The previous chapter presented a discussion on heart-to-heart connections, the primacy of the nurse-client relationship. The Modeling and Role-Modeling theory and paradigm are based on the belief that how we connect with our clients will impact, if not effect, their well-being. Most nurses embrace the concept of caring and support the need for a strong interpersonal relationship with their clients, yet many have difficulty connecting in a way that will enhance the well-being of both nurse and client.

This chapter discusses the importance of such a relationship, explores factors that interfere with our ability to connect, and presents specific factors that influence our ability to connect. The first section discusses the trusting, functional relationship and includes a brief description of Watzlawick's axioms of communication. The next section presents three communication strategies, *Establishing a Mindset, Creating a Nurturing Space,* and *Facilitating the Story,*[2] which I have derived from personal experience.

The last section discusses issues related to modalities commonly used by nurses as a way to connect. The nature and merits of communication strategies, facilitating and impeding factors, and the differences between communication strategies and complementary modalities are also presented. While the first two strategies might be common for many professionals, Facilitating the Story is only useful for those who value Self-care Knowledge as defined by Modeling and Role-Modeling.

A TRUSTING, FUNCTIONAL RELATIONSHIP

Carolyn Kinney, proposed that heart-to-heart communication helps nurses create a spiritual connection with clients. Spiritual connections help us transcend numerous factors that constitute human life. For example, appearance, odors, voice tones, clothing, and other attributes that sometimes interfere with our ability to connect with another human. When we connect at the spiritual level, human factors disappear, and the *essence of the human being* emerges. We are able to put aside our biases and focus on the needs of another human being. In doing so, we learn and grow; we become more of whom we have the capability of being. A spiritual connection is the basis of a *trusting, functional* relationship.

Nearly all nurses would say the client-nurse relationship is built on trust, but we don't often talk about what that means. I have heard nurses say clients should trust them because they are the experts. Others have said they need to learn to trust the client, and until they do they are cautious, believing some of what the client says, but not everything. Still others have agreed a healthy nurse-client relationship is reciprocal, the nurse has to learn to trust, and so does the client.

When we wrote the original book on Modeling and Role-Modeling (Erickson, Tomlin & Swain, 1983), we purposefully used language to depict that the relationship had to "work" between the two people. We said the first Aim of Nursing was to Build Trust (p.170), and the related intervention goal was to "Develop a *trusting and functional relationship* between yourself and your client" (p.171). We also said that these were based on the Principle, "The nursing process requires that a trusting and functional relationship exist between nurse and client" (p. 170).

We discussed the use of technical skills (p. 53) and respectful language (p. 143) as ways of building a trusting relationship and expanded on these and other possibilities in our section on Nursing Interventions (pp.173-186). We also argued a trusting relationship was necessary for the nurse to nurture growth and facilitate healing, and alluded to the nurse's ability to connect with clients as a prerequisite for such a relationship. Yet we didn't clearly state what that meant or how to do it. Many nurses have told me they agree with these ideas, but have difficulty connecting.

I emphasize connecting as the first step in building such a relationship. The greater the connection, the more meaningful the relationship. *Connecting requires synchrony of two individual energy fields. When this happens, the two people involved create a shared energy field in which they become a "whole" that is different from either one separately—a whole that is greater than the sum of the parts.* This is the basis of a trusting, *functional* relationship. Nurses who have had this experience know it is very powerful; it can change how we view life and how we think about nursing.

Yet, connecting is easy for some and not for others. Some nurses know how to relate at a spiritual level, others have more difficulty. Nevertheless, I think all nurses who *want* to have such a relationship with their clients can learn to make deep meaningful connections. It just requires they truly believe that the first goal of a nursing interaction is to build a trusting, functional relationship. It isn't to teach clients how to take care of themselves or what to do to be healthy. Once nurses firmly embrace this idea, it is easier for them to learn strategies that will enhance their ability to make heart-to-heart connections.

Why Bother?

Some Holistic Nurses, who use complementary modalities, have informed me they don't bother with "collecting all that data and all that other stuff." According to them, their use of the modalities nurtures growth and facilitates healing. I think these nurses have mastered the art of nursing, and therefore, connect with their clients without fully understanding what is happening or why it happens because of their mind set. They probably create a nurturing space without thinking about it. When this happens, these nurses serve as an energy conduit and bring restorative energy from the environment to the client. Their modality strategies enhance the client's ability to use these resources. Growth and healing are initiated and the *client's own restorative capabilities take over.*[3]

In many cases, a modality-focused practice is sufficient because the clients select the provider and the providers use self-restorative techniques, so they have the resources necessary to facilitate their clients. On the other hand, nurses practicing in a system where clients have little control over who is assigned to provide their care, and nurses working with a wide range of people, experience a different situation. The natural inclination toward connecting with people who "choose" one another is missing.

There is little time to do more than what is required in such an environment. Nurses need to understand their clients' thoughts and beliefs, so they can plan focused nursing care and not waste time with trial and error, or with creating a negative relationship. They need to know how to get meaningful data from their clients in a hurry. Facilitating the client to tell their story may be the only way these nurses can get the information needed to determine appropriate interventions. To do this, they have to be able to create a connection.

Why Can't I Connect?
Some nurses have said they "know all about *Modeling and Role-Modeling (MRM)* and *believe* in it, but just can't connect with the clients." There are several reasons this might happen. For example, although they believe in the MRM way of nursing, they may still be focused on "doing something." They haven't learned *being* is more important than *doing*. They haven't learned, yet, that their *spirit and the energy disseminated from their spirit* can be a more powerful intervention than any other *technique* or *treatment*. Nor have they learned that energy, which comes from their spirit, is often what is needed to "jump start" their clients' own healing resources.

Being is Important

These nurses have to learn *Being is more important than doing and doing without Being is often ineffective.* I think some nurses connect when they first interact with their clients, but as soon as they focus on doing, they inadvertently disconnect. That is, they focus on *doing the task*, which changes the energy patterns. Rather than transferring energy into the client's energy field, they transfer it into the field of the object they are attending to. Clients can often feel the difference between the two types of energy experiences although they are usually not able to express it. Instead, they simply say the nurse "cared" or didn't "seem to care."

> Nurses who have learned that *Being* is more important than *doing* have already learned how to connect with their clients. Doing without Being is often ineffective.

Take, for example, a nurse who has to insert a urinary catheter. This nurse might enter the client's space, make eye contact, talk gently, observe nonverbal responses as she or he initiates a relationship, and then tell the person what needs to be done. During this interaction, *if the nurse is focused on the client and responds to the client's nonverbal communication cues,* they will likely merge their separate energy fields into one. However, if the nurse *refocuses on the catheter tray and the client's anatomy, the energy shifts. They become disconnected.* This nurse simply needs to learn how to stay focused on the *person* while doing something with or to the person. We do this by talking with them about what is happening, attending to their breathing and other nonverbal cues, and responding to these cues as part of the interaction. While this sounds difficult for the beginning nurse, with practice, nurses can learn to stay connected with their clients even as they perform complex interventions.

Self-Restoration

Another reason these nurses might have trouble connecting is they may have forgotten or not learned that they must take care of themselves before they can facilitate growth and healing in others. Since the human spirit is more important than anything else that can be used in the caring of people, it is important for the nurse to know how to reenergize her spirit.

Our desire to help others is not enough; we have to actively reenergize ourselves. This is very important because nurses serve as an *energy conduit.* Energy from the universe can be used to help us help ourselves. It can also be transferred from us to the client through our shared energy fields (as described in Chapter 2). However, the nurse's ability to serve as a conduit is influenced by her own internal resources. Metaphorically speaking, a nearly burned out light bulb will give off only a little light. Our ability to connect with our clients is directly related to our ability to create an interactive energy field between them and us.

Resistance

Most of the time, nurses want to help their clients. They want to connect in ways that will facilitate growth and healing, but sometimes it seems very difficult or nearly impossible. And then there are times when we simply might not *want to connect!* We may be too busy, too tired, too focused on something else, or the client just doesn't "resonate" with us—we don't like her language, the way she does things, and so forth. I remember Mr. Brown, presented at the beginning of the chapter, who helped me learn that there is no such thing as impossible and that connecting is basic to nursing.

Long before we had ICUs, DRGs, or early discharge, I worked as a staff nurse on a medical-surgical unit in a large tertiary hospital where most patients were quite sick. Mr. Brown, presented at the beginning of the chapter, was one who wasn't so sick, but taught me many things. After the experience described above, I had many thoughts.

As a nurse, I had failed to think about Mr. Brown as anything other than a condition. When he was first admitted, his medical condition wasn't nearly as critical as that of many others on our unit. Initially, I thought of him as a "hip repair," and then gradually, my orientation changed to one of frustration, and finally annoyance. He mandated time that I needed to take care of others who "really needed my help!"

I knew some of his history, but didn't consider it important. He was not one of those people with whom nurses automatically connect. He did not consider the needs of the nurses or other patients, nor was he well-educated, handsome, or charismatic. He didn't hold an important position at the university nearby, in the city, or anywhere. He seemed to be just Mr. Brown, a hip repair. The doctors and we nurses treated him as such. We really didn't try to connect with him; we didn't try to understand his view of life. We didn't talk about what it must be like to live in the streets when the temperature was often well below freezing, when it was hard to find food. We just didn't think about it.

That night, I felt I had failed as a nurse. I had forgotten the age-old rule: look at the face, then the body, then the equipment.[4] I had forgotten this was a person who needed my assistance just like the others; his need to be cared about and comforted had not been on my mind. Instead, I had focused on how to get through the evening shift without totally exhausting myself, and that meant giving him the physical care he needed, but no more.

Following the incident described above, I had a few moments of introspection, and then I remembered what I knew to be true about nursing and myself. I remembered that, generally, I cared more about the person than the disease, and my aim as a nurse was to facilitate my client's sense of control, hope, and self-worth. I decided I needed to find a way to connect with Mr. Brown, to try to discover what he REALLY needed. I knew if I did that, I could relate to him as a person, not as a "hip repair."

When I entered his room, he looked worried—I'm sure he wondered what punishment he was going to get for his "bad behavior." After all, he had called the police! When I sat down by his bedside, he looked even more worried. For him, this was unexpected. Why would a nurse sit down in his room? Who knows what he might have expected? I don't know what the police had told him, but I suspect they weren't very sympathetic. They might even have told him he shouldn't call them again or he'd be in trouble with them. If they did, he was really alone now; he had no back-up resources.

I tried to center myself and then said I knew we had not had a good relationship. He had done many things to get our attention and we had not responded in ways that were helpful to him. I commented he had managed to get lots of attention, but none of it had really helped him. He commented that he didn't care; at least it was warm in the hospital, he had three solid meals a day, and he didn't really care if the nurses liked him. For the first time in more than two months of working with Mr. Brown, I heard what he was saying—I began to connect. I remember looking into his eyes, seeing a person, and knowing this was a human being—someone who needed to be connected, have someone see his view of the world, and help him find his way. That was the beginning of a wonderful relationship between Mr. Brown and myself.

Rediscovering the *person* changed how I talked to and about him, what I suggested for his care, whom I asked to come see him, and so forth. With simple person-focused nursing care, Mr. B. was able to mobilize the resources he needed to recover and leave the hospital. While I had resisted connecting with him, when I did, I discovered things about him and myself that will always be a part of my life. Nevertheless, resistance is normal; we all do it sometimes. But we can learn to be proactive and make purposeful choices.

Making Choices

I know we can connect and we can disconnect: we can also choose to NOT connect. It makes a difference in how we interact with our clients, how we relate to them, and what happens to them.

Our choices also make a difference in what happens to us. Our own emotional and spiritual growth is either enhanced or hindered by our choices. They also influence how we think about people. Marsha Walker (2006) (Appendix A) describes Heart Touch as a way to help nurses make choices and develop relationships founded in trust. Trusting relationships that spring from a sense of "connectedness", nurtures growth, and facilitates healing. They are the precursors to spiritual relationships.

USING COMMUNICATION STRATEGIES

Communication Considerations

Nurses use communication strategies to build trusting, functional relationships, so they can nurture growth and facilitate healing. When communicating, it is important to keep this in mind. Without the aim of nurturing growth, relationships might be based on a status quo outcome. That is, clients may trust we care about them as they are, but fear rejection if they grow and change. Without considering our clients' world-view, what we communicate might have a negative effect on their well-being. For example, a number of clients have told me they dare not get too well because they will no longer be able to come see me. I simply respond that they can grow as much as they want, and they can *still* come see me if they want. If, on the other hand, I had said they didn't *need* to see me, some would decide they were right, they couldn't get *too well* or they would be "cut off." Others would decide they were right after all, they couldn't trust me to understand their needs.[5] How and what we communicate verbally is important, but what we communicate nonverbally is more important. Our attitudes, beliefs, and intent will be carried to others through our energy, and they will experience these nonverbal messages at a deeper level.

Wazlawick's Theory

We've said synchrony of energy fields is necessary if we want to build trusting relationships. One way to facilitate synchrony of energy fields is to consider communication theory. Watzlawick (1967) proposed four key communication axioms listed in Figure 10.1.

1. We cannot not communicate.
2. Every communication has both affect and content.
3. Communication between two people is an uninterrupted, ongoing sequence.
4. Every communication is symmetrical or not.
Figure 10.1 Watzlawick's communication axioms.

<u>We Cannot Not Communicate.</u> Watzlawick (1967) stated we cannot not communicate. He explained saying two people, visually near one another, are communicating, if *one* of the two perceives they are communicating. It is impossible to *not* send a message! For example, Mary enters the room, and preoccupied by an earlier discussion, fails to notice Jill looking at her, waiting to be recognized. Mary moves past Jill to another person. She did not intend to ignore Jill; she was just preoccupied and didn't see Jill. Nevertheless, Jill *perceived Mary was sending her a message!* How Jill interprets the message depends on Jill's world-view. We cannot not communicate when another person

perceives we are communicating with them. This is because, communication has two components: verbal and nonverbal. Some say at least 65% of what we communicate is nonverbal. The rest is verbal. This means when people *perceive* we are communicating, we *are* communicating even though we don't know we are! When we walk down the hall and ignore people looking out the door at us, we are communicating something to them. What we communicate depends on how they perceive the message. The bottom line, we are communicating any time someone else is attending to us, either directly or indirectly.

<u>Communication has Affect and Content.</u> Every message we send has two components: affect and content. Affect includes the feelings communicated by voice tones, body stance, facial expressions, hand signals, and so forth. Think of how you feel when someone uses soft, kind voice tones and a smiling face and compare that to how you feel when you hear angry voice tones, loud words harshly spoken, and so forth. Add to that, eyes narrowed so they seem like slits, tight, hard mouth lines, and you will have very different responses. The affective component of our messages is very powerful because it often overrides the content of what we say. The content is simply that—the words used in our communications. Consider the time you heard someone say, "Hi, how are you?" While the content asked a question that would appear to invite a response, the affect communicated suggested the message was a formality, a socially accepted way of recognizing another person. It was not intended to stimulate a response other than, "Fine, thank you." This message has implied social norms that help us decode it in a meaningful way for both members.

Now, consider the nurse who stands in her patient's doorway, chart clasped to her chest, tight "hurried" look on her face and states, "Everything looks good in here. You need anything?" She sounds like she is in a hurry although her tones are pleasant enough. Overall, this nurse is probably communicating, "I'm really busy. It doesn't look like you need anything; I think you're okay right now. I'll get on to the next one." But, that is not what she said. She asked if the client needed something. The client will receive these messages, incorporate both content and affect, decode within their own context, and respond. And the process goes on.

<u>Communication is Uninterrupted.</u> Communication is a sequence of messages sent, decoded, and returned between two people. When two people have meaningful series of interactions, the messages to and from one another may be interrupted by time, but continue from where they left off. This is because communication has a strong affective component as described above. Consider that you had feelings before you had words! Feelings were a part of you even before you could understand concepts. As a result, affect is a major aspect of all communication. As we read in Chapter 3, our feelings release chemicals stored in our cells. How we *perceive* messages determines how they are stored. When we communicate with the same person over time, it is as though the messages were never interrupted by time. We cannot start over unless we consciously decode and

recode messages. Otherwise, communication between two people is an uninterrupted sequence of messages.

<u>Communication is Symmetrical or Not</u>. Messages sent and received are coded and decoded based on how the two members perceive the relationship. When one person perceives they have authority, are better, smarter, or more clever, than the other, the messages they send will have affect and content that relay these perceptions. Vice versa, when one person feels inferior to another, they will also send and receive messages within that context. And when both people feel equal, their messages sent through affect and content will relay this perspective, too. When we have unconditional acceptance for another person, we communicate a message different than when we perceive we are the experts, we aim to teach, or have other attitudes of authority or power. People will also receive messages and decode them based on how they perceive themselves within the context of the other.

Since symmetrical communication is a component of synchrony, it is important to think about how we communicate, send nonverbal cues so they "say" what we want, and what our communication goal might be. As we discuss the three Communication Strategies that facilitate connecting with clients, Watzalawick's communication axioms will serve as a context for understanding their importance.

COMMUNICATION STRATEGIES TO FACILITATE CONNECTING

While I'm sure many strategies can be used, when practicing Modeling and Role-Modeling, I always use three that I have found to be most useful: *Establishing a Mind Set, Creating a Nurturing Space, and Facilitating the Story.* This section describes them. While I may appear to present them as though they are implemented *sequentially,* in reality, they are reinforced and enhanced *continuously.* That is, while we start with Establishing a Mind Set, move into Creating a Nurturing Space, and then Facilitating the Story (See Figure 10.2), we are, in reality, doing all three at once. As the relationship deepens, we recycle back to Creating a Nurturing Space, and continue on.

Establishing a Mind Set

The interdependent caring-healing processes are based in a reciprocal relationship between nurse and client. The feelings, attitude, behavior, and language used by one member will influence those of the other. Together, two people create a unit (or a dyad) that is greater than the sum of the two individuals. Each person has a significant role; each makes a contribution to the process, and each influences the outcome. However, as healthcare providers, we have to bring to the relationship resources that will complement those of the client, and sometimes counterbalance the *lack of resources of the client*. When we enter the dyadic relationship with depleted resources, it is very difficult to reinforce those of our clients. We need to learn to take care of ourselves first. There are several ways we can do this.

Establishing a Mind Set
  Self-Care Preliminaries
  Moving Forward
    •Centering
    •Focusing
    •Opening
Creating a Nurturing Space
  Sources of Stimuli
  Respecting their Space
  Spirit-to-Spirit Contact
Facilitating the Story
  Tapping Self-care Knowledge
    •Addressing the Stimuli
    •Only the Client Knows
    •Word to the Wise

Figure 10.2 Three Strategies that Facilitate a Trusting Relationship.

Self-care Preliminaries

We need to be open to discovering not only our strengths and desires, but also our limitations, prejudices, likes, and dislikes. We need to spend time thinking about our values, beliefs, and what makes *us* unique; we need to learn to differentiate our *sense-of-self* from our *Essence of Self* (see Chapter 1) and plan ways to further uncover and enhance our Self.

To do this, we need to find ways to get our basic needs met through relationships with friends and families, not through relationships with our clients. Our ability to know ourselves well, to know our strengths and limitations, and to know how to get our needs met through appropriate relationships is an important aspect of preparing ourselves for the caring process.

Moving Forward[6]

Once you feel comfortable with who you are and your role in the caring-healing processes, you are ready to focus on developing techniques that will help you connect with your clients. They are Centering, Focusing, and Opening. Together, these three create Presence.

Centering. If you haven't already developed this technique, you will need to start at home or in a private, quiet space where you won't be interrupted for a few minutes. While there are multiple ways to learn to center yourself, many have found the one described in Appendix D to be useful.

> Center yourself before you focus your intention. Centering helps organize your own energy field, so you can send helpful, healing energy to your client.

Once you have learned how to center yourself, you can do it anytime and anywhere. All you have to do is take a deep breath, blow it out, relax all parts of your body and your being, let go of all tension, and replace it with white energy that is relaxing, refreshing, restoring and, healing. Then, with the next few breaths, continue to energize yourself. As you move toward your client, remind your Self that you can stay centered, even as you refocus your attention. With that, focus on your *intent to connect* with your client's energy field, facilitate growth, and nurture healing.

Focusing. The *intent* to facilitate growth and healing in another is a necessary component of Presence. Figure 10.3 offers seven steps that will enable you to focus your attention, connect with your client, and set your intent.

---

1) Focus your attention on your client. Note his or her posture, body language, facial expressions, and general demeanor.

2) Send energy to your client; look at the person's face, focus on the eyes, and smile with your eyes.

3) Remind yourself that you can facilitate healing and growth by being present, accepting the essence of the other without conditions, and by communicating love and respect.

4) Continue to breathe regularly and deeply, stay relaxed and focused, let healing energy pass through your body, and connect with your client.

5) Continue to send loving, respectful energy to your client, introduce yourself, and explain the purpose of your visit.

6) Remind yourself that you know what you need to know, you will remember what you know, and you will be able to use what will be most helpful.

7) Finally, draw energy from the Universe to help you, keep you energized, and guide you.

Figure 10.3 Steps to focus attention and set intent.

As you practice the steps listed in Figure 10.3, you may notice that the energy around you seems to change. This happens because you have already initiated the merging of the two energy fields, yours and your client's. By focusing on your own energy field, you are able to shift vibrations, so it can synchronize with the energy field of your client. *You have changed the energy around you!* As you focus your attention on your client, you direct *your energy field to vibrate at a level consistent with the energy field of your client.* When you have healing, helping *intent*, you *send* healing, helping energy. Positive *Intention* initiates *Presence*. On the other hand, when you have hurtful intent, you send negative energy.

You have energy you can use to help others help themselves. When you focus on sending that energy to them, to help them grow and heal, you are using *intention*. As you connect with another, you can learn to *focus your intention*, the second step in creating Presence. The third is Opening Yourself.

> Our goal is to be Present, to have Presence, so we can help our clients help themselves. We do this first by centering ourselves; this organizes our energy. Next, we focus our intent, which helps us direct our energy and draw from the Universe. Finally, we open ourselves to our client, so our energy fields can merge. When this happens, we have Presence.

Opening. We have to "open" our energy field, so it is receptive to the energy field of another. When we do that, we prepare ourselves to hear and understand what the other person wants to communicate. It is important we be willing to hear what is being said, and know that people do the best they can, given their circumstances.

We have to keep in mind that all people need to be affiliated and individuated. They also need to be able to present their story and know that they (and their story) will be perceived as important and worthwhile. When this happens, they can find meaning in the interaction.

We also have to remember that nature or the Universal Field connects all people. We are all part of a larger energy field. So, when you open yourself to your client and your client's story, you are connecting with not only your client, but with others through the Field. When you do this, you send positive energy into the world—energy that is needed by many, energy that will help many *even without their knowing and even without your knowing.*

As we open ourselves to others and their stories, we also need to remember we cannot "fix" anyone, not even ourselves. We can only help people grow, develop, and heal. We are facilitators, not fixers.

> Keep in mind that our intent is to facilitate growth and healing. We are involved in the caring process in order to mobilize resources, build resources, and facilitate healing in our clients.

While it appears that developing Presence might take too much time, once you have learned to Center, Focus, and Open yourself, you can do it all within seconds. Soon it will become natural, a way of Being. You will do it without thinking. As this happens, you will gain comfort in your role as nurturer of growth, and discover that the healing process takes less time. It will no longer be the focus of your interactions; it will be the byproduct! The focus of your work will be the *working relationship between the two of you. As described in Chapter 9, that, in itself, facilitates growth and healing in both members of the dyad.*

Now that we have the necessary mindset, we are ready to move on to the next Strategy. We are ready to Create a Nurturing Space.

Creating a Nurturing Space

The bottom line for this strategy is: *We cannot force growth in another person. We can only create an environment that nurtures growth. With sufficient growth, people will heal themselves.*

Our aim is to create an environment that promotes a sense of safety, security, and connectedness in our clients. We can do this in any setting, as long as we focus first on the client's needs and sources of stimulation.

How we do this depends on whether we enter their space or they enter ours. If you are in private practice or see clients in your own space, it is possible to create space that is conducive to growth before you meet with them. Asking clients what would help them relax and enjoy being with you in your space also helps. And, then, be prepared to accommodate their wishes whenever possible.

Sources of Stimuli. When creating a nurturing space, it is important to remember we have five sources of stimulation: hearing, seeing, feeling, smelling, and tasting. We aim toward *decreasing adverse stimulants and increasing positive stimulants.* Our aim is to create an environment that will facilitate our clients to focus on their inner knowing, not on stimulants outside themselves.

Sometimes objects such as candles, pictures, pillows, soft toys, or music help people quiet themselves, and move into their inner space where they can get in touch with their spirit. We need to remember, however, this is very personal, so what helps one person may be a major detriment to another. For example, trees and a garden surround my home office situated in a sunroom with large windows. While most people love the view, one little girl told me she was afraid of the trees; she was worried a wolf would come get her. Another client mentioned that he quit going to another nurse therapist because she always had candles burning and the smell made his nose itch so bad he couldn't focus on anything except trying to avoid sneezing!

Respecting Space of Others

Whenever you enter your client's space (and all space is theirs unless it is your office or personal space), you need permission to arrange or rearrange the environment. While it may seem appropriate for you to close the door, pull a room divider, turn down the radio, open windows, fluff pillows, light candles, etc., it is not your space to manipulate. Unless you ask your client what would be helpful before you initiate your plans, you may create a feeling of being invaded rather than helped. Types of questions or statements that might help you in this area are shown in Figure 10.4.

- Hello, my name is Karry Raj. I'm a nurse; I'm interested in finding ways to help you feel more comfortable.
- I wonder if that would be all right with you?
- May I come into your room, closer to your bed, sit in this chair?
- Where would it be best for me to sit (make some suggestions, but leave the decision to the client)?
- Before I do anything else (or say anything else), I wonder if there is anything I can do to help you be more comfortable? (You might make suggestions, but wait for affirmation before you act.)
- Are you comfortable?
- It seems a bit noisy (hot, cold, etc.) here. I wonder if you would enjoy (a quieter space, more warmth, light, coolness, etc.)
- I have some ideas about how we might get started, but first I'd like to hear your thoughts on how I might help you.

Figure 10.4 Examples of comments, questions that initiate a trusting relationship.

Facilitating Healing Energy

Our intent is to create an environment that facilitates clients to take in positive energy, so they feel safe, secure, and connected. It is not necessary to block out all stimuli to be able to create this space, but it is necessary to decrease adverse stimuli, and help them feel safe and secure. When people experience feelings of safety and security, they start connecting with the source of the experience and their natural healing abilities emerge. They are then able to screen out other sounds, smells, sights, etc., and continue to focus on their own internal experience and inner knowing. When additional help is needed, two modalities, guided imagery and hypnosis can be used to achieve the goal of creating a nurturing space.

Eye contact helps us connect Soul-to-Soul. It sends the message that the person is worthy, important, and lovable.

Spirit-to-Spirit Contact

Once you have permission to enter your client's space, it is important to try to deepen the relationship established when you prepared the environment. Eye contact is very helpful for most people. When we take time to look into (not just at, but into) another person's eyes, we are connecting with his or her inner Self. Some say we connect with the Soul. While Soul-to-Soul connections are fleeting, they have an important impact; they help us establish spirit-to-spirit relationships.

Some people avoid eye contact. There can be many reasons for that. For some it is a cultural issue. Others are embarrassed, some afraid. Some worry such an intimate interaction might show how unworthy they are or that you might rob them of their line of defense. Others avoid eye contact because they have a Sensory Integration Disorder, so we need to be careful about judging a person's behavior without first understanding their world. Nevertheless, when we can use eye contact, we help people learn life is about Being, rather than doing. This "knowing" may be fleeting, but even so, it initiates growth. It is a "seeding" of worth and dignity. You build on this "growth" as you move into the next Strategy, Facilitating the Story.

Facilitating the Story

Facilitating the story is an important strategy, since story telling helps clients uncover and clarify needs, discover barriers to needs satisfaction, and identify what will be helpful in resolving problems. It also helps the story teller elucidate and sometimes set goals that are growth-directed. Story telling allows the teller to *contextualize* life experiences and present them in a way that softens associated feelings. Sometimes, these experiences are presented symbolically; other times they are clearly stated. In all cases, once the experiences are told, the burden for solving related problems has been shared with another. This, in itself, instills hope for most people.

Tapping Self-care Knowledge

While there are a number of ways to initiate story telling, the easiest and most efficient way is to use naturalistic communication techniques drawn from the hypnosis modality developed by Milton Erickson (Rossi, 1980). Since all synchronized communication has hypnotic potential, naturalistic trance induction techniques are very helpful in bypassing resistance (or fear) of disclosure.

I usually start this process by inviting my client to get comfortable, take a few deep breaths, and let out the tension that accumulates in us as part of living. I then tell him when he is ready, he can begin to relax even more and this will help in many surprising ways. (Remember to maintain eye contact, use soft voice tones, and softened facial muscles.)

Going Inward. I observe my client's response to my suggestions, noting physical changes that suggest an increase in comfort level, feelings of safety, and connection. Sometimes the person is invited to pay attention to the breathing and notice how the breaths go in and out (repeating the words in and out as they inhale and exhale) and how it slows down as they relax and become more comfortable.

Addressing the Stimuli. While it is ideal to work with people in a quiet, beautiful milieu, it isn't always possible. To compensate, you can comment on the sounds and lights around you, mention how they continue to be present, but as you and the client focus more and more on your breathing and relaxing, these sounds and lights will actually slip into the background. These messages give clients permission to internalize your positive energy and attend to their own needs. This in turn helps them experience a nurturing space and know you are concerned with their wellbeing.

As you continue to relax and find your own synchrony, comment that you understand people know what they need, what interferes with their wellbeing and what will help them more than anyone else could possibly know.[7] Then, return to encouraging relaxation, and breathing.

<u>Only the Client Knows.</u> It is important to continue building your relationship, to help your clients focus internally, so they have full access to their Self-care Knowledge. As their comfort increases, it is time to proceed.

I often start by saying there are many things we know about ourselves, and there are some things *we 'know,' but don't know we know.* However, it is interesting that all things 'known' and known, but not 'known' are important and helpful to KNOW. I add that all things 'known' are a part of our life journey, all are important, and when we are ready, we know what we want to know.[8] The key point is that *only* the client knows, and only the client understands how self-knowing (see Chapters 1 and 4) impacts their current situation.[9]

As you continue to observe your clients, note their comfort with where they are at this time. If they seem comfortable, haven't changed physical posture to indicate blocking of communication, and still seem to be connected, it is time to invite them to start telling the story. Suggesting that they start describing their situation does this. (E.g., "Why don't you tell me a little about what is going on with you now, what is happening in your life?") Encourage details, using communication skills to facilitate this process. You might use words such as, "Can you tell me more about that?"

Always allow clients to continue with their stories even when they don't seem to be related in any obvious way. Sometimes, stories will include what seems to be related to the situation, what is expected to happen, and what the client perceives can be done about it. If not, explore each of these issues (Erickson et al., 1983).

Remember, life is contextual; there will be linkages and associations described by your client that may not seem rational or real to you. While you may keep these thoughts in the back of your mind, it is most helpful to your client if you can *fully understand this is your client's reality.* This is your client's life situation and view of the world. These views affect how they respond as holistic people: how they feel, how their body reacts, and how they relate to others. They also affect the neurotransmitters excreted, and the energy field patterns.

<u>Word to the Wise.</u> Your clients' self-assessment is necessary before you can begin to understand their world-view. Once you have this data, you will be ready to proceed with the rest of the Modeling Process, described in Erickson et al., 1983, pp. 148-231, and expanded in this book in Chapters 11-13.

Keep in mind our job is to empathize, not sympathize. You want to understand, but not feel obligated to fix the situation.

Don't rush this process. It is necessary in order to build a strong relationship. Personal experience has shown me clients don't always trust the health care system or its providers, but will often agree with the providers in order to maintain the relationship with the system and its providers. Without a trusting, functional relationship, you will have difficulty facilitating a deep, contextualized self-assessment (in your client). Your ability to understand without assuming responsibility is important if you wish to stay connected with your client through challenging times.

> It is very important for us to learn to take care of ourselves before, during, and after working with people. Without such Self-care, we lack the ability to serve as energy conduits and energy transformers when working with clients.

MODALITIES AS A WAY OF CONNECTING

Can Nurses Bypass Communication Strategies?

Many health care providers, as a way of connecting or merging energy fields, use complementary modalities. Some think the strategies identified above are not necessary, that they can go directly to modalities. I disagree. I think the first step in a mutual relationship is the development of trust. Some do this without thinking about it. They have learned to synchronize their energy systems with their clients in such a way that the client feels safe and secure. I think this can happen when clients seek us out and ask for our services. Usually, when they do this, they know, in advance, which modalities we use. Obviously, there is enough trust to seek our assistance with an unstated acceptance of the type of modality. The trust is partially established before they walk into our office.

But the situation differs for those who are in a more vulnerable position, such as hospitalized clients, or those we have been asked to work with by someone else. When this is the case, we need to be careful to establish a trusting, functional relationship (i.e., to be sure that our energy fields are in synchrony) before we move forward. Under these circumstances, I think it is very important for us to use strategies, such as those described above, before introducing modalities. Colleagues have told me stories about clients, referred by nurses or doctors, who have refused their service even when offered as a gift. I think this happens when we fail to build a trusting relationship before we offer a modality. That is, we offer to *do something* before we have demonstrated we are trustworthy.

To compound the problem, not all people want "whatever we have to offer." Some people enjoy energy work, and some don't! Some like guided imagery and some don't, and so forth. We need to remember all people have preferences, and when we respect their wishes, their bodymind responds differently than it does when they feel the need to protect themselves.[10] When they feel safe, they release multiple biophysical chemicals that create an internal healing environment. When they don't, the opposite happens—they use up resources needed to cope with stress, grow, and heal, and release stress-related chemicals.

What About Modalities and the Setting?

I've heard advocates of complementary modalities say some settings are more conducive to specific modalities, and therefore, these modalities should apply to all clientele in the setting, without consideration of the clients' unique needs. Perhaps there are settings where this is true, but I think too often when this happens, the advocates might be subscribing to specific modalities as an *alternative* to either nursing or medicine, not as a *complement* to either profession. For example, during a conversation with a colleague, I was asked to "sanction" healing touch for all persons in the hospital's coronary care unit. My colleague's argument was the medical staff had approved this modality. A group of physicians had agreed nurses could use healing touch on their patients to see if it would expedite recovery. This approval had occurred after a long, difficult debate between nurses and doctors where one of the doctors had said, "Well, I don't think it will help them one bit, but it won't hurt them, so why not let the nurses do it if they want to? Maybe it will make my job easier—as long as the nurses keep doing their work. Let's just try it out." My colleague, elated with the victory, viewed this as a breakthrough, an opportunity that needed to be "snatched."

Although I can understand the physician's attitude, "it won't hurt them, so why not try it out," and the nurse's view that nurses need to take opportunities to alter the power bases when they arise, it seemed that a major issue was missing. I asked what the nurses hoped to accomplish by using Healing Touch? Did they hope to complement medical practice or nursing practice? Since their goal would determine how they measured the effect of healing touch, this was an important question. Would they use length of stay, or cardiac status outcomes or would they use nursing outcomes such as stress levels, well-being, and quality of life? And, would they measure the client's perspective on the value of the modality? What if some didn't *want* healing touch? Would they be given a choice or would healing touch be built in as part of the everyday treatment plan?

While healing touch would most likely be very helpful to most clients, some might not find it helpful, and some might even have adverse reactions. Since our nursing goal is to create a nurturing environment, so the clients' natural healing abilities can take over, *all interventions,* including complementary modalities, should be used based on our clients' perspectives of what they need to help them help themselves.

There is one other issue related to the use of modalities in nursing. Some colleagues identify themselves as healing touch therapists, reiki therapists, hypnotherapists, and so forth. My position is that we are nurses who *use* complementary modalities, skills, and techniques in our nursing practice. While some might think they have more prestige as an expert in a modality than they do as a nurse, I disagree. We have a contract with the public to be nurses and, as such, to use whatever modalities, techniques, and skills we can to help them be healthy. While there may be more money (and possibly, even more recognition by some health care providers) when we identify ourselves as a modality expert, we may lose track of the philosophy and beliefs of the nursing profession itself.

> Nursing is contextual. We have to be cognizant of the social context where we practice. This context includes the clients' and the families' orientation, their needs, and their goals before we worry about those of other disciplines. Unless we keep this in mind, we can easily slip into a practice that is based on the needs of another discipline rather than the needs of our clients. Communication strategies are used with each client to facilitate the development of a trusting relationship; modalities are used based on the situation, client need, and care provider's expertise. When practitioners define themselves based on their modality expertise, they may be practicing within the context of that modality, not nursing.

You may think I am advocating against modalities; I am not. I simply want us to remember we are nurses first. It is important for us to continue to learn new techniques, modalities, and skills that we can use as we practice. But, it is equally important to remember the essence of nursing, and know that we are learning new things, so we can practice nursing better, not so other disciplines or groups can recognize us.

I have used a number of techniques in my own practice, but I have been careful to do these based on the client's needs and requests. Take for example, the following case:

> *Mr. M, a middle-aged university professor, presented himself in my office declaring he wanted help with his blood pressure. He said he was taking medications, but his pressure reading continued to be a "bit higher" each time he visited the doctor's office. He was getting worried about his situation, so he had decided to come see me. While he had presented himself to my secretary as someone who needed my help because he was taking too much medicine for hypertension, he did not mention the drugs nor did he mention hypertension as most health care providers think about it. Instead, he told me he was hyper-tense all the time because his wife nagged him too much. He described her as a loving wife without whom he couldn't get along, but he didn't like the nagging. He continued to describe their relationship in detail, always returning to the conflict between being affiliated and individuated.*
>
> *He told me he had heard I used "different ways to help people." When asked to clarify, he told me he'd heard I used some kind of touching, foot massaging, and that I talked a lot with people (therapeutic touch, reflexology, hypnosis). He went on to say he had been seeing his doctor*

weekly, and that the nurse and doctor just talked at him all the time, but it wasn't helping. As I listened to him, I decided he was struggling to achieve Intimacy, but lacked sufficient positive residual from Trust, Autonomy, and Identity to complete this work. He perceived he had to choose between being connected and being isolated. When he felt connected to his wife, she nagged him and didn't support his individuality. On the other hand, when he separated from her, he felt isolated and alone. The stress caused by the conflict was affecting his physical well-being. When I asked him what he thought would help him, he said he wanted to talk on a regular basis; he wanted to learn how to "have his cake and eat it too!" He did not ask for, nor mention touching or foot massaging again. Agreeing that talking might be a good idea, we decided he'd come back a couple of times a week to talk, to get to know himself better, and find ways to be healthier and happier. Over a few weeks, he was able to find alternative ways to contend with his stress and cope with life events. His blood pressure returned to normal and he was able to discontinue his medications.[11]

My work with this client was primarily nursing based on Modeling and Role-Modeling theory, supplemented with hypnotherapy techniques that facilitate communication. Mr. M. wanted to "talk" and that is what we did. Others might have chosen another alternative. I have had some who have chosen music therapy, some who prefer bibliotherapy, meditation, exercise, and so forth.

Some might say this case is not a good example since many nurses don't have the time to work with someone like this. I would agree. This is not a short-term nursing intervention. Many times, we only have a few seconds or minutes at best. Sometimes, we only see someone once. What about those times? I think in those situations it is most important to attend to our communication strategies and nursing skills first, and then add whatever else we have learned that will help us with our clients. Let me give you another example:

My husband had undergone a mitral valve replacement, followed by several complications that warranted follow-up procedures including the insertion of a pacemaker. He was having considerable difficulty in getting sufficient sleep. Each nurse who came in his room asked what he needed; he told them he had a little cough, so he couldn't sleep. Each gave him something new. First he got pain medication, then a sleeping pill, then another pillow, then he was set on the edge of the bed and told he wasn't getting enough exercise, and then he was taken to the bathroom to void. Not one of these activities had been in response to his request. After nearly 20 hours of such nursing care, the shift changed, and in came James Brown. When he entered the room, I noticed he seemed to center himself, then focus on my husband. He looked into my husband's face and said he had heard he was having a bit of a problem. My husband responded as he always did, "I need sleep, and I can't get any because I have this little cough." James immediately stated that it seemed like he needed to have his cough taken care of, so he could sleep. He left the room, came back a few minutes later with some cough syrup, which he gave my husband. Then James asked him what else he needed, and my husband responded that he needed his back rubbed. James positioned him, rubbed his back, and before he was finished, my husband was asleep. He slept for the next 4 hours without difficulty. It took James about 4 minutes from the time he came into the room until he finally left. And then James had 4 hours without needing to come back, and my husband had time to start replenishing some of his resources.

James used many of the strategies described above. He also used some naturalistic hypnotic techniques, which helped my husband trust him. He demonstrated his ability to *be* and *do* at the same time. He was able to connect with his client the minute he walked into the door, stay connected while manipulating intravenous tubing, checking dressings, and managing other necessary technical and physical care of the body. He used Presence as he interacted, and was able to comfort my husband so he could restore his own resources.

CONCLUSIONS

Carolyn Kinney proposed that our relationship with another person is primary. I would add that it is the *core of* the healing process. People need others in order to grow and become the most they can be. Our relationships influence how we perceive our worth, our contributions, and our Life Purpose. Connecting is the link between our Intentions and the effects of our relationships.

The Principles of Nursing, first proposed in the original book (Erickson et al., 1983, p. 170), help us understand why we do what we do as professionals. For example, the Principle *"The nursing process requires a trusting and functional relationship exist between nurse and client"* indicates that our goal is to be in an ongoing process with one another. This is accomplished by doing what is needed to communicate that we are trustworthy. Sometimes we use modalities to facilitate this process. When we do, the important thing to keep in mind is not the modality, but the Aims of Nursing and related Principles.

Table 10.5 provides a few examples of relations among the Aims of Nursing, Nursing Principles (Erickson et al., 1983, p.170) Communication Strategies, and types of techniques, strategies, and modalities that enhance our work.

Table 10.5 Relations among aims of nursing, strategies, modalities.

AIMS	STRATEGY	PRINCIPLE	GOAL & MODALITIES
Prepare self	Establish a Mind-set	We have to take care of ourselves first so we can facilitate the well-being of others.	Increase self resources through meditation, self-hypnosis, centering, Walker & Kinney techniques. Set the stage with Intentionality, Unconditional Acceptance. Use hypnotic techniques, guided imagery, client selected alternative therapies to build relationship
Build trust	Creating a nurturing space	The nursing process requires that a *trusting* and *functional* relationship exist between nurse and client.	Decrease adverse stimuli and enhance healing stimuli. Use Presence, Intentionality, Unconditional Acceptance to maintain and enhance relationship. Use hypnotic techniques, guided imagery, client-selected alternative therapies to nurture growth.
Promote positive orientation	Create a nurturing space	A-I is dependent on individuals perceiving they are acceptable, respectable, and worthwhile human beings.	Promote self-worth, dignity and spiritual awareness. Use hypnotic techniques, healing touch, therapeutic touch, reiki, Maintain Presence, Intentionality, Unconditional Acceptance to deepen the connection, encourage client self-care knowledge.
Promote perceived control	Facilitate the story	Human development is dependent on individuals perceiving they have some control while experiencing affiliation.	Facilitate clients' sense of intra and interconnectedness, enhance Self awareness. Use empathy, Presence, Unconditional Acceptance and purposeful Intentionality to create safe environment. Use healing touch, therapeutic touch, reflexology, hypnotic techniques to mobilize & build resources and enhance awareness of Self-care Knowledge with inner voice.
Affirm and promote strengths	Nurture growth	There is an innate drive toward holistic health that is facilitated by consistent and systematic nurturance.	Facilitate dynamic, adaptive mind-body-spirit holism with Self-knowing. Maintain Presence, Intentionality, Unconditional Acceptance to maintain & enhance safe environment. Use communication and selected hypnotic techniques, guided imagery in conjunction with selected energy therapies to mobilize and build resources, enhance Self–knowing and develop Self-awareness.
Set mutual goals that are health directed	Nurture growth	Human growth is dependent on satisfaction of basic needs and facilitated by growth-need satisfaction.	Facilitate healthy problem solving and coping. Maintain Presence, Intentionality, and Unconditional Acceptance to further enhance sense of affiliated-individuation. Use communication techniques and guided imagery to facilitate goal setting.

We start by connecting, heart-to-heart. This synchronizes our energy fields, helps us draw energy from the Universe and get in touch with Universal Consciousness. This is a state of *Being*. We continue deepening the relationship by using Presence, Intentionality and Unconditional Acceptance. This helps others perceive that they are acceptable, respectable, worthwhile human beings. It also helps us connect spirit-to-spirit. This expedites the healing process because healing happens at the spiritual level. When we aim to connect, sprit-to-spirit, we maximize the experience of affiliated-individuation. This inspires hope and encourages people to become more fully themselves.

As we *aim* to help people gain control over their lives, we encourage them to tell their story. We do this by helping them stay connected with us *and* by exploring their uniqueness as they tell their story, no matter where it begins. This encourages them to discover what impedes their growth and what they need in order to heal. These understandings provide the bases for setting mutual goals for the interpersonal, healing process.

Connecting and initiating the healing process doesn't take a lot of time. In fact, I think it saves more time than it takes. But, before you are comfortable with this idea, you need to be fully comfortable with the notion that you have the ability to help another person initiate the healing process, and it can go on, even in your absence. You do this by *knowing* you are a source of wisdom because you are connected with the Universe, and therefore, Universal knowledge. Within your being lies the greatest gift that can be offered to any other human. It is the gift of your Self.

ENDNOTES

[1] Remember, he lived on the streets. We lived in a northern state at the time, and it was the middle of the winter.

[2] Each strategy has implications for the nurse and the client. It is important to attend to both if our goal is to "Develop a trusting and functional relationship between nurse and client" (p. 170). Each strategy is also an important precursor to Modeling the client's world.

[3] I know this because I practiced nursing like this for 16 years before I realized I needed to label and articulate what I was doing, so I could do it more purposefully.

[4] I learned this as a student from a wonderful teacher, Velma Phillips. I will always be grateful to her. She taught me wonderful technical care, but she also taught me to think of the client as a person first.

[5] This type of communication with clients is based on a belief, supported by years of experience, that they *won't need me* and will choose, on their own, that they can get along just fine if they don't perceive they have been disconnected, cut off, rejected, or abandoned.

[6] You may ask how these processes are like and different from hypnotic techniques. The answer is they are the same. These same steps are taken when we plan to enter a relationship with another and induce a trance state. They are typically called naturalistic trance induction processes. They focus on establishing a relationship and helping the other person find their core, discover what they need, and rework negative residual.

[7] These comments are called embedded suggestions and seeding, and are discussed in more detail in Chapter 11.

[8] Actually, this is an interesting confusion technique that helps people who get in the NO state to bypass it. As they try to follow what is being said, they usually move past the No because they have been told they No, but they don't KNOW what they NO. Of course, it can be taken many ways, but interestingly, often opens doors for people that are important in their healing process.

[9] Sometimes it is like solving the "cold case"!

[10] See Chapter 3 for elaboration on this topic. For the time being, remember, our feelings and thoughts trigger various chemical responses, depending on our perceptions.

[11] A detailed description of this case can be found in Erickson, 1990b.

CHAPTER 11

NURTURING GROWTH

HELEN L. ERICKSON

Looking back, I remember the night the desk clerk announced that Mr. M, one of the new patients to be admitted during the evening shift, had just arrived. When I looked up to make a cursory assessment, I saw a tall, sturdy man holding his slim, straight body in such a way that I immediately knew he was a proud, independent person. My cursory assessment, that he perceived himself as the head of the family and very much in control of his life, was later confirmed. Mr. M., a well-known professor in a nearby university, was being admitted with shoulder pain of unknown etiology. The year was 1967.

Over the next two years, Mr. M returned to our unit a number of times. What had initially appeared to be a severe case of bursitis was later diagnosed as cancer of the bone. Every effort was made to save his life. Repeated surgery, chemotherapy, and radiation seemed to have no effect on the persistence of the tumor invading his body and draining his life force. His original weight of 210 pounds shrunk to less than 100 pounds. His height seemed to shrink proportionately. This man, once 6'3", now appeared very small and fragile. Ultimately, to relieve his intense pain, a cordotomy was selected as the medical treatment. However, Mr. M. rejected the idea of a cordotomy. He wanted to be in charge of his own body. The thought of being unable to control his bowels and bladder was intolerable. While he had severe, relentless pain, he perceived pain as the lesser of two evils. He would often comment that his pain was less severe on the evenings I took care of him. At the time, I was grateful his disease occasionally gave him a respite, and relieved those occasions were the evenings I worked.

One evening, I arrived on the unit and found Mr. M.'s entire family in the hall outside his door, leaning against the wall, or sitting on the floor. Their appearance had changed. This family always maintained dignity, appeared well-groomed, and planned their visits one or two at a time in order to comply with visiting hours and avoid tiring their loved one. Now, all four children, Mr. M.'s wife, and brother were here and all looked like they had been here for several days. Their wrinkled clothes, messed hair, and totally fatigued faces and bodies reflected a family in crisis.

During report, I learned a cordotomy had been done several days before. Mr. M. had given in to the doctor's and nurse's need to "make him more comfortable." However, since that time he had not allowed his family to reenter his room. The family was desperate—they wanted to be with him. After report, I went to see the family, confirmed the report and nursing diagnosis, and went to Mr. M. When I told him I was glad to see him and pleased to be with him that evening, he looked at me with very sad eyes. I took his hand and asked him what was happening. He responded that he didn't want his family to see him in this condition. Then he cried and said he had always taken care of his family and now, under these circumstances, he couldn't even take care of himself. I knew Mr. M. saw his role in the family as the provider, the caretaker, the bread-winner. He now perceived he no longer had a role to perform, therefore, he refused to let his family near him—the loss was great; the pain intolerable.

I continued holding his hand and quietly told him he was very important to his family. I reiterated that in the past he had been the provider, the one who went to work, so he could take care of those he loved, but now, unable to do this, it was understandable that he felt great loss, and with loss came terrible pain. I then told him he had continued caring for his family as his illness had progressed, that he had been very methodical in assuring his finances and business were in order, and that he should be very proud of this. After a few quiet seconds, I added that it was possible for him to continue taking care of his family. They no longer needed him to be the "bread-winner," they now only needed to share his life with them—they only wanted to be with him. He was important because he loved them and they loved him. I went on to say that it was not his ability to work or provide for them that mattered now; it was his ability to continue to love and be loved. He looked at me, seeking confirmation of my words. Nodding my head, I held his hand and stroked his arm.

Over the next two days Mr. M. and his family rested quietly. One family member was always tucked into the chair near his bed, so they could see one another as they each woke from their naps. When he died quietly, Mrs. M. was holding his hand. She gently told him good-bye, left the room, and called the children.

The family members arrived, one by one, and grieved with dignity and peace.

I did not see nor hear from the family members for the next eight years. Then, suddenly, one day, the following letter arrived in the mail:

> *Dear Mrs. Erickson,*
>
> *I am sorry to be so late in writing you; as you will perhaps understand, I have procrastinated—but I am sorry, because it is unfair to you. My mother, as you probably knew, had lympho-sarcoma; when it became more than she could bear this past spring, she chose not to struggle for every last breath, as had my father, but to let go. The experience with my dad was infinitely painful for her—as with the rest of us—but worst for her; and she refused to re-enact that torture. As in life, she thought of others before herself; so, too, in dying. Her suffering was, I believe, kept to a minimum.*
>
> *In the year my Dad was with you people in Ann Arbor, you were of incalculable aid and comfort to both my parents—you gave them confidence in you and your staff, and the dignity and respect which makes life worth living; no one else could, or did, more genuinely have their gratitude and respect. When I would come down and all seemed to be lost, the one bright spot was that Mrs. Erickson would be coming on, and we could breathe a little more easily as Dad's anxiety visibly receded. Your kindness and humanity made the world a better place at that time and without you the experience would have been more difficult than you probably believe.*
>
> *Thank you.*
> *J.M.*

OVERVIEW

Growth is a strange thing. It is crucial for survival, precedes development, and is necessary before healing can occur. Yet, it comes in tiny increments, sometimes undetected by the observer. Often, we are unaware it will happen, it just doesn't occur to us. But it does happen. It shows us where we are and where we have been. It acts like a ray of sunshine, bringing us hope and nurturing our spirit. Without it we wither; we cannot *not* grow and still survive. We cannot stand still or stay the same over time. Seconds, minutes, hours, days, months, and years all come and go—time marches on, and we either grow or stagnate. Without growth we fall behind, like a withering bud on a vine; a bud that has the potential to grow and develop into a beautiful flower, but is unable to do so because it lacked the resources.

When we think of growth like this—as a positive change toward the expected—it seems easy to know when it has or has not occurred. Still, growth is difficult to assess. Although we might think of growth as a positive change in biophysical, psychological, social, or cognitive, status, sometimes what we perceive as a positive change is really not! Rarely do we think of growth as an increase in *negative behavior,* even though some of the most important growth processes are demonstrated by an increase in assertive behavior perceived to be negative actions! As in everything in life, it is all a matter of perspective.

This chapter is about nurturing and facilitating growth. Several issues are addressed including the nature of growth, the difference between growth and growth needs as described by Maslow, and implications for practice.

THE NATURE OF GROWTH

Growth is a Positive Change

Growth is a positive change that occurs as our needs are met. With growth, we build and mobilize resources needed to contend with daily life. Growth can be minimal or extensive. When minimal, it is often difficult for the observer to notice the change, yet it is there. When sufficient growth occurs, the change is more obvious.

I am not talking about growth that is unhealthy, such as a tumor that "grows," or negative residual that builds over time. I *am* talking about positive changes that create healthy resources needed as we move through life, seek meaning, and try to accomplish our Life Purpose. While there may be a better term for this concept, it escapes me. So, for the purpose of this book, *growth is the positive changes in body, mind, and spirit that occur naturally when a person's needs are met.*

> *To grow is to expand or become larger in any way; to increase in degree; move from one condition to another; and to produce something as part of a natural process or to allow it to be produced. Growth can be thought of as the process of increasing in numbers, size, power or intensity* (Encarta Encyclopedia, 2003).

Growth is Gradual

Growth is often viewed as change that is obvious, but most of the time it is invisible. In fact, most of the time we may have difficulty recognizing growth until it has happened repeatedly. This confusion occurs because we mix up the concepts of growth and development. Simply stated, growth usually occurs in minutia, while development is an aggregate of growth over time. Growth can occur and then seem to disappear, while development is a constant. That is, growth is temporary (or a state resource), while development is more stable. Sometimes, we talk about growth when we see it start to "pile up" or aggregate—this is an appropriate way to think about it. But, this type of growth is usually obvious. What is more difficult to observe, assess, or even understand is growth in the minutia; but it is the most important. Without tiny increments of growth, there would not be the opportunity for growth in the aggregate. In other words, people are more likely to grow a little at a time, and over time, accumulate the results (i.e., growth) than they are to grow in big spurts all at one time. When the latter happens, it is usually an *integration and synthesis* of resources (produced by growth). Such an integration and synthesis usually transpires when development occurs.

Growth is a Product

The Modeling and Role-Modeling theory (Erickson, Tomlin & Swain, 1983, pp. 158-59) states that need satisfaction *produces growth*. We also refer to higher-level needs as growth needs. Thus, the word "growth" was used in two different ways: as a product of need satisfaction, and as a type or category of needs. This confusion occurred because we wanted to credit Maslow appropriately (Erickson et al., 1983, pp. 56-61). In hindsight, I realize it might have been better to label the two categories of needs as Basic and Higher-levels. Maslow also talks about Higher-level needs as Being and Self-actualizing needs. Interestingly, Goble (1970), who wrote about Maslow's theory, identified them all as basic needs, but distinguished among physiological, safety, belonging and love, esteem and self-actualizing needs (pp. 37-48). This classification is more consistent with the idea that satisfaction of all needs (to some extent) is necessary for the growth of our Soul. Nevertheless, the confusion still exists for some. Therefore, this section is designed to specify the differences between *growth as a product* of both Basic and Higher-level need satisfaction, and *higher-level needs* that are a prerequisite for self-actualization.

> Basic needs satisfaction is necessary for survival and precedes *emergence of Higher-level needs*. Higher-level needs satisfaction is necessary for self-actualization and precedes *transcendence, a precursor to self-actualization.*

More specifically, we can think of growth as a product when we consider the outcome of need satisfaction. That is, satisfaction of any needs at all levels produces growth. On the other hand, when we talk about growth needs, we are addressing an issue of motivation. People are motivated to not only survive, but to thrive, to move toward self-actualization. Growth happens when both types of needs are met. So, hereafter, to avoid confusion, we will call our need to thrive, (previously known as growth needs), higher-level needs to assure the distinction between growth as a product of need satisfaction and the motivation to become the most that we can be—to self-actualize.

Since we are grounded in human form, needs that relate to the growth of our biophysical-psychosocial self are fundamental, while Higher-level needs are necessary for self-actualization. Both are necessary for Soul-work.

Growth is Unique to the Individual

Growth is also personal; it only occurs when we *perceive* our needs are met. Sometimes, growth occurs in spurts and is obvious, but usually it happens in tiny increments, often invisible to the observer. It builds new resources, strengthens available resources, and enhances our ability to mobilize resources. Each of these attributes of growth is common across all living creatures, yet growth is also unique in each human being. This is because every human has needs that are identical in *type,* but how and what will meet them varies according to the individual. Take as an example, the differences in babies. Some like to be held tightly, wrapped in blankets, and cradled in the arms of the caregiver. Others may choose to be held over the shoulder, loosely wrapped, and still others may prefer others ways of being handled, comforted, and nurtured. Yet, each baby needs to develop a sense of trust with feelings of being safe, secure, and connected. Each human has a need to feel valued, to be perceived as a worthy individual; yet, how these needs are met depends entirely on the individual and their Life Purpose and Reason for Being.

No one can know what is in the heart and Soul of another person. No one can know what another person needs in order to grow; it is very personal knowledge. All we *can* know about others is that all people have an inherent drive toward growth, all want to be the most they can be, all want to find meaning in their lives, and all need others to help them with these processes.

Growth is Ordered

Interestingly, although growth is personal, there is an overall 'design" to it. In Chapters 2 and 3 we talked about energy and proposed that we are energy first, that energy templates determine the structure of all things as they transform into matter, and that there is order in our universe. Brian Greene (2003) calls this *symmetry,* defined by Encarta Encyclopedia (2003) as "harmony or beauty of form that results from balanced proportions".[1]

We know from normal growth and development that this is true. The growth of humans is consistently similar, one to another; there is a master design. When the ova is fertilized by the sperm, somehow the cells find their way to the proper place, so all humans more or less look alike, eyes in the face, teeth in the mouth, liver on the right side, heart on the left, and so forth. Over time, we are able to see the result of "growth by design," yet it is still difficult to see growth happen!

> While there is a natural "plan" for how and when people might grow, our ability to follow the plan varies. Some take more time than others. Yet, with a little help, our natural abilities emerge and we grow. It is the nature of holistic humans.

We could compare human growth with that of a fully-formed, healthy acorn planted in a cup of dirt. If the dirt has the proper nutrients (such as vitamins and minerals), the proper acidic content necessary to create a "growth environment," and gets energy from the sun and water, *as needed,* then the acorn will gradually change, a bit at a time, cracking through the acorn shell, sending down roots, sending up sprouts, and with time, the sprout becomes a trunk, branches are formed, leaves develop and a new oak tree exists. Although no two trees will ever look alike, there is a distinct similarity among them. Growth of humans is the same; there is a predictable sequence of growth of the holistic person, and of the systems and subsystems of the human. Nevertheless, the predictability varies by individual. While there are norms for growth patterns, no two people follow those patterns exactly.

Growth is Evasive

I have stated that it is not always easy to recognize growth or evaluate it. While physical growth might be assessed by factors such as height, weight, bone density, chemical blood levels, and so forth, and psychological, cognitive, social, and spiritual growth by standardized tools, the assessment of holistic growth is more difficult. Nevertheless, if we define growth as *evidence of moving in a healthy direction* rather than defining it as *evidence of strengths and virtues* (i.e., developmental residual), then we might be able to recognize growth. Take, as an example, the growth of the oak tree described above.

If we watch our cup of dirt, hour upon hour, we would most likely miss the minute-by-minute changes; they happen too slowly, and we don't have the endurance to stay focused. However, if we were to videotape the process with a camera that could see through the dirt and inside the acorn shell, and then watch it in slow motion, we would probably be able to see minute changes happening, a bit a time. We could see the growth. As it happens, instead of watching the acorn shell absorb the water, take in the sun's energy to make the nourishment needed to transform the inside of the acorn into a tiny sprout that soon cracks through the acorn, all we see, one day, is a tiny new tree!

Interestingly, if we watch our tree grow, we will notice it takes on the form of what we call an "oak tree." We can recognize it in its entirety, all the parts in the right place, all parts functioning in the expected manner for an oak tree, yet, we cannot see the individual parts grow! We can only see the growth of the whole tree. People are like that, too. That is why it is important to think of growth from a holistic perspective rather than from a systems view.

There is another issue related to assessment of growth: learning to recognize growth that "unbinds negative residual."[2] Often, we think of growth only within the context of a healthy person under ideal conditions. We know everyone is unique in how they exhibit need satisfaction, and, therefore, growth will *look* different in different people. All we have to do is to learn how to distinguish various forms of healthy growth, as they relate to positive developmental residual. Nevertheless, we forget we have both positive and negative residual as an outcome of developmental processes. When this happens, recognition of growth within the context of negative residual is more difficult.

Take for example, the adolescent who has learned people are unreliable, untrustworthy, and that they often want a relationship for the sole purpose of meeting their own needs. Nevertheless, when first encountered, this person seems to have control of his life, to be very independent, and to not need others. After a short period of nurturance from a caring person, this individual might suddenly demonstrate suspicion, caution, and challenge the other's motivation. Some people would be surprised at such behavior and see it as unwarranted, out of context, and a negative reaction. However, our attitude would be different if we understand that someone with negative residual, as described above, will only *let down their façade* and behave in such a way when they have had an opportunity *to experience the feelings of being cared about as a worthy human being, i.e., to experience temporary need satisfaction.* This behavior can be evidence of growth because this person has learned there are people in the world who care about him *without conditions.* This knowing is different from where the individual started; a change has occurred. We could consider this an "unbinding of negative residual." It is possible this adolescent experienced some growth related to positive residual, such as a beginning sense of trust, as well as beginning to unbind negative residual.

When it seems confusing, the simplest way to assess whether growth has occurred is to evaluate whether or not needs have been met from the individual's perspective. Need satisfaction is always a prerequisite for growth. When need satisfaction occurs, growth will result.

Growth is Contextual

A final consideration regarding the nature of growth in human beings is *context.* We stated in earlier chapters that people live in a context, and that we have to understand their context if we are to help them grow. Our *external* context includes anything and everything in our environment. From a broader perspective, we could say that context includes everything in the Universe. On the other hand, we can narrow our parameters, discuss context from a more personal perspective, and say it is everything and anything around us that has a direct influence on our lives. This view of context would include such things as where and how we live, whom we live with, our social networks, the social norms and so forth. Our *internal* context includes our perceptions of the external context: what we do, how we live, how we think others see us, their perceptions of our worth, and our reactions to these perceptions. It also includes how we see ourselves, given *our perceptions* of how others view us. For example,

Many people consider 48 year-old Zelda a very strong, independent, and competent woman. She runs a non-profit agency created to help the underprivileged. She is loved and valued by friends, family, and others she has helped through the years. Many people have commented they don't know what the community would be like without Zelda. Nevertheless, Zelda perceives that her worth is linked to her ability to constantly take on more responsibilities, help more people, and sacrifice her own needs for the well-being of others. Even though many tell her she is valued because she has "a good heart" and because she "cares," she perceives she cannot say "no" to any request, that she has to keep taking on new responsibilities, and always be strong.

While Zelda has enjoyed her work for the past 20 years, she has noticed, recently, that she is often tired. She feels as though she never has time for herself, and feels guilty if she takes a few days off. After all, there is always more to do! Unfortunately, Zelda tends to surround herself with people who reaffirm her worst fears. Such people want Zelda to continue taking care of them, always be responsible, and be in charge. When Zelda responds to these individuals as a source of input to validate herself, her beliefs about herself are reaffirmed. She discounts others who say she needs to slow down, refocus, or take care of herself. She doesn't trust their comments and thinks they don't apply to her.

Zelda's ability to grow is personal; it depends on her orientation and her environment. Her life is contextual, and, hence, her ability to grow also depends on her willingness to continue accepting her perceptions of that context and internalizing them. Until she learns that she needs a balance of affiliation and individuation, of being connected and loved for who she *is*, and being strong, independent, and valued for what she *does*, she will have trouble accepting help from others. At present, Zelda attends to her sense-of-self and ignores her Essence of Self (See Chapter 1). While she may be fulfilling her Life Purpose, she will not be able to discover it until she learns to listen to her "inner voice," and she cannot do that until she alters her perceptions of her context. There are two ways Zelda can be helped.

First, she needs someone to consistently nurture her growth at the stages of Trust and Autonomy, so she can learn she is a good human being, worthy of being loved and valued, and that it is okay for others to help her. She also needs to learn that she will not be rejected for being dependent and needing others. Moreover, she needs help learning to make choices that are good for *her*, practice saying "no" to those who request she take care of them, and learn that she will not be abandoned or rejected by making these choices. Fortunately for Zelda, (at some level) she has a need to know—a *need to know* more about herself, her relationships, her purpose in life, and the meaning of her life. So with a little help, she will *discover* what she needs.

A second way to help Zelda is to remind her that she is energy first, and is here for a purpose. Like most of us, Zelda may believe she has a Soul, and she needs to attend to her Soul on occasion. But she has lost sight of her Soul as a reason for her being here, for her living this lifetime. Perhaps, she doesn't know she was energy first—Soul energy—and that she has a Reason for Being (or shall I say, a Reason for *Becoming human)*. Her Reason for Being, or more precisely, her Life Purpose has gotten lost in her effort to *do* what she thinks is valued by others. This would help her with her work at the stage of Integration. While this is listed as the second way to help Zelda, it is really the first thing we would do, even as we move into the work described above.

Since growth is contextual, it would be helpful for Zelda to think about the "outer limits" of her context, rather than the "inner limits." If she were to do that, she might be able to discover two things: First, that her energy field ripples out and affects the energy fields of others, both near and far. It has the potential to affect things, animate and inanimate, reach beyond her immediate environment, and out into the Universe. Secondly, if Zelda refocuses on the extent of her context, she might be able to discover that it works both ways: energy comes from the Universe and goes back to the Universe. We are all part of a Unified Field of Energy. The only difference is that our energy field vibrates at a different level the closer we get to incarnate form. This type of thinking might help Zelda reorient herself. She might be able to refocus from her current emphasis on *doing* to an understanding that she is here to *be,* so she can do her Soul-work—work that was determined before she entered this lifetime in human form.

> Since need satisfaction precedes growth, and need satisfaction depends on our internal environment, growth is contextual. Our ability to grow depends on our view of our external world as well as our view of ourselves in that outside world.

If Zelda experiences human caring that would nurture her growth in the first three developmental stages, *and reorients herself* regarding which came first—her body or Soul, she would be able to find her Reason for Being, her Life Purpose, and would *know* how to use her energy to take care of herself.

Need to Know
According to Maslow, we have a need for information that is related to unmet basic or higher level needs. This means we have a need to know because "not knowing" threatens us, or creates unmet basic needs. Other times, our need for information is related to higher level needs, we want more self-actualizing type of information. In any case, our search for "knowing" relates to our unmet needs.

Information that increases our unmet need status depletes resources while information that helps us satisfy needs creates new resources. Since need satisfaction produces growth, and information helps meet our needs, it is important to consider the context of the desired information. Without such information, it is possible we will "teach" people things that will further create unmet needs rather than meet their needs. Let me give you an example:

Jimmy, who lived in a remote community with his family, was diagnosed with a patent ductus arterious when he was about 8 years old. His doctor advised surgery within the year and referred him to the Health Science Center about 350 miles from his home. His parents were told that they should plan to be away for about 2 weeks. This meant both parents had to take vacation time, arrange for care of the other children in the family, and coordinate finances needed to cover the costs of the surgery and their time away from home. Finally, the date was set. Jimmy and his parents drove for nearly 9 hours to arrive at our house in preparation for Jimmy's admission the following day. Upon entering my home, Jimmy looked at me, smiled and announced he had a cold, so he couldn't go to the hospital the next day. His mother and I looked at him, checked his throat and nasal passage and affirmed that he did not; he had no evidence of a cold whatsoever. We reassured him that he would be just fine and that he would be able to go to the hospital and get his new toys (he had been promised new toys for his hospital stay).

The next day, he was admitted, and later that day, he started sniffling. At first, no one paid attention, but as the evening wore on, the nurses started to show concern. The doctors were called; the cold got worse. He coughed, his nose ran, and he seemed to have a full-blown cold. He was started on antihistamines and other medications, as well as IPPB treatments. Everyone wanted to continue with plans if possible. The next day, he looked miserable, yet, the play-therapist nurse came to his room to do his preoperative teaching. He was put on NPO status for surgery the next day. When dawn came, he looked too sick to take to surgery; it was cancelled, and he was discharged with orders to reschedule.

Upon return to my house he looked at me and said, "See, I had a cold, so now I don't have to have surgery." Within an hour, his cold was gone! His parents were upset and called the hospital, but were told he couldn't come back for at least two weeks. Arrangements were made for 2 months later. About 1 week before he was to return, he developed a sore throat and runny nose. His doctor diagnosed strept throat and started him on antibiotics. Nevertheless, his surgery was cancelled.

By this time the pattern was obvious, so I called him and asked him why he thought he had a sore throat and runny nose. He said he had it because he didn't want to have a zipper put in. When I asked him about his zipper, he explained that the nurse who had done the preop teaching told him all about what would happen, including that he would have a zipper on his chest after the doctors fixed his heart. He then went on to say that a zipper was a bad thing because one of the boys at school was a bully and he would unzip him and his heart would fall out. He commented that without a heart he couldn't live. (Keep in mind that he had probably been told at one point in time that he couldn't live without getting his heart fixed—now it was just one more step. You can't live without a heart.)

The situation became clear. Jimmy needed to know how to be safe. When the information we gave him didn't fit into his view of the world, he created his own. You may remember children this age often have biophysical responses to stress. Jimmy did; he got a "cold" without a virus! The solution was fairly simple. First, he needed to understand there are some things we can't avoid. We talked about how he felt when his first tooth fell out, that he was scared because it hurt a little bit and bled, but soon it was all over and he got a reward from the tooth fairy AND he got a new tooth. He remembered. Then we talked about how he felt about that. He confirmed it had been scary, but he felt good now and liked his new teeth. Next, we talked about what he had to do to help his loose tooth come out (wiggle it, pull just a little, and then rinse his mouth after it came out). He remembered. We talked about how he had done so many important things to take care of himself and that now that he was such a big boy, he could do even more important things. He agreed he was big, but he was scared. I promised him a teddy bear that would make him feel safe and told him his mother and I would work on lots of good things for him to do to help himself with his heart and with his zipper, and asked if he could do some things like he had done before. He agreed he could. I suggested that he start by wiggling his toes and fingers and then confirmed with him that he could do that. Silly me, he said, of course he could. He needed something harder. So, we talked about taking big deep breaths and blowing them out. He could do that, too. Then we talked about how to relax his body, one part at a time and to notice how nice it felt when he was relaxed. He could do that, too. Next, he and I agreed that his mother could also help him and she was informed of the plan: daily practice on "things to do to help him get better." Finally, I told him I knew the nurses and doctors, and I would ask them to put staples and super glue on his zipper, so it never, ever came open. He liked the idea.

He arrived for surgery, was given his Magic Teddy Bear, and was told that whenever he wanted to be more comfortable, he could hold it tightly to his chest. He went through the procedure without incident. When he returned from OR, he opened his eyes, looked at us, and said, "Give me something easy to do!" I told him to wiggle his fingers and toes and take a little breath and blow it out. He said, "Thanks." His recovery was faster than anticipated. Today, he is a very resourceful young professional who remembers, at some level, what he needed to know more than 25 years ago. He still has his teddy bear.

People have a need to know, so they can grow. What they need is contextual and so is their growth; we cannot understand their need without first understanding their view of the world and we cannot know when growth has occurred without considering the context. Because Jimmy was a holistic being, stressors in one subsystem created a stress response in another. He knew, at one level, there are some things that cannot be avoided, but he didn't know that this information applied to his current situation. Once he understood that, he was ready to build on other knowledge he had acquired. I simply had to recognize the signs, understand that people have an inherent need to grow and that growth is orderly. We all go through common experiences we can draw from, but we have to individualize the information for the individual. Helping people grow is not a difficult thing to do, it just requires believing in the human's inherent drive to grow, understanding the nature of growth, and having faith in our ability to nurture and facilitate people to do what they can do naturally.

ENHANCING GROWTH

Nurturance

Nurturing and facilitating often seem to be the same thing, but there are important differences. Nurturing, a state of Being, has two key components: acceptance and intent. That is, nurturing happens when we unconditionally accept another person and purposefully send positive energy to that person. The dictionary says that *to nurture* is to encourage somebody or something to grow, develop, thrive and be successful, or to keep a feeling in the mind for a long time, allowing it to grow or deepen, while *facilitate* is to make something easy or easier to do (Encarta Encyclopedia, 2003). This definition suggests that nurturing can produce both rapid and gradual growth with immediate and long-term outcomes.

The Nature of Nurturing

Nurturing is what we do because of our beliefs about people, our professional goals, and ourselves. When we realize people have an inherent need to grow, growth depends on need satisfaction, and need satisfaction occurs when people perceive their needs are met, then we might be motivated to find ways to meet those needs. When we add this knowledge to our understanding of ourselves as human beings who need to be accepted and valued, and realize that the most important interactions we have with others are when we are able to transcend the physical environment and simply connect at a spiritual level (as described in Chapter 9), then we are motivated to accept others as they are, and to simply *Be with them*. And, when we understand nursing differs from other disciplines because we are committed to caring for holistic persons and helping them grow, and add this knowledge to knowledge about people and ourselves, we fully understand nurturing is the crux of our profession; it is the primary way we help people grow.

In the original book we identified nurturance as one of the key actions of the nurse. We stated:

> *Nurturance fuses and integrates cognitive, physiological and affective processes, with the aim of assisting a client to move toward holistic health....Being accepted as a unique, worthwhile, important individual—*

with no strings attached—is imperative if the individual is to be facilitated in developing his or her own potential (Erickson et al., 1983, pp. 48-49).

This definition, indicating that nurturing has a powerful effect, was the basis for one of the five principles of the Modeling and Role-Modeling theory: "There is an innate drive toward holistic health that is facilitated by consistent and systematic nurturance" (p. 170). This definition suggests that knowing how to nurture others is basic knowledge for those who practice Modeling and Role-Modeling. It also indicates the need to discuss the relationship between nurturance and facilitation.

> We need to learn how to *be* and how to have *intent* before we can learn to connect.

Facilitation

Facilitation, described in our original book (Erickson et al., 1983), is defined as:
> *"Making easier or less difficult; helping forward. The nurse-client relationship is an interactive process that helps the individual to identify, mobilize, and develop the individual's own strengths in his or her own movement toward health"* (p. 252).

This definition suggests that the key difference between nurturing and facilitation is the action of the nurse in the latter. When we facilitate, we *make it easier or less difficult for people to grow*. We do this with purposeful strategies artistically designed for the individual. This is the essence of unique, individualized interventions (Campbell, Finch, Allport, Erickson, & Swain, 1985; Erickson, 1983, 1984, 1988, 1990a, 1990b, 1996, 2002; Erickson et al., 1983; Erickson & Swain, 1982, 1990).

> Nurturance can happen without facilitation, but facilitation cannot happen without nurturance. Nurturance is necessary for growth. Both are necessary for healing.

Let's use the story of Mr. M at the beginning of the chapter to illustrate the relationship between nurturance and facilitation. You may have noticed that I did not discuss any specific interaction with J.M.,[3] Mr. M's son. That is because I did not do anything other than nurture the family using the strategies described in the previous chapter on ways of connecting. I prepared myself, focused on their situation, and opened myself to "experience" their condition (which is no doubt the same as interacting with their energy fields and connecting spirit to spirit).

Yet, several years after his father's death, J.M. wrote to me, addressing me as though we shared a meaningful relationship and had been in recent contact. He also indicated that since I cared a great deal about him and his family, I would want to know about their situation. Specifically, he said, "*I am sorry to be so late in writing you; as you will perhaps understand, I have procrastinated—but I am sorry, because it is unfair to you. My mother, as you probably knew...",* indicating I would know about his mother's condition although I hadn't seen the entire family since his father's death. Later in his letter, he articulated the specifics of the interventions that were meaningful, *"...you were of incalculable aid and comfort to both my parents—you gave them confidence in you and your staff, and the dignity and respect which makes life worth living; no one else could, or did, more genuinely have their gratitude and respect. When I would come down and all seemed to be lost, the one bright spot was that Mrs. Erickson would be coming on, and we could breathe a little more easily as Dad's anxiety visibly receded. Your kindness and humanity made the world a better place at that time and without you the experience would have been more difficult than you probably believe."*

Please understand that Mr. M. was a very sick man who required intensive nursing care, but this is not what JM mentioned. He mentioned only "aid," "comfort," "kindness" and "humanity." He also talked about the outcome of these nursing actions such as "confidence," "dignity," "respect," "life worth living," "one bright spot," "easier breathing," "receded anxiety," and ease in living through a very difficult time in that family's life. Finally, it is important to point out that Mr. M. was the focus of my care and that I rarely saw JM who was only 16 at the time of his father's death.

These few sentences summarize the essence of nurturance: it is not difficult, it doesn't take a lot of time, yet, it has a profound impact on the person who perceives they have been nurtured, and it has a long-term effect. Furthermore, it doesn't require anything except one human being who cares about another, who *knows* that the most important things we can do for others is to care about their life experience and intentionally use our own energy field to help them mobilize and build resources. When we know these things and use ourselves as an energy conduit, we are able to nurture people, helping them grow in ways only they will know and understand. Those of us who act on what we *know* are often fortunate enough to learn the value of nurturance—our clients tell us.

> While nurturing is determined by how we use *our energy fields to enhance growth in another,* facilitating is more proactive. Nurturing is primarily an exchange of positive energy that enhances growth in another. It may include basic communication that empowers people, but it is primarily an energy intervention.

The Role of Facilitation

So, one might ask, how does facilitation relate to the story of Mr. M.? To explore this question, let's go back to the story itself. While there are other examples of proactive care and caring in this story, this is the most obvious:

I continued holding his hand and quietly told him he was very important to his family. I reiterated that in the past he had been the provider, the one who went to work, so he could take care of those he loved, but now, unable to do this, it was understandable that he felt great loss, and with loss came terrible pain. I then told him he had continued caring for his family as his illness had progressed, that he had been very methodical in assuring his finances and business were in order, and that he should be very proud of this. After a few quiet seconds, I added that it was possible for him to continue taking care of his family. They no longer needed him to be the "bread-winner," they now only needed to share his life with them—they only wanted him to let them be with him. He was important because he loved them and they loved him. I went on to say that it was not his ability to work or provide for them that mattered now; it was his ability to continue to love and be loved. He looked at me seeking confirmation of my words. Nodding my head, I held his hand and stroked his arm.

Mr. M. needed to be nurtured *and* facilitated to remember that his worth was about *Being* not about doing. But, before he could hear that, it was important to remind him that he had continued to *do*, to take care of his family even after he was too sick to work. Once I had affirmed his worth as a "doing person," I was able to use basic communication skills to facilitate him to *doing something easy, something new, and something he could still do;* I was able to facilitate him to share himself and accept his family's love.

Facilitation requires more active interventions, but does not have to be time consuming, complex, or difficult. It just requires that nurses recognize the power of nurturance, implement the three strategies (*Establishing a Mindset, Creating a Nurturing Space, and Facilitating the Story*) discussed in the previous chapter, and then address the client's expressed needs.

> As you acquire attitudes and skills needed to enhance growth, you will discover the healing process takes less time. It will no longer be the focus of your interactions; it will be the byproduct! The focus of your work will be *the working relationship between you and your client. That, in itself, facilitates growth in both members of the dyad and healing in the client.*

Nurturance and facilitation can be done while carrying out complex technical tasks if and when we remember that the client, not the task, is the focus of the care. I could just as easily have told a story about a man in a surgical intensive care unit who required multiple technical interventions. The issues remain the same; we nurture and facilitate growth by using Presence, Intent, and Unconditional Acceptance.

Presence and Intent

Presence is the holistic existence of an individual who is fully open to another human's energy system. *Intent* is the purposeful use of our holistic selves to enhance growth in another person. I first learned about Presence and Intent about 50 years ago when I was being treated for bilateral pneumonia.

I was a student nurse at the time; capping ceremony was a few days away, but I didn't care. It was our first spring; I was very sick—sick enough that the doctors called my parents and told them to come to the hospital, that I might not live through the night. While the doctors had diagnosed pneumonia, they were puzzled. Life-threatening pneumonia was rare in young, healthy adults. They thought I might have contracted some strange, contagious disease, so I was put in isolation. Few people entered the room, since they had to wear isolation garb and had to have the doctor's permission.

Nasal oxygen-prongs were not an option at that time, so I was in an oxygen tent. Breathing was very difficult. I had trouble moving without becoming exhausted. I really couldn't do much for myself, so I was considered "Complete care." Three nurses were assigned to my care. The first two shared a model of care. They came into my room like a whirlwind, turned on the lights that shined down and into my eyes, and busily prepared the room for their "work." They started by propping the door open, so the noise from the hall permeated the room. Next, they snatched my food tray off the bedside stand with comments to the effect that I should have eaten something. Then they tossed me from side to side as they washed my body, changed my linen, and gave me medications. Finally, they were gone.

I remember learning that I had to prepare myself when they entered my room, and thinking, "Brace yourself, here she comes, hang on tight, don't let her take away all your breath, try to hold on long enough— she will soon be gone. Then you can relax and get in some new air." They seemed to "grab" me when they rolled me, spoke in tones that were harsh and cold, and seemed to be focused on getting done; I might as well have been a bag of dirty laundry. I knew they would deplete me even though they intended to clean my body, tidy my bed, and put medicine into me. I just hoped I could endure their "care."

The third nurse was a gift. She seemed to float around my room filling it with energy. Somehow, it seemed like she didn't even touch the ground; she never made the "thud, thud" noise so common with nurse's shoes. She used a small bedside lamp, not the overhead lights, and always closed the door, so my room was left with a quietness that restored my being. I didn't experience the brisk movements the others used when they cleaned the room, rolled me in bed, washed me, or gave me medications. Instead, she was always gentle, her movements efficient, her touch soft and caressing. She always seemed to "bathe" me, rather than wash me! Her touch never hurt; it comforted. I've often thought that she saved my life. Her Presence gave me energy. Her intent to comfort and restore me helped me build and mobilize resources I needed to heal myself. Later, when I thanked her for her care, she told me nursing was about "being with the person in spirit while doing tasks necessary to nurture the body.

She knew the importance of being and doing long before I read about it in books. She personified Presence and Intent.

Unconditional Acceptance

I've thought about the concept of Unconditional Acceptance for many years. Ages ago, I concluded that Unconditional Acceptance is what we do when we accept, without provisions or conditions, the human being with whom we are interacting. This means that we *accept and have the intent to connect to that person's spiritual being.* It does not mean we accept or approve behavior, but that we accept and respect the holistic person as a worthy human being. It also means we perceive all people have the need for dignity and respect, a sense of worth. This can be achieved when one person unconditionally accepts another as a worthy human being.

Unconditional acceptance of another has the potential to set the healing-cascade in motion. People have a natural potential to heal themselves when they experience acceptance by another. Pert (2003), a leading scientist in mind-body interactions, presents a conversation illustrating the importance of these interactions.

> Pert, *"It's true, we do store some memory in the brain, but by far, the deeper, older messages are stored in the body and must be accessed through the body. Your body is your subconscious mind, and you can't heal it by talk alone."*
>
> Brian, *"But, it's true. The body becomes the battlefield for the war games of the mind. All the unresolved thoughts and emotions, the negativity we hold on to, shows up in the body and makes us sick. Forgiveness is about opening up the heart and learning to love, which is why I think we're all here on this planet. So simple, yet such a difficult lesson to learn"* (p. 306).

I wonder whether it is as simple as Pert's colleague suggests. Is it just a matter of "opening up the heart and learning to love..."? Is that what Carolyn Kinney suggests in Chapter 9, as she talks about heart-to-heart connections and proposes that true heart-to-heart connections create spiritual connections? (According to Kinney, this is the primacy of the nurse-client relationship.) If so, then we need to clarify what is meant by the words *to love.* Since these words have many meanings, depending on the context, what would it mean *to love* our clients?

In Chapter 6, M. Erickson and Jensen discussed two types of motivational orientation: being and deficit. According to them,

> *People with Being Motivation exhibit a drive to learn and grow, to find meaning in their lives, and to relate to others with true reciprocity. They are not concerned with safety issues and are not seeking relationships to meet safety needs. They have the ability to focus on others*

rather than themselves. Their Growth Needs can be met when they are able to facilitate the growth in others. However, they don't focus on others or facilitate others at their own expense! They actually gain a deep sense of enjoyment when they observe growth in others; they do not perceive that another person's growth is their loss.

They enjoy receiving but also have their needs met when giving to others. Although needs gratification seems to be very egocentric, the healthy self-actualized individual is typically both self-confident and altruistic. They can satisfy their own needs without being driven by what others think or say; and are far more likely to be concerned about the welfare of others than those who have Deficit- Type Motivation. They have a healthy ratio of affiliated-individuation.

Persons with Being Motivation often transcend the physical plane; they are able to see potential good in others and in our world. They simply seem to have a storehouse full of need assets so it takes little to get unmet needs satisfied. It takes little for them to change a negative experience into a positive one, and little to find the strengths in their significant others. They are happy people with a high level of well-being (M. Erickson and B. Jensen, Capter 6).

These comments provide a basis for understanding the nature of *unconditional loving,* the precursor to Unconditional Acceptance of the worth of another human being. Interestingly, three of the definitions of the word *love* found in Encarta Encyclopedia (2003) "An intense feeling of tender affection and compassion; something that elicits deep interest and enthusiasm in somebody; the mercy, grace and charity shown by God to humanity" are consistent with M. Erickson and Jensen's discussion of the Being Motivated person. To extrapolate, behavior exhibited by Being-oriented people is the same as what we would see in people who have unconditional acceptance of another human being. When applied to clients, nurses who unconditionally accept the worth of their clients would likely demonstrate an interest in their well-being and show compassion for their human state.

The consequences of experiencing Unconditional Acceptance are: a sense of worth and dignity, trust in the provider, the discovery that one's Self is what is important, the ability to listen to one's Inner Voice, and the initiation of a natural self-healing process.

When we think of Unconditional Acceptance in these terms, it would seem to be the basis of all nursing care, but we know it isn't. We also know there are some who would like to be more accepting of others, but have difficulty. Sometimes nurses question themselves because of their difficulty in this area. It is important, then, to consider a few things that interfere with our becoming what we want to be. These are discussed below.

Unconscious Knowing

Remember, we all know things we don't know we know. We have many stored memories that influence our thinking and, therefore, our behavior. Often we aren't even aware of these memories or this kind of knowing. For example, the story about my search for the "right place to build our home," reported in Chapter 4. Consider the decisions I made about our lives without being aware of the stored memories and their impact on my thinking.

Also, consider the negative residual we carry with us, negative residual that consists of stored memories, and know that these memories have potential to affect our thoughts and feelings. Because of these stored memories, we sometimes behave in ways we sometimes regret, but have difficulty changing.

Often this happens because of early learning about our selves that we project on to others. For example, toddlers who are told they are "bad" because they don't do as told, learn that they and their behavior are not separated, but are the same. Unless this "knowing" is reframed, it will carry into adulthood. Unfortunately, what we learn about ourselves is often what we project on to other people.

Since our past experiences are related to our stored memories, it may seem redundant to discuss them as a factor in impacting our behavior. However, sometimes our past experiences aren't stored only in our unconscious knowing, but also in our conscious knowing. I have had nurses who told me they cannot work with a particular client because he or she is too much like another person from the past. We all have these experiences. It is very difficult at times to separate the person from the person's behavior, particularly if we don't approach the relationship with the *intent* to connect and facilitate growth. It is always easier to connect with another person heart-to-heart if we take care of ourselves first and if we set the intent, before we try to interact professionally.

> Unconditional acceptance of the person as a human in the process of Being and Becoming is basic to the Modeling and Role-Modeling paradigm. It is prerequisite to facilitating holistic growth and movement toward eudemonistic health. Unconditional Acceptance of the person as a human being who has an inherent need for dignity, respect from others, and for connectedness—that kind of Unconditional Acceptance is based on Unconditional Love. When we have Unconditional Love, it is only one step more to Unconditional Acceptance.

Nevertheless, there will be days when we seem to synchronize with our clients, understand their world-view, and everything goes well. There will be other days that aren't so smooth. It is important we learn from our experiences, grow, and continue to aim to be the most we can be. What we believe about others we should apply to ourselves first. We have to learn to unconditionally accept our own worth and need for dignity, our own Self as we are meant to be.

IMPLICATIONS FOR PRACTICE

I have stated that growth is always a positive change that can happen in tiny increments or in spurts. However, while we can anticipate growth will occur, we cannot always anticipate what it will look like, or recognize it when it happens. Sometimes what appears to be a step backwards is actually growth. It all depends on how you interpret the behavior.

> *I remember a friend who was very distressed when her 2 1/2 year old child took a magic marker and drew circles on her freshly painted white wall. Her comment was that he had never done anything like that before. When I asked what she meant, she said he'd never made circles before! As she was speaking, she turned to me with a surprised look on her face and said, "Wow, I hadn't thought about that! He's learned something new!" Then she commented, "Guess I just have to teach him where to do his new thing!"*

Clearly, her first interpretation was that her son had demonstrated bad behavior (because of what it meant to her), but she soon appreciated what he had learned, and had to decide how she could guide his behavior, so it was more consistent with her personal needs.

When we work with clients, we need to remember growth is also contextual. Behavior that represents growth for one person may seem to be a step backwards for another. It all depends on the context. Let's refer back to the example of Rebecca in Chapter 9. Carolyn describes a time when she had offered Rebecca a book to read, thinking she would benefit from the information. Rebecca angrily threw the book at Carolyn and stormed out of her office. At first Carolyn was perplexed, but then realized two things: First, Rebecca was still working on Trust, so she was not ready for Autonomy type activities, and second, Rebecca *trusted her enough to show her anger.* When Rebecca's behavior was interpreted within this context, Carolyn realized how much Rebecca had grown. She also knew what she had to do to facilitate further growth.

While we might inadvertently do many things that will interfere with our well-intentioned plans, if we have developed a trusting, functional relationship with our clients, we will be forgiven! And the trust will continue to build as soon as our client's understand we also make mistakes, but want to help in whatever way we can. It is important for clients, family members, and colleagues to remember that we recognize we have limitations, and that we, too, can grow and learn from our mistakes. When they understand this, it is easier for them to learn from us, understand that our behavior is well-intentioned, and that we are just human beings, doing the best we can. This is all that can be expected, one human to another.

ENDNOTES

[1]*When applied to theories of energy, supersymmetry is proposed as a way of thinking about the relationship of the subatomic particles with energy forces.*

[2] A possible explanation for this process is that not only does need satisfaction help reframe earlier perceptions, but in doing so, it also alters the energy field.

[3] *I don't remember ever actually communicating directly with JM; yet, he obviously thought I was. That was because my verbal comments to his mother and father, and perhaps to all of them, in general, plus my nonverbal actions "said" many things to him. We cannot not communicate when another person perceives we are communicating with them. Every verbal and non-verbal cue sends a message to the one who perceives a relationship exists.*

CHAPTER 12

FACILITATING DEVELOPMENT

HELEN L. ERICKSON

Thirty-two year-old Bill drove himself to the emergency room (ER) thinking he was having a heart attack. After careful assessment, his physician diagnosed hyperventilation and stress hypertension, and referred him to me. She was concerned he might "work himself into a heart attack or stroke if he didn't get help." She also said he needed to get his blood pressure under control; he had been hypertensive for the last 6 months.

During our first meeting, Bill asked why the doctor had sent him to me. I explained that we are a system with many parts, but our mind and body know how to work together, so we can learn a lot about our body if and when we let our mind give us the information. He seemed satisfied with this response, so after helping him choose a comfortable chair and a place to put it (in my office), I asked him about his ER experience. He said while driving home, he suddenly got dizzy, had trouble breathing, and felt tightness in his chest; he thought he was having a heart attack. With that in mind, he drove to the ER.

I asked him whether he had had a similar experience before. He said no, so I reframed the question and asked if he had ever experienced a time when he felt dizzy, had trouble breathing, or his chest was tight. He said it had happened once when he was working, shingling the roof of a house. He said he looked down, got dizzy, and couldn't breathe. He had to sit down, so he wouldn't fall off the roof. When asked to elaborate, he said there wasn't anything more to tell, but within a few seconds, he narrated the following story: When he first came home from Vietnam, he wanted to put his war experiences behind him and get on with his life. So, he started working for his father, who owned a construction business. One day, he was on the roof and when he looked down he saw "all those men running around—they looked like ants rolling down the hill." He took a deep sigh and looked very sad. I touched him gently and asked if he had had such an experience before. He started to cry and said yes, and added the following:

His best high-school friend and he decided it was their American duty to join the army and go to Vietnam. Soon, they found themselves in the middle of a major offensive drive; they were supposed to take over a company of N. Vietnamese just over the hill. Bill, as the leader of his squad, had to lead the way. He remembered climbing the hill, hearing explosions around him, being very frightened, but still climbing. Then, suddenly, he heard a huge explosion just behind him. When he turned, he saw his best friend flying through the air and the others in his squad rolling around on the ground. He had led his men through a minefield and everyone had stepped on one or been injured by one. His next memory was of himself rolling down the hill. Then everything went black. He was discharged and sent home due to extensive injuries incurred that day.

When he finished his story, I talked quietly with him about adolescents—that they are idealistic and believe they can change the world. I also talked about friendship and how important it is. Then I slowly, carefully, said, "You ARE NOT responsible for the death of your friend or the other men in your squad. An awful thing happened, but you were not responsible. You are a good man, a good friend, and a good citizen, and you can be a good leader again if you want. But, most importantly, you were not responsible for their deaths." He looked at me, put his head on the table, and cried quietly. I sat with my hand on his back. When he was finished, he apologized, and I told him I was honored he had shared his thoughts and feelings and thanked him. We checked his blood pressure and were pleased to notice it was only 122/78. I suggested he come back the next week, so he made another appointment.

He arrived on time, found his chair, sat down, and began to talk. He said there was one other time he had felt dizzy, angina, and breathless—the day his father died. I asked if he wanted to talk about it, and once again, he recounted his story.

On first coming home from Vietnam, he just wanted to forget, find a life, have a family, and start again. He worked hard to overcome his injuries, and then married the woman he'd dated before and again after Vietnam. They bought a house, started a family, and were happy. His father, who owned a construction company, hired him as a roofer. Life was good. Then, one Sunday morning his mother called and said his father wasn't feeling well; he had indigestion. She asked Bill to come over and see him. Bill said he didn't want to. He wanted to stay home with his wife, watch TV, and just hang out. His mother called again in the morning and then in the afternoon, so Bill decided he needed to see what "she" wanted.

When Bill entered his parents' home, his father stood up, made a funny noise, and fell to the floor. Bill ran to him and started chest compression. His father made a "gurgling sound" and died. Bill claimed he had killed his father, and he knew he would die just like his father, from a heart attack.

We talked about the sounds people sometimes make when they die, and that indigestion is a sign of a pending or ongoing heart attack, so it was probably going on all day. He said he should have gone earlier, so I asked whether he thought his father would have gone to the hospital if he had left sooner. After thinking about it he said no, his mother had tried to get him to do it, and he had said it was just indigestion. He said he probably couldn't have done anything differently, even if he had gone earlier. We then talked about the loss, his grief, and how normal it is to have many different feelings. I then said that his father's death wasn't his fault anymore than the deaths of his friends. But, it was normal to feel sad, to be angry, and to take a few months to work it out. I suggested he was doing what he needed—working on a healthy, loving relationship with his wife and finding ways to deal with his losses and grief without hurting himself. Again, he cried. When he was finished, he thanked me, said goodbye, and left.

I talked with his physician a number of times over the next four years. She said his blood pressure was normal. He had no more physical problems and was the proud father of a little boy. About ten years later, he called to tell me his wife and he were just fine. They now had two children, and he simply wanted to say thanks.

OVERVIEW

Encouragement offers hope, confidence, and courage. When we encourage people by nurturing growth and facilitating healthy development, we help them become more fully who they are naturally. This chapter addresses issues of facilitating development. In previous chapters we proposed growth precedes development. In the last chapter, I said we could enhance growth by using Presence, Intent, and Unconditional Acceptance of the person we are trying to help. Often, people only need us to *be there*, to care about them. And when we do, they are able to mobilize resources and grow.

Chapter 5 presented a discussion about human development and some aspects of its nature. This chapter builds on the discussion of the nature of development and how we can facilitate it. The previous three chapters prepared you for learning more about facilitating development in people. Chapter 9 presented the idea that the nurse-client relationship can be a spiritual experience. Kinney discussed how the five Aims of Intervention interface with our Soul needs and what happens when we connect with others at the spiritual level. She proposed this as the essence of the Nurse-client relationship.

Chapter 10 discussed connecting with another person and suggested three strategies to enhance a connection: Establishing a Mind Set, Creating a Nurturing Space and Facilitating the Story. Chapter 11 discussed issues related to nurturing growth. I suggested two key factors: 1) Using ourselves as conduits of energy through Presence and Intent, and 2) Unconditional Acceptance of others and ourselves to maximize our ability to be Present and have loving, helpful Intent.

This Chapter adds to the work presented in earlier chapters. Specifically, I will build on M. Erickson's work on the nature of development and present important issues related to facilitating development.

MORE ABOUT
THE NATURE OF DEVELOPMENT

Growth and Development

We have commented, in other chapters, that development occurs after growth has accrued. This suggests development is different than growth, but there is more to development. Growth and development are so closely linked it might seem development is just an extension of growth, but that is inaccurate. *While growth precedes development, development occurs even when growth doesn't exist.* This is the nature of negative developmental residual, which is laid down *because needs are not met!* Unmet needs leave sediment or residue just as met needs. The difference is the nature of the residual. Consider the positive residual that occurs after considerable growth and you will note the difference between residual resulting from repeated need satisfaction and residual resulting from unmet needs. Yet, the two types of residual exist; they just have different chemical composition and different types of energy fields.

> Our developmental residual impacts our ability to seek growth, build meaningful relationships, find joy in our work, and search for our Life Purpose. Growth is necessary for us to survive while healthy development is necessary for us to thrive.

Specifically, growth can occur in the blink of an eye, but can be temporary; development takes time, but is stable. Growth is a positive change;

development has both positive and negative results. Growth can be anticipated, but is not predictable; development is predictable. Growth has minimal influence on how we view the world, how we experience our relationships, and the nature of our character. Development determines how we view the world, how we experience relationships, and the nature of our character.

Development Residual is Stored Memories

The developmental process takes time. However, the time frame for specific task work varies. As indicated in Chapter 5, some developmental tasks can be accomplished in 10-12 months, while others take years. While people seem to move from one stage to another as though a switch had been flipped, coming to the point of movement takes a long time. During that period of time, multiple memories are created and laid down in our cells, creating developmental residual. These memories are not just in our brain; they reside throughout our body. They contribute to our intuition, gut knowing, inner voice, and "knowing without knowing we know"—our Self-Care Knowledge!

As stated in Chapters 2 and 3, our emotions, feelings and thoughts produce chemicals stored in our cells as "memory." These "stored memories" can be accessed when we have similar experiences or encounter a situation that triggers an association with any of the original feelings or thoughts. When this happens, the experience stimulates the release of more chemicals that are sent around our body, seeking receptor sites, ready to bind with cell walls, and change the interiors of the cells. Sometimes these new messages reinforce previous "learning"; sometimes they send contradictory messages. In both cases, they have the potential to build on our residual—a storage of memories.

Pert (2003) describes it as follows:

> The receptor, having received a message, transmits it from the surface of the cell deep into the cell's interior, where the message can change the state of the cell dramatically. A chain reaction of biochemical events is initiated as tiny machines roar into action and, directed by the message of the ligand (i.e., binding chemical) begin any number of activities—manufacturing new proteins, making decisions about cell division, opening or closing ion channels, adding or subtracting energetic chemical groups like the phosphates–to name just a few. In short, the life of the cell, what it's up to at any moment, is determined by which receptors are on its surface, and whether those receptors are occupied by ligands or not. On a more global scale, these minute physiological phenomena at the cellular level can translate to large changes in behavior, physical activity, and even mood (p. 24).

In Chapter 2, Brekke and Schultz reminded us that matter and energy interchange continuously. They said, "at the subatomic level, mass and energy change unceasingly into each other, (therefore) these particles can manifest as mass or energy." These "stored memories" then can also be thought of as energy. In this case, residual might be thought of as "bound energy." So, there are at least two ways to think of developmental residual: as the chemical composition of the cells and as energy.

> Embedded in the residual are emotional and cognitive "memories." The binding of chemicals within our cells, chemicals that create energy fields, creates these "memories." Therefore, we might say residual is "bound energy fields" or energy fields so densely integrated they are fairly stable.

In either case, the developmental process produces residual—residual embedded with our emotional and cognitive memories, feelings and thought patterns, information about how we view our selves and others, and our overall view of the world. This residual affects how we experience our lives, our receptivity to change, our health and well-being, and our ability to grow. It also affects our ability to impact the well-being of others.

INITIATING DEVELOPMENT

General Considerations

Before discussing data interpretation and developmental facilitation, we will review two interrelated considerations: development is sequential and predictable, and development is contextual.

Sequential, predictable development

Development is sequential. There is a time frame for initiating the task work of each stage; there is also a time frame for moving on to the next stage. As part of human nature, these stages are built into our biological makeup. All humans follow the same sequence although the task work is influenced by culture.

This makes it possible to predict (with some variance for individuality), when people will enter and exit a given stage *and* what developmental residual they will carry as they work through the stage-related task and move on to the next. Although residual varies by individual, several factors can be predicted. For example,

•Development always occurs sequentially, stage Zero through stage Nine. Although someone may seem to fly through a stage using less time than anticipated, each stage occurs in its proper place and time in the life cycle.

•When a person enters a stage with a healthy balance of (positive and negative) residual, encounters minimal losses during the stage, and experiences repeated need satisfaction, we can predict "healthy residual" will grow substantially and negative residual will grow minimally. Since we know what healthy balance of residual occurs *by stage*, we can predict expected outcomes.

•Because development is sequential and predictable, and because we know what positive and negative residual includes, development is also obvious. It can be clinically assessed and measured using well-designed research tools.

These three commonalities across people provide a frame of reference to think about what people say, how they behave, and their world-view. Even though people may be working on similar developmental tasks, we also need to consider culture, which has a significant impact on behavior.

Development is Contextual

Growth and development are both contextual. This is important in order to interpret behavior and world-views, and encourage or facilitate the developmental process. Often, we assume all people living in a local community share beliefs; therefore, the citizens of the community share a context. This is both accurate and inaccurate. When we consider the community and its resources the context is shared, but consider the difference between the milieu of a private school and a public school, or even the schools on different sides of town or in the inner-city area. The larger community may have many commonalities, but the *places where people live, work, and play* vary by socioeconomic status, ethnic makeup, family history, religious beliefs, and many other factors which create a context in which development will occur.

While developmental residual is sequential and predictable, the context in which it was built is very important and may vary considerably by groups. For example, some cultures believe dating teenagers need chaperones until they are old enough to marry. Teenagers searching for Identity and living in a home where parents share this belief will behave differently from those living in a "latch key" type of home. It is important for us to understand the motivation behind the needs (which drive the behavior), before we draw conclusions about their developmental residual.

When I lived in Michigan, I remember having a discussion about this issue with one of my students. She was working with teenagers in college, and was surprised to find that one young lady who planned to attend a party with her boyfriend was adamant she needed her sister to go with her. My student interpreted this desire as a need for safety and security related to the stage of Trust. She was perplexed because this young lady seemed to be very healthy in all other ways, so she (the student) wondered how she could be healthy (meaning she had a healthy balance of positive and negative residual) when she had basic unmet needs at the Trust level?

> *Mothers create a sense of trust in their children by that kind of administration which in its quality combines sensitive care of the babies' individual needs and a firm sense of personal trustworthiness within the trusted framework of their culture's life style* (Erikson, 1963, p. 249).

As we explored the young lady's cultural background, it became clear the student was simply looking at data from her own cultural perspective. In our culture, most young people are ready to branch out on their own, and attend parties by the time they are in their late teens. That is because our culture approves of the behavior. As Erikson said, there is a "cog wheeling effect" (1963, pp. 249-251) from generation to generation that creates cultural norms, and these norms impact how we work through our developmental stages. This doesn't change the sequence of the stages; it just changes the behavior typical to the stages. This young lady was perfectly healthy; she just needed and wanted to do what was appropriate (in her culture) for a respectful, respectable unmarried young lady.

> *Parents must not only have certain ways of guiding by prohibition and permission, they must also be able to represent to the child a deep, an almost somatic conviction that there is a meaning to what they are doing* (Erikson, 1963, p. 249-50).

In the few paragraphs above, I have added to the information presented in Chapter 5 regarding the nature of development. Now we can turn to interpretation of data, which is the first step in learning to Facilitate Development.

Learning to Interpret Data

In the original book on Modeling and Role-Modeling we said, "Once you have compiled the data, you will search for relationships within the data that will lead to interpretations, diagnoses, and the formulations for (intervention) goals" (Erickson et al., 1983, p. 148). We offered many suggestions for doing this work of aggregating, etc. Later I built (Erickson, 1990a) on this work and stated the need to look for "patterns of relationships among the data or phenomena observed" (p. 2). Some of my other writings provide ways for us to "think" about the data (see bibliography, Chapter 11). Rather than repeating what has already been said, I wish to offer a few guidelines for data interpretation.

Guidelines

Once you have learned what to expect in the various developmental stages and get past the idea that people should behave in certain ways at certain ages, data interpretation is easier. However, at first learning, it may seem formidable. The following basic principles can help.

<u>Caring Has a Long-Arm Effect.</u> First of all, remember, the MRM logo was designed with a purpose in mind. Looking at it, you will notice the hand (which represents the nurse or the significant other) has a long arm—an arm that seems to go beyond the immediate nurse-client relationship. This is because that long arm was designed to symbolize our ability to impact the future well-being of others. We never know when someone is growing, but we know when we "seed" or plant ideas about another person's worth, growth may occur—growth that has the potential to change the individual's life over time. We have "long arms" because people need others to help them find their way in life. Since our needs are greater when we are vulnerable, the nurse has the potential to impact another person's life in ways that don't always exist between two strangers.

<u>Do More Good than Harm.</u> We have the potential to help people grow; we also have the potential to stilt their growth. We discussed this briefly in Chapter 3. It depends partly on how we think and feel, and how we communicate what we think and feel. It also depends on our intent. When we interact with another human being, we are sending messages. Some messages reinforce their worth, affirm their need for dignity and contributions, and others don't. No matter what we intend or do not intend to communicate, decoding the message depends on the other person's perspective.

Since we are human, we can't always be what we strive to be. We also know we can't be all things to all people, and we can't always do what we know is best. However, if we are aware of the linkage between what we think and feel and the well-being of others, we might become more aware of our own attitudes, and try to be patient, understanding, and accepting. Nevertheless, as humans, we may have the best intentions, and still need something simple to hold on to, something to help us keep our intent in our mind. Therefore, some benefit from a simple guideline: *Do more good than harm.* Thinking like this offers us a way to evaluate our successes and compare them to the times when we are less successful in carrying out our intent.

<u>Judge a Book by Its Contents.</u> Since growth precedes healthy development, and has to occur repeatedly before healthy residual can be constructed, it is important to nurture growth in clients without anticipating immediate results. Sometimes this is difficult. Some clients seem to hang onto a developmental task long after it might seem appropriate. In doing this, their behavior may appear inappropriate for their age. Sometimes significant others and health care providers are annoyed by their observations. They fail to recognize opportunities to nurture growth—growth that might be the last tiny increment before development occurs.

We never know what compels someone else's life, what motivates their behavior or why they think and act the way they do, but we can try. When we look at the bigger picture, it is often clear that what appears to be negative behavior is really a sign of growth; it just isn't what we expected. When we hasten to label behavior without understanding the underlying dynamics, we may miss the opportunity to facilitate reworking negative residual from earlier stage work.

Implications

A common problem nurses have when working with people is failing to recognize their behavior as an indication of their sequential, predictable developmental residual—something that will grow if and when we facilitate it. Below is a fairly simple case scenario that shows how *every* interaction we have with others has potential. How we use that potential determines what happens next in our lives and the lives of others. It is like a ripple out effect on water. We can't always see what causes the ripple, but as time goes by, it reaches further and further, touching and changing, creating new ways of being. We may have clouded vision and not see what surrounds the ripple, but with faith, we know it will happen.

Case Presentation

> *Thirty-two year-old Jim has been married for 4 years to a nurse, has a 2 year-old son, a Masters degree from a prestigious institution, and successfully holds an administrative position in a large company. When Jim was admitted to the emergency room with a fractured arm, acquired when he was doing "stunts" on his bicycle to entertain his son, his wife commented she had two children—their son and Jim. She said he acted just like a teenager and that is how he got hurt. The nurse in charge of Jim's care was overheard telling another nurse the wife was "dead-on"; he did act just like a teen. She said she would have expected more of him, given his age and job. After that her interactions with Jim were detached and brusque; she told him she had many patients and didn't have time to fool around with someone who wasn't really sick. Jim looked worried and asked if he had come to the wrong place. He thought his arm might be broken, but he could wait until the doctor's office opened the next day. The nurse responded that he was not the only person in the ER. She also said that they would get to him when they could, and that he just needed to learn to ride his bike like an adult.*

Jim provides a common example of our opportunities to facilitate people. Without knowing more about Jim, I would interpret the data as follows:

Data Interpretation

<u>Data:</u> Jim is chronologically in the stage of Intimacy, yet his behavior, according to the wife and nurse, is more like an adolescent.

<u>Interpretation</u>: Jim's stage of development and chronological years are not in synchrony. This means he may have had trouble acquiring a positive balance of residual in an earlier developmental stage.

<u>Data:</u> Jim has acquired an educational degree from an institution that mandates high performance, and he has a work position usually not earned for another ten or more years.

<u>Interpretation</u>: During the stage of Industry, Jim learned he was intelligent and if he worked hard he could get good grades. This pleased his caregivers. As a result, he learned to achieve at school, worked diligently to succeed as a "student," finished high school with good grades, entered college where he worked hard and continued to achieve (good grades). But, all of these were for the benefit of others more than for him. Or, all of these achievements were because others "valued" him when he earned good grades, achieved, and did the "right thing."

<u>Data:</u> After college, he did the next "right thing"; he got married and had a child.

<u>Interpretation:</u> Jim was 28 when he got married, the age of Identity for most young people today. He has done all the things he probably thought would make him worthy: good grades, good job, good wife, and a baby. An alternative view is that his "good wife" was selected because he wanted someone who would "love him," (which can also be interpreted as take care of him), someone who would encourage his affiliation needs, perhaps at the Trust level, possibly at the Autonomy level.

<u>Data:</u> Jim's wife commented that she had two kids—her husband acts like a teenager.

<u>Interpretation:</u> Jim's wife indicates their relationship is a child-adult relationship, rather than an adult-adult one. She feels a lack of intimacy, probably feels Jim wants her to take care of him, but he doesn't reciprocate. While there are two of them, they haven't been able to find the "Us," (or the separate unit made by the merging of their energy fields.) This suggests one or both of them probably have inadequate residual to work on the task of Intimacy. Since Jim has been labeled as "acting like a kid" and is the direct client, it is appropriate to consider him first, but we need to remember relationships take two people, and his wife is a major contextual factor in Jim's life.

Looking for a pattern

Jim seems to be "stuck" in Identity even though his chronological stage is Intimacy. Since he has been married for four years, the problem is probably long-standing. He also seems to have become an achiever for the sake of achieving rather than for his own growth. This might suggest an imbalance in residual before the stage of Industry or at least during that stage.

<u>More data:</u> The nurse rebuffs Jim, indicating he is not worthy of her time and Jim admits he has a problem, and maybe he'd made the wrong decision about how to handle it.

<u>Reassess the pattern:</u> Jim continues to show residual with a negative balance, but now it appears to include the stage of Autonomy as well.

An Evaluation

After we interpret the data, it is important to make an assessment. My initial assessment of this case is as follows.[1]

> *The problem started around 9-10 months of age to mid toddlerhood. I think Jim has a fairly healthy sense of early trust, but probably has an insecure attachment, which came about due to the change in the caregiver-child interaction that occurs around this time. Consider the caregiver-infant relationship where the baby changes and grows, but is primarily dependent upon the caregiver(s) for need satisfaction. The caregiver learns to synchronize with the infant, respond, and "be there" when the infant needs the connection. And then, the baby learns to comfort itself, to some degree. By 8-9 months most babies are able to crawl; they start showing more independence, i.e., taking steps or walking, and interact more with their environment.*
>
> *When this is coupled with a child who is biologically ready to move into Autonomy, parents are often confused about the "sudden" changes and decide it is time to take charge. They want to be good parents, but lack understanding of the toddler's need to learn to exercise judgment and make good decisions. So, life often becomes a power struggle. They are seen as "getting big," as being 1 or 1 1/2 years old, rather than 12 or 18 months. The implications are profound. The baby is no longer a baby and has to start acting like a child. In our society this often means a responsible, industrious person who respects authority!*
>
> *My guess is Jim came out of Trust with a reasonable balance between Trust and Mistrust, but with an insecure attachment.[2] When this happens, work on Autonomy can be difficult. Jim's comments to the nurse suggest he doubts his ability to make decisions: 'Jim looked worried and asked if he had come to the wrong place. He thought his arm might be broken, but he could wait until the doctor's office opened the next day'. This suggests the negative balance in residual started at an early age, long before the stage of Industry. These are comments of doubt with minimal shame, residual from the task of Autonomy. Interestingly, it is those characteristics that seem to stand out in this case, not his successes or innate ability to learn! Often this is the case—we see what is wrong or not-right before we can see what is normal or strong.*
>
> *Unless Jim is helped, he is a prime candidate for a midlife crisis with potential for an onset of physical problems. This happens because*

"somatic responses" are normal for the stage of Initiative, a stage where Jim learned to step forward and take charge because others expected or wanted it from him. The strain between doing what others want or expect, and getting his needs met in a way that will nurture his discovery of Self is sufficient to cause maladaptive responses. He is the type of person who might draw from his physiological subsystem to cope with unmet psychosocial and spiritual needs (see Erickson et al., 1983, pp. 47-49, and Chapter 8 in this book).

Opportunities

Unfortunately, the ER nurse did not understand the importance of nurturing growth in people and its impact on their ability to rework developmental residual. Growth can occur in a flash. When someone is cared for and treated with respect, they can acquire new resources needed to rework existing residual. The ER nurse had three opportunities to help Jim *and* his wife.

The first was when the wife commented that *she had two children—their son and Jim. She said he acted just like a teenager and that is how he got hurt.* The nurse could have responded something like, "Sounds like your husband knows how to play. That is wonderful. So many adults lose that quality." Such a comment sometimes helps the significant other reframe their perceptions. It is very possible Jim's playfulness is one of the characteristics she was attracted to before marriage. But, now, they are married, have a child, and are "older"; what was once exciting and fun is now a burden. By offering an alternative perspective on the behavior of others, people are often able to change how they view the behavior. This of course, would change the energy fields. When people want to be connected, their energy fields 'work' to synchronize with one another. When they are irritated, frustrated, or detached, they disconnect. Both people can feel a disconnection in energy fields. Those seeking the approval of another can feel the withdrawal and experience a subtle rejection or abandonment.

The second opportunity missed by this nurse was because of how she viewed human nature, and specifically, Jim's behavior. Because she probably made a flash decision that Jim was immature and irresponsible, she labeled his behavior "like a teen."

This type of comment has several implications: First she implied teen behavior is bad: that it is not to be embraced or encouraged, which shows a lack of respect for normal processes across the lifespan. It also suggests there is a time to be a kid and a time to be an adult, and the two should not mix. Adults are not supposed to be playful, but serious. Most important of all, the nurse's orientation communicated disapproval of Jim and his behavior. The minute she made her "decisions" about Jim, she was not only detaching from him, but possibly sending his wife and him nonverbal messages that Jim was not worthy, not to be respected, valued, and most certainly, not to be unconditionally accepted.

The third opportunity was missed when Jim exposed vulnerability through his comments that expressed doubt. If the nurse had, suddenly, become aware of her own actions, and then used the three strategies (Establishing a Mind Set, Creating a Nurturing Space, and Facilitating the Story) as recommended in Chapter 10, she might have been able to *change the energy between them*. If this had happened, it is possible Jim would have built new resources on the spot; resources that had the potential to change his residual. As stated by Pert (2003), "On a more global scale, these minute physiological phenomena at the cellular level can translate to large changes in behavior, physical activity, and even mood" (p. 24).

While these interactions took only a few minutes, Jim learned some things about himself and others. He acquired knowledge that becomes memories and will be stored in his residual. He learned he cannot always trust nurses to care about him, his life, and his needs. In fact, he might have learned nurses can be hurtful, so it is better to protect oneself. These understandings may build Mistrust within the context of the stage of Intimacy. Let me explain.

Implications

The developmental processes are epigenetic; we rework each stage with every new task. We build on what we came with, and leave the stage with more residual, positive and/or negative. When we are chronologically at the stage of Intimacy (as Jim is), and we deal with Trust issues, we learn about Trust as it relates to the chronological stage. So, Jim has not only learned that nurses cannot be trusted to care about him (as the infant would want in the first stage of life), but also that nurses are not available for a respectful, caring relationship as an adult in Intimacy would want.

This problem may be compounded by the fact that Jim's wife is a nurse. Jim may have just reinforced what he already knew: that nurses really don't care about his Self. This would probably support what he had learned as a child—that in order to be accepted, valued, and loved, he needed to behave in ways pleasing to others.

In these few moments, the nurse missed the opportunity to help another person build the new resources needed to rework residual, so he could become more fully alive and integrated. She also missed the opportunity to help herself. When we give from the heart, or reach out to touch the Soul of another person, we enrich our own Spirit. We connect with Universal energy, and come closer to understanding our Life Purpose.

Jim would, probably, have benefited from a Spirit-to-Spirit[3] interaction accompanied by a few comments about his situation, his needs, and his ability to enjoy his son and have fun. When we remember these simple actions of *mutuality,* we enrich not only the lives of others, but also our own. *We* grow because we *feel good about what we have done. At an energy level, we experience a connection to the Universe where love and compassion exist, and where our Spirit thrives.* At a humanistic level, we have met our own needs for self-esteem and growth. Usually, we also receive energetic feedback (nonverbal), that we are decent, worthwhile, human beings—information that meets our esteem needs. In some ways, we may benefit more than the clients, but that is not for us to decide, since we can never fully know what another person is experiencing. All I can say is the need for healthy affiliated-individuation is inherent in others and we often miss the opportunity to meet those needs because we are preoccupied with other "more important" things, or simply forget the epigenetic model of development exists in all human beings.

ER nurses are too busy to have lengthy communications, but they do have time to center themselves, focus their attention, and have intent of sending healing, loving energy to those around them. This, in itself, has the potential to change energy fields and the potential to help people rework their developmental residual.

Considerations

If I were to work with Jim as the ER nurse, I would start by simply nurturing growth in him at the most basic level where human interactions are necessary: the stage of Building Trust. If I am inaccurate in my assessment, Jim will let me know immediately[4] by responding in ways that tell me Trust isn't the issue. Later in this chapter I will talk about Trust strategies nurses can use that go beyond the strategies discussed in Chapter 10.[5]

I would also build on what I already know as two of Jim's strengths: he is a fast learner, and he wants to achieve. This information is evident in our data interpretation. We know he has achieved, academically, at a very high level at an early age, suggesting cognitive strengths. When we take this information and consider the patterns he projects, we also know he has not learned to use his strengths to build resources in other subsystems. He's stuck. At this point, I wouldn't worry about him being an over-achiever. Instead, I would focus on his learning *to trust others* and *feel good about his decision-making* about his Self, his holistic being.

Cognitive Development

Cognitive development is the final factor we need to discuss as a facilitation consideration. According to Piaget (Phillips, 1969), cognitive development is sequential, like psychosocial development, but it is not chronological. The original book on Modeling and Role-Modeling (Erickson et al., 1983) presented a lengthy discussion on cognitive development including tables illustrating the stages and related characteristics (pp. 63-68).

Cognitive development tends to parallel psychosocial developmental residual. Therefore, persons with considerable negative residual often have cognitive thinking consistent with the age-range in which the residual was created. For example, adults who had difficulty in the stage of Trust or Autonomy may use magical thinking or early concrete thinking when faced with situations, which trigger memories stored during these stages. Appendix D provides general guidelines for those who wish to build on the work presented in the original book.

STAGE-RELATED CONSIDERATIONS

In this section, I will present a few suggestions for nurturing growth at each stage of development. The focus will be on the developmental task since the aim is to nurture sufficient growth to produce a healthy balance of residual. As we consider these issues, we need to remember helping relationships require that the energy fields be in synchrony. This means it starts with us. We need to take care of ourselves, so we can be centered and focused: we need to be Present, so we can use Intent and Unconditional Acceptance of the worth and uniqueness of the human with whom we work.

> When we center ourselves, we organize our energy field, so it is focused rather than disseminated. When we use Intent, we synchronize our energy field with that of the other. These are simple things we can do to help others work and rework their developmental tasks.

Integration

This stage was proposed in Chapter 5 as the Zero Stage, the beginning of life on earth in human form. I believe Integration is an important stage of human development, which we can facilitate by caring for the mothers who provide the environment for healthy growth.

M. Erickson stated in Chapter 7 that a healthy uterine environment was a facilitating factor. Many women have not learned they need to care for themselves before they can care for others; this is true about the growing intrauterine fetus. A nonstressed environment produces chemicals different from a stressed environment. We know chemicals circulating in our blood are stored as memories. This suggests the mother's feelings have the potential to enhance or impede the growth of the fetus. We also learned, in Chapter 9, that the heart sends out major electrical pulses and facilitates coordination of the multiple energy fields, physical and spiritual, in the human.

Integration is the merging of the spiritual energy field with the physical body (the biophysical psychosocial energy field). When the mother is healthy, feels safe, secure, loved, valued, and connected, we can assume she will produce a different type of energy field. The developing human body will be more receptive to the merging of another energy field, the spirit. All in all, the fetus will have an intrauterine experience different from when the opposite happens: when the mother is not healthy, and does not feel safe, secure, loved, valued, and connected.

With this in mind, the best way to facilitate this developmental task is to do what I heard John Bowlby say one time: "We need to mother the mother, so she can mother the baby" (1977). We need to help mothers learn to care for themselves, be securely connected to a significant other, and welcome the oncoming addition to their life experience.

> **Principle**: *Nurture the mother, so she can nurture her baby* (Quoted from John Bowlby, 1977).

Building Trust

"The general state of trust implies not only that one has learned to rely on the sameness and continuity of the outer providers, but also that one may trust oneself and the capacity of one's own organs to cope with urges..." (Erikson, 1963, p. 248).

General Guidelines

Voice tones and volume, facial expressions, touch, and eye contact are all important when building Trust in others. We instinctively know this when working with infants, but forget it also applies to older persons. During the first few months of life, infants need eye contact,[6] soft voice tones, consistent, gentle, comforting handling, close contact (for example, blanket binding and snuggling), and friendly, happy faces to observe. These actions help the infant feel safe and secure. They begin to learn they belong to a group and are loved: actions that meet affiliation needs. This behavior also affirms the babies' existence, worth, and family membership, and are important as they learn they are not just extensions of their mothers, but unique human beings with a mind and spirit of their own.

> *To the human infant, his mother is nature. She must be that original verification, which will later come from other and wider segments of reality* (Erikson, 1964, p. 117).

Infants possess the need to learn, to be stimulated, and to discover their own uniqueness; they have the inherent need for individuation. Ironically, a happy balance of affiliated-individuation is not always easy to achieve. We are not all good at facilitating both. Often caregivers who are wonderful with affiliation needs do not understand individuation needs.

I remember one 5 month-old boy who was described as "always crying."[7] When his grandmother brought him to our house to visit, he was happy for a few minutes and then started crying. She tried a number of tactics to soothe him, but nothing worked. She laid him down and said that was how he was. The doctor had said to just put him down; he'd outgrow it.

When she agreed to let me hold him, I picked him up and started talking to him, then walked him around our house and told him about various things a slightly older child might be interested in. For example, I said, "See the pretty flower. It is pink." He stopped crying and didn't start again. Instead, he wore himself out exploring (with his eyes), while being held comfortably and being talked to in soothing tones. He was bored, but he needed to be connected. At the age of 5 months, he showed unusual affiliated-individuation. I told his parents to move him around the room a lot. He was very intelligent and needed lots of new stimulation, but he also needed to be held and comforted just like any other 5 month-old. He read at the age of 3 and 1/2. Today, he is nearly 5 and continues to demonstrate his eagerness to learn.

Interestingly, other babies may be over-loaded by too much stimulation. All children are unique, and all have a need to individuate in their own way. We have to model their world to understand their uniqueness. Then we try a strategy designed specifically for that individual, and reassess. We need to know if it worked. While some children like to be held on the shoulder, others prefer nestling in the chest muscles. Still others prefer to be held face out, with their backs against the chest.

We know all babies need both affiliation and individuation, and it behooves us to try to balance the two needs simultaneously. We do this best with consistent, loving interactions designed to model the child's world. We need to remember infants don't have the ability to understand all the words we use, but they learn fast.

When we interact with the Intent to facilitate continued integration of the spirit with the human form which is learning to organize and regulate itself, we are preparing individuals to be future oriented. They are learning to experience *mutuality,* and the rudiments of Hope, "...the most indispensable virtue inherent in the state of being alive" (Erikson, 1964, p. 115).

> **Principle**: Build Trust by nurturing integration of the spirit with the human form, so the individual will know, at some level, that they are a unique, worthy person. We do this by unconditionally accepting their holistic nature and need for affiliated-individuation.

Trust Work Beyond Infancy

Because development is an epigenetic process, it is important to think about the nature of Trust within the context of other stages. Even the healthiest children require continued assistance in building Trust during Autonomy, Initiative, Industry and so forth. While the principles remain the same as described above, some differences warrant discussion. These are due to two issues: First, the task of the new stage, and second, the residual brought into the new stage.

The chronological task of each stage is the focus of the work to be done during that stage. Development is also an epigenetic process. Therefore, when working on Trust during a later stage of development, we focus first on the chronological task and aim to develop Trust within that context. Let's take Autonomy as an example. During this stage of development, individuation needs are predominant. Nevertheless, soft, gentle interactions with face-to-face and eye contact are important, and so are words that gently direct toward something interesting, rather than away from something desired. To understand these differences, consider your own feelings when someone says you *can't do something* in comparison to when you are told there are options or choices of what you can do.

Learning to use positive language that confirms both the *being* aspect of the human and the need for *doing* is not easy to remember in a pinch. For example, picture the two-year-old racing across your neighbor's backyard, aiming to "hug" their dog (or from the dog's perspective, terrorize it) even after being told to stay with the mother. When the mother redirects the child with calm voice tones that communicate worth and esteem while still guiding good decision-making, the child learns about himself and his worthiness. Now, suppose the child has reached the dog, which turns, barks loudly, and bares its teeth. Most children would crumble on the spot, crying with fear. If the mother can calmly comfort the child, confirm the experience was scary, and help him learn how to interact appropriately with the dog, she will be building Trust within the context of Autonomy.

If, on the other hand, in the heat of the moment, the frustrated mother scolds the child for leaving her side, or says something to the effect that this happens when you don't listen, the child learns two things: 1) he can't trust himself to make good decisions, and 2) he can't depend on his mother for comfort when he feels unsafe and insecure.

> **Principle**: When working with older people who need help with Trust, focus on the chronological task and facilitate Trust within that context.

When we work with people who exhibit a need to start with the task of Trust and have excessive negative residual, the problem gets increasingly complicated with time. We have to unbind the negative residual while reworking the positive! This means we have to "unbind" or alter stored memories in the negative residual before we can change them. We have to do this while continuing to work on building positive resources. I have found Mistrust (negative residual) to be very difficult to alter in older people, but it can be done. It is difficult because they have had many years to practice not trusting people! Now, they have to test and retest the relationship to see if it is *really* trustworthy! Often this will go on for several weeks or even months before they are certain at least one person is trustworthy! After that, they have to be helped to transfer their learning to others. This requires significant others to be involved in the plan.

Many people repeatedly return to the clinical setting, each time in worse condition than before because they haven't followed the medical care plan. Many of these people have deep-seated mistrust (Finch, 1987). Many have told me they don't dare get well because if they do, they can't come see me. I have to assure them they can come see me *even when they don't need me!* Of course they deny the possibility exists, but then, when they build healthy positive residual in the stages of Trust and Autonomy, they discover they really *don't need me the same way.*

So how can we help these people? First of all, the same issues apply as when working with infants and building trust: they need consistent, caring voice tones, facial expressions, touch, and energy. They need to be unconditionally accepted as holistic beings and nurtured, so they learn they are worthy humans who have contributions to make to society, and that they will not be abandoned if they do. We always start with ourselves, using strategies necessary to build our resources and prepare ourselves to merge energy fields. We can think of these folks as people with discharged batteries; the potential to charge them exists, but because their battery has been discharged for so long, it may not take the charge well! We may have to charge and recharge before it sticks. This takes a lot of "caring energy" on our part, so we have to start with a ready source of loving energy and be prepared to recharge ourselves along the way.

We also have to know things change. When working on Trust with an adult who is also chronologically in the stage of Intimacy, it is important to start with Trust as it exists in the first stage, and be prepared to recognize success when it comes. It will look like Trust within the context of Autonomy! Now rather than testing and retesting to see whether we will abandon them or not, they will test and retest to see if we will reject their decision-making! Many students I've worked with have not recognized progress. Instead, they have called it a new problem. So, be prepared. When you are successful, you will see each of the later stages emerge, sequentially, and you will have to continue nurturing growth within the context of that stage. It is extremely important to assure your clients this is what is happening. They aren't getting worse or gaining more problems; they are getting better, and gaining more strengths. If you do this, you will discover they grow out of their need to have you as their trusted affiliate.

Autonomy

General Guidelines

In comparison to Trust, building Autonomy is a flip-flop. We emphasize affiliation needs with Trust, and individuation needs with Autonomy. Children working on this task learn to use good judgment while making decisions. In the previous stage, according to Erikson, they learn to control their own physical urges (such as delay the need for food). In this stage, they learn to control impulsive urges related to behavior. This is very difficult for some children. To accomplish their task work, they need the freedom to explore, try various options, make mistakes, and try again. At the same time, they need to feel safe and protected (affiliated). Without clear understanding of the accepted parameters, children don't feel safe in their explorations. They need to know there is someone else they can "fall back on," someone who will protect them from their own impulsive behavior. This is the essence of Trust in Autonomy.

Erikson (1964) describes this as the child facing "the double demand for self-control and for the acceptance of control from others" (p. 118). When we think about Autonomy in this way, it is important to remember healthy "acceptance of control from others" does not mean others rule our lives, but that we have an inherent need for affiliated-individuation, and we have to learn to compromise with others, so we can be both affiliated and individuated.

The caregiver's role is to provide the child with opportunities to explore, choose options, and *experience results* within parameters set by the caregiver. The point is, clearly established limits or parameters will be tested during this stage. Caregivers need to kindly, clearly, and repeatedly affirm that limits will be maintained. They also need to create an "illusion of control" for the child (Lefcourt, 1965, 1973). That is, they need to give children *options within the context of parameters.* This way they can practice making decisions, but not be required to use judgment in areas where they lack the maturity or experience needed to make appropriate decisions. For example,

> *Twenty-six months old, Mary woke up one morning and saw snow on the ground. Jumping out of bed, she ran to the door. She was going to play in the "white fluffy stuff." Her mother suggested she get dressed first, stating the snow was cold. Mary said, "No, (she is eager if not impulsive, and a bit obstreperous), Mary go now!" Her mother said it was too cold to go outside without her clothes. Mary ran to the closet, got her jacket, and ran back to the door. Her mother pointed out that her feet were bare. Mary put on boots and headed for the door again. At this point, her mother recognized Mary was following directions by putting on clothes that would protect her from the cold even though she was still in her pajamas. She decided all Mary really needed was something on her legs and feet. So, she told Mary her legs and feet would still get cold; she needed socks and long pants, leggings with feet, or tights before she would be ready.*
>
> *Mary immediately put on her tights and rushed outside, leaving the door wide open. She stayed outside for all of 4 minutes, dressed in her pajamas, hooded coat, boots, and tights. She said her hands were cold and she was ready to come back in. When she came in, her mother asked if her feet were cold and she said no because she had her tights and boots on. She said she was going to have breakfast and go back out with all her "warm clothes." Then, looking at her mother, she smiled and said she was going to wear mittens, too.*

Mary learned she needs assistance that defines the parameters *that will allow her to make decisions.* She also learned some of her decisions fell short of the mark; she can do better. And then she planned for the next practice! Mary's mother did not need to say, "I told you so," nor did she need to discipline Mary for being obstreperous or leaving the door wide open. With time and patience (on the part of Mary's mother), Mary will learn *all the steps in the decision-making process.* And with her mother's guidance, she will learn to use good judgment.

If Mary's mother had perceived she wasn't "minding" or was being bratty, the outcome would have been very different. When we take such attitudes about a person who is struggling to find their way through Autonomy, they have to choose between pleasing us and becoming more of who they have the capability to be. They have to choose between affiliation that doesn't support individuation and individuation with limited affiliation. Neither of these is growth directed; neither will facilitate healthy autonomy residual. If Mary's mother and other care providers continue to work with her as described above, Mary will learn about herself, acquire a healthy sense of doubt or introspection, and move on to Initiative without difficulty.

The principles I've described in this scenario apply to all humans, at all stages. Often, health care providers get confused when people don't seem to "do what they are supposed to do." They are labeled as non-compliant, bad, unwilling to cooperate, and so forth. The problem, actually, is not the client's; it is the health care provider's! The health care provider simply doesn't understand the nature of Autonomy. We need to remember people don't usually say no just for the sake of rebelling; they say no because they perceive they don't have control over their lives. They are learning to have control by *being in control.* Once they learn to make worthy decisions (which means they are worthy), they can learn to have control without always being in control of what they do, where they go, and how they live. They learn that having control is an internal way of *being* rather than a way of *doing.*

Principle: Building healthy Autonomy residual requires that we care about the growth of the human Self and use techniques that facilitate emergence of the Self within the context of others. This means we facilitate people to continue being affiliated with caregivers as in Trust, but now with a growing understanding of how they are unique human beings.

Autonomy Beyond Toddler-hood

Trust and Autonomy are the basis for psychosocial development across the lifespan. As we grow, we rework these stages over and over. Once we acquire healthy Trust and Autonomy residual, the next two tasks are less difficult unless we encounter a major loss, which is difficult to resolve. Unresolved losses and their impact on development is a different issue and will be addressed in Chapter 14. Here, I simply want to talk about the work of Autonomy in later stages, under more normal conditions. Since Autonomy involves learning about one's Self as it relates to the sense-of-self, problems can emerge later in life with which significant others are often unprepared to understand. One such example is learning to please, and doing what is expected for the sake of affiliation. This issue, *pleasing for the sake of affiliation* can become a major issue as time goes by.

When children focus on pleasing others at the expense of perceiving control over their lives, they begin to build a stronger sense-of-self rather than an understanding of who they are as unique human beings. Since the toddler is still young, dependent upon its care providers, *and has a limited world*, this isn't as great a problem as it is in later life, such as during adolescence. During adolescence people seek relationships with their peers. It is necessary for them to break away from the immediate group (i.e., their family) and move into society. If the sense-of-self is stronger than an understanding of their Self, they tend to seek approval from and can be heavily influenced by their peers. They will rebel against parents in order to do what is natural—establish their own Identity. When parents or care providers don't understand this issue, there is often a serious threat of withdrawal of the support needed to discover one's Self. For example,

> *Seventeen year-old Jannie had diabetes from the age of 3. She came into the clinic for a check up; I saw her a few minutes after her MD. She was very distraught and sent everyone out of the room, except me. After they left, she said the doctors wanted to raise her insulin because her blood glucose was too high. She didn't want them to; she didn't think she needed it. I asked her why her blood glucose was so high. She told me she was mad at her mother the evening before, so she ate a bag of Snicker bars. My response was that it is very normal for teens and their parents to disagree, so it was good to know she is normal, but we needed to find some other way for her to tell her mother she was upset: a way that didn't hurt her.*

Jannie was a typical teenager, struggling through her own personhood; she was dealing with Autonomy once again, but from a slightly different perspective. Now, she had to do it within the context of the stage of Identity. Because she had learned she was "bad" when she ate candy or didn't do what she was supposed to do when on a diabetic diet, she didn't want the other health care providers to know what she had done. Yet, she had sufficient trust in our relationship and sufficient positive residual to know she would be better off telling someone, so she told me.

I believe she trusted I would unconditionally accept her and help her find a way to solve her problem. I had told her there is no bad or good behavior, there is only behavior that is efficient or not. And whether it is efficient or not depends on what we hope to accomplish. Eating candy bars the night before she came to the clinic was not an efficient way of dealing with her anger.

By revealing her decision to eat candy to get even with her mother, she was able to avoid choosing between doing what the doctors wanted her to do (i.e., increase her insulin), *and* telling them she would increase her insulin, and then not doing it. From her perspective, telling them about the candy was not an option because she knew her mother, the doctors, and even many of the nurses would disapprove of her behavior. This is the same as saying they would disapprove of her judgment and decision-making abilities. In Jannie's case, her mother was an extension of the doctors, so she would have difficulty choosing to agree to an increase in insulin and then not following through. Her mother was her watchdog and would probably raise a fuss if Jannie didn't comply.

In my experience, many clients tell their health care providers they will do something even when they know it is not right for them, and then won't do what they have agreed to do. I also know many health care providers are unaware of this behavior; instead, they are confused because their clients are so hard to "regulate."

How can health care providers help people in stages other than Autonomy who are working hard learning to make decisions using good judgment? To start with, we have to believe people really *do* want to grow and fulfill their potential, and their needs motivate their behavior. All people working on Autonomy issues want to be affirmed for their choices and for their decisions, and they want to be assured their judgment is okay. They want control over their lives, their need for control affirmed, and positive feedback on the results of their decisions.

This means the person needs multiple opportunities with options to choose from (remember 'illusion of control'), opportunities to make decisions, *and see the results of the judgment*. They also need to be *affirmed each step in the process: considering options, setting priorities, making decisions, and evaluating results.* Often, they don't realize the decision-making process requires multiple steps, which provide multiple opportunities for making mistakes. As toddlers, they didn't have the opportunities to learn this, so they cannot carry these skills into their later years.

It isn't hard to tell someone he is courageous because he tried! Nor is it difficult to find something positive about results. When we affirm *"the results,"* we affirm the person who made the decision that produced the results. Nevertheless, healthcare providers do not usually offer affirmations of unsuccessful attempts.

No Such Thing as Failure. Often, I hear the word "failure" used by older people working on Autonomy. When a client uses such language, I usually tell them there are no failures—only decisions, acts, or plans (which ever they have 'failed' at) more successful than others. And if they keep trying, they will learn some things work better; it is just a matter of patience and courage. Patience is needed because we sometimes have to try again; courage is needed, so we don't get discouraged when it takes multiple tries.

Another useful follow-up strategy is to remind the person of times when they had to be patient and have courage, such as when they learned to crawl, walk, etc. It is best to use as an example some skill they have learned well, and which they use without thought. It is important to follow-up with details about what they had to learn in order to do this, comment on the decisions made, the value of their judgment, and the outcomes. Break the process down into the steps listed above: considering options, setting priorities, making decisions, and evaluating results. You may recognize this type of language reframes the underlying feelings of the statement from negative to positive.

Controlling Others' Behavior. Some people act as if they not only want to control their lives, but also the lives of others. They feel safe only when *in control* of their environment. This is because they don't feel they have control over themselves, and depend on others to feel safe, loved, connected, and valued. They perceive the only way to *have* control, is *to* control everything and everyone around them.

They missed the opportunity of exploring, choosing, making decisions, and learning they have good judgment. So, as adults, they have to control everything—they are unable to discriminate, recognize parameters, or see themselves separate from their significant others. At the same time, those around them often see them as domineering, negative people. While they may have authority and even control over people, they lack the ability to attract companions, so they feel lonely and isolated. Most people tend to stay at a distance from such people; sometimes they fear them, other times they are just repelled.

If we choose to work with someone like this, we have to realize the underlying dynamics: lack of trust, excessive mistrust. They need to be connected spirit-to-spirit, and they need parameters. We, as care providers, have to purposefully make an energetic, spirit-to-spirit connection and *stay* connected. This is difficult with this type of person; they try to overpower, take charge, or push us away. If we allow this to happen, they learn that we cannot be trusted, just as others in the past; that they dare not attach to us, because we will abandon them, and that the only way to survive is to continue their controlling behavior.

Providing Personal Space. There are several things we can add to our arsenal of strategies when working with people who have excessive negative residual and minimal Autonomy. First, they need personal space and have difficulty if they perceive it has been invaded. They can *feel* the invasion; it is a matter of change in energy. We need to respectfully request permission to enter it. This means the area around them, the immediate physical space surrounding their bodies, and their bodies. When we do not have time to obtain permission, it is important to tell them in respectful, firm tones what we are doing, so they *perceive control.* While these are good things to do with all people, they are very important for this type of clientele. Remember, they don't feel safe unless they perceive they have control. If we are respectful of this need for "space," they will gradually learn we are trustworthy because we help them feel safe.

Setting Parameters. Second, they need parameters; they need to know what is okay and what is not, but they need to hear it without being "disconnected" or threatened with punishment or ridicule. We disconnect when we change our Intent. Remember when we use Intent, we direct positive energy toward another person with a specific purpose in mind. Disconnection alters the energy flow, so the person *feels* a change, a withdrawal. If we set parameters and disconnect at the same time, people perceive it as a rejection.

When setting parameters, it is always helpful to distinguish between the person and the behavior. That is, if we can remember needs motivate behavior then we can separate the two by accepting the needs (i.e., the human), but not necessarily accepting the behavior. Sometimes this is most easily done by describing the underlying philosophy of Modeling and Role-Modeling. I do this by explaining that all people have needs; needs drive behavior. People want to be the best they can be, but sometimes their needs get in the way. I also state the difference between the person and the behavior. All people have strengths and are inherently good, but sometimes people do things that are not okay. And then, kindly, firmly, set the parameters. There are no mistakes, no exceptions; they cannot do things that hurt themselves, and they cannot do things that will hurt others.

Contracts. Sometimes we have written contracts to this effect (Erickson, 1990b). Usually they include what *can be done* as well as the parameters within which they can be done. Sometimes they are more to the point, and simply say a specific behavior is not acceptable. There is always a reward of the client's choosing (and my mutual agreeing) to a contract that is kept. Reward examples have included such things as an extra 10 minutes time in conference; a picture of myself with the client; the client "gives himself permission" to go to the movies, take a nap on Sunday, call a friend, and so forth. It is always amazing to see what clients choose as rewards. Often, they are simple things many people do every day without thinking. Simple things that make them feel more worthy, less stressed, and so forth.

Contracts serve two purposes: First, they establish the parameters, and second, they inform clients that you care enough to follow through, "protect them from themselves," and not reject them as people. When using contracts, it is important that only absolutely unacceptable behavior be written with no options. For example, when using contracts with people who physically hurt themselves through cutting, sexual activity, etc., there are no options—it has to stop. On the other hand, with people who do things harmful to themselves (because they interfere with their health, such as overeating), the contract is written for 3 or 4 out of 7 days. It is usually easier for people to give up hurting others or themselves than it is to give up behavior that is comforting, even when the comforting behavior is self-destructive. I usually add a sentence in the contract for those who have the most serious problems. It reads: "I also agree that I will call Dr. Erickson if at any time I feel that I cannot keep my contract. I will not break it until we have talked."[8]

In the many years I have worked with clients, including those who have sexually abused their children, purposefully overdosed with insulin, stabbed a wife, and had multiple serious accidents, I have never had a single person break their contract. Instead, I have had a few who called me to "just talk, so they could keep going" and I have had several who told me they really struggled, but were able to wait until our appointment.

Transitional Objects. I have repeatedly said staying connected is important. A cancelled appointment, late arrival, unexpected telephone call during a discussion, and other types of "being rejected or disconnected" are upsetting. Since these people have few resources, they are unable to understand when we say we have other things to do. It simply means we have more important things to do than be with them. However, they can tolerate the separation if two things happen: first, a connection has been made between their care provider and them, and second, if their care provider gives them a transitional object.

This concept was presented in Chapters 7 and 9. To refresh your memory, a transitional object is anything that represents the attachment object. But, transitional objects must be consistent with the client's world, and be given with the clear message that you value the recipient, and want the object to remind them you care about them and your voice will go with[9] them.

Seeding. People can't grow too fast, or too much at one time. So, seeding can be used to help them start thinking about the future. Seeding involves making suggestions such as "Some people like to….," "Maybe some day you will be interested in…," "I know you don't care now, but it is possible someday you will want to know about…," etc.

Seeding is a powerful technique because it offers an option without any need to commit, has no personal feelings attached, and holds no possibilities for being unsuccessful. For those working on Autonomy, options are very important, particularly options that will facilitate their growth. Seeding gives people an opportunity to let the idea settle in, become part of who they are, and ultimately emerge as their own idea. It helps people develop decision-making skills and use good judgment. Each of these helps change cellular memories, and, therefore, developmental residual.

Reframing. Another technique to help people rethink past decisions works well in building autonomy in older people. Reframing is what we do when we change the definitions of words used by clients to describe their attributes or behavior. For example, it is not unusual to hear someone use the word stubborn to describe another person. When we reframe this term, we can say something like, "So, you have a strong will! That is wonderful! That is why you keep going even though you have had some tough times!" There is a big difference when you compare a "stubborn" person, and a "strong-willed" person. The implication for the first is the individual is always cantankerous or difficult while the second implies the individual is strong and has the will to persevere. If you consider the difference such terminology has on visceral reactions, you can appreciate the implications for changing "stored memories" or developmental residual.

Indirect Suggestions. Some people have created a coping pattern in which the only way to feel safe is to always be right, to always be in control. They tend to be argumentative and very resistant to suggestions that might help them feel better. They might also demonstrate the same underlying dynamics by being passive resistant. That is, they may *appear to* agree completely with what is being said, but never follow through. They exert their will and take control even though it might not be healthy.

When we work with such people, indirect suggestions are often helpful. This is best achieved by choosing the message, and sending it to someone nearby. You continue looking at the other person, but say it so the first person can hear. For example,

> *I was recently sitting with a support group of women for weight management. One lady repeatedly commented about the program and why it didn't work for her. Although she had paid money to attend, she was unable to participate. Several other things she said suggested she ate for comfort and would not give up over-eating until she had something else to comfort her.*
>
> *After a couple of sessions, I turned to the lady sitting about three seats away and said, "Eating is such a comfort for some of us that it is hard to give up. We often don't realize giving up is hopeless; we have to learn to let go. But, that, too, takes time. The trick is to find something else that will comfort us." The lady I was looking at agreed, but then said she didn't think she ate for comfort, but maybe she did. She then commented about the big difference between giving up and letting go.*
>
> *The next week, the lady I had aimed my comments at spoke up and said she had no idea why it had happened, but when she got home that day she just decided to stop eating some of her junk food when she was down on herself, and to eat vegetables instead. She went on to comment she had given up on herself, but when she decided to let go of the junk food, she had felt like a new woman. She looked like one too! She looked happy and proud of her decision.*

Indirect suggestions bypass all the superficial resistance people put up to protect themselves. When someone they trust provides the suggestions, they are assimilated into the subconscious and stored in their Self-care Knowledge.

Embedded Commands. Yet another technique that can be used for this population is the embedded command. This technique is used when we want to dislodge negative residual, but know direct confrontation will produce resistance. For example, people worried about self-discovery often resist examining why they make the choices they do or the implications of their decisions. They are afraid they will uncover what they think is the truth, that they have poor judgment, are stupid, or simply no good.[10] When we say something like, "One of these days you'll know what you already know, but don't know you know! Then you can decide what to do about it," we are saying several things. Table 12.1 analyzes this simple statement.

Table 12.1 Examples of embedded commands and implied messages

Comment: "One of these days" means "not now, but soon."
Implication: What I am about to say will happen.

Comment: "You'll know"
Implication: Means "*you WILL* know." It will happen; you will understand this and know it consciously, even though you don't believe me now.

Comment: "What you already know."
Implications: Means at some level, most likely the subconscious, you already know the answer to the problem.

Implication: YOU are the one in control, not I; you are the one who will do the problem-solving, not I; and you are the one who can use good judgment in making decisions; you don't need me.

Comment: "But don't know you know" means "you know at some level, but you aren't ready to understand yet."
Implication: You have the answer yourself; it's not a mystery.

Comment: "Then you can decide" means "you are in control."
Implication: You trust the person will take charge of his or her own life.

Comment: "What to do about it" means "you will decide and take action."
Implication: You will do something about this issue that needs to be resolved.

The above techniques, seeding, reframing, indirect suggestions, and embedded commands are all communication techniques first introduced to me by my father-in-law, Milton Erickson. Today, they are commonly discussed in hypnotherapeutic literature. While this may intimidate some readers, I have provided them because they are *communication techniques* you can use to help people grow and resolve Autonomy issues. They are neither complicated nor difficult. You just have to believe communication is an appropriate tool for you to use. You also have to practice, and then practice some more. Remember, you always need to build a trusting, functional relationship first, and you do this with Presence, Intent, and Unconditional Acceptance.

Initiative

General guidelines
Just as in all other states, work on Initiative depends on the residual at the outset of the stage. Assuming the person is healthy and well-balanced, the most important aspect of Initiative is to provide opportunities so the child can move

into new social circles, try new relationships, and continue practicing skills learned during Autonomy. Now the emphasis is on learning to use these skills in unknown territory. Children require opportunities to play with others outside their immediate circle so they can learn to live by the rules created by peers rather than adults, and have purpose in their play.

We can facilitate Initiative easily by creating opportunities for children to develop new skills, continuing to set parameters for interactions, and encouraging their independence by supporting them until they become comfortable with the experience. We should remember a child's play is a child's work, and that too much "work time" is exhausting. So, while children need opportunities to learn to purposefully use their decision-making skills with peers, they also need time to recover. Parents often comment that their children who go to play group in the morning just seem to hang out in the afternoon. They are giving themselves the opportunity to integrate everything they have learned with past information.

> **Principle**: Building healthy Initiative residual requires that people continue to feel connected to their "safety anchor"—the person who has unconditionally accepted their inherent need to become the most they can be.

Initiative Beyond Middle Childhood

While older people have multiple needs while working through Trust and Autonomy, it seems Initiative is not a major problem for them. That is, even those who need considerable help with Trust and Autonomy, once they have developed better balanced residual, their natural propensities to grow and develop take over. They start moving into new circles. Now, they just need to know that the significant other who helped them grow will continue to stand by to provide reinforcement and affirmation. As one client told me when he reached this stage, "the umbilical cord isn't cut yet, it is just stretched a long way" (Erickson, 1990b, p. 479). My response was it was like a very long telephone cord; I would always be at the end of it. Today, I would have remarked, "Now that we have wireless, our options are greater than ever before. You have the freedom to go as far as you want, and still be close to me. "

Simply stated, working with older people means those who are fearful of taking initiative are usually people who either have inadequate Trust and Autonomy or are fearful that *if they take* initiative, they will lose their support base. This happens because care providers often perceive that once a child or older person can be autonomous (often called independent), they should be able to go out on their own. They no longer need the support base. These care providers have forgotten people need affiliated-individuation; we all need to be connected, so we can become more of our natural Self.

You will run into people who need a little help, a little nudge that will enable them to broaden their social circles and practice their newly acquired decision-making skills. If you work with them enough so they learn to trust you, and then give them a transitional object, they will feel safe enough to take the initiative needed to grow.

I remember one colleague confronted with her first day of teaching a large group of students. While she had mastered teaching small groups, she lacked the experience to teach large groups. Extremely anxious, she came to see me. I reminded her she had developed all the skills she needed over the past few years while working with small groups of people. Now she was ready to go into a large group, use the same skills, and even build on them. She agreed that was what she needed to do, but she would feel much better if I would go and sit in the front row so she could see my face.

I told her that wasn't possible, but a piece of me could go with her in her pocket. I had a number of small objects I used for just such a time sitting on my desk. I suggested she choose one, put it in her pocket, and when a little nervous, she could reach in and feel it. When she did that, she would remember my voice, see my face, and she would be just fine. She selected an object, left my office, and taught her class. Her class evaluations at the end of the semester were excellent. When I left that university, I received her note, thanking me for helping her grow and stating she still carried the object when she went out into new situations.

Industry

General Guidelines

By this stage, most healthy children simply need clear parameters or directions about their limits, opportunities to practice goal-setting and strategy development independently and with peers, and a "safe harbor" to return to after a busy day in the outside world. The parameters should also include guidance, so they learn to balance their competence and be good workers in projects that serve the needs of society and the needs of their spirit, or Self.

Principle: Building healthy Industry residual requires helping people build competence while learning to work with others.

Industry in Adults

When working with older people who need help with Industry, we need to distinguish between those who work too much because they are self-actualized and those who work too much because their identity is tied to their work. As we discussed earlier, people who enter this stage without sufficient positive residual learn that hard work makes them respectable, important people. They haven't learned industry; they ward off inferiority by workingBut, they never seem to do enough to feel safe; they don't balance their lives, and they don't really enjoy their work. They simply work because it makes them worthy. These people are typically called workaholics.

I have also heard self-actualized people called workaholics, but they aren't. They set goals, create strategies, and work diligently to meet their goals. They are happy at work, and with their work, even though their families sometimes perceive they work too much.

Working with the two types of people requires different strategies. The first group needs help developing skills, solving problems, setting goals, and creating strategies. They often lack confidence in their judgment, so they overwork to ensure they "do it right." They are usually not very efficient, but work very hard. They need help learning to be more efficient and need affirmation for learning. It is usually best to teach them to break down the steps and take one at a time, since they often lack these skills. As they develop better decision-making and goal-setting skills, some people are ready to assess their work environment and decide whether they can handle it in other more enjoyable ways.

When working with self-actualized people who work excessively, the problem is not industry, but often intimacy on the part of their partner. Because of their commitment to their life work, some partners feel left out. Many of these self-actualized people will attempt to spend more time with the partner if they are reminded that it might make him or her happy. It should be remembered, however, that these people are very content with their lives and will alter their behavior only when they feel the need to do it for someone else.

Identity

General Guidelines

Since this is the first stage in which reworking of all previous stages is a major aspect of the task itself, we have to recognize that all task issues previously addressed will emerge. Unfortunately, they don't emerge sequentially. At one moment, the teen may be working on Initiative within the context of Identity and the next it will be Autonomy. Caregivers often get confused; they say such things as, "One minute he was acting like a responsible teenager taking out the trash, planning how he could earn extra money for college, and the next minute he was demanding we let him go to a rock concert and take his friends! He knows he isn't allowed to drive his friends without supervision. One minute he acts like an adult and the next like a two year old!"

We need to help parents understand the teen is experiencing typical teen growth patterns. They are not adults, but are on the edge. What they learn about themselves now will influence how they manage their adult lives.

They continue to need help making decisions and using good judgment as they take initiative. They naturally want to do things on their own, often with their peers. They need "reserved guidance" as they try various possibilities. As in all other stages, it is helpful if the teen is given clear guidelines or parameters. Now, however, it is necessary to expand the nature of the guidelines. There needs to be room for negotiation. For example, a family rule may be that teens will be home by 10:00 PM on school nights and by midnight on weekends. *If* it becomes clear these timelines won't be met, there is to be a phone call home explaining where they are and what they are doing. Guidelines are to be observed. However, *if and when* they are not met, a follow-up discussion is important. During this time, caregivers should remember that teens who are respected, valued, and trusted will do their best to retain that trust. Family discussions need to keep that in mind. Teens are struggling to learn to behave as adults. They need to be treated as emerging adults, with the same respect and appreciation we might have for any human being doing their best. At the same time, they need a clear understanding of what is expected of them. They will try to rise to our standards and values if we keep in mind this stage of life is like learning to walk again. They will stumble and fall, acquire a few bruises along the way, and in doing so, learn about themselves, who they are, and where they fit into the larger scheme of life.

> **Principle**: Building healthy Identity residual requires helping people discover their true nature and become aware of their Self as it relates to others.

Identity in Older People

Bill's story, at the beginning of this chapter, is an example of working with someone (at a later stage in life) who continued to have Identity issues and as a result, ran into difficulty in the stage of Intimacy. Since his difficulty was compounded with major losses, he demonstrated more serious behavior than many others might at his age. Often, when difficulties in the stage of Identity are carried into later life, it is because parents or caregivers expected too much of their teens. Rather than observing physical problems, as described with Bill, we would more likely see problems in these people emerge during Generativity. These people try to do the right thing because they have learned affiliations require commitment to the needs of others. They have a strong sense-of-self, but missed the opportunity to learn about their Self, an opportunity that goes hand in hand with the task of Identity.

They make work commitments guided by others, relationship commitments that seem "right," and try to be loyal to both. However, when they reach Generativity and ask themselves what they have produced, they realize their "product" is not satisfying. Their lives feel empty and they are confused when others point out they have everything anyone could want: a good job, loving family, nice home, and so forth. But, at some level, they know they are not happy. What they haven't learned, yet, is happiness comes when we do what is right for our Self, not what is right from the perspective of others.

To help these people, we need to give them permission to have their feelings, affirm that while others might think they have the "world in a hand basket", we recognize it is the wrong world for them. It is very important to affirm their feelings and reassure them that their worth is not tied to what they have been doing, but how they choose to live their lives. Sometimes they need to make major life changes which involve their families. They need help learning to communicate with their loved ones, to express their feelings, and needs.

Throughout the process of working with these people, it is important to assure them that at some level they know what they need, how they can get those needs met, and what they can do differently to help themselves grow. I remember, many years ago, I interviewed a gentleman who had just been admitted to the hospital with a new diagnosis of leukemia. When asked to tell me a story, any story that came to his mind. His story went like this:

Well, when I was about 16, my parents decided to move to a farm a long way away from where we lived. I had nothing to say about it. I had lots of friends I had to leave behind. I was really mad about that. The day we moved, my parents needed to go into town to get groceries. They asked me to watch my younger sister. While they were gone, she decided to ride one of our horses. I let her. The horse spooked and ran under a tree; she hit her head on a branch and was killed.

I don't know why this story came to my mind! I haven't thought of it for years. (silence for about 40 seconds). Well, maybe that is why I got sick. Maybe I've been thinking about my life and think that I have not really made much of a mark. I've always tried to make up for that, but I've never been able to. Once you're dead, you are dead. I don't think my parents ever forgave me. I guess I'll probably die, too.

I haven't seen or heard from this man for years, but I did work with him for about three years after that interview. After he finished his story, we talked about his family, which consisted of two teenage sons. I asked him his philosophy on raising teens. He said he had learned too much responsibility was not a good thing for kids, so he tried to help them make better decisions than he had as a kid. This gave me an opportunity to present (seed) the idea that kids want to do the best they can, but they are kids. They need help, and sometimes they will make mistakes, and sometimes things will happen when they "take charge." It was really great that he was teaching his sons they could make mistakes or that things might happen (indirect suggestion to his Self), sometimes very serious things, and they needed to think them through and sort out *exactly* what part of the outcome they were responsible for. I also commented that sometimes tragic things happen, not because we are responsible, but just because we are there, we feel responsible (reframe). I then said it is very important for us, as parents, to let our teenagers know they have done the best they can under the circumstances, *and* they can learn important lessons about themselves from the experiences, so they can do it differently the next time (learning to use better judgment). I also said as we practice these skills, it is amazing what we can learn about ourselves, things that will help us be who we want to be and to be healthy (embedded command).

The last time I talked with this gentleman, he had been in a four year remission, had changed his job so he had more time with his wife and children, and was feeling good about the way his children were developing. He commented that marrying his wife was the smartest thing he had ever done and raising two great kids was the best work he had ever done.

This gentleman is not atypical of older adults who need help reworking the stage of Identity. However, whenever we work with such people, it is always important to *start at a stage below where you think the problem emerged.* If it is at the stage of Identity, then start lower. I almost always start with Trust and work forward as fast as possible. That way I won't make the mistake many care providers do, which is start too high in the sequence of task work. When we do this, we reinforce previously established perceptions and increase negative residual.[11] I will further address related issues in the last chapter of this book, Chapter 14.

Intimacy

General Guidelines
When people enter this stage with a healthy balance of residual, they need little help working through the task of Intimacy, but there are a few things we can do. First is reassuring couples that it takes time to learn to be a couple. People often get confused about the difference between physical love and interpersonal intimacy. While the two complement one another, there is a difference. Interpersonal intimacy is built on a strong, healthy base of trust and autonomy. Without this, it is impossible to acquire a relationship with another where there is a healthy balance of affiliated-individuation. Work on intimacy requires learning to negotiate (as in the stage of Initiative), set goals, and plan strategies (Industry) that are consistent with who we think we are and what gives us pleasure (Identity), *but now it has to be done within the context of the "us"* (described in Chapter 5). Couples often need help with this. Sometimes one gets ahead of the other and tries to force the process, for example, when to start a family; the two people struggle to maintain their own identity while also trying to build an intimate relationship. Sometimes they seek help from outsiders, such as parents or best friends.

As caregivers, it is important to help them understand outside support is important, but before they talk to anyone else, they need to talk with their significant other. They need to be reminded no two people are alike, even as no two trees, no two flowers, and so forth, are alike. But, nature has a way of complementing differences and humans are part of nature. I often acknowledge that beauty in nature is created by the differences. It is the same in human nature. The more we learn to be true to ourselves while trying new ways to think and act, the more rewards we find in life.

It is also important for couples to understand they need other people, too. That is, they need other people to help them meet their needs. Neither member of the dyad should expect their partners to be interested in everything they are or to want to do all things they want. At the same time, the two of them also need to identify common interests and set priorities for the relationship.

The priority for the couple is to find ways to reciprocally meet the needs of their partner, affirm the worthiness of their partner, be the safe anchor, create a sense of belonging, and respect and value the other, no strings attached. This is the work of Intimacy. But, for many, this is not easy to do. Some are impatient. They think they shouldn't have to do anything to build a relationship; it should just happen. Others are worried about losing their own identity if they "give in" to their partner. In both cases, they need help sorting through the type of relationship they want and understanding the difference between one that is short-lived and one that is more enduring.

Many people can accomplish this task more easily when reminded that important things take time. We don't learn by simply existing day to day, anymore than we learned to ride a bike, or drive a car; these skills had to be learned, and mastered. People have *to work* at each and every developmental task. Often, all they need from us is reassurance that this is normal, and that if they keep working and seek new resources or information to help them, they too will be successful.

Bill's Story

Before we move on to Intimacy in Older People, let's revisit Bill, described at the beginning of the chapter. I first determined that Bill had negotiated each of the first few stages of development without difficulty. He had acquired healthy developmental residual, as expressed by his orientation to the future, decision-making abilities, willingness to explore beyond his secure base, and ability to set goals and work toward balanced goal-achievement.

His difficulty came about because he was working on the task of Identity when he decided to join the military to go to Vietnam. Typical of the teen, he was idealistic; he had a cause and he answered it. Also, typical was his need to "do his own thing" at the same time that he chose to do something that would be valued by others. He carried strong, healthy residual that helped him adapt to the rigor of military life and demonstrate leadership among his peers. He showed the virtues and strengths that grew out of healthy developmental residual. But, still, he was in a crisis when I was asked to see him.

His problem was not what had occurred during the first few stages of life, but what happened to him as he worked on the stage of Identity coupled with the task of his current stage of life. He had entered the army with a way of thinking about himself. He had demonstrated an immature, but healthy, sense of Identity. Under other circumstances, he would have probably finished the task-work of the stage without difficulty if he had not encountered two episodes that reinforced his self-evaluation based on immature logic. He needed help in two ways.

First, he needed help resolving the task of Identity, so he could go on to Intimacy with a healthy balance of residual. Otherwise, he would continue to build negative residual. He also needed to be facilitated to focus on his current (and chronologically predicted) developmental task. He needed *permission* to have affiliated-individuation with his parents, and to work on Intimacy with his wife.

Once he was reminded of his abilities and offered a new way to think about his feelings and actions, he was able to move on. Since development is an epigenetic process, we could predict he would continue to work through some of the experiences he had encountered during the stage of Identity. We could also predict that he would be successful and maneuver his life journey in growth-directed ways.

> **Principle**: Building healthy Intimacy residual requires that people maintain their Self while creating, with another person, a unique unit, different than either member of the dyad. This unit has at its core a relationship based on respect and compassion for the other.

Intimacy in Older People

Usually, people beyond this age who have reworked earlier stages and are now ready to work on Intimacy need little more than those who are dealing with Intimacy for the first time. They may need help breaking old habits of relating, which were unhelpful, but once they have developed new communication skills, they move along fairly quickly. Sometimes they benefit from a structured experience like that offered by Marriage Encounters or other workshops in which communication between two people is the focus. The most important thing to remember for this group is they haven't had extensive practice with their recently acquired skills while reworking earlier stages, so they may need "home work assignments."

Home work assignments are helpful for people reworking any of the tasks starting with Autonomy and on. Because there are two people involved in the assignment, home work assignments from a third person are particularly helpful for an older couple working on Autonomy. This way there are no points to negotiate other than how they will complete the assignment. For example,

> *One gentleman I worked with over a period of months had trouble with Trust when he first came to see me. As time went by, he grew remarkably, and ultimately hit the stage of Intimacy. When this happened, it became necessary for us to involve his wife within this context. (Earlier she had been involved with his work on Trust, Autonomy, etc.). When they arrived for their appointment, I invited them to find chairs that were comfortable. I noticed they sat opposite one another (oppositional behavior is suggestive of the stage of Autonomy). When I asked them what they wanted, they said they wanted to learn to have a "loving relationship where we are equal partners." They both had discussed this and that was why they had made an appointment.*
>
> *I affirmed this would be very nice; it would be like growing two different flowers in the same patch, two flowers that complemented one*

another. I then commented it would be interesting to see if they became a hybrid (indirect suggestion that they might create an "us" or unit different from the two separate people). I also said such a thing takes time and work, so we would start with a home work assignment. I asked if that would be okay with them. They both agreed. So, I sent them home to figure out how they could sit next to one another and enjoy it.

They came back saying they had trouble, but figured out that sitting next to one another was really nice when they shared popcorn and a movie. This week they sat next to one another in my office. I affirmed their discovery, reminded them again that what they were undertaking required work and commitment, and again suggested they would benefit from another assignment. They again agreed. I told them to go home and find some way they could be near one another and touch.

At the next visit, they were holding hands during the meeting. The same routine followed. The home work assignment was to find some way to do something interesting together, something where they were near one another, touched sometimes, and something that made them laugh. Off they went.

When they came back, the wife said they thought they had it figured out, but they just wanted to be assured. Then they looked at each other and laughed. Finally, they said they had decided I wanted them to go to the kitchen and "make hanky panky"! So, they did. They then revealed that their son walked in just as mom was lying on the floor, covered with whipping cream and maraschino cherries! They laughed again and said you never saw anyone get out of there so fast! We all laughed. When I asked them what they had learned, they said they needed to lock the door next time! When leaving, they told me they didn't need any more assignments; they could handle things on their own. I totally agreed!

While this case may raise your eyebrows, I report it here to remind you we cannot tell people how to do what is natural for them, we can only give them permission and some general guidelines. Most people will find what works for them.

Generativity

General Guidelines

Often comparatively healthy people get to this stage and, suddenly, struggle with the big question—what is my life about? They get confused, worry they have lost interest in their relationship with the significant other (Intimacy), and feel something is wrong with them. They need reassurance that they are very normal and that they haven't lost interest. They just need to feel safe and loved, so they are able to go on to the next big thing, discovering their Life Purpose.

Now, before we can reassure anyone that this is the case, we need to briefly assess their Intimacy to be sure we aren't missing something. What we want to know is whether they are actually working on the task of Generativity, or do they have trouble with Intimacy, but are now confronted with Generativity because of their biological clock?   Four easy questions can help you with this assessment:

1) *When you think of your partner, is that person boring to be around? A yes or no answer suggests there might be a problem, so you will want more information. The answer you want to hear is a qualified answer, like maybe. Or yes and no: yes, because she doesn't seem to need me like she used to, and no, because she is an interesting person to be around. She seems to know what she wants. This suggests this person perceives the partner knows the "secret of life"! The partner has discovered how to be happy, feel productive, and stay engaged with life. Now, your client wants the same thing, but not at the cost of the relationship. There is concern that refocusing on one's Life Purpose will take away from the intimacy they have built over the years.*

2) *Can you image ways in which you can continue to have a relationship with your partner while working on something very interesting to you? With this question you are suggesting that individuation is acceptable, even desirable. You are also asking this person to consider how they can achieve the proverbial "Have your cake and eat it too!" This means they will have to continue to enjoy Intimacy while revisiting their own Identity, this time focusing more intently on the nature of their Self. When listening for this answer, note if their response includes both affiliation and individuation needs. Responses emphasizing one at the expense of the other suggest they need help sorting through the two.*

3) *Imagine yourself ten years from now. How would you like to think about yourself and what would you like to feel about yourself? This helps people practice their industry skills, only now within the context of what their life work is and has been. This will help them sort out what they have done that relates to their obligations and responsibilities (sense-of-self) as compared to their Life Purpose. Sometimes people have the experience of discovering that the obligations and responsibilities they had always thought as superimposed by others were really those things they wanted to do for themselves.*

4) *How do you imagine getting to the point you would like to be at in ten years? Again, this helps people work on Industry skills within the context of fulfilling their Life Purpose. As they think through the steps, they might need help learning that their Presence (Being) is more important to their loved ones than their ability to Do. This is important for the aging adult whose body is no longer limber and able to tolerate*

physical activity. Again, as in all other stages, they may need help letting go of old ways of coping and taking on new strategies.

Principle: Building healthy Generativity residual requires that people value the product of their life work.

Generativity in Older People

People in the last two stages of life sometimes need help with this task as well. If they have sufficient, balanced residual from earlier stages, then this work is not too difficult. For example,

> *The couple discussed above that learned how to play with one another (e.g., hanky panky in the kitchen) later appeared at my doorstep; they just came by to say hello. However, when they settled into my "therapy chairs" as they had called them earlier, I knew there were other reasons for the appointment. When asked how they were doing, and how life was going, they hesitated and then commented that now that they were both retired, they had traveled and had fun, but they were both wondering if there was something else they should be thinking about. When I asked, "Like what?" the wife spoke up and said they were enjoying themselves so much, they were afraid they were selfish, and that, maybe, they lived hollow lives. I said it was time for another assignment. They agreed. I sent them home to think about the most important things they had done in their lives, what the purpose of their lives might have been, and how they felt about it.*

> *They called two weeks later and said they both agreed: the best thing they had done with their lives was to teach their children to love and play at the same time. They wanted to know if that counted. I affirmed that this was a very important accomplishment, and just as a stone thrown in a pond will cause a ripple out effect, so will their life work. They thanked me and hung up. That was the last time I heard from them, although I received a note from their son after they both passed. He said they had talked about me a number of times, so he knew I would want to know they passed on within a few months of one another, just as they had wanted. He also said he thought his father had a smile on his face when he died and was surprised, because he had always thought he was afraid of dying.*[12]

Ego Integrity

General Guidelines

This is the stage of revisiting how we have lived our lives. We can help people with this by reaffirming that we all made mistakes in our past, but that is the nature of human beings. The most important thing is to learn from our mistakes. Sometimes people need help revisiting the lessons and remembering what was learned. They also need help figuring out how they have applied their lessons in later life, most importantly during the stage of Generativity. We can always affirm that they have had productive lives and that they will go on across time by making such statements as, "You have taught me so many things, you will always be a part of my life. And I will remember you as I try to help others." You can be more specific too, if you understand the individual's world-view. For example,

> *I remember one lady I worked with who was dying of breast cancer. Although only 67, she was working on Ego Integrity. (Developmental processes are epigenetic, so we work on all at the same time, even though there is a key focus, i.e., the task). She had discovered a lump in her breast just before her scheduled trip to Washington, DC, so she delayed seeking medical assistance. Her trip was the culmination of her life-plan to have a high-rise facility where seniors could live independently.[13] She had worked diligently for months to create the plan, get city approval, raise seed money, and now it was time to go to Washington to get Federal assistance. When I cared for her, just a few days before she passed, the television news was full of the opening of this facility. I walked into her room and noticed her watching the "cutting of the ribbon" with pure satisfaction on her face. When she saw me, she took my hand, and told me she was happy that I knew what I wanted to do with my life and was doing it.*
>
> *She then commented that she would not have done one thing differently as far as her life-work was concerned, but she didn't know if she had lived a good life or not. I was young and unknowing, but somehow understood what she was saying. While she knew her work project was good, did that make her life worthy? As with so many times in my life, I was guided to respond in a helpful way. I told her these are personal things, but from my perspective, her life would go on in many ways that were important, most of which only she knew about. Two examples were that there would be people who would live happy, healthy lives in her "Home for Seniors" for generations—probably long after both of us were somewhere else. I also told her I could not begin to explain how much I had learned from her, but her caring about others would always influence my thinking and actions. She seemed very satisfied with these ideas. The next day, her daughter arrived; they exchanged love and respect for one another and the following day she was gone. My writing this story is testimony that she has influenced me throughout my life; she continues to live through these words.*

Principle: Building healthy Ego Integrity residual requires that people accept their life as they have lived it, and feel satisfied that they have lived it well.

Transformation

I have written about facilitating Transformation earlier. You may remember the story about Mrs. Cook in Chapter 1, and my brother in Chapter 5. Neither of these addressed the issue of Hope, the virtue derived from healthy residual during Stage 1, Building Trust. Hope is described by Erikson as "...the most indispensable virtue inherent in the state of being alive" (Erikson, 1964, p.115). Hope, when talked about in Transformation, is the hope of continued life even after physical death. Our Soul knows there is life hereafter, but many people have not been able to reconnect with their Soul so that they *know* what they know! They often need help with this process. Some seek reassurance from their faith; others turn to those near them.

Your decision regarding how you work with someone during this stage is very personal. How we view this stage of life depends on personal beliefs. There are no right or wrong perspectives, just different views. You may feel comfortable with the suggestions I discuss below. You may not. Either case is perfectly fine. You just need to be honest with yourself. If you are not comfortable, perhaps you can offer to find someone else who is more comfortable, such as a chaplain, friend, colleague, and so forth. Your comfort with facilitating Transformation is not a criterion for being a good nurse, mother, daughter, husband, or anything else. It is just who you are.

> *That is, our spirit, like a vaporous ghost, inhabits the mechanical vehicle we call the physical body. At the time of death, our spirit moves on, leaving behind only a lifeless shell* (Gerber, 2001, p. 12).

General Guidelines.

For those who seem to need help, the first question to ask is whether their significant others have given permission. If not, this is the first step. Families often need help in letting go. This is different from giving up; they need to tell those who are at this stage of life that they love them, they will miss them, but it is okay to go on their way. Whenever possible, it is helpful if they can be guided to *help* their loved one in the process. By this statement, I mean singing songs, playing music, and other ways we let people know we are okay, and that they will be, too. This is the nature of facilitating Hope.

Sometimes, significant others aren't available to grant permission; yet, it is time. Under these circumstances, the best you can do is reassure the person they will be able to come back in spirit and comfort their loved ones, and that they will discover it will be wonderful to be free of the physical form that restricts movement. Such reassurance often comforts people. It tells them their loved ones will be okay, and that they can check and see, if need be.

Once you are comfortable permission has been granted, some people need reassurance the journey will be toward light, not darkness. Each of us has our own personal beliefs about the hereafter; most believe there is a tunnel through which the spirit passes, a tunnel filled with bright light. What happens after that is where different views come into play. In any case, you can reassure them that there will initially be light, if they look for it. There will also be other spirits waiting to guide them on the next phase of their journey. You can also reassure people that God (or the Universal Force, Higher Power, the Divine, or other language within their world-view) is intelligent, loving, kind, and understanding of our frailties and vulnerabilities, and will be forgiving if we forgive ourselves. They need to accept their lives as they lived them, acknowledge they did the best they could under the circumstances, and embrace the peace and freedom that comes with letting go. Most people are able to take this step more easily if they have someone who can be with them that will give them permission to separate energy fields, to acknowledge their Life has had meaning, and to stand by as their spirit leaves the body, moves on, and reconnects with the Soul and Universe.

> **Principle**: Transformation is most easily accomplished when we have Hope that there is life hereafter.

CONCLUSIONS

Throughout this chapter I've emphasized the importance of the epigenetic process of development. That is, the ongoing work on developmental residual. While there are specific ages in which a given task becomes the focus of our attention, we rework each task again and again. Each time a task is reworked, it is done so within the context of the current stage-related task. For example, we build Trust early in life, and then, as we go along, we rework Trust within the context of Autonomy, Initiative, Industry, etc. At the same time, we are working on each of the other tasks. Again, using the stage of Trust as an example, while building Trust, we are already beginning to learn about ourselves in respect to each of the other tasks. We're laying down rudimentary residual that we will build upon as time goes by. The nature of the residual will determine what we have to draw from and what we have to build on. You can relate these ideas to growing a garden. Plants have a natural tendency to grow, but they need good soil for their roots. If we start a garden with nothing but a thin layer of poor soil, not many plants will grow or flourish, no matter how much water we add. The base is important. If plants do grow, they usually have shallow roots and are destroyed with minimal exposure to rain, sun, cold, heat and so forth. Human development is similar, so we have to learn to facilitate growth from the inside out or from the bottom up.

Sometimes health care providers get discouraged because they think the process takes too much time, expertise, or resources. I have already stated that it is important to remember three things: *Caring has a long-arm effect*[14]*,* we should aim to *Do more good than harm,* and remember to *Judge a book by its contents.* The first is important because it suggests that a simple act of compassion has the potential to change a person's life. A few days ago Oprah Winfrey interviewed a gentleman she'd talked with a number of years before. Both of them acknowledged that they had looked at one another that first day, made a Spirit-to-Spirit connection and that both of them had changed because of that connection. Numerous people have told me that some simple thing I've done has helped them change their lives. Caring can have an effect on others long after the event, and sometimes without our knowing it. We have to believe that simple techniques such as seeding and reframing are often all that is needed to facilitate healthy task work.

The second of these, try to *Do More Good Than Harm,* was written because too many health care providers disparage themselves since they can't be all things to all people. It is very important for us to *try* and to know that we won't always feel, act, or think in ways that are true to our Self. That is because we are human! If we were perfect (whatever that means) we wouldn't be human! So, we have to learn to *try* to do the best we can, and accept that in *trying* we will be more effective sometimes, but not at other times, and that is okay. The more we learn to accept our limitations, the easier it is for us to grow and to help others grow. So, today, tell yourself you have done the best that you could, and tomorrow you will try again. That is all that we should expect of ourselves.

The last of these, *Judge A Book By Its Contents*, applies to ourselves as well as those we care about. This relates to the previous thought as well. The more we look for the good in the people we interact with, the more we can find the good in ourselves. We just have to acknowledge that each human is unique, each has his or her journey, and each knows at some level, what is needed to help make the journey one of meaning. From the beginning to the end of holistic existence, we work and rework the developmental tasks of incarnate life. We do this in order to become the most we can be, so we can fulfill our Life Purpose.

---

[1] It should be noted that I have said Initial Assessment. That is because it is important to continue to assess and reevaluate your data. If you don't do that, you become stuck and fail to observe or understand new data that might help better understand developmental residual.

[2] The need to "please the care-giver," succeed for the caregiver, and an overwhelming 'sense-of-self,' is often linked to insecure attachment. The trust is there, so the affiliation exists, but the permission to be individuated, to be one's Self is often conditional. The conditions were probably met when Jim started achieving in school. He was a 'good boy.'

[3] Please review Chapter 9 for information about this concept.

[4] A number of clients have come straight out and told me that I'd missed the guess! This is because I started *below* where the problem started. If I start with a stage *above the problem* (e.g., start with Autonomy when Trust is the issue), they simply smile and thank me, and go about their business. When this happens they have learned *one more time* they are not worthy of my time and attention and that they have to take care of themselves.

[5] As we think about this, it might be helpful to remember Watzlawick's axioms of communication, discussed in Chapter 10. Keep in mind, we cannot not communicate. Since Jim is anticipating something from the nurse, no matter what else happens, the nurse is communicating with Jim. Since 65% or more of her communication is nonverbal, she is clearly communicating her

disapproval of Jim. She has initiated a non-accepting relationship, teaching Jim he can't trust the nurse (and possibly nurses at large) to care about him unconditionally.

[6] It should be noted some children have sensory integration trouble, so they are uncomfortable with eye contact. I have been told some children are unable to focus clearly, so close eye contact makes them feel like the other object is moving back and forth at a very rapid rate. Thus, they may tend to look at people and things from an angle rather than straight on. This possibility should be considered when assessing an individual's behavior in respect to normal development.

[7] I haven't mentioned this before, but there seem to be many babies that cry a lot, but can't seem to be soothed. I have heard dozens of parents say the doctor simply doesn't know what to do, that there really isn't anything wrong, and it is just the baby's personality. Many of them have been advised to let the baby cry, that they will outgrow it. I have learned through the years that some of these babies just need to be handled differently, but others seem to have a different problem. Some are allergic to milk, some have parents who are exhausted or up tight, and the baby picks up on the parents' energy fields. And then there are many that fall into the "None of the Above" category! Many of these babies seem to do much better when given infant doses of acidophilus, which can be found in the local health food store of People's Pharmacy.

[8] I learned this technique from a wonderful book called, "Can You Wait Till Friday?" by Kenneth Olson (1975).

[9] This is a hypnotic technique that helps the person "remember", at a cellular level, the caring they have experienced during the interaction. It helps anchor the growth into place, so more can be built upon it.

[10] These are all words people have used in describing themselves after they have grown enough to no longer be threatened by the implications.

[11] I discussed such a case in the article listed as Erickson, 1990b. If you are interested, read case pages 283-289.

[12] Keep in mind his son had grown up during the years this man carried considerable negative residual. He probably had impressed upon his young son that he was afraid of death, a natural fear when you don't know your Self.

[13] This was one of the first in the nation and was later used as an exemplar by many other cities.

[14] See Chapter 10 for more information on the Long Arm Affect.

CHAPTER 13

FINDING MEANING IN OUR LIFE JOURNEY

DA'LYNN KAY CLAYTON, HELEN L. ERICKSON
AND SHARON ROGERS

James, a devoutly religious 30 year-old man, was married and had one child. His wife was pregnant again. They were happily settled in their church community, surrounded by friends. One Sunday morning, just after James had finished delivering a sermon to his congregation, the 'unthinkable' happened. Suddenly, an unknown man appeared before James and shot him three times, twice at point blank range after he had fallen to the ground.

Within seconds James went from a state of serenity to one of chaos. Seconds before, he had been standing before his beloved congregation and talking about the love of God and then, suddenly he was lying on the floor, bleeding and struggling for his life. The paramedics, who had seemed to appear out of nowhere, were cutting his clothes and trying to treat him. He was aware his congregation was watching. He felt 'naked,' and 'alone'. James had also experienced numerous invisible wounds; wounds missed by the healthcare team because they went deeper than the flesh, wounds on his psyche and soul. James was taken to a trauma center where the healthcare team worked to save his life and treat his visible wounds. But his invisible wounds were ignored.

OVERVIEW

Nothing stands still. Time moves on, and with it, we too must continue down the pathway of a journey—the journey we call life. Each of us will traverse multiple pathways, searching for understanding, acceptance, and love. Sometimes, we actively choose pathways; other times we are thrust in a direction we had never imagined. Sometimes, we purposefully choose a pathway thinking it will help us in our search for meaning; other times we find ourselves on a pathway by serendipity. It just seems to be what we need to do at the time, or it is the lesser of two unattractive options! But what about the times we are thrust in a direction we had not imagined, had not wanted, and did not know how to handle, *and* we have no choice! How can we make meaning of this type of experience? What happens when resources are available and what happens when they are not?

This chapter describes some of these possibilities. Cases will be used to illustrate real life events that have the potential to jeopardize our health and well-being. They will also be used to illustrate how we can find meaning in every day life, and how that impacts our well-being. We will talk about these issues from the perspective of the healthcare provider as an individual and their work with others.

Life is a journey. Illness and alterations in health create chaos and send us into crisis. They can also provide an impetus for growth and transformation. Nurses can offer theory-based holistic nursing care to persons experiencing health changes; they can also facilitate opportunities for growth and discovery of meaning. People are able to let go, reframe, and move on. This "way of being" with clients and families not only helps clients, it enhances our sense-of-self and understanding.

LIFE IS A JOURNEY

Pathways

Life is a journey. We start with minimal awareness of where we are and where we want to go. Still, each of us will discover that we cannot stop time, nor can we reverse our lives and go back to a previous place. Life marches on and we *must go with it.* If we are to *be alive and in physical form,* we must take *the journey.* We must encounter events that have the potential to bring joy and delight. We will also encounter events that have the potential to bring sadness and despair. How we experience the *journey* varies by person and events.

Most people, if asked, would wish to live a meaningful life, be able to have loving relationships, and find ways to cope and move on after difficult life experiences. In a life that is not always easy, each of us is confronted with events that seem to tax our ability to respond in healthy ways. The people we encounter and their response to us during these times affect what happens next.

Many people are able to *reframe*[1] difficult life experiences with little assistance. When they do, they are often able to assign meaning to the experiences. However, some events are too traumatic for most of us to handle without help. Sometimes health care providers are able to recognize the *visible wounds, but miss the invisible wounds.*

The Invisible Wounds

The story presented at the beginning of this chapter describes James and his visible wounds, but misses the important *invisible wounds.* It's time now to tell you some more of the story.

Over the next several months, James went through numerous surgeries and experienced multiple complications. The health care providers continued to focus on his visible wounds, probably thinking that the physical wounds were the most important. After all, they had worked hard to save his life! But what about the invisible wounding of being shot, of being stripped naked in front of those you work with, of wondering why the God you were working for did not protect you from such an experience?

Without their knowing, the well-meaning, but distant manner used by the nurses and doctors resulted in additional wounding. He suffered multiple complications, seeming to take a long time to get better. James stated that he silently endured these 'treatments' by repeating to himself, 'It doesn't matter, it doesn't matter, it doesn't matter, I am just a piece of meat. It doesn't matter.' Slowly, his body recovered, but the rest of him did not. Later, James reflected on those times, saying he had many questions, 'ugly questions,' such as 'Why did this happen to me? Why did God allow this to happen to me?'

During the entire time, the members of the congregation were also deeply troubled by what had happened; many of them had witnessed the assault. They looked to James's family for support; after all James had been one of the Church leaders. Now the burden of helping the members of the congregation fell on the family. But James's extended family was having their own troubles.

They wanted to help and support James, but they were at a loss. They did not understand his intense anger and spiritual pain. They were worried about him and his wife. After all, she was pregnant. The distress could result in her losing the unborn child. They also had to 'take care of the congregation,' find their way through their own feelings, and assimilate the impact this had had on their own lives. They did their best, but the pain continued for everyone, much of it invisible.

A few years later, family members shared these events with a nurse researcher. They described their experiences and expressed their pain. They talked about their need for a professional who would willingly walk with them through this very difficult physical and spiritual experience. They said that they had needed someone who would share their journey, not necessarily someone who could provide answers, but someone who was willing to listen, support, and encourage them on their journey through undiscovered land with an uncertain destination. They said that just being able to tell our story, in our own way, has had a healing effect on us.

> Each person must find meaning in significant life events. No one can tell another person what the meaning of an experience is but nurses can help by listening, supporting, and accepting unconditionally people's emotions/feelings as they move through the often painful and difficult process of spiritual growth.

Finding Meaning

Loss, Resource Availability, and Chaos

James, his family, and his congregation had not chosen the pathway of loss and grief; it had been thrust upon them. While health care providers recognized their need for emergent physical care, they lost sight of the holistic beings involved in the process. They saw the visible wounds and treated them, but they missed the invisible wounds. As a result, James and his loved ones found themselves alone, emotionally confused, and filled with spiritual pain. It took years to make sense of the events and incorporate them into their understanding of their journeys.

Because James is a holistic person, failure to recognize and treat his *invisible wounds* made it difficult for his body to mobilize the resources needed to deal with visible wounds. Previously, Walker and H. Erickson described relations among the mind-body-sprit (Chapter 3), Benson described the coping process (Chapter 8), and these authors as well as Hertz and Baas (Chapter 4) talked about "stored memories." Suffice to say, James, his family, and congregation experienced multiple traumas that affected them in numerous ways. Each had unresolved losses, each had a depressed immune system secondary to feelings of hopelessness, and each was vulnerable and had difficulty mobilizing resources.

Unexpected life events that are perceived as losses are difficult to resolve without adequate resources. They often result in a Chaotic Crisis for those who come together to help one another. There is an urgency in tending to the tasks at hand. Unfortunately, the resources available are inadequate to attend to all the tasks, take care of one another, and take care of themselves. When this happens, something has got to give, and sometimes people perceive they are not doing enough or have failed to help the one they love, which further drains both internal and external resources. They have difficulty moving on. Sometimes they get stuck in the chaos, experience morbid grief, and have trouble incorporating the experience into the fabric of their lives. Instead, it remains as an event that was thrust upon them, with no meaning and no relationship to their life journey.

Meaning from Chaos

When people mobilize sufficient resources, they are able to initiate the slow process of piecing together what has happened, integrate the experience into their lives, and move forward. They move toward contextualizing the experience, creating order out of chaos, and finding meaning in the events. Thus, spiritual growth occurs, which allows people to see self, life, others, the world, and the Creator in new ways. Life opens up for them and becomes more meaningful.

We can facilitate these processes by allowing people to reflect on their experiences. Each person needs to tell his or her story, often over and over again.[2] The story may sound chaotic to the listener. Stories of great pain are told in bits and pieces, by jumping around, and not following the events chronologically, but as they are remembered (Frank, 1995).

While the reporting may seem chaotic, with fragmented thoughts, there is an order to the recitation. The storyteller is "remembering" the pieces as he or she has the resources needed to remember. When the health-care provider is fully present, uses active listening skills, and does not try to "fix" the problem, storytellers are able to better understand what has happened, and embed the experiences within the context of their lives. In doing this, they are able to assign meaning to the experiences.

James and his family needed an opportunity to tell their story, create meaning out of chaos, and move on. They indicated that the nurse's active listening, a couple of years after the event, had helped them in this process.

Facilitating Discovery

The road of discovery is a lonely one. Each of us has to contextualize our life experiences for ourselves and discover their meaning. We have to do it *for ourselves, but we do not have to do it by ourselves.* When other people connect with us, listen to our pain, support us by letting us be ourselves, and allow us to feel what we feel without judgment, most people are able to initiate the healing process on their own.

When people unconditionally accept others who are trying to find their way through the fog and pain of major traumatic life events, the love and respect reflected in unconditional acceptance of the person and their experience is extremely important. We cannot fix people, nor can we tell them what is right for them to do or think, but we can love them, empathize with them, and stay connected spiritually.

It is essential for nurses to respect the person, the family, the pain, the experience, the process, and the spiritual forces that help us in this world. Nurses do not have to solve these problems but trust that with empathy and unconditional acceptance, each person will find their way. It is important for us to find our own answers to difficult and complex life questions. When we let go of "fixing it" or "making it better," we can learn to help others resolve their problems and heal their Souls. But, first, we have to find the courage to walk with them through the unknown without fixing the problem. This is our greatest challenge.

While this sounds simple, it is not. It takes courage to walk with another through unknown territory without trying to provide answers or solutions. It seems mundane to say that love is sufficient under these conditions, but sometimes all we have to offer is love, compassion, and caring. How wonderful it would be if we could learn that love, compassion, and caring may be more important than any other single thing we can do.

Contextualizing Life Experiences

H. Erickson stated:

We need to remember that there are times that people need more help with spiritual healing and growth than they do with physical healing. They need help contextualizing their life experiences. Until this happens, people cannot find meaning in the event that relates to their Life Purpose. Instead, they may assign meaning, but it will be outside their own Reason for Being and, therefore, will not seem to have anything to do with their Life Purpose (Personal communication, November 30, 2005).

Most nurses know people have to find meaning in their life events if they are to let go of the trauma and move on. But, many nurses have trouble applying these concepts. Some say it is not what they think nursing is about. They may agree nurses are concerned with health and health processes, but they believe helping people with spiritual healing is not the nurse's role. This is because their definition of health is different from the one we are describing. The Modeling and Role-Modeling theory and paradigm support Smith's eudemonistic model of health.

Models of Health

Smith (1981) described four models of health—*clinical, role-performance, adaptive,* and *eudemonistic.* These models are a progressive expansion of the idea of health ranging from the absence of disease to a person's potential for spiritual growth and well-being.[3] Nurses' views of health influence the type of data collected, how the data is interpreted, and how care is prioritized, implemented, and evaluated (Erickson, 1990a).

Erickson and Swain (1985) conducted a twenty-two month study to explore the relationships among nurses' conception of health, their conceptual framework for practice, and clinical outcomes. Nurses who worked within the context of the *clinical* model of health assumed chronic diseases would continue to progress despite nursing interventions. The nurse's focus was directed towards minimizing disease progression, management of signs and symptoms, and related effects. The nurses using the clinical model of health interpreted changes in social roles, adaptation, and a lack of self-fulfillment as effects of their diseases. The second group of nurses worked within the context of the *eudemonistic* model of health and used the MRM theory of nursing. They focused on the person rather than the disease. These nurses worked to build and restore resources needed to contend with life stressors and aimed at increasing a person's ability to maintain social roles, adapt, and experience a greater sense of self-fulfillment. The nurse's conception of health influenced clinical judgment and clinical outcomes. The second group of patients had fewer complications, better disease management, and more satisfaction with life over the period of the study.

The way the nurse views health makes a difference (Erickson, 1990a, 1990b; Erickson & Swain, 1985; Smith, 1981). Health care providers can inhibit or prevent spiritual growth when illness is viewed and treated as an isolated or random event, i.e., something that is caused by bacteria, virus, or genetics. When we focus on the disease and causative factors, we miss the opportunity to help people find meaning in the event.

Illness as an Opportunity

Illness is an opportunity for reflection, understanding, and spiritual growth. However, before this can happen, it has to be contextualized. That is, it must be viewed within the context of what is going on in a person's life at the time of the event and just prior to the event.

We are all exposed to viruses and bacteria, but only become ill at specific points in time. What makes the difference between health and illness is what else is happening at the time of exposure. It is important for the person, family and health care providers to examine the context of the illness experience. What else is going on? How is the illness event related to other life experiences? What pattern can be seen or identified?

Illness and health are important indicators of what else is happening in a person's life. The body has an amazing ability to heal itself without assistance under some circumstances (Cousins, 1983). When nurses recognize the holistic nature of their clients, they are more likely to perceive health as a state of well-being. When this happens, they can learn that helping people find meaning in their experiences is as important (if not more important) than helping them learn how to take care of their physical disabilities. When we help people find meaning in their life experiences, we help them cope with stressors, resolve losses, choose healthy alternatives, to grow, and to find meaningful pathways for their life journey. Lives are changed.

> Illness experiences are an opportunity for healing, spiritual growth, and transformation when the nurse views illness within the context of a person's life experience rather than as an isolated event or something caused by disease progression. Holistic approaches include more than interventions for immediate symptoms such as medication, diet changes, exercise, etc. While these treatment options can be important, the holistic nurse knows that if care stops there, growth and transformation will be inhibited.

It is essential for the holistic nurse to ask questions such as: "What is this illness experience about?" "What is this illness experience telling the person and family?"[4] Interestingly enough, even when nurses do not specifically ask these questions, people often offer this information. The nurses' orientation toward health will determine how they listen and how they respond. When we hear such information and recognize that this is the key to understanding how the holistic person thinks and feels, we are able to use it to plan interventions. We know that we have the essential elements needed to address underlying causes of illness, to treat invisible wounds, and to promote personal growth. We can help people heal.

CROSS ROADS

Each of us will occasionally find ourselves at a crossroad, faced with the dilemma of choosing between alternative pathways. If we have the resources needed to contend with the dilemma, we might be able to move on and make meaning of the experiences encountered along the pathway. If, on the other hand, the event is outside our experience, outside what we know and how we think and feel, we may have difficulty.

It is during such times that we need others to join us, to help us find meaning, so we can move on. Without such help, we are vulnerable to additional losses. We have more difficulty adapting to the losses, finding new ways to adapt, heal and grow.

Sometimes we cope, but at the expense of our overall well-being. We become maladaptive. Sometimes we get stuck and cannot move on. Sometimes the losses are overwhelming, so people sink into feelings of helplessness and ultimately hopelessness. They have morbid grief and are *impoverished* (Erickson, 1976, 1990a; 1990c; Erickson, Tomlin, & Swain, 1983). Still other times we are able to grieve and let go. We move into a state of Adaptive Equilibrium. Each of these concepts has been discussed in detail in earlier work (Erickson, 1976, 1990b; 1990c; Erickson et al., 1983) and in Chapter 8 in this book. Here, we will provide examples.

Threatened Loss and Unexpected Outcomes (Maladaptation)

Sometimes we have losses (real, threatened, or perceived) that produce unexpected or unanticipated outcomes.[5] This is because we are holistic and as holistic beings, we mobilize resources to cope with stress in whichever way we can. When resources directly related to the losses are not available (or perceived to be available), we draw from another part of ourselves. We do what is necessary in order to reduce the feelings of distress and satisfy the unmet needs. Sometimes we do not choose the healthiest option, but we do the best we can under the circumstances. *Rarely are these processes conscious; usually they take place at the holistic, unconscious level.*

These processes have several ramifications. First, when we are ill, there may be psychosocial or spiritual responses that are directly due to biophysiological stressors. When this happens, there are unanticipated responses to the perceived problem.

Another possibility is that we may see unanticipated responses that are not due to the perceived problem, *but are secondary to other things occurring simultaneously*. Other things that are a part of our life, but we are unaware of their existence.

In either case, we note that *something is amiss! The cause and effect do not seem to fit. What we see as a problem seems to be an unlikely cause of the responses we observe.* What we do know is that people seem to have trouble mobilizing resources in a healthy, growth directed way. We need to think why this might happen.

Using Theory to Understand

When we use the Modeling and Role-Modeling theory, our mind goes in two directions. First, we observe unmet needs and ability or inability to mobilize resources to contend with those needs.[6] Second, since needs are related to attachment objects, there may be a loss related to those objects. Either or both of these issues are important in understanding the problem and what will help resolve it.

Both of these concepts were discussed in earlier Chapters, so we will not go into detail here. However, to refresh your memory, stressors are unmet needs; they produce *stress responses*. Our ability to mobilize resources needed to contend with the stress response, determines our ability to cope with the stressor and stress response. Furthermore, any object that meets our needs repeatedly becomes an attachment object. Real, threatened, or perceived loss of such an object produces a grief response (stress response). Resolution of the grief response depends on the availability of another object that can meet our needs repeatedly. Simply stated, when people are unable to mobilize resources needed to contend with their losses, they are unable to let go of the lost object and move on. Since people can only resolve loss when they are able to find a new *attachment object* that will meet their needs, it is important to assess what meaning is attached to the loss (or lost objects).

Application

When people have unexpected response to illness or treatment, it is not only important to determine if there is a physiological reason for the response, but to also consider other possibilities. People are holistic. No matter how the response might be exhibited, we need to remember what we are seeing is the stress response, not the stressor. Stressor can occur in any of the subsystems; simultaneously, stress responses can show up in any of the subsystems. Sometimes the stressor is in one and the stress response is in another. We will not know without first talking with our clients.

This means we need to explore what our clients' perceive is related to the response and what can be done to help them. We need to explore their Self-care Knowledge.[7] When we fail to explore the holistic person's Self-care Knowledge (including what has caused the problem, what is currently happening, and what can help them) unwanted health outcomes will most likely be seen.

Esther

Esther provides an example of real and threatened losses and unexpected responses. Esther, a 67-year-old woman, experienced a severe cerebral vascular accident (CVA) during a Sunday morning church service. She survived, underwent rehabilitation and three months later was discharged home. The first night at home Esther fell and broke her right foot. She was re-hospitalized for surgery and rehabilitation. After successful rehabilitation, she was discharged home again. A few months later, Esther drove to church, but before putting the car in 'Park,' she stepped on the gas pedal, driving her car over a curb, onto the sidewalk, and into the church building.

Esther's family noted that several things had happened to their loved-one over the past several months. As they began to contextualize these experiences (i.e., put them into the context of Esther's life), they began to recognize some relationships. Since she had been widowed for the last five years, she lived alone. Her family noted that she seemed to enjoy her independence. While she had several risk factors for having a CVA – hypertension, obesity, and Type II diabetes, she seemed to have external resources to help her. She was very active in her community and she had a number of friends. She also had children and grandchildren nearby.

Given these resources, they wondered, 'Why now?' What might have caused the CVA to happen when it did? And why did she fall and break her foot? Was that fall caused by the weakness on her right side due to her CVA, or was it more complicated? Was there meaning when Esther ran her car into the church building? What was going on?

A nurse interested in these questions began to explore the experience. Esther's children reported their mother was frantic – getting busier and busier, sleeping less and less for the three week period before her CVA. The nurse discovered that Esther's older sister, Irene, had been severely ill with an undiagnosed health problem for several weeks before the onset of the Esther's CVA. Was there a connection between these events?

Irene and Esther were the only living members of their family of origin. Despite the fact that they had lived hundreds of miles away from one another for many years, they had always been very close. The nurse also learned that Irene and Esther had talked by phone minutes before Esther fell and broke her foot. During that conversation, Irene had told Esther she had been diagnosed with liver cancer.

The nurse wondered, "Did Esther fall because her body was in a weakened state from the CVA? Or did Esther fall as a response to her sister's diagnosis of cancer? Was her fall a symbolic way of saying "I can't stand this any more?" Remember, Irene is a significant contributor to Esther's affiliation needs. Perhaps the threat of losing Irene also threatens her affiliation needs so much that she is now having trouble with her individuation needs.[8]

While answers to these questions will not change the fact that Esther needs treatment for her broken foot, they might provide direction regarding Esther's other needs. If Esther is responding to what is happening to her sister, and nurses do not recognize this and intervene appropriately, what will happen as Esther's sister's condition worsens? Without proper intervention, Esther might continue to decline with one health problem after another until she is no longer able to cope.

Five months after Esther had learned her sister had cancer, her sister called again saying the chemotherapy and radiation were not working – the cancer was spreading. The doctors had told her, "Nothing more could be done." The following morning was the day Esther drove to church and had her accident.[9]

As the family put Esther's "accident" within the context of her life experiences, it seemed that Esther's health crises were related to Irene's situation. The family recognized the need to actively intervene. With direction from a nurse, they made plans. Her children called frequently and asked their mother what was happening. They encouraged her to process her feelings while they listened.

As Irene's condition worsened, they recognized the need to be proactive. When hospice was called in to take care of Irene, they knew that death was imminent. They also knew Esther was not strong enough to make the lengthy trip to see her sister or attend the funeral. Her children decided they needed another plan. One of Esther's daughters went to stay with Irene for a few days, telling her mother that she was going as a surrogate. They reassured Esther that she was vicariously helping her sister through her daughter's visit. Irene died a couple of weeks later. As previously planned, Esther's family gathered around Esther and had a memorial service for Irene in Esther's living room. Esther was encouraged to tell stories and share memories of Irene. The service was recorded for Esther to review; copies were sent to Irene's children. Esther had no additional illnesses, health crises, or accidents. She resolved her losses and moved into an adaptive equilibrium.

Unresolved Loss and Impoverishment

Impoverishment has been discussed briefly above, in earlier work (Erickson, 1976; 1990; Erickson et al., 1983) and in Chapter 8 in this book. For the purpose of this chapter, we want to emphasize the potential outcome. People who are impoverished have diminished resources needed to contend with stress and stressors. They seem to be depleted. They have difficulty contending with ongoing stress; new stressors seem to throw them into a depleted state. While we know that every nurse can tell a story about an impoverished client who just could not get better, we want to tell Avery's story to illustrate this point.

Avery

Avery, a man in his 50's, was diagnosed with lymphoma–a generally treatable form of cancer. He was a deeply religious man, had a loving wife and children, and work he enjoyed. While one would expect him to do well with treatment, he did not. He died within a couple of months of diagnosis. Family and friends could not help but notice that he died ten months to the day after his best friend's sudden death. He laid in state in the same room his friend had laid ten months earlier, and was buried just a few hundred feet away from his friend.

A few years later, Avery's wife, Elena, commented to a nurse that twenty years before, another of Avery's friends had passed. He was a physician with a chronic condition, so he medicated himself. He died tragically after taking an overdose of pain medication. The insurance companies initially treated the death as a suicide. As his friend did not have a will, the estate took years to settle in court. The friend's wife had been pregnant with their first child, complicating the problem. Avery and his wife supported their friend's wife through this grueling and deeply painful experience. Then Avery had another loss. In less than a year after this friend's death, his mother died. Avery's wife described this as "a real turning point in his life. Avery just couldn't get over that."

The grief of suddenly losing a second friend combined with unresolved grief from the loss of his first friend and then his mother was more than Avery could endure. His life journey came to an end in an untimely manner despite having a strong and loving family, devout religious beliefs, and a seemingly curable illness.

Apparently health care providers had failed to understand Avery's illness within his life context. A key question that might have been asked is, "Is Avery's illness a symptom of unresolved loss and grief?" In the absence of asking such a question, it is natural to ask, "Could his death have been avoided if a nurse had known how to help Avery recognize the unresolved losses and process these experiences?" Neither of these will ever be answered, but we can hypothesize. In both cases, the answer would be, "Most likely." As we learn to contextualize illness experiences, we will be better able to see the hidden or underlying elements of the experience. This will lead to a different type of caring and more proactive and purposeful interventions for such clientele.

While all clients benefit from creative and holistic interventions, these interventions are essential for clients who are impoverished and have unresolved losses. Holistic nurses look beyond the physical symptoms to identify unresolved losses, facilitate grieving and letting-go, thus they promote discovery and healing.

Losses and Equilibrium

In the preceding paragraphs we have talked about people who have difficulty contending with stress. In the first case we presented Esther, who coped, but needed help finding ways that would not jeopardize her overall well-being. With help, she was able to move from a *maladaptive* to an *adaptive* state of stress. We also talked about Avery, who despite spending the last few months of his life surrounded by professional nurses, was unable to find resources needed to contend with his losses. He became more *impoverished* and died.

In this section we want to talk briefly about those who are able to experience loss, work through the grieving process, let go of the lost object, and move on. When asked to comment on this topic, H. Erickson said;

All of us have times when we move into a state of maladaptive equilibrium or impoverishment. Some people have great difficulty mobilizing resources and so they spend months and sometimes years without ever being able to move on. Others, who at first glance seem to be at heightened risk, are able to mobilize resources and move on. Take for example, the magnificent young man, Mattie Stepanek. Mattie suffered from a rare type of muscular dystrophy, lived confined to a wheelchair, required nasal oxygen for years, and was in and out of the hospital from early childhood until his death at age of 14. Still, Mattie wrote hundreds of poems, published several books, was identified by many as a 'hero' and a 'peacemaker' of our time. Mattie Stepanek was able to cope with multiple stressors, and still kept going. He influenced thousands of people, lived a memorable life, and he was only a child.

My father-in-law[10] was like that too. Although he had polio as a young man, he was able to overcome his physical handicaps, breathe with accessory muscles, and participate fully in life until his death at the age of 79. While the easiest way to describe such people would be to say that they have the resources needed to cope and move on, this is just too simplistic. I think these people have found meaning in their experiences. In doing so, they have discovered their Reason for Being and are able to fulfill their Life Purpose. For some reason, some people are able to transcend their physical being. Of course, I think these people have considerable positive (developmental) residual with strong holistic Integration as described in Chapter 5. They have an awareness of their needs, have great access to their Self-care Knowledge, and are able to mobilize both internal and external resources without much trouble. We need to learn from them! (Personal communication, January 10, 2006).

These comments indicate that facilitating clients to uncover their Self-care Knowledge is key to helping them find meaning in their life experiences.

SELF-CARE KNOWLEDGE: KEY TO FINDING MEANING

Knowing, But Ignoring

Self-care Knowledge was first introduced in Erickson et al. (1983), and further described in Erickson (1990a), and in Chapter 4 in this book. It is the personal knowledge, both conscious and unconscious, about what facilitates our health and growth, what interferes, and what we need to cope.

For those who use Modeling and Role-Modeling as their theory and paradigm for practice, Self-care Knowledge is the primary source of data. As such, it is essential for them to recognize value, interpret, and validate Self-care Knowledge. Interestingly, many clients and families do not fully understand the value of the self-care information they disclose. While they *know* what they are saying is related to what is happening in their lives, they have been socialized by others to reduce sickness to a causative factor such as a virus, bacteria, injury, and so forth.

People need nurses who are able to hear what is being said, interpret the meaning within the context of holism, reinforce the importance of their comments, and intervene appropriately. Too often, people have the opposite experience: they *know* and they report what they *know,* but significant others (including health care providers) discount their knowledge. So, they ignore or refute what they know about themselves.

The following case is a good example of this *knowing, but not being reinforced to know.*

> *Sarah, three months pregnant with her second child, began to leak fluid. Initially, she was told not to worry, it was only urine. But, Sarah was uneasy; she was not sure the fluid was urine. A month later, it was determined that the fluid was not urine, but amniotic fluid. Furthermore, most of it had leaked out. Her doctors advised an abortion. Sarah and her husband rejected this option on spiritual grounds. Sarah began asking God to reveal what was going to happen to her unborn baby. Her interpretation of God's response was that the child would die.*
>
> *Sarah's close and deeply religious friends discouraged her interpretation, insisting her baby would live. Sarah acquiesced to their insistence; she decided she was wrong and that her baby would live. She was confined to strict bed rest. Although she was very careful, labor began around 6 months gestation. The baby died a few hours after delivery. Sarah was devastated. How could God do this?*

Later, as Sarah reflected on the entire experience, she decided that God had been trying to prepare her for this outcome. When she came to this understanding, she found great comfort in her discovery that she had known that she would lose the baby, even when those around her did not support her "knowing" and did not give her permission to express it. Perhaps Sarah was able to find meaning in this entire experience because she was able to validate her Self-care Knowledge.

Often Self-care Knowledge can be hard to accept when it reveals an unwanted outcome, such as death. Denying it or wishing that it was different does not help the client or the nurse. In this case, if Sarah had the support needed to prepare for this outcome, her journey would have been easier. At the least, it would not have been so lonely.

Nonverbal Cues

Sometimes nurses pick up nonverbal cues that provide information about clients' Self-care Knowledge, but they are hesitant to act on such information. No one else seems to notice, the clients have not said anything, so they ignore the cues. Sometimes there are serious repercussions, sometimes not. The following case provides an example.

Nursing students were on a Labor and Delivery unit when a staff nurse announced that there would be an emergency C-section within a few minutes. She invited the faculty to bring a student for observation. When the faculty and student asked permission from the patient, she agreed. As the faculty observed the patient, she noted something deeply disturbing in the woman's eyes – she noticed a type of fear she had not seen before in a woman preparing for a C-section. The woman said nothing about her fear to the teacher. Wondering what this fear could mean, the teacher stayed nearby. To the teacher's amazement, nothing out of the ordinary seemed to happen during the delivery. After the baby was born and all seemed well, the teacher and student left. The clinical day was over. As the teacher was leaving the unit, the woman's mother approached her and in frantic tones asked, "How is SHE?" Disturbed again by a level of fear and concern not seen before, the teacher responded, "Mother and baby were doing well when I left the room." Those words did not ease the fear of this woman's mother.

The next week, the staff nurse approached the teacher and said, "Wow you left just before things got interesting." The nurse went on to explain that after the delivery of the placenta, the mother began to bleed out. The nurse stated, "We almost lost her." The teacher has said that she wonders to this day if this woman or her mother verbalized their fears and concerns to the staff nurse or doctor. It was clear that she picked up on the cues, but because no one else seemed to notice, and nothing was said, she discounted her intuition.

Nurses often pick up on clients' cues, but are hesitant to act on them because they do not seem to fit the expected responses. As we learn to better understand the meaning of such cues, we can learn more about modeling a client's world. As has been stated repeatedly by those who use Modeling and Role-Modeling, modeling the client's world is essential if we are to plan purposeful interventions that will help people find meaning in their life experiences.

Modeling the World of Others

Before we can help others find meaning in their lives, we have to understand their perspectives on life. We have to step into their world and see life from their perspectives. We have to understand how they view themselves and their significant others. Erickson et al., (1983) called this "Modeling their world." They provided detailed instruction on how we can Model the world of another. H. Erickson has expanded on these processes in Chapters 10-11 in this book.

We contend that individualized and personalized interventions are necessary. However, we also believe that there are times when we can aggregate clinical cases and discover similarities among a group of clients that will help us better understand what we are observing when we model the world of another. That is, sometimes when we work with a similar group of people over time, patterns emerge. In the work of one of us (DaLynn Clayton) with hospitalized children, some commonalities observed are as follows:

Small children repeatedly express the need for love and security, for information about what is happening to them, what we are doing to them, what is going on around them, and their parents' location when the parents cannot be with the child.

Older children express needs for play. When asked what they would like to do today, many children say, "PLAY." It is best to follow the child's lead on what to play and how to play. Play is a very intriguing form of Self-care Knowledge.

Family members' staying with the child, frequently describe needing to care for personal needs such as resting, taking a break, getting a shower, washing clothes, etc. Family members of chronically ill children often need respect for what they know about their child and their child's care. They also need understanding when they act as though their child's hospitalization is a normal event. In their world, hospitalization is often to be expected.

Understanding these patterns has been useful in Modeling the worlds of hospitalized children and their families. They help us move more quickly to Role-Modeling, or the phase of planning and delivering purposeful care. However, it is always important to take time to listen and validate our understandings before we intervene. Otherwise, we may plan care inappropriate for the individual.

Role-Modeling Facilitates Growth

Role-Modeling is defined as "facilitation of the individual in attaining, maintaining, or promoting health through purposeful interventions" (Erickson et al., 1983, p. 95). In essence, nurses creatively design and deliver holistic care based on their clients' view of the world. Their aim is to facilitate their clients' growth, development and when necessary, healing. This is in contrast to care provided by nurses who believe they know what is best for their patient. When we use Modeling and Role-Modeling, we take into consideration the Five Aims of Nursing as described by Erickson et al. (1983, pp. 170-222).

Build Trust

Nurses join people and their families on their journeys. The nurse facilitates, guides, accepts, supports, advocates, and also learns along the way as a fellow traveler. A central component of nurse's relationship with a person is to facilitate "individuals to identify, mobilize, and develop his or her own strengths" (Erickson et al., 1983). The nurse's primary focus is on what is "right" with someone, what is working, what a person's strengths are rather than what is "wrong" with someone, what is not working well, or what is lacking. As we build trust, we create a Heart-to-Heart connection, nurse and client. This type of relationship helps people feel safe, respected, and valued.

Promote Positive Orientation

Holistic nursing care is given within the context of relationship. Halldorsdottir (1991) identified helpful and harmful ways of being with others. The most helpful way to be with another is the *life-giving mode* in which the nurse connects to the true essence of the other person. Healing love, mercy, compassion, interconnectedness, and responsiveness create a healing climate for clients. This is comparable to the Heart-to-Heart relationship described by Kinney in Chapter 9.

The *life-sustaining mode* is also helpful, but not as healing as the prior mode. In the life-sustaining mode, the nurse acknowledges the personhood of the other, offering support, encouragement, and reassurance, but not necessarily within the context of the individual's world-view.

Two harmful ways of interacting with others are life-restraining and life-destroying modes. In the *life-restraining mode*, the nurse is insensitive or indifferent, treating the person as a nuisance. Force, control, and blame are used. However, the most caustic and detrimental way of being with others is the *life-*

destroying mode. In this mode the nurses' interactions depersonalizes another, uses coercion, threats, manipulation, and humiliation during interactions. (Halldorsdottir, 1991). The implications are obvious. The Modeling and Role-Modeling paradigm argues for a life-giving mode of relationship, or, as described by Kinney, a Heart-to-Heart connection that creates a spirit-to-spirit relationship.

Affirming Strengths

Holistic care is delivered within the *context of love, unconditional acceptance, respect, presence, advocacy,* and *selective normative disregard* (Erickson et al., 1983; Rodgers, Vardey, 1995). At times providing care within the *context of love* will be easy for the nurse and at other times it may be quite challenging. The nurse may find a person difficult to care for. It is the responsibility of the nurse, however, to work through the issues and challenges, so the care needed is provided. This often requires *"soul work"* on the part of the nurse – a working through of what is bothering the nurse and why. *Unconditional acceptance* involves accepting each person as important and worthwhile – with no strings attached (Erickson et al., p. 49). *Respect* is given to each person as a fellow human being. Respect is also given for what others know about their care and the care of their family members. When we fully respect our clients, it is much easier to recognize and affirm their positive attributes and characteristics.

Promote Control

Presence involves being fully aware and mindful of the person and their family while delivering nursing care (Rodgers, 1996). *Advocacy* involves facilitating individual self-determination as well as interacting on behalf of the person when he or she does not have the necessary resources to act on their own behalf (Rodgers, 1996). *Selective normative disregard* is used "when the nurse understands and values the need for rules, policies, and procedures, but also recognizes that there are situations in which disregarding those policies is essential for creating an individualized intervention designed to meet the needs of the person" (Rodgers, 1996, p. 177). When we want to promote a sense of control in our clients, we may need to find creative, innovative ways to work within the system or even change the system. Advocacy implies that we have the client's best interest at heart, that we facilitate their perception of having control over their own lives.

Mutual Goals

The nurse recognizes and facilitates growth and when needed, the healing process. Healing is an inward discovery of truth and understanding that results in seeing life in new ways and in transformation (Clayton, 2001; Epstein, 1994). Healing experiences come in a myriad of forms – relationships, nature, spiritual encounters, discoveries, enlightenment, and simple ordinary acts of love.

If we listen, people will describe these deeply profound and powerful experiences. *At the wedding of one of my former students, I sat near an elderly man who was a local physician. I asked him how he knew the groom. He got very quiet and said almost in a whisper, "Awhile back I was in the hospital for a few weeks. Every morning this young man would come into my room with a hot cup of coffee." As the man spoke, tears streamed down his cheeks and the look of gratitude in his eyes was unmistakable. This seemingly simple act had a profound effect on this gentleman.*

The nurse listens to the person's verbal and nonverbal communication and responds in a healing manner. Self-care Knowledge and unmet needs are used to create holistic interventions for clients and their families. The nurse knows how to listen, pace, reframe, and use embedded commands–communicating within the context of language and movement. Setting mutual goals is only one more aspect of helping people heal and grow.

Growth Precedes Discovery

We are each on our own journey. Each searching for a meaningful life. Most of us have moments when we can pause and reflect, and while doing so, capture a glimmer of our potential, our strengths, and embrace the Essence of our Self. When we have these transcendent experiences, we know life is about Being, it is about relationships, learning to love, and to be connected. For those few seconds or moments, we know that our work is to find meaning in every day experiences, both the good and the bad. When we are able to do that, we are able to continue on the journey; we are able to keep searching for our Reason for Being. We also know we cannot do this work without the help of others, others who love, support, and facilitate us. Others who unconditionally accept us for all that we are and all that we are not (H. Erickson, personal communication, November 29, 2005).

ENDNOTES

[1] See Chapters 10-12 for more detail on reframing.

[2] Chapter 11 provides more guidelines on facilitating the story.

[3] Smith's model includes the Clinical model (health is the absence or control of disease), the Role-performance model (health is one's ability to carry out the roles of life), the Adaptive model (health is one's ability to cope with stress) and the Eudemonistic Model (health is quality of life, one's ability to enjoy life and find ways to interact with others in meaningful ways).

[4] For more detail on how collect data, interpret, and analyze it, and what to do with it, see Erickson et al., 1983 pp. 99-120.

[5] When this happens, we need to remember that loss can be real, threatened, or perceived (see Chapter 7) and loss is always related to some type of attachment object. That is, the lost *object* has met our needs repeatedly; the loss results in unmet needs.

[6] Approaches to nursing care vary based on the Adaptive Potential Assessment Model (APAM) and its three stress states (Erickson, 1976; 1990; Erickson et al., 1983). When a person is in *equilibrium*, the nurse can focus care on establishing rapport, building trust, following the person's

lead. Sharing knowledge with the person and family is fairly easy as long as the nurse follows the person's lead for information. When a person is in *arousal*, building trust and promoting control are essential. When a person is in *impoverishment* anticipating needs, building and restoring inner resources, promoting strengths and promoting a future orientation are essential. It is important for the nurse to recognize people moving towards impoverishment. *Conservative withdrawal* is at the end of *arousal* just before moving into *impoverishment*. The person still has some resources left, but is saving them until such a time as someone comes along to facilitate the person to mobilize their dwindling resources. It is important to build trust and focus on helping the person to build or to restore inner resources. *Protective withdrawal* is at the beginning of *impoverishment*. The person is attempting to protect self from people or situations that are causing depletion of the few resources that remain. These individuals are likely to express hopelessness and despair, if asked.

[7] For more detail on Self-care Knowledge, see Chapter 4 in this book. For more information about collecting Self-care Knowledge as primary data, see Erickson et al., 1983.

[8] See Chapter 6.

[9] Of course there are other factors to consider. One family member wondered if this accident reflected Esther's feeling of anger and a sense of abandonment by God. She had been asking God to restore Irene's health, but God had not answered her prayer as she had expected. Esther said she was angry with God and questioned His love for her and her family.

[10] Milton Erickson, H. Erickson's father-in-law, is one of the well-known leaders in the nature and use of hypnosis. He published more than 150 articles, several books, and has been the source of many other books by his followers.

CHAPTER 14

THE HEALING PROCESS

HELEN L. ERICKSON

Mr. B., a tall burly man who carried himself as though he could plow down anything and anyone getting in his way, swaggered into my office for his appointment, his stance and gaze designed to intimidate. He bellowed out, in very colorful language, that my office was sure hard to find and he didn't know how I could be of 'any good to him'. My secretary suggested I leave my door open just 'to get some air'. Assuring her we would be okay and she could close it without concern, I took my seat and offered him a choice of chairs. As soon as he landed in his chosen chair, he started his tirade. In loud threatening tones, he told me he was mean and tough, he could hurt people and enjoy it, he had been in the navy, had killed a man in a street fight, and was proud of it. He proceeded to tell me he wouldn't take any nonsense, and I'd better watch my step. As the profanity and voice tones increased, my secretary poked her head in and asked if I needed anything. I said both of us would probably enjoy some water, but otherwise, we were just fine.

As I spoke, I looked at Mr. B., smiled and focused on staying connected with him. He looked shocked, turned to the secretary, somewhat subdued, and said he would like some water. Then he started again, but this time he spoke in slightly quieter tones and used far less profanity as he focused on why he was in my office. He revealed he had diabetes, and it was 'so bad' he couldn't work, couldn't socialize, and his wife would leave him if he didn't shape-up. He then commented (in soft, wistful tones) that the only one that could stand him was his dog. With that, he launched into a saga about his dog, a little character that sat on his lap, ate breakfast with him, licked his face and hands, and was always happy to see him. During this discussion, he opened his body stance: arms uncrossed, legs opened, face softened, and voice tones quiet and peaceful.

After about a 10 minute talk about his dog, his only friend, he crossed his arms and legs, sat back in the chair, raised his head, projected his chin, and asked what I was going to tell him he had to do about his diabetes—after all he didn't have all day to mess around in my office. He repeated several profane adjectives describing his attitude toward his condition. Then he added his condition was, after all, the purpose of the appointment. I informed him the time was his to talk about anything he wanted, and if and when he wanted to talk about his physical condition, I was ready to listen, but something else might be of more interest to him right now. To this, he again looked surprised and said something about me being 'a little lady that knows her business'. I responded that I recognized he had learned to act tough and hide his feelings, but he really couldn't fool me. I told him I knew he was tough on the outside, but inside he had a very soft spot—he was like a big teddy bear. He could be scary if you didn't know what was really there. Again, he looked surprised. Changing positions in the chair, with his upper body bent toward me, and in softened voice tones, he recounted the following story.

He was found a few hours after birth, wrapped in a towel and placed in a box on the steps of the church. He was raised in an orphanage where 'many ugly things happened'. When he was 16 he left, lied about his age, and joined the navy. While in the navy he acquired a reputation for being tough, able to take care of himself, and someone to stay away from. After he left the Navy he married the first "decent" woman who came along. They had a daughter. He thought everything was fine until he came home and found a letter saying she had left and he shouldn't try to find her. He commented, sadly, face tilted toward the floor, that he had been abandoned again.

Then he looked at me, sat straight, head up, chest and chin out, and said that was enough and he was leaving. As he stood, I told him I was honored he had shared some of his story with me, and we could talk again if he wanted. Moving toward the door, he turned and commented that he didn't know what had gotten into him, he never talked to anyone like that, and said, 'At least, I don't intend to talk with you like that again!' And left.

The following day, he called my office for another appointment. Over the next several weeks, he came to see me off and on. At the end of our time together, Mr. B.'s diabetes was under control. He had taken a custodial job working for a thrift store, had joined a church, and was enjoying a good relationship with his wife.[1]

OVERVIEW

Mr. B. is only one of the many people I have worked with through the years using the Modeling and Role-Modeling theory and paradigm. Many have had serious physical problems that stymied their healthcare providers. In a few cases, attending physicians have referred clients insisting they come for help. In nearly all such cases, the clients have developed multiple layers of negative developmental residual, maladaptive coping patterns, and need help healing. They need help unbinding and peeling off layers of negative residual, while building positive residual. This takes time. *It always has to start at the beginning, or with the first loss.* Sometimes, I have worked with people over a period of weeks, either visiting with them as they come to a clinic for care, or other times when they have made appointments to come to my office. There are, however, many people I interacted with only one or two times in acute care settings, doctors offices, over the phone, and even in the grocery store. Yet, I have received letters or calls from them later, telling me the interactions helped them immensely and sometimes even changed their lives. *This is because healing can be started in a single interaction and, sometimes, individuals can do the rest on their own.*[2]

Healing always involves loss. While some people have experienced a recent loss, those who have long-standing, unresolved losses with morbid grief are the most challenging. They have learned to adapt by drawing resources from one subsystem to contend with losses in another. It has become part of their fabric; the process is no longer acute, and in most cases, the loss is not obvious to the casual observer.

This book is about helping people grow, develop, and when needed, heal. This chapter focuses on the healing process. While healing takes place in another person and we need to understand that process and how it works, nurses play a unique role in initiating and facilitating the process, so we also need to understand what we can do to help ourselves as we aim toward facilitating healing in others.

The first section addresses the nature of healing. The second addresses factors related to our ability to facilitate the healing process. The third section focuses on the nurse, and how to think about ourselves, so we can help people heal. Deepak Chopra's *The Seven Spiritual Laws of Success* (1996) guides this section.

HEALING IS INHERENT

Loss is a natural part of life; so are grief and healing. Loss produces a grieving response we have to work through in order to resolve the loss. We also have to work through grief, so we can move on and find happiness in life. Healing occurs as we work through the grieving process. It is both the means and the end; it creates a link between loss and healthy, holistic being.

Loss creates disorder and disruption in our holistic being. It produces multiple unmet needs, associated pain, and drains energy. Unresolved loss interferes with our ability to grow toward our maximum potential. On the other hand, healing restores order, synchrony, and creates need satisfaction and need assets. It provides an opportunity to learn, and a base for growth, development, and self-actualization.

> We have to attach to objects to be healthy, but we also have to let them go if we are to continue to grow. Our drive to restore harmony and synchrony, become holistic, and be in touch with our Self creates a need to heal after losses occur.

Healing Opportunities

Health care providers frequently talk about healing wounds, suggesting the wound or loss comes first and healing is a way to eradicate or fix it. Other times, common language implies healing is necessary, so we can let go of the past and grow. Both orientations are accurate; *healing bridges the gap between loss and Self-discovery.*

Health care providers, particularly nurses and social workers, have unique opportunities to help people discover their Self. This is because we interact with people when they are most vulnerable and need help restoring and building their strengths, defining their uniqueness, and healing from life experiences. When vulnerable, we naturally seek respite from discomfort and pain.[3] At such times, we are more open to new ways of thinking and acting. Health care providers who purposefully make heart-to-heart connections have opportunities to offer alternatives. Often, these opportunities coincide with physical care of the acutely ill. For example, I have instructed students to ask post-operative patients if they want something to help them be *more comfortable* rather than if they want something for *pain.*

The difference in the language we use affects how we respond and which stored memories are triggered. When we think about receiving something for pain, our mind automatically goes in one of several directions, with the focus on the pain. Either we are thinking of *feeding* the pain, *diminishing* the pain, or *eradicating our ability to experience* the pain. Each option results in the excretion of chemicals, affecting our entire being.

Now, consider the word, *comfort*. If we feel comfort, we enhance our ability to be comfortable. On the other hand, if in pain, few people would want to *diminish or eradicate* comfort. This narrows the choice of possible responses at all levels, biophysical (which triggers stored memories), emotional (which affects excretion of neurotransmitters), and spiritual (which enhances search for Self). The use of language is important when we aim to help people heal.

> Basic Principle: Use language, whenever possible, that has a positive, growth-directed innuendo associated with it.

Other examples include those often used when health care providers introduce themselves to their clients, "I'm the wound therapist," "I'm the phlebotomist," or "I'm the inhalation therapist." When I hear such language, my mind automatically goes to the many wounds and blood draws I've seen or done, and the labored breathing I've observed. These visions (which affect my biophysical responses) don't have *people* attached, just bodies. Imagine the effect this has on my energy fields. If we want to help people *heal holistically,* we should learn to use language that stimulates healthy excretion of neurotransmitters and heart-to-heart connections, even when we are providing complex technical care.

The healing process can be initiated anywhere—in the intensive care unit, at the water fountain in the mall, in a client's home, in our backyard—anywhere two people interact. The healing process starts with a change in the way we think and feel and continues on through time. It doesn't happen in split seconds although it can be initiated in split seconds. Sometimes it takes little time, and other times it takes longer. Remember, seeding works, but it takes time. In any case, healing can happen and when it does, it creates changes in the holistic person, changes that move the person closer to Self-discovery, self-actualization, and fulfillment of Life Purpose. This is important no matter what type of loss we are experiencing.

Who Needs to Heal?

We all need help growing and becoming our unique Self. That is why we are here, in human form. We have to live a physical life, so we can have human experiences as we take the journey. These experiences help us discover our Self, and identify our Life Purpose and our Reason for Being.

As humans, we need to be both connected and individuated; we have an inherent drive for affiliated-individuation. Therefore, to gain the most from the journey, we have to attach to people and things; we also have to learn to let go and move on. This means each of us has to experience the joy of attachment, the pain of loss, the emotion of grief, and the hope of new beginnings. We have to experience the peaks and valleys, so we can learn about ourselves, who we are in relationship to others, and who we are as unique human beings. This helps us with our Soul-work; it helps us achieve our Reason for Being.

We cannot do this alone; we have to do it with others. Therefore, loss, grief, and healing are not only experiences each of us must manage in our own time and way, but also experiences we must have by traveling with others as they have similar experiences. To have the full human experience, we need to learn through our own joy, pain, hope, and through the joy, pain, and hope of others. Each of us has to travel our pathway, but each of us needs others to accompany us on our journey. We also need to travel with others as they take their journey. In the first case we learn about our self within the context of our own life journey while in the second we learn about our Soul-work in respect to others. We need both types of experiences to fully understand our Self and how we relate to and impact others and the Universe.

> Loss, grief, and healing are part of our life journey. We learn from them, gain understanding of who we are, and in the long run, find our Life Purpose by fully living each phase.

At the Beginning of Life

Loss and grief occur repeatedly from birth to when we separate from physical life. Consider, for example, the prenatal infant secure in the womb, acquiring nutrition and other necessary resources without much effort. Suddenly, the environment changes. The soft, comfortable surroundings become rigid and constricting. The infant may be confronted with several hours of being squeezed, pushed, and perhaps, physically traumatized (it is believed it hurts to have the head and body molded as the infant moves through the birth canal). What was once a safe, secure environment is no longer experienced the same way. To top it off, after passage through what would have seemed a small space, the infant is thrust into the cold, bright lights, and a new world. The infant has to let go of the object (the warm, cuddly environment with all its sounds and tastes) that met physiological, safety and security needs, and reattach to a new object (perhaps the same human, but in a different form) if it is to thrive. The need to 'heal' has begun and continues throughout the lifespan. The infant has to learn to regulate its own body even as it continues spiritual integration. It needs help with these processes. Yet, it has already started its journey, initiated its Life Purpose, and established its individuality in the human world. As others help the infant heal, both will benefit. The infant will proceed on the journey of life and the others will experience the joy of sharing the journey with another.

Saying Goodbye

At the other end of the continuum, people often need help letting go of physical life. Several stories, previously reported, describe the healing process at this stage of life. For example, Mrs. Cook (Chapter 1), my brother (Chapter 5), and Mr. M. (Chapter 11) each provide an example of someone who needed help in the last stage of life. Healing, in the last stage of life, does not mean the individual is suddenly, physically revitalized. It means the person has learned we are more than a physical body—we are also spiritual beings. When this happens, people are willing to let go of the physical form and material life, and move on. Reconnected with their spirit, they have achieved the maximum in healing; they are ready to reunite spirit with Soul. Just as the infant needs help learning to come into physical life, people often need help learning to leave physical life. Both the beginning and the end are times of healing because healing is about integration of body, mind, and spirit.

> The need to heal is preceded by one or more losses. When loss occurs, dynamic, interactive processes among the multiple parts of the holistic being are affected. Chemicals are released creating cascades of responses through the body. Synchrony among the energy fields is disrupted, and coping responses are initiated. Healing restores harmony and synchrony among the multiple parts of the human being.

Healing Ability

Healing is essential for us to do our Soul-work because it helps us understand what is possible. Nevertheless, at times, people have trouble healing and need more help. Our need is partially related to our ability to mobilize resources.

Sometimes we have adequate resources, so the grieving and healing processes are accelerated and almost effortless. For example, there are times when we can negotiate our way through transitions without difficulty, including moving from infancy to toddler-hood, being promoted from second to the third grade, taking a new position at work, replacing an old piece of loved furniture with a new one, moving from a one-bedroom home to a three-bedroom home, and so forth. While we experience loss during these transitions, it is minimal and almost unrecognizable. This often happens because we look forward to the change. Our natural propensity to grow takes over, the grieving process is almost nonexistent, and healing happens almost spontaneously.

On the other hand, everyone also has life experiences that exceed their ability to mobilize resources. Sometimes, the loss is unexpected; sometimes, there is no anticipated exchange, and sometimes it is simply a matter of resources. When this happens, we might get stuck in the grieving process for a short period of time. Frequently, we are able to mobilize resources, heal, and move on. Other times, healing requires more resources than we can mobilize. When another person helps us, we may be able to work through the process. But, then there are times when both internal and external resources are inadequate, and we are stuck in the grieving process.

Healing and Sense-of-self

Sometimes, people get stuck in the grieving process because they have focused on their *sense-of-self* rather than searched for their *Essence of Self.*[4] Often an entire life is built around our sense-of-self, and then something happens that disrupts the patterns we've developed, our habits, values, and expectations. When this happens, we have to revisit who we are and what we value. Sometimes it is easy for people to make the changes; they value the opportunity to *get back on the right track.* Other times, they are confused, even distraught. They get stuck in morbid grieving. Sorting through the difference between our sense-of-self and our Essence of Self is necessary for healing to occur. Sometimes people get into maladaptive coping that interferes with their growth.[5]

Maladaptive Coping Mechanisms

Unresolved losses are unresolved stressors. Stressors produce stress, and we have to contend with the stress if we are to survive. Any coping mechanism that reduces the stress is better than none at all. However, resources in one subsystem are often inadequate or unavailable, so we draw from another subsystem. When this happens, we use a maladaptive coping mechanism. We tax one subsystem to maintain another. This is usually an unconscious process.

When people use maladaptive coping mechanisms, they experience some relief from the stress, but do nothing to alleviate the stressor. Ultimately, the stressor resurfaces, and again, resources are drawn from the alternative subsystem.[6] These resources will reduce the stress, but less effectively each time. Nevertheless, patterns emerge. The person with maladaptive coping may feel stuck, but they endure the discomfort even though it may get so bad they suffer from mind, body, and spirit dissonance. This can go on for years.

Often family members are confused by these patterns of behavior. Sometimes family members perceive the condition so severe and incapacitating that there is no hope, nothing can be done. They try different doctors, different medications, and sometimes seek alternative health strategies, and yet, their loved one gets worse. Sometimes families get annoyed with their sick member, believing they aren't doing what is needed to get better. They don't understand people cannot give up on coping mechanisms that worked in the past unless they have something to replace them.

Mistaken Labels. Health care providers are also confused by these clients. They are often treated aggressively at first, and as time goes by, are frequently labeled as non-compliant, unresponsive, difficult to control, or brittle. Here's one such example:

> *A number of years ago a cardiologist asked me to see one such client. She had been hospitalized for an impending myocardial infarct (MI). She had severe chest pain, elevated enzymes, and a history of a MI the year before. The cardiologist called me because this woman had a history of being admitted to the hospital for the past four years around*

Thanksgiving time with similar signs and symptoms. Her family had gathered to support her the first three years, but now they were disgusted. They insisted she "did this on purpose to ruin our holidays." According to them, she never followed the doctor's orders and "enjoyed being sick."[7] The doctor said she was difficult to control, non-compliant, and seemed to have many unrelated physical problems that emerged, one after the other.

<u>*Primary Data.*</u> *When I entered her room and asked her to describe her situation for me* (Erickson, Tomlin & Swain, pp. 116-167), *she stated she had chest pain, and afraid she'd have another heart attack or pulmonary emboli, she had driven herself to the emergency room. I told her I admired her knowing what she needed. She responded that someone had to take care of her, and no one wanted to, so she took care of herself. Then she added that she always got sick when she was stressed, and she got stressed because she had too much to do, and it wasn't her fault. She commented that the holidays were particularly hard because everyone wanted so much from her. This statement resulted in her family rolling their eyes and looking disgusted. When I asked her to tell me more about this, she provided numerous examples where she had been stressed and then got sick. Often, the stress was preceded by someone asking her to do something for someone else, such as bake cookies for an event, watch a grandchild, or get herself ready for a trip.[8] In her recitation, she was clearly making the point that the stress came first and was followed by an illness.*

As I stayed connected with her, listened, and affirmed her stories and identified her strengths when they emerged, she proceeded to move back in time, describing multiple incidents where she had been stressed and then gotten sick. As she reached her childhood, her voice tones became more defensive, and then she recounted her experience as a three year old. Her family had moved to a farm; everyone had to work. Her assignment was to go to the barn and pick up the eggs. She described the barn as a big, empty, scary place filled with noises and other things. The first day she had trouble getting out there, but she did. She looked, found a few eggs, and took them back to her mother. Her mother insisted there were many more, she had to go look. So, she dragged herself back out there again. This time she made the mistake of trying to take the eggs from a "sitting hen."[9] The hen pecked her arms, face, legs, and chased her out of the barn. Her mother told her she didn't have to go back that day, but the next day, she sent her out again. On the way to the barn, she fainted. Her mother decided the sun was too hot on her head (remember, the barn was a long way from the house). So, she made a sunbonnet to protect her from the heat. Nevertheless, the little three-year-old fainted on the way to the barn. She didn't have to go back again. As she finished her story, she looked at me defiantly and repeated that ever since that time, whenever she got stressed, she got sick.[10]

The Secondary Source. *Her family met me in the hall and chorused that they had heard that story a thousand times and were sick of it. When they were all together, they said, their mother was just fine. She cooked meals, took care of the children, and so forth. The problem occurred when she was expected to "act like an adult and do things on her own."*

Interpreting Data. *This lady had learned how to get her basic psychosocial needs for safety and security met, but at the cost of her physical health. Now her maladaptive coping pattern was also threatening her relationship with her family. What had worked in the past was becoming ineffective. She had learned as a small child how to be safe, but it interfered with her ability to grow. She had learned that being sick was a way of avoiding taking risks on her own. She was stuck in the stages of Autonomy and Initiative. She would not willingly give up maladaptive coping mechanisms that worked when it meant that her safety needs would no longer be met. I had to offer her something that would meet those same needs, and do it in a way that she would know I could be trusted. I also had to believe that once I helped her feel safe, her natural drive to grow would "kick in."*

Testing Interpretations. *My response to her was that she was very smart, had learned how to take care of herself, and knew what she needed. I casually commented that all people need to feel safe, respected, and loved, and included myself in the statement by placing my hand on my chest. Then, I added that maybe she and I (hand moving slowly back and forth between the two of us, creating a link) could work together so she could learn even more ways to get her needs met and not be stressed. With a little humor, I suggested it might be similar to learning how to eat your cake and have it too. She looked leery, but agreed. At the close of our meeting, I gave her my business card with my office telephone number and told her I'd come by the next day to see her, and she could call me if she wanted. Before I left, I asked if I could help her be more comfortable in her bed by fluffing her pillows, tightening her sheets, or getting her some water. The family stood by and watched with arms crossed.*

The next day when I arrived, she was preparing to go home. The staff agreed she could go with me to the conference room for a few minutes. As we walked down the hall, I asked her if she wanted help walking and she refused, but wanted me to "just stay nearby." That session was dedicated to learning more about her and building trust. As I talked with her I learned she was the third of four girls and one boy. Her older sisters were approximately 2 1/2 years apart; she was born 20 months after the second. The fourth sister was born 11 months later and then within 2 years, the baby brother was born. She saw herself as the one who didn't fit in, the one who was supposed to be the boy, and the one whom no one wanted. This suggested she might have had trouble in the stages of Integration and Trust.

Interventions. Over the next few weeks, I saw her for a few minutes weekly in the doctor's office. Our work started at the Trust level and worked forward. Each week, I gave her a new transitional object, symbolic of the stages of Trust, Autonomy, and Initiative, respectively. The first transitional object was the business card (described above), and the second was my penlight. As I gave her this, I asked if she still had the business card; she showed me that she did. I then offered the penlight from my lab coat pocket and asked if she would like it. I had selected this because she had frequently used language such as, "I'm not sure I see it that way" or "I don't know how to see things differently" and "I'm in the dark about that." Giving it to her, I maintained eye contact and told her I liked the pen because it was just the right size to carry around with me; it wasn't too small or too big, and I wanted her to have it because it reminded me of her, and so she could find her way and be safe no matter where she was or who she was with. Finally, I added that she should know she would never be alone because I was giving her something of myself.

The third item was a picture postcard of a child walking through a field of flowers. When I gave her this picture, I suggested she see the wild spring flowers blooming in the fields. We had talked about her ability to leave the house, do things without worrying she would get too far away from the house at one time or get sick again, and what she could do to protect herself[1] before she went on her adventure. The fourth transitional object was a small Guardian Angel pin I gave her as she was beginning to take small Initiative-type steps. I told her, at that time, I would always be with her, and she with me, and when she was scared of doing new things, she just needed to remember she would never be alone again. I also told her the more things she learned to do, the more she would discover what she liked to do, and what would make her feel whole. Finally, I suggested she might surprise herself as she discovered who she really was, that from my perspective, there was a really delightful, capable woman just waiting to be discovered.

Evaluation. Upon conclusion of our work, she was taking small Initiative-type steps, reaching out to members of the church to help her be independent of her family, and was physically stable. I have not seen this lady for many years although I talked with her physician sometime later and learned she was doing well physically and hadn't had any more emergency admissions.

I am confident our work together helped her learn new coping mechanisms. As she grew, she peeled negative residual and replaced it with positive residual. She had learned to trust others to be there when she needed them, and she had learned that even in my absence, we would stay connected. She had started the healing process. From years of experience and feedback from numerous clients, I believe my intent to stay connected helped her feel safe when she needed it even though we were separated by space and time. I also believe her natural propensity to heal propelled her forward on her healing pathway. Even in my physical absence, I could help her feel a sense of affiliated-individuation. This is the advantage of using healing energy with intent.

THE PRIMACY OF HEALING

The preceding paragraphs were designed to help you better understand healing within the context of the Modeling and Role-Modeling theory and paradigm. They were intended to build on previous chapters and provide practical information. This section is dedicated to exploring the centrality of healing in health care. This is not to discount the marvel of technical care. Technical care is necessary to maintain and promote physical life. But, technical care cannot promote well-being, help people build strong interpersonal relationships, or help them discover their Self and their Life Purpose. Technical care gave my husband a new mitral valve, but nurturing, facilitating, and healing saved his life and gave him the opportunity to fulfill his Life Purpose.

In the first three chapters of this book we proposed we are energy first, that our Soul comes to reside in human form because it has a Reason for Being, or work to do. The second section focused on the nature of people, concepts we need to understand before we can use the Modeling and Role-Modeling theory to guide our practice. This last section addresses concepts related to the healing process. This chapter focuses on the healing process, per se.

Healing As Core

Many healthcare providers argue that healing is within their professional domain; nursing is no exception. The notion of nurses participating in the healing process was first introduced by Nightingale (1860) when she argued that nurses create a healing environment, so the human can repair itself. While we got sidetracked for a number of years building the science of nursing, many nurses continued to practice using healing principles.

Fenton (1997) observed some of their behavior during an ethnographic study of Clinical Nurse Specialists (CNS) and described what she called Underground Nursing (p. 560). She states, "Behind closed doors, and sometimes in full view, they used their listening, presencing, comforting, and touching skills in ways that were not always apparent to other professions" (p. 561). She provides an example of a CNS who interacted with a man undergoing chemotherapy and his wife. She describes their fear at the outset of the interaction, the nurse's attitude and actions, which demonstrated caring, presence, comforting, and active listening. Fenton ends the scenario with, "My last picture of this episode was as they left. The man's wife stopped and hugged the CNS with tears in her eyes. She was laughing and crying with relief about her husband's prognosis and for having experienced a truly healing encounter" (p. 561).

Beverly Hall (2005) recently published *The Art of Becoming a Nurse Healer,* in which she states:

Healing derives from a sense of hope, a view that in every single instance, there is always something we can do to alleviate suffering, and that we own the responsibility to think through the alternatives. Therefore as Quinn (1996) helps us realize, the healing model is always optimistic because nurses can always heal even when patients cannot be cured. Healing develops out of learning how to be right with self and others. It is based on intentionality, compassion, and the focused attention of nurse toward the patient. Patients who cannot be cured of their disease can be healed because healing...means to make whole. A state of wholeness exists...separate from the patient's disease (p. 3).

Later Hall says, "nursing frameworks allow a focus on the human spirit as well as the mind and body" (p.15) indicating that the whole person is multi-dimensional. Although she doesn't explicitly discuss the interaction of dimensions, she implies in her work that she believes the whole is greater than the sum of the parts, or holistic.[12] Others have also written about healing. For example, Kritek (1997) edited *Reflections on Healing: A Central Nursing Construct* containing 48 chapters, each describing an aspect of the healing process. Waters and Daubenmire (1997) stated, "The endogenous healing process is a natural phenomenon that moves one toward harmonious energy patterns and expanded consciousness" (p. 58). Another author, Branum (1997), wrote about healing in people diagnosed with terminal disease. She stated, "Healing, within this context, is a matter of restoring hope and relieving unnecessary suffering. It is not the false hope of immortality, but the realistic hope of the soul for meaning and resolution in the time one has to live" (p. 330). Clearly, facilitating the healing process should be an upfront goal of nursing, not something done Underground. Nevertheless, it is often put aside as something extra or something someone else does.

> As health care providers and as recipients of health care, we should revolt against the notion that healing is done underground, and take the position that the *most* important thing a nurse can do is facilitate healing in another human. What is the value of physical life if we can't live a quality life? And what is the purpose of physical life if we can't fulfill our Life Purpose? Facilitating healing should be the major aim of the nursing profession.

Watson (1993) cautioned us to make certain we maintain a balance between the science of nursing and the "caring and healing arts" (p. 19). This statement is consistent with my belief about the balance between the art and science of nursing. However, I would argue that anything as important to the well-being of human beings as the healing process should not only be considered an art of nursing,[13] but should be thrust mainstream into the science of nursing.[14]

American Holistic Nurses Association

During the early 1980's, several nurses who believed holism and healing form the core of nursing[15] came together to discuss how they might move these concepts forward in health care. Under the tutelage of Charlotte McGuire, they organized and created The American Holistic Nurses Association (AHNA).[16] Recognizing that mainstream nursing had drifted from the work of Florence Nightingale, nurse leaders such as Barbara Dossey, Lynn Kegan, Cathie Guzzetta, Noreen Frisch, Johanne Quinn, Veda Andrus, Marie Shanahan, and others, helped articulate the nature of Holistic Nursing. Several publications resulted including *AHNA Standards of Holistic Nursing Practice: Guidelines for Caring and Healing* (Dossey, Guzzetta, Quinn, & Frisch, 2000); *Holistic Nursing: A Handbook for Practice (*Dossey, Keegan, & Guzzetta, 2005), *Core Curriculum for holistic nursing,* (Dossey, 1997). A series entitled *Nurse as Healer* was commissioned with Lynn Keegan as the series editors. Several books, authored by Shames (1995), Frisch and Kelley (1995), Keegan and Dossey (1997), Umluf (1997), Keegan (2002), and Olson (2000) included in the series, helped further define the essence of Holistic Nursing and healing as a core component of nursing.

By the mid 1990's, a sufficient number of nurses and health care agencies were interested in holistic nursing to warrant national certification. In 1997, the American Holistic Nurses Certification Corporation (AHNCC)[17] was established. Today, two types of national certification processes are overseen by AHNCC. One is for nurses with a baccalaureate degree and the second is for graduate level nurses. Holistic Nursing (HN-BC) and Advanced Holistic Nursing (AHN-BC) are the respective credentials for the two levels.

Caring and Healing

Although some nurses and other health professionals get sidetracked by the pull of the treat-the-disease model and the demands of health care systems, most understand we do not aim to treat or cure disease. Instead, we aim to facilitate growth and healing. While we continue to discuss caring as key to nursing, we now differentiate between caring and healing. Caring is what we do as human beings, interfacing heart-to-heart, with others; healing is what we aim to facilitate in our clients. It is the focus of our intent. We cannot cure people, we cannot heal them, but we can aim to facilitate the healing process, inherent in each of us. If we have intent to help others build resources, and mobilize them for the purpose of growing and becoming the most they can be, we have the intent to facilitate healing. As Nichols (2000) succinctly puts it, "Energy follows thought" (p. 13). We have the ability to facilitate healing by our intent. However, we must understand healing is not curing, and does not always occur in the way we anticipate.

The case presented at the beginning of the chapter is an example of someone who has developed maladaptive coping patterns, reducing resource availability and making it more difficult to build new resources. Facilitating the healing process is more complicated for someone like this in comparison to a person experiencing a single grieving experience. While many health care providers might be tempted to focus on the caring process, caring without a focus on facilitating healing would not have helped this gentleman.

Previous chapters provide information that can assist people of all ages who need help to grow and heal. Chapter 12 provides some guidelines on how to support people who are working on developmental tasks consistent with their chronological age as well as those working on tasks inconsistent with their age. I have not provided lists of guidelines because we cannot know exactly how they would be applied until we understand the world-view of the person with whom we are working. The following comments are offered instead. They are guidelines for you to consider and adapt within your own world context.

Getting Connected

The primary principles to consider are that people need to be facilitated in normal, healthy, grieving processes. First, we need to remember the importance of heart-to-heart connections. Many times, we simply need to be Present and have Intent. When we take time to prepare ourselves (Chapters 9 and 10), focus on empowering our client's natural healing abilities through the use of Presence and Intent, and then actively listen to their story, it is often amazing how people are able to grow and heal. They don't need complex interventions because they are able to mobilize necessary resources. But they do need time. As health care providers, it is important to remember healing takes time. We have to believe we have the ability to initiate a healing process that will continue over time if we do not disconnect our energy.

Stay Connected

This brings me to the second issue: disconnection of energy or intent. Many people have told me they have limited energy, so they can't get too involved with others and, when they do, they cannot continue to stay involved. These statements indicate a lack of understanding of the nature of energy fields and our ability to use them. For example, when we perceive we have to give our energy to another to help them, we forget we are connected to the Universe where there is an infinite amount of energy. We don't have to give our energy away! We simply have to learn how to serve as a conduit. I like to think of myself as a transformation station. I can draw from the Universe, transform energy, so it synchronizes with the fields of others, and pass it on. I really don't have to do anything, except be open to the Universe and have the Intent to pass on helpful, healing energy. Some would say this is love and loving energy. I think it is learning how to Be. Whatever one chooses to call it, I believe it is powerful.

The second factor related to this issue is the notion of staying "involved." When we use this language, we imply actively *thinking* about what we will *do* next. I rarely do this with clients. Instead, I do two things. First I speak to the Universe (and myself) and ask for healing energy to continue flowing through me to the client, and second, I ask for the wisdom to understand the client's world-view. Some would say this is an auto hypnotic technique that stimulates my unconscious and subconscious processes to stay alert. I think this is possible, but I also believe it brings me collective knowledge (Consciousness, as described in Chapter 3), so I can work more purposefully. Staying involved need not mean you continue spending time doing something, it just means you don't disconnect your energy from others.[18]

Seed

When we connect with others, send healing energy, and have the Intent to unconditionally accept them, we automatically encourage them to express their needs. Affirmation of a human's needs is powerful; it is the same as affirmation of the essence of the person. Again, most of the time we don't have to do much— we simply need to connect, stay connected, and occasionally seed possibilities. For example,

> *Not too long ago, I was standing by a water fountain in a local exercise facility when a lady I had never seen before walked up to get a glass of water. She approached, breathing hard, face pinched tight, looking tired, and sad. Her face was aimed at the water fountain. I thought she would get a drink and move on. I said nothing and did not move, but opened myself to send her some energy. Suddenly, she looked at me face softened slightly, then looked at my shirt, and said (face again getting tight and voice sounding disappointed), "Oh, so you're a nurse. I suppose you're going to tell me I need to quit smoking, too!"*
>
> *I responded by sending more energy, smiling slightly, and said, "Yes I am a nurse, but no, I'm not going to tell you to quit smoking. That is a personal thing between you and your Self." She looked surprised and said she knew she should quit, but she'd rather die smoking than getting hit by a car! I agreed getting hit by a car would not be any fun, and then added that I believed people did the best they could, that each of us had to find a way to live our own life, and sometimes we just needed someone to talk to. She immediately launched into a story about her family—how they tried to tell her what to do, but didn't take care of themselves, and always wanted something from her. Then she gradually moved on and talked about how she needed them and how she guessed they didn't mean to hassle her, they were just worried about her.*
>
> *As she talked, I just listened, smiled slightly, staying connected, sending energy, and occasionally nodding my head. Doing so, I noticed her breathing had slowed considerably, her body was straighter, and her*

face was gradually softening. Suddenly, she stopped, saying she wasn't as tired as she had thought, and was surprised she wasn't having any trouble breathing, so maybe she should go exercise some more. As she wandered back to the machines, she turned, smiled, and said, "Thanks, I feel a lot better now."

Most people would say nothing happened at the water fountain that day. It certainly didn't take much from me other than 1-2 minutes, and purposeful Being. I suspect, however, the next time I see that lady, she will smile and say hello.[19] While those moments may not have made a big change in this woman's life, they may have started a healing process that will result in a change. Sometimes small changes lead to even more change; combined they can make a difference in another human's life. People only need to get started.

> As humans, we have a natural propensity to heal and become more fully integrated. Sometimes, it is just a matter of getting started. We help others heal through heart-to-heart connections, seeding, and reframing.

Contextualize

One factor which impedes our capability to initiate or start the healing process is our inability to place behavior in a context. Instead, it is viewed as isolated actions or reactions without any specific meaning. Since needs drive all our behavior, all behavior is contextual. When we understand this simple principle of human nature, we no longer observe behavior in isolation. For example,

A number of years ago I was asked to consult with the nursing staff regarding a lady who had recently experienced a mastectomy. They didn't know what to do with her. She was first day post-operative, and, according to the head nurse, "Raising a fit!" She had told her assigned nurse to get out of her room and leave her alone, refused to listen to another nurse who was trying to teach her how to cough, and seemed out of control.

When I entered her room, I observed a lady sitting on the side of her bed, hospital gown hanging around her neck and hanging down, hair uncombed, eating her breakfast. Her husband and daughter were with her. After I introduced myself and told her the head nurse had asked me to see her, I asked if she was willing to tell me what had happened. She immediately reported she had expected to go to surgery for a lumpectomy and had returned with a full mastectomy.[20] Her voice was loud, forceful, and filled with anger. I said most people go through feelings of shock and anger when they have such experiences, and I wondered if I could help her in any way. She said she was going to be angry all day, and then she'd be fine. She pointed out that her husband and daughter were with her, and she knew she could get through the whole experience. She then thanked me, finished her breakfast, and asked to walk in the hall. As we walked in the hall, she talked about getting better, going home, and getting back to work.

I returned to the staff and reported that she was in a normal state of grieving because of her losses, but she would be fine if the nurses simply supported her grieving process. I indicated it was important they avoid trying to fix her, or teach her where she had made her mistakes, e.g., she had signed the consent form for a radical mastectomy if needed. I also said that she would ask about these issues when she entered the next stage of grief, i.e., bargaining. Right now she was in Arousal and was able to mobilize resources. Her behaviors suggested that she was in the Anger stage of grief which supported the notion that she was mobilizing resources. The head nurse told me that I obviously didn't understand. She recommended that I go visit the other lady who had also had a total mastectomy the day before.

When I entered this lady's room, I found her lying on her side in a fetal position. She had on a pink negligee, her hair was nicely combed and her nails were painted. She was very quiet. When I introduced myself and asked her if there was anything I could do for her, she looked away, then started to cry. She said, no, there was nothing anyone could do. She then added that her husband had been seeing other women before she had the mastectomy; now there was no hope for their marriage.

Again, I talked with the staff and commented that the first lady was doing well while the second was not. The second, in the state of Impoverishment, was having difficulty mobilizing resources. She was at risk for developing physical complications and morbid grief. They could not understand these differences because the patients acted so differently. The first was angry and aggressive; she didn't care about her appearance, she just cared about her process. Her behavior was not acceptable, they did not understand it, and did not know what to do to help her. The second lady was quiet, wanted to look "pretty," and didn't make demands on the nurses. Her behavior was easier for the nurses to accept because she only wanted to look nice, to have her hair combed and nails polished. She didn't make demands on the nurses that they didn't understand.

The nurses had failed to put the behavior of these two women in a context. The context includes their world-view, life experiences, culture and current situation. Behavior is always contextual, never isolated. But, we often fail to understand the importance of contextualizing behavior, attitudes, values, and ways of being. I remember a story my father-in-law told me about context. He described a family that went to a doctor for some help.

The parents had a small boy who seemed to be acting strangely. The doctor sent the little boy out to play and then invited the parents to join him at the window to watch. The boy walked around the yard, looking at the ground. Suddenly, he swooped down and pulled up an angle worm. Then he stretched it out, took a stick, and cut it in two parts. The doctor immediately commented about the child's destructive behavior; it indicated serious pathology. The mother protested, but to no avail. They brought the child back into the office as the father and doctor were discussing what needed to be done to fix this child. As he arrived in the office, the mother turned to the child and asked him what he was doing in the yard. He said he was looking for something to play with. The doctor assumed that this child's play was to destroy a living creature, which was more evidence of pathology. But, the mother continued. She told him she had noticed he found a worm. He agreed. Then she said that she had also noticed he had cut it in two parts, and asked him why he had done that. The child innocently looked at her and said, "He was lonely. He needed a friend to play with."

How easy it would have been for this family and doctor to make the mistake and misunderstand the behavior if the mother had not believed in her child. A simple question revealed the truth about most children in Initiative, they need friends. It is as natural as the sun rising. But, without consideration of the context, we often misunderstand. When we understand the context, it is easier to know what we need to do. We gain an understanding of the context by using the nursing assessment protocol described in Erickson et al., (1983) and Erickson (1990).

Helping People Heal

Initially, it is important to evaluate an individual's ability to mobilize resources so we can decide how to spend our time. People who are in Arousal need help mobilizing their resources, sorting through options, and affirming their decisions. They need someone who will listen to them. People in Impoverishment need interventions that will build resources. They feel helpless and hopeless, and are at risk for immune system depression, unexpected complications, and delayed recovery. They need to know that we care, and we will help them find ways to heal. They often don't know how to help themselves. When we work with them, we have to do an assessment of their developmental residual, so we can understand where the problem started.

Longstanding Losses

Sometimes the problem is long-standing.[21] Recent losses only serve to mobilize stored memories with feelings of loss and helplessness from an earlier time. These people usually need extensive help healing. They have more tasks to work through, more negative residual to unbind, and more positive residual to build. This kind of work takes time. It isn't impossible, but it does require that the healthcare provider understand it takes time, and growth occurs slowly and in small increments.

Healing always has to start with the original loss. This principle holds true with all situations, including those where maladaptive coping patterns exist. If we don't start with the original, we may help the person cope temporarily, but we don't help them heal. The wound remains with all of its stored cellular memories, disrupted energy, and negative residual, impeding growth and well-being. Additional negative residual will build on top of it, creating an even more complex situation. For example,

> *Mrs. Jones, aged 59, had recently lost her husband; she was obviously grieving. The nurse working with her stated that she was having difficulty helping her get past the stage of Anger. While she had initially seemed to do better and had moved on to feelings of sadness, within a few days she was again expressing anger that seemed almost hostile.*
>
> *I asked her to explore earlier losses with Mrs. Jones and explained that a classic sign of morbid grief was bouncing from hostility to depression and back again. Sometimes the feelings were focused, and sometimes they were not. When the nurse asked Mrs. Jones if she had ever had anything like this (the death of her husband) before, Mrs. Jones immediately commented that her mother had died when she was 5, and the death of her husband was just like losing her mother all over again.*

Mrs. Jones needed help grieving for her mother and healing before she could move on. The nurse working with Mrs. Jones commented that she never would have imagined that her mother's death would have anything to do with her husband's, and she was surprised when Mrs. Jones raised the topic. She said that she had an urge to tell her that her mother's death had occurred a long time before, but she remembered that doing this would only result in yet another loss, the loss of hope that the nurse could help.

People live in *a context. The context is their life. It often starts before their birth and goes* across their entire life time. Unless we understand this, we often miss an opportunity to help another human heal.

We don't always have to know the entire story. We just have to be aware that the story exists.[22] If we try to help people based on the obvious loss, and they respond well, then there is no need to know the rest of the story. Usually these people don't even offer other life experiences. But any time client's don't respond within the usual time frame, we need to explore for more details.

One technique I have found that helps people tell their story is to ask them to tell me something about themselves, any story that just pops into their mind. If they have trouble getting started, I suggest that they might *start* with something from their childhood. I have found that the story that emerges is nearly always the core of the problem, but it doesn't always come out directly. However, when they are validated for sharing and *remembering*, they often tell the rest. Most of the time we don't have to take much time, or ask many questions. People want to heal and they want help with healing. When they know they can trust us, they provide the information we need to help them. We just have to listen and let them peel away the layers in their own way and their own time.

Maladaptive Coping Patterns

Other people need extensive help healing. These people have developed maladaptive coping patterns in order to contend with stress in an alternative subsystem. While this can happen in any of the subsystems, my primary emphasis has been on those who have biophysical problems secondary to psychosocial losses. Through years of experience, I have come to believe many mid-life diseases we see in health care are related to unresolved losses and morbid grief. Linked to these losses are stored memories (Chapters 2, 3, and 4), which alter the chemical makeup of the cells, and produce alternative energy fields within and around the cells of the organs. I think long-term stress on the biophysical subsystem results in breakdown during the mid-life years because developmental residual comes to the point of inefficiency and people develop chronic diseases.

Interestingly, when their losses are resolved, these people enjoy a superior quality of life for long periods of time, with minimal side effects. In some cases, the condition seems to disappear. For example, one cardiologist[23] told me she had three patients with long-standing insulin-dependent diabetes who were able to go off their insulin after their spouses died. She reported that in each case, the spouses were chronically ill, mandated extensive care on the part of the patient, and were no longer perceived as companions by the patients. She was also able to model their world and understand their need for her assistance that was outside the usual medical model prototype.

Healing and Curing

Healing does not cure physical conditions. However, when people heal, their physical conditions often diminish or disappear. This is because many physical conditions are the result of maladaptive coping responses. These create stored cellular memories that are unleashed when we have a new experience that reminds us of the first experience at a conscious or unconscious level. The story of Bill, the 32 year-old Vietnam veteran presented at the beginning of Chapter 12 provides an example. You may remember Bill's trouble started in Vietnam when he led his men through a minefield, resulting in the death of several people including his best friend. He, too, was injured at the time. If you can, imagine Bill climbing the hill, frightened, but brave, fully aroused, heart beating fast. Then, something made him turn and look over his shoulder (probably the sounds of mines exploding and men screaming in fear and pain). As he did (heart beating faster), he noticed he was on top of a hill and men were rolling down, around, and on the ground. No doubt thousands of chemicals were released into his blood stream at that moment; the experience was embedded throughout his body as chemically stored-memories. Secondary memories were laid on top as he himself was injured and rolled down the hill.

Later in life, as he sat on the roof, looked down, and saw men walking around, unconscious associations were made, chemicals were unleashed, and Bill once again had a rapid heart beat, difficulty breathing, and tightness in his chest. That is, he experienced (at an unconscious level) an association with that day in Vietnam; this psychosocial experience produced an autonomic response that affected his heart. While the response was to be expected and perfectly human, it was maladaptive. The stressor was psychosocial and the stress response was physical. Over time, it took its toll; he developed hypertension and precursor symptoms of a myocardial infarct and had difficulty with the task of Intimacy. He needed help healing. And, as he healed, his physical symptoms dissipated and ultimately disappeared. He was able to move on and work on a healthy relationship with his wife and family.

The case of Mr. B. reported at the beginning of this chapter is a different example of the linkages between healing and curing. When I first met him, his diabetes was very unstable. He experienced frequent insulin reactions, was fatigued, and unable to work. He had maladaptive coping patterns from an early stage of life. While they had "worked for him" for a number of years, they had also produced considerable negative residual. His coping patterns interfered with his ability to successfully establish happy, healthy relationships with significant others. After a few weeks of working with him, his diabetes became much more stable. While it did not disappear, it was easily manageable. He was able to live a higher quality of life including enjoying relationships with significant others.

As we heal, we let-go of the lost object and attach to new objects. This makes it possible for us to mobilize alternative resources and produce different chemical responses which alter biophysical patterns. When this happens, unhealthy physical signs and symptoms diminish while healthy signs increase. Our work with people who have hypertension (Erickson & Swain, 1990) provides an example. We did not cure hypertension, but we did help people heal. As they found alternative ways to handle their stress, they were able to move into more harmonious, synchronous mind-body relationships. Their blood pressure readings decreased and they perceived themselves healthier.

> Healing is always necessary following a loss. We have multiple real, threatened, or perceived losses as we travel through life. Losses threaten our ability to be holistic, to be integrated, body, mind, and spirit. We need to work through the grieving process, so we can resolve our losses and recover our holistic abilities.

It is important to remember what was said in Chapter 3 about mind, body, and spirit relationships and the importance of recognizing this as an issue of understanding, not of fault and blame. When we understand possible linkages between loss and stored memories, we cannot blame people for their health conditions. People do the best they can under their circumstances. There is no fault and no blame. There is just understanding. The more we understand, the more we can help people find their way. That is my purpose.

WHAT TO DO?

This book, about helping others become the most they can be, was written for health care providers. But, we need to take care of ourselves first. You might say it is difficult to charge the battery of another person if our own is run down! We need to understand what interferes with our natural ability to heal ourselves when needed and how to apply this knowledge to the practice of nursing

This section, then, is dedicated to what we can do to help ourselves *be and become*. To that effect, I have drawn from Deepak Chopra's work, which has inspired me for years. You may wish to explore some of his writings for personal enrichment. In the interim, I offer you my application of his work, drawn specifically from his book, *The Seven Spiritual Laws of Success*. While I may have taken a little license with his ideas, originally written to help people learn how to acquire affluence, it seems to me that these ideas apply to the *affluence* of everyday life and particularly to those times when we work as professionals.

The Law of Pure Potentiality

Earlier, I said *healing creates changes in the holistic person, changes that move us closer to Self-discovery, self-actualization, and fulfillment of Life Purpose.* This implies that healing entails becoming aware of our core and discovering who we are as holistic beings. When we connect with our core, or our spirit, it helps us better understand our Self, for that is the source of knowing or consciousness.

Landis talks about it like this:

> *The human spirit, although empirically indefinable, is conceptualized as our inner-most resource (Ellison, 1993). Within the spirit are two dimensions—a vertical component representing a religious orientation related to God or a higher power and a horizontal component representing an existential orientation related to sense of purpose and satisfaction in life. The vertical and horizontal dimensions are interrelated, bi-directional, and interact together to form our human spiritual component* (Stoll, 1989) (Landis, 1997, p.74).

Landis goes on to discuss the nature of the spirit, suggesting that the two dimensions need to not only interface, but to align with one another. She claims,

"Humans need to experience God or a higher power as the source of meaning and purpose for life, love, forgiveness, and hope (Fish & Shelly, 1978) (Landis, 1997, p. 74). She adds that

> *The healing experience, like any experience is difficult to explain. However, it is an active process of mobilizing one's inner resources toward achieving balance and wholeness. Thus everything necessary for healing lies within the human person....My position is that the human spirit is the source of our healing and the innate spiritual force is the energy that permeates our psychosocial and biophysical components promoting their healing and wholeness* (p. 76).

I believe that healing is central to nursing. Yet, many nurses claim they do not have time to facilitate healing, they are busy *doing what they have to do*. Deepak Chopra (1996) offers one way to think about this. He states, "When you discover your essential nature and know who you really are, *in that knowing itself* is the ability to fulfill any dream you have, because you are the eternal possibility, the immeasurable potential of all that was, is and will be." He goes on to say that *unity* is what connects everything and everyone; there is no separation between you and this energy field (p. 10).

I believe the most important thing we can *do* for others is to uncover our Self so we can learn how to draw from the Universe. When we learn how to do this, there is no limit to our potential. Our lack of understanding of our own potential interferes with our ability to help people heal.

> *The first spiritual law of success is the Law of Pure Potentiality. This law is based on the fact that we are, in our essential state, pure consciousness. Pure consciousness is pure potentiality; it is the field of all possibilities and infinite creativity. Pure consciousness is our spiritual essence....This is our essential nature* (Deepak Chopra, 1996, p. 9).

The Law of Giving and Receiving

By nature, humans want to be holistic with integrated mind, body, and spirit. Most nurses I've talked with agree with this statement, yet they have trouble. They often tell me they are so busy *doing* what they *have* to do, they don't have time to think about helping people heal, or *find their Self,* and all that stuff! Furthermore, they are just too tired. Nursing is hard physical work; it depletes resources, doesn't pay much, and takes a lot to keep up with the technical aspect of nursing care.

I understand this position, but I do not accept it as valid. My counter statement is that as busy nurses, we don't have time to just *do. We have to learn how to use our energy to create heart-to-heart connections using Presence and Intent.* If we can do this, we can facilitate healing because healing comes naturally. I think we waste a lot of time focusing on the wrong thing. What we focus on is where our energy will be sent, so we would be better off focusing on the human rather than the parts. When we learn how to use ourselves as a bridge between the Universe and our clients, we will discover why people sometimes talk about *angels of mercy.* Our spiritual being has an unlimited potential, a potential to help others heal.

Furthermore, the universe is dynamic. When we give, we will receive. I suspect some of you are saying, "Oh, yeah, that old cliché! Well, you just don't know what it is like working a 12 hour shift in an acute care setting." My response to you is, "Yes I do. I've done it." I think the problem many nurses face is that they don't really understand the concept of universal exchange. They give, and give, and give until they are exhausted. What they have forgotten is to receive! We must use ourselves as conduits of energy, as receivers of universal energy if we are to be able to send energy. This is why so many people write about nurses learning how to take care of themselves. It is basic to holistic nursing. However, we cannot just take care of ourselves by exercising 3 days a week, doing yoga 4 days a week, meditating every morning, praying at meals or bedtime, and so forth. We have to learn the basic rule—we have to be able to reenergize ourselves while we are giving. When we do this, we will still get physically tired, but we will not become spiritually or emotionally drained. Chopra (1996) says we should think about this constant energy exchange like a circulation system. When the blood stops flowing, it stagnates or clots. Energy exchange is like that too. When we forget to receive, we stagnate, and get plugged up. He states, "Every relationship is one of give and take. Giving engenders receiving and receiving engenders giving" (p. 29).

As health care providers, we have to learn how to give and receive even as we interact with others. Through our experiences we will be energized and learn about our Self.

> The second spiritual law of success is the Law of Giving. This law could be called the Law of Giving and Receiving, because the universe operates through dynamic exchange. Nothing is static. Your body is in dynamic and constant exchange with the body of the universe; your mind is dynamically interacting with the mind of the cosmos; your energy is an expression of cosmic energy (Chopra, 1996, p. 27).

The Law of Cause and Effect

As nurses become more influential in health care and take on more advanced practice roles, it is more important than ever for us to proactively set our intent. Our energy follows our intent. When our practice focuses on what we do, our energy follows. It doesn't connect with the whole person, but the part we are attending to. If our focus is on diagnosing and treating a disease, condition, ailment or even health exercises, then that will be where our energy interacts. This does not help people heal. In fact, it sometimes reinforces maladaptive coping patterns.

We make many decisions every day about what we will attend to, where we will *put* our energy, how we will live the next few moments. Many of these decisions are stimulated by what is happening to us at the time. We need to remember that what is happening to us at any second in time is because of decisions we made in the past. Chopra (1996) says, "Whether you like it or not, everything that is happening at this moment is a result of the choices you've made in the past. Unfortunately, a lot of us make choices unconsciously, and therefore, we don't think they are choices—and yet, they are" (p. 40). This is because our choice to set our intent (or choice to not set it!) is a decision.

As healthcare providers, the more we learn to set our intent on nurturing, facilitating, and promoting the well-being of others, the more we will discover ways to make it happen. Sometimes, it may be because we are in a given spot at a given time. Other times, opportunities will come to us when least expected. The more we practice this, the better we get. What we choose to do with our lives is our business, but we have to remember all things are connected.

> The third spiritual law of success is the Law of Karma. "Karma" is both action and the consequence of that action; it is cause and effect simultaneously, because every action generates a force of energy that returns to us in like kind...Therefore, karma implies the action of conscious choice-making (p. 39). Transcend Karma by 1) paying your debt, 2) transform karma by asking, what can I learn from this experience, and 3) transcend by connecting with true Self, the Spirit (p. 45-46).

The Law of Least Effort

Chopra says, "Nature's intelligence functions effortlessly, frictionlessly, spontaneously. It is non-linear; it is intuitive, holistic, and nourishing. And when you are in harmony with nature, when you are established in the knowledge of your true Self, you can make use of the Law of Least Effort" (pp. 54-55). He describes this by discussing nature "at work," saying, "Grass doesn't try to grow," it just does. "Flowers don't try to bloom," they just do. "Fish don't try to swim," they just do. He tells us we need to let ourselves follow that which is natural. He states when we seek power over others, we waste energy, because it is not natural to have power over others. He asserts that nature "is held together by the energy of love" (pp. 53-55).

He goes on to say that our body "can generate, store, and expend energy." When we free up our energy to be creative, we can create whatever we want. He has identified three components to the Law of Least Effort. The first is acceptance of the moment. We need to learn that we are doing what we are supposed to do at the moment, and we are responsible for finding meaning in that moment. The second is learning to assume responsibility by not blaming anyone or anything for our lives, not even ourselves. Instead, we need to learn to experience the moment as an opportunity to learn and grow. The third component of the law relates to defenselessness. That is we have to learn we don't have to convince anyone of our point of view, our way of thinking. He states that learning to be defenseless in respect to our way of viewing the world frees up energy that is reserved for the "fight." When we learn to think like this our energy can follow the natural path of the Universe and we all benefit.

> *The fourth spiritual law of success is the Law of Least Effort. This law is based on the fact that nature's intelligence functions with effortless ease and abandoned carefreeness. This is the principle of least action, of no resistance. This is therefore, the principle of harmony and love. When we learn this lesson from nature, we easily fulfill our desires* (p. 53).

The Law of Intention and Desire

As health care providers, we usually don't have opportunities to follow our clients' progress. This is difficult for some because we want immediate feedback. When someone has a sore throat and takes antibiotics, they are usually better the next day. We can see the immediate results. We have to learn to trust ourselves, understand who we are at the core, and be willing to discover our Self and our Life Purpose. When we do that, it is easy to know that our intent to help people will influence their well-being, and in return we will grow and become more fully what we want to be.

Chopra (1996) states it like this, "Attention energizes, and intention transforms. Whatever you put your attention on will grow stronger in your life. Whatever you take your attention away from will wither, disintegrate, and disappear. Intention, on the other hand, triggers transformation of energy and information. Intention organizes its own fulfillment" (p. 70). He goes on to say, "Intention is the real power behind desire. Intent alone is very powerful, because intent is desire without attachment to the outcome. Desire alone is weak, because desire in most people is attention with attachment" (p. 73). Later, when discussing how to have intent without being attached to the outcome, he states, "Attachment…is based on fear and insecurity—and the need for security is based on not knowing the true Self" (p. 84).

> *The fifth spiritual law of success is the Law of Intention and Desire. This law is based on the fact that energy and information exist everywhere in nature. In fact, at the level of the quantum field, there is nothing other than energy and information. The quantum field is just another label for the field of pure consciousness or pure potentiality. And this quantum field is influenced by intention and desire* (p. 67).

The key here is to learn how to have intent without being attached to the outcome. Frequently, we think we know what is best. We pray for divine intervention, but just as we want it. This idea of having intent, but without attachment to the outcome is very difficult. We have to learn we might not always understand the way of the Universe, but there is order, and things will work out in a way that is best for all involved. For example, when people get sick, their loved ones often pray for recovery. What if they prayed for comfort and wisdom instead? Or what if we needed help with a client and asked for wisdom and guidance rather than an extra pair of hands! We need to learn how to have intent and desire, without having detailed expectations of the fruition of our intent. We also need to learn how to recognize the fruition of our intent. This is what helps us learn about our Self and our Life Purpose.

The Law of Detachment

The Law of Detachment builds on the Law of Intention. This means it is important for us to create our dreams, to have desires, to have intent, but we have to learn how to let our life take its own course. According to Chopra, "detachment is based on the unquestioning belief in the power of your true Self" while attachment is "based on fear and insecurity." To detach from the outcome means we trust our Self will guide us in making choices, following the best pathway, choosing relationships, and so forth. He also advises that when we choose attachment, we will chase our dreams all our life and never find them because they take us away from our Self. On the other hand, when we learn to detach from the outcome, uncertainty enters, and this creates opportunities for creativity, which is boundless. Creativity comes from our connection to the Universe.

> *The sixth spiritual law of success is the Law of Detachment. The Law of Detachment says that in order to acquire anything in the physical universe, you have to relinquish your attachment to it. This doesn't mean you give up the intention to create your desire. You don't give up the desire. You give up your attachment to the result* (p. 83).

The Law of Purpose in Life

The last of Chopra's spiritual laws for success addresses finding a purpose in life. According to Chopra, there are three components to this principle or law as he calls it. The first component says that each of us is here to discover our true Self, to find out on our own that we are spiritual beings who have taken manifestation in physical form. The second component is to learn to express our unique talents, to be fully who we have the capability to be. The third component is to find ways to service humanity (pp. 97-99). He argues that by learning these three we will find meaning in our lives and understand why we are here.

> *The seventh spiritual law of success is the Law of Dharma or Life Purpose. Dharma is a Sanskrit word that means "purpose in life." The Law of Dharma says that we have taken manifestation in physical form to fulfill a purpose. The field of pure potentiality is divinity in its essence and the divine takes human form to fulfill a purpose* (p. 95).

CONCLUSIONS

I started this book with a chapter describing my thoughts and beliefs about our Reason for Being, Life Purpose, and finding Meaning in Life. I hoped the reader would identify with some aspect of that chapter and realize that as health care providers we have the best of all possibilities. We have chosen careers or pathways that make it possible for us to interact with others in ways most people are unable to do in the course of everyday life. We are privileged to have opportunities, day after day, year after year, to learn about ourselves through our interactions with others and help others learn about themselves. This is a blessing.

Chopra (2000) said,

> *Everything that we experience as material reality is born in an invisible realm beyond space and time, a realm revealed by science to consist of energy and information. This invisible source of all that exists is not an empty void but the womb of creation itself. Something creates and organizes this energy. It turns the chaos of quantum soup into stars, galaxies, rain forests, human beings, and our own thoughts, emotions, memories, and desires* (pp. 1-2).

Each of us has to decide the extent to which our work is what helps us learn about ourselves. Last night I listened to Jeffrey Brown interview Art Buchwald (Jim Lehrer, March 29, 2006) regarding his last thoughts. Approximately one month ago Art Buchwald's physicians told him he would die within two weeks if he didn't start renal dialysis. Buchwald decided against dialysis and checked into a hospice for the duration. Last night he was laughing, joking, and reviewing his life and life work. When asked what he hoped to be remembered for, he commented that the better question was "What am I doing here in the first place!" Then he proceeded to say he hoped people would remember him for his ability to make people laugh. What a worthy Life Purpose!

But finding our Soul-work is not easy. Sometimes we need help. As stated by Chopra (2000),

> *God has managed the amazing feat of being worshiped and invisible at the same time. Millions of people might describe him as a white-bearded father figure sitting on a throne in the sky, but none could claim to be an eyewitness. Although it doesn't seem possible to offer a*

single fact about the Almighty that would hold up in court of law, somehow the vast majority of people believe in God—as many as 96 percent, according to some polls. This reveals a huge gap between belief and what we call everyday reality. We need to heal this gap (p.1).

Chapters 2 and 3 provided information needed to understand how the Modeling and Role-Modeling helps you, in human form, draw closer to bridging the gap of believing and knowing. We wanted to provide information you could use in everyday life, information needed in everyday *reality*.

Chapters 4-8 were also designed with this in mind. We wanted to help you learn more about the nature of the human form so that you can think about your work more purposefully. Finally, Chapters 9-14 were designed to help you learn *how to do your work while being your own unique Self.*

> Without understanding, life is shallow—there is no purpose. Without meaning, life is empty—there is no reason for being.

We've now come full circle. We are at the end of the book and the beginning of the rest of your life and have just talked again about Life Purpose. I hope you were able to learn something about yourself and your chosen profession. I also hope we have contributed to your understanding of what lies in the gap between beliefs and reality. Only you can choose what you believe and what it means to have those beliefs. Only you can decide what the meaning of life is for you. I wish you well.

A wonderful realization will be the day you realize that you are unique in all the world. There is nothing that is an accident. You are a special combination for a purpose—and don't let them tell you otherwise...You are that combination so that you can do what it is essential for you to do. Don't ever believe that you have nothing to contribute. The world is an incredible unfulfilled tapestry, and only you can fulfill that tiny space that is yours.

Buscaglia, L. (1983). *Living, Loving, and Learning.* New York: First Ballantine Books, p. 117.

ENDNOTES

[1] He was one of several people I worked with as a part of a research project designed to help people with diabetes. The Primary Investigator of that project was Mary Ann Swain.

[2] As an example, I have presented to large audiences of people and later received letters from individuals stating that what I said to them changed their lives. *One person I particularly remember is a physician who looked me up at a conference, handed me a letter, and disappeared. In his note, he told me that based on what I had said to him, he had changed his practice, moved to another city, knew for the first time in his life who he really was, and was very happy! He thanked me profusely, stating that my comments will always be with him. I do not remember our specific interaction, I just remember him asking a question in an audience of over 200 people.* While there might have been 200 people in that audience, if we connect with an individual heart-to-heart we can initiate healing.

Another interesting example of this situation happened many years ago when I was speaking at a STTI Theory Conference about Modeling and Role-Modeling. *Again, a lady asked a question, which I answered with a heart-to-heart connection. After I finished speaking, I asked for questions and this lady stood up, came straight up to the stage, and as she did she started telling me she now knew why she couldn't have a normal sexual relationship with her husband. Fortunately, for both of us, Carolyn Kinney was with me, so I was able to turn the QA session over and deal with this lady's needs. She told me a wonderful story about the beginning of her life, one that she had never known until she heard me talk, and then suddenly, she knew. She was astounded with what she was telling me and needed help thinking about it. I worked with her for about 15 minutes. Nearly 2 years later, she saw me again at a conference. I did not recognize her. She reminded me of the incident, and then told me she had confirmed her story, and no one was more surprised than she, but now she was happy and as normal as could be. She wanted to heal, needed help getting started, and then just took off.* That's how it often works. And she's not alone. There are many other such stories. So, when nurses say they don't have time, I just say, "That's because you want to fix people. Let it go!"

[3] While many nurses might argue that pain is biophysical, application of the content presented in Chapters 2 and 3 indicates pain is an aggregate of mind, body, and spirit interactions. I like to think of the difference between physical pain and psychic pain. Jean Johnson's early work showed that people are able to separate the two when they are informed there is a difference. My experience has shown me that not only are they able to separate the two, but almost every time they do, psychic pain is greater than physical pain. Yet, we commonly use medications to treat this pain, medications that dull the senses, making it possible for health care providers to avoid the real issues.

[4] If you've forgotten the difference between these two, you might want to review that section of Chapter 1. Briefly, sense-of-self is how we see ourself based on the perceptions of others, while Essence of Self is our view of our true Self at the Soul level.

[5] Sometimes, maladaptive coping is the only option. It is the best of all possibilities. For example, someone who has lost control of the muscles usually used to breathe because of a disease (such as polio), might develop the use of accessory muscles to breathe. This is better than not breathing! While this isn't the usual example of maladaptive coping, it is an example, since the stressor (need to breathe), in the best of situations, would stimulate the normal breathing mechanisms, but due to an inability to do so, alternatives have to be used.

[6] We learn fast! What works one time is usually used again and again, unless we consciously change the response.

[7] When working with someone like this, it is important to sort out the difference between those who have secondary gain, from those who don't. Those with secondary gain have learned that being sick is an acceptable way to get affiliation needs met. It is helpful to understand these

dynamics, because you know there is a deep need to be protected, safe, and cared about underlying secondary gain. Often those with secondary gain present themselves as strong people who don't need other people. They just "happened" to get sick. It requires considerable work to rebuild Trust before Autonomy can be initiated. I didn't see secondary gain in this lady. She emphasized the relationship between being asked to do something for someone else on her own and being stressed (or overwhelmed). This is more consistent with insecure attachment (Trust Stage) and difficulty in Autonomy.

[8] Her history included numerous major surgeries and illnesses starting with an appendectomy, and including hysterectomy, cholecystectomy, pulmonary emboli, and others.

[9] A sitting hen is one who has laid a number of eggs, and was trying to hatch them. Sitting hens are very protective of their eggs and will attack anyone who tries to remove them.

[10] Remember malingering is normal for this age group. But, when it becomes a way of coping, patterns are created that can become a way of coping across the lifetime.

[11] Remember her trouble started when she walked across a barnyard (which is field-like), to the barn (which was far away), was pecked by the chickens (got sick) and felt unprotected, unsafe. To help her learn to take risks, make decisions, and develop and demonstrate some autonomy, she needed to feel safe, protected, and connected. I also wanted her to reframe her thinking about her ability to get out of the house.

[12] Hall talks about a caring relationship and states, "Caring is not an action, per se, but a state of mind and an attitude" (p. 57). In the last part of her book, Hall talks about "Healing in Action" and briefly discusses the "Wisdom of Caring" stating, "Wisdom surfaces when involvement overrides the reaction to create distance from patients in order to avoid pain....Clearly the way that we face up to the suffering we encounter, including our own, can lead to highest wisdom or lowest forms of despair" (p. 71). She provides direction for the nurse, so burnout can be avoided. Hall's final chapters provide guidelines and exercises that facilitate nurses in developing the art of nursing. While many of Hall's suggestions have been presented in this book, they are presented in a different context. They are concise and provide an opportunity to focus on the act and implications of the art of healing.

[13] I believe the art of nursing is the application of science within the context of the uniqueness of the human being. That is, we use the science to help people. How we use the science varies by individual, depending on their world-view, likes, dislikes, and cultural considerations.

[14] I recognize the extensive use of the word "should" in this section. Usually, I say we "Shouldn't should on ourselves," but in this case, maybe it is the best word possible.

[15] It should be noted that a core group of physicians, who believed that holism is central to the practice of medicine, created the American Holistic Medical Association in 1978.

[16] AHNA can be contacted through their website: www.ahna.org

[17] The website is ahncc@flash.net

[18] An interesting way to learn this is to actively and purposefully imagine an energy field around yourself, running through you, coming in through either your head or feet, and moving out through your hands toward another person. You need not look directly at the other person. You may, if you wish, but do it unobtrusively, so the other doesn't perceive you are staring. Do not say anything, just watch the other person, and feel the energy flow. Then stop the flow and feel the difference in yourself. Try this several times; then, ask the other person if they noticed any difference in their warmth.

[19] This text was originally written several days ago. Today, I returned to the same place. There were only two of us in the room and about 25 pieces of equipment. A few moments after I walked in and starting exercising, this lady arrived. She promptly came to a piece of equipment one over from mine, looked at me, and smiled using most of her face muscles. She greeted me as though we were old friends and proceeded to exercise, talking as she went. After about 5-8 minutes, I turned away and talked with the other person in the room, on the opposite side of me. After about 3 minutes, I looked back and she was breathing heavily. I commented that it looked like she was

working pretty hard. She breathed shallowly and said she couldn't breathe very well. I suggested she slow down just a little, and see how that worked. Again, I sent her energy and stayed focused on her. Her breathing changed, she continued her exercising, started talking and continued for the next 20 minutes without difficulty. When I finished my routine, she came to me and said, "Can you believe it, a woman told me she'd give me $30.00 if I quit smoking!" I responded the same as I had the last time, indicating this was a personal thing, that it was between "you and yourself" and added that she knew what she needed to take care of herself. As we left, I patted her on the back, telling her I'd see her "the next time."

[20] When I checked the consent form, she had been advised that a lumpectomy was the plan, but if the pathology report so indicated, a total resection would be done.

[21] When I talk about this issue, I'm always reminded of a scene in a movie starring Alan Alda. He and his wife and another couple are in the backyard enjoying a barbeque. The men were in Vietnam together. Everyone is laughing, having a good time, and then the topic changes and war stories emerge. At first, there is laughter, and then it gradually becomes more sober. Within a short time, Alda goes inside and starts to cry. When his wife comes and puts her arms around him, he tells her about a tragic incident in the war. She is shocked, comments he had never mentioned it before, and she had never seen him cry before. She asks him why. He simply states, "I was afraid if I ever started crying, I would never stop." This is the classic feeling people express about long standing losses. They are too painful to talk about.

[22] This is another lesson I learned from my father-in-law. Years ago when I asked his advice regarding a client, he gave me a homework assignment. I was to read a fiction book, chapter by chapter. After reading the first chapter, I was to predict what would happen in the next, then read that chapter and see where I was correct and where I had made mistakes. It took a long time, but when I was finished, I thought I was pretty good. He then assigned me to read another book. This time, I had to read the last chapter first, predict what came before, and figure out where I'd made my mistakes. By the time I finished this book, I understood. There is no such thing as just a moment in time; it is always part of a bigger picture. Since that life-learning experience, I have never been able to think of a client without considering their context.

[23] I worked with this cardiologist for about one year when doing research with people who have hypertension.

BIBLIOGRAPHY

Chapter 1

Chopra, D. (2000). *How to know God: The soul's journey into the mystery of mysteries.* New York: Three Rivers Press.

Chopra, D. (2004). *The book of secrets: Unlocking the hidden dimension of your life.* New York: Harmony Books.

Erickson, H. (1976). Identification of states of coping utilizing physiological and psychological data. Master's Thesis, The University of Michigan.

Erickson, H. (1988). Modeling and role modeling: Ericksonian approaches with physiological problems. In J. Zeig, & S. Langton (Eds.), *Ericksonian psychotherapy: The state of the art.*

Erickson, H., & Swain, M.A. (1982). A model for assessing potential adaptation to stress. *Research in Nursing and Health* pp. 93-101.

Erickson, H. C., Tomlin, E. M., & Swain, M. A. P. (1983). *Modeling and role modeling: A theory and paradigm for nursing.* Englewood Cliffs, NJ: Prentice-Hall. Second-eighth printing, 1988-2005; EST Co: Austin, TX.

Frankl, V. (1984). *Man's Search for Meaning.* (Revised and updated). New York: Washington Square Press, Simon & Schuster Inc.

Freidman, M. and Rosenman, R. (1964). Predictive study of coronary disease: The western collaborative group study. *Journal of American Medical Association, 189, 15-25.*

Keegan, L. & Dossey, B. (1998). *Profiles of nurse healers.* New York: Delmar Publishers.

Kinlein, M.L. (1977). *Independent nursing practice with clients.* New York: J. B. Lippincott Company.

Kinney, C. (1996). Transcending breast cancer: Reconstructing one's self. *Issues in Mental Health Nursing,* 17:201-216.

Lesser, E. (1999). *The seeker's guide: Making your life a spiritual adventure.* New York: Villard.

Lindberg, J., Hunter, M., & Kruszewski, A. (1983). *Introduction to person-centered nursing.* Philadelphia: J.B. Lippincott Company.

Maslow, A.H. (1963). Further notes on being psychology. *Journal of Humanistic Psychoanalysis,* III, 120-35.

Maslow, A.H. (1982). *The Farther Reaches of Human Nature.* New York: Penguin Books.

Moore, T. (1992). *Care of the soul: A guide for cultivating depth and sacredness in everyday life.* New York: Harper-Collins Publishers.

Orem, D. (1971). *Nursing concepts of practice.* New York: McGraw Hill.

Zukav, G. (1989). *The seat of the soul.* New York :Simon & Schuster, Inc.

Chapter 2

About electromagnetic fields (n.d.). Retrieved November 2, 2005, from *The world health organization.* http://www.who/int/peh-emf

Alligood, M. R., & Tomey, A. M. (2002*). Nursing theory utilization and application,* (2nd ed.). St. Louis: Mosby.

Anderson, M. (2005). Is jiggling vacuum the origin of mass? *New Scientist, 8(2520).*

Bache, C. M. (2000). *Dark night, early dawn.* Albany: State University of New York Press.

Bell, J. (1987). *Speakable and unspeakable in quantum mechanics.* Cambridge: Cambridge University Press.

Benor, D. (April 24, 2005). *Wholistic healing research.* Retrieved March 4, 2006, from http://www.wholistichealingresearch.com

Benor, D. Editors Musings. (September, 2001, Vol.1, No. 1). *The International Journal of Healing and Caring*—On Line Wholistic Healing Publications. Retrieved March 4, 2006 from http://www.IJHC.org

Braud, W., and Anderson, R. (1998). *Transpersonal research methods for the social sciences: Honoring human experience.* Thousand Oaks, CA: Sage.

Brennan, B. (1987). *Hands of light: A guide to healing through the human energy field.* New York: Bantam Press.

Brennan, B. (1994). *Light emerging: the journey of personal healing.* New York: Bantam.

Brofman, M. (2003). *Anything can be healed.* Scotland: Findhorn Press.

Bohm (1980). *Wholeness and the implicate order.* London: Routledge & Kegan Paul.

Byrd, R. C. (1989). Positive therapeutic effects of intercessory prayer in a coronary care unit population. *Southern Medical Journal,* 81(7), 826-829.

Bruyere, R. (1989). *Wheels of Light: A Study of the Chakras.* Sierra Madre, Calif: Bon Productions.

Bruyere, R. (1994). *Wheels of Light: A Study of the Chakras.* Arcata, Calif: Bon Productions.

Chopra, D. (1989). *Quantum healing: Exploring the frontiers of mind-body medicine.* New York: Bantam.

Chopra, D. (1990). *Quantum healing: Exploring the frontiers of mind-body medicine.* (2nd ed.). New York: Bantam.

Chopra, D. (1992). *Ageless body, timeless mind: The quantum alternative to growing old.* New York: Bantam.

Chopra, D. (1994). *The seven spiritual laws of success.* San Rafael, Calif: New World Library and Amber-Allen Publishing.

Chopra, D. (2000). *How to know God: The soul's journey into the mystery of mysteries.* New York: Three Rivers Press.

Chopra, D. (2004). *The book of secrets: Unlocking the hidden dimension of your life.* New York: Harmony Books.

Clarke, A. (1997). *3001: The final odyssey.* Toronto: Del Rey Book.

Dale, C. (2003). *New chakra healing.* St. Paul: Llewellyn Pub.

Dossey, L. (1992). But, is it energy? Reflections on consciousness, healing and the new paradigm. *The International Society for the Study of Subtle Energies and Energy Medicine. Vol. 3 (3).*

Dossey, L. *(1993). Healing words: The power of prayer and the practice of medicine.* San Francisco: HarperSanFrancisco.

Dossey, L. (1999). *Reinventing medicine: Beyond mind-body to a new ear of healing.* San Francisco: HarperSanFrancisco.

Dossey, L. (2002). Samueli conference on definitions and standards in healing research: Working definitions and terms. *Alternative Therapies,* 9(2), A10 -A 12.

Dyer, W. (1989). *You'll see it when you believe it: The way to your personal transformation.* New York: Avon Books.

Eden, D & Feinstein, D. (1998). *Energy medicine.* New York: Penguin Books.

Einstein, A. (1972). Quoted in *New York Post.* November 28, 1972.

Emoto, M. (2004). *The hidden messages in water.* Hillsboro, OR: Beyond Words Publishing.

Erickson, H. C., Tomlin, E. M., & Swain, M. A. P. (1983). *Modeling and role-modeling: A theory and paradigm for nursing.* Englewood Cliffs, NJ: Prentice-Hall Second-eighth printing, 1988-2005; EST Co: Austin, TX.

Gerber, R. (1988). *Vibrational medicine.* Santa Fe, N.M: Bear & Company.

Gerber, R. (2000). *Vibrational medicine for the 21st Century.* New York, NY: HarperCollins.

Gerber, R. (2001). *A practical guide to vibrational medicine; energy healing and spiritual transformation.* New York, New York: Quill, HarperCollins Publishers.

Grad, B. (1965). Some biological effects of laying-on of hands: a review of experiments and implications. *Pastoral Psychology,* 21: 19-26.

Grayson, S. (1997). *Spiritual healing.* New York: Simon & Schuster.

Green, B. (2003). *The elegant universe.* New York: Vintage Books, Random House, Inc.

Gordon, R. (2002). *Quantum-touch: The power to heal.* (Rev. ed.). Berkeley, CA: North Atlantic Books.

Gupta, M. (2001). *Healing through reiki.* Delhi: Pustak Mahal.

Haisch, B., Rueda, A., & Puthoff, H. (1994). Inertia as a zero-point field Lorentz force. *Physical Review A,* 49(2):678-94.

Haisch, B., Rueda, A., & Putoff, H. (1997). Physics of the zero point field: implications for inertia, gravitation and mass. *Speculations in Science and Technology.* 20: 99-114.

Hunt, V. (1995). *Infinite mind: The science of human vibrations.* Malibu, Calif: Malibu.

Jonas, W. (2002). The science behind healing. In B. Horrigan (Ed.) *Voices of integrated healing.* St. Louis: Churchill Livingstone.

Jones, J. E., & Bearley, W. L. (2000). *Facilitating team development: A view from the field, 2001.* Sydney Australia: AimBooks.

Kargulla. B., & Kunz, G. (1989). *The chakras and the human energy fields.* New York: Quest.

Lidell, L., Thomas, S., Cooke, B., & Porter, A. (1984). *The book of massage: The complete step-by-step guide to eastern and western techniques.* Simon & Schuster, Inc.: N.Y.

Lilly, S., & Lilly, S. (2004). *Healing with crystals and chakra energies.* London: Anness Publishing Ltd.

McKivergin and Daubenmire (March, 1994). The healing process of presence. *Journal of Holistic Nursing,* 12(1), 65-81.

McTaggart, L. (2002). *The field: The quest for the secret force of the universe.* New York: HarperCollins.

Oka, R., Gortner, S., Stotts, N., & Haskell, W. (1996). Predictors of physical activity in patients with chronic heart failure secondary to either ischemic or idiopathic dilated cardiomyopathy. *American Journal of Cardiology,* 77(2), 159-163.

Oschman, J. (1990). Bioelectromagnetic communications. BEMI Currents, *The Newsletter of the Bio-Electro-Magnetics Institute,* 2(2): 11-14.

Oschman, J. (1997). What is healing? part 3: silent pulses. *Journal of Bodywork and Movement Therapies*, 1(3), 179-94.

Oschman, J. (2000). *Energy medicine: The scientific basis*. Edinburgh: Churchill Livingstone.

Oschman, J. (2003). *Energy medicine in therapeutics and human performance*. Amsterdam, the Netherlands: Butterworth Heinemann.

Motoyama, H. (2001). *Theories of the chakras: Bridge to higher consciousness*. New Delhi, New Age Books, p. 291.

Napier, T. (2004). *Facing fiction with PhACT* (n.d.). Retrieved March 6, 2006, from http://www.phact.org/terns.html

Page, C. (2000). *Frontiers of health for healing to wholeness*. Essex, UK; C.W. Daniel Company.

Palmer, L. D. (2005, April). The soundtrack of healing. *Spirituality & Health*. 8:2. 42-47.

Pearsall, P. (1998). *The heart's code*. New York, NY: Broadway Books.

Pert, C. (2002). *Molecules of emotion: The science behind mind-body medicine*. Schribner, New York: NY.

Pert, C. (2003). *Molecules of emotion: the science behind mind-body medicine*. Schribner, New York: NY.

Puthoff, H. (2003). *On the feasibility of converting vacuum electromagnetic energy to useful form*. Paper presented at International Workshop on the Zeropoint Electromagnetic Field. Cuernavaca, Mexico. March 29-April 2, 1993.

Quinn, J. (1989). Healing: the emergence of the right relationship. In R. Carlson & B. Shields (Eds.), *Healers and healing*. (pp. 139-144). Putnam: New York.

Rossi, E. (1986). *The Psychobiology of mind-body healing: New concepts in therapeutics hypnosis* New York: W.W. Norton & Company.

Russek, L., and Schwartz, G. (1996). 1996 energy cardiology: a dynamical energy systems approach for integrating conventional and alternative medicine. *Advances: The Journal of Mind-Body Health,* 12 (4): 4-24.

Sarter, B. (2002). *Evolutionary healing*. New York: Jones and Bartlett Publishers, Inc.

Sheldrake, R. (1999). *Dogs that Know When Their Owners are Coming Home*. New York, NY: Crown.

Slater, V. E. (2005). Energetic healing. In B. Dosssey, L. Keegan, & C. Guzetta, *Holistic nursing*, (4th ed.). Boston: Jones and Bartlett Publishers.

Stenger, V. (1990). *Physics and psychics: The search for a world beyond the senses*. Amherst, N.Y.: Prometheus Books.

Talbot, M. (1991). *The holographic universe*. New York, NY: HarperCollins.

Sugano, H., Uchida, S., & Kuramoto, I. (2005). A new approach to the studies of subtle energies. *The International Society for the Study of Subtle Energies and Energy Medicine, Vol. 5*, (2).

Targ, R. & Karta, J. (1999). *Miracles of mind: Exploring nonlocal consciousness and spiritual healing*. Novato, Calif.: New World Library.

Todaro-Franceschi, V. (1999). *The enigma of energy*. New York: the Crossroad Publishing Company.

Trivieri, L. (2001). *The American holistic medical association guide to holistic health*. New York: John Wiley & Sons, Inc.

Tomey, A. M., & Alligood, M. R. (2002). *Nursing theorists and their work*. (5th ed.). St. Louis: Mosby.

Watson, J. (2005). *Caring science as sacred science.* Philadelphia: FA Davis.

Wang Chong, (AD 27-97). *Lung-Heng, Part I, philosophical essays of Wang Ch'ung* (Alfred Forke , Trans.). Luzac, London. 1907, p. 11.

Watson, J. (1999). *Nursing: human science and human care: A theory of nursing.* New York: National League for Nursing.

Waters, P., & Daubenmire, M. J. (1997) Therapeutic capacity: The critical variance in nursing practice. In P.B. Kritek (Ed), *Reflections on healing: A critical nursing construct.* (pp. 56-68). New York: NLN Press.

Weiss, S. (2002). Kneeling at the axis of creation. In B. Horrigan (Ed), *Voices of integrative healing.* St. Louis: Churchill Livingstone.

Wirth, D. (1990). The effect of non-contact therapeutic touch on the healing rate of full thickness dermal wounds. *The International Society for the Study of Subtle Energies and Energy Medicine.* Vol. 1, No.1.

Wright, L. M. (2005). *Spirituality, suffering, and illness.* Philadelphia: F. A. Davis.

Zukav, G. (1979). *The dancing wu li Masters.* New York: Bantam Books, p. 22.

Chapter 3

Ader, R. (1981). *Psychoneuroimmunology.* New York: Academic Press.

Ader, R., & Cohen, N. (1975). Behaviorally conditioned immunosuppression. *Psychosomatic Medicine, 37(4),* 333-339.

Alexander, F. (1950). *Psychosomatic medicine.* New York: W.W. Norton & Co.

Aspect, A., Dalibard, J., and Roger, G. (1982). Experimental test of Bell's inequalities using time-varying analyzers. *Physics Review Letters, 49,* 1804.

Arenzo-Seisodos F, et. al. HIV blocked by chemokine antagonist. *Nature,* 1996 Oct 3; 383(6599):400.

Blalock, E., Harbour-McMenamin, D., and Smith, E. (1985). Peptide hormones shaped by the neuroendocrine and immunologic systems. *The Journal of Immunology,* 135(2), 858-861.

Bell, J. (1987). *Speakable and unspeakable in quantum mechanics.* Cambridge: Cambridge University Press.

Benor, D. (1990). Survey of spiritual healing research. *Complementary Medical Research, 4 (1),* 9-33.

Benor, D. (1992a). Lessons from spiritual healing research & practice. *The International Society for the Study of Subtle energies and Energy Medicine Journal.* Vol. 3, (1).

Benor, D. (1992b). *Healing research,* Vol.*1.* Deddington, England: Helix Editions Ltd.

Benson, H. (1996). *Timeless healing.* New York: Simon and Schuster.

Benson, H., & Friedman, R. (1996). Harnessing the power of the placebo effect and renaming it 'remembered wellness.' *Annual Review of Medicine, 47,* 193-99.

Bohr, N. (1961*). Atomic theory and the description of nature.* Great Britain: Cambridge at the University Press.

Calabria, M., & Macrae, J. (1994). *Suggestions for thought by Florence Nightingale.* Philadelphia: University of Pennsylvania Press.

Cannon, W. (1932). *The wisdom of the body.* New York: W.W. Norton & Co., Inc.

Capra, F. (1983). *The tao of physics.* Boston: New Science Library.

Chew, G. (1968). 'Bootstrap': A scientific idea? *Science, 161*,762-765.

Childre, D. & Martin, H. (1999). *The heartmath solution.* San Francisco: Harper-Collins Publishers.

Chopra, D. (1990). *Quantum healing: Exploring the frontiers of mind-body medicine.* New York: Bantam.

Chopra, D. (2000). *How to know God: The soul's journey into the mystery of mysteries.* New York: Three Rivers Press.

Chopra, D. (2004). *The book of secrets: unlocking the hidden dimension of your life.* New York: Harmony Books.

d'Aquili, E., & Newberg, A. (1998). The neuropsychological basis of religions, or why God won't go away. *Zygon-The Journal of Religion and Science, 33(2),* 187-201.

Dossey, L. (1993*).* *Healing words.* San Francisco: HarperCollins Publishers.

Dossey, L. (1997). *Be careful what you pray for: You might just get it.* San Francisco: HarperCollins.

Dyer, W. (1989). *You'll see it when you believe it: The way to your personal transformation.* New York: Avon Books.

Einstein, A. (1961). Quoted in M. Capek, *The philosophical impact of contemporary physics.* New Jersey: D.Van Nostrand.

Engel, G. (1962). Anxiety and depression-withdrawal: The primary affects of unpleasure. *International Journal of Psychoanalysis.* 43, 89-97.

Erickson, H., & Swain, M. (1982). A Model for Assessing Potential Adaptation to Stress. *Research in Nursing and Health, 5,* 93-101.

Erickson, H. C., Tomlin, E. M., & Swain, M. A. P. (1983*).* *Modeling and role-modeling: A theory and paradigm for nursing.* Englewood Cliffs, NJ: Prentice-Hall, Second-eighth printing, 1988-2005; EST Co: Austin, TX.

Funkenstein, D., King, S., & Drolette, M. (1957). *Mystery of stress.* Cambridge: Harvard University Press.

Gordon, R. (2002). *Quantum-touch: The power to heal.* (Rev. ed.). Berkeley, CA: North Atlantic Books.

Green, B. (2003). *The elegant universe.* Vintage Books, Random House, Inc. N.Y: N.Y

Grinberg-Zylberbaum, J., Delaflor, M., Attie, L., Goswami, A. (1994). The Einstein-Podolsky-Rosen paradox in the brain: The transferred potential. *Physics Essays,* 7, 4, 422-28.

Haisch, B., Reuda, A., & Puhoff, H.E. (1994). Inertia as a zero-point field Lorentz force. *Physical Review A,* Vol. 49, No. 2, p 678-694.

Herbert, N. (1985). *Quantum reality.* Garden City, N.J.: Anchor Press.

Hughes J, Kosterlitz HW, Leslie FM. Effect of morphine on adrenergic transmission in the mouse vas deferens. Assessment of agonist and antagonist potencies of narcotic analgesics. *British Journal of Pharmacology.* 1975 Mar; 53(3):371–381.

Jahn, B., & Dunne, R. (1987). *Margins of reality.* New York: Harcourt Brace Jovanovich.

Janis, I. (1958). *Psychological stress.* New York: John Wiley & Sons.

Kaye, J., Morton, J., Bowcutt, M., Maupin, D. (2000). Stress, depression, and psychoneuroimmunology. *Journal of Neuroscience Nursing, 32 (2),* 93-100.

Kunz, D. (1991). *The personal aura.* Wheaton, IL: Quest Books.

Lesser, E. (1999). *The seeker's guide: Making your life a spiritual adventure.* New York : Villard.

Matthews, D., & Larson, D. (1995). *The faith factor: An annotated bibliography of clinical research on spiritual subjects:* Vol. III. Rockville, MD: National Institute for Health Care Research.

McTaggart, L. (2002). *The field: The quest for the secret force of the universe.* New York: HarperCollins.

Nichols, L. (2000). *The soul as healer: Lessons in Affirmation, Visualization, and Inner Power.* St. Paul, MN: Llewellyn Publications.

Pert, C. (1986). The wisdom of the receptors. *Advances* 3, No 3.

Pert, C. (1997). *Molecules of emotion. The science behind mind-body medicine.* New York: Scribner.

Pert, C. (2003a). *Molecules of emotion. The science behind mind-body medicine.* (First trade book). New York: Scribner.

Pert, C. (2003b). Paradigms from neuroscience: When shift happens. *Molecular Interventions, 3*: 361-366.

Pert, C. & Synder, S. (1973). Opiate receptor: demonstration in nervous tissue. *Science.* 179.

Pert, C., Ruff, M., Weber, R., & Herkenham, M. (1985). Neuropeptides and their receptors: a psychosomatic network. *Journal of Immunology.* 135, (2). August 1985.

Pinel, J. (1993). *Biopsychology.* (3rd Ed). Boston: Allyn & Bacon.

Polianova, M., Ruscetti, F., Pert, C., Tractenberg, R., Leoung, G., Strang, S., Ruff, M. (2003). Antiviral and immunological benefits in HIV patients receiving intranasal peptide T (DAPTA). *Peptides, 24(7),* 1093-1098.

Rein, G. (1995). The in vitro effect of bioenergy on the conformational states of human DNA in aqueous soltions. *Acupuncture Electrotherapy Research, 20(3-4),* 173-80.

Schiff, M & Braud, W. (1997). Distant intentionality and healing: assessing the evidence. *Alternative Therapies.* 3 (6), 72-73.

Schmidt, S., Schneider, R., Utts, J., Walach, H. (2004). Distant intentionality and the feeling of being stared at: Two meta-analyses. *British Journal of Psychology, 95,* 235-247.

Selye, H. (1936). A syndrome produced by diverse nocuous agents. *Nature.* 138, 32.

Sicher, F., Targ, E., Moore, D. & Smith, A. (1998). A randomized double-blind study of the effect of distant healing in a population with advanced AIDS: report of a small scale study. *Western Journal of Medicine,* 168(6):356-64.

Simantov R., Childer, S.R., Snyder, S.H. The opiate receptor binding interactions of 3H-methionine enkephalin, an opioid peptide. *Eur J Pharmacol.* 1978. Feb 1; 47(3):319–331.

Soloman, G., & Moos, R. (1964). Emotions, immunity, and disease: A speculative theoretical integration. *Archives of General Psychiatry,* 11, 657-674.

Song, L., Schwartz, G., Russek, L. (1998). Heart-focused attention and heart-brain synchronization: Energetic and physiological mechanisms. *Alternative Therapies in Health and Medicine, 44(5),* 44-62.

Walker, M., & Walker, J. (2003). *Healing massage: a simple approach.* New York: Delmar Thomson Learning.

Walker, M. (2006). The effects of nurses practicing the hearttouch technique on perceived stress, spiritual well-being, and hardiness. *Journal of Holistic Nursing,* (In press)

Chapter 4

American College of Sports Medicine (ACSM). (2005). *Guidelines for exercise testing and prescription.* (7th ed.). Philadelphia: Lea Febinger.

American Association of Cardiovascular and Pulmonary Rehabilitation (AACVPR). (2004). *Guidelines for cardiac rehabilitation and secondary prevention programs.* (4th ed.). Champaign, IL: Human Kinetics.

Baas, L. S., Beery, T. A., Allen, G. A., Wizer, M., & Wagoner, L. E. (2004). An exploratory study of body awareness in persons with heart failure or transplant. *Journal of Cardiovascular Nursing.* 19(1), 32-40.

Baker, C. A. (1989). Recovery: A phenomenon extending beyond discharge. *Scholarly Inquiry for Nursing Practice: An International Journal.* 3:181-197.

Bandura A. (1982). Self-efficacy mechanism in human agency. *American Psychologist,* 37:122-147.

Beery, T. A., Baas, L. S., Fowler, C., & Allen, G. (2002). Spirituality in persons with heart failure. *Journal of Holistic Nursing.* 20:5-26.

Benson, H., & Klipper, M. Z. (1976). *The relaxation response.* New York: Avon Books.

Blazer, D. G. (1982). Social support and mortality in an elderly community population. *American Journal of Epidemiology,* 1982;115:684-689.

Bickerstaff, K. A., Grasser, C. M., & McCabe, B. (2003). How elderly nursing home residents transcend losses of later life. *Holistic Nursing Practice, 17*(3), 159-165.

Borg, G. (1973). Perceived exertion: A note on "history" and methods. *Medicine Science & Sports,* 5:90-93.

Charles, S. T., Mather, M., & Carstensen, L. L. (2003). Aging and emotional memory: The forgettable nature of negative images for older adults. *Journal of Experimental Psychology, 132,* 310-324.

Christman, N. J., Kirchhoff, K. T., & Oakley, M. G. (1992). Concrete objective information. In G. M. Bulechek & J. C. McCloskey (Eds.), *Nursing interventions: Essential nursing treatments.* (2nd ed., pp.140-150.) Philadelphia: W.B. Saunders Company.

Cioffi, D. (1991) Beyond attentional strategies: a cognitive-perceptual model of somatic interpretation. *Psychological Bulletin* 109(1), 25-41.

Curl, E. D. (1992). *Hope in the elderly: Exploring the relationship between psychosocial developmental residual and hope.* Dissertation Abstracts International. 53(4):1782.

Dossey, B. M., Keegan, L., & Guzzetta, C. (2005). *Holistic nursing: A handbook for practice,* (4th ed.). Boston: Jones and Bartlett Publisher.

Erikson, E. (1963). *Childhood and society.* (2nd ed.). New York: Norton.

Erickson, H. C., Tomlin, E. M., & Swain, M. A. P. (1983). *Modeling and role-modeling: A theory and paradigm for nursing.* Englewood Cliffs, NJ: Prentice-Hall; Second-eighth printing, 1988-2005; EST Co: Austin, TX.

Erickson, H. C. (1984). *Self-care knowledge: Relations among the concepts support, hope, control, satisfaction with daily life and physical health status.* Unpublished dissertation, University of Michigan, Ann Arbor, MI.

Frankl, V. E. (1985). *Man's search for meaning* (Revised and updated). New York: Pocket Books.

Fontana, J.A. (1996). The emergence of the person environment interaction in a descriptive study of vigor in heart failure. *Advances in Nursing Science.* 18(4), 75-82.

Hertz, J. E. (1996). Conceptualization of perceived enactment of autonomy in the elderly. *Issues in Mental Health Nursing, 17*(3), 261-273.

Hertz, J. E., Rossetti, J., & Nelson, C. M. (2006). *Self-care activities reported by older adults living in senior apartments.* Unpublished manuscript, Northern Illinois University, DeKalb, IL.

Hertz, J. E. G. (1991). *The perceived enactment of autonomy scale: Measuring the potential for self-care action in the elderly.* Unpublished doctoral dissertation, The University of Texas at Austin, Austin, TX.

Johnson, J. E. (1999). Self-regulation theory and coping with physical illness. *Research in Nursing and Health,* 22:435-48.

Johnson, J. E., Babbs, J.M., Leventhal, H. (1970). Psychosocial factors in the welfare of surgical patients. *Nursing Research,* 19:18-29.

Johnson, J. L., Morse, J. M. (1990). Regaining control: The process of adjustment after myocardial infarction. *Heart and Lung,* 19:126-135.

Kabot-Zinn, J. (1985). The clinical use of mindfulness mediation for the self-regulation of chronic pain. *Journal of Behavioral Medicine,* 8:163-191.

Kinney, C. K., Mannetter R., & Carpenter M. A. (1992). Support groups. In: G.M. Bulechek & J.C. McCloskey (Eds.), *Nursing Intervention: Essential nursing treatments,* (2nd ed.). Philadelphia: WB Saunders Co. 1992: 326-339.

Krumholz, H. M., Butler, J., Miller, J., Vaccarino, V., Williams, C. S., Mendes de Leon, C. F., et al. (1998). Prognostic importance of emotional support for elderly patients hospitalized with heart failure. *Circulation*, 97, 958 -964.

Leenerts, M. H., Teel, C. S., & Pendleton, M. K. (2002). Building a model of self-care for health promotion in aging. *Journal of Nursing Scholarship, 34*(4), 355-361.

Levine, L. J., & Bluck, S. (1997). Experienced and remembered emotional intensity in older adults. *Psychology and Aging, 12,* 514-523.

Maddox, M. (1999). Older women and the meaning of health. *Journal of Gerontological Nursing, 25*(12), 26-33.

Mather, M., & Carstensen, L. L. (2003). Ageing and attentional biases for emotional faces. *Psychological Science, 14,* 409-415.

Moser, D. K., Dracup, K. (1995). Psychosocial recovery from a cardiac event: The influence of perceived control. *Heart and Lung,* 24:273-280.

Noble, B. J., & Robertson, R. J. (1996). *Perceived exertion.* Champaign, IL: Human Kinetics.

Norbeck, J. S. (1998). Social support. *Annual Review of Nursing Research* .6:85-105.

O'Malley, P., & Menke, E. (1988). Relationship of hope and stress after MI. *Heart and Lung,* 17:184-190.

Rideout, E., & Montemuro, M. (1986). Hope, morale and adaptation in patients with chronic heart failure. *Journal of Advanced Nursing,* 11:429-433.

Roglieri, J., Futterman, R. & McDonough, K. (1997). Disease management intervention to improve outcomes in congestive heart failure. *American Journal of Managed Care,* 1831-1839.

Rossi, E. (1986). *The Psychobiology of mind-body healing: New concepts in therapeutics hypnosis.* New York: W.W. Norton & Company.

Rossi, E., & Cheek, D. (1988). *Mind-body therapy: methods of ideodynamic healing in hypnosis.* New York: W.W. Norton & Company.

Selye, H. (1976). *The stress of life* (Rev. ed.). New York: McGraw-Hill Book Company.

Singleton, J. K. (2000). Nurses' perspectives of encouraging clients' care-of-self in a short-term rehabilitation unit within a long-term care facility. *Rehabilitation Nursing, 25*(1), 23-35.

Smith, J. A. (1981). The idea of health: A philosophical inquiry. *Advances in Nursing Science, 3* (3), 45-50.

Stewart, M. J. (1989). Social support intervention studies: A review and prospectus of nursing contributions. *International Journal of Nursing Studies*, 26(2):93-114.

Stewart, M. J. (1993). *Integrating social support in nursing.* Newbury Park: Sage Publishers.

Suls, J. & Wan, C. K. (1989). Effects of sensory and procedural information on coping with stressful medical procedures and pain: a meta–analysis. *Journal of Counseling in Clinical Psychology*, 57:372-379.

Tilden, V.P., Galen, R.D. (1987). Costs and conflict: The darker side of social support. *Western Journal of Nursing Research*, 9(1):9-18. Chapter 6.

Wang, H. H., Hsu, M. T., & Want, R. H. (2001). Using a focus group study to explore perceptions of health-promoting self-care in community-dwelling older adults. *Journal of Nursing Research, 9*(4), 95-104.

Watson, J. (1999). *Nursing: human science and human care: A theory of nursing.* New York: National League for Nursing.

Watson, J. (2005). *Caring science as sacred science.* Philadelphia: FA Davis.

Weber, B. A., Roberts, B. L., Resnick, M., Deimling, G., Zauszniewski, J. A., Musil, C., & Yurandi, H. N. (2004). The effect of dyadic intervention on self-efficacy, social support, and depression for men with prostate cancer. *Psycho-Oncology, 13*, 47-60.

Wilberding, J. Z. (1985). Values clarification. In G. M. Bulechek & J. C. McCloskey (Eds.), *Nursing interventions: Treatments for nursing diagnoses* (pp. 173-184). Philadelphia: W. B. Saunders.

Witvliet, C. (1997). Traumatic intrusive imagery as an emotional memory phenomenon: A review of research and explanatory information processing theories. *Clinical Psychology Review, 17,* 509-536.

World Health Organization. (1948). *Constitution of the World Health Organization.* Retrieved February 3, 2006, from http://www. policy.who/int.

Chapter 5

Baranowski, M., Schilmoeller, G., & Higgins, B. (1990). Parenting attitudes of adolescent and older mothers. *Adolescence*, 25, 781-790.

Bowlby, J. (1960). Grief and mourning in infancy and early childhood. *The Psychoanalytic Study of the Child,* VX, 3-39.

Elster, A., McAnarney, E., & Lamb, M. (1983). Parental behavior of adolescent mothers. *Pediatrics*, 71, 494-503.

Erickson, H. (1988). Modeling and role modeling: Ericksonian approaches with physiological problems. In J. Zeig, & S. Langton (Eds.), *Ericksonian pychotherapy: The state of the art.* New York, New York: Brunner/Mazel Publishers.

Erickson, H. (2002). Facilitating generativity and ego integrity: Applying Ericksonian Methods to the Aging Population. In B. B. Geary and J. K. Zeig, (Eds.). *The Handbook of Ericksonian Psychotherapy.* New York, New York: Brunner/Mazel Publishers.

Erickson, H. C., Tomlin, E. M., & Swain, M. A. P. (1983). *Modeling and role-modeling: A theory and paradigm for nursing.* Englewood Cliffs, NJ: Prentice-Hall; Second-eighth printing, 1988-2005; EST Co: Austin, TX.

Erikson, E. (1963). *Childhood and society.* New York: W.W. Norton.

Erikson, E. (1964). *Insight and responsibility.* New York: W.W. Norton.

Fraiberg, S. (1967). *The magic years: Understanding and handling the problems of early childhood.* (2nd ed.). New York: Charles Scribner's Sons.

Fraiberg, S. (1977). *Every child's birthright: In defense of mothering.* New York: Basic Books, Inc.

Gilligan, C. (1993). *In a different voice: Psychological theory and women's development.* Harvard, Conn: Harvard University Press.

Henry, O. (1992). The Gift of the Magi and Other Short Stories. New York, New York: Dover Publishing, p. 2.

Klein, H., & Cordell, A. (1987). The adolescent as mother; Early risk identification. *Journal of Youth and Adolescence*, 16, 47-58.

Mahler, M. S. (1975). *The Psychological Birth of the Human Infant: Symbiosis or Individuation .* New York: Basic Books.

McAnarney, E., Lawrence, Ricciuti, Polley, & Szillagyi. (1986). Interactions of adolescent mothers and their one-year-old children. *Pediatrics*, 78, 585-90.

Montagu, A. (1960). Constitutional and prenatal factors in infant and child health. In M. Haimowitz & N. Haimowitz (Eds.). *Human development: Selected Readings.* New York: Thomas. F. Crowell Company.

Panzarine, S. (1989). Interpersonal problem solving and its relation to adolescent mothering behaviors. *Journal of Adolescent Research*, 4, 63-74.

Parks, P. & Arndt, E. (1990). Differences between adolescent and adult mothers of infants. *Journal of Adolescent Health Care,* 11, 248-253.

Ragozin, A., Basham, R., Crnic, K., Greenberg, M., & Robinson, N. (1982). Effects of maternal age on parenting role. *Developmental Psychology*, 18, 627-634.

Reis, J., & Herz, E. (1987). Correlates of adolescent parenting. *Adolescence*, 22, 599-609.

Schuster, C., & Ashburn, S. (1986). *The process of human development: A holistic life-span approach.* Boston: Little, Brown, & Company.

Seymore, C., Frothingham, T., Macmillan, J., & Durant, R. (1990). Child development knowledge, childrearing attitudes, and social support among first- and second-time adolescent mothers. *Journal of Adolescent Health Care*, 11, 343-350.

Showers, J., & Johnson, C. (1985). Child development, child health and child rearing knowledge among urban adolescents: Are they adequately prepared for the challenges of parenthood? *Health Education*, 16, 37-41.

Tornstam, L., 1997, Gerotranscendence: The contemplative dimension of aging. *Journal of Aging Studies*, Vol 11 2:143-154.

vonWindeguth, B., & Urbano, R. (1983). Teenagers and the mothering experience. *Pediatric Nursing*, 15, 517-520.

Weiss, R. (1977). *Loneliness: The experience of emotional and social isolation.* Cambridge, MA: MIT Press.

Weiss, R. (1982). Attachment in adult life. In C. M. Parkes & J. Stevenson-Hinde (Eds.), *The place of attachment in human behavior* (pp. 111-184). New York: Wiley.

Chapter 6

Erickson, H. (1976). I*dentification of states of coping utilizing physiological and psychological data.* Master's Thesis, The University of Michigan.

Erickson, H. (1996). Holistic Healing: Intra/Inter Relations of Person and Environment. (Guest Editor). I*ssues of Mental Health Nursing,* Vol. 17, 3, 1996.

Erickson, H. C., Tomlin, E. M., & Swain, M. A. P. (1983). *Modeling and role-modeling: A theory and paradigm for nursing.* Englewood Cliffs, NJ: Prentice-Hall; Second-eighth printing, 1988-2005; EST Co: Austin, TX.

Goble, F. (1973). *The third force.* New York: Pocket Books.

Harlow, H. (1960). The nature of love. In M. L. Haimowitz & N. R. Haimowitz (Eds.), *Human development: Selected readings* (pp. 190-205). New York: Thomas F. Crowell, Company.

Krugman, S. & Dubowitz, H. (2003). Failure to thrive. In *American Family Physician,* Vol. 68 (No. 5), p. 879.

Mahler, M. S. (1975). The psychological birth of the human infant: In M. Mahler, *Symbiosis or individuation .* New York: Basic Books.

Maslow, A. (1968). *Toward a psychology of being.* (2nd ed.). New York: D. Van Nostrand.

Maslow, A. (1982). *The farthest reaches of human nature.* New York: D.Van Nostrand.

Maslow, A. H. Conflict, frustration, and the theory of threat. *Journal of Abnormal Psychology,* 1943, 38, 81-86.

Spitz, R. (1960). Motherless infants. In M.L. Haimowitz & N.R. Haimowitz (Eds), *Human development: Selected readings.* Thomas Y. Crowell, Company New York, pp. 106-172.

Merk manual: diagnosis and therapy, (2002), pp 262-263.

Chapter 7

Ainsworth, M. (1968). Object relations, dependency and attachment: a theoretical review of the infant mother relationship. *Child Development,* 40, 969-1025.

Avant, K. (1981). Anxiety as a potential factor affecting maternal attachment. *Journal of Obstetrical, Gynecological, and Neonatal Nursing,* 10, 416-419.

Baranowski, M., Schilmoeller, G., & Higgins, B. (1990). Parenting attitudes of adolescent and older mothers. *Adolescence,* 25, 781-790.

Bowlby, J. (1958). The nature of the child's tie to his mother. *International Journal of Psychoanalysis,* XXXIX, 1-23.

Bowlby, J. (1969). *Attachment.* Harper, New York: Basic Books, Inc.

Bowlby, J. (1973). *Separation* Harper, New York: Basic Books, Inc.

Bowlby, J. (1977). *The nature of parenting.* An invited lecture presented at The University of Michigan, Ann Arbor Michigan.

Bowlby, J. (1982). *Loss.* (2nd ed.). Harper, New York: Basic Books, Inc.

Cranley, M. (1981). Development of a tool for the measurement of maternal attachment during pregnancy. *Nursing Research,* 30, 281-284.

Elster, A., McAnarney, E., & Lamb, M. (1983). Parental behavior of adolescent mothers. *Pediatrics,* 71, 494-503.

Engel, G. (1964). Grief and grieving. *American Journal of Nursing,* 64, p. 93.

Engel, G. (1968). A life setting conducive to illness: the giving-up: given-up complex. *Annals of Internal Medicine,* 69, 293-299.

Erickson, H. C. (1976). *Identification of States of Coping Utilizing Physiological and Psychological Data.* Unpublished Master's thesis, University of Michigan, Ann Arbor, MI.

Erickson, H. (1983). Coping with new systems. *Journal of Nursing Education,* 3, 132-136.

Erickson, H. (1990a). Theory Based Nursing. In C. Kinney, & H. Erickson (Eds.), *Modeling   and Role-Modeling: Theory, Practice and Research.* Society for Advancement of Modeling and Role-Modeling. Vol. 1(1), 1-27.

Erickson, H. (1990b). Self-care knowledge: A exploratory study. In C. Kinney, & H. Erickson, (Eds.), *Modeling   and Role-Modeling: Theory, Practice and Research.* Society for Advancement of Modeling and Role-Modeling. Vol. 1(1), 178-202.

Erickson, H. (1997). *Intensive training in hypnosis.* The Psychology of Health, Immunity and Disease: The Definitive Practitioner's Conference on the clinical Application of Psychoneuroimmunology and the Mind-Body Connection. The National Institute for Clinical application of Behavioral Medicine. December 8-14, 1997. Hilton Head Island, South Carolina. Intensive Training Institute Audio cassettes

Erickson, H. (2002). Facilitating generativity and ego integrity: Applying Ericksonian Methods to the Aging Population. In B.B. Geary and J.K. Zeig, (Eds) *The Handbook of Ericksonian Psychotherapy.* New York: Brunner/Mazel.

Erickson, H. (2007). *Modeling and Role-Modeling: Research Findings and Measurement Issues.* Cedar Park, TX: Unicorns Unlimited. To be published.

Erickson, M. (1994). *Development of a theoretical model of factors among maternal bonding, attachment and infant well-being.* Unpublished manuscript. The University of Texas at Austin, Austin, TX.

Erickson, M. (1996a). Factors that influence the mother infant dyad relationship and infant well-being. *Issues in Mental Health Nursing,* 17, (3), 185-200.

Erickson, M. (1996b). Predictors of maternal-fetal attachment: An integrative review. *Online Journal of Knowledge Synthesis for Nursing,* Sigma Theta Tau, 3, 32.

Erickson, M. (1996c). The relationships among need satisfaction, support, and maternal attachment in the adolescent mother. Unpublished Dissertation. The University of Texas, Austin TX.

Erickson, H. C., Tomlin, E. M., & Swain, M. A. P. (1983*). Modeling and role-modeling: A theory and paradigm for nursing.* Englewood Cliffs, NJ: Prentice-Hall; Second-eighth printing, 1988-2005; EST Co: Austin, TX.

Fairbairn, W. (1952). *An object-relations theory of the personality.* New York: Basic Books.

Fraiberg, S. (1967). *The magic years: Understanding and handling the problems of early childhood.* (2nd ed.). New York: Charles Scribner's Sons.

Freud, S. (1920/1955). The psychogenesis of a case of homosexuality in a woman. In E. Strachey (Ed. and Trans.). *The standard edition of the complete psychosocial works of Sigmund Freud* (Vol. 18, pp. 145-172). London: Hogarth Press. (Original work published 1920).

Harlow, H. (1960). The nature of love. In M. L. Haimowitz & N. R. Haimowitz, (Eds.). *Human development: Selected Readings.* Thomas Y. Crowell Co: New York, pp. 190-205.

Kinney, C. (1990a). The attachment-loss-reattachment life-span development model. An unpublished manuscript.

Kinney, C. (1990b). Facilitating growth and development: A paradigm case for modeling and role-modeling. *Issues in Mental Health Nursing, 11*: 375-395.

Kinney, C. & Erickson, H. (1990). Modeling the client's world: A way to holistic care. *Issues in Mental Health Nursing*, Vol. 11 (2), 93-108.

Klein, H., & Cordell, A. (1987). The adolescent as mother; Early risk identification. *Journal of Youth and Adolescence*, 16, 47-58.

Klein, (1952). Some theoretical conclusions regarding the emotional life of the infant. In J. Riviere (Ed.) *Developments in Psychoanalysis*. London: Hogarth.

Kuebler-Ross, E. (1969). *On death and dying*. London: Tavistock.

Leifer, M. (1977). Psychological changes accompanying pregnancy and motherhood. *Genetic Psychology Monographs*, 95, 55-96.

Lindemann, E. (1952). Symptomatology and management of acute grief. *American Journal of Psychiatry,* 101, 141-48.

McAnarney, E., Lawrence, Ricciuti, Polley, & Szillagyi. (1986). Interactions of adolescent mothers and their one-year-old children. *Pediatrics*, 78, 585-90.

Montagu, M. (1960). Constitutional and prenatal factors in infant and child health. In M. L. Haimowitz & N. R. Haimowitz (Eds.), *Human development*. Thomas Y. Crowell Co: New York. Pp. 124-143.

Muller, M. (1993). Development of the Prenatal Attachment Inventory. *Western Journal of Nursing Research*, 15, 199-215.

Panzarine, S. (1989). Interpersonal problem solving and its relation to adolescent mothering behaviors. *Journal of Adolescent Research*, 4, 63-74.

Parks, P. & Arndt, E. (1990). Differences between adolescent and adult mothers of infants. *Journal of Adolescent Health Care*, 11, 248-253.

Ragozin, A., Basham, R., Crnic, K., Greenberg, M., & Robinson, N. (1982). Effects of maternal age on parenting role. *Developmental Psychology*, 18, 627-634.

Reis, J. & Herz, E. (1987). Correlates of adolescent parenting. *Adolescence*, 22, 599-609.

Robertson, J. & Robertson, J. (1969). Quality of substitute care as an influence on separation reponses. *Journal of Psychosomatic Research.* 16, 261-265.

Seymore, C., Frothingham, T., Macmillan, J., & Durant, R. (1990). Child development knowledge, childrearing attitudes, and social support among first- and second-time adolescent mothers. *Journal of Adolescent Health Care*, 11, 343-350.

Showers, J. & Johnson, C. (1985). Child development, child health and child rearing knowledge among urban adolescents: Are they adequately prepared for the challenges of parenthood? *Health Education*, 16, 37-41.

Spitz, R. (1960). Motherless infants. In M. L. Haimowitz & N. R. Haimowitz (Eds.), *Human development*. Thomas Y. Crowell Co: New York, pp. 166-172.

vonWindeguth, B. & Urbano, R. (1983). Teenagers and the mothering experience, *Pediatric Nursing.* 15, 517-520.

Winnicott, D. (1953). Transitional objects and transitional phenomena: a study of the first not-me possession. *International Journal of Psychoanalysis, 34;* 89-97

Zukav, G. (1989). *The seat of the soul*. New York : Simon & Schuster, Inc.

Chapter 8

Aiken, L. H., Clarke, S., Sloane, D., Sochalski, J., & Silber, J. (2002). Hospital nurse staffing and patient mortality, nurse burnout, and job dissatisfaction. *JAMA, 288*(16), 1987-1993.

Ajzen, I., & Fishbein, M. (1980). A theory of reasoned action. In I. Ajzen & M. Fishbein (Eds.), *Understanding attitudes and predicting social behavior* (pp. 1-17). Englewood Cliffs, NJ: Prentice-Hall.

Antonovsky, A. (1979). *Health, stress, and coping.* San Francisco: Jossey-Bass Publishers.

Antonovsky, A. (1987). *Unraveling the mystery of health: How people manage stress and stay well.* San Francisco: Jossey-Bass Publishers.

Arrow, H., McGrath, J. E., & Berdahl, J. L. (2000). *Small groups as complex systems: formation, coordination, development, and adaptation.* Thousand Oaks, CA: Sage Publications.

Bandura, A. (1997). *Self-efficacy: the exercise of control.* New York: W.H. Freeman.

Barker, V. E., Abrams, J. R., Tiyaamornwong, V., Seibold, D. R., Duggan, A., Sun Park, H., et al. (2000). New contexts for relational communication in groups. *Small Group Research, 31*(4), 470-504.

Barnfather, J. S. (1987). *Mobilizing coping resources related to basic need status in healthy, young adults.* Unpublished dissertation, University of Michigan, Ann Arbor, MI.

Barnfather, J. S. (1990). An overview of the ability to mobilize coping resources related to basic needs. In H. C. Erickson & C. Kinney (Eds.), *Modeling and role-modeling: theory, practice and research* (Vol. 1 (1), pp. 156-169). Austin, TX: The Society for the Advancement of Modeling and Role-Modeling.

Barnfather, J. S., Swain, M. A., & Erickson, H. C. (1989a). Construct validity of an Aspect of the coping process: Potential Adaptation to Stress. *Issues in Mental Health Nursing, 10*, 23-40.

Barnfather, J. S., Swain, M. A., & Erickson, H. C. (1989b). Evaluation of two assessment techniques for adaptation to stress. *Nursing Science Quarterly, 2*(4), 172-182.

Beaton, R. D., Murphy, S. A., Pike, K. C., & Corneil, W. (1997). Social support and network conflict in firefighters and paramedics. *Western Journal of Nursing Research, 19*(3), 297-313.

Beehr, T. A., & Bowling, N. A. (2005). Hardy personality, stress, and health. In C. Cooper (Ed.), *Handbook of stress medicine and health* (2nd ed., pp. 193-211). New York: CRC Press.

Beehr, T. A., & McGrath, J. E. (1992). Social support, occupational stress and anxiety. *Anxiety, Stress & Coping: An International Journal, 5*(1), 7-19.

Benson, D. (2003). *Adaptive potential assessment model applied to small groups.* Unpublished Dissertation, University of La Verne, La Verne, CA.

Bliese, P. D., & Britt, T. W. (2001). Social support, group consensus and stressor-strain relationship: Social context matters. *Journal of Organizational Behavior, 22*(4), 425-436.

Boyers, A. E. (2000). The influence of cognitive-behavioral stress management, optimism, and coping on positive growth in women with breast cancer. Unpublished dissertation, University of Miami, Coral Gables, FL.

Brissette, I., Scheier, M. F., & Carver, C. S. (2002). The role of optimism in social network: Development, coping, and psychological adjustment during a life transition. *Journal of Personality and Social Psychology, 82*(1), 102-111.

Burt, R. S. (2001). Attachment, decay, and social network. *Journal of Organizational Behavior, 22*, 619-643.

Campbell, D. G., & Kwon, P. (2001). Domain-specific hope and personal style: Toward an integrative understanding of dysphoria. *Journal of Social and Clinical Psychology, 20*(4), 498-520.

Cannon, W. B. (1935). Stresses and strain of homeostasis. *The American Journal of American Sciences, 189*, 1-14.

Cannon, W. B. (1939). *The wisdom of the body.* New York: W. W. Norton and Company, Inc.

Capra, F. (1996). *The web of life: A new scientific understanding of systems.* New York: Anchor Books.

Chansler, P. A., Swamidass, P. M., & Cammann, C. (2003). Self-managing work teams: An empirical study of group cohesiveness in "natural work groups" at a Harley-Davidson Motor Company plant. *Small Group Research, 34*(1), 101.

Cline, R. J. (1999). Communication in social support groups. In L. R. Frey (Ed.), *The handbook of group communication theory and research* (pp. 516-538). Thousand Oaks, CA: Sage Publications.

Cohen, J. A., & Welch, L. M. (2000). Attitudes, beliefs, values, and culture as mediators of stress. In V. H. Rice (Ed.), *Handbook of stress, coping, and health: Implications for nursing research, theory, and practice* (pp. 367-366). Thousand Oaks, CA: Sage Publications.

Cooper, C. (Ed.). (2005). *Handbook of stress medicine and health* (2nd ed.). New York: CRC Press.

Cooper, C., & Dewe, P. (2004). *Stress: A brief history.* Malden, MA: Blackwell Publishing.

Densten, I. L. (2001). Re-thinking burnout. *Journal of Organizational Behavior, 22*, 833-847.

Emmons, R. A. (1991). The repressive personality and social support. In H. S. Friedman (Ed.), *Hostility, coping, and health* (pp. 141-151). Washington DC: American Psychological Association.

Engel, G. L. (1962). *Psychological development in health and disease.* Philadelphia: W. B. Saunders.

Erickson, H. C. (1976). *Identification of states of coping utilizing physiological and psychological data.* Unpublished Master's thesis, University of Michigan, Ann Arbor, Michigan.

Erickson, H. C. (1984). *Self-Care knowledge: Relations among the concepts support, hope, control, satisfaction with daily life and physical health status.* Unpublished dissertation, University of Michigan, Ann Arbor, Michigan.

Erickson, H. C., & Kinney, C. (Eds.). (1990). *Modeling and role-modeling: Theory, practice, and research* (Vol. 1). Austin, TX: Society for the Advancement of Modeling and Role-Modeling.

Erickson, H. C., & Swain, M. A. (1982). A Model for assessing potential adaptation to stress. *Research in Nursing and Health, 5*, 93-101.

Erickson, H. C., Tomlin, E. M., & Swain, M. A. P. (1983). *Modeling and role-modeling: A theory and paradigm for nursing.* Englewood Cliffs, NJ: Prentice-Hall; Second-eighth printing, 1988-2005; EST Co: Austin, TX.

Erikson, E. (1964). *Insight and responsibility.* New York: W.W. Norton.

Fenlason, K. J., & Beehr, T. A. (1994). Social support and occupational stress: Effects of talking to others. *Journal of Organizational Behavior, 15*(2), 157-175.

Fishbein, M., & Ajzen, I. (1975). *Belief, attitude, intention, and behavior: An introduction to theory and research.* Reading, MA: Addison-Wesley Publishing.

Folkman, S. (1997). Positive psychological states and coping with severe stress. *Social Science and Medicine, 45*(3), 207-221.

Ford-Gilboe, M., & Cohen, J. A. (2000). Hardiness: a model of commitment, challenge, and control. In V. H. Rice (Ed.), *Handbook of stress, coping, and health: Implications for nursing research, theory, and practice* (pp. 425-436). Thousand Oaks, CA: Sage Publications.

Frazier, P. A., Tix, A. P., Klein, C. D., & Arikian, N. J. (2000). Testing theoretical models of the relations between social support, coping, and adjustment to stressful life events. *Journal of Social and Clinical Psychology, 19*(3), 314-335.

Frey, L. R. (Ed.). (1999). *The handbook of group communication theory and research.* Thousand Oaks CA: Sage Publications.

Friedman, H. S. (1991a). Understanding hostility, coping, and health. In H. S. Friedman (Ed.), *Hostility, coping, and health*. Washington DC: American Psychological Association, (pp. 3-9).

Friedman, H. S. (Ed.). (1991b). *Hostility, Coping, and Health*. Washington DC: American Psychological Association.

Frisch, N. C., & Bowman, S. S. (2002). The modeling and role-modeling theory. In J. George (Ed.), *Nursing Theories* (5th ed., pp. 463-487). Upper Saddle River, NJ: Prentice-Hall.

Frisch, N. C., & Kelly, J. (1996). *Healing life's crises: A guide for nurses.* Albany: Delmar Publishers.

Garber, J., & Seligman, M. E. P. (Eds.). (1980). *Human helplessness: theory and applications*. New York: Academic Press.

Gillis, A. (1993). Determinants of a health-promoting lifestyle: an integrative review. *Journal of Advanced Nursing, 18*(3), 345-353.

Granstrom, K., & Stiwne, D. (1998). A bipolar model of groupthink. *Small Group Research, 29*(1), 32.

Halm, M., Peterson, M., Kandels, M. B., Sabo, J., Blalock, M., Braden, R., et al. (2005). Hospital nurse staffing and patient mortality, emotional exhaustion, and job dissatisfaction. *Clinical Nurse Specialist, 19*(5), 241-251.

Herth, K. (1989). The relationship between level of hope and level of coping response and other variables in patients with cancer. *Oncology Nursing Forum, 16*(1), 67-72.

Herth, K. (1990). Fostering hope in terminally-ill people. *Journal of Advanced Nursing, 15*(11), 1250-1259.

Hobfoll, S. E. (1998). *Stress, culture, and community: the psychology and philosophy of stress.* New York: Plenum Press.

Hobfoll, S. E., & Shirom, A. (1993). Stress and Burnout in the workplace: conservation of resources. In R. T. Golembrewski (Ed.), *Handbook of Organizational Behavior.* New York: Marcel-Dekker, Inc.

Holahan, C. J., Moos, R. H., & Schaefer, J. A. (1996). Coping, stress resistance, and growth: conceptualizing adaptive functioning. In M. Zeidner & N. S. Endler (Eds.), *Handbook of coping: theory, research, applications* (pp. 24-43). New York: John Wiley & Sons.

Holden, G. (1991). The relationship of self-efficacy appraisals to subsequent health related outcomes: a meta-analysis. *Social Work in Health Care, 16*(1), 53-93.

Hopkins, B. A. (1994). *Development and validation of a content analysis tool to identify adaptive potential.* Unpublished dissertation, The University of Texas at Austin, Austin, TX.

Horsburgh, M. E. (2000). Salutogenesis: "origins of health" and sense of coherence. In V. H. Rice (Ed.), *Handbook of stress, coping, and health: Implications for nursing research, theory, and practice* (pp. 175-194). Thousand Oaks, CA: Sage Publications.

Irvin, B. L. (1993). *Social support, self-worth and hope as self-care resources for coping with caregiver stress.* Unpublished dissertation, The University of Texas at Austin, Austin, TX.

Irvin, B. L., & Acton, G. J. (1997). Stress, hope and well-being of women caring for family members with Alzheimer's disease. *Holistic Nursing Practice, 11*(2), 69-79.

Janis, I. L. (1982). *Groupthink* (2nd ed.). Boston: Houghton-Mifflin.

Jones, J. E., & Bearley, W. L. (2000). *Facilitating team development: A view from the field,* 200. Sydney, Australia: AimBooks.

Kaba, E., Thompson, D. R., & Burnard, P. (2000). Coping after heart transplantation: a descriptive study of heart transplant recipients' methods of coping. *Journal of Advanced Nursing, 34*(4), 930-936.

Katzenbach, J. R., & Smith, D. K. (1999). *The Wisdom of Teams.* New York: Harper Perennial.

Keck, V. E. (1989). *Perceived social support, basic needs satisfaction, and coping strategies of the chronically ill.* Unpublished dissertation, University of Michigan, Ann Arbor.

Keyton, J. (1999). Relational communication in groups. In L. R. Frey (Ed.), *The handbook of group communication theory and research* (pp. 192-222). Thousand Oaks CA: Sage Publications.

Kleinbeck, S. V. (1977). *Coping states of stress.* Unpublished Master's Thesis, University of Michigan, Ann Arbor, MI.

Kobasa, S. C. (1979). Commitment and coping in stress resistance among lawyers. *Journal of Personality & Social Psychology, 42*(4), 707-717.

Kobasa, S. C. (1985). Stressful life events, personality and health: An inquiry into hardiness. In A. Monat & R. S. Lazarus (Eds.), *Stress and coping: An anthology* New York: Columbia University Press, (pp. 174-188).

Krause, N. (1995). Assessing stress-buffering effects: A cautionary note. *Psychology and Aging, 10*(4), 518-526.

Kylma, J., & Vehvilainen-Julkunen, K. (1997). Hope in nursing research: a meta-analysis of the ontological and epistemological foundations of research on hope. *Journal of Advanced Nursing, 25*(2), 364-371.

Landrum, D. R. (1999). *A comparison of the effects of cardiac rehabilitation programs on coping levels and outcome measures in cardiac patients.* Unpublished dissertation, University of Texas, Austin, TX.

Langfred, C. W. (1998). Is group cohesiveness a double-edged sword? *Small Group Research, 29*(1), 124-143.

Langfred, C. W. (2000). The paradox of self-management: individual and group autonomy in work groups. *Journal of Organizational Behavior, 21,* 563-585.

Lazarus, R. S. (1999). *Stress and emotion: A new synthesis.* New York: Springer Publishing Company

Lazarus, R. S. (2000). Evolution of a model of stress, coping, and discrete emotions. In V. H. Rice (Ed.), *Handbook of stress, coping, and health: Implications for nursing research, theory, and practice.* Thousand Oaks, CA: Sage Publications, (pp. 195-222).

Lazarus, R. S., & Folkman, S. (1984). *Stress, appraisal, and coping*. New York: Springer.

Leidy, N. K. (1989). A physiologic analysis of stress and chronic illness. *Journal of Advanced Nursing, 14*, 868-876.

Leidy, N. K. (1990). A structural model of stress, psychosocial resources, and symptomatic experience in chronic physical illness. *Nursing Research, 39*(4), 230-236.

Leidy, N. K. (1999). Psychometric properties of the Functional Performance Inventory in patients with chronic obstructive pulmonary disease. *Nursing Research, 48*(1), 20-28.

Leidy, N. & Darling-Fisher, C. (1995). Reliability and validity of the modified Erikson psychosocial stages in diverse clinical samples. *Western Journal of Research, 17* (2), 168-187.

Leidy, N. K., Ozbolt, J. G., & Swain, M. A. (1990). Psychophysiological processes of stress in chronic physical illness: a theoretical perspective. *Journal of Advanced Nursing, 15*, 478-486.

Leidy, N. K., & Traver, G. A. (1995). Psychophysiologic factors contributing to functional performance in people with COPD: are there gender differences? *Research in Nursing and Health, 18*(6), 535-546.

Lyon, B. L. (2000). Stress, coping and health. In V. H. Rice (Ed.), *Handbook of stress, coping, and health: Implications for nursing research, theory, and practice*. Thousand Oaks, CA: Sage Publications.

Maddi, S. R., & Kobasa, S. C. (1984). *The hardy executive: health under stress*. Homewood, IL: Dow Jones-Irwin.

Maddi, S. R., & Kobasa, S. C. (1991). The development of hardiness. In A. Monat & R. S. Lazarus (Eds.), *Stress and coping: An anthology* (2nd ed. pp. 245-257). New York: Columbia University Press.

Maslach, C., & Leiter, M. P. (2005). Stress and burnout: The Critical research. In C. Cooper (Ed.), *Handbook of stress medicine and health* (pp. 155-191). New York: CRC Press.

McEwen, B. S. (1998). Protective and damaging effects of stress mediators. *New England Journal of Medicine, 338*(3), 171-179.

McEwen, B. S., & Lasley, E. N. (2003). Allostatic load: when protection gives way to damage. *Advances in Mind-Body Medicine, 19*(1), 28-33.

Mechanic, D. (1985). Some modes of adaptation: defense. In A. Monat & R. S. Lazarus (Eds.), *Stress and coping: An anthology* (2nd ed. pp. 208-219). New York: Columbia University Press.

Mikhail, A. (1985). Stress: a psychophysiological conception. In A. Monat & R. S. Lazarus (Eds.), *Stress and coping: An anthology* (2nd ed. pp. 30-39). New York: Columbia University Press.

Monat, A., & Lazarus, R. S. (Eds.). (1985). *Stress and Coping: an anthology* (2nd ed.). New York: Columbia University Press.

Natterlund, B., & Ahlstrom, G. (1999). Experience of social support in rehabilitation: a phenomenological study. *Journal of Advanced Nursing, 30*(6), 1332-1341.

Parker, J. D., & Endler, N. S. (1996). Coping and defense: a historical overview. In M. Zeidner & N. S. Endler (Eds.), *Handbook of coping: Theory, research, applications* (pp. 3-23). New York: John Wiley & Sons.

Pellitier, 1997. *Mind as healer:mind as slayer*. New York: Delta Publishing Co.

Peterson, C., Maier, S. F., & Seligman, M. E. P. (1993). *Learned helplessness : A theory for the age of personal control*. New York: Oxford University Press.

Pierce, G. R., Sarason, I. G., & Sarason, B. R. (1996). Coping and social support. In M. Zeidner & N. S. Endler (Eds.), *Handbook of coping: theory, research, applications* (pp. 434-451). New York: John Wiley & Sons.

Poole, M. S., Keyton, J., & Frey, L. R. (1999). Group communication methodology: Issues and considerations. In L. R. Frey (Ed.), *The handbook of group communication theory and research* (pp. 2-112). Thousand Oaks, CA: Sage Publications.

Porth, C. M. (2002). *Pathophysiology: Concepts of altered health states*. Philadelphia: Lippincott, Williams, & Wilkins.

Raleigh, E. D. H. (2000). Hope and helplessness. In V. H. Rice (Ed.), *Handbook of stress, coping, and health: Implications for nursing research, theory, and practice* (pp. 437-459). Thousand Oaks, CA: Sage Publications.

Rice, V. H. (2000). Theories of Stress and relationship to health. In V. H. Rice (Ed.), *Handbook of stress, coping, and health: Implications for nursing research, theory, and practice* (pp. 27-45). Thousand Oaks, CA: Sage Publications.

Roth, S., & Cohen, L. J. (1986). Approach, avoidance, and coping with stress. *American Psychologist, 41*(7), 813-819.

Rotter, J. B. (1966). Generalized expectations for internal versus external control of reinforcement. *Psychological Monographs: General and Applied, 80*, 1-26.

Rozell, E. J., & Gundersen, D. E. (2003). The effects of leader impression management on group perceptions of cohesion, consensus, and communication. *Small Group Research, 34*(2), 197.

Ruiz-Bueno, J. B. (2000). Locus of Control, Perceived Control, and Learned Helplessness. In V. H. Rice (Ed.), *Handbook of stress, coping, and health: Implications for nursing research, theory, and practice* (pp. 461-482). Thousand Oaks, CA: Sage Publications.

Seligman, M. (1974). Helplessness. In R. Friedman & M. Katz (Eds.), *The psychology of depression: Contemporary theory and research* (pp. 83-125). Washington, D.C.: V.H. Winston and Sons.

Seligman, M. E. P. (1975). *Helplessness: On depression, development, and death*. San Francisco: Freeman Press.

Selye, H. (1974). *Stress without distress*. Philadelphia: J. B. Lippincott Company

Selye, H. (1976). *The stress of life* (Rev. ed.). New York: McGraw-Hill Book Company.

Selye, H. (1985). History and present status of the stress concept. In A. Monat & R. S. Lazarus (Eds.), *Stress and coping: An anthology* (pp. 17-29). New York: Columbia University Press.

Selye, H. (Ed.). (1980). *Selye's guide to stress research* (Volume 1 ed.). New York: Van Nostrand Reinhold Company.

Semmer, N. K., McGrath, J. E., & Beehr, T. A. (2005). Conceptual issues in research on stress and health. In C. Cooper (Ed.), *Handbook of stress medicine and health* (2nd ed., pp. 1-44). New York: CRC Press.

Siela, D., & Wieseke, A. W. (2000). Stress, Self-Efficacy, and Health. In V. H. Rice (Ed.), *Handbook of stress, coping, and health: Implications for nursing research, theory, and practice* (pp.495-516). Thousand Oaks, CA: Sage Publications.

Stetler, C., Murali, R., Chen, E., & Miller, G. E. (2005). Stress, immunity, and disease. In C. Cooper (Ed.), *Handbook of stress medicine and health* (pp. 131-154). New York: CRC Press.

Stewart, M., Davidson, K., Meade, D., Hirth, A., & Makrides, L. (2000). Myocardial infarction: survivors' and spouses' stress, coping, and support. *Journal of Advanced Nursing, 31*(6), 1351-1361.

Stotland, E. (1969). *The psychology of hope.* San Francisco: Jossey-Bass Publishers.

Triandis, H. C. (1995). *Individualism and collectivism.* Boulder, CO: Westview.

Tsigos, C., Kyrou, I., & Chrousos, G. P. (2005). Stress, endocrine manifestations, and diseases. In C. Cooper (Ed.), *Handbook of stress medicine and health* (2nd ed. pp. 101-129). New York: CRC Press.

Underwood, P. W. (2000). Social support: The promise and the reality. In V. H. Rice (Ed.), *Handbook of stress, coping, and health: Implications for nursing research, theory, and practice* (pp. 367-392). Thousand Oaks, CA: Sage Publications.

Wallenstein, G. (2003). *Mind, stress, & emotions: The new science of mood.* San Francisco: Commonwealth Press.

Welch, J. L., & Austin, J. K. (2001). Stressors, coping and depression in haemodialysis patients. *Journal of Advanced Nursing, 33*(2), 200-207.

Westburg, N. G. (2001). Hope in older women: The importance of past and current relationships. *Journal of Social and Clinical Psychology, 20*(3), 354-365.

Zautra, A. J. (2003). *Emotions, stress, and health.* New York: Oxford University Press.

Zeidner, M., & Saklofske, D. (1996). Adaptive and maladaptive coping. In M. Zeidner & N. S. Endler (Eds.), *Handbook of coping: Theory, research, applications.* (pp. 505-531). New York: John Wiley & Sons.

Zellars, K. L., Hochwarter, W. A., Perrewe, P. L., Miles, A. K., & Kiewitz, C. (2001). Beyond self-efficacy: Interactive effects of role conflict and perceived collective efficacy. *Journal of Managerial Issues, 13*(4), 483-499.

Chapter 9

Armour, J. A. (1991). Anatomy and function of the intrathoracic neurons regulating the mammalian heart. In I. H. Zucker and J. P. Gilmore, (Eds.) *Reflex control of the circulation* (pp. 1-37). Boca Raton, FL: CRC Press.

Armour, J. (1999). Neurocardiology: Anatomical and functional principles. In R., McCraty, D., Rozman, & D., Childre, (Eds.) *Heartmath: A new biobehavioral intervention for increasing health and personal effectiveness – Increasing coherence in the human system.* Amsterdam: Harwood Academic Publishers.

Barrios-Choplin, B., McCraty, R., & Cryer, B. (1997). A new approach to reducing stress and improving physical and emotional well-being at work. *Stress Medicine, 13*:193-201.

Buber, M. (1970). *I and Thou.* New York: Scribner's Sons

Childre, D. and Martin, H. (1999). *The HeartMath solution.* San Francisco: HarperSanFrancisco.

Dale, C. (2003). *New chakra healing.* St. Paul: Llewellyn Publishers.

Erickson, H. C., Tomlin, E. M., & Swain, M. A. P. (1983). *Modeling and role-modeling: A theory and paradigm for nursing.* Englewood Cliffs, NJ: Prentice-Hall; Second-eighth printing, 1988-2005; EST Co: Austin, TX.

Friedman, M. & Rosenman, R. (1964). Predictive study of coronary heart disease: The western collaboration group study. *Journal of American Medical Association* 189, pp. 15-25.

Gerber, R. (2001). *A practical guide to vibrational medicine; Energy healing and spiritual transformation.* Quill, HarperCollins Publishers, NY: NY

Gerber, R. (2001). *Vibrational Medicine: The number one handbook of subtle-energy therapies.* (3rd ed.). Rochester, Vermont: Bear and Company.

Judith, Anodea (1996). *Eastern body, western mind: Psychology and the chakra system as a path to the self.* Berkeley, CA: Celestial Arts.

Jung, C.G. (1933). *Modern man in search of a soul.* New York: Harcourt, Inc.

Kingman, D. R. (1998). *The future of love: The power of the soul in intimate relationships.* New York: Doubleday.

Kinney, C. K. (1990). Facilitating growth and development: A paradigm case for modeling and role-modeling. *Issues in Mental Health Nursing, 11*: 375-395.

Kinney, Carolyn K. (1996). Transcending breast cancer: Reconstructing one's self. *Issues in Mental Health Nursing, 17*: 201-216.

Lacey, J. I. & Lacey, B. C. (1978). Two-way communication between the heart and the brain: Significance of time within the cardiac cycle. *American Psychologist* (February): 99-113.

McCraty, R., Atkinson, M., & Tomasino, D. (2001). *Science of the heart: Exploring the role of the heart in human performance.* www.heartmath.org/science. Retrieved February 20, 2005.

Maslow, Abraham (1996). *Toward a psychology of being.* New York: Van Nostrand Reinhold.

Moore, Thomas (1992). *Care of the soul: A guide for cultivating depth and sacredness in everyday life.* New York: HarperCollins.

Moore, Thomas (2002). *The soul's religion: Cultivating a profoundly spiritual way of life.* New York: HarperCollins Books.

Ornish, D, Gotto, A., Miller, R. (1979). Effects of a vegetarian diet and selected yoga techniques in the tratment of coronary heart disease. *Clinical Research*: 27:270A.

Saint-Exupery, A. (1943). *The little prince.* San Diego: Harcourt Brace Jovanovich.

Schwartz, Gary E. (1997). Information and Energy: The soul and spirit of mind-body medicine. *Advances: The Journal of Mind-Body Health,* Vol. 13 No. 1, 75–77.

Thurston, Mark (1989). *Soul-purpose: Discovering and Fulfilling Your Destiny.* New York: Harper & Row.

Weil, Andrew (1995). *Spontaneous healing.* New York: Random House.

Wilber, Ken (2005). Foreword. In A. Ardagh. *The translucent revolution: How people just like you are waking up and changing the world.* Novato, CA: New World Library, pp. xviii-xix.

Williamson, Marianne (1992). *A return to love.* New York: HarperCollins.

Chapter 10

Erickson, H. C., Tomlin, E. M., & Swain, M. A. P. (1983). *Modeling and role-modeling: A theory and paradigm for nursing.* Englewood Cliffs, NJ: Prentice-Hall Second-eighth printing, 1988-2005; EST Co: Austin, TX.

Rossi, E. (1980). *Hypnotic alteration of sensory perceptual and psychophysiological processes by Milton H. Erickson: The collected papers of Milton H. Erickson on hypnosis.* Vol. I-IV. New York: Irvington Publishers, Inc.

Goble, F. (1970). *The third force: The psychology of Abraham Maslow: A revolutionary new view of man.* New York: Pocket Books. See page 453.

Maslow, A. (1968). *Toward a psychology of being.* D. Van Norstrand Co: New York.

Maslow, A. (1969). *The psychology of science: A reconnaissance.* Chicago: Henry Regnery Co.

Walker, M. (2006). The effects of nurses practicing the hearttouch technique on perceived stress, spiritual well-being, and hardiness. *Journal of Holistic Nursing.* In press.

Watzlawick, P. (1967). *Pragmatics of human communicaton. A study of interactional patterns, pathologies, and paradoxes.* New York: W.W.W. Norton and Company.

Chapter 11

Encarta World English Encyclopedia, (2003). Microsoft Corporation. Bloomsbury Publishing Co.

Barnfather, J., Swain, M. A, & Erickson, H. (1989). Evaluation of two assessment techniques. *Nursing Science Quarterly.* 4, 172-182.

Barnfather, J., Swain, M. A., Erickson, H. (1989). Construct validity of an aspect of the coping process: Potential adaptation to stress. *Issues in Mental Health Nursing*, 10, 23-40.

Campbell, J., Finch, D., Allport, C., Erickson, H., & Swain, M. (1985). Modeling and role-modeling: A nursing assessment format. *Journal of Advanced Nursing*, 10, 111-115.

Erickson, H. (1983, March). Coping with new systems. *Journal of Nursing Education*, 132-136.

Erickson, H. (1984). Political aspects of compassionate care. Published in *Proceedings from a call to create.* Loyola University of Chicago, June 1-4, 1984.

Erickson, H. (1985, March/April). New challenges for nurses. *DCCN*, 99-100.

Erickson, H. (1986). *Synthesizing clinical experiences: A step in theory development.* Ann Arbor, MI: Biomedical Communications, University of Michigan.

Erickson, H. (1988). Modeling and role modeling: Ericksonian approaches with physiological problems. In J. Zeig, & S. Langton (Eds), *Ericksonian pychotherapy: The state of the art.* New York: Bruner/Mazel.

Erickson, H. (1990a). Theory based nursing. In H. Erickson, C. Kinney (Eds.), *Modeling and role-modeling: Theory, practice and research.* Vol.1(1). Austin, TX: Society for the Advancement of Modeling and Role-Modeling, pp. 1-27.

Erickson, H. (1990b). Self-care knowledge: Theory based nursing. In H. Erickson, C. Kinney (Eds.), *Modeling and role-modeling: Theory, practice and research.* Vol. 1(1). Austin, TX: Society for the Advancement of Modeling and Role-Modeling, pp.178-202.

Erickson, H. (1990c). Modeling and role-modeling with psychophysiological problems. In J. K. Zeig & S. Gilligan. (Eds.), *Brief therapy: Myths, methods, and metaphors* (pp. 473-491). New York: Brunner/Mazel.

Erickson, H. (1996). Holistic healing: Intra/inter relations of person and environment. (Guest Editor). *Issues in Mental Health Nursing*, Vol. 17, 3, 1996.

Erickson, H. (2002). Facilitating generativity and ego integrity: Applying Ericksonian methods to the aging population. In B.B. Geary and J.K. Zeig, (Eds.), *The handbook of Ericksonian psychotherapy.* New York: Brunner/Mazel.

Erickson, H., & Swain, M. A. (1982). A model for assessing potential to adapt to stress. *Research in Nursing and Health*, 5, 93-101.

Erickson, H. & Swain, M. A. (1990). Mobilizing self care resources: A nursing intervention for hypertension. *Issues in Mental Health Nursing*. Vol. 11 (3), 217-236.

Erickson, H. C., Tomlin, E. M., & Swain, M. A. P. (1983). *Modeling and role-modeling: A theory and paradigm for nursing.* Englewood Cliffs, NJ: Prentice-Hall; Second-fifth printing, 1988-2000; EST Co: Austin, TX.

Goble, F. (1970). *The third force: The psychology of Abraham Maslow: A revolutionary new view of man.* Pocket Books: New York.

Kinney, C. & Erickson, H. (1990). Modeling the client's world: A way to holistic care. *Issues in Mental Health Nursing*, Vol. 11 (2), 93-108.

Chapter 12

Bowlby, J. (1977). *The nature of parenting*. An invited lecture presented at The University of Michigan, Ann Arbor Michigan.

Erickson, H. (1990a). Theory Based Nursing. In H. Erickson, C. Kinney (Eds.), *Modeling and role-modeling: Theory, practice and research*. Vol. 1(1). Austin TX. Society for Advancement of Modeling and Role-Modeling, pp. 1-27.

Erickson, H. (1990b). Modeling and role-modeling with psychophysiological problems. In J.K. Zeig & S. Gilligan (Eds.), *Brief therapy: myths, methods, and metaphors* (pp. 473-491). New York: Brunner/Mazel.

Erickson, H. C., Tomlin, E. M., & Swain, M. A. P., (1983). *Modeling and role-modeling: A theory and paradigm for nursing.* Englewood Cliffs, NJ: Prentice-Hall; Second-eighth printing, 1988-2005; EST Co: Austin, TX.

Erikson, E. (1963). *Childhood and society.* (2nd ed.). New York: W.W. Norton.

Erikson, E. (1964). *Insight and responsibility.* New York: W.W. Norton.

Finch, D. (1987). *Testing a theoretically based nursing assessment.* Unpublished Masters Thesis. The University of Michigan. Ann Arbor, MI.

Gerber, R. (2001). *A Practical guide to vibrational medicine; Energy healing and spiritual transformation.* New York, New York: Quill, Harper-Collins Publishers.

Lefcourt, H. (1965). Internal versus external control of reinforcement. *Psychological Bulletin*, 65(4), 206-220.

Lefcourt, H. (1973). The function of the illusion of control and freedom. *American Psychologist*, 28, 417-425.

Olson, Kenneth (1975) *Can you wait till Friday?* Greenwood, Conn: A Fawcett Crest Book.

Pert, C. (2003). *Molecules of emotion: The science behind mind-body medicine.* New York, New York: Schribner.

Weiss, R. (1977). *Loneliness: The experience of emotional and social isolation.* Cambridge, MA: MIT Press.

Weiss, R. (1982). Attachment in adult life. In C.M. Parkes, & J. Stevenson-Hinde (Eds.), *The place of attachment in human behavior* (pp. 111-184). New York: Wiley.

Winnicott, D. (1965). *The maturational process and the facilitating environment.* New York: Internation Universities Press.

Watzlawick, P. (1967). *Pragmatics of human communicaton. A study of interactional patterns, pathologies, and paradoxes.* New York: W.W.W.Norton and Company.

Chapter 13

Clayton, D. K. (2001). *Journeys through chaos: Experiences of prolonged family suffering and evolving spiritual identity.* Unpublished dissertation. The University of Texas at Austin, Austin, TX.

Cousins, N. (1983). *The healing heart: Antidotes to panic and helplessness.* New York: W.W. Norton.

Epstein, G. (1994). *Healing into immortality.* New York: Bantam Books.

Erickson, H. (1976). *Identification of states of coping utilizing physiological and psychological data.* Unpublished Master's Thesis, The University of Michigan, Ann Arbor, MI.

Erickson, H. (1990a). Self-care knowledge: An exploratory study. In H. Erickson & C. Kinney (Eds.), *Modeling and Role-Modeling: Theory, Practice and Research* (Vol. 1). Austin, TX: Society for Advancement of Modeling and Role-Modeling, pp. 78-101.

Erickson, H. (1990b). Theory based practice. In H. Erickson, C. Kinney (Eds.), *Modeling and role-modeling: Theory, practice and research.* Vol. 1(1). Austin, TX: Society for Advancement of Modeling and Role-Modeling, pp 178-202.

Erickson, H. Modeling and Role-Modeling with Psychophysiological Problem (1990). In J. K. Zeig & S. Gilligan. (Eds.), *Brief therapy: Myths, methods, and metaphors* (pp. 473-491). New York: Brunner/Mazel.

Erickson, H.L. & Swain, M.A. (1985) *Exploring relations among health conception, clinical judgments and clinical outcomes.* Unpublished manuscript. The University of Texas at Austin, Austin, TX.

Erickson, H. C., Tomlin, E. M., & Swain, M. A. P. (1983). *Modeling and role-modeling: A theory and paradigm for nursing.* Englewood Cliffs, NJ: Prentice-Hall; Second-eighth printing, 1988-2005; EST Co: Austin, TX.

Frank, A.W. (1995). *The wounded storyteller.* Chicago: The University of Chicago Press.

Halldorsdottir, S. (1991). Five basic modes of being with another. In D. A. Gaut & M. M. Leininger (Eds.), *Caring: The compassionate healthier person* (pp. 37-49). New York: National League for Nursing Press.

Rodgers, S. (1996). Facilitative Affiliation: Nurse-client interactions that enhance healing. *Issues in Mental Health Nursing, 17,* 171-184.

Smith, J.A. (1981). The idea of health: A philosophical inquiry. *Advances in Nursing Science, 3* (3), 45-50.

Vardey, L. (1995). *Mother Teresa: A simple path.* New York: Random House.

Chapter 14

Branum, K. (1997). Healing in the context of terminal illness. In P. B. Kritek (Ed.), *Reflections on healing: A central Nursing construct.* (pp. 330-348). New York: NLN Press.

Brown, Jeffrey (Interviewer). (March 29, 2006). *The Jim Lehrer Show.* (Television Broadcast). New York: Public Broadcasting System.

Buscaglia, L. (1983). *Living, loving, learning.* New York: First Ballantine Books.

Chopra, D. (1996). *The seven spiritual laws of success: A practical guide to the fulfillment of your dreams.* New Delhi: Shri Jainendra Press.

Chopra, D. (2000). *How to know God: The soul's journey into the mystery of mysteries.* New York: Three Rivers Press.

Dossey, B., Guzzetta, C., Quinn, J., Firsch, N. (2000). *AHNA standards of holistic nursing practice: guidelines for caring and healing.* New York, New York: Jones & Bartlett Publishers.

Dossey, B., Keegan, L., Guzzetta, C. (2005). *Holistic nursing: A handbook for practice* (4th ed.). New York, New York: Jones & Bartlett Publishers.

Dossey, B. (1997). (Corporate Editor). Core curriculum for holistic nursing by American Holistic Nurses Association. New York: Aspen Publishers.

Erickson, H. (1990). Theory based nursing. In H. Erickson & C. Kinney (Eds.), *Modeling and role-modeling: Theory, practice and research.* Vol. 1(1). Austin, TX: Society for Advancement of Modeling and Role-Modeling, pp. (1), 1-27.

Erickson, H. & Swain, M.A. (1990). Mobilizing self care resources: A rursing intervention for hypertension. *Issues in Mental Health Nursing*, Vol. 11 (3), 217-236.

Erickson, H. C., Tomlin, E. M., & Swain, M. A. P. (1983). *Modeling and role modeling: A theory and paradigm for nursing.* Englewood Cliffs, NJ: Prentice-Hall; Second-fifth printing, 1988-2000; EST Co: Austin, TX.

Fenton, M. (1997). Healing: The underground experience. In P. B. Kritek (Ed.). *Reflections on healing: A central nursing construct.* (pp. 559-565). New York: NLN Press.

Fish, S., & Shelly, J. (1978). *Spiritual care: The nurse's role.* Downers Grove: InterVarsity Press.

Frisch, N., & Kelley, J. (1995). *Healing life's crises: A guide for nurses; nurse healer series.* Boston, MA: Delmar Publishers, An International Thomson Publishing Company.

Hall, B. (2005). *The art of becoming a nurse healer.* Orlando, FL: Bandido Books.

Hover-Kramer, D., & Shames, K. (1997). *Energetic approaches to emotional healing.* Boston, MA: Delmar Publishers, An International Thomson Publishing Company

Keegan, L. (1994). *The nurse as healer.* Boston, MA: Delmar Publishers, An International Thomson Publishing Company.

Keegan, L. (2001). *Healing with complementary & alternative therapies.* Boston, MA: Delmar Publishers, An International Thomson Publishing Company.

Keegan, L. (2002). *Healing nutrition.* Boston, MA: Delmar Publishers, An International Thomson Publishing Company.

Keegan, L., & Dossey, B. (1997). *Holistic nursing.* Boston, MA: Delmar Publishers, An International Thomson Publishing Company.

Kritiek, P. (1997). *Reflections on healing: A central Nursing construct.* New York: NLN Press.

Landis, B. (1997). Healing and the human spirit. In P. B. Kritek (Ed.). *Reflections on healing: A central nursing construct* (pp. 72-80). New York: NLN Press.

Nichols, J. (2000). *The soul. as healer: Lessons in affirmation, visualization, and inner power.* St. Paul, MN: LLewllyn Publications.

Nightingale, F. (1860). *Notes on nursing: What it is and what it is not.* London: Harrison.

Olson, M. (2002). *Healing the dying.* Boston, MA: Delmar Publishers, An International Thomson Publishing Company.

Shames, K.(1995). *Creative imagery for nurse healers: Nurse as healer series.* Boston, MA: Delmar Publishers, An International Thomson Publishing Company.

Stoll, R. (1989). The essence of spirituality. In V. B. Carson (Ed.), *Spiritual dimensions of nursing practice* (pp. 4-23). Philadelphia: W.B. Saunders.

Umlauf, M.G. (1997) *Healing meditation: Nurse as healer series.* Boston, MA: Delmar Publishers, An International Thomson Publishing Company.

Waters, P. & Daubenmire, M. (1997). Therapeutic capacity: The critical variance in nursing practice. In P. B. Kritek (Ed.), *Reflections on healing: A central Nursing construst.* (pp. 56-68). New York: NLN Press.

Watson, J. (1993). *Rediscovering caring and healing arts. American holistic nursing Standard* 7 (38).

STORIES USED IN THIS TEXT

Chapter 1

A child, searching for Self
A spiritual child, observed by his teacher
Fear of a can of worms, finding caterpillars
Mrs. Cook's Transformation
Trusting our inner voice
Learning that we're here for a purpose
Learning the importance of articulating what we know

Chapter 3

Premature twins and energy therapies
Distant healing
M. Walker and connecting with the Universe or God
M. Walker and an experience with expectations

Chapter 4

Anna Martin, cigarette smoker
Knowing but not knowing we know

Chapter 5

Multiple stories about healthy/unhealthy developmental residual
Bud, transformation, spiritual growth
The Gift of the Magi by O'Henry

Chapter 6

Adam's life story
But, I have no refrigerator
Jane, learning to transfer knowledge
Jay and Bill, two adolescents
My dog needs food
Faith as a self-actualized woman

Chapter 7

My box of books
My brother's old shoes
Anne lets go
Old couple that died one year apart
I've been sick since my husband died 25 years ago
A Vietnam vet searching for Self
Growth during the last few weeks of life (loss resolution)

Chapter 8

Harvey, a happy man

Chapter 9
Rebecca

Chapter 10
Mr. Brown breaks his hip

Mr. M's blood pressure goes up

Lance has a cough

Jimmy doesn't want a zipper

Chapter 11
Mr. M and his son

Zelda searches for her life purpose

Learning about Presence

Chapter 12
Bill comes home from Vietnam

Jim breaks his arm riding a bike

The five month old needs help, he's bored

Mary sees snow

Janie eats the Snickers bars to get even with mom

He had to move to the farm

Chapter 13
James, shot and wounded

Esther has multiple threatened and real losses

Avery has morbid grief

Sarah

Nursing students

Mattie Stepanek & Milton Erickson

Chapter 14
Mr. B. a tough old Teddy Bear

It all started with the chicken-attack

Seeding can happen by the water fountain

Who is in trouble here?

Someone is lonely and needs a friend

Mrs. Jones loses her mother again

The lady learns about her beginnings

The veteran is afraid to cry, he might not be able to stop

GLOSSARY

Adaptation: The process by which an individual responds to internal and external stressors in a health and growth directed manner.

Adaptive equilibrium: State in which people who have a potential for mobilizing coping resources use them in a growth and health directed manner that leaves no subsystem in jeopardy.

Affiliated-Individuation: The need to be dependent on support systems while simultaneously maintaining independence from them. The drive for healthy AI exists across the lifespan, but is demonstrated differently depending on the developmental stage.

Anticipatory loss: Occurs when the loss is anticipated. If the person perceives the object no longer meets his needs, only minimally meets them, or the person feels in control of the situation, feelings of loss will be minimized and loss resolution will be much easier.

APAM: Abbreviation for Adaptive Potential Assessment Model, which identifies three states of coping: arousal, equilibrium, and impoverishment. Each state represents a different potential for mobilizing resources needed to contend with stressors.

Arousal: One of the states of the APAM, a stress state.

Attachment objects: Objects that repeatedly meet our needs. They are specific to the person. People may attach to animate objects such as a person or pet, inanimate objects like a book or bicycle, abstractions such as an idea, or even a life goal.

Attachment: An outcome of bonding. It can be either secure or insecure. Insecure attachment takes two forms: clinging and push-away behavior. Insecure attachment can interfere with our ability to produce healthy developmental residual, while secure attachment helps us produce healthy residual.

Basic needs: Basic needs exist in a four-level hierarchy with biophysical needs at the first level, followed by the need for safety and security, love and belongingness, and esteem and self-esteem, respectively. Basic needs are somewhat hierarchical and necessary for growth.

Being (v): Acting from our spiritual core and using intentionality to be connected with another being. Being enhances synchrony of energy fields between two people. It involves the integration of spirit with human form.

Being (n): The holistic person with mind-body-spirit relations, all connecting, interacting, and shaping the essence of who we are as holistic beings.

Being Orientation: People with Being Motivation exhibit a drive to learn and grow, find meaning in their lives, and relate to others with true reciprocity. They have the ability to focus on others rather than themselves and gain a deep sense of enjoyment when observing growth in others. It takes little for them to change a negative experience into a positive one, and little to find strengths in their significant others. Overall, they are happy people with a high level of well-being.

Bodymind: The notion that the body has a mind of its own. First proposed by Diane Connely, the term refers to the effects of chemicals excreted throughout the body that influence our thoughts and feelings.

Bonding: Starts with the first sensation of being connected because our needs are met and continues until attachment occurs. It can occur without attachment, but attachment cannot occur without bonding.

Caring Field: According to Watson (1999) when the nurse is fully present with the client, nurse and client connect on an energetic level, creating a Caring Field—a new field of consciousness and possibilities. It is the basis for helping people grow, develop, and heal.

Cellular Memory: An aspect of energy transformation in which chemical molecules are stored after a specific life experience. These chemicals are released again during life experiences that are associated, through the senses, with the original event. It is an ongoing, dynamic process that provides insight into mind-body relations.

Challenging losses: Losses experienced because of the choices we have made. When we experience losses as opportunities or challenges, we move through the stages of grief more rapidly, with more positive anticipation, and less conflict.

Conflict: A situation or event that creates two or more types of unmet needs and requires choosing between two or more outcomes. Maslow discusses four types of conflict: Approach-Approach, Approach-Avoidance, multiple Approach-Avoidance, and Avoidance-Avoidance.

Consciousness: A Universal intelligence, created by a merging of all energy fields, human, and other, that provides information about the structure of our Universe, and all knowledge about our nature. It is "a kind of energy itself" (Gerber, 2001, p.10) which is in us and around us.

Coping: The process of contending with stressors. Coping can be adaptive (health and growth-directed) or maladaptive (sickness-directed). Factors that influence our ability to cope include our perception of the stressor, the nature of the stress response, and the ability to mobilize resources.

Deficit Orientation: Develops in people who experience prolonged difficulty with need satisfaction. Deficit-oriented people have difficulty meeting their own needs in a healthy manner. Instead of building relationships based on mutual trust, they build relationships hoping to get their own needs met. Self-oriented and unable to perceive the world through other people's eyes, their behavior and interactions with others are driven by their unmet needs.

Development: The holistic synthesis of the growth-produced increasing differentiations of a person's body, ideas, social relations, and so forth. People have an inherent drive to develop. The Modeling and Role-Modeling theory holds that development is chronological and age-related; sequential and predictable; contextual; stage specific; task-focused; and epigenetic. This theory argues that growth and development are inter-related, but not the same.

Developmental losses: Losses related to stages of development. These losses are a normal part of life, they must happen for us to be able to move on and work on the next task. The ability to resolve them depends on the resources available.

Developmental Residual: The products of the task-work carried or taken as we move from one developmental stage into the next. It helps us with the task of the new stage and helps us rework the previous stages. There are two types of residual: positive and negative. We need a healthy balance between the two if we are to continue to grow and become the most we can be. Developmental residual includes stored memories.

Distant healing: Distant healing is the attempt to benefit another rather than to simply have an effect. It includes prayer, directed thoughts and feelings, and spiritual healing techniques.

Distant Intentionality: Distant intentionality is the intent to have an effect on another from a distance and includes the effects of mental intention on "non-living" and living systems through energy exchange.

Distressor: A stimulus that is experienced as threatening or one that mounts (either directly or indirectly) a maladaptive response.

Energy: The capacity to do 'work' and create change. It is categorized as either potential or kinetic and can be found in numerous forms. While it cannot be created or destroyed, it can be transformed from one type to another. Energy can be transformed to matter, and matter to energy.

Enlightenment: Cosmic understanding acquired when the spirit is reconnected with the Soul as it enters the Universal Energy Field. Consciousness and the Universal Force, integrated in the Universal Field, produce Enlightenment.

Epigenesis: The ability to continue to grow across a lifetime. The reworking of the original task within the context of the current, chronologically based task is the essence of developmental epigenesis.

Equilibrium: A state of the APAM, wherein people have a good potential for mobilizing coping resources.

Essence of Self: The nature of our spirit defined by the context of a lifetime. It is who we are without the influence of others. It does not change, but it does evolve in how it is expressed.

Facilitation: Making easier or less difficult; helping forward. The nurse-client relationship is an interactive process that helps the individual identify, mobilize, and develop the individual's own strengths in his or her movement towards health. The key difference between nurturing and facilitation is the action of the nurse in the latter. When we facilitate, we make it easier or less difficult for people to grow. We do this with purposeful strategies artistically designed for the individual.

G-APAM: The Group Adaptive Potential Assessment Model is the product of a Delphi study looking at the assessment of adaptive potential in groups. G-APAM uses coping potential and stress level to create quadrants of group behavior within an encompassing context.

Grief: Is always a result of loss. The normal grief process should last no more than 12-14 months. When loss is significant, there is usually an acute phase of grief that lasts 1-4 months.

Growth needs/Higher-level needs: Growth Needs emerge when Basic needs have been met to some degree. Although there are many types of Growth needs, they are not organized hierarchically. Since we have an inherent need to explore, be creative, and expand our horizons, Growth needs emerge when we feel safe, connected, and somewhat self-sufficient. Growth Need satisfaction is necessary for us to move toward self-actualization.

Growth: Growth includes the physical, psychosocial, cognitive, and spiritual *changes* that people experience as their needs are met. It precedes healthy development and comes from healthy development. Survival of the human being depends on some growth. The degree of growth determines the developmental residual we carry as we move on to another developmental stage.

Healing: A concept related to health, which means to move toward holism or integration of spirit with the human form.

Heart-to-heart connections: An energy-field connection between two people.

Holistic being: The intermixing of Spiritual energy with the energy field of the biophysical-psychosocial being (and all of its genetic predispositions) creates a *holistic being.*

Human being: The spirit in human form.

Human energy field: Human beings interact with the Unified Field by way of the Human Energy system, which consists of three key components: the meridians, chakras, and the aura.

Human form: the predetermined biophysical-psychosocial-cognitive form of people.

Impoverishment: A state of the APAM wherein persons have diminished, if not depleted, resources available for mobilization.

Inner Voice: Present in each one of us, some refer to this as "intuition." It is not our conscience; it is not massaged or shaped by society or social norms. It comes directly from our Self-knowing. It speaks to us when we ask for insight, and also at unexpected times. Since it doesn't always send messages we understand, we often ignore or pass them off as irrelevant thoughts.

Integration: The task of Integration starts pre-birth and continues until birth or shortly after. The task is integration of the spirit with the biophysical-psychosocial body of the human being. The Developmental Residual dimensions are: Unity and Duality. The Strength is Awareness and the Virtue is Groundedness.

Intent: Intent is the purposeful use of our holistic selves to enhance growth in another person.

Life Purpose: The work we have to do in human form in a given lifetime to enhance the Soul. Finding Meaning in our life and a purpose for our existence help us discover our Life Purpose. It can only be discovered by finding meaning in day-to-day experiences.

Living Matrix: Coined by Oschman, the term, the *living matrix* refers to the dynamic interaction that starts at the cellular level, moves out to the subsystems, and into the entire 'body' of the person. This view of holism is consistent with MRM. It helps further our understanding of linkages between chemical and electrical energy, mind-body relations, and the importance of Self-care

Knowledge as the primary source of information.

Maladaptation: The process an individual uses to cope with a stressor within one subsystem by taxing energies from another.

Maladaptive equilibrium: A relatively steady state wherein an individual is coping with stressors, but at the cost of draining energies from another subsystem or subsystems.

Meaning-in-life: The significance or importance of our existence as human beings in our day-to-day lives.

Meaning-of-life: The significance, importance, and nature of our Soul-work. The Meaning of Life is discovered as we connect with our Self/Soul. Some say the Meaning of Life is to love and be compassionate.

Morbid Grief: Occurs when there is an unresolved conflict, ambivalence, or guilt associated with the loss or there is inadequate transference of attachment to another object. It interferes with the resolution of developmental tasks, the reworking of earlier tasks, and moving on with our lives.

Neuromodulation: Communication by way of neurotransmitters which are released directly into the body fluids. The primary way we are able to have a dynamic, interactive web of communication among all parts of the body. This exchange of information can impact multiple receptor sites grouped together as well as multiple sites located throughout the body. Although it can happen in milliseconds, it can also take longer.

Neurotransmission: The neuron-neuron exchange of information which can take milliseconds; the primary way the central nervous system communicates with the peripheral nervous system.

Nonlocality: Based on John Bell's theory of interconnectedness that once subatomic particles have established a connection, they remain connected energetically over distance and can communicate with and affect each other. The term 'nonlocal' refers to phenomena that demonstrate that our minds can observe and even influence individuals, objects, and events widely separated from the observer by distance and time (Gerber, 2000, pp. 382-383).

Nurturance: The fusing and integrating of cognitive, physiological, and affective processes with the aim of assisting a client to move toward holistic health. Nurturing, a state of Being, has two key components: acceptance and intent. Nurturing happens when we unconditionally accept another person and purposefully send positive energy to that person. Nurturing is what we do because of our beliefs about people, our professional goals, and ourselves. Nurturance can happen without facilitation, but facilitation cannot happen without nurturance. Nurturance is necessary for growth. Both are necessary for healing.

Perceived Enactment of Autonomy (PEA): Coined by Judith Hertz (1996), a prerequisite to Self-Care Action. It precedes Self-care Action and represents the potential for SCA. PEA is a sense of being able to do what is best for one's self .

Presence: Presence is the intentional use of energy to help others feel connected. Presence can help people feel cared about, mobilize their resources, and grow. It is the holistic existence of an individual who is fully open to another human's energy system, and is an important factor in facilitating growth and healing. It is a combination of the techniques of Centering your energy field, Focusing on your intent, and Opening yourself to your client, so your energy fields can merge.

Reason for Being: The reason for us to exist in human form, to become a human being. Our Reason for Being is to continue a specific aspect of our Soul-work.

Reframing: A hypnotherapeutic or communication technique that facilitates a change in the perception of an event, situation, condition, and so forth.

Seeding: A hypnotherapeutic or communication technique that instills an idea at the conscious or unconscious level. Seeding is a way of initiating growth in another human being.

Self: The nature of our Soul. It is closely linked to the Essence of Self, but is removed from incarnate life.

Self-actualization: The process of self-actualization includes moments or episodes of transcendence; moments when we become more connected to our Self, more holistic with mind-body-spirit integration. It is the process needed to discover our Essence of Self and to connect with our Self.

Self-actualizing: The actualizing of our Life Purpose. It requires that we merge our sense-of-self with our Essence of Self.

Self-care Actions: The mobilizing and use of Self-care Knowledge and Self-care Resources in order to meet our needs. In MRM theory, Self-care Action is based on personal meaning to the individual. It includes anything we do to take care of ourselves.

Self-care Knowledge: The personal understanding of what is needed to help us grow, develop, or heal. It includes awareness of personal needs and goals, as well as strengths, capabilities, characteristics, values, and liabilities. It also includes recognition of what is *not needed*.

Self-care Resources: The internal and external resources which help us through difficult situations and are used to help gain, maintain, and promote an optimum level of holistic health. They are needed to survive and thrive.

Self-care: The ability to take care of oneself in multiple ways—ways that facilitate holistic growth and development.

Self-knowing: Knowledge drawn from our personal reservoir as well as a greater source: our Soul, and the Universe. It is an aggregate of specific knowledge drawn from our Soul and cosmic knowledge drawn from the Universe.

Sense-of-self: Our understanding of who and what we are as defined by the perceptions of others mixed with our own perceptions. Sense-of-self can change over the lifetime, depending on our relationships.

Situational Losses: Losses that occur because of a situation or life event and are different from developmental losses, since usually, there is no opportunity for growth prior to the loss. We all experience situational losses, some of which are more obvious, and some more obscure.

Soul: The seat of our Self. It is linked to our mind and body by way of spiritual energy. Our Soul is composed of energy, which vibrates at a very high level. It is our Reservoir. It contains information about who we are, what fulfills us, what drains us, what makes us unique, and what gifts we have to offer. It resides within the Universal Energy Field.

Soul-work: The reason our Soul manifests in a holistic, human form. Soul-work is what must be accomplished for growth of the Soul.

Spirit: A type of energy that connects our Soul with our human form. It is the energy that transforms purposefully, is manifested in the dimensions of the person, and transcends person.

Spiritual Drive: A force that pulls the Soul and body together. It starts before our biophysical existence, continues through our lifetime, and culminates during Transformation. It is always present and pervades our subsystems. It inspires our search for the Essence of Self. It draws from the Universe and gives back to the universe, representing the continual exchange of energy. Our spiritual drive is *greater* than any of the subsystems and has a bigger influence on our total well-being.

Spiritual energy: Soul energy converted to a lower vibratory level. Spiritual energy has to synchronize its vibrations with the human body so they can integrate.

Spiritual Enhancement: The ongoing process of finding meaning in our life experiences. It occurs repeatedly across the lifespan; it helps us uncover our Reason for Being or Soul-work for this lifetime.

Spirituality: Spirituality, or belief in the importance and meaning of life, is seen as the core of the holistic individual in Modeling and Role-Modeling Theory. This belief lays the foundation for a hopeful outlook or positive orientation.

Spirit-to-spirit connection: A connecting of two people that transcends the physical sphere of life.

State Resources: One way of thinking about Internal resources. They are derived from need satisfaction and are necessary to help us live and grow. However, they are not stable; they develop in a short period of time and disappear just as fast.

Stress: The nonspecific response of the holistic person to any demand or stressor. Eustress, good stress, and Distress, bad stress, are the two types of stress.

Stressor: A stimulus that precedes and elicits stress. Stressors in one subsystem have the potential to create a stress response in another.

Threatening losses: Losses that are outside our control, so we feel threatened. These may be real or not, i.e., they can actually happen, or be perceived as happening. They are more difficult to resolve.

Trait Resources: A second way of thinking about Internal resources. There are three types of trait residual that can become Self-care Resources: Genetic Resources, Stored memories, and Psychosocial Development.

Transcendence: The experience of being fully connected with our spirit and temporarily with our Soul. Transcendence is the act of self-actualizing.

Transformation: The task of transformation involves our ability to separate our spiritual energy from our physical body, transform to Soul energy, and become part of the Universal Field–that from which we came. During this process, the journey of life comes full cycle, and our spiritual energy returns to its original source.

Transitional objects: Objects specific to the person that *represent* or *symbolize* an attachment object, and are usually age-specific. They serve a two-fold purpose: they meet the needs in lieu of the attachment object, and they facilitate normal, healthy developmental processes. They enhance transitions.

Unified Energy Field: A theoretical field of energy in which all forces (and, therefore, all types of energy) interface and transform from one type of energy to another. The Universal Energy Field.

Universal Force: The life-giving force or energy that comes from *the* Universal Field; God, the Divine. Provides the primary energy source for Consciousness and Enlightenment.

Unified Field Theory: See Unified Energy Field.

Zero Point Energy: Accepted by some physicists as real energy which we cannot directly sense since it is the same everywhere, even inside our bodies and measuring devices. It is believed to exist in an empty space (the Zero Point Field) where subatomic particles can continue to move even at a temperature of absolute zero. The potential for understanding how the Soul connects with our mind and body may lie in understanding Zero Point Energy and its connection with other types of energy fields.

Zero-point energy: Energy that moves at zero point Kelvin degrees.

Appendix A
Heart-Centered Awareness
©Marsha Walker, 1998

A. Heart Touch

1. Centering—Take 3 slow, deep breaths (similar to a sigh) in a slow, comfortable rhythm. Focus your attention on the inhale and exhale, bringing your conscious thoughts to the present time and to your body in the room. Let go of all thoughts when they arise and return your attention to the exercise.

2. Imagine a small circle of light in the center of your forehead and watch it move slowly down your face, neck, chest, and see it come to rest in the area of the heart. Allow the circle to grow in size with each inhale until it is a sphere encircling and permeating the entire chest area.

3. Recall a situation where you felt very loved or where you felt very loving toward another individual, whether person, animal, plant, or place. Relive the situation, feeling the feelings and experiencing the sights, sounds, smells, tastes, and touches, including any movement that was occurring in the situation.

B. Loving-Touch

1. Send the feeling of love that you are feeling to an individual by imaging the love as a stream of light moving from your heart area to the heart area of the other individual, and then see the light and love filling and surrounding the other individual. If you are touching the other individual in your image, or in real life, visualize the love as a stream of light moving down your arm to your hand, filling and surrounding the other individual.

2. Mentally identify something about the other individual that you can love and/or appreciate.

C. Connecting with Higher Power

Finally, while maintaining the connection with the other individual, create a connection with your view of a Higher Power, a Source of Love, Light, Truth, and/or Wholeness, whether it be through prayer, meditation, or another personal method that is comfortable for you. Having created a connection with the other individual and Higher Power, image a three way connection between the individual, yourself, and a Higher Power, which might look like a triangle or circle of light. The researcher suggests that the feeling of love is the connecting energy between nurse, other individual, and Higher Power that creates balance, wholeness, and health.

Appendix B
An Operational Taxonomy of Human Needs
© Helen L. Erickson, 1975

I. Primary Needs

A. Basic Needs
1. Physiological

    a) Survival needs include biological necessities which must be satisfied for biological homeostasis. Partially unmet or unmet needs in this category can result in disequilibrium in the body processes, and if continued, death.

        1) food
        2) water
        3) oxygen
        4) elimination of waste products
        5) rest and sleep
        6) temperature regulation
        7) pain avoidance
        8) biological homeostasis.

    b) Stimulation needs are not necessary for survival of life although unmet needs in this area may result in retardation of physical and emotional growth.[1] Types include:

        1) sexuality
        2) activity
        3) exploration
        4) manipulation
        5) novelty.

2. Social[2]

    a) The need for safety and security is necessary for healthy growth. These include a need for:

        1) a predictable, consistent world
        2) fairness and justice
        3) freedom with limits
        4) safety from harm
        5) protection of personal items
        6) nurturing care.

    b) The need to be loved and to belong[3] is also necessary for healthy growth. These include a need for:

        1) affection
        2) warmth
        3) kindness
        4) consideration in human relationships
        5) to be understood and accepted as an individual
        6) mutual trust
        7) identity.

    c) The need for esteem and self-esteem is also necessary for healthy growth. These include a need to/for:

        1) feel adequate

2) mastery and competitiveness
3) strength
4) achievement
5) confidence
6) independence
7) respect from others
8) status
9) attention
10) importance
11) dignity.

B. Growth Needs (Higher-level Needs)

1) Need for meaningfulness in life
2) Need for self-sufficiency
3) Need for effortlessness
4) Need for playfulness
5) Need for enrichment
6) Need for simplicity
7) Need for completion
8) Need for aliveness
9) Need for goodness and truth
10) Need for beauty.

II. Secondary Needs[4]

1)   The need for coping mechanisms
2)   The need for cognitive skills sufficient to perceive and understand stimuli
3)   The need to receive stimuli in a cognitive form, i.e., information
4)   The need to provide input and receive feedback
5)   The need for freedom of speech
6)   The need for freedom of action, such as choice in own destiny.

---

[1] Studies have shown that deprivation of stimulation can result in disorientation in the psychological processes and can result in retarded physical and emotional development. Other studies have shown that sensory stimulation results in long-range changes in body chemistry.

[2] Social needs are not necessary for the life of the organism. As shown by Erikson (1963), if these needs are not met in the most desirable way during human maturation, the organism (human) will adapt and the result will dictate a personality characteristic. This is to say that the organism has the ability to adapt to an unmet need at this level by using various methods in his repertoire of coping if his basic needs have been met to some degree.

[3] Although these needs are not necessary for the life of the organism, studies have shown that a lack in fulfilling them can result in depression and regression of the physical and psychological processes. Sullivan describes the need for love as a need for intimacy; Rogers describes love as having unconditional positive regard for the person; Maslow describes love as a closeness between two people. The need to belong is a different entity. It refers to the need to belong with or to be able to identify with another person or group.

[4] While Maslow called these secondary needs, I think they are better described as inherent instincts or drives basic to humankind.

Appendix C
A Preliminary Taxonomy of Eriksonian Developmental Attributes
© Helen L. Erickson, 1980

I.   TRUST

Characteristics

Confidence
Optimism
Reliance on self and others
Faith that the world can satisfy needs
Sense of hope or belief in the attainability
  of wishes in spite of problems,
  without overestimation of results

As an adult

Optimistic, confident, reliance on self
Faith that needs will be met somehow
Sense of hope of attaining wishes without
  overestimation of results

MISTRUST

Lack of self-confidence
Pessimism
Dependent on others, clingy
Suspicious
Feeling that things won't turn out right

Withdrawn
Easily hurt

Controlling, sarcastic, aggressive,
  pathologically optimistic, never
  satisfied emotionally, lack of
  self-confidence, suspicious.
Bitterness towards others
Antagonistic

II   AUTONOMY

Characteristics

Self-control over motor and sphincter muscles
Ability to make & carry out decisions
Can cope adequately with problems
Can wait patiently
Can give generously & can hold as
  indicated
Can distinguish between own &
  other's wishes and possessions
Has feelings of good will and pride

As an adult

Perceives ability to control own life,
Self-directed, strong will, persistent

SHAME AND DOUBT

Feelings of embarrassment, exposed,
  small, impotent, dirty
Feelings of being fooled
Feelings of wanting to hide
Feelings of rage against self
Defensive behaviors
Uncertainty and mistrust
Fear of unknown
Lack of self-confidence

Feels nothing one does is good.
Feels that others control one rather
Than one's control of self.
Overly compliant but angry,
Stubborn, aggressive, obstinate
Impulsive
Lack of responsibility
Wants to get away with things

III   INITIATIVE

Characteristics

Enjoys activity
Assertive
Interest in learning
Dependable

As an adult

Assertive, able to take initiative, can
  delay gratification; a problem-solver

GUILT

Hesitates to participate in groups
Defeatist attitude, hostile
Feelings of being deterred
Feels responsible when not
Feelings of shame, being bad.

Conflict between ideal and real self
Rigid superego, self-punishing.
Bitterness toward restrictive adults

IV	**INDUSTRY**		**INFERIORITY**

Characteristics
Interest in doing the work of the world, feeling
  one can learn and solve problems.
Responsible work habits and attitudes.
Mastery of age-related tasks
Perseverance
Diligence
Self-control
Cooperation
Compromise versus competition

Feels inadequate

Feels defeated.
Unable to learn tasks easily
Appears lazy to others
Unable to stick to plan
Unable to compete, compromise,
  cooperate

As an adult
Able to use logic and problem-solve well
Able to set goals and work toward them

Doesn't enjoy work or try new tasks.
Aggressive, bossy, hypercompetitive
Lacks perseverance, meek, isolated

V   **IDENTITY**   **ROLE-DIFFUSION**

Characteristics
Feelings of internal stability
Feelings of sameness
Feelings of continuity
Feelings of wholeness
Feelings of uniqueness
Responsible
Loyal
Commitment to a value system

Self-conscious.
Doubtful of self.
Confused about social role
Impotent
Insecure
Disillusioned
Alienated

As an adult
Know how to fit into society.
Sense of consistency with real and ideal self

Vacillates in decision-making
Appears brazen
Avoids adult company and behavior
Fears loss of uniqueness

VI   **INTIMACY**   **ISOLATION**

Characteristics
Mutual trust
Sharing of feelings
Responsibility to significant others
Shares identity without loss of self
Loving, patient, kind
Not jealous, boastful, arrogant or rude

Self-absorption
Unable to be intimate, spontaneous
Withdrawn, lonely, conceited
Behaves in stereotypical way
Repeated, unsuccessful relations
Overextends without real interest in
  activity
Lives a façade
Makes pretentious claims
Distrustful, pessimistic, ruthless
Vacillates in behavior

As an adult
Has warm, sharing relationships with adults
Willing to commit to others

Lacks close relationships
Feelings of loneliness
Often bitter

VII   GENERATIVITY

Characteristics

Concern for providing for others is as great as
  concern for providing self
Sense of enterprise
Charity, altruism, perseverance
Collaborates well with others
Receives gratification from jobs well done,
What can be given to others.
Accepts self in total (i.e., body and personality)

SELF-ABSORPTION

Regression to adolescence or earlier
Behavior characterized by physical
  and psychological invalidism.
Dislikes own body.
Feels inept at handling self
physically or interpersonally.
Operates on "slim margin" therefore
easily burned out
Withdrawn
Resigned
Isolated
Rebellious
Unable to give to others

VIII   EGO INTEGRITY

Characteristics

Accepts life as own
Defends meaning and dignity of own life style
Anticipates peaceful transition
Accepts spiritual self

DESPAIR

Wants another chance at life
Hypercritical of others
Fearful of death
Projects own self-disgust
Feels inadequate
Chronic hostility

Compiled from a variety of sources.
Not to be reprinted without permission of author.

Appendix D
Notes on Piaget's Cognitive Theory
© Helen L. Erickson, 1994

NOTES ON PIAGET

	SYMBOLISM	CAUSALITY	PREDICTING THE FUTURE
Sensorimotor	cue that something is to come	object-action sequence are intertwined	no variability in sequence
	no discrimination between cue and response	one link relates to next	
	no object permanence totally a private experience	dreams, etc. experienced as real	
Preoperational	connects cue and response	reasoning is particular to particular (transductive)	expects identical occurrence of events
egocentrism	classification is based on personal experience	non-reversibility of relationship	
irreversibility	objects are related to self experience with missing elements new classifications	no differentiation of self and actions animism and artificialism	
		magic	
Concrete	classification goes beyond appearance	relationship based in empirical observations	predictions possible
ordering	both private and shared signs exist	reversibility in relations	
conservatism hierarchy		separation of self's actions	
Formal	classification by combinations mostly shared signs	hypothetical relations	if, then

Notes:
1) Any response (behavior) is equally a representation of what is inside the individual as well as what is in the environment.
2) If the stimulus can not be assimilated, it does not exist; to be assimilated the individual needs sufficient biological development to assimilate/accommodate.
3) Structuring is the beginning of meaningful knowing behavior.
4) Schema include reflexes, perceptions, motor behavior.
5) Regarding signifiers: sign has social implications, language is a social vehicle, and symbols are idiosyncratic.

Appendix E
Heart-to-Heart Techniques
© Carolyn K. Kinney, 2006

Listening with Heart

1. Focus attention on your heart. Take a few minutes to give your attention to your heart and the area immediately surrounding your heart. Imagine a sense of warmth filling the space and think loving thoughts such as appreciation and compassion for yourself and other people important to you. Breathe gently and quietly as you maintain your attention in this way for 2-3 minutes or as much time as you have available to you. (Note: The Institute of HeartMath[1] has a technique called *HeartLock-In* that when practiced on a regular basis has shown to help reduce anxiety and stress and increase the ability to maintain focus.)

2. Then, shift your loving attention to the client with whom you wish to connect.

3. Be clear in your intention. Consciously identify that your intention is to connect your spirit with your client's spirit. Clearly say to yourself what you wish to happen, such as be open to client's needs, be non-judgmental, respect client's wishes, be of help in whatever way the client needs. Clear intention invites input from your soul and your client's soul, especially when accompanied with a conscious internal request.

4. Still your mind. Be in a receptive mode. Slow down. The more you are able to quiet yourself and are open to listening, the clearer the information you receive will be.

5. Allow time for the connection to form with your clients and your clients' spirit. Do not force your intent. Be patient and receptive to what they offer. Let go of the need to have a specific outcome or preconceived idea of what your clients need. Let them be the guide and follow their lead.

6. Use silence to allow your clients to feel you are receptive to what they want to say. Silence also makes it possible to hear messages from your inner voice. In other words, it creates a space for the soul's communication.

7. Listen with your heart and all your senses. This means you are fully present and are giving your undivided attention to your clients and what they need. This type of listening requires you to convey, by your actions, that you have all the time your clients need. With practice, you will be able to convey this attitude genuinely and convincingly even when you have other commitments. This type of listening invites an expansion of awareness for both nurses and clients.

8. Convey active involvement. Ask appropriate questions and provide requested information following your client's lead. Ask questions such as, 'Is there anything more....?' or 'Let me see if I understand.....'

9. Confirm what your clients have communicated. Make sure you have understood them and repeat back your understanding. Assure them that you want them to be comfortable and you value them 'just because they are.'

10. Check in with your heart area periodically to make sure you are maintaining heart-based feelings and a sense of warmth.

****

Connecting with Breathe

1. Focus attention on your breathing. Notice how your body feels and how your breath feels as you inhale and exhale naturally for at least 30 seconds.

2. Take a few deep breaths, and as you inhale, do it in a loving way, nourishing and nurturing yourself with each breath, feeling the loving energy flowing throughout your body.

3. As you exhale, imagine you are releasing all the tension in your body.

4. Now turn your attention to your client.

5. Match your inhalation and exhalation with your client's. Do so quietly and subtly. A good time to do this is during a period of silence described in the Heart Listening strategy. This can also be effective during quiet conversations.

6. Visualize a wave of clear energy and relaxation moving gently into your body and observe how this affects the rhythm of your breathing and your client's breathing.

7. Be receptive to any thoughts and messages that come into your awareness. Be open to your inner voice and your client's inner voice.

8. Continue interacting with your client as appropriate and trust that in one way or another you are receiving guidance from your soul and your client's soul.

---

[1] Institute of HeartMath's website: www.heartmath.com.

Appendix F
A Note from Evelyn Tomlin, Co-author of *Modeling and Role-Modeling: A Theory and Paradigm for Nursing (1983).*

Some of you know I believe self-sacrificing Love is at the core of the Universe. God the father, Son and Holy Spirit revealed to humans that He, Himself is the very Essence of Love. Since He is our Creator, our SuIstainer and Master Comforter while we live in an increasingly difficult, flawed world, we ignore Ultimate Reality when we do not include Him in our thoughts and deeds.

I dare to say that Modeling and Role-Modeling as a Theory and Paradigm for Nursing operationalizes God's love to the extent that we limited humans, created in His Image, can with His help, imitate our triune God. If we have no way to validate self-evident truths, we are left to flounder on a sea of post-modern relativism. We have no reason to follow anyone else's ideas, or trust inevitably imperfect descriptive research.

In the years preceding 1983, so far as I was able, I sought to make my contributions to the theory and paradigm in reliance on God's specific help. I sought consistently to bring our written thoughts into harmony with God's broader self-revelation recorded in the world's Best Seller. I sought to be a Christ-follower in every way possible, imperfect as I am—and ever will be—until the day I am taken to live joyfully—and ever more creatively—with Christ and His other followers in His promised New Heaven and New Earth.

As colleagues together, embarking on this latest and most ambitious multibook project, you have my heartiest best wishes! Godspeed and congratulations.

Evelyn Tomlin, M.S., R.N.
Generva, IL
March 17, 2006
rntomlin@wans.net

INDEX

INDEX

INDEX

INDEX

INDEX